30-11

SOCIAL PROBLEMS
AND PUBLIC POLICY
Deviance and Liberty

SOCIAL PROBLEMS AND PUBLIC POLICY
Deviance and Liberty

EDITED BY Lee Rainwater HARVARD UNIVERSITY

 ALDINE PUBLISHING COMPANY / *Chicago*

ABOUT THE EDITOR

Lee Rainwater, Professor of Sociology in the Department of Sociology and
the John F. Kennedy School of Government at Harvard, received his M.A.
and Ph. D. in sociology from the University of Chicago. He is Principal
Investigator in the Research Program on Family Behavior and Social Policy,
Joint Center for Urban Studies, Harvard and M.I.T. and is currently on the
Board of Associate Editors of *Journal of Marriage and the Family,* and a
member of the Advisory Board of the *Journal of Afro-American Studies.*
Professor Rainwater's books include *The Moynihan Report and the Politics
of Controversy* (senior author with William L. Yancey), *Behind Ghetto Walls:
Black Families in a Federal Slum* (Aldine, 1970), and *What Money Buys: In-
equality and the Social Meanings of Income* (In press).

Article 25

American Youth Gangs; Past and Present, by Walter Miller:
Copyright ⓒ 1974 by Alfred A. Knopf, Inc. Reprinted from
Current Perspectives in Criminal Behavior, *edited by*
Abraham S. Blumberg, by permission of the publisher.

First published 1974 by
Aldine Publishing Company
529 South Wabash Avenue
Chicago, Illinois 60605

Library of Congress Catalog Card Number 72-97244
ISBN 202-30263-6 cloth; 202-30264-4 paper

PREFACE

THIS BOOK is designed as an introduction to social science perspectives on a broad range of social issues in American society. It is one of two companion volumes, dealing respectively with problems of inequality and justice and with problems of deviance and liberty; the volumes have been organized so that each can stand independently of the other.

Any one of the problems dealt with here is complex enough to merit the attention of a cadre of specialists. A book that seeks to survey contemporary social issues, therefore, cannot hope to provide an exhaustive or definitive analysis of each one. But there is a role for a survey that deals with the many different kinds of social problems of concern to American citizens and with the many different policy initiatives that are used to cope with these issues. From such a survey one can learn something about the common themes, predilections and quandaries that characterize this nation's response to its complexities, its patterns of inequality and injustice.

Given the tremendous variety of social problems of concern in our society, each selection in these volumes has to do several different kinds of duty. They have been chosen to cover as fully as possible the range of substantive problematic issues, the range of social science perspectives that can be brought to bear on issues of all kinds, and the range of social science methodologies used in studying modern society. Finally, the selections have been chosen to emphasize the contributions that can be made to understanding social problems by intensive and rigorous social science research.

Because these problems are of concern to so many in our society and because we all have available a good deal of information about many if not all of them, informal and impressionistic approaches often tell us a good deal about them. In this sense, every man is his own social scientist. Journalists and popular writers using this common sense approach to social problems may present in the mass media essays that are imaginative and incisive. As interpreters of social reality, they are formidable competitors to the social scientist, whose "ivory tower" and plodding approach often seems to yield less illumination than a good police reporter's work. Increasingly, however, the tools of social scientists are enabling them to produce information and analyses that contribute far more to our understanding than even the most insightful journalist can achieve. The selection in these volumes are designed to highlight the deeper and more fundamental understanding of social issues that can come from the rigorous analysis of government statistics, or from special sample surveys, or from in-depth ethnographic studies.

■ My editorial introductions to each selection appear in sans serif type (as here) and are set off from the text of the selections themselves by squares like those preceding and ending this paragraph. To assist the reader who wants to explore more fully the topics that are covered in this book, I have included suggestions for further reading at the end of each introduction. ■

The perspective on social problems that guided me in preparing this book was developed while working with a number of valued colleagues, in particular Irving Louis Horowitz and David J. Pittman during my years at Washington University, and Phillips Cutright, Herbert J. Gans, and Martin Rein during our time together at the Joint Center for Urban Studies of M.I.T. and Harvard. My wife, Carol Rainwater, has been an important contributor to this work, both in discussions over the years of most of the social issues covered here and more concretely through her assistance in selecting and assembling the articles included.

As on other occasions, I have benefited greatly from discussions with Aldine's publisher, Alexander J. Morin. Janet Braeunig of Aldine has responded magnificently to my not-so-orderly approach to editing this collection. And I thank Sally Nash for her competent handling of the complex process of manuscript preparation involved in preparing this book.

LEE RAINWATER

CONTENTS

INTRODUCTION: THE STUDY OF SOCIAL PROBLEMS

"A social problem is a condition which is defined by a considerable number of persons as a deviation from some social norm which they cherish." This definition offered by Richard C. Fuller and Richard R. Myers some 30 years ago characterizes with considerable economy the kinds of issues sociologists typically study under the rubric of "social problems." As will quickly become apparent below, the "field" of social problems has a very different character from most of the substantive areas of sociology, such as social stratification or interaction processes or the family.

In their efforts to define what social problems as traditionally studied have in common, Fuller and Myers noted that there is always a dual reference in the assertion that something is a social problem: (a) a reference to an objective condition, and (b) a reference to a subjective evaluation which defines that condition as in some way undesirable, destructive, or immoral. They note further that the objective condition is verifiable, in the sense that impartial or trained observers can describe its nature and extent. But in order for a particular objective condition to be reasonably characterized as a social problem, it is necessary that members of the society see it as an undesirable departure from the ordinary course of things.

One could relax this latter condition somewhat and broaden the definition to include objective conditions that have or are believed to have consequences which, if understood, would be regarded as deviating from some social norm. These might be called "hidden social problems." I raise this issue not simply to make a pedantic point but to observe that one important consequence of living in a complex society like ours is that new undesirable consequences are constantly being discovered. Before these situations are fully communicated, the existence of the

This introduction is identical in both volumes of *Social Problems and Public Policy*, the first dealing with *Inequality and Justice* and the second with *Deviance and Liberty*. Nevertheless, I suggest that the reader of both volumes may wish to read the introduction again, to recapitulate the setting for the subsequent discussion.

problem may be known only to a few specialists; after they have been fully communicated, these situations are recognized as social problems by many people. Some aspects of environmental issues present particularly dramatic examples of this—for example, the dangers of nuclear fall-out.

The relationship of the social scientist to social problems is ambiguous; it has plagued research in this area from its inception and involves issues that are not really resolvable. Sometimes the social scientist is interested in studying the problem itself—for example, he may be interested in studying patterns of crime, understanding who commits crimes, and why and what their fate is. When he does this, he generally takes for granted the definition of crime as a social problem, although he may not fully share the social evaluations of crime that are prevalent at the time he does his work. On the other hand, and increasingly, social scientists have been interested not so much in studying the problem itself as in studying the processes by which society defines and takes action about problems. Here the social scientist focuses on the characterization of a given objective condition as a social problem. Indeed, as Howard S. Becker has noted, the social scientist may have to address the question of whether the objective condition which society defines as a problem really exists at all (as in the case of witchcraft, for example).

There are solid theoretical, policy, and ethical reasons for selecting either of these approaches to particular social issues, but they are really quite different, and this has frustrated all attempts to develop a closely reasoned "theory" of social problems. For our purposes here, we will certainly be better off if we start with the understanding that there is no "field" of sociology with theoretical coherence that can be called "social problems." We must look elsewhere for the vitality of this subject of study. Throughout the whole of sociology's growth from early in this century to the present, social problems consistently have attracted high interest among researchers, writers, teachers, and students. As we will see, the existence of the field has allowed many creative scholars to sharpen their analytic tools in the process of trying to understand particular problems. But trying to invest the study of social problems with theoretical precision has come to naught. We are left finally with the understanding that the subject is attractive because those who study society inevitably are also concerned with changing it, and naturally pay especial attention to its problematic aspects. Since social scientists are very much representative of their own society, they tend to bring to their work exactly the same range of subjective definitions about "problems" that others in the society have.

In short, practicing sociologists and students study social problems because they are concerned about them and they wish to use the tools of their discipline to illuminate them.

If the sociologist's interest in a particular problem is in its definitional aspect—that is, in how society comes to define a particular condition as a problem and how that definition is incorporated into ongoing social transactions—then he can achieve an adequate account within the bounds of the discipline itself. This approach is eminently sociological. If, however, one's interest is in the social problem itself, it is not possible to get very far by using only the tools of sociological analysis. Social problems are not simply *sociological* problems, but always involve other aspects of human behavior—economic, political, psychological, and historical. If we want to understand the problem itself rather than the process by which society defines it as a problem, then we must seek understanding from a broader perspective than that provided by the sociologist's expertise alone.

In these two volumes, the emphasis is primarily on the social problems themselves, although many of the selections deal with the social processes of problem definition because those processes in turn often create problems. We have not confined our selections to the work of sociologists; instead, selections from all the social sciences have been chosen in order to illustrate the broad range of social science theory and method that must be applied to gain the fullest understanding of social problems.

The range of social problems traditionally covered by sociology, however, has not been of equal concern to the other social sciences. It is in that sense that this field of study has seemed to "belong" to the discipline of sociology. Although in fact all such problems involve economic or political or psychological aspects, few of them have been subjected to study by specialists in those fields. In general, issues related to economic and political inequality, for example, have been heavily and creatively studied by the nonsociological disciplines. However, until recently there were many areas of deviant behavior and some areas of inequality that were almost exclusively the concern of sociologists and psychologists. It is only recently that we have begun to see interesting work on the economics of drugs or crime or the political aspects of abortion or "gay liberation." If a lively interest continues in research on these kinds of social problems from the perspective of different social sciences, we can look forward to an increasingly good understanding of them. In this way some of the disciplinary parochialism that has characterized much sociological work on social problems will be corrected.

FIVE SOCIOLOGICAL PERSPECTIVES ON SOCIAL PROBLEMS

Although sociology from its inception has been deeply involved in describing and analyzing social problems, the approach of sociologists to the subject has shifted markedly from time to time. Earl Rubington and Martin S. Weinberg have analyzed the development of five different sociological perspectives: (1) social pathology, (2) social disorganization, (3) value conflict, (4) deviant behavior, and (5) labelling.

Early sociologists, working in the period before World War I, tended to see social problems as manifestations of one or another departure from "normality" in society. They regarded society as an organism, and as with other organisms, it was possible to speak of its state of health and to point to particular conditions that were pathological. This view came easily at the time since it was consistent with deeply established assumptions about the importance of biological factors in social behavior, ranging from the role of inheritance in establishing mental superiority or inferiority to the role of climate in determining which nations prospered and which nations declined. The social pathologist tended to locate the causes of social problems in individuals who were defective in some way, who caused problems because they were feeble-minded or had criminal constitutions or some other weakness, or who gave in to immoral impulses or preyed on the weakness of others.

In more recent times, sociologists who find the *social pathology* perspective meaningful have spoken of society and its institutions as "sick." The causes of that sickness are generally located in the predatory character of particular classes or institutions within society. In this form, the social pathology perspective shades imperceptively into the two approaches that succeeded it in the development of sociology—social disorganization and value conflict. The emphasis on social pathology is perhaps best thought of as a primitive first approximation of a social scientific view of widely recognized problems in society. As the theoretical tools available to sociologists for analyzing social life have improved, this naive approach has been supplanted.

The second sociological perspective on social problems to gain ascendancy was that of *social disorganization*. After World War I, sociologists—particularly those associated with the University of Chicago—concentrated their attention on the dynamics of social life in the American city. They came to see the many social problems in the cities as the result of rapid social change, of the impact on social life and individuals of two major processes: urbanization from abroad and from rural areas within the United States, and the technological change attendant on advanced industrialization and the development of new products such as the automobile. The "Chicago School" sociologists who studied social pathologies such as crime, truancy, suicide, and tuberculosis made the surprising discovery that over a half a century of waves of immigration to the city, the same neighborhoods manifested continuing high rates of these problems although the immigrant groups that inhabited them changed from one generation to the next. They concluded that these environments somehow disorganized and disrupted the lives of their inhabitants. This social disorganization compounded the breakdown of rules and the inability of individuals to depend on a familiar set of expectations that could successfully guide their actions.

Just as the perspective of social pathology implicitly assumes an obverse condition of social normalcy, the perspective of social disorganization implicitly assumes the existence of social organization. Indeed, the latter perspective became of central importance for much of sociology between the two world wars because of a growing conviction on the part of sociologists that they were beginning to develop a scientific theory of how societies were put together. The central role of rules—of recipes for doing the work of society—in the theory of social organization sets up social disorganization as an everpresent companion. If the rules do not work, or if they are unclear or contradictory, then the group has a problem because it cannot carry forward its activity.

Much of the empirical research done during this period fit neatly into a framework emphasizing the central role of normlessness and cultural conflict. However, as time went on, more and more sociologists began to observe that many situations involving social problems did not fit under the rubric of social disorganization. In fact, much socially problematic behavior seemed highly organized and tightly integrated into the ongoing activity of society. Observations of this kind considerably strengthened a growing skepticism about the proposition that "bad things" in society or in individuals were producing the bad effects we call social problems.

This skeptical impulse eventually produced a third approach, usually called the *value conflict* perspective. It is this perspective on which we have drawn for our own general definition of social problems, accepting the position originally enunciated by Fuller and Myers (Rubington and Weinberg, 1971) who first brought into sharp focus the view that central to all such problems are "conflicts in the value scheme of the culture." In this view, problems occur not because things fall apart socially but because different groups in society have different interests, these interests conflict, and these conflicts precipitate conditions that at least some people regard as undesirable.

Fuller and Myers distinguish three kinds of social problems. First, there are *physical problems* which everyone regards as a threat to their welfare. Value conflict does not cause such problems (earthquakes, hurricanes, floods, droughts, etc.), but our way of adapting to them does involve conflicting interests, and disagreements arise concerning what should be done to cope with them.

A second kind of social problem they call the *ameliorative problem*. Here there is general consensus that an objective condition is undesirable, but people "are unable to agree on programs for the amelioration of the condition." Examples include crime, physical and mental disease, accidents, etc. These problems, unlike physical problems, are fully social in that both the objective condition and our responses to it are full of potentials for interest or value conflict.

A third kind of problem they call the *moral problem*. Here there is no agreement that the problematic condition itself is undesirable. Some groups in society believe it is a problem and others argue with equal vehemence that it is not, that it is in some way a "normal" social situation. Many of the conditions and processes we have included under the rubric of problems of inequality are of this type, in that there is not universal agreement that they are in fact problematic.

There is a kinship between this perspective and the social disorganization approach. For both, the central factor in social problems is that there is no homogeneity of social values. The notion that social problems were greatly heightened by the trends of urbanization and industrialization which was so obvious in earlier views is muted but nevertheless present here, as in the observation by Willard Waller that "social" problems in the modern sense did not exist when every primary group cared for its own helpless and unfortunate. Social problems as we know them are a phenomenon of secondary group society in which the primary group is no longer willing or able to take care of its members."

More systematic attention to sociological theory as the starting place for sociological perspectives, in contrast to a conceptual apparatus inductively developed from empirical work, bore important fruits in the 1950's for the study of social problems. Ideas developed by Robert K. Merton as part of his more general interest in structural-functional theory were applied to a wide range of social problems, under the general rubric of "anomie" in a new theory of *deviant behavior*. A 1939 article by Merton on "Social Structure and Anomie" some fifteen years later had been applied in a fairly systematic way to studies of crime and delinquency and later even more broadly to other social problems ranging from drug use to poverty. Merton's theory was of considerable generality, seeking to account for all behavior that deviates from customary expectations. Instead of regarding social problems as manifestations of a lack of rules, he saw them as situations in which individuals learned the values of their society, but because they did not have access to approved ways of making those values effective for themselves, sought other ways of gaining culturally approved ends. Those "deviant" ways brought them into conflict with the dominant conceptions of conventional behavior. "Racketeering" is a particularly clearcut example. Poor but ambitious young men, lacking access to legitimate careers became gangsters, thus winning, by illegitimate means, the success denied them by their impoverished backgrounds.

In this perspective, the norms of society are taken for granted; what is problematic is the individual's response in terms of those norms. If he has access to approved ways of achieving goals, he is unlikely to engage in deviant behavior; if he does not have access to achievement consistent with culturally approved models, he is likely to violate the rules and thus lay himself open to punitive responses on the part of society. Deviant behavior is seen as the product of strains built into society, stemming from a disjunction between what the culture offers as desirable and what the social structure actually makes available to all members.

This perspective encourages the student of social problems to pay close attention to the situation of individuals engaging in deviant behavior, to determine what kinds of stresses they are subjected to by their position in relation to the "opportunity structure" of society, and to point policy-makers toward altering that position in such a way that individuals can achieve their goals in more conventional ways. While a conflict between the "deviant" and the "normal" is recognized, that conflict is regarded as a secondary consequence of the fact that the deviants have not had an opportunity to become normals in the first place.

A strong reaction against this conception of the dynamics of deviance and social problems has informed the work of sociologists who have developed our final perspective—that of societal reaction or *labelling*. The labelling theorists want to attend not to the behavior of deviants so much as to the behavior of the normals who are engaged in labelling behavior *as* deviant. Their starting place is the process by which members of society select certain kinds of behavior that are labelled as rule violations out of the many kinds of behavior individuals present to those around them. Their criticism of the deviant behavior theorists is that their conception of rule violation is too mechanical. It assumes that the labelling process is automatic and highly predictable, given the details of the deviant's behavior. In fact, such writers as Lemert and Becker observed that exactly the same behavior may variously be ignored by society, mildly sanctioned, or subjected to the most intense and dramatic moral reaction (for example, the consumption of alcohol).

The process by which this reaction is established and the purpose of the process for society, the labelling theorists argue, is far more interesting than the evaluation of the deviant act itself. Further, they observe, the reaction of the deviant to his situation is not simply a matter of his choices as determined by the opportunity structure but is also adapted to the societal reaction. Thus, Lemert's concept of "secondary deviance" refers to those aspects of the behavior of the deviant that are generated by his effort to adopt to the fact that he is (or potentially may be) labelled by the larger society as deviant. For example, much of the behavior of the drug user is seen as adaptive to the illegal situation in which he finds himself rather than as a result of drug use as such. The "deviant subculture" that grows up when persons engaged in a given kind of deviant behavior spend considerable time with each other is as much a product of their cooperative endeavor to defend themselves against the responses of society as it is intrinsic to their initial deviant commitment.

In summary, the perception of social problems in these five perspectives has differed dramatically. For the social pathologist, the problem is the defective character of individuals in society (or in a later version, the defective character of social institutions). For the sociologist who focuses on social disorganization, the problem is the ineffectiveness of rules for organizing constructive social processes. For the value conflict theorist, the problem can be understood only as a result either of conflicts among groups in society or of conflicting interests held by a single individual. For the deviance theorist, the problem lies in the instigations to rule violation created by the unequal distribution of opportunities for self-realization in society. For the labelling theorist, the problem is very much in the eye of the beholder, and in the process by which society separates its members into the moral and the immoral, the conforming and the deviant.

The theorists who developed these different perspectives have tended to emphasize (and perhaps to exaggerate) their incompatibility. To some extent the differences are more a result of preferred subject matter than anything else. Many modern investigators have combined at least the last three perspectives—those of anomie theory, labelling theory, and value conflict—in ways that yield a much more richly detailed and subtle picture of socially problematic situations and behavior than any investigator working only within one tradition is likely to be able to do.

ANALYZING SOCIAL PROBLEMS

The analysis of particular social problems requires that the analyst learn something of how the problematic situation came to be defined as it is, and how the particular actions that make up the problem came to be established. In their analysis of "the natural history of a social problem," Fuller and Myers offer the view that all social problems go through three definable stages—one might say three logically necessary stages—for the complete development of an "institutionalized" problem. These stages are (1) awareness, (2) policy determination, and (3) reform. With respect to most problems of concern to society and to social scientists, these stages are not observable separately, since society has long ago reached the third ("reform") stage of concern with problems such as crime, economic dependency, political corruption, etc. However, since what the problem is and how it is to be dealt with changes in its details over time (the definition of "crime," for example), Fuller and Myers' admonition to be sensitive to the sequence of stages is still very useful.

In the beginning there must be the definers—those who offer in some vigorous and convincing way a definition of particular conditions as a social problem, as a situation that challenges important values and produces undesired consequences. Then there will generally follow discussion about what should be done about the newly-diagnosed problem. Once decisions are made about what should be done, there is a final stage of doing it. Fuller and Myers call this "reform," but we might adopt the more general term of "policy action." Since in the real world problems seldom go away, most social action on social problems has to do with changing slightly the definition of what is the problem or the prescription of what might be done about it or, even more commonly, changing slightly the procedures by which a policy is administered and executed within a general social prescription.

The social scientist who is interested in a given social problem needs to start with a concern about how and to whom that problem is salient. There are several different levels of salience that one can readily observe. In terms of increasing breadth of concern, these may be categorized as follows:

1. *Detached scholarly diagnosis.* It sometimes happens that scholars (not only social scientists but also biological and physical scientists, legal scholars, etc.) observe social situations they believe can be defined as problematic in the light of established values and norms. They may write or speak about their diagnoses, without engaging a wider audience than their own colleagues. Some of the earliest work that eventuated in a broader concern with automotive safety, for example, can be seen as having begun at this level.

2. *The voice in the wilderness.* Somewhat more public and at the same time more individual is the activity of persons who undertake to publicize and dramatize situations which they and perhaps only a small group of others see as a problem. The most dramatic example of this kind in recent times is that of Rachel Carson, whose book, *Silent Spring,* first announced to a wide audience the environmental threat posed by pesticides. History is full of examples of voices in the wilderness who were initally treated as crack-pots (and, of course, for many voices in the wilderness that evaluation never changes).

3. *Pressure-groups.* Here those involved in asserting the existence of a problem encompass a broader group than either specialized scholars or the friends of a voice in the wilderness. A group of individuals, for reasons that seem sufficient and compelling to them, vigorously assert the existence of a problem against what they see as the indifference or resistance of society. Sometimes such groups persist over long periods of time with no apparent effect on the way society deals with the problematic situation. Then for reasons that may be quite difficult to disentangle the circumscribed issue may find itself augmented in the following ways:

4. *Pervasive elite concern.* The most significant transition in the evolution of a social problem may take place when the issue comes to be defined as important by individuals who conceive of themselves as part of the elite, as "knowledgeable persons." Racism in America, for example, was more the province of pressure groups than otherwise until the early 1960's, when it became an issue which could not be ignored by any individual who wished to claim that he was knowledgeable, judicious, and constructive-minded about society.

5. At the broadest level, a social problem may evoke considerable *society-wide concern;* it may be considered important not just by the elite (or sometimes not even by the elite) but by the man in the street. Some of the most interest-

ing political situations in a democratic society occur where the elite misperceive the concerns of the man in the street, and his concerns come to represent a political embarrassment to the elite. A recent example is the case of crime as a social problem, which achieved apparently very high salience among the public before that fact was clearly perceived by most of the elite. This disjunction of perceptions provides an important avenue of opportunity for aspiring politicians to move into more powerful positions.

These different levels of saliency in terms of the variable of "awareness" can be used to analyze not only social problems as such but also issues of policy determination and execution. A given policy approach may be confined to a particular set of scholars or a voice in the wilderness or a particular pressure group, or it may be the conventional wisdom within the elite or the wider society. Similarly, particular approaches to policy execution may be localized in each of these different groups. The social scientist who wishes to understand the pattern of social action involved in a given problematic issue needs to examine the varieties of awareness, policy determination, and policy execution that exist among these different levels of society at any given time.

For each group that has some awareness of the problem, or for all groups taken together, one can raise the following kinds of questions, and answers to each of them are necessary if we are to have a full understanding of the problem.

What is the problem? That is, what is the objective condition to which those who define the problem direct our attention?

Who are the people whose behavior constitutes the problem, and what are their characteristics?

How broad is the domain of the problem? That is, is it highly circumscribed ("teenagers vandalizing high schools during the summer vacation"), is it extremely pervasive in its penetration of various aspects of social life ("moral breakdown and permissiveness in our society"), or is it in between?

How much policy thinking is there about the problem? Is it one which, whatever the level of awareness, is not being much attended to by those with the power to make policy, or is it regarded as already routinely handled and therefore not subject to policy reassessment, or is it very much on the agenda of those who initiate policy?

What is in fact being done? Is this a social problem for which policy is more symbolic than actual, is political rhetoric the principal form of policy, or is the problem subject to considerable bureaucratic institutionalization and ongoing activity?

Given the level of policy action, to what extent does policy in fact affect the problem, either in terms of decreasing or increasing its prevalence or altering its form through the mechanisms we have discussed above as "secondary deviance?"

The social scientist whose interest in a social problem is not substantive, in the sense that he does not wish to make an independent contribution to public policy on the issue, may address himself to these questions simply to contribute to basic knowledge about how societies in general or a particular society operates: defining and taking action to understand social problems is itself of the essence of the ongoing life of human societies. But as we have noted, social scientists have generally studied social problems in good part because they wish to contribute to their constructive resolution.

Sometimes the upshot of the social scientist's study has been to suggest that "the problem itself is the problem," that is, that there is no real damage done to society by the condition causing complaint and that society would be better off if it were simply redefined as not a problem. As we will see, the social scientists on the U.S. Commission on Pornography essentially came to that conclusion. Or the social scientist may take the problem as seriously, or more seriously, than society in general, and set about seeking to develop knowledge that will be useful in coping with it.

What kinds of contributions can social science make? Howard S. Becker has suggested five areas in which social scientists can contribute. First, he says, the social scientist can help by "sorting out the differing definitions of the problem." Because problems are defined in different ways by different groups in society (and have been defined in different ways at different times in the history of the same society), discussion often produces more confusion than necessary because participants operate on the incorrect assumption that theirs is the only way of stating the issue. The social scientist who spells out different definitions of the problem and shows how they are related or contradictory provides the raw material for reconciling those differences in ways that could lead to more useful policy consideration.

Second, the social scientist can assist by analyzing the assumptions made by interested parties about how the problematic situation is constituted and operates. Those who are participants in policy determination and execution processes all operate on the basis of implicit models about what goes on in the world. These assumptions may conflict, just as definitions of the problem may conflict, and they may or may not be accurate. They are generally not complete or accurate over the whole range of social action entailed in the problem. The social scientist therefore seeks to make explicit the implicit models held by different participants in the problem-defining and resolving process.

Then he is in a position to make a third contribution, the one that is most distinctively a product of his expertise: testing various assumptions about the problem against empirical reality. The social scientist brings to bear a set of methodological and theoretical tools to assess the facts of the matter. This is simply said, but the complexity of the social facts involved in even the most apparently simple social problem is formidable indeed. As many social scientists and philosophers of science have observed, facts are not neutral. Students and activists concerned with any problem acquire interests in their particular definitions of its nature, definitions which analysis often shows are more a product of the organizational requirements of those involved than of their detached assessment of the reality with which they deal.

The structure of putative facts that shores up conventional ways of dealing with problems is extremely complex, and a great deal of social science activity involves simply demonstrating the inaccuracy of pieces of this structure. This is a fairly dismal task; indeed in recent times it has seemed that sociology may replace economics as "the dismal science." Over and over again sociologists seem able to demonstrate that various institutions designed to do something about a problem do not work—job training programs don't cure poverty, prisons do not rehabilitate criminals, more money spent on schools doesn't increase learning, etc. In the long run, however, social scientists are committed to the belief that a necessary though not sufficient condition for dealing constructively with social problems is a more accurate model of the social processes involved in each of them.

Becker observes that an accurate model of social processes makes possible the social scientist's fourth contribution—that of "discovering strategic points of intervention in the social structures and processes that produce the problem." The sociologist's assessment of the various kinds of social transactions that add up to the problematic situation allows him to imagine interventions which might have the effect of ameliorating the problem or doing away with it entirely. If he understands the dynamics of the problem, he is in a better position to predict the consequences of policy innovations. Recently there has been considerable interest among social scientists in large-scale experiments to test innovations and in particular to test the effectiveness of small variations in them. The New Jersey negative income tax experiment that was completed in the early 1970's is the largest example of such experimentation to date. Here different amounts of guaranteed income and different tax rates on the earnings of persons who received benefits from the plan were tested against each other and against a control group of low-income families who received no benefits. The experiment's designers hoped that analyzing the results of this experiment will yield greater precision in dealing with some aspects of the poverty problem. Some social scientists, particularly economists and political scientists, have for some time been involved in an effort to design intervention strategies to deal with social problems. Sociologists have been less involved in such activity, but it seems likely that in the future they will be more concerned with this kind of innovation design and testing research.

Many social scientists evince considerable ambivalence about a fifth contribution they can make toward the solution of social problems. They can, Becker notes, "suggest alternative moral points of view from which the problem can be assessed." Sociologists have long struggled to dissociate themselves from social philosophy and to establish their detachment as scientists. Yet involvement with the pragmatic issues of social problems often pushes them imperceptibly toward that earlier role. The social scientist often discovers when he offers alternative policy recommendations for dealing with a problem that he runs up against moralistic objections to his proposed innovations. In this situation, he often shifts his attention from the facts as such to analyzing the relationship between particular moral prescriptions ("crime should be punished") and the broader moral and humanitarian values to which those prescriptions are related as means to ends. He may suggest that in terms of these more basic moral views, a different set of operational moral standards might prove more constructive. These different standards, in turn, may serve to legitimate policy innovations that have not been previously considered acceptable. Since moral standards often conflict, this kind of analytic work generally proves crucial to resolving the policy impasses that often characterize serious social problem issues.

THE ORGANIZATION OF THESE VOLUMES

I have organized my coverage of social problems issues under two main rubrics: problems of inequality and problems of deviance. Problems of inequality are defined in terms of the values having to do with justice, equal treatment, equal humanity, which are supposed to inform public policy in the United States. The issues subsumed under the rubric of deviance involve another established natural value, that of liberty, of individual choice, of the determination of one's own best interest, free from arbitrary interference by the state, and with the security to exercise it.

The focus of these volumes is firmly substantive rather than disciplinary. That is, we are interested in social problems as areas of application of the social sciences to important social issues. We take it that it is their interest in problems and policy that brings students to a course in social problems, and that an interest in application characterizes an increasing number of sociologists. In pursuing this focus, however, we have made extensive use of the work of sociologists whose interest in social problems is perhaps more for what their analysis can tell one about the basic dynamics of human society than for policy purposes. It is commonly true in the social as in the physical sciences that an interest in research important for the development of the discipline in fact turns out to provide knowledge that is crucial for understanding some quite practical matter.

Many students of social problems end up pursuing careers in the public professions. It is important that before they specialize in a particular area (housing, welfare, education, health, corrections, etc.), those who are going to pursue such careers understand something of the general nature of social problems and the many themes that tie them together, themes having to do both with the problematic behavior itself and with the common responses on the part of political and administrative institutions.

Already public service work directed to social problems is a major industry in America, and all indications are that it will become even larger in a generation's time. Yet one major conclusion from research on these activities over the last decades is that they have a great capacity for dehumanizing those they are designed to serve, and very little capacity for resolving the social issues that lead to their establishment. I hope the germs of better kinds of intervention can already be found in the knowledge of today's social scientists.

A most convenient compendium of articles representative of different perspectives on social problems can be found in Earl Rubington and Martin S. Weinberg (eds.), *The Study of Social Problems: Five Perspectives* (Oxford University Press, 1971). The editors' analysis of the history and interrelations of the perspectives discussed above is particularly useful for the student. The articles by Fuller and Myers referred to above are included in this compendium, as is the article by Willard Waller. The reader also will be interested in the editor's introduction in Howard S. Becker (ed.), *Social Problems: A Modern Approach* (John Wiley and Sons, 1966).

Another overview of the relationship between sociology and social problems analysis, representing a structural-functional approach, is Robert K. Merton's

"Social Problems and Sociological Theory," in Robert K. Merton and Robert A. Nisbet (eds.), *Contemporary Social Problems* (Harcourt, Brace, 1961). One of the most incisive analyses of the relationship between the personal, political, and professional ideologies of sociologists and their work on social problems is in C. Wright Mills, "The Professional Ideology of Social Pathologists" (*American Journal of Sociology*, September 1943). For a more recent analysis of some of these issues, see Irving Louis Horowitz, "The Sociology of Social Problems: A Study in the Americanization of Ideas," in his *Professing Sociology: Studies in the Life Cycle of Social Science* (Aldine, 1968). See also Alvin W. Gouldner, "Anti-Minotaur: The Myth of a Value-Free Sociology" (*Social Problems*, Volume 8, Number 3, Winter 1962, pp. 199 ff.), and the contributions by the editors in *Alvin W. Gouldner and S. M. Miller, Applied Sociology* (The Free Press, 1961).

I.

MODERN PERSPECTIVES ON DEVIANCE AND SOCIAL PROBLEMS

DEVIANCE IS BY DEFINITION a social problem. Because deviant behavior violates the normative expectations of a given group, deviance must be regarded as a problem for that group, since all groups of people want their norms to be enforced. As Kai Erikson notes in the first selection, norms that are not enforced cease to be norms. We shall see, however, that detached analysis of the range of behavior called deviant suggests that in terms of actual disruption of social life the social problem sometimes lies more in the norm's existence than in its violation.

This book's title suggest the basic values by which one can assess whether the social problem ultimately is norm or deviance. Many modern societies place considerable value on personal liberty, so that interference with personal choices can be justified only in terms of the potential damage that particular kinds of behavior might do to the legitimate interests of others. Sociological research suggests that the social problem associated with deviance is often and exactly the victimization of individuals who violate norms, which cannot be justified in terms of basic values of liberty, social order, or justice. Several kinds of deviance in which these issues arise are discussed in Part II, "Deviant Exchanges," which deals primarily with the so-called "crimes without victims."

In other kinds of deviance, though, the victims are obvious. Basically the social problem here is that people or, in a more organized way, social institutions interfere with individual liberty and self-realization. Selections in Part III deal with the violation—which establishes the deviance—of norms that involve personal control. Sometimes the principal victim is the deviant person himself, as in mental disorders, and the social problem lies in society's inability either to prevent or to ameliorate that condition. In crimes of violence or against property, however, the liberty lost is that of the victim, who by virtue of the crime is deprived of some of his ability to go about his affairs unmolested.

15

In Part IV the focus moves to people defined as deviant because of some characteristic of the way they live rather than because they violate a particular norm (as in the commission of a crime). Here we deal with the extent to which social institutions can make certain individuals unable to exercise their liberty or to realize themselves fully—for example, individuals who are labeled as mentally retarded and therefore subject to special treatment even though they are capable of living in a normal way. Howard Becker points out that one of the functions of social science is to provide new perspectives by which a social problem is defined. "Mental retardation" as a problem begins with considering how society can cope with "defective" persons, but Jane Mercer shows in Selection 23 that eventually the problem must be redefined in more complicated terms: How can society help the small proportion of severely mentally retarded persons without at the same time damaging the life chances of others who (for many reasons) may have low intelligence test scores but can grow up normally if society treats them as normal individuals?

Another social issue concerns the relative costs and benefits of particular ways of enforcing norms. As we consider (in Part V) the institutions that deal with deviants, we begin to get some insight into the very high social and personal costs in the American way of enforcing norms; we are confronted with what might be called the pathologies of enforcement and correction. These are social problems almost classic in the applicability of the framework of value or interest conflict. Hard-liners tend not to see these issues as problems, or to see the problems only in terms of the number of violators who slip through the net of law enforcement and punishment. Soft-liners see the problem, instead, as one of institutional inhumanity and ineffectiveness either in reducing the prevalence of deviant behavior or at least in reducing the rate of recidivism on the part of those who are caught in the detection net.

1. NOTES ON THE SOCIOLOGY
OF DEVIANCE

KAI T. ERIKSON

Reprinted by permission from Social Problems *9 (1962): 307-14. Copyright 1969 by The Society for the Study of Social Problems. Kai T. Erikson is Professor of Sociology at Yale University. The following selection sketches the theoretical orientation used in* Wayward Puritans *(Wiley, 1966), a historical and sociological study of deviance among the Massachusetts Bay Puritans in the 17th century, which won the 1967 MacIver Award of the American Sociological Association. In this book and other articles Erikson has contributed significantly to our knowledge of the processes by which society screens behavior and attributes deviance.*

■ In this selection Erikson challenges a traditional sociological approach that considers deviant behavior as a straightforward interaction between individuals (who for social or personal reasons engage in deviant behavior) and society (which reacts because its norms are violated). Erikson approaches the issue the other way around: How and why, out of all the many different acts many individuals engage in, does society choose some few acts and individuals to call deviant?

Erikson takes as his point of departure for this work the propositions of a founding father of modern society, Emile Durkheim, who observed in *The Rules of Sociological Method* (Free Press, 1958) that crime is a natural event, "an integral part of all healthy societies." Erikson suggests that acts of deviance and persons who engage in deviance serve the purposes of society by marking out the bounds of conduct that accord with the group's sense of itself, thus contributing to its solidarity. In his book on deviance in Puritan New England, Erikson used historical examples to show that sometimes the depth of conflict over deviant behavior in a society may be almost imperceptible to a distant observer because the norms involved are so subtle, but he suggested that the issues around which especially notable outbreaks of deviance occur tell us something about the aspects of the culture that are most salient to the group's definition of itself and to its conception of what makes it unique. For the Puritans these issues revolved around religion, around God and the Devil. Looking at the most notorious forms of deviance in modern American society, what might we say about its central focus?

Other discussions of deviance that share much with Erikson's approach include Howard S. Becker, *Outsiders: Studies in the Sociology of Deviance* (Free Press, 1963); and Edwin M. Lemert, *Human Deviance, Social Problems, and Social Control* (Prentice-Hall, 1967). Harold Garfinkel has analyzed the importance of ceremonies for making the attribution of deviance stick in "Successful Degradation Ceremonies," *American Journal of Sociology* 61 (1956): 420-24. Erikson's analysis applies to any level of group life, not just to society as a whole. Thus one can analyze deviance from group norms even in very small groups of friends or co-workers, as in Robert A. Dentler and Kai T. Erikson, "The Function of Deviance in Groups," *Social Problems* 7 (1959): 98-107; and Kenneth Westhues, "Social Problems as Systemic Costs," *Social Problems* 20 (4) (1973): 418-30. ■

IT IS COMMON PRACTICE in sociology to picture deviant behavior as an alien element in society. Deviance is considered a vagrant form of human activity which has somehow broken away from the more orderly currents of social life and needs to be controlled. And since it is generally understood that this sort of aberration could occur only if something were wrong within the organization of society itself, deviant behavior is described almost as if it were leakage from machinery in poor condition: it is an incidental result of disorder and anomie, a symptom of internal breakdown.

The purpose of the following remarks will be to review this conventional outlook and to argue that it provides too narrow a framework for many kinds of sociological research. Deviation, we will suggest, recalling Durkheim's classic statement on the subject, can often be understood as a normal product of stable institutions, an important resource which is guarded and preserved by forces found in all human organizations.

According to current theory, deviant behavior is most likely to occur when the sanctions governing conduct in any given social setting seem to be contradictory—as would be the case, for example, if the work rules posted by a company required one course of action from its employees and the longer range policies of the company require quite another. Any situation marked by this kind of ambiguity, of course, can pose a serious dilemma for the individual: if he is careful to observe one set of demands imposed upon him, he runs the immediate risk of violating some other, and thus may find himself caught in a deviant stance no matter how earnestly he tries to avoid it. In this limited sense, deviance can be viewed as a "normal" social response to "abnormal" social circumstances, and we are therefore invited to assume that every act of deviation results from some imbalance within the social order—a condition of strain, anomie, or alienation.

This approach to the study of deviant behavior has generated a good deal of useful research, but it has at least one serious drawback for investigators who share an interest in what is known as "social problems." The "anomie" theory (if we may use that convenient label for a moment) is designed to account for all behavior which varies in some technical way from the norms of the community, whether or not that behavior is considered a problem by anyone else. For example, the bank teller who becomes a slave to routine and the armed bandit who relieves him of the day's receipts both register as deviants according to the logic of this scheme, since each is deviating in his own way from the ideal standards of the culture. Yet the most important difference between these men is one that the "anomie" theory cannot easily take into account: the bank teller, no matter

how desperate his private needs, does not ordinarily create any concern in the rest of the community, while the bandit triggers the whole machinery of social control into vigorous action. In short, the "anomie" theory may help us appreciate the various ways in which people respond to conditions of strain, but it does not help us differentiate between those people who infringe the letter of the norm without attracting any notice and those who excite so much alarm that they earn a deviant reputation in society and are committed to special institutions like prisons and hospitals.

From a sociological standpoint, deviance can be defined as conduct which is generally thought to require the attention of social control agencies—that is, conduct about which "something should be done." Deviance is not a property *inherent in* certain forms of behavior; it is a property *conferred upon* these forms by the audiences which directly or indirectly witness them. The critical variable in the study of deviance, then, is the social audience rather than the individual actor, since it is the audience which eventually determines whether or not any episode of behavior or any class of episodes is labeled deviant.

This definition may seem a little indirect, but it has the advantage of bringing a neglected sociological issue into proper focus. When a community acts to control the behavior of one of its members, it is engaged in a very intricate process of selection. After all, even the worst miscreant in society conforms most of the time, if only in the sense that he uses the correct spoon at mealtime, takes good care of his mother, or in a thousand other ways respects the ordinary conventions of his group; and if the community elects to bring sanctions against him for the occasions when he does misbehave, it is responding to a few deviant details set within a vast array of entirely acceptable conduct. Thus it happens that a moment of deviation may become the measure of a person's position in society. He may be jailed or hospitalized, certified as a full-time deviant, despite the fact that only a fraction of his behavior was in any way unusual or dangerous. The community has taken note of a few scattered particles of behavior and has decided that they reflect what kind of person he "really" is.

The screening device which sifts these telling details out of the person's overall performance, then, is a very important instrument of social control. We know very little about the properties of this screen, but we do know that it takes many factors into account which are not directly related to the deviant act itself: it is sensitive to the suspect's social class, his past record as an offender, the amount of remorse he manages to convey, and many similar concerns which take hold in the shifting moods of the community. This may not be so obvious when the screen is dealing with extreme forms of deviance like serious crimes, but in the day-by-day filtering processes which take place throughout the community this feature is easily observable. Some men who drink too much are called alcoholics and others are not, some men who act oddly are committed to hospitals and others are not, some men who have no visible means of support are hauled into court and others are not—and the difference between those who earn a deviant label and those who go their own way in peace depends almost entirely on the way in which the community sifts out and codes the many details of behavior to which it is witness. In this respect, the community screen may be a more relevant subject for sociological research than the actual behavior which is filtered through it.

Once the problem is phrased in this way we can ask: How does a community decide what forms of conduct should be singled out for this kind of attention? The conventional answer to this question, of course, is that society sets up the machinery of control in order to protect itself against the "harmful" effects of deviation, in much the same way that an organism mobilizes its resources to combat an invasion of germs. Yet this simple view of the matter has not always proven to be a very productive one. In the first place, as Durkheim and Mead pointed out some years ago, it is by no means clear that all acts considered deviant in a culture are in

fact (or even in principle) harmful to group life. In the second place, it is gradually becoming more evident to sociologists engaged in this area of research that deviant behavior can play an important part in keeping the social order intact. This raises a number of interesting questions for sociology.

In recent years, sociological theory has become more and more concerned with the concept "social system"—an organization of society's component parts into a form which sustains internal equilibrium, resists change, and is boundary maintaining. In its most abstract form, the "system" concept describes a highly complex network of relations, but the scheme is generally used by sociologists to draw attention to those forces in the social order which promote a high level of uniformity among human actors and a high degree of symmetry within human institutions. The main organizational drift of a system, then, is seen as centripetal: it acts to draw the behavior of actors toward those centers in social space where the core values of the group are figuratively located, bringing them within range of basic norms. Any conduct which is neither attracted toward this nerve center by the rewards of conformity nor compelled toward it by other social pressures is considered "out of control," which is to say, deviant.

This basic model has provided the theme for most contemporary thinking about deviation, and as a result little attention has been given to the notion that systems operate to maintain boundaries. To say that a system maintains boundaries is to say that it controls the fluctuation of its constituent parts so that the whole retains a defined range of activity, a unique pattern of constancy and stability, within the larger environment. Because the range of human behavior is potentially so wide, social groups maintain boundaries in the sense that they try to limit the flow of behavior within their domain so that it circulates within a defined cultural territory. Boundaries, then, are an important point of reference for persons participating in any system. A people may define its boundaries by referring to a geographical location, a set of honored traditions, a particular religious or political viewpoint, an occupational specialty, a common language, or just some local way of doing things; but in any case, members of the group have some idea about the contours of the niche they occupy in social space. They know where the group begins and ends as a special entity; they know what kinds of experience "belong" within these precincts and what kinds do not.

For all its apparent abstractness, a social system is organized around the movements of persons joined together in regular social relations. The only material found in a system for marking boundaries, then, is the behavior of its participants; and the kinds of behavior which best perform this function are often deviant, since they represent the most extreme variety of conduct to be found within the experience of the group. In this sense, transactions taking place between deviant persons on the one side and agencies of control on the other are boundary-maintaining mechanisms. They mark the outside limits of the area within which the norm has jurisdiction, and in this way assert how much diversity and variability can be contained within the system before it begins to lose its distinct structure, its cultural integrity.

A social norm is rarely expressed as a firm rule or official code. It is an abstract synthesis of the many separate times a community has stated its sentiments on a given kind of issue. Thus the norm has a history much like that of an article of common law: it is an accumulation of decisions made by the community over a long period of time which gradually gathers enough moral eminence to serve as a precedent for future decisions. And like an article of common law, the norm retains its validity only if it is regularly used as a basis for judgment. Each time the group censures some act of deviation, then, it sharpens the authority of the violated norm and declares again where the boundaries of the group are located.

It is important to notice that these transactions between deviant persons and agents of control have always attracted a good deal of attention in this and other cultures. In our own past, both the trial and punishment of deviant offenders took place in the public market and gave the crowd a chance to participate in a direct, active way. Today we no longer parade deviants in the town square or expose them to the carnival atmosphere of Tyburn, but it is interesting to note that the "reform" which brought about this change in penal policy coincided almost precisely with the development of newspapers as media of public information. Perhaps this is no more than an accident of history, but it is nevertheless true that newspapers (and now radio and television) offer their readers the same kind of entertainment once supplied by public hangings or the use of stocks and pillories. An enormous amount of modern "news" is devoted to reports about deviant behavior and its punishment: indeed the largest circulation newspaper in the United States prints very little else. Yet how do we explain what makes these items "newsworthy" or why they command the great attention they do? Perhaps they satisfy a number of psychological perversities among the mass audience, as commentators sometimes point out, but at the same time they constitute our main source of information about the normative contours of society. In a figurative sense, at least, morality and immorality meet at the public scaffold, and it is during this meeting that the community declares where the line between them should be drawn.

People who gather together into communities need to be able to describe and anticipate those areas of experience which lie outside the immediate compass of the group—the unseen dangers which in any culture and in any age seem to threaten its security. Traditional folklore depicting demons, devils, witches, and evil spirits, may be one way to give form to these otherwise formless dangers, but the visible deviant is another kind of reminder. As a trespasser against the group norms, he represents those forces which lie outside the group's boundaries: he informs us, as it were, what evil looks like, what shapes the devil can assume. And in doing so, he shows us the difference between the inside of the group and the outside. It may well be that without this ongoing drama at the outer edges of group space the community would have no inner sense of identity and cohesion, no sense of the contrasts which set it off as a special place in the larger world.

Thus deviance cannot be dismissed simply as behavior which *disrupts* stability in society but may itself be, in controlled quantities, an important condition for *preserving* stability.

This raises a delicate theoretical issue. If we grant that deviant forms of behavior are often beneficial to society in general, can we then assume that societies are organized in such a way as to promote this resource? Can we assume, in other words, that forces operate within the social order to recruit deviant actors and commit them to deviant forms of activity? Sociology has not yet developed a conceptual language in which this sort of question can be discussed with any ease, but one observation can be made which gives the question an interesting perspective— namely, that deviant activities often seem to derive support from the very agencies designed to suppress them. Indeed, the institutions devised by society for discouraging deviant behavior are often so poorly equipped for that task that we might well ask why this is considered their "real" function at all.

It is by now a thoroughly familiar argument that many of the institutions built to inhibit deviation actually operate in such a way as to perpetuate it. For one thing, prisons, hospitals, and similar agencies of control provide aid and shelter to large numbers of deviant persons, sometimes enhancing their survival chances in the world as a whole. But beyond this, such institutions gather marginal people into tightly segregated groups, give them an opportunity to teach one another the skills and attitudes of a deviant career, and often provoke them into employing these skills by reinforcing their sense of alienation from the rest of society. It should be pointed out, furthermore, that this process is found not only in the institutions which actually confine the deviant, but throughout the general community as well.

The community's decision to bring deviant sanctions against an individual is not a simple act of censure. It is a sharp rite of transition, at once moving him out of his normal position in society and transferring him into a distinct deviant role. The ceremonies which accomplish this change of status ordinarily have three related phases. They provide a formal *confrontation* between the deviant suspect and representatives of his community (as in the criminal trial or psychiatric case conference); they announce some *judgment* about the nature of his deviancy (a verdict or diagnosis, for example); and they perform an act of social *placement*, assigning him to a special role (like that of prisoner or patient) which redefines his position in society. These ceremonies tend to be events of wide public interest and usually take place in a dramatic, ritualized setting. Perhaps the most obvious example of a commitment ceremony is the criminal trial, with its elaborate formality and ritual pageantry, but more modest equivalents can be found everywhere that procedures are set up to judge whether someone is deviant or not.

Now an important feature of these ceremonies in our own culture is that they are almost irreversible. Most provisional roles conferred by society—like those of the student or conscripted soldier, for example— include some kind of terminal ceremony to mark the individual's movement back out of the role once its temporary advantages have been exhausted. But the roles allotted to the deviant seldom make allowance for this type of passage. He is ushered into the deviant position by a decisive and often dramatic ceremony yet is retired from it with hardly a word of public notice. And as a result the deviant often returns home with no proper license to resume a normal life in the community. Nothing has happened to cancel out the stigmas imposed upon him by earlier commitment ceremonies; from a formal point of view, the original verdict or diagnosis is still in effect. It should not be surprising, then, that the members of the community seem reluctant to accept the returning deviant on an entirely equal footing. In a very real sense, they do not know who he is.

A circularity is thus set into motion which has all the earmarks of a "self-fulfilling prophecy," to use Merton's fine phrase. On the one hand, it seems obvious that the community's reluctance to accept the deviant back helps reduce whatever chance he might otherwise have for a successful readjustment. Yet on the other hand, everyday experience seems to show that this reluctance is entirely reasonable, for it is a well-known and highly publicized fact that large numbers of ex-convicts return to criminal activity and that many discharged mental patients suffer later breakdowns. The common assumption that deviants are not often cured or reformed, then, may be based on a faulty premise, but this assumption is stated so frequently and with such conviction that it often creates the facts which later "prove" it to be correct. If the returning deviant has to face the community's apprehensions often enough, it is understandable that he too may begin to wonder whether he has graduated from the deviant role—and respond to the uncertainty by resuming deviant activity. In some respects, this may be the only way for the individual and his community to agree as to what kind of person he really is, for it often happens that the community is able to perceive his "true colors" only when he lapses momentarily into some form of deviant performance.

Moreover, this prophecy is found in the official policies of even the most advanced agencies of control. Police departments could not operate with any real effectiveness if they did not regard ex-convicts as an almost permanent population of offenders, a pool from which to draw suspects; and psychiatric hospitals could not do a responsible job in the community if they were not alert to the fact that ex-patients are highly susceptible to relapse. Thus the prophecy gains currency at many levels within the social order, not only in the poorly informed opinions of the community at large but in the best informed theories of most control agencies as well.

In one form or another, this problem has been known in Western culture for many hundreds of years, and the single fact that this is so becomes a highly significant one for sociology. If the culture has supported a steady flow of deviant behavior throughout long periods of historical evolution, then the rules which apply to any form of functionalist thinking would suggest that strong forces must be at work to keep this flow intact—and this because it contributes in some important way to the survival of the system as a whole. This may not be reason enough to assert that deviant behavior is "functional," in any of the many senses of that term, but it should make us wary of the assumption that human communities are organized in such a way as to prevent deviance from occurring.

This in turn might suggest that our present models of society, with their emphasis on the harmony and equilibrium of social life, do a one-sided job of representing the situation. Perhaps two different and often competing currents are found in any well-functioning system: those forces which promote a high overall degree of conformity among its members, and those forces which encourage some degree of diversity so that actors can be deployed throughout social space to patrol the system's boundaries. These different gravitational pulls in the social system set up a constant tension of opposites, outlining the area within which human life, with all its contradiction and variety, takes place. Perhaps this is what Aldous Huxley had in mind when he wrote:

> Now tidiness is undeniably good—but a good of which it is easily possible to have too much and at too high a price. . . . The good life can only be lived in a society in which tidiness is preached and practised, but not too fanatically, and where efficiency is always haloed, as it were, by a tolerated margin of mess.

These brief remarks are no more than a prelude to further thinking and research, and in the remaining paragraphs we will try to indicate some of the directions this line of reasoning might take.

In the first place, this paper has indirectly addressed itself to one of the oldest problems in sociology. It is all very well for an investigator to conclude that something called a "system" has certain "requirements" in respect to its participants, but the major problem for research is to ask how these needs are imposed upon the people who eventually satisfy them. Ordinarily, the fact that deviant behavior is not evenly distributed throughout the social structure is explained by declaring that something called "anomie" or "disorganization" prevails at certain sensitive points. Deviance leaks out through defects in the social structure; it occurs when the system *fails* to impose its needs on human actors. But if we consider the possibility that even the best organized collectivity needs to produce occasional episodes of deviation for the sake of its own stability, we are engaged in quite another order of inquiry. Perhaps the coherence of some social groupings is maintained only when a few juvenile offenders are enlisted to balance the conformity of an adult majority; perhaps communities can retain a sense of their own territorial identity only if they keep up an ongoing dialogue with deviants who mark and publicize the outer limits of group space; perhaps some families can remain intact only if one of its members becomes a visible deviant to serve as a focus for the rest. If these suppositions prove useful, we should try to learn how a social system appoints certain of its members to deviant roles and how it encourages them to spend a period of service testing the group's boundaries. This is not to suggest that a system necessarily creates the crises which impel people into deviant activity but that it deploys these resources in a patterned, organized way.

In the second place, it is evident that cultures vary in the way they regulate deviant traffic moving back and forth from their outer boundaries. We might begin with the observation, for example, that many features of the traffic pattern in our own culture seem to have a marked Puritan cast: a defined portion of the population, largely drawn from young adult groups and from the lower economic classes, is stabilized in deviant roles and often expected to remain there indefinitely. The logic which prevails in many of our formal agencies of control and in the public attitudes which sustain them sometimes seems to echo earlier Puritan theories about predestination, reprobation, and the nature of sin. Be this as it may, different traffic patterns are found in other parts of the world which offer an interesting contrast. There are societies in which deviance is considered a natural mode of behavior for the young, a pursuit which they are expected to abandon once they move through defined ceremonies into adulthood. There are societies which give license to large groups of people to engage in deviant behavior during certain seasons or on certain days of the year. And there are societies which form special groups whose stated business is to act in ways contrary to the normal expectations of the culture. Each of these patterns regulates deviant traffic differently, yet each of them provides some institutional means for a person to give up a deviant career without any kind of permanent stigma. In other of these cases, the person's momentary commitment to deviant styles of behavior is easily reversed—when the group promotes him to manhood, declares a period of festival to be over, or permits him to give up the insignia which marked his membership in a band of "contraries." Perhaps the most interesting problem here from the point of view of pure research is to see whether these various patterns are functionally equivalent in any meaningful way. Perhaps the most interesting problem for those of us who lean over into the applied areas of the field, however, is to ask whether we have anything to learn from those cultures which permit reentry into normal social life for persons who have spent a period of time in the deviant ranks and no longer have any special need to remain there.

2. STIGMA AND SOCIAL IDENTITY

ERVING GOFFMAN

From Erving Goffman, Stigma: Notes on the Management of Spoiled Identity, *pp. 1-19,* © *1963. Reprinted by permission of Prentice-Hall, Inc., Englewood Cliffs, New Jersey. Erving Goffman, Professor of Sociology and Anthropology at the University of Pennsylvania, has tried throughout his career to develop a rich and subtle microsociological theory of face-to-face interaction. In his work he is always simultaneously concerned with the taken-for-granted culture individuals carry with them into interactions (by which they give meaning to what goes on there) and the developing process of social exchange within a situation where individuals simultaneously seek their own ends and accommodate themselves to face-to-face reality. His books include* The Presentation of Self in Everyday Life *(Doubleday-Anchor, 1959),* Encounters: Two Studies in the Sociology of Interaction *(Bobbs-Merrill, 1961),* Behavior in Public Places *(Free Press, 1963),* Interaction Ritual *(Double-day, 1967),* Relations in Public *(Basic Books, 1971). One other book of particular interest to students of deviant behavior is* Asylums *(Doubleday, 1961), which analyzes the "moral career" of the mental patient as he is eased out of ordinary society and confined to a mental hospital.*

■ We saw in the first selection how society organizes itself to make use of deviance as a resource. Here Goffman discusses the processes by which "normals" and "deviants" assume their respective roles, protect or expose themselves, and come to terms with their situations. In so doing they all start from the central cultural reality that individuals in any society maintain definitions of normal social behavior and conceptions of undesirable departures from the to-be-expected. Goffman shows how stigmatizing processes operate at both the trivial and the tragic level of human relations, how ultimately "normal" and "stigmatized" identities are not complete but only temporary roles and partial identities, so that each of us is in some sense deviant and in other senses normal and hence intimately acquainted with both kinds of social position. It is from the building blocks of stigmatization in intimate encounters that the larger and more permanent consequences of deviance are constructed.

An evaluation of the sociology of deviance that is quite useful and extends Goffman's analysis is in John Lofland, *Deviance and Identity* (Prentice-Hall, 1969). A classic book on stereotyping and prejudice, from which Goffman draws to some extent, is Gordon W. Allport, *The Nature of Prejudice* (Doubleday-Anchor, 1958). Anselm L. Strauss has fully developed the concept of social identity and

its role in interaction processes In *Mirrors and Masks: Research for Identity* (Free Press, 1959). A series of experimental social psychological studies of deviance that touch on many of these ideas is Jonathan L. Freedman and Anthony N. Doob, *Deviancy: The Psychology of Being Different* (Academic Press, 1968). Irving L. Horowitz and Martin Liebowitz develop the idea of a merging of social deviance and political marginality in "Social Deviance and Political Marginality: Toward a Redefinition of the Relation Between Sociology and Politics," *Social Problems* 15 (Winter 1968): 286-96. For an excellent discussion of physical disability as a form of social deviance see Eliot Friedson, "Disability as Social Deviance," in *Sociology and Rehabilitation,* ed. Marvin B. Sussman (American Sociological Association, 1965). A useful discussion of the influence of the sociologist's own sympathies on his conclusions about deviant and other groups is in Howard S. Becker, "Whose Side Are We On?," *Social Problems* 14 (Winter 1967): 239-47. ■

THE GREEKS, who were apparently strong on visual aids, originated the term *stigma* to refer to bodily signs designed to expose something unusual and bad about the moral status of the signifier. The signs were cut or burnt into the body and advertised that the bearer was a slave, a criminal, or a traitor—a blemished person, ritually polluted, to be avoided, especially in public places. Later, in Christian times, two layers of metaphor were added to the term: the first referred to bodily signs of holy grace that took the form of eruptive blossoms on the skin; the second, a medical allusion to this religious allusion, referred to bodily signs of physical disorder. Today the term is widely used in something like the original literal sense, but it applied more to the disgrace itself than to the bodily evidence of it. Furthermore, shifts have occurred in the kinds of disgrace that arouse concern. Students, however, have made little effort to describe the structural preconditions of stigma, or even to provide a definition of the concept itself. It seems necessary, therefore, to try at the beginning to sketch in some very general assumptions and definitions.

PRELIMINARY CONCEPTIONS

Society establishes the means of categorizing persons and the complement of attributes felt to be ordinary and natural for members of each of these categories. Social settings establish the categories of persons likely to be encountered there. The routines of social intercourse in established settings allow us to deal with anticipated others without special attention or thought. When a stranger comes into our presence, then, first appearances are likely to enable us to anticipate his category and attributes, his "social identity"—to use a term that is better than "social status" because personal attributes such as "honesty" are involved, as well as structural ones, like "occupation."

We lean on these anticipations that we have, transforming them into normative expectations, into righteously presented demands.

Typically, we do not become aware that we have made these demands or aware of what they are until an active question arises as to whether or not they will be fulfilled. It is then that we are likely to realize that all along we had been making certain assumptions as to what the individual before us ought to be. Thus, the demands we make might better be called demands made "in effect,"

and the character we impute to the individual might better be seen as an imputation made in potential retrospect—a characterization "in effect," a *virtual social identity*. The category and attributes he could in fact be proved to possess will be called his *actual social identity*.

While the stranger is present before us, evidence can arise of his possessing an attribute that makes him different from others in the category of persons available for him to be, and of a less desirable kind—in the extreme, a person who is quite thoroughly bad or dangerous or weak. He is thus reduced in our minds from a whole and usual person to a tainted, discounted one. Such an attribute is a stigma, especially when its discrediting effect is very extensive; sometimes it is also called a failing, a shortcoming, a handicap. It constitutes a special discrepancy between virtual and actual social identity. Note that there are other types of discrepancy between virtual and actual social identity, for example the kind that causes us to reclassify an individual from one socially anticipated category to a different but equally well-anticipated one, and the kind that causes us to alter our estimation of the individual upward. Note, too, that not all undesirable attributes are at issue, but only those which are incongruous with our stereotype of what a given type of individual should be.

The term stigma, then, will be used to refer to an attribute that is deeply discrediting, but it should be seen that a language of relationships, not attributes, is really needed. An attribute that stigmatizes one type of possessor can confirm the usualness of another and therefore is neither creditable nor discreditable as a thing in itself. For example, some jobs in America cause holders without the expected college education to conceal this fact; other jobs, however, can lead the few of their holders who have a higher education to keep this a secret, lest they be marked as failures and outsiders. Similarly, a middle class boy may feel no compunction in being seen going to the library; a professional criminal, however, writes:

I can remember before now on more than one occasion, for instance, going into a public library near where I was living, and looking over my shoulder a couple of times before I actually went in just to make sure no one who knew me was standing about and seeing me do it.[1]

So, too, an individual who desires to fight for his country may conceal a physical defect, lest his claimed physical status be discredited; later the same individual, embittered and trying to get out of the army, may succeed in gaining admission to the army hospital, where he would be discredited if discovered in not really having an acute sickness. A stigma, then, is really a special kind of relationship between attribute and stereotype, although I don't propose to continue to say so, in part because there are important attributes that almost everywhere in our society are discrediting.

The term stigma and its synonyms conceal a double perspective: Does the stigmatized individual assume his differentness is known about already or is evident on the spot, or does he assume it is neither known about by those present nor immediately perceivable by them? In the first case one deals with the plight of the *discredited,* in the second with that of the *discreditable.* This is an important difference, even though a particular stigmatized individual is likely to have experience with both situations. I will begin with the situation of the discredited and move on to the discreditable but not always separate the two.

Three grossly different types of stigma may be mentioned. First there are abominations of the body—the various physical deformities. Next there are blemishes of individual character perceived as weak will, domineering or unnatural passions, treacherous and rigid beliefs, and dishonesty, these being inferred from a known record of, for example, mental disorder, imprisonment, addiction, alcoholism, homosexuality, unemployment, suicide attempts, and radical political behavior. Finally there are the tribal stigma of race, nation, and religion, these being stigma that can be transmitted through lineages and equally contaminate all members of a family. In all of these various instances of stigma, however, including those the Greeks had in mind, the same sociological features are found: an individual who might have been received easily in ordinary social intercourse possesses a trait that can obtrude itself upon attention and turn those of us whom he meets away from him, breaking the claim that his other attributes have on us. He possesses a stigma, an undesired differentness from what we had anticipated. We and those who do not depart negatively from the particular expectations at issue I shall call the *normals.*

The attitudes we normals have toward a person with a stigma, and the actions we take in regard to him, are well known, since these responses are what benevolent social action is designed to soften and ameliorate. By definition, of course, we believe the person with a stigma is not quite human. On this assumption we exercise varieties of discrimination, through which we effectively, if often unthinkingly, reduce his life chances. We construct a stigma theory, an ideology to explain his inferiority and account for the danger he represents, sometimes rationalizing an animosity based on other differences, such as those of social class. We use specific terms such as cripple, bastard, moron in our daily discourse as a source of metaphor and imagery, typically without giving thought to the original meaning. We tend to impute a wide range of imperfections on the basis of the original one, and at the same time to impute some desirable but undesired attributes, often of a supernatural cast, such as "sixth sense," or "understanding." Further, we may perceive his defensive response to his situation as a direct expression of his defect, and then see both defect and response as just retribution for something he or his parents or his tribe did, and hence a justification of the way we treat him.

Now turn from the normal to the person he is normal against. It seems generally true that members of a social category may strongly support a standard of judgment that they and others agree does not directly apply to them. Thus it is that a businessman may demand womanly behavior from females or ascetic behavior from monks, and not construe himself as someone who ought to realize either of these styles of conduct. The distinction is between realizing a norm and merely supporting it. The issue of stigma does not arise here, but only where there is some expectation on all sides that those in a given category should not only support a particular norm but also realize it.

Also, it seems possible for an individual to fail to live up to what we effectively demand of him and yet be relatively untouched by this failure; insulated by his alienation, protected by identity beliefs of his own, he feels that he is a full-fledged normal human being, and that we are the ones who are not quite human. He bears a stigma but does not seem to be impressed or repentant about doing so. This possibility is celebrated in exemplary tales about Mennonites, Gypsies, shameless scoundrels, and very orthodox Jews.

In America at present, however, separate systems of honor seem to be on the decline. The stigmatized individual tends to hold the same beliefs about identity that we do; this is a pivotal fact. His deepest feelings about what he is may be his sense of being a "normal person," a human being like anyone else, a person, therefore, who deserves a fair chance and a fair break. (Actually, however phrased, he bases his claims not on what he thinks is due *everyone* but only everyone of a selected social category into which he unquestionably fits—for example, anyone of his age, sex, profession, and so forth.) Yet he may perceive, usually quite correctly, that whatever others profess, they do not really "accept" him and are not ready to make contact with him on "equal grounds." Further, the standards he has incorporated from the wider society equip him to be intimately alive to what others see as his failing, inevitably causing him, if only for moments, to agree that he does indeed fall short of what he really ought to be. Shame becomes a central possibility, arising from the individual's perception of one of his own attributes as being a defiling thing to possess, and one he can readily see himself as not possessing. . . .

The central feature of the stigmatized individual's situation in life can now be stated. It is a question of what is often, if vaguely, called "acceptance." Those who have dealings with him fail to accord him the respect and regard which the uncontaminated aspects of his social identity have led them to anticipate extending and have led him to anticipate receiving; he echoes this denial by finding that some of his own attributes warrant it. . . .

The stigmatized individual can also attempt to correct his condition indirectly by devoting much private effort to the mastery of areas of activity ordinarily felt to be closed on incidental and physical grounds to one with his shortcoming. This is illustrated by the lame person who learns or relearns to swim, ride, play tennis, or fly an airplane; or the blind person who becomes expert at skiing and mountain climbing. Tortured learning may be associated, of course, with the tortured performance of what is learned, as when an individual, confined to a wheelchair, manages to take to the dance floor with a girl in some kind of mimicry of dancing. Finally, the person with a shameful differentness can break with what is called reality, and obstinately attempt to employ an unconventional interpretation of the character of his social identity.

The stigmatized individual is likely to use his stigma for "secondary gains," as an excuse for ill success that has come his way for other reasons.

For years the scar, harelip or misshapen nose has been looked on as a handicap, and its importance in the social and emotional adjustment is unconsciously all embracing. It is the "hook" on which the patient has hung all inadequacies, all dissatisfactions, all procrastinations and all unpleasant duties of social life, and he has come to depend on it not only as a reasonable escape from competition but as a protection from social responsibility.

When one removes this factor by surgical repair, the patient is cast adrift from the more or less acceptable emotional protection it has offered and soon he finds, to his surprise and discomfort, that life is not all smooth sailing even for those with unblemished, "ordinary" faces. He is unprepared to cope with this situation without the support of a "handicap," and he may turn to the less simple, but similar, protection of the behavior patterns of neurasthenia, hysterical conversion, hypochondriasis or the acute anxiety states.[2]

He may also see the trials he has suffered as a blessing in disguise, especially because of what it is felt that suffering can teach one about life and people.

But now, far away from the hospital experience, I can evaluate what I have learned. [A mother permanently disabled by polio writes.] For it wasn't only suffering; it was also learning through suffering. I know my awareness of people has deepened and increased, that those who are close to me can count on me to turn all my mind and heart and attention to their problems. I could not have learned *that* dashing all over a tennis court.[3]

Correspondingly, he can come to reassess the limitations of normals, as a multiple sclerotic suggests.

Both healthy minds and healthy bodies may be crippled. The fact that "normal" people can get around, can see, can hear, doesn't mean that they are seeing or hearing. They can be very blind to the things that spoil their happiness, very deaf to the pleas of others for kindness; when I think of them I do not feel any more crippled or disabled than they. Perhaps in some small way I can be the means of opening their eyes to the beauties around us: things like a warm handclasp, a voice that is anxious to cheer, a spring breeze, music to listen to, a friendly nod. These people are important to me, and I like to feel that I can help them.[4]

And a blind writer:

This would lead immediately to the thought that there are many occurrences which can diminish satisfaction in living far more effectively than blindness, and that lead would be an entirely healthy one to take. In this light, we can perceive, for instance, that some inadequacy like the inability to accept human love, which can effectively diminish satisfaction of living almost to the vanishing point, is far more a tragedy than blindness. But it is unusual for the man who suffers from such a malady even to know he has it and self-pity is, therefore, impossible for him.[5]

And a cripple:

As life went on, I learned of many, many different kinds of handicap, not only the physical ones, and I began to realize that the words of the crippled girl in the extract above [words of bitterness] could just as well have been spoken by young women who had never needed crutches, women who felt inferior and different because of ugliness, or inability to bear children, or helplessness in contacting people, or many other reasons.[6]

The responses of the normal and of the stigmatized that have been considered so far are ones which can occur over protracted periods of time and in isolation from current contact between normals and stigmatized. This book, however, is specifically concerned with the issue of "mixed contacts"—the moments when stigmatized and normal are in the same "social situation"—that is, in one another's immediate physical presence, whether in a conversation-like encounter or in the mere copresence of an unfocused gathering.

The very anticipation of such contacts can, of course, lead normals and the stigmatized to arrange life so as to avoid them. Presumably this will have larger consequences for the stigmatized, since more arranging will usually be necessary on their part.

Before her disfigurement [amputation of the distal half of her nose] Mrs. Dover, who lived with one of her two married daughters, had been an independent, warm, and friendly woman who enjoyed traveling, shopping, and visiting her many relatives. The disfigurement of her face, however, resulted in a definite alteration in her way of living. The first two or three years she seldom left her daughter's home, preferring to remain in her room or to sit in the backyard. "I was heartsick," she said; "the door had been shut on my life."[7]

Lacking the salutary feedback of daily social intercourse with others, the self-isolate can become suspicious, depressed, hostile, anxious, and bewildered. Sullivan's version may be cited.

The awareness of inferiority means that one is unable to keep out of consciousness the formulation of some chronic feeling of the worst sort of insecurity, and this means that one suffers anxiety and perhaps even something worse, if jealousy is really worse than anxiety. The fear that others can disrespect a person because of something he shows means that he is always insecure in his contact with other people; and this insecurity arises, not from mysterious and somewhat disguised sources, as a great deal of our anxiety does, but from something which he knows he cannot fix. Now that represents an almost fatal deficiency of the self-system, since the self is unable to disguise or exclude a definite formulation that reads, "I am inferior. Therefore people will dislike me and I cannot be secure with them."[8]

When normals and stigmatized do in fact

enter one another's immediate presence, especially when they there attempt to sustain a joint conversational encounter, there occurs one of the primal scenes of sociology; for, in many cases, these moments will be the ones when the causes and effects of stigma must be directly confronted by both sides.

The stigmatized individual may find that he feels unsure of how we normals will identify him and receive him. An illustration may be cited from a student of physical disability.

Uncertainty of status for the disabled person obtains over a wide range of social interactions in addition to that of employment. The blind, the ill, the deaf, the crippled can never be sure what the attitude of a new acquaintance will be, whether it will be rejective or accepting, until the contact has been made. This is exactly the position of the adolescent, the light-skinned Negro, the second generation immigrant, the socially mobile person and the woman who has entered a predominantly masculine occupation.[9]

This uncertainty arises not merely from the stigmatized individual's not knowing which of several categories he will be placed in, but also, where the placement is favorable, from his knowing that in their hearts the others may be defining him in terms of his stigma.

And I always feel this with straight people —that whenever they're being nice to me, pleasant to me, all the time really, underneath they're only assessing me as a criminal and nothing else. It's too late for me to be any different now to what I am, but I still feel this keenly, that that's their only approach, and they're quite incapable of accepting me as anything else.[10]

Thus in the stigmatized arises the sense of not knowing what the others present are "really" thinking about him.

Further, during mixed contacts, the stigmatized individual is likely to feel that he is "on," having to be self-conscious and calculating about the impression he is making, to a degree and in areas of conduct which he assumes others are not.

Also, he is likely to feel that the usual scheme of interpretation for everyday events has been undermined. His minor accomplishments, he feels, may be assessed as signs of remarkable and noteworthy capacities in the

circumstances. A professional criminal provides an illustration.

"You know, it's really amazing you should read books like this, I'm staggered I am. I should've thought you'd read paperbacked thrillers, things with lurid covers, books like that. And here you are with Claud Cockburn, Hugh Klare, Simone de Beauvoir, and Lawrence Durrell!"
You know, he didn't see this as an insulting remark at all; in fact, I think he thought he was being honest in telling me how mistaken he was. And that's exactly the sort of patronizing you get from straight people if you're a criminal. "Fancy that!" they say. "In some ways you're just like a human being!" I'm not kidding, it makes me want to choke the bleeding life out of them.[11]

A blind person provides another illustration.

His once most ordinary deeds—walking nonchalantly up the street, locating the peas on his plate, lighting a cigarette—are no longer ordinary. He becomes an unusual person. If he performs them with finesse and assurance they excite the same kind of wonderment inspired by a magician who pulls rabbits out of hats.[12]

At the same time, minor failings or incidental impropriety may, he feels, be interpreted as a direct expression of his stigmatized differentness. Ex-mental patients, for example, are sometimes afraid to engage in sharp interchanges with spouse or employer because of what a show of emotion might be taken as a sign of. Mental defectives face a similar contingency.

It also happens that if a person of low intellectual ability gets into some sort of trouble the difficulty is more or less automatically attributed to "mental defect," whereas if a person of "normal intelligence" gets into a similar difficulty, it is not regarded as symptomatic of anything in particular.[13]

A one-legged girl, recalling her experience with sports, provides other illustrations.

Whenever I fell, out swarmed the women in droves, clucking and fretting like a bunch of bereft mother hens. It was kind of them, and in retrospect I appreciate their solicitude, but at the time I resented and was greatly embarrassed by their interference. For they assumed that no routine hazard to skating—no stick or stone —upset my flying wheels. It was a foregone conclusion that *I* fell because I was a poor, helpless cripple.

Not one of them shouted with outrage, "That dangerous wild bronco threw her!"—which, God forgive, he did technically. It was like a horrible ghostly visitation of my old roller-skating days. All the good people lamented in chorus, "That poor, poor girl fell off!"[14]

When the stigmatized person's failing can be perceived by our merely directing attention (typically visual) to him—when, in short, he is a discredited, not discreditable, person—he is likely to feel that to be present among normals nakedly exposes him to invasions of privacy, experienced most pointedly perhaps when children simply stare at him. This displeasure in being exposed can be increased by the conversations strangers may feel free to strike up with him, conversations in which they express what he takes to be morbid curiosity about his condition, or in which they proffer help that he does not need or want. One might add that there are certain classic formulas for these kinds of conversations: "My dear girl, how did you get your quiggle"; "My great uncle had a quiggle, so I feel I know all about your problem"; "You know I've always said that Quiggles are good family men and look after their own poor"; "Tell me, how do you manage to bathe with a quiggle?" The implication of these overtures is that the stigmatized individual is a person who can be approached by strangers at will, providing only that they are sympathetic to the plight of persons of his kind.

Given what the stigmatized individual may well face upon entering a mixed social situation, he may anticipatorily respond by defensive cowering. This may be illustrated from an early study of some German unemployed during the Depression, the words being those of a 43-year-old mason.

How hard and humiliating it is to bear the name of an unemployed man. When I go out, I cast down my eyes because I feel myself wholly inferior. When I go along the street, it seems to me that I can't be compared with an average citizen, that everybody is pointing at me with his finger. I instinctively avoid meeting anyone. Former acquaintances and friends of better times are no longer so cordial. They greet me indifferently when we meet. They no longer offer me a cigarette and their eyes seem to say, "You are not worth it, you don't work."[15]

A crippled girl provides an illustrative analysis.

When . . . I began to walk out alone in the streets of our town . . . I found then that whenever I had to pass three or four children together on the sidewalk, if I happened to be alone, they would shout at me. . . . Sometimes they even ran after me, shouting and jeering. This was something I didn't know how to face, and it seemed as if I couldn't bear it. . . .
For awhile those encounters in the street filled me with a cold dread of all unknown children . . .
One day I suddenly realized that I had become so self-conscious and afraid of all strange children that, like animals, they knew I was afraid, so that even the mildest and most amiable of them were automatically prompted to derision by my own shrinking and dread.[16]

Instead of cowering, the stigmatized individual may attempt to approach mixed contacts with hostile bravado, but this can induce from others its own set of troublesome reciprocations. It may be added that the stigmatized person sometimes vacillates between cowering and bravado, racing from one to the other, thus demonstrating one central way in which ordinary face-to-face interaction can run wild.

I am suggesting, then, that the stigmatized individual—at least the "visibly" stigmatized one—will have special reasons for feeling that mixed social situations make for anxious unanchored interaction. But if this is so, then it is to be suspected that we normals will find these situations shaky, too. We will feel that the stigmatized individual is either too aggressive or too shamefaced, and in either case too ready to read unintended meanings into our actions. We ourselves may feel that if we show direct sympathetic concern for his condition we may be overstepping ourselves, and yet if we actually forget that he has a failing we are likely to make impossible demands of him or unthinkingly slight his fellow-sufferers. Each potential source of discomfort for him when we are with him can become something we sense he is aware of, aware that we are aware of, and even aware of our state of awareness about his awareness; the stage is then set for the infinite regress of mutual consideration that

Meadian social psychology tells us how to begin but not how to terminate.

Given what both the stigmatized and we normals introduce into mixed social situations, it is understandable that all will not go smoothly. We are likely to attempt to carry on as though in fact he wholly fitted one of the types of persons naturally available to us in the situation, whether this means treating him as someone better than we feel he might be or someone worse than we feel he probably is. If neither of these tacks is possible, then we may try to act as if he were a "nonperson," and not present at all as someone of whom ritual notice is to be taken. He, in turn, is likely to go along with these strategies, at least initially.

In consequence, attention is furtively withdrawn from its obligatory targets, and self-consciousness and "other-consciousness" occurs, expressed in the pathology of interaction —uneasiness. As described in the case of the physically handicapped:

Whether the handicap is overtly and tactlessly responded to as such or, as is more commonly the case, no explicit reference is made to it, the underlying condition of heightened, narrowed, awareness causes the interaction to be articulated too exclusively in terms of it. This, as my informants described it, is usually accompanied by one or more of the familiar signs of discomfort and stickiness: the guarded references, the common everyday words suddenly made taboo, the fixed stare elsewhere, the artificial levity, the compulsive loquaciousness, the awkward solemnity.[17]

In social situations with an individual known or perceived to have a stigma, we are likely, then, to employ categorizations that do not fit, and we and he are likely to experience uneasiness. Of course, there is often significant movement from this starting point. And since the stigmatized person is likely to be more often faced with these situations than are we, he is likely to become the more adept at managing them. . . .

NOTES

1. T. Parker and R. Allerton, *The Courage of His Convictions* (London: Hutchinson & Co., 1962), p. 109.

2. W. Y. Baker and L. H. Smith, "Facial Disfigurement and Personality," *Journal of the American Medical Association,* CXII (1939), p. 303.

3. E. Henrich and L. Kriegel, eds., *Experiments in Survival* (New York: Association for the Aid of Crippled Children, 1961), p. 19.

4. Ibid., p. 35.

5. H. Chevigny, *My Eyes Have a Cold Nose* (New Haven, Conn.: Yale University Press, paperbound, 1962), p. 154.

6. F. Carling, *And Yet We Are Human* (London: Chatto & Windus, 1962), pp. 23-24.

7.

8. H. S. Perry, M. L. Gawel, and M. Gibbon, eds., *Clinical Studies in Psychiatry* (New York: W. W. Norton & Company, 1956), p. 145.

9. R. Barker, "The Social Psychology of Physical Disability," *Journal of Social Issues,* IV (1948), p. 33.

10. Parker and Allerton, p. 111.

11. Ibid.

12. Chevigny, p. 140.

13. L. A. Dexter, "A Social Theory of Mental Deficiency," *American Journal of Mental Deficiency,* LXII (1958), p. 923.

14. L. Baker, *Out on a Limb* (New York: McGraw-Hill Book Company, 1946), p. 73.

15. S. Zawadski and P. Lazarsfeld, "The Psychological Consequences of Unemployment," *Journal of Social Psychology,* VI (1935), p. 239.

16. K. B. Hathaway, *The Little Locksmith* (New York: Coward-McCann, 1943), pp. 155-157.

17. F. Davis, "Deviance Disavowal: The Management of Strained Interaction by the Visibly Handicapped," *Social Problems,* IX (1961), p. 123.

3. THE PLACE OF FORCE IN HUMAN SOCIETY

WILLIAM J. GOODE

Reprinted from American Sociological Review 37 *(October 1972): 507-18. William J. Goode is Professor of Sociology at Columbia University. He has made theoretical and substantive contributions to a wide range of sociological subjects. He is known best for his comparative work on family behavior, represented by a series of articles on illegitimacy, and by his books,* World Revolution and Family Patterns *(Free Press, 1963) and* After Divorce *(Free Press, 1966).*

■ In Selection 1 Erikson observed that to stay alive norms must be enforced, at least periodically. In this selection Goode seeks to rectify a curious fact about sociological theory: although it is replete with discussions of power, authority, social conflict, and the like, it contains little in the way of a general theory of the role of force in human relationships. Goode argues that force is one of the four great social control systems, along with prestige, wealth, and love. Each system is part of the effort to control deviant behavior and to dramatize transgressions. Each of the four also produces its own distinctive kind of deviance, because societies have expectations about the amounts and appropriate expressions of these resources. Of all the sanctions brought to bear on deviant behavior, and of all the ways of symbolizing and dramatizing transgression and punishment, systems of force loom the largest. Therefore, an understanding of how society manages force, how it assembles, distributes, and brings to bear resources of force, is crucial to understanding processes of deviance.

Goode also has developed the theoretical implications of love as a social control system in "The Theoretical Importance of Love," *American Sociological Review* 24 (February 1959): 30-47; and he has discussed patterns of violence in "Violence Between Intimates," in *Crimes of Violence,* ed. D. J. Mulvihill and M. Tumin (Government Printing Office, 1970). Another theory of the role of power and force is in Talcott Parsons, "Some Reflections on the Place of Force in Social Process," in *Sociological Theory and Modern Societies* (Free Press, 1967). Still other important discussions of this subject include E. V. Walter, *Terror and Resistance* (Oxford University Press, 1969); and

Earling E. Bow and Russell M. Church, eds., *Punishment* (Appleton-Century-Crofts, 1968). A general theory of sanctions regarded as social exchanges is found in George C. Homans, *Social Behavior: Its Elementary Forms* (Harcourt-Brace, 1961). ■

HUMAN BEINGS learn early that almost everything they want can be obtained only through each other's cooperation, whether their need or goal is a mother's breast or a love potion, a slave uprising or a new colony, a Nobel Prize or protection against a bullying policeman. Everyone learns, consciously or not, accurately or not, various ways of controlling others for one's own ends. Few people spend much time calculating how to control others, but everyone does so part of the time.

Whatever people do, for whatever goals, will be evaluated by others, who will become thereby more or less willing to cooperate, more or less likely to resist, more or less likely to continue in the relationship. We all interact with others, engage in a flow of transactions with others; and whatever we do has some effect on others, to our advantage or not, in conformity with our wishes or not, and whether or not we will it so.

Consequently, however else we might classify the wide range of human acts, we can also view them as samples of social control processes—i.e., the ways by which people shape the flow of each other's behavior. Almost all can be grouped into a small number of types of social control forces. One of these is force and force-threat, which I shall henceforth simply call "force"; when I mean only "overt force," I shall so label it.

The use of force—and I repeat, I mean by this term both force-threat and overt force—is as ubiquitous as the preachments against it. Whatever else social systems are, they are also force systems. Force constitutes one of the major foundations of all social structures. The processes by which the command of force is expended, exchanged, accumulated, or lost, are universal in social interaction, because force is one of the fundamental resources people and groups need to elicit cooperation, help, and conformity from one another.

Force constitutes one of the four great social control systems in all societies. For two millennia, social analysts have given much attention to three of these—which they have variously termed force, prestige, and wealth—because these underlie all stratification systems. The fourth, which may be called love, friendship, or personal attraction, has less often appeared in grand theory, more often being viewed as an accidental or intrusive set of forces; and no one has ascertained whether its impact is as systematic as the other three.

Every person and group participates in these control systems, gaining or losing in one or more, investing wisely or foolishly, with few or great results. Over time, some accumulate far more resources and are better able to obtain whatever pleasures and comforts, dignities and treasures may be available. Both individuals and groups, families and corporations, social strata and nations may enjoy this fate; although of course most do not.

It is necessary to separate each of these four systems from the other. Force, prestige, wealth, and love should not be confused under the slippery term *power* because they differ both concretely and theoretically. That they differ concretely is proved by our own acts in the course of the day: in order to persuade others to do something, we may here decide to threaten a lawsuit and there praise another for a fine performance; or in

still another situation simply offer money. Theoretical analysis will reveal many parallel patterns partly because at the psychological level these factors are experienced as rewards and punishments. A full exposition of their differences would take us far afield, but let me note such theoretically important differences as the following.

1. It is possible to expand almost indefinitely the number of one's economic customers as well as the number of people one rules by force; but one cannot do so for friendship and love.

2. One can make explicit contracts in economic exchanges, enforceable by law, and explicit contracts or exchanges to gain a command of force, often not enforceable by law; but one cannot by contract obtain another's love or friendship, respect or esteem.

3. One can retire from production for the economic market, but one's actions continue to be evaluated by prestige criteria as long as one lives.

4. A social organization that relies on overt force (e.g., a slave system, a prison) differs substantially from one that relies on affection or esteem, with reference to such characteristics as its members' normative commitment to collective goals, their belief that the system is just, their willingness to leave the organization, how well they work if not supervised, and so on.

5. Overt force can expropriate whatever wealth is available, but it cannot extort love; for we cannot love another or cause another to love us by willing it.

6. Overt force can command the external trappings of honor and deference, encomiastic speeches, and the kowtows and obeisances of even unwilling subjects; but it cannot by fiat elicit respect in those subjects' minds.

Although these differences are not here presented systematically, and their implications are not all self-evident, they suggest that it might be theoretically profitable to examine each of these four realms or processes separately. They may well be viewed as distinct elementary processes, which in interaction shape much of our social behavior, but whose patterns and characteristics are best understood if we see them as analytically separable. They may be viewed, in fact, as crude parallels to different types of physical forces whose analysis yields relationships that parallel one another in some ways, forces that cannot yet, even in that most advanced of fields, be analyzed by an integrated field theory.

The systematic study of force as a distinct phenomenon or set of processes has been singularly neglected in the history of social thought, partly because its use has been viewed as deplorable, and therefore occurring mainly in unusual, deviant, criminal, or evil circumstances.

Philosophers and rulers have joined in deploring force, the former because they correctly perceived that its use implies an unjust demand, the latter because they were convinced that their just reign required no force. After all, subjects happy with their government obey because they want to do so. Doubtless, rulers have also guessed that subjects who are persuaded violence is wrong are easier to command.

Against the view that political or social systems do not rest on force except in deviant circumstances is a recurring theme, largely expressed (though not often publicly) by dissidents, women, slaves, children, and the lower orders generally, that force is the foundation of rule. This may seem to be a self-serving view, since they are precisely the most likely victims of force and force-threat. Nevertheless, since neither of these opposing views has been investigated systematically, we should now examine both.

We sociologists have neglected such an examination because we share a long humanistic tradition whose biases deny the ultimate importance of force. We have been taught to believe in man's unconquerable soul, his often mute but always staunch resistance to tyranny. We can observe over the panorama of the past five hundred years

in Western nations, and more recently in others, the slow advance of human rights and freedom against monarchy and imperialism, dictatorship and despotism, propaganda and news control. Consequently, we continue to feel, whatever the evidence before our eyes, that somehow human beings do resist force and force-threat over time, and that man's will to freedom not only endures but also prevails.

In addition, as sociologists and culturologists, we harbor the bias that force will have little effect on a cultural or social system, that organic life somehow resists or survives the rude threats of a mortar gun, or the blazing pain of napalm. After all, the Chinese swallowed their Mongol and Manchu rulers, the Indonesians pushed out the Dutch, the Indians did not become English, and so on.

However, that sanguine view of history should not be allowed to obscure other facts. For example, Rome did impose its cultural patterns on a wide area; indeed, we are all molded to some degree by Roman conquests. The Islamic conquest not only shaped the Arab world, but its heritage also spread far beyond to Spain and Portugal in the West and Indonesia in the East. The Iberian conquerors of the New World imposed their culture and social system on that area, undermining or destroying most of the native cultures encountered along the way. Both they and the Anglo invaders of the New World imposed their culture and social system on the slaves they imported from Africa.

But leaving aside such grand examples of cultural clash, that sanguine view overlooks the cruel fact that a human being lives but a short time, while such conquests and tyrannies may last for centuries. To say that they are ineffective because they will ultimately fail to impose their social and cultural systems ignores the truth that temporarily they do so; and "temporarily" may well outlast the life of an individual.

Sociologists have always agreed that all societies must be able to command enough force to kill or restrain those who cannot be controlled by other means. For anyone can at least be stopped by overt force from doing something. However, sociologists have mainly focused, for the past half-century, on the other means of control. They have explored mainly the impact of the normative order, explaining social action by reference to values and value consensus. They have shown that people obey the rules of the society, group, or family because they have been socialized to believe the rules are right. For example, it is not merely unprofitable to defraud, steal, or kill; it is morally repugnant.

Sociologists have urged, correctly I think, that if people and groups acted only with a rational view to their personal profit and with no inner normative controls, then group structures, goals, and controls would be unsupported and a war of all against all would result.

On the other hand, as I and others have noted, this essentially Lintonian view is partly incorrect, since the observable consensus and normative commitment are not total enough to create the necessary social controls. Some opinion is set against almost any normative rule; people alter their faith when they change social positions; beliefs vary among social strata; and so on. Such observations suggest, at a minimum, that if social control systems are to succeed they require far more support than internal moral commitment can yield. That support may come from gains and losses in wealth, or from affection or force, but surely not alone from normative commitment.

With that bias toward moral commitment as an explanation, sociologists have felt, along with most social analysts, that force is a weak reed to lean on, and that no regime or society can rest on force alone. Indeed it cannot; but neither must it do so. None ever need try; rulers and conquerors, like teachers and husbands, army officers and employers, always command other resources. We have rejected an empty claim. On the other hand, no sensible person would argue that any society, organization, or group has tried to operate without that most potent weapon.

If this is properly the territory of our sister discipline, political science, they have not bothered to cultivate it; and we shall not be usurpers. Indeed, force has been analyzed mainly as overt force, in criminal violence or the repression of criminal violence, or in war and war games of various kinds.

Much more important, force processes may be so general that we can view their analysis as a distinct task, like that of market processes in economics. That is, they are to be observed or guessed at in all social systems and pervade all continuing social relations to some degree. Thus, no existing intellectual field can claim any better right to study them than any other.

We shall understand these phenomena more clearly if we stop thinking of them as occurring only in despotisms and tyrannies, among criminals, or in war, and instead begin to observe that in any civil society—e.g., England and Scandinavia—everyone is subject to force. All are engaged in it daily, not alone as victims but as perpetrators as well. Everyone controls some force and offers some force-threat to others. We are all potentially dangerous to one another. Once we see that, and the pervasiveness of such dynamics in our social life, we shall be better able to observe their regularities and to measure their effects.

In this view, and by this definition, force is very human, not simply an animal heritage to be eventually overcome. Indeed, force exhibits a very different structure in other animal societies, even among predators, whose killing propensities seem so like our own. The differences can be briefly summarized.

1. Within such societies, animals will not fight to the death, and will not kill when they have vanquished another.

2. The leader or dominant animal does not give orders to subordinates to use force on recalcitrant members.

3. Members do not organize to support or to kill leaders.

4. Weaker animals cannot kill dominant animals.

Given these structural differences, it seems plausible to view human force systems as worthy of study in their own right, not as a leftover from our animal past, or processes that occur when a social system or subsystem has broken down into a jungle chaos.

CONCEPTS AND MEASUREMENT

Not all the conceptual and methodological problems of this challenging proposal can be adequately discussed here; and some central ones cannot, I believe, be solved in this decade. To touch on a few will, however, clarify the theoretical orientation I urge.

As a first step in conceptual clarification I suggest eliminating the term *power* from sociological analyses for the next decade. We have too long avoided dealing seriously with force by shoving it under that grand label. The term is both too broad and too narrow, even in its most popular, Weberian definition: i.e., one has power to the degree that one can impose his will even against resistance. It is too narrow, because even if one *can* impose one's will, the other person or group commands power, too. As Machiavelli wisely remarked over four centuries ago, even a victory is not absolute.

It is too broad because one can impose one's will through all sorts of resources, from bribery or love to the thrust of an army corps. A child may impose its will by a smile, or a respected colleague by a lifted eyebrow.

Still more important, because this allusive, adumbrative label conveys a penumbra of domination by bayonets and coercion, we feel we have dealt with force and force-threat without examining the processes by which, for example, money can purchase a force-threat, or civil societies or economic or family systems may at various points be supported by force.

For similar reasons, we should no longer use the terms *forced compliance* or *coercion* to mean overt or physical force. We feel coerced or forced to comply when we do not wish to do something but feel the other person can make our resistance too costly to bear. Such a lopsided bargaining situation can occur when we are frightened by the anger of our beloved or the possible contempt of our friend, and not alone when we face a hoodlum's knife or a despot's gun.

On the other hand, we may not feel coerced even when we do confront overt force, simply because we believe we can overcome it, or because we are willing to pay that price. Thus, it is not overt force that defines a situation of coercion but our desire not to obey the command, and our perception that the cost of resistance is too high, whether in physical punishment, the loss of esteem, money, or affection.

Next, we should note that force is empirically and definitionally not limited to punishment or deterrence. We can reward another by backing that person in a conflict with whatever forces we command. Force protects each individual, as, for example, various of our civil rights are, or can be, backed by a court order enforceable by a marshal, or as a wife can be protected by force against the threats of her husband. Force can persuade others to *do* something, not merely to stop doing something. Physical force and its threat can alter another's cost reward calculations, and thus move him or her toward the action we desire.

All this is true for other resources as well. Love or affection can turn into hate. A salary can be reduced or raised, and profit turned into loss. One can be hired or fired. We can be esteemed for our action, or denigrated. We can experience force, then, as punishment or reward, as we do other important resources that shape our behavior. It is a philosophical bias, not empirical observation, that views force as only punishment and deterrence.

The problem of observation in this realm is acute, because the influence of force is shown precisely by the difficulty of observing it in ordinary civil life. It is not visible because it has been effective. Indeed, a fruitful working hypothesis about social and biological life is that some forces are not less powerful for being less visible, not unimportant because they are called into play less often; some phenomena are striking for their absence. With reference to such factors, we can guess that if they are rare, or rarely visible, it is because other complex and efficacious processes reduce their frequency of appearance, or change them into less threatening forms. We live in a sea of deadly germs, yet remain healthy; our heart rarely fails to adjust to extreme variations in demand for blood flow; killer animals almost never kill members of their own species when they fight. In these and similar cases, it is profitable to ask why an apparently likely outcome does not occur frequently.

In social life, all of us have felt murderous rages, but few of us have murdered. I have previously argued that love is kept under control, is prevented from appearing as often or as devastatingly as it might by a wide range of social patterns. We might be fooled into supposing that the imperious drive of sex is weak, since no society we know was a hotbed of fleshly pleasure; but we know, from our own lives, that numerous controls bar the creation of so happy a state.

Following this working guess, I assert that the importance of force and force-threat in human behavior is richly demonstrated by the rarity of its use. Living as we do in protected environments, we rarely see anyone manhandled, or hear an overt threat—except from fellow drivers. Nevertheless, every social system is a force system. The two statements do not make a paradox, because every social system contains mechanisms, processes, and patterns whose result and often intention is to prevent the outbreak of overt force. Even in systems with a high overt force component, such as a prison, such outbreaks are infrequent.

Thus a U.S. businessman does not ship arms to a belligerent country because he knows they will be confiscated. Nor does a divorced husband remove his children from the custody of his wife. He knows that she could haul him into court. Indeed, the use of physical force betokens a failure of the force-control processes.

Partly for that reason, we cannot solve our methodological problem by gathering a sample of violent episodes on a frontier. The problem is not merely that cases of overt physical force are relatively rare. It is rather that short of actual killing or jailing, *most cases of even overt force* are instances of force-threat, promises of more to come. In few robberies is the victim physically subdued. Instead, he is threatened. If a bullying policeman shoves a citizen, the latter correctly perceives the action less as force than as a threat of more force, a possible escalation to death. In a country with a settled electoral and judicial tradition, a vote count almost always signals that the loser must step down, under a threat of overt force rarely expressed; and a court order to vacate the office is a command backed by overt force. So well is this understood that in the United States, rife at times with corruption and often violent in its reactions, no defeated major officeholder, with whatever police forces at his or her command, has ever denied his or her office to the winner of an election.

The cases of the businessman who obeys government regulations, the husband who accepts a custody arrangement, or the defeated officeholder who vacates his or her office, sharpen the observational problem, while showing how overt force shades into force-threat, and most often is felt as a threat of more force. In instances of force *not* immediate and physical, the individual may be unaware that he or she has been moved by such a threat and in fact not even calculate how far he or she could resist without overt force being applied. Much force appears to people not as a threat of violence but simply the rules of the game, the obvious reality of the cosmos, to which one must bow unthinkingly.

Moreover, where the use of overt force is almost certain, those who conform may do so for other reasons. For example, we do not walk into an office of General Motors and begin using an idle calculating machine because we believe it is morally wrong, or even because we would be quickly ejected, but more immediately and consciously because our friends would consider us foolish or bizarre. Or, again, we may refuse to race on the highway, saying we could be carted off to a village jail, when in fact we are much more fearful of a wreck.

The methodological problem is, in short, how to measure the variance accounted for by force and force-threat, in an action or set of actions in which the participant may not have an accurate idea of its impact, and may not have considered force a possibility; or, if aware, may be unwilling to confess it.

But though I do not yet see how such problems of observation and measurement can be solved at present, our theoretical explorations should not await their resolution. Rather, they are more likely to be worked out if we can offer interesting or fruitful propositions that can be tested only when those problems have been solved.

I suggest, therefore, that inquiry into the control processes of force might be worthwhile. It follows from this orientation that all highly industrialized societies are high force systems, by comparison with almost all societies that have gone before them. No dissident groups of substantial size can hide out and engage in armed resistance, set up a competing regime, or impose a radically different system on these nations. There are no earls or dukes whose armed and loyal retainers might be a threat to the social or political system.

More significant, their citizens support the social and political systems and would back them with force were they attacked by dissident groups. This is as true of Holland and Sweden, with their low homicide and crime rates and low frequency of army attacks against civilians, as it is of the United States, with its somewhat higher rates.

By contrast, some Latin-American countries, such as Bolivia and Colombia, whose governments over the past decade have had to muster soldiers to protect themselves against rebels or competing subgovernments, would be placed much lower on this scale. Some African countries with a high use of overt governmental force, and some countries in the east of India would fall still lower on such a scale. Most bloody despotisms of the past would rank only modestly high on this scale, supported as they were by only a palace guard and their own soldiers. A neat demonstration of the low position of some Latin-American countries is the fact that only rarely have the masses risen in armed support of an overthrown regime.

In general, the widespread use of physical force by the regime or dominant groups in a society is probably negatively correlated with that country's position on the scale of the force it commands, because the application of overt force tells us that many people in the society oppose the political or social system and are unwilling to back it by force—i.e., by informal controls over dissidents.

However, the negative correlation may be a modest one because: (1) dominant groups are not necessarily wise and may use more or less than the optimum amount of physical force for the control they seek, just as parents may use more or less force on their children than would be most effective or rational (perhaps, for historical reasons, rulers of contemporary Russia use more overt force than necessary); (2) leaders may command much physical force and force-threat yet use their overt force to increase still more control; and (3) rulers may, knowing their support or force resources are modest, wisely accept the situation and refuse to risk their positions by embarking on a course of armed repression. Despite these qualifications, the general negative correlation between a regime's command of force and use of physical force seems evident.

Since this view insists that everyone commands some force, if only because others may protect him or her, and everyone is potentially a threat or a support, we need ask not only how much force the regime or the dominant strata enjoys but also how much counterforce the citizenry can muster. We may imagine a low force regime with a high force citizenry (although I believe this unlikely), or a high force regime with a high-force citizenry. Let us consider the latter.

Although there is some truth in Casanova's comment (which he attributed to a Jesuit) that no nation suffers heavy taxation where its citizenry is armed, and in Machiavelli's comment that a wise man who becomes ruler of a city will arm its citizens to gain their support in exchange for the trust and respect he has thus given, there is little truth in the parallel insight that an armed citizenry is free, or will not tolerate despots.

Harsh and even terrorist rulers have abounded in West and East African kingdoms where almost every adult male is a warrior. The Germans were both free and armed when they clashed with Rome, if Tacitus reported correctly; but the Asiatic steppes and the Islamic countries from the Punjab westerly to Africa have been both armed and victims of autocrats for a thousand years of recorded history. Switzerland and Iceland were both armed and free; but during much of Latin America's chaotic political and social life its populace has been armed and unfree.

All this follows from our theoretical conception; for a society's total force is not a summation of the individual capacity to kill but a function of the social organization of force. Consequently, armed but unorganized citizens may be, and indeed usually are, helpless before the organized might of a tyrant's army and police, even when these are few in number.

The force of a free citizenry is not, then, determined by how many guns they possess but by their collective determination to resist. This in turn is primarily a function of their faith that their fellow human beings will not let them stand alone against the physical force of a ruler but will, rather, risk individual injury to prevent collective injury. Thus, in ranking a citizenry

by the force it commands, the question is not so much whether it owns more guns than the government but whether its members can count on each other for support against encroachments on their freedom. That is the measure of its force. With that capacity, guns can be obtained; without it, guns have historically been of little use.

Thus, we can argue that political and social systems like the Scandinavian and Anglo countries, Iceland, Switzerland, or Holland do command high force since they would be militarily supported by their citizenry against any physical force that sought to impose radical changes against their will, and because technically they command a vast quantity of military and police equipment. But they are also systems in which the citizens themselves command high force, although in most the homicide and crime rates, and the amount of violence used by citizens and the government is low.

The citizens of such countries can and do reject leaders, in the strict sense that they can and do vote them out, and their verdict is backed by force. Again, the verdict is not settled by armed conflict, because those concerned are certain of the outcome.

Our own country falls into this category too, but since some will reject this description, let me be more specific. In face of the cynicism or despair about the trend of our time, feelings which I often share, I assert that: (1) certainly in this country we have suffered encroachments on our liberties over the past three years; (2) but, over a longer span, perhaps a generation or more, our freedoms have been strengthened; (3) whether we look at the past few years or the past generation, the world as a whole has witnessed an expansion of civil freedoms and rights unparalleled throughout history; (4) in any event, as my analysis shows, freedom is never absolute, to be acquired once and for all. Precisely because it is a relationship, based on collective trust and buttressed by one's fellow citizens' willingness to back it with force, it varies over time, forever being lost or regenerated. What we have lost in the United States in the past three years we shall regain.

The foregoing analysis contains several concrete and theoretical hypotheses, and leads to a technical formulation, which I shall briefly expound. First, Americans will in fact resist with overt force large encroachments on their freedom, and this fact will weigh heavily in the calculations of those who might wish to embark on a program of repression.

Second, whether a businessman, a potential criminal, a pupil, a colony, will risk death, jail, or other forms of physical violence—in short, will violate a rule or refuse to accept social control—is not a function alone of the firepower or physical strength of such controls and of the visibility of the dereliction but of whether in either side's evaluations the cost of submission outweighs the threat of force. In short, how much are the alternative actions worth as goals? And their worth is a function of their values.

In older terminology, military analysts spoke of "the will to battle," an imponderable that has more than once outweighed firepower. In less disciplined form, this differential evaluation of submission can appear as a culture's joy in violence, a theme observable in Plains Indian cultures, Norse sagas, the Song of Roland, and Arab conquests in the early Mohammedan period. Such an evaluation makes the threat of violence less costly and the cost of submission higher. It therefore affects the calculation of alternative costs in a wide range of control decisions, not alone those affecting liberty. . . .

In the remainder of the paper I should like to . . . present some hypotheses that focus on overt force. These are drawn from more extended analyses, but I shall try to make them as clear as I can in briefer form. That is, I will be laconic, but I hope not cryptic.

1. The less the value consensus within a group, the more efficacious is overt force, as against other resources of reward and punishment, especially prestige or friendship. On the other hand, the less the consensus, the less stable is the rule or command likely to be if the physical force exercised by a commander or ruler weakens

temporarily. Force is more useful, since the group lacks direction until it can agree on some set of goals, and it will therefore not agree on the goals set by the ruler. On the other hand, because they agree on no alternative set of goals they will show less resistance to force.

Few will back the ruler's authority if it is challenged, because they do not share his goals or values, and of course no organization of subordinates would arise to support him. On the other hand, it is less likely that subordinates can organize, since they do not have collective goals or shared values, except in their desire to kill or depose the leader. This situation has roughly characterized Latin America, where the masses were typically not united in values and could unite only to unseat a leader or simply watch while a set of opposing forces engaged in battle, participating as little as possible.

2. The greater the value discrepancy between the rulers and the ruled—note that the previous proposition simply referred to a general lack of consensus in a group—the less effort the leaders will invest in a program to socialize the ruled or to use other social control variables such as friendship, money, or prestige. Instead, they will use overt force and strong threats of it. Consequently, in a conquest it is not likely that the ruled will ever willingly be incorporated into the conqueror's system. One of the few exceptions is Rome, but note that Rome gradually extended the advantages of Roman citizenship to an ever-increasing set of groups and tribes. By contrast, even over long periods of time most conquests have failed in that the conquerors were eventually thrown out and the conquered not assimilated into their system of values.

3. The higher the level of management tasks to be accomplished, the less efficacious is a strong component of overt force. It is less efficient because it requires, relative to the output, a greater or closer supervision if the worker is unwilling; and in turn the worker is almost always unwilling if much overt force is used. There are too many

junctures and phases where slackness and sabotage are not visible, in contrast with simpler tasks. Of course, as we know, scientists can be made to work at modest task levels under threat of overt force; but I remind you that even the scientists depicted in Solzhenitzin's *The Inner Circle* were given far greater privileges than ordinary prisoners, and viewed themselves as lucky. Correspondingly, a strong component of overt force is more efficient when the task is simpler, and there is no need for long periods of nonsupervision.

The above relationship has been noted by many analysts; but we may now consider an unnoted corollary, that the greater the component of overt force, the less the managerial costs in dollars and time, even though the task must be less sophisticated. In concrete terms, 8 or 10 guards can be used to supervise the work of a hundred or more agricultural workers. Note in this connection that had the feudal lord of the manor tried to elicit maximum productivity from his serfs he would also have had to spend far more time and energy in management. He would have had to plan more, and he could not have devoted as much time to falconry, stag hunting, and other courtly pleasures.

4. Because the use of force is generally deprecated, the greater the approximation to using overt force on others, the more likely that those who do so will develop and offer moral justifications for using it. Moreover, experimentation in social psychology has reported that when observers see that an individual has suffered, or has been made the victim in an experiment, they are more likely to deprecate him or her, or feel that he or she has deserved the misfortune.

5. The greater the likelihood that force is used overtly by authorities, the more likely it will be viewed by those authorities and outsiders as necessary and therefore approved. Note that this view is taken when force is used by stronger on weaker parties, as by parents on children, policemen on adolescents, on prisoners as against work-ers, marine trainees as against navy recruits, felons as against misdemeanants, lower classes as against upper classes, blacks as against whites, and so on. It is, then, approved more when used on those who command less overt force or force-threat and on those who are thought to require it more.

6. Those segments of the population on whom the use of overt force by authorities is more approved because other means are thought not to be available or efficacious may in fact respond to other means, but the society or its ruling groups typically disapprove of such de-escalation. They view the costs of getting conformity as too high to them in prestige, money, or affection, compared with the cost of using force. They may even refuse to consider that their policies are unwise. They believe the cost of using overt force on such groups is relatively low, since they doubt they can gain their allegiance. Presumably, public opinion surveys might test this hypothesis. I am of course suggesting that this widespread "folk sociological belief" may be wrong, but people do act in this fashion.

7. When an individual or group uses overt force on the more advantaged segments of the population, who are generally thought to require no force since they usually co-operate anyway, others will disapprove and withdraw their force-threat backing unless it is shown that the group's violation (typically, some protest) was greater than the conflict situation justified. When authorities use overt force on more advantaged people, they must argue persuasively in its favor, or they will suffer a range of reprisals from social disapproval to the loss of their jobs.

8. Let me offer a final proposition, focused again on overt force. People lose prestige—i.e., gain disapproval—the more they apply force in situations where acts are thought to be properly guided by values, norms, or shared goals—e.g., sit-ins or robberies. By contrast, those who use force in situations already defined as potentially violent will not lose as much esteem. Thus, one loses more prestige by fighting in a business office than in a lower class bar or a slum.

The slave overseer lost more respect for brutality on a long-settled or conquered plantation than on one newly carved from the wilderness. A peace officer in a middle class suburb loses more respect for using violence than did the frontier sheriff.

This relationship has a corollary: social anger, hostility, or deprecation directed against an individual increases the more that individual proves by resistance that conformity and stability in a social institution are maintained by overt force. That is, by compelling others to use overt force to gain compliance the resisters prove that some people feel little moral commitment to the system, or feel that it is very unjust. An extreme case of course is the violent reaction of slave owners to slave rebellions, but note recent student riots and sit-ins.

FINAL REMARKS

In proposing the systematic study of force as a set of control processes, I have moved from considering large-scale structures to smaller units, and from situations in which overt force is very much in the background to those where it plays a prominent part. I have done so not merely to meet in part the challenge I have offered, to share the task, but also to show that this general theoretical orientation can generate testable hypotheses that will further our understanding of social structures.

I have offered several conceptual clarifications, notably abandoning the loose term *power* and analytically separating the main realms or types of control processes—i.e., force, prestige, wealth, and affection.

I have pointed out some methodological problems, most importantly that those who are moved by force may not know that they are. However, not only is that problem already widespread in existing analyses of power but we also are more likely to try to solve these problems when we see that this approach helps in developing interesting propositions. In accord with that hope, I have tried to develop several such hypotheses.

I should like to close with a few, by no means all, of my prejudices about social structures. Like other people's they may be empirically incorrect in part; yet they may lead to uncovering relationships we might otherwise overlook.

I have already referred to one of these, the working guess that a phenomenon may have important consequences or may be a crucial element in the social structure, though rarely observed; and indeed its rarity may suggest how important it is that the social processes keep it in check.

Let me suggest a few more. Although I applaud the kindly bias of modern social analysts who argue that rewards are powerful in eliciting desirable behavior from others, while punishments confuse or hinder one's efforts, I believe that research will increasingly disclose the powerful effect of punishment in inducing conformity, and even change in values. Correspondingly, although I, too deprecate the use of overt force, the historical record shows that regimes with even a fairly high component of overt force can be stable for a long period; and when force patterns are embedded in the system of understandings about reality that people share, overt force can be efficacious indeed. This embeddedness need not be based on moral consensus or a belief that overt force is just. However, precisely how we come to accept that embeddedness should be a focus of our inquiries.

Next, people on whom overt force is used, or who feel its threat severely, can better judge its efficacy than those whose privileges are supported by it. In line with this prejudice, I suggest that although the imposition of an unwanted system, regime, or control pattern on a population almost always requires overt force, we cannot deduce from observing the use of a low amount of force that all or most subordinates approve the system or share its values. Correspondingly, those who are disadvantaged, whose traits or talents are little rewarded, do not and historically have not accepted this arrangement as just and right. If they accept it at times, they do not affirm it, and feel little commitment to it.

Finally, the past decade exhibits a worldwide revolutionary temper, in which the disadvantaged have increasingly come to perceive, and to articulate, that much of the social structure is not only unjust and can be changed but is also held in place by force, wielded by human beings. Thus, they have come to be less willing to comply with its rules. One might, then, as a challenge to rulers everywhere, point out that we can in fact test their claim that their system is based on justice and on people's allegiance to it by reducing the use of physical force to buttress it. Thus my final prejudice: that system which requires the least physical force would more closely approximate justice than any we now know.

4. THE SOCIOLOGY OF THE DEVIANT ACT: ANOMIE THEORY

ALBERT K. COHEN

Reprinted from American Sociological Review *30, no. 1 (February 1965): 5-14. Albert K. Cohen is Professor of Sociology at the University of Connecticut. He has specialized in deviant behavior theory and research, and research on lower class behavior. He is the author of an influential book,* Delinquent Boys *(Free Press, 1955), which began a major reevaluation of sociological theories of delinquency, and of many other articles dealing with delinquency, social disorganization, and deviant behavior generally. He has summed up his views about deviance theory in* Deviance and Control *(Prentice-Hall, 1966).*

■ Before the ascendance of the societal response school of deviance theory, represented here by Erikson, Goffman, and others, the most influential theory guiding empirical research in the United States was that advanced by Robert Merton in his famous essay, "Social Structure and Anomie." Emile Durkheim had argued that increasing division of labor tends to create a condition of normlessness in which the members of society are uncertain about what models of life to follow and consequently do not have a sense of the just regulation of their desires. In anomie, then, there is a lack of moral integration in the society; at least some individuals have a sense of being dislocated in social space.

Durkheim applied the concept of anomie in an analysis of suicide, arguing that "anomic suicide" resulted from situations in which individuals lost the sense that their lives were subject to moral regulation. In using the concept of anomie to explain high rates of suicide among wealthy persons and those who are divorced, he argued that rapid upward changes in the standard of living as well as the breakup of marriages put norms into flux. A similar explanation applied to an increasing suicide rate during economic depressions.

Robert Merton modified Durkheim's theory, shifting the focus from the moral regulation of personal impulses to situations of conflict between the cultural goals society holds out to individuals and the social and institutional means it provides for achieving them. Merton argued that anomie characterizes a situation in which a disjunction or disequilibrium exists between cultural goals and the institutionalized means for achieving those goals. Specifically he argued that in American society one goal is held out to all persons—the goal of success,

of achievement, of high social and financial status—but many persons do not in fact have access to approved means for achieving it. Individuals may respond to this disjunction by developing one or another deviant adaptation. They may retreat from society, rejecting both goal and means; they may rebel and seek to replace both goal and means; they may engage in an unrealistic adherence to the means of society while secretly rejecting its goal; or they may seek to achieve the goal but reject the socially approved means. The criminal is the characteristic innovator: he pursues success by illegal means. The drug addict is the characteristic retreatist: he moves away into his own, different world.

Thus in the Mertonian framework deviant behavior is seen as an adaptation to anomie, arising from the fact that the deviant individual lacks access to opportunities that allow him to achieve the cultural goals held out for everyone. In this selection Albert Cohen reassesses the vast literature on deviant behavior informed by the Mertonian paradigm and seeks to match it with empirical studies derived from the symbolic interactionist perspective. Cohen's sources were plentiful, since well over 100 empirical studies applying Merton's paradigm have appeared since its initial publication in 1949.

Merton's essay appears in *Social Theory and Social Structure* (Free Press, 1957). Richard A. Cloward develops the most influential elaboration of that theory in "Illegitimate Means, Anomie, and Deviant Behavior," *American Sociological Review* 24 (April 1969): 164-76; and it is applied to the study of delinquency in Richard A. Cloward and Lloyd Ohlin, *Delinquency and Opportunity* (Free Press, 1960). A set of critical essays evaluating anomie theory from the perspective of symbolic interaction is in Marshall Clinard, ed., *Anomie and Deviant Behavior: A Discussion and Critique* (Free Press, 1964). David Matza's effort at synthesizing the structural-functional view found in Merton's work with the symbolic interactionist view is *Becoming Deviant* (Prentice-Hall, 1969). A more formal and abstract theory of deviance as part of a general theory of the social system is in Talcott Parsons, *The Social System* (Free Press, 1951), pt. 7, "Deviant Behavior and the Mechanisms of Social Control". ■

MY CONCERN in this paper is to move toward a general theory of deviant behavior. Taking "Social Structure and Anomie" as a point of departure, I shall note some of the imperfections and gaps in the theory as originally stated, how some of these have been rectified, some theoretical openings for further exploration, and some problems of relating anomie theory to other traditions in the sociology of deviance. It is not important, for my purposes, how broadly or narrowly Merton himself conceived the range of applicability of his anomie theory. Whatever the intention or vision of the author of a theory, it is the task of a discipline to explore the implications of a theoretical insight, in all directions. Many of the points I shall make are, indeed, to be found in Merton's work. In many instances, however, either they appear as leads, suggestions, or *obiter dicta*, and are left undeveloped, or they appear in some other context and no effort is made systematically to link them with anomie theory.

THE ANOMIE THEORY OF DEVIANT BEHAVIOR

Merton's theory has the reputation of being the preeminently *sociological* theory of deviant behavior. Its concern is to account for the distribution of deviant behavior among the positions in a social system and for differences in the distribution and rates of deviant behavior among systems. It tries to account for these things as functions of system properties —i.e., the ways in which cultural goals and opportunities for realizing them within the limits of the institutional norms are distributed. The emphasis, in short, is on certain aspects of the culture (goals and norms) and of the social structure (opportunities, or access to means). The theory *is*, then, radically sociological. And yet, as far as the formal and explicit structure of Merton's first formulation is concerned, it is, in certain respects, atomistic and individualistic. Within the framework of goals, norms, and opportunities, the process of deviance was conceptualized as though each individual—or better, role incumbent—were in a box by himself. He has internalized goals and normative, regulatory rules; he assesses the opportunity structure; he experiences strain; and he selects one or another mode of adaptation. The bearing of others' experience—their strains, their conformity and deviance, their success and failure—on ego's strain and consequent adaptations is comparatively neglected.

Consider first the concept of strain itself. It is a function of the degree of disjunction between goals and means, or of the sufficiency of means to the attainment of goals. But how imperious must the goals be, how uncertain their attainment, how incomplete their fulfillment to generate strain? The relation between goals as components of that abstraction, culture, and the concrete goals of concrete role incumbents is by no means clear and simple. One thing that is clear is that the level of goal attainment that will seem just and reasonable to concrete actors, and therefore the sufficiency of available means, will be relative to the attainments of others who serve as reference objects. Level of aspiration is not a fixed quantum, taken from the culture and swallowed whole, to lodge unchanged within our psyches. The sense of proportionality between effort and reward is not determined by the objective returns of effort alone. From the standpoint of the role sector whose rates of deviance are in question, the mapping of reference group orientations, the availability *to others* of access to means, and the actual distribution of rewards are aspects of the social structure important for the determination of strain.

Once we take explicit cognizance of these processes of comparison, a number of other problems unfold themselves. For example, others, whom we define as legitimate objects of comparison, may be more successful than we are by adhering to legitimate means. They not only do better than we do but they also do so "fair and square." On the other hand, they may do as well as we or even better by cutting corners, cheating, using illegitimate means. Do these two different situations have different consequences for the sense of strain, for attitudes toward oneself, for subsequent adaptations? In general, what strains does deviance on the part of others create for the virtuous? In the most obvious case ego is the direct victim of alter's deviance. Or ego's interests may be adversely but indirectly affected by the chicanery of a competitor— unfair trade practices in business, unethical advertising in medicine, cheating in examinations when the instructor grades on a curve. But there is a less obvious case, the one which, according to Ranulf, gives rise to disinterested moral indignation. The dedicated pursuit of culturally approved goals, the eschewing of interdicted but tantalizing goals, the adherence to normatively sanctioned means—these imply a certain self-restraint, effort, discipline, inhibition. What is the effect of the spectacle of others who, though their activities do not manifestly damage our own interests, are morally undisciplined, who give themselves up to idleness, self-indulgence, or forbidden vices? What effect does the propinquity of the wicked have on the peace of mind of the virtuous?

In several ways, the virtuous can make capital out of this situation, can convert a situation with a potential for strain to a source of satisfaction. One can become even more virtuous letting his reputation hinge on his righteousness, *building his self out of invidious comparison to the morally weak*. Since others' wickedness sets off the jewel of one's own virtue, and one's claim to virtue is at the core of his public identity, one may actually develop a stake in the existence of deviant others and be threatened should they pretend to moral excellence. In short, another's virtue

may become a source of strain! One may also join with others in righteous puritanical wrath to mete out punishment to the deviants, not so much to stamp out their deviant behavior as to reaffirm the central importance of conformity as the basis for judging men and to reassure himself and others of his attachment to goodness. One may even make a virtue of tolerance and indulgence of others' moral deficiencies, thereby implicitly calling attention to one's own special strength of character. If the weakness of others is only human, then there is something more than human about one's own strength. On the other hand, one might join the profligate.

What I have said here is relevant to social control, but my concern at present is not with social control but with some of the ways in which deviance of others may aggravate or lighten the burdens of conformity and hence the strain that is so central to anomie theory.

The student of Merton will recognize that some of these points are suggested or even developed at some length here and there in Merton's own writing. Merton is, of course, one of the chief architects of reference group theory, and in his chapter on "Continuities in the Theory of Reference Groups and Social Structure," he has a section entitled "Nonconformity as a Type of Reference Group Behavior." There he recognizes the problems that one actor's deviance creates for others, and he explicitly calls attention to Ranulf's treatment of disinterested moral indignation as a way of dealing with this problem. In "Continuities in the Theory of Social Structure and Anomie," he describes how the deviance of some increases the others' vulnerability to deviance. In short, my characterization of the earliest version of "Social Structure and Anomie" as "atomistic and individualistic" would be a gross misrepresentation if it were applied to the total corpus of Merton's writing on deviance. He has not, however, developed the role of comparison processes in the determination of strain or considered it explicitly in the context of anomie theory. And in general, Merton does not identify the complexities and subtleties of the concept strain as a problem area in their own right.

Finally, in connection with the concept strain, attention should be called to Smelser's treatment of the subject in his *Theory of Collective Behavior.* Although Smelser does not deal with this as it bears on a theory of deviance, it is important here for two reasons. First, it is, to my knowledge, the only attempt in the literature to generate a systematic classification of types of strain, of which Merton's disjunction between goals and means is only one. The second reason is Smelser's emphasis that to account for collective behavior one must *start with* strain, but one's theory must also specify a hierarchy of constraints, each of which further narrows the range of possible responses to strain, and the last of which rules out all alternatives but collective behavior. If the "value-added" method is sound for a theory of collective behavior, it may also be useful for a theory of deviance, starting from the concept strain, and constructed on the same model.

Now, *given strain,* what will a person do about it? In general, Merton's chief concern has been with the structural factors that account for variations in strain. On the matter of choice of solution, as on other matters, he has some perceptive observations, but it has remained for others to develop these systematically. In particular, in the original version of his theory each person seems to work out his solution by himself, as though it did not matter what other people were doing. Perhaps Merton assumed such intervening variables as deviant role models, without going into the mechanics of them. But it is one thing to assume that such variables are operating; it is quite another to treat them explicitly in a way that is integrated with the more general theory. Those who continue the anomie tradition, however—most notably Merton's student, Cloward—have done much to fill this gap. Cloward, with Ohlin, has accomplished this in large part by linking anomie theory with another and older theoretical tradition, associated with Sutherland, Shaw and McKay, and Kobrin—the "cultural transmission" and "differential association"

tradition of the "Chicago school." Cloward and Ohlin also link anomie theory to a more recent theoretical development, the general theory of subcultures, and especially the aspect of the theory that is concerned with the emergence and development of new subcultural forms. What these other theories have in common is an insistence that deviant as well as nondeviant action is typically not contrived within the solitary individual psyche but is part of a collaborative *social* activity, in which the things that other people say and do give meaning, value, and effect to one's own behavior.

The incorporation of this recognition into anomie theory is the principal significance of Cloward's notion of illegitimate opportunity structures. These opportunity structures are going social concerns in the individual's milieu, which provide opportunities to learn and to perform deviant actions and lend moral support to the deviant when he breaks with conventional norms and goals.

This is the explicit link with the cultural transmission—differential association tradition. The argument is carried a step further with the recognition that even in the absence of an already established deviant culture and social organization a number of individuals with like problems and in effective communication with one another may join together to do what no one can do alone. They may provide one another with reference objects, collectively contrive a subculture to replace or neutralize the conventional culture, and support and shield one another in their deviance. This is the explicit link to the newer theory of subcultures.

There is one more step in this direction that has not been so explicitly taken. Those who join hands in deviant enterprises need not be people with like problems, nor need their deviance be of the same sort. Within the framework of anomie theory, we may think of these people as individuals with quite variant problems or strains which lend themselves to a common solution, but a common solution in which each participates in different ways. I have in mind the brothel keeper and the crooked policeman, the black-marketeer and his customer, the desperate student and the term paper merchant, the bookie and the wire services. These do not necessarily constitute solidary collectivities, like delinquent gangs, but they are structures of action with a division of labor through which each, by his deviance, serves the interests of the others. Theirs is an "organic solidarity," in contrast to the "mechanical solidarity" of Cloward and Ohlin's gangs. Some of Merton's own writing on functionalism—for example, his discussion of the exchange of service involved in political corruption—is extremely relevant here, but it is not explicitly integrated into his anomie theory.

THE ASSUMPTION OF DISCONTINUITY

To say that anomie theory suffers from the assumption of discontinuity is to imply that it treats the deviant act as though it were an abrupt change of state, a leap from a state of strain or anomie to a state of deviance. Although this overstates the weakness in Merton's theory the expression, "the assumption of discontinuity," does have the heuristic value of drawing attention to an important difference in emphasis between anomie theory and other traditions in American sociology, and to the direction of movement in anomie theory itself. Human action, deviant or otherwise, is something that typically develops and grows in a tentative, groping, advancing, backtracking, soundingout process. People taste and feel their way along. They begin an act and do not complete it. They start doing one thing and end up by doing another. They extricate themselves from progressive involvement or become further involved to the point of commitment. These processes of progressive involvement and disinvolvement are important enough to deserve explicit recognition and treatment in their own right. They are themselves subject to normative regulation and structural constraint in complex ways about which we have much to learn. Until recently, however, the dominant bias in American

sociology has been toward formulating theory in terms of variables that describe initial states, on the one hand, and outcomes, on the other, rather than in terms of processes whereby acts and complex structures of action are built, elaborated, and transformed. Notable exceptions are interaction process analysis, the brand of action theory represented by Herbert Blumer, and the descriptions of deviance by Talcott Parsons and by Howard Becker. Anomie theory has taken increasing cognizance of such processes. Cloward and Merton both point out, for example, that behavior may move through "patterned sequences of deviant roles" and from "one type of adaptation to another." But this hardly does justice to the micro-sociology of the deviant act. It suggests a series of discontinuous leaps from one deviant state to another almost as much as it does the kind of process I have in mind.

REPONSES TO DEVIANCE

Very closely related to the foregoing point is the conception of the development of the act as a feedback, or, in more traditional language, interaction process. The history of a deviant act is a history of an interaction process. The antecedents of the act are an unfolding sequence of acts contributed by a set of actors. A makes a move, possibly in a deviant direction; B responds; A responds to B's responses, etc. In the course of this interaction, movement in a deviant direction may become more explicit, elaborated, definitive—or it may not. Although the act may be socially ascribed to only one of them, both ego and alter help to shape it. The starting point of anomie theory was the question, "*Given* the social structure, or ego's milieu, what will ego do?" The milieu was taken as more or less given an independent variable whose value is fixed, and ego's behavior as an adaptation, or perhaps a series of adaptations, to that milieu. Anomie theory has come increasingly to recognize the effects of deviance upon the very variables that determine deviance. But if we are interested in a general theory of deviant behavior we must explore much more systematically ways of conceptualizing the *interaction* between deviance and milieu. I suggest the following such lines of exploration.

If ego's behavior can be conceptualized in terms of acceptance and rejection of goals and means, the same can be done with alter's responses. Responses to deviance can no more be left normatively unregulated than deviance itself. Whose business it is to intervene, at what point, and what he may or may not do is defined by a normatively established division of labor. In short, for any given role—parent, priest, psychiatrist, neighbor, policeman, judge—the norms prescribe, with varying degrees of definiteness, *what* they are supposed to do and *how* they are supposed to do it when other persons, in specified roles, misbehave. The culture prescribes goals and regulates the choice of means. Members of ego's role set can stray from cultural prescriptions in all the ways that ego can. They may overemphasize the goals and neglect the normative restrictions, they may adhere ritualistically to the normatively approved means and neglect the goals, and so forth. I have spelled out the five possibilities on alter's side more fully elsewhere. The theoretical value of applying Merton's modes of adaptation to responses to deviant acts is not fully clear; yet it seems worthy of exploration for at least two reasons.

First, *one* determinant of ego's response to alter's attempts at control, and of the responses of third parties whom ego or alter might call to their aid, is certainly the perceived legitimacy of alter's behavior. Whether ego yields or resists, plays the part of the good loser or the abused victim, takes his medicine or is driven to aggravated deviance depends in part on whether alter has the right to do what he does, whether the response is proportional to the offense, and so on.

Normative rules also regulate the deviant's response to the intervention of control agents. How the control agent responds to the deviant, after the first confrontation, depends on his perception of the legitimacy of the deviant's response *to him* and not only on the nature of the original deviant act. For example, this perceived legitimacy plays an important part in police dispositions of cases coming to their attention.

This approach also directs attention to strain in alter's role, the adequacy of *his* resources relative to the responsibilities with which he is charged by virtue of his role, and the illegitimate opportunities available to *him*. A familiar example would be the normative restrictions on the means police may consider effective to do the job with which they are charged, and variations in the availability to them of various illegitimate means to the same end.

The disjunction between goals and means and the choice of adaptations depend on the opportunity structure. The opportunity structure consists in or is the result of the actions of other people. These in turn are in part reactions to ego's behavior and may undergo change in response to that behavior. The development of ego's action can, therefore, be conceptualized as a series of responses on the part of ego to a series of changes in the opportunity structure resulting from ego's actions. More specifically, alter's responses may open up, close off, or leave unaffected legitimate opportunities for ego, and they may do the same to illegitimate opportunities. The following simplified table reduces the possibilities to four.

RESPONSES OF THE OPPORTUNITY STRUCTURE
TO EGO'S DEVIANCE

	Legitimate Opportunities	Illegitimate Opportunities
Open up	I	II
Close off	III	IV

I. *Open up legitimate opportunities.* Special efforts may be made to find employment opportunities for delinquents and criminals. On an individual basis this has long been one of the chief tasks of probation officers. On a mass basis it has become more and more prominent in communitywide efforts to reduce delinquency rates.

Black markets may sometimes be reduced

by making more of the product available in the legal market or by reducing the pressure on the legal supply through rationing.

Several years ago the Indiana University faculty had a high rate of violation of campus parking regulations, in part because of the disjunction between the demand for parking spaces and the supply. The virtuous left early for work and hunted wearily for legitimate parking spaces. The contemptuous parked anywhere and sneered at tickets. One response to this situation was to create new parking lots and to expand old ones. Since the new parking spaces were available to all, and not only to the former violators, this provides a clear instance where the virtuous— or perhaps the timid—as well as the deviants themselves are the beneficiaries of deviance.

II. *Open up illegitimate opportunities.*
Alter, instead of fighting ego, may facilitate his deviance by joining him in some sort of collusive illicit arrangement from which both profit. The racketeer and the law enforcement officer, the convict and the guard, the highway speeder and the traffic policeman may arrive at an understanding to reduce the cost of deviance.

Alter, whether he be a discouraged parent, a law enforcement official, or a dean of students, may simply give up efforts to systematically enforce a rule and limit himself to sporadic, token gestures.

An important element in Cloward and Ohlin's theory of delinquent subcultures is that those who run the criminal syndicates are ever alert for promising employees, and that a certain number of those who demonstrate proficiency in the more juvenile forms of crime will be given jobs in the criminal organization.

III. *Closing off legitimate opportunities.*
The example that comes most readily to mind is what Tannenbaum calls the "dramatization of evil." A deviant act, if undetected or ignored, might not be repeated. On the other hand, others might react to it by publicly defining the actor as a delinquent, a fallen woman, a criminal. These definitions ascribe to him a social role, change his public image, and activate a set of appropriate

responses. These responses may include exclusion from avenues of legitimate opportunity formerly open to him and thus enhance the relative attractiveness of the illegitimate.

IV. *Closing off illegitimate opportunities.*
This is what we usually think of first when we think about "social control." It includes increasing surveillance, locking the door, increasing the certainty and severity of punishment, cutting off access to necessary supplies, knocking out the fix. These measures may or may not achieve the intended effect. On the one hand, they make deviance more difficult. On the other hand, they may stimulate the deviant, or the deviant coalition, to ingenuity in devising new means to circumvent the new restrictions.

The table is a way of conceptualizing alter's actions. The same alter might respond simultaneously in different cells of the table, as may different alters, and these responses might reinforce or counteract one another. Responses might fall in different cells at different stages of the interaction process. In any case, as soon as we conceive of the opportunity structure as a dependent as well as an independent variable, this way of thinking suggests itself as a logical extension of the anomie schema.

Parsons' paradigm of social control is in his opinion applicable not only to deviance but also to therapy and rehabilitative processes in general. According to this paradigm, the key elements in alter's behavior are support, permissiveness, denial of reciprocity, and rewards, judiciously balanced, and strategically timed and geared to the development of ego's behavior. To exploit the possibilities of this and other paradigms of control, one must define more precisely these categories of alter's behavior, develop relevant ways of coding ego's responses to alter's responses, and investigate both theoretically and empirically the structure of extended interaction processes conceptualized in these terms.

Finally, the interaction process may be analyzed from the standpoint of its consequences for stability or change in the normative structure itself. Every act of deviance can be thought of as a pressure on the normative structure, a test of its limits, an exploration of its meaning, a challenge to its validity. Responses to deviance may reaffirm or shore up the normative structure; they may be ritual dramatizations of the seriousness with which the community takes violations of its norms. Or deviance may prompt reexamination of the boundaries of the normatively permissible, resulting in either explicit reformulation of the rule or implicit changes in its meaning, so that the deviant becomes redefined as nondeviant, or the nondeviant as deviant. Thus deviance may be reduced or increased by changes in the norms. These processes go on within the household, courts of law, administrative agencies, and legislative chambers, but also in the mass media, the streets, and the other forums in which "public opinion" is shaped. Although these processes may be punctuated by dramatic, definitive events, like the passage of a new law or the promulgation of a new set of regulations on allowable income tax deductions, the pressure of deviance on the normative structure and the responses of the normative structure to deviance constitute continuing, uninterrupted, interaction processes. One goal of deviance theory is to determine under what conditions feedback circuits promote change and under what conditions they inhibit change in the normative structure.

In this connection, one of Merton's most perceptive and fruitful distinctions is that between the "nonconformist" and other types of deviant. Whereas the criminal and others typically *violate* the norms in pursuit of their own ends, but in no sense seek to *change* those norms (though such change might very well be an unanticipated consequence of their cumulative deviance), the nonconformist's objective is precisely to change the normative system itself. This distinction suggests, in turn, the concept of the "test case" (which need not be limited to the context of legal norms and the formal judicial system)—i.e., the act openly committed, with the intention of forcing a clarification or redefinition of the norms. What we must not overlook, however, is that *any*

deviant act, whatever its intention, may, in a sense, function as a test case.

DEVIANCE AND SOCIAL IDENTITY

There is another piece of unfinished business before anomie theory, and that is to establish a more complete and successful union with role theory and theory of the self. The starting point of Merton's theory is the means-ends schema. His *dramatis personae* are cultural goals, institutional norms, and the situation of action, consisting of means and conditions. The disjunction between goals and means provides the motive force behind action. Deviance is an effort to reduce this disjunction and reestablish an equilibrium between goals and means. It issues from tension; it is an attempt to reduce tension. Roles figure in this theory as a locational grid. They are the positions in the social structure among which goals, norms, and means are distributed, where such disjunctions are located and such adaptations carried out.

Another starting point for a theory of deviant behavior grows out of the social theory of George Herbert Mead. This starting point is the actor engaged in an ongoing process of finding, building, testing, validating, and expressing a self. The self is linked to roles, but not primarily in a locational sense. Roles enter, in a very integral and dynamic way, into the very structure of the self. They are part of the categorical system of a society, the socially recognized and meaningful categories of persons. They are the kinds of people it is possible to be in that society. The self is constructed of these possibilities, or some organization of these possibilities. One establishes a self by successfully claiming membership in such categories.

To validate such a claim one must know the social meaning of membership in such roles: the criteria by which they are assigned, the qualities or behavior that function as signs of membership, the characteristics that measure adequacy in the roles. These meanings must be learned. To some degree, this learning may be accomplished before one has identified or even toyed with the roles. Such learning Merton has called anticipatory socialization. To some degree, however, it continues even after one has become more or less committed to a role, in the process of presenting one's self, experiencing and reading the feedback, and correcting one's notion of what it is to be that kind of person. An actor learns that the behavior signifying membership in a particular role includes the kinds of clothes he wears, his posture and gait, his likes and dislikes, what he talks about and the opinions he expresses—everything that goes into what we call the style of life. Such aspects of behavior are difficult to conceptualize as either goals or means; in terms of their relation to the role, at least, their function is better described as expressive or symbolic. But the same can be said even of the goals one pursues and the means one employs; they, too, may communicate and confirm an identity.

Now, *given* a role, and *given* the orientations to goals and to means that have been assumed because they are part of the social definition of that role, there may be a disjunction between goals and means. Much of what we call deviant behavior arises as a way of dealing with this disjunction. As anomie theory has been formally stated, this is where it seems to apply. But much deviant behavior cannot readily be formulated in these terms at all. Some of it, for example, is directly expressive of the roles. A tough and bellicose posture, the use of obscene language, participation in illicit sexual activity, the immoderate consumption of alcohol, the deliberate flouting of legality and authority, a generalized disrespect for the sacred symbols of the "square" world, a taste for marihuana, even suicide—all of these may have the primary function of affirming, in the language of gesture and deed, that one is a certain kind of person. The message-symbol relationship, or that of claim and evidence, seems to fit this behavior better than the ends-means relationship.

Sexual seduction, for example, may be thought of as illicit means to the achieve-ment of a goal. The point is, however, that the seduction need not be an adaptation to the insufficiency of other means, a response to disjunction. One may cultivate the art of seduction because this sort of expertise is directly significant of a coveted role. Indeed, the very value and meaning of the prize are conferred by the means employed. One could, of course, say that the expertise is itself the goal, but then it is still a goal that expresses and testifies to a role. Finally, one could say that the goal of the act is to validate the role, and all these kinds of behavior are means to this end. I think this statement is plausible and can be defended. If it *is* the intent of anomie theory, then the language of tension reduction does not seem to fit very well. The relation I have in mind, between deviant act and social role, is like the relation between pipe and elbow patches and the professorial role. Like the professor's behavior, it is not necessarily a *pis aller*, a means that one has hit on after others have failed. It commends itself, it is gratifying, because it seems so right—not in a moral sense but in the sense that it fits so well with the image one would like to have of oneself.

One important implication of this view is that it shifts the focus of theory and research from the disjunction and its resolution to the process of progressive involvement in, commitment to, and movement among social roles and the processes whereby one learns the behavior that is significant of the roles. One may, like the child acquiring his sex identity, come to accept and identify with a role before he is quite clear what it means to be that sort of person, how one goes about being one. But once one has established the identity he has an interest in learning these things and making use of that learning. Thus Howard Becker's dance band musicians arrive at that estate by various routes. For many of them, however, it is only as this identity is crystallizing that they fully learn what being a musician means within the world of musicians. They discover, so to speak, what they are, and what they are turns out to be highly unconventional people. We seek roles for various reasons, some of them having little to do with tension reduction, and having found the role, come into unanticipated legacies of deviant behavior.

The same processes operate in movement in the other direction, toward restoration to conformity. They are most dramatically illustrated in religious conversion. As the sinner is born again, with a new identity fashioned out of new roles, whole bundles of behavior, not all of them deviant, are cast aside, and new bundles are picked up. Relatively little may be learned by examining, one at a time, the items these bundles contain, the sense in which they constitute means to ends, and their adequacy to their respective goals. The decisive event is the transformation of self and social identity. At that moment a wholesale transformation of behavior is determined.

Anomie theory is, perhaps, concerned with *one* structural source of deviance, while the ideas just presented are concerned with another. Neither one need be more faithful to reality than the other, and the defense of one need not be a challenge to the other. But those who are interested in the development of a general theory of deviance can hardly let matters stand at that. Is it possible to make any general statements about the kinds of deviance that may be attributed to anomie and the kinds that may be attributed to role

validation through behavior culturally significant of membership in the role? Or may two instances of *any* sort of deviant behavior, identical in their manifest or "phenotypic" content, differ in their sources or "genotypic" structure?

Ultimately, however we must investigate the possible ways in which the two kinds or sources of deviance interact or interpenetrate. For example, does role symbolism function as a structural constraint on the choice of means, and instrumental or means-ends considerations as a structural constraint on the choice of expressive symbolism? Does behavior that originates as a characteristic adaptation to the anomie associated with a particular role come in time to signify membership in that role and thereby to exercise a secondary or even independent attraction or repulsion, depending on one's orientation toward the role itself? Finally, is it possible that in any instance of deviant behavior, or, for that matter, *any* behavior, both processes are intertwined in ways that cannot be adequately described in terms of presently available modes of conceptualization? I suggest that we must bring the two schemes into more direct and explicit confrontation and try to evolve a formulation that will fuse and harness the power of both.

5. LABELING, MORALS, AND PUBLIC POLICY

EDWIN M. SCHUR

Abridged from Labeling Deviant Behavior, pp. 148-53, 159-66, 169-73 by permission of Harper & Row, Publishers, Inc. Copyright © 1971 by Edwin M. Schur. Edwin M. Schur is Professor of Sociology at New York University. His Crimes Without Victims, published in 1965, has had a major impact on the sociology of deviant behavior, on legal thinking about criminal justice, and on public policy. Professor Schur specializes in the sociology of deviance and the sociology of law and public policy.

■ In Crimes Without Victims Schur argued that the criminalization of certain kinds of deviant behavior created a wide range of social problems and resulted in destructive interference with individual liberty. A "crime without victim" is a form of deviant behavior called criminal in law but engaged in voluntarily by all parties so that no "victim" or complainant is involved. Schur's examples of such crimes (to which we will turn in Part II) are abortion, homosexuality, and drug addiction.

Schur is concerned here with the implications of the labeling approach to deviance as Erikson and Goffman discuss it and especially with its practical implications for public policy. He observes that conflict is the essence of the process by which behavior is labeled deviant and by which those so labeled respond to society's treatment of them. He argues that the influence of labeling theory at the pragmatic level of policy can be liberating or stultifying, depending on how it is interpreted.

Alvin W. Gouldner has vigorously critized the labeling approach as a conservative influence on sociology in "The Sociologist as Partisan: Sociology and the Welfare State," *American Sociologist* 3 (May 1968): 103-16. Books that emphasize the individual's freedom of action and "rationality" in engaging in deviance include Frank Hartung, *Crime, Law, and Society* (Wayne State University Press, 1965); and Thomas S. Szasz, *Psychiatric Justice* (Macmillan, 1965). Several excellent articles on the tenuousness of the border between deviant and normal behavior are in Jack D. Douglas, ed., *Deviance and Respectability* (Basic Books, 1970). ■

CONFLICT, LABELING, AND RESISTANCE TO LABELING

WE HAVE ALREADY OBSERVED that an analysis of aspects of social conflict must be included in any labeling approach to deviance and control. At each of the three levels of analysis mentioned earlier, elements of conflict are inherent in the social reactions to deviation and in efforts at social control. At each level and for any particular kind of deviation or potential deviation, what Lofland has called "conflict games" are present. Opposing "forces"—be they pressure groups or subcultures at the collective decision-making level, actors and others on the interpersonal level, or "clients" and control agencies at the organizational-processing level—struggle to define situations, types of behavior, specific acts, and the essential "character" of particular individuals. Through these conflict processes emerge the various "outcomes" that we noted earlier. Some types of behavior come to be defined as conformist, some as deviant. Through interaction with significant others some individuals learn to see themselves as "normal," whereas others begin to see themselves as abnormal or as wrongdoers. Still other individuals come to be publicly and officially defined as deviators, perhaps even as "criminals," whereas some to whom formal labeling processes are initially applied eventually are exonerated of the "charges" leveled against them.

In considering factors affecting the development of deviant identity, Lofland has remarked, "other things being equal, the greater the *consistency, duration* and *intensity* with which a definition is promoted by Others about an Actor, the greater the likelihood that an Actor will embrace that definition as truly applicable to himself." Unfortunately, this statement (though perhaps basically sound) does not take us very far, for we must recognize one or the other of two important qualifications: first, we know full well that "all other things" are rarely if ever equal; second, the factors that influence the consistency, duration, and intensity with which a definition is imposed vary, depending upon the situation. Although we can make some kinds of broad generalizations about probable deviance outcomes, they are thus uncertain guides to prediction of specific types of deviation or particular categories of individuals.

For example, Table 5.1 shows the general relation between *resources* (for the moment unspecified) and *outcomes* at the various levels of analysis. Clearly groups and individuals with high resources are more likely than are those with low resources to be able to avoid or resist negative labeling. But the crucial question remains: What are the relevant resources? The answer is not obvious. We immediately think, of course, of "standard" sociological variables that might influence these outcomes: socioeconomic status, age, sex, education, and so on. Indeed, we have already noted Becker's comment that by and large the poor, racial minorities, women, and the young in our society tend to have rules imposed on them by the more powerful segments of the population. Similarly, Lofland has suggested that "When low education and youth or old age are combined in the same Actor . . . it seems apparent that he becomes especially vulnerable to escalation [to deviant identity]." But there are several problems in using such standard variables to analyze specific deviance situations. The first is that the salience of a particular variable in determining the probability of deviating acts or the susceptibility to labeling varies with the type of deviation being considered. A youth

may thus appear to have a relatively high probability of "vagrancy" and high susceptibility to labeling as "vagrant" yet a relatively low probability of committing forgery and of being labeled a forger (or a tax evader or an embezzler). Although this example suggests the effect of a combination of personal status characteristics and "opportunity," not all variations in susceptibility are attributable to such combinations. For example, the probability that Blacks will engage in armed robbery (and be labeled "robbers") is relatively high, yet for homosexual behavior the probability is approximately the same as that for Whites. Presumably, opportunity is not a key factor in this variability. On the contrary, it seems that race has little or no importance in determining either probability of homosexual activity or susceptibility and resistance to labeling as homosexual. Other factors, including perhaps the strength of masculine self-concepts, particular family background and early socialization factors, and the like may be more salient in this kind of deviation.

A second major complication is that the effects of a given variable may not always work in the same *direction* in determining the probability of engaging in a particular deviation, on one hand, and susceptibility to labeling as that kind of deviator, on the other. The variable of race appears to operate in the same direction in both aspects for the deviation of armed robbery, whereas for drug addiction the occupational status of a doctor seems to operate in different directions. When other things are equal, doctors have a higher probability of becoming addicts than do others; yet they also have greater resistance to (higher probability of avoiding) being labeled addicts, at least officially. One explanation may lie in doctors' greater "opportunity"—that is, their easy access to drugs. Opportunity, rather than high occupational status, is thus the salient variable. These observations, in turn, suggest a possible generalization: status characteristics of the individual tend to operate in one direction in determining the probability of a specific deviation and the susceptibility to negative labeling, whereas opportunity factors tend to

TABLE 5.1

RELATION BETWEEN SALIENT RESOURCES AND DEVIANCE OUTCOMES

	Interpersonal Reactions	*Organizational Processing*	*Collective Rule-making*
High resources (of individual or group)	High ability to resist imputations of deviant identity *or* to "manage" *desired* deviant roles successfully	High resistance to processing efforts Low rates of "official" deviance	Dominant social perception of individual or group norms as "conformist" High ability to impose rules
Low resources (of individual or group)	Low ability to resist imputations of deviant identity *or* to manage *desired* deviant roles successfully	Low resistance to processing efforts High rates of "official" deviance	Dominant social perception of individual or group norms as "deviant" Low ability to impose rules

operate in opposite directions in determining the two aspects.

This difference seems to result from conditions in which opportunity is a salient factor in determining initial deviation, conditions that imply a certain amount of protection, or insulation, for the deviator. As the doctor has both access to drugs and insulation from detection (*because of* his legitimate access to drugs), so the bank teller has both opportunity to embezzle and some protection against discovery; the youth immersed in a delinquent subculture is to some extent shielded by his membership even as it affords him special opportunities for deviating. In a sense, then, a certain amount of resistance to negative labeling is built into what we call "opportunity."

When we turn to a third major category of variables traditionally used to "explain" the deviating acts of individuals—social psychological factors like individual alienation, weak masculine self-concepts, various personality traits attributed to particular family situations, and so on—we find that they, too, seem to operate in one direction in determining the likelihood of initial deviating acts and the susceptibility to negative labeling. For example, the strength or stability of sexual identity seems to be a highly salient characteristic in determining homosexual behavior. Presumably males with strong masculine self-concepts are less likely to engage in homosexual activities and are also relatively unsusceptible or resistant to labeling as "homosexual." The same unity of direction seems typical of other social psychological variables as well. The individual whose psychological problems or personality state increases the probability of his engaging in some form of deviation probably has, at the same time and because of this condition, weaker resistance to any labeling efforts directed against him than does the person with greater psychological "stability."

Of course, additional problems intrude between these broad generalizations about relative probabilities and more specific efforts at prediction. For purposes of analysis we have treated these variables as if they acted separately and as if for each particular kind of deviation only one were salient. Yet we can assume that this simplicity is not accurate. Just as individuals display various constellations of possibly relevant characteristics in the three categories, so may some combinations be salient for the generation of particular kinds of deviating behavior (and the susceptibility to particular kinds of negative labeling). Furthermore, we must remember that an individual's or a group's resources for resisting labeling processes do not remain constant. On the contrary, such resources tend to be affected by those very same processes. Although the strength of an individual's sexual identity may partly determine his resistance to labeling as a sexual deviant, active efforts to define him thus (even efforts that are not totally "successful") may, in turn, affect his sexual identity. At the level of collective decision making, the pressure groups or segments with greatest power tend to impose the rules, but any "political" setbacks that such groups experience will in turn reduce their power (and thus indirectly diminish their ability to impose rules or to resist the rules that others would impose upon them). . . .

LABELING AND PUBLIC POLICY

What, if any, are the distinctive moral and policy implications of the labeling approach? It is interesting that the orientation has received quite contradictory interpretations in this regard; indeed, it is even tempting to suggest that the meaning of labeling analysis itself lies "in the eye of the beholder." Some commentators consider the approach as reflecting a kind of social radicalism that calls into question conventional definitions and institutions; others claim that its concentration on individual social psychology and small-scale interactions renders it nearly apolitical (if not, by indirection, politically conservative). Some critics charge labeling analysts with romantic sentimentalizing of wrongdoers and unwillingness to recognize the responsibility of such individuals for their own behavior. On the other hand and somewhat paradoxically, labeling analysts themselves sometimes view the approach as a vehicle for denying older "determinisms" and a basis for reasserting the values of personal freedom and individual responsibility.

In this apparent confusion one point seems certain: whatever its more specific implications, the labeling approach does highlight the value-laden nature of deviance and control problems. As we have seen, both the growing attention of American sociologists to this general topic and the development or revival of the orientations considered in this book are partly attributable to discontent with the apparent results of adopting a natural science model for social research, of attempting to confront problems of deviation from a narrowly quantitative, "value-free" perspective. The labeling approach makes clear in a number of ways that some consideration of values is essential to an analysis of deviance. The central theme, that men "create" deviance by defining certain forms of behavior and certain individuals as such, amounts to a radical restatement of Willard Waller's earlier insistence that social "problems" occur only through the making of value judgments. As we have also noted, the labeling approach highlights the significance of conflict elements in these definitional processes, thus showing the basically "political" nature of deviance. The labeling analyst's recognition that, from the deviator's point of view, the conformist may be considered the "outsider," or "deviant," emphasizes still further the crucial role of values in this area. . . .

The moral and policy questions involve the extent to which personal "responsibility" for his behavior ought be imputed to the deviator. How far we wish to go in that direction depends, in turn, partly upon the kind of balance we believe exists between the individual's freedom of action and the ability of reactors to control his situation. Some labeling-oriented or symbolic-interactionist writers seem to attribute considerable freedom of action to the deviator, even though they also usually seek to avoid entanglement in the conventional controversy over freedom

and determinism. In reaction to what David Matza has characterized as the "hard determinism" underlying early criminological studies, some analysts of deviance have thus adopted a rather extreme version of what might be called "hard antideterminism." For example, in recent writings by Frank Hartung on criminality and by Thomas Szasz on mental illness, we find strong declarations of rational bases for deviations that previously had been viewed from a deterministic vantage point, as well as considerable willingness to impute to actors "responsibility" for their behavior. Szasz has argued in support of his belief that mental illness is a "myth," that people who are troublesome because of various "problems of living" should not be subjected to involuntary psychiatric "treatment" or commitment. Unless they themselves seek psychiatric help voluntarily, they should be either left alone or (if their actions create real danger to others) be held accountable and punished under the criminal law.

Other labeling analysts apparently seek a middle path between viewing deviators as either "sick" or "bad" and considering them as "simply different" (Szasz also makes this effort, but with perhaps limited success); they speak of "residual deviance" and of processes in which the individual "drifts" into deviance. Yet Matza, in describing the latter processes has spelled out how delinquency may be activated among youths in such a state of "drift" and has defined the role of "will" in such a way that his analysis veers toward "hard antideterminism." Will, he has declared, "is something that may or may not be exercised. Will is an option."

Matza's attribution of freedom of action to the deviator has become even more pronounced in his recent *Becoming Deviant*. In reanalyzing Howard Becker's study of marihuana use, Matza presents his own central theme at the outset: ". . . the process will be rendered *easy* and open; it becomes apparent that *anyone* can become a marihuana user and that *no one* has to." Continuing in this vein, he returns to the notion of "option" from his earlier work. Exposure to the op-

o use marihuana does not force one
nt activity; rather, one experiences
ption to use it or not. Both the be-
f deviant activity and its continua-
nd upon the individual himself.

ing willing, the subject may begin a
that neither holds him within its grip
olds without him. Without the subject,
cess has no meaning since it must be
ed through him and take its form from
o enter the process, the invitational edge
deviant phenomenon must somehow be
ed. To do that a leap is required—an act
ill; the phenomenon is engaged, but not
ractly. The subject is actually doing the
g—an immersion in concrete activity which
essential. The remainder of the process of
coming deviant can hardly happen if the sub-
ct continues to gaze at a phenomenon kept
at a distance.

Matza has described the individual's participation in even more active terms, claiming
that at certain stages in the process of becoming deviant the subject "makes up his mind,
literally." Although he has recognized that
the individual "does sometimes have empty
authority, a subjectivity oppressed by context
or circumstance," he has undercut this recognition with the claim that peer influence is
"a matter to be considered by the subject. . . ."
Although it is, of course, true that the individual reflects to some extent upon the circumstances and individuals affecting his behavior, the implication that he can decide
how much influence they will have seems
rather extreme. Matza has provided no real
evidence that the process that he has described
actually occurs, either invariably or even frequently, and he has certainly adduced no
data in support of its primacy. Furthermore,
the example of marihuana use seems a loaded
one, for this type of deviation is one in which
fairly free choice is known to be frequently if
not typically a significant factor. It is not at
all clear that Matza's interpretation would be
valid if applied to other types of deviation.

At least in the absence of hard data, such
an interpretation remains largely academic.
What may be more to the point is the fact
that varying notions about freedom of action
and personal responsibility for behavior are
held by individuals who deviate and by individuals who respond to deviation. Efforts
have been made to determine empirically
what such notions are, and there is thus at
least a partial basis for assessing their significance. At least two different patterns of
individual deviators' views on responsibility
for their acts seem to exist. On one hand, as
we have seen, there is sometimes a running
struggle between those reactors who view a
type of deviation as evidence of sickness or
maladjustment and the deviators themselves,
who seek to define their behavior as simply
different from that currently dominant. The
implication seems to be that such deviators
consider themselves "responsible" for their
actions, which they view as morally acceptable. On the other hand, there are times
when deviating individuals or groups seek to
project images of their behavior as "beyond
their control," either applying a "medical
model" to their actions or conditions or
stressing the impact of other external "determinants." For example, a recent study of
Alcoholics Anonymous has noted the extent
to which that organization has employed an
"illness" interpretation of alcoholism to elicit
relatively favorable public response. At any
rate, it does often seem that deviators are
alert to the possible "responsibility implications" of their behavior and that they may
engage in "performance" designed to project
certain images of themselves in this regard.
As Judith Lorber has commented, "the deviant often more or less deliberately conveys
an impression which he hopes will lead to
the imposition of a certain label by his
audience."

As for the views of reactors to deviation,
Stoll has cited various research findings showing that individuals and agencies that hold
deterministic views tend to be less punitive
in their reactions than are those that adopt
voluntaristic interpretations. It seems clear
that the reactors' assumptions about freedom
and responsibility will affect policies toward
deviation and, at least indirectly, individual
deviant "careers" as well. Perhaps the clearest example has been the underlying philosophy of the juvenile court movement and its
impact on the processing of delinquents. As

we have noted, the application of a "rehabilitative ideal" (itself based heavily on deterministic assumptions about the initiation of delinquency) has been a substantial factor affecting the processing and labeling of delinquents. This example also suggests that academic theories about freedom and responsibility can have an impact in the real world, to the extent that they come to be translated into the ideologies and everyday practices of social control organizations. . . .

Although its challenge to the credibility hierarchy seems to suggest that labeling analysis is somewhat "radical" in its political leanings, Alvin Gouldner has argued that, on the contrary, its research focus implies a rather conservative perspective on the problems of modern society. Admitting that a "sociology of the underdog" is justified because deviants undergo much suffering that is both unnecessary and largely hidden from public view, Gouldner has nonetheless considered the labeling approach (in particular the work of Becker) as romanticizing certain nonpolitical deviations and avoiding a truly radical critique of the social system as a whole. Labeling analysis, he has claimed, focuses unduly upon the activities of local officials, while avoiding direct scrutiny or analysis of the national establishment. Even if this accusation were justified, Gouldner's interpretation of the reasons for this focus is not very convincing. Declaring that the new perspectives on deviance may afford an easy avenue to professional attention for young sociologists and that "sociologists with liberal ideologies will more likely adopt underdog perspectives when they experience these as compatible with the pursuit of their own career interests," Gouldner has related these perspectives to the alleged concentration on local officialdom: ". . . the respectables who are being resisted, and whose hierarchy of credibility is disputed, are those local officials who, for most part, do not control access to large supplies of research funds." According to Gouldner, the new underdog sociology is "the sociology of young men with friends in Washington." . . .

On balance, then, what is our assessment of the moral and policy implications of label-ing analysis? First, we reemphasize the roots of the labeling approach in certain basic formulations of classic sociological theory. Whatever changes in moral outlook and public policy may be promoted by labeling research cannot be attributed solely to its unique features. At the same time, the labeling orientation does have some distinctive emphases, and they may well exert an impact on attitudes and policies toward deviance and social control. Among such major policy effects we may cite at least five.

First, its strong relativism reinforces the growing challenge to conventional thinking about problems of deviation, a challenge that has itself, as we have seen, partly contributed to the current popularity of the labeling approach.

Second, by stressing conflict elements, and by focusing on rule-making processes, labeling analysis makes clear that problems of deviance and control are also "value" and "political" problems.

Third, through research on social control processes and agencies, the labeling approach has attracted a great deal of public attention to deficiencies in our control apparatus.

Fourth, by dramatizing the stigmatizing nature of negative labeling, the approach has probably led to somewhat greater caution in the use of negative labels and to less glib resort to euphemistic terminology for processes that are not less harsh or punishing.

Fifth, the voluntaristic theme underlying some labeling analyses may have served a useful purpose in causing various specialists to reassess earlier, largely unquestioned deterministic assumptions about the causes of deviance.

Apart perhaps from promoting a very broad injunction to "avoid unnecessary labeling," the orientation does not seem to provide a clear-cut general direction for public policy toward deviating behavior. On the contrary, the policy impact of labeling-oriented research is probably going to vary, depending upon the type of deviance involved, the specific nature of existing control policies and practices, and the other social forces affecting the course of policy in that particular area.

For example, although research on labeling processes has helped to promote changes in the juvenile court system, such changes also have reflected new outlooks derived partly from other sources, like arguments long advanced by legal critics of the system.

Overall, the labeling orientation carries the potential to generate either broad-scale and basically "political" or narrowly social psychological and essentially "apolitical" studies —or both. Gouldner has recently captured this dual potential in a comment on Erving Goffman's work.

On the one side, it has an implication of being *against* the existent hierarchies and hence against those advantaged by them; it is, to this extent, infused with a rebel vision critical of modern society. On the other side, however, Goffman's rejection of hierarchy often expresses itself as an *avoidance* of social stratification and of the importance of power differences, even for concerns that are central to him; thus it entails an accommodation to existent power arrangements.

Which type of impact the labeling school will have will depend largely upon which version of labeling analysis receives greater emphasis. If the broad focus on conflict and rule-making prevails, then we can expect the orientation to contribute significantly to the formulation of public policies. If, on the other hand, microsociological attention to relevant social psychological processes gains ascendance, then the approach probably will contribute little in the policy realm, though it may, of course, make very useful contributions to sociological theory.

In conclusion, it should be clear that the labeling approach to studying deviance and control is likely neither to undermine the legitimacy of workable, sensible, and humane rules and control processes nor to provide a panacea for the problems created by disturbing and offending behavior. It is not a revolutionary new approach to the analysis of social problems but rather a reordering of emphases in such analysis, a reordering that may help us to view deviance and control in a realistic, comprehensive, and sociologically meaningful light. It will thus continue to deserve our serious attention.

II.
DEVIANT EXCHANGES: GAMBLING, DRUGS, AND SEX

PEOPLE ENGAGE daily in innumerable transactions with one another. They exchange not only goods, services, and money but also friendship, help, intimacy, and deference. All these exchanges are complex blends of choice and constraint; all are affected by the prevailing social definition of what is desirable, but society also says that some exchanges between people are not permitted. Such exchanges are regarded as deviant behavior; the norms may proscribe such exchanges entirely or may proscribe only particular exchanges for certain categories of persons. An example of the second kind is the incest taboo, which proscribes sexual activity with persons in certain kinship relations but not with persons outside them. To engage in sexual relations that can be labeled as incest is to engage in a deviant exchange.

For present purposes, we will confine our attention to voluntary deviant exchanges in which no harm is done to third persons—the so-called "crimes without victims." Obviously some deviant transactions damage third parties, as when two individuals conspire to take another person's property. The exchange is regarded as deviant exactly because it does harm to a third person; if no harm were done, no conspiracy could be said to exist.

In crimes without victims, however, the exchange itself is regarded as deviant, quite apart from any effect it may have on third parties and even though it meets with the wishes of both participants. "Vice" is the old-fashioned name for such exchanges. The moralist's argument is that no matter what the wishes of the persons involved, the exchange is vicious or immoral and does damage to and affronts society (or in a less secular time, God).

When the sociologist uses any concept he is obviously making an assertion about the real world. Here he is saying that nothing intrinsic to exchanges of this kind damages other individuals so that they may legitimately claim to be its victims. We include under this rubric many voluntary exchanges commonly regarded as deviant in American society—in particular, gambling, the use of drugs, and a wide range of proscribed sexual behavior, including heterosexual relationships outside marriage, homosexuality, pornography, and the various issues that arise as a consequence of the connection between heterosexual relations and conception—contraception, abortion, and illegitimacy.

These activities are often said to harm some parties and so can be labeled as deviant. What the sociologist observes, however, is that other activities that have equal potential for harm to third parties are tolerated if not encouraged. Thus the specialist in drugs points out that we permit cigarette but not marihuana smoking, though overwhelming evidence shows that cigarettes harm the individual more than does marihuana. We permit alcohol consumption but proscribe the use of other drugs, though the evidence on damage to third parties demonstrates that alcohol is by far the greater problem. Similarly, we sometimes proscribe gambling on the grounds of damage to third parties—the gambler's wife and family—but any man is free to be a spendthrift in a nightclub or a sporting goods store, thereby equally damaging his family exchequer.

Deviant exchanges of this victimless kind must be understood simply as offenses against morals. For a variety of reasons these particular exchanges contravene the moral values of enough people with enough power to enforce their proscription. Often it doesn't really matter whether many people engage in the deviant behavior so long as everyone clearly understands that it *is* deviant. Those who for some reason hold strong feelings about what they consider the self-indulgence of drug use or gambling, the unnaturalness of homosexuality, or the immorality of premarital heterosexual relations, manage to create a situation in which their moral preferences are ratified by the deviants' stigmatization and, occasionally, more formal punishment. Thus the deviants pay the costs of the moral gratification of those who disapprove of the deviant exchange.

It is not merely this interference with the liberty of others that leads to the sociologist's interest in the social problem of victimless crimes. In addition, much research has suggested that the proliferation of prohibitions against these activities and the concentration of law enforcement attention on them militate against effective law enforcement when it comes to crimes that clearly have victims. Thus researchers have developed in considerable detail the intimate connection between crimes of vice and police corruption. Because these crimes have no complainant, the police decide very much on their own whether or not to enforce the law, thereby creating an uncertainty that policemen and local political organizations may use to extract a price for overlooking violations. Illegal gambling can exist only with police cooperation, and the same is true of any but the most discreet prostitution. The patterns of accommodation that grow up between police and other officials and persons engaged in deviant exchanges constitute a continuing source of political vulnerability, and because corruptness and laxness are widely understood, the legitimacy of government is undermined.

Given the complex relationships that grow up among those engaged in deviant exchanges and between them and officials and ordinary persons, the sociologist has been able to range widely in choosing particular subjects for study. Thus some have devoted a great deal of attention to the processes of the deviant exchanges themselves, while others have concentrated on the exchanges between the deviants and officialdom, and still others on the process by which society establishes or disestablishes a particular exchange as deviant. The selections in this part also show the wide range of methods that can be brought to bear on these issues, from participant observation to survey research to demographic analysis, from interviews with key informants to documentary study to social psychological experiments in the laboratory.

An extremely useful analysis of the problem that victimless crimes create for rational law enforcement is Herbert L. Packer's *The Limits of the Criminal Sanction* (Stanford University Press, 1968). A related approach to the issue of organized crime is Thomas C. Schelling, "Economic Analysis and Organized Crime," in the President's Commission on Law Enforcement and the Administration of Justice, *Task Force Report: Organized Crime* (Government Printing Office, 1967). Another interesting effort to analyze the relationship between law and morality is H. L. A. Hart, *Law, Liberty, and Morality* (Stanford University Press, 1963).

6. GAMBLING IN NEW YORK CITY: THE CASE FOR LEGALIZATION

JOAN RANSOHOFF WYNN AND CLIFFORD GOLDMAN

Reprinted from Joan Ransohoff Wynn and Clifford Goldman, "The Case for and Against Legalized Gambling in New York," from Legal Gambling in New York: A Discussion of Numbers and Sports Betting, *Fund for the City of New York, 1972, pp. 1-19. Copyright 1972 by Fund for the City of New York. Joan Ransohoff Wynn, former head of the Housing Planning Unit of the New York City Bureau of the Budget, and Clifford Goldman, former executive director of the Hackensack Meadowlands Development Commission, acted as consultants to the Fund for the City of New York in compiling the report presented here.*

■ One response to the difficulty and wastefulness of trying to enforce laws against crimes without victims is to remove the criminal label entirely. This suggestion often is made about gambling, which is difficult for many to accept as a "real" crime given the many circumstances in which it is either legal or openly tolerated. Arguments for converting gambling from a crime to a state monopoly seem to have gained ground in recent years, particularly with respect to lotteries, which now exist in several states, as does off-track betting on horse races.

In this study, organized by a New York foundation concerned with better public decisions, an effort is made to assess systematically both the extent of gambling under illegal auspices and some of the consequences were gambling to become a legal state monopoly. The study is distinctive not only for the high professional level at which the analysis is carried out but also for the use of a sample survey to determine the size of the New York City "market" for illegal gambling and its dollar volume. The results provide a basis for policy recommendations on the kinds of gambling that might usefully be legalized and how legal gambling would have to be designed to compete effectively with illegal gambling and drive it out of business.

A useful collection of studies of gamblers and gambling activities is Robert D. Herman, ed., *Gambling* (Harper & Row, 1967). Discussions of organized crime and gambling are in Donald R. Cressey, *Theft of the Nation* (Harper & Row, 1969); Ralph Salerno and John S. Thompkins, *The Crime Confederation* (Doubleday, 1969); the President's Commission on Law Enforcement and the Administration of Justice, *Task Force Report: Organized Crime* (Government Printing Office, 1967); and Marvin B. Scott, *The Racing Game* (Chicago: Aldine, 1968). ■

IN THE TWO CENTURIES of this nation's history, the tide of public opinion has surged back and forth between permissive and restrictive attitudes toward gambling. The actions of a number of legislatures suggest that this tide is now running strongly in favor of lawful betting. State after state, usually on the recommendation of a select study commission, has legalized bingo, pari-mutuel horserace betting, lotteries, and—most recently, in New York—off-track betting. Now under consideration are proposals to legalize the numbers game, sports bookmaking, casinos, and other gambling activities.

Objections to gambling on moral or social grounds in most cases have been overcome by state and local governments' pressing need for additional revenue and legislators' attraction to new, relatively painless sources of such funds. The most efficient, productive levy, the progressive income tax, is largely preempted by the federal government, which up to now has returned little of the money to the localities where it was raised. Legal gambling, an essentially voluntary revenue source controlled by the states, thus has a powerful appeal. And this appeal is enhanced by the astronomical estimates of the size of the betting handle and the profits to be made from taxation or government operation.

Some advocates of legal gambling also contend that it will yield important social benefits. One is to relieve the courts of the onerous, corrupting, and generally futile task of enforcing unpopular laws against gambling. Betting, they argue, is a victimless crime—a diversion that harms only its practitioner and that the public demands. In the face of public ambivalence, or even indifference, the courts tend to be lenient toward accused gamblers, and police are ineffective in any serious attempt to curb the activity. As a result, illegal gambling operators have succeeded in corrupting the law enforcement system.

For this reason, the Knapp Commission recommended:

The criminal laws against gambling should be repealed. To the extent that the legislature deems that some control over gambling is appropriate, such regulation should be by civil rather than criminal process. The police should in any event be relieved from any responsibility for the enforcement of gambling laws or regulations.

Most police reformers regard the elimination of a powerful temptation to corruption as the most compelling argument in favor of repealing laws against betting. Too often, however, they ignore some important consequences. Organized crime* now controls the overwhelming majority of illegal gambling activities. If all gambling is simply declared legal, present operators will have an enormous advantage over legitimate new competitors. Almost certainly the profits of gambling will continue to support criminal organizations whose other activities will still plague the police and the public. It is more than possible, moreover, that organized crime would meet the threat of competition with violence, posing new and more serious law enforcement problems. Unless the police are

* The authors use the term "organized crime" with extreme reluctance and only because of the unwieldiness of the more precise descriptive phrase: large-scale, diversified criminal organizations. By definition, illegal gambling alone is organized crime. Worse, the label has been both romanticized and made the center of controversy about the existence of a national, or international, conspiracy of criminals. So much attention has been focused on the question of whether there is a Mafia or Cosa Nostra that too little study has been made of the way professional criminals function. In this report the term *organized crime* refers in every instance to a large-scale, diversified criminal organization.

prepared to turn their backs on the problem of organized crime, complete legalization of all forms of gambling is not a cure for the disease of corruption.

Some legal gambling proponents argue that a properly designed and operated alternative to present criminal betting would in fact capture the business. In that case, it would deprive organized crime of a large, steady source of income that is its financial mainstay. It would also eliminate employment opportunities for an army of criminals who are now regularly supported by gambling but are available for other jobs. The mere existence of a legal game, however, would not automatically accomplish this objective.

The problems of revenue, corruption, and organized crime, together with declining respect for the law, are among today's most pressing public policy issues. All of them were cited in the February 1972 report of the New York State Commission on Gambling.

From all of this activity and disposition of New York dollars, [illegal gambling] this state and its local governments have derived little or nothing except losses—losses in the form of the expense of largely futile policing and prosecuting activities involving endeavors to enforce our anti-gambling laws; losses in the form of burdensome and disruptive court calendar congestions; losses in the form of debased integrity of officialdom subjected and succumbing to bribery and corruption; losses of public confidence in and respect for the law, its enforcement, the judicial processes, our institutions of government and society in general.

The principal beneficiaries of this illicit but widespread utilization of New York dollars within this state have been the criminal elements (organized crime) [sic]. They reap the harvest therefrom and sow it in other fields which they also soon come to control. Illicit gambling comprises one of the largest business enterprises in this state. It grows by leaps and bounds. Yet, for all intents and purposes, it is not taxed; it contributes virtually nothing to government but headaches and disintegration. We feel that it is time to ensnare it, control it, and devote its enormous profits to legitimate public needs.

The ideal legal betting game would accomplish all of the major objectives. It would attract substantially all of the illegal game's customers. At that point the illegal game would cease to be a problem for the police and the courts. All of the profits would be denied to organized crime and would flow into government coffers to be used for worthy purposes.

This suggests that the trick is simply to design such a game. Unfortunately, it can't be done. The three main policy goals do not necessarily reinforce one another, and they may be competitive. Public officials will have to be certain of what they most want to achieve from legalized gambling.

Even if the government runs the legal game, it is important to recognize the competitive advantages of the established, illegal activity. It has a generally satisfied clientele. It is run by experienced, generally efficient operators. It is free from legal accountability and financial regulation, which enables it to operate in a fluid and convenient manner. It can provide credit to players. It pays no taxes on its profits and neither do its customers on their winnings.

A legal game would have an edge in its ability to operate openly and to engage in aggressive promotion. It would attract some new customers who refuse to bet illegally. But a game that hopes to capture the present business must offer gamblers an appreciably more appealing proposition. For most, that means a higher payout in a game of equivalent convenience. (See Figure 6.1.)

Here the inherent conflict between revenue-raising and competitiveness becomes plain. Higher prizes, unless offset by lower operating costs, must reduce revenues. In order to overcome the natural advantages of an established game, the new legal alternative must spend more and keep less. Thus it is too simple to assume that a legal game, by capturing the illegal market, will return to the government as much money as the present criminal activity yields its operators.

The easiest and most profitable way for legal gambling to grow is to exploit its promotional opportunities and create new customers. But the likely result of such a policy is the creation of two separate and parallel games: the illegal game, continuing to thrive on the business of its present customers; and the new legal game, largely dependent on bettors who do not now gamble regularly —almost certainly mostly smaller bettors.

In such a situation, the job of enforcing the law against illegal gambling would be even more difficult. Agents of the legal game must be protected. And unless it is made clear that legalization of some popular forms of gambling is part of a drive against organized crime's illegal betting activities, greater public acceptance of gambling could prompt the courts to be even more lenient in their attitude toward accused illegal operators. The police would be asked in effect to protect a new revenue source with no new tools and in an even less supportive environment.

When gambling is legalized for the sake of its revenue potential, officials are tempted to devise new betting variations that face no competition. The New York State Lottery is a case in point. Lottery players as a group get back no more than 45 percent of their aggregate wager in prizes. This is a lower payoff than that received by numbers bettors, whom operators and police regard as suckers. Thus the lottery has had no appreciable effect on the illegal numbers game. Indeed, lottery profits are so high that organized crime is invading the market by counterfeiting tickets and selling them in competition with those offered by the state.

The consequences of striving for high profits can also be seen in the experience of OTB, the only legal form of gambling that seeks to compete directly with criminal operators. At least a third of OTB's handle is in exotic wagers (e.g., the Superfecta) in which a small bet against high odds returns a large prize to the winner. Such bets appeal mostly to small players, who usually do not bet with bookies. Not surprisingly, since OTB faces little or no competition for these wagers there has been discussion of cutting the winner's share from 83 to 75 percent in order to increase government revenues. And as a consequence of this cultivation of a new and different market, police estimate that bookies in New York still handle upward of $150 million a year in horse race bets.

There is an important lesson in this. Legal

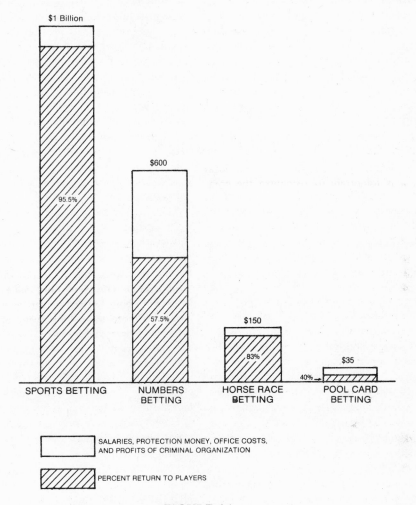

FIGURE 6.1

Size and payout of major illegal gambling operations in New York City (in millions)

gambling, even if it matches the prize structure of its illegal counterpart, will not necessarily capture all of the business. It may take a share of the business, as OTB unquestionably has, but it does not go to the heart of the problems of organized crime and corruption. Unless the legal game replaces the illegal activity, moreover, the public revenues generated can only approach those of illegal gambling by creating a new and parallel market. The consensus of law enforcement officers interviewed for this study is that OTB and the city's bookmakers are presently functioning in just such parallel markets.

This is an unsatisfactory situation for several reasons. It fails to deal effectively with organized crime and corruption. The dollars earned lack the added value of having been denied to organized crime. And because the huge profits in illegal gambling cannot be captured, the results are disappointing even to those whose primary concern is revenue.

Perhaps most important, the thrust of a legal game in a parallel market is the addition of new bettors and an increase in the volume of gambling. But there is an important difference between accepting the public's impulse to gamble and encouraging it for the sake of raising money. The government taxes liquor and tobacco, but it does not—and should not—promote their use.

From a practical standpoint, moreover, there are other objections to legalizing gambling primarily for revenue. Legal gambling is an unreliable revenue source that requires constant promotion. Compared with other forms of taxation, it is wasteful of human and financial resources. It requires valuable skills, and administrative costs are relatively high. In most cases, the burden of gambling is likely to be regressive. To a considerable degree, gambling is a form of entertainment. If the government is to provide such entertainment, it should strive to offer its purchasers the fairest possible deal. In no case should government exploit bettors' ignorance.

The best case for legalizing any form of gambling rests on its potential effect on organized crime and official corruption. The social and law enforcement impact of widespread government-sponsored gambling is not necessarily outweighed by the money it might generate for public use. But if legal gambling can help to eliminate other, more serious and intractable evils, a good argument can be made for it apart from any revenue considerations.

The foregoing analysis suggests three major conclusions.

First, the primary objective of any legal form of gambling should be the elimination of its illegal counterpart. Success should be measured by police intelligence reports, arrests, convictions, sentences, and periodic surveys to determine the extent of illegal betting. Even after illegal gambling is ended, revenue must not assume too much importance as a goal. An increase in the government's bite, and the accompanying decrease in prizes, could provide an incentive for criminal entrepreneurs to revive the illegal game.

Second, legal gambling should be viewed as a *tool* of law enforcement, not as a substitute for it. Legal gambling that furnishes an attractive alternative outlet for the public's betting impulse will make it easier for the police and the courts to put pressure on illegal activity. At first, even a competitive legal game will require the assistance of the law to overcome the advantages of its illegal competitors. In the long run, if the legal game is successful the police will be relieved of the burden of enforcing antigambling laws. In the short run, however, the police must be more diligent. Legalization should be accompanied by stiffer actions against illegal gambling and an educational campaign to enlist the support of the public.

Third, the purpose of a legal game should be to attract current players, not to create new customers. This principle should strictly limit promotional efforts of a legal game. Rather, a legal game should be made obviously more appealing to the practiced player. Some forms of gambling, like the numbers game, are especially exploitative. For reasons that we shall explain, they also tend to be the easiest games for the government to operate. But it is one thing for the government to eliminate the illegal operators of these exploitative games and quite another simply to take their place.

Having set forth our general principles, we shall now summarize the findings of our studies of numbers and sports betting.

NUMBERS BETTING

Numbers (or policy) is a lottery in which a player bets on the number of his choice. There are several variations, but the conventional and most prevalent form in New York is a wager on a 3-digit number from 000 through 999. Winners receive high payoffs, but the odds are heavily against them. The chances that any given number will win are 1 in 1,000. A winner is paid off at advertised odds of 500 or 600 to 1 in most games, but several factors (e.g., tips to runners and reduced payoffs on special or frequently played numbers) cut the actual payoff to 540 to 1 or less.

New York City residents bet about $600

million a year on numbers each year. Over 1.4 million people—24 percent of the adult population—play the game. While the game is thus widely known, many popular beliefs about it are incorrect. For example, numbers is not a game played exclusively by Blacks, Puerto Ricans, or the poor. Fifty-five percent of all players are White, and three-fourths are employed. Play is *proportionately* much heavier among Blacks and Puerto Ricans. Roughly 20 percent of the city's White adults bet on numbers, compared with 40 percent of Blacks and Puerto Ricans.

There is, however, a strong feeling in Black and Puerto Rican neighborhoods that numbers is "their" game. Its lore is part of the community fabric. Runners and controllers are well-known figures. A recent study of Bedford-Stuyvesant has shown how organized crime siphons money from the community through the numbers game. The profits from the numbers game are used to support other activities of organized crime, including narcotics, hijacking, and the theft and sale of securities. While the game's revenues are largely drained off from the community by organized crime and used to finance other syndicate-controlled activities, this fact is not generally perceived by local residents.

The proprietary attitude of local communities is a problem that must be faced squarely by those who have to design a legal numbers game. A good deal of apprehension has been expressed by Black and Puerto Rican communities that legalization would mean a government (i.e., White) takeover of a profitable enterprise that is now viewed as their own.

The numbers organization is three-tiered: many runners report to a much smaller group of controllers, who in turn are associated with a handful of bankers. Runners accept and record bets and pay off winners; they are the sales representatives of the business. Controllers are the equivalent of district managers. Bankers finance the game, assume the risks and receive the profits, which are estimated at roughly $60 million annually. The entire U.S. airline industry makes less money each year.

In New York, the game is controlled by large-scale, diversified criminal organizations to which individual bankers are connected. Individual numbers organizations and the larger criminal group benefit mutually from this arrangement. Operators gain access to money to finance large hits, protection from the law, and a mechanism for allocating territory and controlling price levels and competition. Organized crime receives profits, either through direct operation or in the form of tribute from bankers. The game also provides criminal organizations with a large number of jobs for its members and associates, as well as a network of contacts within the law enforcement system that is useful for protecting other illegal activities.

SPORTS BETTING

There are two major types of sports betting: poolselling and bookmaking. The former, like numbers, is based on many small bets. The Quayle study found that New Yorkers bet $25 million a year on football pools and another $10 million on baseball and basketball pools. This handle is augmented by the bets of commuters and other nonresidents.

Pools pay off even more poorly than numbers. A player tries to pick the winners of from 3 to 16 games. The odds against his picking 16 games correctly are more than 65,000 to 1. But a winner's prize is only 5,000 to 1, with a consolation prize of 200 to 1 for the player who gets 15 out of 16. The probabilities are that the operator keeps more than 90 percent of the money in such bets. For the player, the best strategy is to pick four games. In this case, the operator's advantage is only 37.5 percent. The poolseller also wins all tie games. On the whole, he should retain from 60 percent to 80 percent of his total handle.

Police and bookmakers alike regard poolsellers as petty operators. The same agencies that have confiscated voluminous bookmaking records have only fragmentary examples of poolselling paraphernalia—an accurate indication of this activity's rank among law enforcement concerns. The aggregate proceeds of poolselling are anything but petty. Operators keep as much as $28 million of the $35 million bet each year. Because of high sales costs and the proliferation of loosely organized small operators, however, probably less than $3 million a year reaches the upper levels of organized crime.

Poolselling is a mechanical enterprise that demands efficiency and a widespread sales effort but no particular ingenuity. Because of its low risks and small bets, it requires neither the financial backing nor reinsurance service supplied to bookmakers by diversified criminal organizations. Nevertheless, poolselling is believed, by some police officials, to be controlled by organized crime.

In terms of volume, bookmaking on sports (football, baseball, and basketball) is the largest illegal gambling enterprise in the city. Police estimate the annual handle at about $1 billion. Bookmakers take another $150 million to $200 million a year in horse racing bets. The bookie charges a commission for brokering bets. On football or basketball, a bettor must wager $11 to win $10. The bookmaker keeps $1 of each $22 bet regardless of which team wins. His commission is therefore 4.5 percent. The amount bet on each team is equalized by the point spread—a handicap for the stronger team. In baseball, bets are equalized by variable odds, but the commission is still about 4.5 percent. Bookies also accept combination bets on sports at about the same commission.

Sports bookmaking is a high-volume, low-commission business. Bets are usually large—one-third of football bettors typically bet $50 or more, 1 in 11 generally wagers $100. On horse racing, the commission is much larger—the same 17 percent that the tracks and OTB withhold from the handle. Bookmaking profits from New York City residents alone amount to about $45 million a year on sports bets, and another $34 million on the much smaller horse racing handle. To a bookie, a dollar bet on a horse race is worth nearly a four-dollar bet on sports.

Organized crime controls bookmaking in several ways. Some offices are operated directly. Small, formerly independent bookies who have been "organized" serve these offices as runners. They keep 50 percent of the losses of their customers. Some independent bookies are permitted to run their own offices in exchange for tribute based on the size of their operations. Such independents often end up inside the organization when they have to turn to organized crime for loans to cover heavy losses.

Bookmaking involves substantial risks and demands adroit manipulation of the devices available to minimize such risks. A bookie's goal is to balance perfectly the bets on each contest. Point spreads, which should be as accurate as possible to start, are shifted as betting develops to attract money to the lightly bet contestant. The more point spreads have to be changed, the greater the possibility that the bookmaker will be "middled"—that is, will lose the heavy bets on one team at the initial spread and those on the other team at the adjusted spread.

The bookmaker can stop taking bets on a game when the wagering is seriously out of balance. But this limits his volume and offends his customers. The alternative is to lay off his excess bets (i.e., bet them with another bookmaker). The layoff process can be complicated, taking several steps through a widespread system. The larger the system, of course, the better the chance that local betting imbalances can be evened out.

Every bookmaker must accept some imbalances, since he loses customers by closing his book and loses commissions by laying off bets. In the long run, he can expect to win as many unbalanced bets as he loses. What he needs is the financial capacity to ride out a losing streak. Association with a large criminal organization can provide this and help him minimize his risks. Thus while affiliation with organized crime may sometimes be dictated by power considerations (e.g., the fear of the law on the one hand or of possible criminal violence on the other), it also flows logically from the economics of illegal bookmaking.

LEGALIZATION

Our studies have brought us to the conclusion that three technical criteria should apply to legalization of any existing unlawful form of gambling. The first is obvious: a legal game should be more attractive than the illegal game to its present customers. The second is equally clear: a legal game should include foolproof safeguards of its fiscal integrity. The government should never be in the position of gambling with taxpayers' money.

The third criterion is that a legal gambling activity should be controlled by the government rather than by private licensees. This is admittedly a more controversial premise, but the experience of privately operated legal gambling—in some states of the United States as well as in foreign countries—makes us share the fear of some law enforcement officials that criminal elements may infiltrate licensed gambling. The result would be continuing corruption and new police problems. The New York legislature, apparently with this possibility in mind, ruled out private operation when it approved a constitutional amendment to authorize legal gambling in the state.

By all our criteria, numbers and poolselling are more suitable for legalization than bookmaking. Both numbers and poolselling have high profit margins to cover operation costs. A legal form of either game could substantially better the prizes now paid by its illegal counterpart even if its expenses proved somewhat higher. Bookmaking, though, now operates on a margin of 4.5 percent. OTB needs 10 percent merely to cover costs and is trying to cut that figure to 7.5 percent. Detailed analysis may show that bookmaking can be run by the government (possibly using OTB's facilities) on a 4.5 percent margin. But we must assume on the present evidence that it cannot—especially since legalized sports betting would attract a high proportion of small bets that are relatively more costly to handle.

Large bettors will not be attracted to legal bookmaking because gambling winnings over $600 must be reported to the Internal Revenue Service for federal income tax purposes. To a bettor in the 40 percent tax bracket (not unrealistic for the typical "high roller"), a winning legal bet of $1,100 would net only $600. An equivalent bet with a bookie would yield $1,000 tax free. To put it another way, for the same legal net return of $600, the bettor would have to risk only $660 in an illegal wager, not $1,100.

Another major tax obstacle to legal sports gambling—but not necessarily to legal numbers or poolselling—is the 10 percent federal excise on the total handle of many forms of gambling. The tax would apply to legal bookmaking unless it were set up on a parimutuel basis. Since the bookie's total margin is only 4.5 percent, the tax would have to be added to the price of a bet. A legal wager that paid $10 would cost $12.10 rather than $11. What this means can already be seen in Las Vegas, where illegal bookmaking continues to thrive in spite of legal competition. The excise tax does not apply to state-operated lotteries whose winning numbers are established by the results of a horse race. A state-operated numbers game could escape the excise tax by using a number selection system similar to that now employed by state lotteries. The excise tax would apply to a sports pool, unless it were set up on a pari-mutuel basis, but pools' margins are so high that the tax could be absorbed.

Finally, a government bookmaking operation—if it were to have any chance to attract present bettors—would have to offer credit. The Quayle study showed that of bettors who wager more than $500 a year on sports one-fourth normally bet on credit and 40 percent bet on credit at least half of the time. The bigger the bettor, moreover, the more likely he is to expect and use credit. By contrast, only 5 percent of numbers players use credit "frequently."

Our second criteria is that legislation to legalize any new form of gambling must include theoretical and practical assurances that the game cannot lose money—in other words, that the government is not gambling. In poolselling, for example, the chances of the operator's losing—even on a given day—are so remote as to be almost impossible. But even this is not good enough for a government-operated activity.

In the state lottery, at horse racing tracks and in OTB, the payout is a fixed percentage of the receipts. There is no practical way for the government to lose.* The state lottery is mathematically secure, because tickets are prenumbered. The number of winners is completely controlled, and total prizes are held to 45 percent of receipts. But players in a legal numbers game must be permitted to pick their own numbers. It is possible that many players could select the same winning number on a given day, so that the game had to pay out more in prizes than it had taken in. Several "break the bank" provisions, detailed later in this report, can be incorporated in a legal game to protect against this remote possibility. Similar safeguards are available for pools. In both cases, the task is not difficult because of the favorable odds of the games.

Assuring the financial safety of a legal bookmaking operation is not so easy. The government could not lay off dangerously heavy bets, and could not easily make the quick entrepreneurial decisions that a successful bookie must make. Sports betting could be put on a pari-mutuel basis; this would have the added advantage of exempting it from the 10 percent federal excise tax. But pari-mutuel betting would not attract many of illegal bookmaking's present customers, who are accustomed to fixed odds. This would be especially true if the government attempted to raise its cut substantially above the present 4.5 percent commission.

Another possibility is suggested in an unpublished paper by graduate students in the New School's Department of Urban Affairs and Public Analysis. They would use computers to set shifting point spreads under fixed odds. Possible losses (i.e., the allowable imbalance in bets on a game or group of games) would be limited to the profit margin. But this would be only 4.5 percent less operating expenses—a very narrow limit indeed. Further study is needed to establish whether betting patterns are regular enough for such a system to work, whether betting could take place freely under its limitations, or even whether it is feasible at all in such a low-margin game. The main point is that it would be a knotty problem simply to design a secure legal bookmaking operation, with no likelihood that it could capture an important share of the present business.

Government sports bookmaking can scarcely be as competitive with illegal activity as OTB now is with illegal horse race bookmaking. OTB faces no federal excise tax, can afford to pay track odds, and doesn't need to limit traditional betting practices to insure its financial security. Yet even OTB has not put the bookies out of the horse race betting business.

Poolselling is better suited to government operation. Its current payoff odds are so low that a legal game could offer much higher prizes without increasing the dangers of loss unacceptably. Blank entry forms could be sold on a commission basis in the same manner as lottery tickets. The only social benefits, however, would be to give players a fairer break and to deny a relatively small amount of revenue to organized crime. Legalization of pools would have little impact on corruption in the law enforcement system, which pays almost no attention to the present illegal operation.

We believe that the numbers game is the best vehicle to test the proposition that control of some important forms of gambling can be wrested from the criminal organizations that now run them, collect their profits, and use the money to support other activity such as the narcotics trade. Because the numbers game attracts large numbers of small players, less affected by federal income taxes on winnings; bcause the federal excise tax need not apply; because credit betting is less extensive than assumed; and because a legal

---

* There is one minor exception. In pari-mutuel horse betting, there is a fixed minimum payment of 10 cents on a winning $2 bet. It is conceivable that a winning horse could be so heavily favored that losing bets would not provide enough to cover this minimum payout. But decades of racing results document the fact that this minor risk can be ignored.

game can be designed that will offer a substantially higher payout, legalized numbers can supplant the present illegal game in certain conditions.

A competitively successful legal game must:

1. Offer the same convenience and betting format. Players must be permitted to choose their own numbers, and must receive fixed-odds prizes.

2. Offer greater prizes. As much as possible (allowing for expenses and government revenues roughly equal in percentage to the sales tax) payoffs should approach the actual odds against winning. A payoff of 825 to 1 would cover operating costs of 10.5 percent and still return 7 percent to government.

3. Respond to the proprietary feeling of Black and Puerto Rican communities toward the present game. A controlled form of community operation is possible, and probably desirable, but unregulated community control would provide the surest opportunities for infiltration by criminal elements. Raising the cash prize payout to players is unquestionably the most direct and perhaps the most effective way of keeping the game's proceeds in the neighborhoods from which they come. Other schemes have been suggested—e.g., reserving a portion of the game's revenue to be administered by neighborhood nonprofit corporations for high-priority projects in heavy-betting neighborhoods. Such schemes probably deserve further exploration, but they present difficult problems of equity and administration without any assurance that they would actually benefit heavy-betting communities as significantly as would returning the cash directly to the people in more liberal prizes.

A successful legal game paying more back to the bettors would not support so many runners as the current illegal game. Bettors now subsidize the employment of more runners and other numbers "employees" than appear to be necessary to bring the game effectively to its players.

A legal game's operation must have a government control mechanism to guarantee its security, but it must also be responsive to the interests of bettors and of local betting communities. The government's role would be to provide financial security and overall policy direction. But the game could be operated locally, by roughly 20 local corporations, profit or nonprofit. Bets should be sold by stationary agents, by mobile runners, and in certain high density betting areas by computerized vending machines.

In spite of the apparently more liberal public attitude toward gambling, we believe that some arguments against it—particularly as a government activity—cannot be lightly dismissed. In our opinion, legal gambling will be in the public interest only if it helps to solve some of the problems associated with illegal gambling. To us, the case for legal gambling as a means of raising revenue is weak. Legalizing some forms of gambling as a contribution to the battle against official corruption and organized crime is worth a try.

To achieve a measure of success, there will have to be sustained pressure on criminal gambling operations from two sides: the economic competition of a higher payout legal game, and the unacceptable costs of stiff fines and jail terms for those convicted of illegal gambling operations. But it would be a mistake to expect too much to result. Real solutions to such basic problems will require much more basic and far-reaching efforts.

7. MARIHUANA USE IN AMERICAN SOCIETY

NATIONAL COMMITTEE ON MARIHUANA AND DRUG ABUSE

Abridged from Marihuana: A Signal of Misunderstanding, *Appendix, The Technical Papers of the First Report of the National Commission on Marihuana and Drug Abuse, vol. 1, pp. 249-86.*

■ In 1970 Congress established the National Commission on Marihuana and Drug Abuse and required it to report to the President, Congress, and the public its findings on the realities of drug use and abuse and to recommend alternatives to present public policy. The first Commission report discussed marihuana use; the second dealt more broadly with drug abuse.

President Nixon sought to give the Commission a conservative bias in line with his own strong views about drugs, and the Commission was obviously sensitive in its work to the gap between these views and those of most drug experts. The media rapidly condensed the issue into the single question of whether the Commission would recommend the decriminalization of marihuana—that is, recommend that laws punishing the use of marihuana be repealed. Instead, the Commission recommended in its first report that possession of marihuana for personal use no longer be an offense but that marihuana possessed in public should remain contraband and subject to summary seizure and forfeit. Further, it recommended that "casual distribution of small amounts of marihuana for no renumeration or insignificant renumeration not involving profit" no longer be an offense, but that its cultivation, sale, or distribution for profit and its possession with intent to sell should remain a felony. More specific recommendations were designed to carry out a "discouragement policy" toward marihuana use while at the same time lifting the burden of criminality from what was obviously a widespread social habit.

These recommendations were not acceptable to President Nixon, but that seems to be the general fate of presidents and their commissions. Congress and the President appoint commissions to investigate complex issues of public policy, such as racial discrimination, violence, population and birth control, obscenity, and pornography. The commissioners often begin their work in a conservative frame of mind, but in the end they typically adopt the perspectives of informed experts on whom they must rely. When these commissions report, they often assert as rational a policy that the politicians find ideologically or politically unpalatable.

Our selection from the technical appendix to the Report of the National Commission on Marihuana and Drug Abuse deals with survey data designed to establish the extent of marihuana use in the country and the characteristics of its use and users. Accurate information of this kind was crucial to the Commission's conclusions about the removal of criminal penalties for marihuana use. If marihuana was in fact widely and regularly used, criminal penalties simply made no sense; their cost was greater than any conceivable gain from criminal sanctions. The survey data were central to what became the principal thrust of the Commission's work on marihuana—that is, how to come to terms with its continued use as a standard part of the culture of late adolescents and young adults. The survey results were used to establish not only the extent of marihuana use but also something about the social process by which marihuana comes to be used—the role of parental drug use, peer group influence, socioeconomic status, personality factors, and the like.

The literature on marihuana is by now quite extensive. The classic sociological work on becoming a marihuana user is that of Howard S. Becker, reported in *Outsiders* (Free Press, 1963). Other books dealing with more recent patterns of marihuana use include Erich Goode, *The Marihuana Smokers* (Basic Books, 1970); L. Grinspoon, *Marihuana Reconsidered* (Harvard University Press, 1971); J. Kaplan, *Marihuana: The New Prohibition* (Pocket Books, 1971); and R. H. Blum et al., *Society and Drugs*, (San Francisco: Jossey-Bass, 1969). ■

APPROXIMATELY 35 YEARS AGO, the use of marihuana in the United States was defined as a social problem of major proportions. At that time, its use as an intoxicant in this country was limited for the most part to jazz musicians, artists, literary figures, merchant seamen, miners, ranch hands, farm laborers, and other individuals defined as social "outsiders" or marginal types. Many of these persons were drawn from minority group, lower socioeconomic segments of the society.

In the late 1920s and early 1930s, marihuana use became publicly linked to crime, violence, insanity, sexual aggression, immorality, and drug addiction. In subsequent years, marihuana control legislation was passed at both the federal and state levels. Provisions for very harsh penalties reflected the belief that marihuana use was harmful to the individual and society. In retrospect we find much of the evidence purporting to establish these links was spurious, scientifically invalid or simply nonexistent.

Seemingly without warning, the problem of marihuana use emerged once again in the 1960s but this time in altered form. The new marihuana users, however, were quite distinct from those of earlier times. They included young men and women from middle class families, many of whom were attending college (and later high school youth as well) who were bred in relative affluence. These were young people who, in the words of two researchers, were "educated to the ideals of individual freedom and intent on forging their own moral rules, released from parental supervision at an early age and dedicated to the serious pursuit of pleasure as well as to the satisfactions of work." More and more middle and upper middle class youth "discovered" marihuana and experimented with the drug while parents, educators, and government officials watched and worried. In the relatively short period from the thirties to the sixties, marihuana use moved from the fringe or marginal members of society, the outsiders, to youthful, educated, affluent "insiders" of the society.

Various explanations and theoretical propositions have been advanced to unravel the relatively widespread use and acceptance of marihuana by young people. At the societal level, theoretical formulations explain marihuana use as being related to alienation among the young. In this explanation, marihuana is posited as being an outward sign of youthful rebellion against authority. At the interactional level, marihuana use is described as behavior related primarily to conformity to peer group expectations. At the individual level, marihuana use has variously been described as a means of coping with emotional problems, as a means of reducing anxiety, as an aspect of youthful curiosity and as part of youth's search for "kicks" or new experiences.

Numerous and diverse consequences attendant to marihuana use have been described. Most individuals who use or have used marihuana describe a feeling of mild euphoria or intoxication that is perceived as pleasurable. Some persons have stated that marihuana use increases the user's chances of "dropping out" of society or "dropping down" in terms of not achieving at his level of potential. Others are concerned that marihuana use increases the chances of experimenting with other and more dangerous drugs, and although the numbers seem to have declined within recent years, a considerable segment of the American public still believes that marihuana produces addiction and leads to heroin, causes crime, can cause death, and makes people lose their desire to work.

Discussion of marihuana inevitably involves a consideration of the demographic as well as the behavioral correlates of marihuana use. Thus, the questions: Who uses marihuana? Under what circumstances and why? How does the process of becoming a marihuana user take place? Under what circumstances is use sustained or discontinued? What is the nature of marihuana use as well as the incidence of use? These and related questions are central to any consideration of the issue of marihuana use.

What must be understood is the overwhelming importance of social and cultural forces operating in all drug use. Human behavior in relation to drugs occurs only within specific social settings which themselves determine the form that behavior will take, and not the drug itself. People do not "escalate" from the use of marihuana to more dangerous drugs because of any property resting within the chemistry of marihuana itself. If and when escalation does occur, it is a function of the kinds of people who use these drugs, their attitudes and values, their friendship networks, activities related to drug use and other related circumstances. Whether we are considering the individual who has just been initiated to marihuana use or the multidrug user, we must bear in mind that people differently located in the social structure, acting out different roles in society, will "escalate" at different rates. In this process it is not the drug acting on the body that produces the changes which occur, but other people acting on their behavior. ...

Surveys have attempted to determine, at the least, the incidence and prevalence of marihuana use; that is, the proportion of individuals who have *ever used* and who *currently use* marihuana.

The surveys, taken together, demonstrate significant overall increases, since about 1965, in the proportion of Americans who have tried marihuana at least once and those who currently use the drug. They also show, however, that substantial proportions of individuals who try the drug on one or more occasions discontinue use and that the overwhelming majority of those who have *never* tried marihuana are unlikely to experiment with it in the future, even if it were to become legal and more readily available.

PERSONS WHO HAVE TRIED MARIHUANA

The most current available estimate of the number of Americans who have ever used marihuana has been obtained from the results of the Commission's National Survey conducted during August of 1971. The findings show that 14 percent of the youth (12 to 17 years of age) and 15 percent of the adults (18 years and over) in the national sample reported they had tried marihuana at least once. Projecting from this nationally representative sample to the total U.S. resident population in 1970, we now estimate that 3,360,000 youth and 20,700,000 adults or a total of roughly 24 million Americans have tried (ever used) marihuana.

This figure is considerably higher than those obtained from other national surveys conducted between October 1969 and February 1971, all of which were limited to *adults* either 18 or 21 years of age and older, and none of which yielded an estimate of "ever use" higher than 6 percent.

The October 1969 Gallup national poll of adults 21 years and over, for example, yielded a figure of 4 percent or 10 million Americans who had tried marihuana. A telephone poll conducted by the Columbia Broadcasting System in August 1970 revealed that 6 percent of a nationally representative sample of 1,128 adults 18 years and over had tried marihuana. The Social Research Group at George Washington University conducted personal interviews with a nationally representative sample of 2,552 adults 18 to 74 years of age. The results of the survey undertaken during late 1970 and early 1971 show that 5 percent of American adults had tried marihuana.

These figures indicate that the proportion of adults in the population who have used marihuana has increased by 300 percent or more between 1969 and 1971. ...

The Commission's National Survey estimated that 44 percent of American college students had ever used marihuana. ...

The most current estimate of "ever use" of marihuana by college students is that recently revealed by the American Institute of Public Opinion. Its interview survey, conducted in December of 1971 among 1,063 students on 57 campuses, revealed that 51 percent had tried marihuana at least once. This figure suggests that while marihuana use among college students continues to increase, the rate of increase may be slowing somewhat from that of previous years. ...

The Commission's National Survey results constitute the most current estimate of marihuana experience among the nation's junior and senior high school age youth. . . .

The survey findings show that 8 percent of those youth with an 8th grade education or less and 11 percent of those in the 9th through 12th grades had tried marihuana. These figures, like those given for age, increase with increasing educational level (8th grade or less = 8 per cent; 9th-10th grades = 11 per cent; 11th-12 grades = 30 per cent). . . .

The surveys clearly demonstrate that the incidence of marihuana use is age related. Persons who have used marihuana are concentrated primarily among young adults of college age (approximately 18 to 24).

Junior high school students appear to be about half as likely as senior high school students to have tried marihuana, and senior high school students seem to be about half as likely as college students to have ever used the drug. The proportion of adults beyond age 25 who have used marihuana seems to mirror, on the downswing, the upward slope of "ever use" by those in the 12 to 17 age category. [See Table 7.1.]

A more thorough examination of the survey findings, however, suggests that age is not the only factor which is significantly correlated with marihuana use. Differential rates of use have also been observed according to sex, socioeconomic status, religious affiliation, political orientation, student status, type of school attended, community type and region of the country in which

one resides. The most significant determinant of marihuana use, however, appears to be knowledge of or association with friends and age peers who have used the drug. . . .

Regardless of the point at which they begin using marihuana most of the ever users terminate the practice of smoking marihuana by the time they reach mature adulthood.

Undoubtedly, this fact raises questions about the motivations for using the drug in the first place, about the reasons why some people continue to use the drug and others terminate its use, and about the reasons the majority of Americans never try it. The survey findings provide rather reasonable and predictable answers to these questions. . . .

BECOMING A MARIHUANA USER

Meaningful discussion of the use of marihuana necessarily involves investigation of the process which occurs prior to marihuana use. Thus, we must ask, "Is the use of legal drugs such as alcohol, cigarettes and prescription drugs related in any way to the use of marihuana and other illegal drugs?" Statements attempting to describe human behavior almost invariably extend beyond the specific subject matter of the statements themselves. When the statement, "marihuana leads to the use of more dangerous drugs" is made, a number of underlying assumptions is that socially acceptable substances do not

TABLE 7.1

MARIHUANA EXPERIENCE AMONG AMERICANS
12 YEARS AND OVER, BY AGE

Age	Ever Use	Current Use	% of Ever Use
12 - 17	14%	6%	43%
18 - 21	40	18	45
22 - 25	38	16	42
26 - 30	24	8	33
31 - 34	11	2	18
35 - 39	13	1	8
40 - 49	7	0	0
50 - 59	6	0	0
60 +	4	0	0

"lead to" dangerous drug use—that the role of marihuana is distinctive and unique. For example, many officials and the public do *not* believe that alcohol and cigarettes "lead to" dangerous drug use; they often do believe, however, that marihuana does. The social and legal acceptance of alcohol and cigarettes is, in large part, responsible for the former; the criminalization and concomitant stigmatization of marihuana, its use and possession would appear to be the basis for the latter belief. Underlying both the hypothesis and conclusion is the issue of legality. Implicit, then, is the notion that only an illicit substance can lead to the use of other and more dangerous substances.

What, then, is the role of legal drugs in the escalation process to marihuana and other, potentially and more dangerous drugs?

Considerable evidence exists which points to the fact that legal drugs do lead to the use of illegal drugs, an escalation from cigarettes and alcohol to dangerous drugs, and an escalation from prescription drugs, such as barbiturates, tranquilizers and amphetamines to marihuana and such dangerous drugs as LSD, cocaine and heroin.

In at least the following three meanings, legal drugs "lead to" the use of illegal drugs: (1) legal parental drug use is statistically correlated with the illegal drug use of their children; (2) young people who drink alcohol and smoke cigarettes have a higher likelihood of eventually using illegal drugs than is true of their age peers who do not use these legal drugs; (3) there is considerable suspicion that pharmaceutical advertising contributes to a climate of tolerance toward drug taking, toward consciousness-altering chemicals and, in addition, produces prescription drugs in such massive quantities that their use outside a medical setting on a widespread basis is almost inevitable.

Drug use is partly an outgrowth of the life-style of one's parents. This statement might appear to contradict common sense. After all, parents overwhelmingly oppose their children's drug use. Yet, how could such a negative sentiment translate into its opposite? Massive generational differences,

especially in regard to drug use, obviously exist, but historical trends take place within a context of continuity.

The political ideology of today's youth is probably a few degrees to the left of that of their parents. But it is the specifically liberal parent who tends to raise (slightly more) liberal children. The parental generation will disapprove of much of the sexual permissiveness of today's young adults, but it is from the somewhat permissive parents that the (somewhat more) permissive children spring.

Young people who use illegal drugs tend to have been raised by parents who, although negative toward their use of drugs, were not nearly so hostile as their neighbors whose children did not use illegal drugs.

PARENTAL DRUG USE

Parents provide a model or example of acceptable behavior for their children. The example conveyed by a liquor drinking, cigarette smoking, prescription taking parent is very different from that of the parent who is a complete abstainer. There is, then, a generational continuity to historical change. The same acts do not mean the same thing in different generations, and likewise, different acts may mean very similar things. In a sense, the illegal drug use of many youth today has a kind of equivalency in the legal drug use of their parent's generation. . . .

In sum, the conclusion seems inescapable that parental example is a powerful force in impelling young people toward illegal drug use. This does not mean that all smoking and drinking parents will raise children who inevitably become involved with illegal drugs; nor does it mean that only drinking and smoking parents will raise drug-using children. But it does mean that there is a statistical relationship between these two forms of behavior; whether or not there is causality in this statistical association is a matter for further investigation. The consistency and significance of the relationship probably does indicate, however, that the legal drug use of adults today is one potent factor in contributing to the illegal drug use of their children.

Too often this issue becomes construed in ideological terms, often rendered in the equation: if the older generation can have their drugs of choice, then why can't members of the younger generation smoke marihuana? It is facile to dismiss this question as a *non sequitur,* but the fact remains that marihuana use, at the very least, grows out of much of the same cultural values and emphases that drinking and smoking did a generation or two ago.

Regardless of the relative harm of the various drugs in the observed relationship, and regardless of the validity of the arguments for or against the legalization of marihuana, it is difficult to avoid the fact that marihuana (which is by far the most frequently used of the completely illegal drugs in America) is *perceived* by the young as an equivalent recreational drug, in much the same way that adults perceive drinking. Mistaken or not, this belief is a fixture of the thinking and ideology of large segments of the young today, and the data appear to indicate that the parental example of the use of (legal) mind-altering drugs is implicated in a significant manner with the use of illegal psychoactive drugs among the young. This is where drug use receives its impetus—this is where it starts. This is how it is sustained. It is naive to assume that the two forms of drug use discussed here exist in two radically different realms simply because one is legal and the other illegal. The evidence points to the fact that, behaviorally and socially, they are remarkably kindred.

PEER GROUP INFLUENCE

Aside from the influence of parents as a primary socializing influence, the social peer group is one of the most significant elements in shaping, reinforcing and modifying the behavior of young people. To a considerable extent the younger the individual is, the more nearly he can be expected to mirror the judgments, opinions, and outlook of his parents. As he grows older and is exposed to new and different experiences, both formally and informally, his opinions and judgments will change. The changes in behavior and perception will be due, in part, to cognitive reasoning of the issues involved, the risks, the moral implications, etc. In no small part, however, the changes in behavior, opinion, and judgment will be related to the individual judgment about the feelings of his peers.

Food and dress fads, speech patterns and vocabulary, demeanor, and other aspects of behavior are all modified by the influence of peers. Whether the individual conforms his ideals or behavior to suit that of his peer group out of concern for social acceptance or because of a belief in the usefulness or appropriateness of the idea is not, in one sense, significant. What is important is the realization that as the individual grows in age and experience his opinions and judgments will shift from his young years, and this shift will be markedly influenced by his social peer group.

The influence of parental values and behavior along with the influence of one's peers are perhaps the two most significant factors in affecting the quality and quantity of youthful behavior.

The Commission's National Survey found that the influence of a friend or friends was the single most significant element present in initiating marihuana use. It is worth noting that this fact applies to both the youth (12-17 year olds) in the survey as well as to the adults (18 years and older). Among the youth, 62 percent indicated that they received their first marihuana from a friend, while 51 percent of the adults reported a similar experience. As we will point out elsewhere in this section, having friends who use marihuana plays a sginificant role in determining whether or not the individual will be likely to try marihuana and to continue its use. . . .

The Survey showed that the initial experience is not planned in advance, but that youths are somewhat more likely than adults to have done some advance planning for their trial of marihuana.

In sum, today's youth are significantly more likely than their elders to have heard or read about, to have known someone who used and to have actually tried it themselves at an earlier age than their elders. For both youth and adults, however, one's initial experience with marihuana generally takes place in the company of friends who introduce them to the drug. Rarely is marihuana purchased the first time it is used and only occasionally is the initial use of marihuana planned in advance. The practice of marihuana use is from its very beginning a social or recreational activity shared by and with one or a few good friends.

THE MARIHUANA USER

The classic image of "turning on" to the use of an illegal drug, including marihuana, for the first time is that of the "seduction of the innocent," a wanton and almost incidental corruption of a basically wholesome but unfortunately weak and naive young person. This view fails to grasp the reality of the drug conversion process in a number of ways. Most importantly, it ignores the basic fact that, even *before* using an illegal drug for the first time, the young person who eventually uses drugs is *already* different from his peer who does not, and will not, turn on to the use of drugs. In other words, drug use is not a process of seducing the completely innocent but a question of at least a partial choice on the future user's part.

When a young person tries a particular drug for the first time, it is not a fortuitous event. It is the outgrowth of a range of structural and cultural realities. One is opportunity. In spite of recent declarations that marihuana is as easy to purchase as bubble gum, the truth is that a young person who has not had experience with drugs is unlikely to be sufficiently motivated to seek out a known dealer, or drug seller, in his school or neighborhood to make a purchase. Nearly all neophytes who use a drug for the first time are offered the drug in a social setting. But marihuana is not offered equally to everyone. Two different young people attending the same school, living in the same neighborhood, but with social, personality, and background characteristics which differ, will encounter quite different opportunities to try marihuana. And quite clearly, being offered a chance to try marihuana is only half of the equation. The characteristics of the young person determine not only being offered opportunities but also the likelihood of accepting. In this section, then, it is necessary to spell out some of the dynamic processes underlying becoming a marihuana user.

Contemporary thinking on the etiology of marihuana use holds that there is no single "cause" impelling a young person toward turning on, or becoming a marihuana user. A wide range of factors contribute to this phenomenon; a multi-genetic approach must be adopted. Several in combination will make the likelihood of any given young person being, or becoming, a marihuana user extremely high. It is necessary to adopt a probabilistic approach in addition to a number of causes or associations. Erich Goode suggests four sets of factors which are empirically correlated with marihuana use. They are not necessarily "causes" although they are associated with the use of marihuana. The first set of factors is made up of *background* variables; some observers might label them *predisposing* factors in marihuana use. Of the many such variables which might be selected, the social class background of one's parents, sex, and religious background, are closely associated with marihuana use. (Interestingly enough, race does not appear to be significantly related to marihuana use.) Second, there are the many *situational features* of an individual's life; they can be thought of as *precipitating* factors. Geographic location, the urbanness of the community in which one lives, whether or not one attends college, the type of college one attends, one's friendship network, and so on, all have a great deal to do with whether any given young person uses marihuana, at least in a statistical sense. Third, there are the many *social and behavioral correlates* of marihuana use. These are connected with marihuana use, but in an almost dialectical manner. None of them is "caused by" marihuana use, and marihuana use does not "cause" any of them, but they reinforce one another. Some social, attitudinal, and behavioral correlates of marihuana use are: cigarette smoking, drinking alcoholic beverages, political attitudes, religious beliefs, and patterns of sexual behavior. . . .

Analysis of data concerning socioeconomic status and marihuana use indicates that children of better educated, more affluent parents with high prestige occupations have a greater likelihood of using marihuana than children of less well-educated parents with lower prestige occupations. This does not mean that no child of less affluent parents will use marihuana. What it does mean is that there are striking and significant differences in frequency and incidence of use along the dimension of income, education, and occupational prestige. . . .

The same sort of relationship which holds true between using marihuana and the social class *background* of an individual also applies to *present* social class position and education. Individuals who themselves have high incomes, are well educated, and work at relatively high prestige occupations (holding constant other important social characteristics, such as age). . . .

The Commission's National Survey found that among adults (18 and over) with marihuana experience there was a striking association between family income and marihuana experience (ever tried). The percent of persons who had ever tried was highest (18 percent) in the $15,000 to $24,999 income category. For those who presently use marihuana, the highest percent was found in those families reporting an income of $25,000 or more. . . .

MARIHUANA USE AND THE USER: 1972

In an attempt to identify patterns of marihuana use in terms of frequency, intensity, and duration and to discern the attitudinal and behavioral correlates of use, the Commission has reviewed numerous surveys conducted in recent years. Due to large differences in the populations addressed, the survey and sampling methods utilized, and the terminology and operational definitions employed no precise comparisons have been possible. A careful sorting and analysis of the research, however, indicates the existence of patterns and regularities along several dimensions. . . .

The Commission found that the majority of persons who use marihuana can be characterized as *experimental* or *intermittent* users. These individuals can best be described as recreational users who utilize the drug for pleasure. For these individuals, the pleasure experienced in using the drug is framed within a casual behavior context; that is, marihuana use is integrated into the social-recreational requirements of the individual. This is in contrast to the drugs which produce compulsive behavior resulting from physiological dependence.

TABLE 7.2

THE RELATIONSHIP BETWEEN MARIHUANA
EXPERIENCE AND FAMILY INCOME
ADULTS (N = 2,405)

Income (family)	Ever Used	Use Now
$ 4,000 or less	12%	4%
$ 5,000 - $ 9,999	16%	4%
$10,000 - $14,999	17%	4%
$15,000 - $24,999	18%	5%
$25,000 - or more	15%	7%

The Commission found that of those persons who have used marihuana, only 2 percent of the adults and 4 percent of the youth could be classified as *heavy* users; that is, they use the drug several times per day. A very small fraction of the heavy user group *may* be *very heavy users* who are intoxicated most of the time. It should be noted, however, that while the Commission did observe such usage patterns in certain foreign countries, no evidence was presented or obtained which indicates the presence of such usage patterns in this country.

In part, drug use among youth appears to be an outgrowth of the life-style and attitudes of parents. Several researchers have demonstrated that a family environment often produces an atmosphere of toleration about drug use which is easily transmitted to youth. Young people whose parents use barbiturates, amphetamines, alcohol, and cigarettes are more likely than those whose parents abstain from drug use to find mood or consciousness altering substances such as marihuana more acceptable. A general sense of liberalism and permissiveness on the part of parents is often related to the sense of increased permissiveness and liberal attitudes on the part of youth. This is especially relevant to the issue of choosing friends and the willingness to share the kinds of activities in which they engage.

Next to that of parents, the peer group exerts the most significant influence on the behavior of young people. The kinds of persons with whom one chooses to associate and interact is, in part, a function of the socializing experiences which individuals bring to a particular social situation. An individual who is eager for new experiences, who finds drug-taking not unacceptable, and who has friends sharing similar attitudes and values is more likely to find himself in social situations where marihuana (or some other drug) might be tried. The Commission found that the influence of friends is of paramount importance in initiating marihuana use.

Data from the Commission's National Survey show that marihuana use is highest between the ages of 17 and 25. The use of marihuana falls off sharply after age 25 and continues to decline with increasing age. The National Survey data confirmed what other researchers have previously found regarding the relationship between using the drug and knowing persons who use it. The data show that as age increased after age 25, the number of individuals who used the drug or who knew someone else who used it steadily declined.

At the present time, marihuana use appears to be an age-specific phenomenon. Whether or not this situation will change in future years with the aging of the present group of marihuana using youth is a matter of conjecture and one that should interest researchers in years to come. For the present, however, we can conclude that marihuana is a practice largely confined to late adolescent and young adults.

The Commission found no evidence to indicate that race plays a substantial role in determining trial or continued use of marihuana. Among adults in the National Survey, 15 percent of White and 14 percent of Black adults had tried the drug. The corresponding figures for present use of marihuana were 5 percent and 3 percent, respectively.

The Commission did find significant differences between the sexes among both youth and adult marihuana users. In all cases, males outnumbered the females in a ratio of about two to one.

The marihuana user is typically liberal in his or her political attitudes, and generally lives in or near a city or major metropolitan area or one of its suburbs. The user is also more likely to be from the Northeast or the West than from the North Central area or South.

One of the situational features relevant to using marihuana is educational status and educational achievement. College youths tend to use marihuana more than their noncollege peers. Research points to the fact that college youth are more likely than high school youth to know someone who uses marihuana. There appears to be greater use of marihuana among students at the more highly selective colleges and universities where academic quality is high. The marihuana user is more likely than not to have more education than his non-marihuana-using peers. This does not mean, however, that the more educated one is the more likely he is to use marihuana.

Simply stated, the demographic profile of the marihuana user shows that the likelihood of having friends or acquaintances who use the drug, thereby increasing one's own chance of trying marihuana, is greater among the better educated, middle to upper middle socioeconomic class of students and young adults.

The marihuana-using college student is not generally an academic failure nor does any valid evidence exist at this time to indicate that marihuana is a causative factor in academic failure. In contrast, a review of available research clearly points to alcohol use by high school and college youth as a correlate of poor academic achievement. More research is needed in this area, however, in order to better understand the roles which alcohol as well as marihuana play in academic achievement.

The data concerning the relationship between socioeconomic status and marihuana use indicate that children of better educated, more affluent parents with high prestige occupations have a greater likelihood of using marihuana than do children of less well educated parents with lower prestige occupations.

Present research points to a complex series of interrelated social, psychological, and economic factors which strongly influence the likelihood of someone, particularly a student, trying marihuana. The educational and economic achievement of the parents plays a significant role in shaping their children's acceptability of marihuana as well as other drugs. The social, educational, and economic status of one's peers also plays an important role in promoting or discouraging certain forms of behavior, including the use of marihuana and other drugs. Finally, present research points to the fact that the longer a young person remains in school, the greater is the likelihood that he will come to know persons who have tried or use marihuana and thus will have a greater opportunity to experiment with marihuana use himself.

Survey findings have generally shown that adolescents and young adults who drink alcoholic beverages and smoke cigarettes stand a higher statistical likelihood of using drugs, including both marihuana and heroin, than do their peers who neither drink nor smoke. Although many persons believe that those who use marihuana are vastly different, and that the drugs (alcohol and marihuana) are competitors, such is not the case. Young people who use illegal drugs, including marihuana, are fundamentally the same people socially and psychologically as those who use alcohol and cigarettes. They are simply somewhat further along the same dimension. . . .

The Commission's National Survey found that religion and religious participation were found to play a significant role in the decision to use or abstain from the use of drugs. Persons who participate in a formal traditional religious practice stand a considerably lower likelihood of trying and using marihuana or any illegal drugs than those who do not. Persons who are either nonparticipating affiliates of a religious group or who claim no religious affiliation or participation stand a much higher chance of using marihuana as well as other drugs than those who are participants and affiliates. It should be understood, however, that religion is not an absolute shield against the use of illegal drugs. Although no causal link is certain, in a statistical sense the religious are less likely to be attracted to drugs.

The data from a number of studies point to the fact that those who have tried marihuana have little or no interest in religion, are without religious affiliation or differ in their religious affiliation from that of their parents. While a number of studies point to the fact that Jewish youth or those who are nonaffiliated with any religion stand the highest chance of trying marihuana, there are numerous individuals who use marihuana and who are affiliated with and participate in religious affairs.

What must be understood when considering data on marihuana use and religious affiliation is that although a substantial number of those who have used marihuana are self-professed nonbelievers or nonaffiliates of any religious group, the majority of persons who use marihuana are reasonably conventional in terms of affiliation with one of the major religious groups.

Although the data concerning religious participation—that is, attendance at services—showed considerable differences between those with marihuana experience, including present users, and those without marihuana experience on the question of *regular* attendance at religious services, the adult National Survey respondents showed *very little difference* on the self-rating scale of religiosity: deeply religious, fairly religious, and not very religious. While it is true that persons with no religious affiiliation may be more likely to have tried marihuana than individuals with some religious affiliation, the nonaffiliated groups do not constitute a numerically significant total of the marihuana users.

Most persons who have tried and now use marihuana have marihuana-using friends. Although the most common reason for trying marihuana is curiosity, the data provide striking evidence that one tries marihuana aside from curiosity because one's friends use it and provide the opportunity to try it. Findings clearly illustrate the marked differences among those experienced with marihuana and those without marihuana experience in terms of having friends who use the drug. The Commission found that persons who have tried the drug as well as those who use it now have many more marihuana-using friends than do those without marihuana experience.

The Commission's National Survey data point to a pattern of initiation to marihuana use in the course of normal social relationships. The respondents did not report seeking out or being sought out by criminal drug pushers. Most respondents did not report using the drug in the company of persons with whom they would not normally associate. The nefarious drug peddler or pusher does not appear to be a major factor in the initiation or use of marihuana by any sizable number of young people.

The marihuana user, especially among college youth and young adults, is more likely to be sexually permissive than his non-marihuana-using peers. A number of studies suggest that the drug-using college student is more sexually active and has a higher frequency of premarital sex. Researchers have also observed that drug users tend to engage in sex earlier in their lives than non-drug users. There is no evidence at present, however, to show that marihuana contains any aphrodisiacal properties. Young people do not engage in sexual behavior *because* they use marihuana or any other illegal drug. They do both because both are accompaniments of patterns of life which are more permissive in a wide variety of ways. Both are part of larger subcultural developments which include a less restrictive and less traditional pattern of behavior, regardless of the specific area in question. One should not draw any inference with respect to causes—that is to say, that marihuana somehow causes sexual permissiveness. Understanding the relationship between the use of marihuana and sexual behavior especially among youth requires an awareness of the complex sociocultural processes which operate to modify the socionormative framework within which behaviors take place. To ascribe complex human behavior to the infrequent consumption of a drug is to deny reality.

While personality factors undoubtedly play a role in marihuana use they probably play a much greater role in the use of the more dangerous drugs such as heroin. There are far too many instances in which a particularly offensive behavior, such as marihuana use, is ascribed to some form of mental illness or pathology. The more widespread an activity becomes and the more it becomes socially accepted within some groups, however, the less necessary it is to invoke personality differences within a mental health context to explain participation in that activity.

Much of the data concerning marihuana use relates more nearly to social rather than personality correlates to explain the process by which individuals experiment with or continue to use the drug. Marihuana use cannot be simply explained, as some would have it, by the "rebellion" thesis. Those who offer this explanation often postulate that individuals try and continue to use marihuana to express their rejection of the dominant cultural values. To accept such an explanation is to neglect the fact that marihuana-using behavior could not be sustained without more positive rewards other than the sense of rebellion. The participants in marihuana use are, in most cases, sustained in their use of the drug in ways which have meaning for them, which bring them pleasure and satisfaction and which extend beyond the mere notion of committing a "deviant" act.

Researchers have found that drug users of all classes tended to rank high on a dimension of seeking new experience. Put in another way, of all persons who value new experience, their likelihood of trying and using a wide range of drugs is somewhat higher than is true of individuals who close themselves off to new experience or who place little importance in seeking new experiences. Characterizations of personality correlates among marihuana users and nonusers should be viewed not as absolutes which are "good" or

"bad," "healthy" or pathological, nor should attitudes toward the two personality "types," users and nonusers, be translated into judgmental terms such as "good" or "bad," "healthy" or pathological. From a comparative standpoint, the personalities of marihuana users and nonusers demonstrate some differences; however, such differences which do exist are only relative to one another. Causal explanations of marihuana use should not be imputed from the personality differences identified. Rather, such personality differences as can be identified are likely to apply only to this point in time, and to this society.

As the marihuana user of today is significantly different from his counterpart of the 1920s and 1930s, so the future marihuana user may differ significantly from today's user. In either case, the drug itself is not responsible for the changes. Rather, the social, political, economic, and moral climate of society will determine the incidence of marihuana use and the characteristics of those who use it.

8. HEADS AND FREAKS: PATTERNS AND MEANINGS OF DRUG USE AMONG HIPPIES

FRED DAVIS WITH LAURA MUNOZ

Reprinted from the Journal of Health and Social Behavior *9, no. 2 (June 1968): 156-63. Fred Davis is Professor of Sociology at the University of California Medical Center, San Francisco. Laura Munoz is a graduate student in Sociology at the University of California, San Francisco. Davis has applied his expertise as a social psychologist in the symbolic interactionist tradition to understanding a wide range of substantive issues, particularly in studies of the medical profession, of stigmatization, and of coping with the crises of illness and disablement. This article is a reflection of his research interest in youth and in San Francisco; he has written more on both subjects.*

■ If by the late 1960s recreational drug use became widespread among the generation of college age, it was in most places a simple addition to relatively conventional student styles of life. Nonetheless many thought that it symbolized a wish for a greater departure from (or a freer adaptation to) the in-between status that modern American society accords to those who are no longer adolescents but not yet regarded as fully adult.

The group that most fully developed these aspirations were the hippies of San Francisco, who burst into the national consciousness in 1966. They were the second generation of a new style of middle class recreational drug use, the first generation of which included the founder of the LSD cult and an assorted group of artists and writers. For the hippies, drugs were not a mere addition to an established life style but a central element in a new style. In this selection Davis and Munoz analyze the ways in which drugs and the drug experience became a focal concern for the hippie subculture. They also show how that subculture itself contained two rather different orientations to withdrawal from conventional society, one concerned with personal development, insight, and discovery—the "heads"—and the other concerned with experience and enjoyment—the "freaks."

A general statement of the relationship between drugs, social situation, and subjective experience is in Howard S. Becker, "History, Culture, and Subjective Experience: An Exploration of the Social Bases of Drug-Induced Experience," *Journal of Health and Social Behavior* 8 (September 1967): 163-76. An analysis of a different pattern of drug use in West Coast youth culture is in James T. Carey, *The College Drug Scene* (Prentice-Hall, 1968); see also Richard Bloom et al., *Utopiates* (Atherton Press, 1968). A recent assessment of the drug scene several years after its burgeoning is Norman E. Zinberg and John A. Robertson, *Drugs and the Public* (Simon & Schuster, 1972). The first well-developed social psychological theory of social factors in drug use was Alfred L. Lindesmith, *Addiction and Opiates* (Aldine, 1968). ■

REGARDLESS of whether the phenomenon is viewed in terms of a bohemian subculture, a social movement, a geographically based deviant community, or some combination of these, there is substantial agreement among those who have studied hippies that drugs (or "dope," the term preferred by hippies) play an important part in their lives. This generalization applies to nearly all segments of the hippie community for the reasons given below.

First, the patent empirical fact of widespread and frequent drug use per se is easily ascertainable through even a brief stay in San Francisco's Haight-Ashbury, New York's East Village, Los Angeles' Fairfax, Vancouver's Fourth Avenue or wherever else hippie colonies have sprung up. Second—and this importantly distinguishes hippie drug use from that of other drug-using subcultures—there are pronounced ideological overtones associated with it. Not only is it frequently asserted by many hippies that there is "nothing wrong" with certain of the drugs favored by them (chiefly marihuana and LSD, along with a number of other hallucinogens), or that their use is less harmful than alcohol or tobacco, but that these drugs are positively beneficial, either as a pleasant relaxant, as with marihuana, or as a means for gaining insight with which to redirect the course of one's life along inwardly more satisfying and self-fulfilling lines (LSD). Among other manifestations, this spirit of ideological advocacy expresses itself in the conviction of some hippies that their ultimate social mission is to "turn the world on"—i.e., make everyone aware of the potential virtues of LSD for ushering in an era of universal peace, freedom, brotherhood and love. The last, and perhaps most crucial, circumstance for making drug use important in the lives of hippies is the simple and stark matter of the drugs' illegality. As contemporary deviance theory of the symbolic interactionist persuasion has shown in so many differing connections, the act by a community of successfully labeling a particular practice deviant and/or illegal almost invariably constrains the "deviant" to structure much of his identity and activity in terms of such imputations of deviance and lawbreaking. Thus, the omnipresent threats of police harrassment, of arrest and incarceration, as well as of a more diffuse social ostracism are "facts of life" which the hippie who uses drugs only occasionally must contend with fully as much as the regular user.

Beyond these rather global observations, all further generalizations concerning hippie drug use must be qualified carefully and treated as tentative. For not only are the actual patterns of drug use quite varied among individual hippies and different hippie subgroups, but the patterns themselves also are constantly undergoing change as the subculture evolves and gains greater experience with drugs.

Further compounding the hazards of facile generalization are the following.

1. The apparent readiness of many hippies to experiment—if only once "to see what it's like"—with almost any drug or druglike substance, be it Hawaiian wood rose seeds, opium or some esoteric, pharmacologically sophisticated psychoactive compound.

2. The periodic appearance on the hippie drug market of new drugs, usually of the hallucinogenic variety, which, like new fashions generally, excite a great flurry of initial interest and enthusiasm until they are either discredited, superseded, or partially assimilated into a more "balanced" schedule of drug use. Thus, in the past year alone, for example, at least three new hallucinogenic-type drugs have made much heralded, though short-lived, appearances in the Haight-Ashbury: STP (dimethoxy-methyl-amphetamine), MDA (methylene-dioxy-amphetamine), and PCP, the "peace pill" (phencyclidine).

3. The vagaries, uncertainties, deceptions and misrepresentations of the illegal drug market as such. Not only is it hard for a buyer to be sure that he is getting the drug he thinks he is getting—indeed, that he is getting any drug at all and not some placebo—but dosages, strengths, and purity of compounding, even when not knowingly misrepresented by dealers, are likely to be unknown or poorly understood by dealer and buyer alike. Thus, the ubiquitous possibility of an untoward reaction in which the user, or a whole aggregate of users, becomes violently ill or severely disoriented.

4. The fact, to be discussed later, that the very same drug (LSD, for example) can, depending on the intent of the user, his mood, the setting, and the group context, be used to achieve very different drug experiences and subjective states. Though this "choice of drug experience" is never fully within the control of even the experienced user (see 3, above), it does exist and thus facilitates differential use by different users as well as by the same user at different times.

Obliquely, these circumstances point to

what is perhaps the chief obstacle to making firm generalizations concerning hippie drug use—namely, that the subculture is not (at least as yet) of a piece, that it includes many disparate social elements and ideational tendencies, and that, to the extent that drug use constitutes something of a core element in it, this must be seen in the context of these varying and constantly shifting socio-ideational subconfigurations. As has been characteristic of almost any expressive social movement in its formative stages, this diversity in the midst of a search for common definition is reflected in the frequent discussions among hippies on who is a "real" hippie, who a "plastic" hippie, and what "genuine" hipness consists of. Moral, behavioral, and attitudinal boundaries of inclusion and exclusion are constantly being assessed and redrawn. But, in the absence of any recognized leadership group capable of issuing ex cathedra pronouncements on these matters, one man's, or one underground paper's, definition is as good as the next's. These ongoing discussions, debates, and polemics extend, of course, to the place and use of drugs in the "new community," as hippie spokesmen like to refer to themselves. Some take a very permissive and inclusive stance, others a more restrictive one, and still others shift their ground from one encounter to the next. Inconclusive as this dialogue may be from an organizational standpoint, it nonetheless is important for the influences, albeit variable, it exerts on drug practices and attitudes within the subculture.

With these reservations in mind we wish to sketch here a rough sociological atlas, as it were, of patterns and meanings of drug use among San Francisco's Haight-Ashbury hippies, at least insofar as these manifested themselves through the summer and well into the fall of 1967. The data were gathered by the methods of ethnographic field work as part of a broader study of the interaction of Haight-Ashbury's hippie community with the larger San Francisco community. Although informed by a close-in familiarity with the hippie community, the data are, strictly speaking, impressionistic inasmuch as time, re-

sources and certain situational peculiarities connected with doing research among hippies militated against any exhaustive study of drug use per se.

LSD AND METHEDRINE

Since much of what follows deals with social psychological aspects of the use of the above two drugs, a few preliminary words are in order concerning the drugs themselves, their direct pharmacological effects, average dosages, modes of administration, and frequency of use. No detailed description can be attempted here; rather, our aim is merely to touch on a few matters pertinent for the subsequent discussion of types of drug users. Inasmuch as we shall not be discussing marihuana, suffice it to say here that it is very widely used by all segments of the hippie community and constitutes the drug staple of the subculture. (Hashish, the purified and condensed forms of cannabis, though much preferred by those who have tried it, appears in the Haight-Ashbury only rarely and commands an exceedingly high price.)

The hallucinogenic LSD (lysergic acid diethylamide), one of a growing family of such drugs, is marketed in the Haight-Ashbury in tablet form. The shape, color and general appearance of tablets will vary considerably, from "well made" to "extremely crude," as new batches are produced by different illegal manufacturers. Taken orally, an average dose, usually one tablet, contains approximately 185 micrograms of LSD. Some users, though, are known to ingest considerably more than this amount—i.e., up to 1,000-1,250 micrograms, when they wish to "turn on." Street prices vary from about $2.50 per tablet in times of plentiful supply to $5 and $6 when supply is short. Typical users in the Haight-Ashbury "take a trip" once a week or thereabouts on the average; again, however, there is a considerable number who "drop acid" much more frequently, perhaps every three or four days, while still others resort to the drug only occasionally or episodically. The characteristic psychopharmacologic effects of the drug are described by Smith as follows.

When someone ingests an average dose of LSD, (150-250 micrograms) nothing happens for the first 30 or 45 minutes, and then after the sympathetic response the first thing the individual usually notices is a change in the way he perceives things. . . . Frequently . . . he notices that the walls and other objects become a bit wavy or seem to move. Then he might notice colors . . . about the room are looking much brighter or more intense than they usually do and, in fact, as time goes on these colors can seem exquisitely intense and more beautiful than any colors he has seen before. Also, it is common for individuals to see a halo effect around lights, also a rainbow effect. . . . There is another kind of rather remarkable perceptual change, referred to as a synesthesia. By this I mean the translation of one type of sensory experience into another, so that if one is listening to music, for example, one can sometimes feel the vibrations of the music in one's body, or one can sometimes see the actual notes moving, or the colors that he is seeing will beat in rhythm with the music.

More pronounced effects of an emotional, meditative, or ratiocinative kind can, but need not, follow in the wake of these alterations in sense perception. In any case, the direct effects of the drug last on the average for an 8- to 12-hour span.

Methedrine (generic name, methamphetamine) is a stimulant belonging to the sympathomimetic group of drugs. Its appearance is that of a fluffy white powder, referred to commonly as "crystals." In the Haight-Ashbury it is sold mainly in spoonful amounts (1-2 grams, approximately) and packaged in small transparent envelopes, prices ranging from $15 to $20 an envelope. Frequently, a user or small dealer in need of cash will repackage the powder and sell it in smaller amounts. Until a few years ago most users of Methedrine took it orally in capsule form. Among Haight-Ashbury hippies, however, the primary and preferred mode of administration is intravenous injection. Hence, the paraphernalia employed is almost identical to that of the heroin user: hypodermic needle, syringe, spoon for diluting the powder in tap water, and candle for heating the mixture. Because needles and associated equipment are often unsterilized or poorly sterilized, cases of serum

hepatitis are quite common among Methedrine users. The physiological effects of the drug are elevated blood pressure, increased pulse rate, dilation of pupils, and blurred vision—these accompanied by such behavioral states as euphoria, heightened spontaneous activity, wakefulness, loss of appetite and, following extended use, suspicion and acute apprehensiveness ("paranoia").

Although there is some disagreement among experts on whether regular use of Methedrine leads to addiction as, for example, in the case of heroin, it is well established that a fair proportion of users become extremely dependent on the drug. Thus, whereas the episodic user will inject 25-50 milligrams for a "high," those who get badly "strung out" on a 2- to 3-week Methedrine binge will by the end be "shooting" as frequently as 6 times a day for a total daily intake of some 1,000 to 2,000 milligrams (1 to 2 grams). Needless to say, were it not for the steep increase in body tolerance levels built up through continuous use of the drug, such high daily dosages might well prove lethal.

HEADS AND FREAKS

A suitable starting point for our ethnographic sketch is those terms and references used by hippies themselves to distinguish certain types of drug users and patterns of drug use. Chief among these is the contrast drawn between "heads" and "freaks," sometimes explicitly, though more often implicitly with reference to a particular drug user or drug practice. While a whole penumbra of allusive imagery surrounds these terms, a "head" essentially is thought to be someone who uses drugs—and, here, it is mainly the hallucinogens that the speaker has in mind—for purposes of mind expansion, insight, and the enhancement of personality attributes; i.e., he uses drugs to discover where "his head is at." For the "head," therefore, the drug experience is conceived of, much as during the first years of LSD experimentation by psychiatrists and psychopharmacologists (ca. 1956-63), as a *means* for self-realization or self-fulfillment, and not as an end in itself. The term *head* is, of course, not new with hippies. It has a long history among drug users generally, for whom it signified a regular, experienced user of any illegal drug— e.g., pot head, meth head, smack (heroin) head. Although still sometimes used in this nondiscriminating way by hippies, what is novel about their usage of head is the extent to which it has become exclusively associated with certain of the more rarified facets of the LSD experience.

By contrast, the term *freak* refers usually to someone in search of drug kicks as such, especially if his craving carries him to the point of drug abuse where his health, sanity, and relations with intimates are jeopardized. Though used primarily in the context of Methedrine abuse ("speed freak"), the reference is frequently broadened to include all those whose use of any drug (be it Methedrine, LSD, marihuana, or even alcohol) is so excessive and of such purely hedonistic bent as to cause them to "freak out"—e.g., become ill or disoriented, behave violently or erratically, give evidence of a "paranoid" state of mind.

Whereas the primary connotative imagery of "head" and "freak" derives mainly from the subculture's experience with drugs, the terms themselves—given their evocative associations—have in a short course of time acquired great referential elasticity. Thus head, for example, is extended to include any person (hip, "straight," or otherwise) who manifests great spontaneity, openness of manner, and a canny sensitivity to his own and others' moods and feelings. Indeed, hippies will claim that it is not strictly necessary to use hallucinogenic drugs—helpful though this is for many—to become a head, and that, moreover, there are many persons in the straight world, in particular children, who are "really heads" but don't know it. Parenthetically, it might be noted that the concept of a *secret union* of attitude and sensibility, including even those ignorant of their inner grace, is a familiar attribute of expressive social movements of the deviant type; among other purposes, it helps to subjectively legitimate

the proselytizing impulses of the movement. Homosexuals, too, are known to construct such quasi-conspiratorial versions of the world.

Similarly, the term freak, while much less fertile in its connotative imagery than head, is also extended to persons and situations outside the immediate context of drug use. Hence, anyone who is too aggressive or violent, who seems "hung up" on some idea, activity, or interactional disposition, might be called a freak. Accordingly, abnormal phases (e.g., high anxiety states, obsessiveness, intemperateness) in the life of one customarily thought a head will also be spoken of as freaking or freaking out.

The two terms, therefore, have acquired a quality of ideal typicality about them in the hippie subculture and have, at minimum, come to designate certain familiar social types. At this level of indigenous typifications, they can be seen to reflect certain ongoing value tensions in the subculture: a reflecting turning inward versus hedonism, Apollonian contentment versus Dionysian excess, a millenial vision of society versus an apocalyptic one. And that these generic extensions of the terms derive so intimately from drug experiences afford additional evidence of the symbolic centrality of drugs in the hippie subculture.

SOME SOCIAL CHARACTERISTICS OF HEADS AND FREAKS

In the more restrictive, strict drug-using sense, who, then, are heads (LSD or "acid" users) and who freaks (Methedrine or "speed shooters")? Lacking accurate demographic data on the subject, our impression is that heads are found more often among the older, more established and less transient segments of the Haight-Ashbury hippie community—i.e., persons of both sexes in their mid-to-late twenties who, while not exactly holding down full-time jobs of the conventional sort, are more or less engaged in some regular line of vocational activity: artists, craftsmen, clerks in the hippie shops, some hippie merchants, writers with the underground press, graduate students, and sometimes mail carriers, to mention a few. It is mainly from this segment that such spokesmen and leaders as the "new community" has produced have come. By comparison, freaks are found more often among the more anomic and transient elements of the community, in particular those strata where "hipness" begins to shade off into such quasi-criminal and thrill-seeking conglomerates as the Hell's Angels and other motorcyclists (known locally as "bikeies"), many of whom now frequent the Haight-Ashbury and have taken up residence in and around the area. Some observers even attribute the growing use of Methedrine to the fact that it and closely related stimulants (e.g., Benzedrine, Dexedrine) were popular with West Coast motorcycle gangs well before the origins of the hippie community in the Haight-Ashbury. Unlike "acid," which is widely used by both males and females, "speed" appears to be predominantly a male drug.

As these observations would suggest, it is our further impression that heads are by and large persons of middle and upper middle class social origins, whereas freaks are much more likely to be of working class background. Despite, therefore, the strong legal and moral proscriptions against both LSD and Methedrine, their differential use by hippies reflects, at one level at least, the basic contrast in expressive styles extant in the American class structure; put crudely, LSD equals self-exploration/self-improvement equals middle class, while Methedrine equals body stimulation/release of aggressive impulses equals working class.

These characterizations, however, afford but a gross approximation of drug use patterns in the Haight-Ashbury. The actual demography of use is complicated considerably by a variety of changing situational and attitudinal currents, some of which were alluded to earlier. Two additional matters especially deserve mention here. The first is the existence of a large, socially heterogeneous class of mixed drug users: persons who are neither heads nor freaks in any precise sense, but who regularly sample both LSD and Methedrine, as well as other drugs. Shifting intermittently or episodically from one to another, they may, save for continued smoking of marihuana, even undergo extended periods of drug abstinence. Of such users it can, perhaps, best be said that the very absence of any consistent pattern is the pattern. Secondly, it should be noted that this nonpattern pattern of drug use (this secondary anomie within a more inclusive deviant life scheme) has grown more pronounced in the Haight-Ashbury in recent months. Whereas prior to the summer of 1967 a newly arrived hippie would in all probability have been socialized into the LSD users' culture of "tripping," "mind-blowing," and meditation —heads then clearly constituted the socially, as well as numerically, dominant hippie group in the area—this kind of outcome became a good deal less certain following the publicity, confusion, congestion, and increased social heterogeneity of recruits that attended the summer influx of youth from across the country. Not only did many of the settled hippies move away from the area in the wake of this massive intrusion, but new styles and tastes in drug use, notably "speed shooting," also quickly established themselves. With the inundation and dispersal of the older head group, it became largely a matter of sheer fortuitousness whether a novice hippie turned to "acid" or "speed," to some other drug or a combination of several. Whose "pad" he "crashed" on arrival or who befriended him the first time he set foot on Haight Street could have as much to do with his subsequent pattern of drug use as anything else. This was conspicuously so in the instance of younger recruits, many of them runaways from home in the 14-17 age group, who, except perhaps for marihuana smoking, were completely naive to and inexperienced in drug use.

THE PRESTIGE GRADIENT OF DRUG USE

Nonetheless, to the extent that the hippie subculture has managed to conserve elements of a core identity and to develop something of a common stance vis-a-vis "straight" society, it is still the head pattern of drug use that is ideationally, if not necessarily numerically, dominant within it. Thus, to be spoken of as a head is complimentary, whereas to be termed a freak or speed freak is, except in certain special contexts, derogating. Similarly, the underground press is forever extolling the virtues of "acid"; but, apart from an occasional piece of somewhat patronizing tone in which the author tries to "understand" what "gives" with Methedrine users, it almost invariably condemns "speed." Numerous posters on display in the Haight Street print and funny button shops announce in bold captions "SPEED KILLS."

The perceived dichotomy between mind expansion and body stimulation represented by the two drugs is sometimes reconceptualized to apply to LSD users alone so as to draw a distinction between those who use the drug mainly for purposes of "tripping" as against "true" or "real" heads who purport to use it for achieving insight and effecting personality changes within themselves. While dosage levels of the drug seem to play some part in determining whether a "tripping" or "mind-expanding" experience will ensue—the larger the dose, the more likely the latter or, alternatively, a "bum trip" (i.e., a panic reaction with severe disorientation)—the intent and setting of the user also appear to have an important bearing on the outcome. Quiet surroundings, a contemplative mood, and interesting objects upon which to focus (e.g., a mandala, a candle flame) are felt to be conducive to a mind-expanding experience; moving street scenes, an extroverted mood, and the intense visual and auditory stimuli of the typical folk-rock dance and light show are thought conducive to "tripping." In any event, he who uses LSD only to "trip" (i.e., to intensify and refract his sensate experience of the environment) is regarded, at best, with a certain amused tolerance by "righteous acid heads." The latter, therefore, frequently counsel beginning users of LSD to move beyond mere "tripping" to where they can realize the higher meditative, revelatory, and religious potentials of the drug. In this connection, a number of hippie groups, particularly those involved in the Eastern religions, advocate dispensing with LSD and other hallucinogens altogether following realization of these higher states; once the "doors of consciousness" have been opened, it is stated, it is no longer necessary to use drugs for recapturing the experience—newly discovered powers of meditation alone with suffice. Be that as it may, because the head—as both a certain kind of drug user and certain kind of human being—has emerged as the model citizen of the hippie movement, there are many who aspire to the status and aim to follow the true path can lead them there.

CONCLUSION

In sum, drug use among Haight-Ashbury hippies reveals a number of contrary tendencies, the chief being the emergent social and symbolic contrast of the head and freak patterns—a contrast which, as we have seen, encompasses cultural elements well beyond the immediate realm of drug use per se. While the two patterns can, though several analytical levels removed, be traced back ultimately to certain historically persistent, subterranean expressive value strains in American society-at-large, their surfacing and intimate co-existence within the hippie subculture serve to aggravate already difficult problems of member socialization, group integration, and ideology that confront the community. Stated otherwise, the process of community formation is hindered, not wholly, or even primarily, by outside forces of repression—for these will often solidify a social movement—but through the generation of anomie from within as well. If illegal and socially condemned drug use did not play so large a part in the subculture, these divisive tendencies could, perhaps, be better contained. As is, however, the pervasiveness of illegal drug use constantly opens up the subculture to a gamut of socially disparate, unassimilable elements and assorted predators, few of whom share the ethos of love, expressive freedom, and disengagement from narrow materialistic pursuits that animated, and still animates, many within the movement. And, since it is highly unlikely that the drugs favored by hippies (again, possibly excepting marihuana) will soon be made legal, this situation is likely to get worse before it gets better.

As to the drug use patterns themselves, it can only be a matter of conjecture as to which—head or freak—if either, will come eventually to clearly prevail in the hippie community. Although the head pattern appears on the face of it to resonate more deeply with those broader philosophical and ideational themes that distinguish the movement, it has, in the Haight-Ashbury at least, already lost much ground to the more exclusively hedonistic "freak" pattern. Should it continue to do so, what did have the earmarks of a culturally significant, expressive social movement on the American scene could easily dissolve into little more than the sociologist's familiar "drug users' deviant subculture."

9. SEXUAL EXPERIENCE OF YOUNG UNMARRIED WOMEN IN THE UNITED STATES

JOHN F. KANTNER AND MELVIN ZELNIK

Reprinted with permission from Family Planning Perspectives *4, no. 4 (October 1972): 9-18. John F. Kantner and Melvin Zelnik are Professors of Population Dynamics, School of Hygiene and Public Health, The Johns Hopkins University. Dr. Zelnik has been a Ford Foundation population consultant in Indonesia. The two have coauthored several other reports based on the survey dealt with in this selection—a survey supported by the Center for Population Research of the National Institute of Child Health and Human Development.*

■ Heterosexual relations outside marriage have traditionally been considered deviant, although at all times with considerable ambiguity about how immoral or deviant the activity is really considered to be. It has long been acknowledged that such behavior is less unacceptable when engaged in by young men than by young women, and much research into attitudes has established the vitality of this double standard.

Even so, over the past half-century social commentators have observed (either approvingly or in alarm) that normative support for premarital sexual abstinence seems to have weakened or collapsed. Simply to list the books and articles that have dealt during this time with "the sexual revolution" would require several pages. Yet all of this discussion of change in sexual habits, decay of morals, and the like has taken place with very little in the way of systematic data. Surveys conducted in the 1920s and 1930s were very much on a catch-as-catch-can basis. The pioneering Kinsey studies of sexual behavior in the human male and female sought for the first time to assess systematically the prevalence of particular patterns of sexual practice and experience.

We shall never know in exact detail what pattern of change in premarital sexual behavior has taken place in this century, because it is impossible to do retrospective surveys. Until the mid-1960s the best estimate that could be made from fragmentary research was that probably no dramatic change in the incidence of premarital sexual relations had occurred since the 1920s—unlikely as that would seem to a reader of the popular literature on the subject. However, it did seem reasonable to believe that attitudes toward premarital sexual behavior were changing, particularly among the young.

In this selection, the first systematic study of premarital sexual experience, Kantner and Zelnik report on a national survey based on a probability sample of young unmarried females, 15 to 19 years of age. This well-detailed survey shows something of the influence of social background factors on premarital sexual behavior.

It is important to understand that this survey came about not to answer general questions about patterns of premarital sexual behavior (the kinds of questions that interest the public and popular writers, as well as sociologists and psychologists of marriage and the family) but in response to very practical questions about policies to prevent premarital pregnancies. As contraception has become increasingly common among married persons, even though problems of its accessibility for poor couples still remain, those concerned with family planning and illegitimacy have shifted their interest toward providing family planning services for the unmarried. As with marihuana, an important datum for policy discussion is the extent of the deviant behavior. If premarital pregnancies are in fact widespread, the often-heard argument that family planning services should not be made available to the unmarried for fear of "encouraging immorality" hardly seems strong. Family planning researchers have long noted that a lack of family planning services does not seem to discourage premarital sexual relations—even if one were to argue that this is a proper objective of public policy—and systematic data make the point much more convincingly.

The pioneering studies of sexual behavior are those of Alfred C. Kinsey and his collaborators, reported in *Sexual Behavior in the Human Male* (Saunders, 1948) and *Sexual Behavior in the Human Female* (Saunders, 1953). Two books by Ira L. Reiss report on premarital sexual attitudes as they have changed over time in the United States: *Premarital Sexual Standards* (Free Press, 1960), and *The Social Context of Premarital Sexual Permissiveness* (Holt, Rinehart & Winston, 1967). Another approach to the evidence is that of Phillips Cutright, "The Teenage Sexual Revolution and the Myth of an Abstinent Past," *Family Planning Perspectives*, January 1972, pp. 24-31. ■

NEARLY 2.4 MILLION never-married young women in the United States aged 15-19—about 28 percent of all such young women—were estimated, as of 1971, to have had some coital experience. This estimate, reported in an earlier analysis, was based upon data obtained through interviews of a national probability sample of the 15-19-year-old female population living in U.S. households. The survey included 3,132 White and 1,479 Black respondents, both married and unmarried. The analysis in that earlier report, as in this article, dealt with 4,240 never-married young women—92 percent of the total—of whom 2,839 are White and 1,401 are Black. In our first effort we employed only such simple demographic variables as age and race to describe the proportion of young women who had had sexual intercourse, the frequency with which they had relations, the number of their sexual partners, their knowledge of the risk of conception with unprotected coitus, their knowledge about contraception, their contraceptive practice, and their experience of and attitude toward out-of-wedlock pregnancy.

This article summarizes some of the conclusions of that earlier report and elaborates on our findings relating to aspects of sexuality and knowledge of the risk of conception. . . .

The socioeconomic status measures include family income as reported by the respondent; education of the man and woman whom the respondent indicated had raised her and a per capita measure of poverty 50 percent higher than the official poverty level derived from relating family income to family size.

Measures of residence include whether the respondent lived on a farm or in a metropolitan area (large or small), and in what region of the country she lived. Religion and relationship of the respondent to the head of the household were also employed as measures, along with other variables where they appeared to amplify the analysis.

SEXUAL EXPERIENCE

Our investigation indicates that the likelihood that a young never-married woman has experienced coitus rises from 14 percent at age 15, to 21 percent at age 16, to 27 percent at age 17, to 37 percent at age 18, and to 46 percent by age 19. We find that roughly twice the proportion of Blacks 15-19 have had intercourse as Whites—54 percent compared to 23 percent. Looking at age of initiation of sexual activity, our research indicates that more than half (51.6 percent) of the never-married women who were 19 in 1971 initiated intercourse at age 18 or later. Blacks, however, appear to initiate intercourse earlier. Thus, three-quarters of the never-married Blacks (74.9 percent) appear to have had intercourse before age 18, compared to two-fifths of the Whites (39.9 percent). There is evidence from the survey, moreover, that premarital intercourse is beginning at younger ages and that its extent among teenagers is increasing. Analyses based only on those girls never married in 1971 can be misleading as to age of initiation of intercourse, since our data show that nearly 6 in 10 of those who in 1971 were married had experienced coitus prior to marriage. From the survey data we have estimated the probability that any young woman married or unmarried and 15-19 in 1971 would engage in premarital coitus by age 15. Our conservative estimate is that a minimum of 3 percent of those 19 in 1971 were likely to have had sexual intercourse by age 15, compared to 9 percent of those who were currently 15. The differential applies for both Blacks and Whites but is much greater absolutely for Blacks: A young Black woman aged 19 in 1971 had at least an 8 percent probability of having had intercourse by age 15, compared to a 22 percent probability if she were currently aged 15. A White girl aged 19 in 1971 had little more than a 2 percent likelihood of having had intercourse by age 15, compared to a 7 percent probability if she were currently 15.

The chief differences between Blacks and Whites appear to be in the proportions who have had sexual experience and the age at which coitus begins. Looking at frequency of intercourse and the number of sexual partners among those with some sexual experience, the differences between Blacks and Whites are not striking. Blacks, however, as we reported earlier, have intercourse somewhat less frequently than Whites and with somewhat fewer partners.

As to frequency, 38 percent of those with sexual experience had not had intercourse in the month prior to the interview; another 30 percent had intercourse only once or twice; 18 percent had intercourse between 3 and 5 times, and only 14 percent had coitus 6 times or more during the month. More Blacks than Whites reported not having had intercourse at all in the previous month (41 percent vs. 37 percent), and considerably fewer Blacks than Whites reported having had relations 6 or more times (7.6 percent vs. 16.1 percent). Frequency tends to increase with age. At age 15, less than one-fourth (23.2 percent) had intercourse 3 times or more in the previous month; by age 19, this proportion is more than two-fifths (42.6 percent).

As to number of partners, three-fifths of the sexually experienced young women had only one partner ever; and of those who had sexual relations in the month prior to the interview, more than 9 out of 10 had relations with just one partner. A somewhat higher proportion of Whites (16 percent) than Blacks (11 percent) had 4 or more partners over their entire sexual lives. Those who are older are somewhat less likely to have had only one partner than are teenagers who are younger. For Blacks, 56 percent of

19-year-olds had only 1 sexual partner compared to 65 percent of 15-year-olds. For Whites, the difference is a little greater: 50 percent of 19-year-olds had only 1 partner compared to 70 percent of 15-year-olds.

The high proportion who had intercourse with only one partner is consistent with the report by half of the young women with sexual experience that they had relations only with the man they intended to marry. This proportion was about the same for all ages and for both Blacks and Whites.

In summary, then, our research shows that sexually experienced teenagers appear to have relatively stable sexual relationships (as judged by the number of partners) restricted, in at least half the cases, to the man they intend to marry, and that they experience coitus with relatively modest frequency (two times or less in the month prior to interview, compared to the nine times a month averaged by married couples where the wife is younger than 25). While sexually experienced Black teenagers were found to have had somewhat fewer partners than Whites, and to have had intercourse less frequently, roughly twice the proportion of Blacks was found to have had intercourse at some time. It was found also that sexually experienced Blacks were more likely to initiate intercourse at earlier ages than sexually experienced Whites.

RACE AND SOCIOECONOMIC STATUS

Socioeconomic measures such as poverty status, education of parent or guardian, or family income do not diminish the differences between the proportions of Blacks and Whites with sexual experience. Blacks in poverty, especially those younger than 18, are more likely than those who are less poor to have had sexual experience. For Whites, poverty status at the younger ages appears to make little difference, but for those 18 and older, Whites who are poorer are less likely to have had sexual experience. However, the differences between Blacks and Whites are large at every age and for each poverty level. Nor is there any tendency for Whites to catch up with Blacks as age increases. Rather, the two curves tend to diverge with increasing age.

A similar picture emerges when sexual experience is examined in relation to family income and to education of the female or male parent or guardian. The large differences in proportions with some sexual experience between Blacks and Whites remain.

For all 15-19-year-olds, the higher the socioeconomic status—whether measured by poverty status, family income, or parental or guardian education—the lower, generally, are the proportions with coital experience. This inverse relationship is consistently characteristic only of Blacks, however, among whom the sharpest differences are evident in relation to education of the male parent or guardian (which may mean only that this is the most discriminating status indicator of the three). There is not much difference in the proportion who have had intercourse between Blacks whose parents or guardians have had an elementary or a high school education. Some college education makes a noticeable difference, however. Indeed, 58 percent of Black 15-19-year-olds whose male parent or guardian has only an elementary school education have had some sexual experience, but when the father or male guardian has gone to college this proportion is 37 percent. What is more, this inverse relationship is found for every age group. (A similar finding, but not so marked or so consistent for each age group, is found when we look at education of female parent or guardian.) For whites this inverse relationship between education of parent and sexual experience of child does not hold true for the female parent or guardian and is only weakly related to the male parent's or guardian's education. If we separate college-educated male parents or guardians into those who did not complete college and those who were graduated, we find that the inverse relationship continues strongly for Blacks, but is reversed for Whites. This reversal in the relationship among Whites occurs at all ages and for education of either the male or female parent or guardian. The difference is greater among Blacks if it is the

male parent or guardian who is the college graduate; and the greatest effect appears to be at ages 16 and younger. The proportion sexually experienced is almost identical among Blacks and Whites whose male parents or guardians are college graduates. . . .

In general, the socioeconomic variables of poverty status, family income and parental or guardian education appear to have only a slight effect on the proportion of Whites with coital experience, although the relationship is generally in the expected direction: The higher the socioeconomic status level, the lower the proportion with sexual experience. Among Blacks this effect is considerably stronger, but not strong enough to appreciably diminish the Black-White differences in coital experience (except where the male parent or guardian has gone to college).

In an effort to test the stability of racial differences in intercourse status several multivariate analyses were run in which the comparisons between Blacks and Whites were, in effect, simultaneously standardized for age, family income, education of the male parent or guardian and relationship to family head. The technique provides a comparison of the deviations in the proportions with coital experience of each race from the overall proportions for Blacks and Whites combined, with comparable deviations adjusted for the effect of the variables identified above. These adjustments do reduce the range of differences by race in proportions with sexual experience, but only slightly. As far as we have been able to describe differences in social status and in family structure, this analysis indicates that race differences in intercourse experience are persistent and not readily reducible to differences in social and economic circumstances. That the explanation will turn out to be sociological in nature we have little doubt.

RESIDENCE

As with the socioeconomic variables, differences in place of residence do not diminish very much the large differences between

Blacks and Whites in proportions who have had intercourse. Within the two groups, however, place of residence does appear to affect the patterns of sexual experience.

There is not much difference in the proportions who have had sexual intercourse among those who live in the major regions of the country (Northeast, North Central, South, and West). Farm background does, however, appear to make a considerable difference. Those who once lived on a farm, but moved away, have the highest proportion with coital experience—for 15-19-year-olds as a group, and for each age group. Fifteen-year-olds who moved away from the farm have the same level of sexual activity as girls 16-17 who always lived in an urban environment, and of 19-year-olds who remained on the farm.

A closer look at patterns of sexual experience within the metropolitan community indicates that the proportions who have ever had intercourse generally are highest for those who live in the central cities of metropolitan areas. The size of the metropolitan areas seems not to matter. Those who live in nonmetropolitan areas have experience levels which, in general, fall between those of central cities and their suburbs. A joint examination of metropolitan residence and poverty status reveals little in the way of systematic differences among Whites. Among Blacks, however, the highest proportion who have ever had intercourse occurs among those at or below 150 percent of poverty who live in metropolitan communities (about one-third of all Blacks) and among those above 150 percent of poverty who live in nonmetropolitan areas (about 10 percent of all Blacks).

FAMILY RELATIONSHIPS

We examined the influence of the respondents' positions in their families on the proportions who have ever had sexual intercourse. Most young women live in families headed by their natural fathers. While this is the case for 7 out of 10 young White women, it obtains for only about two-fifths of Blacks, nearly a third of whom live in households headed by their mothers.

The lowest proportion with coital experience is found among young women living in families headed by their natural fathers. This pattern is much more evident among Whites than among Blacks. Although the proportion of Blacks who have ever had intercourse in father-headed families is lower than that of Blacks living under other conditions, the proportion over all ages is not greatly below that found for those living in families headed by their mothers. For Whites, the proportion who have had intercourse is on the order of 60 percent higher for those living in families headed by the mother rather than the father. The stepfather seems to be a fair substitute for the natural father, except possibly for Blacks 16 and younger among whom the proportion who have had coitus is a third to a half higher when the natural father is not around. The important consideration, perhaps, is the integrity of the family, with its full complement of members to fill the essential roles. Unaided, the mother—especially the White mother—appears to have more difficulty maintaining control over her daughter—if this, in fact, is what she wants to do. Other women serving as family heads and perhaps lacking the mother's claim to authority, appear to be even less successful.

Relatively few young women live alone or in group quarters before the age of 18 or 19. Those who do doubtless have the greatest freedom from family control. It is not surprising, therefore, that the proportions in this group who have had intercourse are the highest of any. What may be surprising to some are the moderate proportions with coital experience among young women who live together (in dormitories, for example).

Since the probability that intercourse will be initiated increases sharply with age, it might be expected that the effect of family relationship would manifest itself most clearly among the older teenagers in our sample. Confining our attention to the father-headed and mother-headed situations, we find that the *relative* difference in proportions with coital experience between these two types of families does not increase with age for either

Blacks or Whites. Considering the full range of family situations for Blacks and Whites together again fails to suggest that sexual experience is less likely in father-headed families among older than younger teenagers. A possibly significant problem of interpretation stems from the fact that the figures on proportions who have had intercourse are cumulative over time, whereas the designation of family type is current. . . .

RELIGION

Analysis of religious differences in sexual experience patterns by age and race is handicapped by small numbers in some categories. For example, over three-quarters of the Black sample reports a Protestant nonfundamentalist affiliation. Whites display a wider religious spectrum. Partly for this reason variation in proportions who have had intercourse is much greater among Whites than among Blacks. There are, however, some similarities by race: For both Blacks and Whites, those who say they subscribe to no religion have the highest proportions with coital experience. This holds true for Blacks and Whites at every age, especially for age 16 and younger where the proportion who had intercourse among those who claim no religious affiliation is about twice the average proportion at those ages. Catholics tend to be below average, Protestants somewhat above in proportions sexually experienced. No doubt some of this is a function of socioeconomic factors associated with religious differences. If so, refined comparisons between Protestants and Catholics would be expected to show only modest if any differences.

Among those who attended church four or more times in the month preceding the interview, the proportions sexually experienced are exceptionally low. And within each race there is a pronounced inverse relationship between faithful church attendance and proportions who have had intercourse—that is, the more regular the church attendance, the lower the proportions sexually experienced. This inverse relationship is more marked for White (nonfundamentalist) Protestants than for Blacks.

BASIC BIOLOGICAL UNDERSTANDING

As we pointed out earlier, a great many teenagers—both those who have had intercourse and those who have not—are considerably misinformed about such basic biological facts as when after menarche a girl can become pregnant and at what time during the menstrual cycle unprotected intercourse is most likely to result in a pregnancy. About three-fifths of respondents believe that a girl can become pregnant as soon as her periods begin; while about two-fifths think it is at some time later. There is little difference in replies to this question between those who had intercourse and those who had not. However, Blacks were somewhat more likely than Whites to reply that a woman does not become fecund until sometime after menarche. While technically the more correct answer, this belief could provide a rationalization for deferring the use of contraception.

Young women who mistake the period of greatest risk of conception during the menstrual cycle for the safe period are prime candidates for an unplanned pregnancy, especially if they are using withdrawal, rhythm, or any coitally related method of contraception.

More Whites (42 percent) than Blacks (18 percent) have a generally correct notion about the period of greatest risk. As Whites grow older, and as they become sexually experienced, their knowledge of the variation of risk within the cycle becomes more accurate. Neither age nor experience has this effect on Blacks. The most common fallacy among both Blacks and Whites is that the period of greatest risk is right before, during or after the menses—a dangerous belief. Nearly half the young Black women believe this, as does an almost equally large proportion of Whites. The second most common view among Blacks is that the risk is uniform over the month; more than one-third hold that view, whereas only 15 percent of Whites do so. The existence of these misconceptions is eloquent comment on the extent and effectiveness of school sex education programs. Such misunderstanding obviously poses an unnecessary hazard to those who wish to avoid pregnancy. . . .

SUMMARY

Of the findings presented here the most important, perhaps, is the persistence of differences by race in the proportion who have had intercourse when allowance is made for differences in socioeconomic status and other sociocultural variables. As expected, there is an inverse association between socioeconomic status and proportions with coital experience —much sharper for Blacks than for Whites— but the differences by race cannot be explained by these measures.

There are not many differences in the proportions who have had intercourse from one region of the country to another, but young women who have always lived n a farm are less sexually experienced as a group than others. The greatest amount of sexual experience is found among those who have moved away from farms and among those living in the central cities of metropolitan areas. The effect of central city residence is greatly attenuated for Whites if account is taken of poverty level; for Blacks the central city milieu seems to retain its influence even under these conditions.

The young women in this study live under a variety of family arrangements—the most common, especially for Whites, being a family headed by the father. Differences in living arrangements are associated with different proportions with sexual experience at all ages— the proportions being lowest in situations where the father is the head of the household. The relationship is not a simple one, however, and there are differences between Blacks and Whites in the way it appears to

operate. It is likely that the simple index of family relationship we have used is inadequate to measure the ability of the family to socialize its young members and to exercise social control. This view is supported by the very sharp differences which appear in connection with the degree to which the young woman confides in her family. A high degree of confidence-sharing is associated with relatively low proportions with sexual experience, and vice versa. This appears to be the case among the younger women in our sample, particularly.

A finding of some interest, and one that is perhaps surprising, is the moderate proportion of young women living in group quarters (specifically in college dormitories) who have had intercourse. Such young women, at age 19, do not differ greatly in the extent to which they have had intercourse from those of the same age living at home in families headed by their fathers.

Nominal religious affiliation makes little difference in proportions with coital experience except among fundamentalist Protestants, whose levels are low. Faithful attendance at church, on the other hand, does make a difference, the relationship being inverse.

The level of knowledge is low concerning the period of greatest likelihood of conception during the menstrual cycle. It is positively associated with socioeconomic status but even under optimal conditions the extent of misinformation is substantial. For example, onethird of 19-year-old Whites whose mothers had a college education cannot identify the period of greatest risk. Whites are better informed than Blacks.

The most poorly informed, whether Black or White, are those young women who have lived both on a farm and in the city. As we have seen, they also have the highest proportion with sexual experience. Catholics are not any better informed than others, although young women who have heard of the rhythm method are better informed. . . .

10. HISTORICAL AND CONTEMPORARY TRENDS IN ILLEGITIMACY

PHILLIPS CUTRIGHT

Reprinted from Archives of Sexual Behavior 2, No. 2 (1972): 97-117. *Copyright* © *1972 by Plenum Publishing Corporation. Phillips Cutright is Professor of Sociology at the University of Indiana. He has made important contributions in several areas of sociology, including cross-national studies of political behavior and of the distribution of income and studies of the effect of military service on the life chances of veterans, and of family behavior. Recently he has carried out extensive demographic research on illegitimate and premarital fertility.*

■ All societies have established customary methods for the social placement of the newborn—that is, for determining to whom a child belongs, which family group he is properly a part of. Illegitimacy refers to situations in which such an assignment cannot be made because the child's parents lack the appropriate marital relationship. In Western countries illegitimacy generally involves a situation in which a child not put up for adoption comes to be identified with the mother's kinship group, since at least that part of social parenthood is firmly established. However, the child is stigmatized by "not having a father." Kingsley Davis has called unplanned conceptions that do not fit within the established norms the "social tragedy birth rate." Thus, illegitimate births and unplanned and unwanted premarital pregnancies that precipitate marriage before the birth of the child represent social tragedies in that the products of these conceptions are not introduced into the community under routinely auspicious circumstances.

In addition, illegitimate births in any number raise important social policy issues. Who is responsible for the child? Who will support the child if the mother and her kindred are unable or unwilling to do so? Illegitimacy plays a role, though not so large a one as is often believed, in creating the need for welfare programs such as Aid to Families with Dependent Children, which is analyzed by Martin Rein in Volume I. In general, when two parents are not available to assume responsibility for the child's care, the state's role becomes more important, so the issue of illegitimacy has long concerned applied social scientists. Because models of social and personal pathology have dominated most research on illegitimacy, many of the studies purport to determine the psychopatho-logical characteristics of unwed mothers. Over time several explanations for rising illegitimacy rates in the United States and elsewhere in Western countries have gained currency, and Cutright has systematically examined these theories, making use of historical and cross-national data to test the plausibility of each.

In the United States the rate of illegitimacy rapidly increased into the 1960s, and the differential in the rate between Blacks and Whites has become a particularly violent policy and ideological issue—an issue that first attracted broad public attention during the so-called "Moynihan Report" controversy. In this selection Cutright summarizes the results of several years of research on illegitimacy and demonstrates how some of the most important factors in increasing illegitimacy rates have been ignored in scholarly writing on the subject.

Cutright's work is most extensively reported in his "Illegitimacy in the United States: 1920-1968," Commission on Population Growth and the American Future, Research Reports, Vol. I, pp. 375-438, and in his article "Illegitimacy: Myths, Causes, and Cures" in *Family Planning Perspectives* 3 (1): 26-48. Kingsley Davis has discussed some policy issues concerning illegitimacy in connection with poverty in Margaret Gordon, ed., *Poverty in America* (San Francisco: Chandler, 1965). Two articles by William Goode have been influential in the development of research on illegitimacy: "Economic Factors and Marital Stability," *American Sociological Review* 16 December 1951): 803; and "Illegitimacy in the Caribbean Social Structure," *American Sociological Review* 25, No. 1 (February 1960): 21-30. Other articles of value include: F. Jaffe, "Toward a Reduction of Unwanted Pregnancy: An Assessment of Current Public and Private Programs," *Science* 174 1971): 119-27; A. Campbell, "The Role of Family Planning in the Reduction of Poverty," *Journal of Marriage and Family* 30 (1968): 236-45; H. T. Christiansen, "Cultural Relativism and Premarital Sex Norms," *American Sociological Review* 25 (1960): 31-39; and Prudence M. Rains, *Becoming an Unwed Mother* (Chicago: Aldine, 1971). ▨

THIS PAPER reviews trends in Western nations since 1750 and discusses some implications of these trends of various theories of illegitimacy. It then summarizes a study of trends in the United States from 1920 to 1968 and discusses the changes in the immediate causes of an illegitimacy rate that may account for the increase in illegitimacy in the United States. From this study is estimated the magnitude of the "sexual revolution" among unmarried women. Also measured is the likely impact of having a first illegitimate rather than a first legitimate birth on the status of unwed mothers some 20 years after the birth. The study concludes with an assessment of alternative means through which deliberate changes in social programs might cause a decline in illegitimacy.

TRENDS IN EUROPE: 1750 TO 1965

Trends in illegitimacy in European nations allow one to divide the years since 1750 into three periods. The first period extends from around 1750 to about 1870, the second from around 1880 to 1940, and the third includes the post-World War II years.

The first explosion of illegitimacy in Western nations occurred after 1750. All across Europe, the rates drove upward, peaking between 1860 and 1880 in most nations. Recent work attributes this long-run rise to social, demographic, and economic changes that resulted in the diffusion of modern ideas of self-expression and individualism to the lower classes, who, for the first time, had moved from a life situation that repressed nonmarital intercourse (and perhaps premarital sex with the future husband) to a situation in

which family and community authorities were no longer able to exercise control. Thus rising sexual activity among couples who would not marry brought with it increasing illegitimacy rates.

After about 1880, illegitimacy rates all across Europe receded. In nation after nation, the rates began a decline that continued through the 1930s. Was this period of declining illegitimacy rates accompanied by other changes that might support traditional explanations of illegitimacy? By "traditional explanations" I refer to common concepts of the deterrent effect of religious sanctions for transgression and the repressing effects of economic sanctions. A traditional theory popular with some social scientists is based on views of social disorganization—and the ill effects of urban life. According to this theory, urbanization, industrialization, wars, depressions, and other periods of social strife will "naturally" be accompanied by rising illegitimacy. These traditional views can be tested against the actual trends after 1880.

If there is a single sentence that can sum up the condition of most European nations from 1880 to 1945, it might be this: a period characterized by devastating and prolonged warfare, massive and repeated economic depression, unprecedented increases in urbanization and industrialization, and a massive secularization of populations which can be measured by the shift away from traditional church authority in matters of marriage, divorce, and birth control. All populations in Europe were affected, in varying degrees, by these enormous changes, which should, according to traditional views, increase illegitimacy. Yet, in all populations, illegitimacy rates began a decline that continued from one decade to the next. Secularization, urbanization, industrialization, and social disorders did not increase or even hold steady the high illegitimacy rates of the 1880s. What explains the decline of illegitimacy after 1880?

The decline in illegitimacy was accompanied by a common change in nearly all European nations—the decline of marital fertility rates. Declining marital fertility was not caused by a decline in coital activity;

rather, the decline was due to increasing use of abortion and contraception—primarily *coitus interruptus* and condom. Increasing use of birth control by the married population during this period created a set of conditions that allowed birth control among the unmarried sexually active population to increase as well. It seems likely that illegitimacy declined in most nations because birth control increased. In some nations, a decline in common-law marriages whose issue were defined as illegitimate may also account for some part of the declining . . . rate for older women. The decline in the rate was less pronounced among teen-age girls, a fact that may be accounted for by a dramatic rise in fecundity among the young after 1880 as well as to improvements in other health conditions that decrease sterility and spontaneous fetal loss. Improvements in health conditions must have moderated the decline in illegitimacy after 1880, but no measures of this effect are available.

The third era in the history of illegitimacy began around 1940. Illegitimacy rates in Europe remained low during World War II; after the war, some nations experienced stable, others declining, and still others rising rates. We can statistically account for most of these different postwar patterns by examining differences among nations in the control of marital fertility and changes in the age at marriage and legitimate childbearing. We included in our analysis of change in post-World War II rates the United States, Canada, Australia, and New Zealand, as well as Japan and 18 European nations that lack legal abortion-on-demand. The results of this study clearly show that illegitimacy rates will tend to rise when marital fertility rates indicate weak efforts to control legitimate childbearing; also, illegitimacy rates will tend to rise when the age at marriage is going down and when, therefore, the age at legitimate childbearing is declining. The postwar rise in illegitimacy in the United States is not at all unusual. Other populations with similar behaviors (e.g., Canada, England and Wales, Scotland, New Zealand, and Australia) also experienced similar rises in illegitimacy.

Nations with an early age at marriage (such as the United States) tend to have higher illegitimacy rates among young girls than do nations that have maintained a late age at marriage. Why should young girls have lower illegitimacy rates in nations in which young girls are not likely to marry? Consider the difference between Swiss and American girls. In Switzerland, women traditionally have not married until age 25 or later; younger girls are just that—girls—and may not be judged by most of the population as old enough to be eligible for sexual intercourse. This is not the case in the United States, where many girls marry and start legitimate childbearing by age 18. Legitimate childbearing at an early age may thus weaken normative controls over non-marital sex at an early age, producing the observed higher levels of illegitimacy among young girls in populations where many young women marry.

If it were the case that early-age-at-marriage populations had weak control over fertility, while late-age-at-marriage nations had strong fertility control, one might argue that the observed difference in illegitimacy rates between the two types of populations was a function of higher use of effective birth control in the late-age-at-marriage nations. However, this is not true. Western nations with an early age at marriage moved from a late- to an early-age-at-marriage pattern because they were the first to practice effective control over family size. Nations that have maintained the late-age-at-marriage pattern tend to have weaker control over fertility. These populations tend to rely on delayed marriage rather than birth control to control completed family size.

Awareness of these historical trends and the changes that appear to explain them do not support traditional explanations of illegitimacy that rely totally on secularization or social disorganization views. Nor do the fluctuations over time give support to some psychological explanations of illegitimacy that view unwed mothers as typically "disturbed," "neurotic," "psychotic," or "acting out" various needs. Also, analysis of illegitimacy rates among women with the same years of birth indicates that the same cohort that had a very high illegitimacy rate at one age may have a low rate in later years; also, the same birth cohort of unmarried women may have a very low illegitimacy rate in their early years of childbearing but then have a high rate in the later years of child-bearing. These findings, when considered along with the cyclical nature of illegitimacy rates, indicate that excessive reliance on psychological characteristics of unwed mothers to explain varying illegitimacy rates is no more useful than would be an effort to explain variation in unemployment rates with psychological variables.

ECONOMIC INCENTIVES AND ILLEGITIMACY

The revival of interest in economic sanctions as a means to control illegitimacy in the United States is, I believe, due to the expansion of the Aid to Families of Dependent Children (AFDC) program. In the "good old days," indigent unwed mothers and their children were—along with many indigent married mothers and their legitimate children—denied access to AFDC. This condition has changed, with the result that in spite of the enormous reduction of poverty in the United States after World War II, we find ourselves with rising welfare rolls. For illegitimate children, by way of example, I have calculated that in 1961 only 54 percent of White and 33 percent of non-White illegitimates were on AFDC; by 1969, these percentages had climbed to 87 percent of Whites and 60 percent of non-Whites. Between 1961 and 1969 74 percent of the rise in the number of illegitimates on AFDC was caused by increasing access or utilization of AFDC in the late 1960s. In 1969, about 1 in 3 AFDC children was illegitimate, and in 1971 the AFDC benefits to these children and their mothers ran about $2 billion—or a third of AFDC expenditures.

Illegitimacy is one major cause of AFDC expenditures, but is AFDC a cause of illegitimacy? The answer to this question is no. We have tested this view by comparing changes in illegitimacy rates and changes in benefits for Whites and non-Whites since 1940. State illegitimacy rates change about equally, regardless of whether benefit levels increase, decrease, or remain stable. A second analysis relating the level of benefits and utilization of the program by poor women to the level of illegitimacy in 26 states for 1960 revealed that White and non-White illegitimate rates were lower in states paying high benefits than in states paying low benefits.

A recent article reviewed 1940 to 1965 trends in family or child allowance benefits and illegitimacy rates within a number of nations. The typical pattern within the same nation was stable or rising illegitimacy accompanied by a declining child benefit (caused by inflation). Comparisons of benefit levels and illegitimacy rates across nations in the same year found no association. As with AFDC, the child allowance type of income maintenance program is not a cause of illegitimacy.

Since neither family allowances nor AFDC benefits stimulate illegitimacy, the view that declining economic sanctions against the unwed mother and her child explain increases in illegitimacy can be rejected. The most plausible explanation of the lack of association between illegitimacy and economic "rewards" for children is that, unlike most legitimate children, illegitimate children are neither planned nor wanted. Unlike the legitimate child, the illegitimate child is the unintended result of coital activity among persons whose characteristics limit effective use of contraception and abortion. These characteristics are discussed in a later section. The irrational nature of illegitimate child-bearing is completely unlike the supposed rational childbearing behavior on which economic models of fertility are based. Thus these economic models may account for high or low fertility in a population of married couples with perfect control over fertility, but they are not useful in understanding illegitimate fertility.

STIGMA

The concept of social stigma as a control over illegitimacy first appeared in Europe and then made its way across the Atlantic. "Stigma" refers to norms concerning illegitimacy rather than to norms about nonmarital sex. Stigma is supposed to affect illegitimacy, not by deterring coitus but by affecting the probability of marriage after an illicit pregnancy has occurred. Low-stigma populations do not hasten to the altar and legitimate the pregnancy before birth. In theory, they get married later. Therefore, illegitimacy rates of low-stigma populations are "high." High-stigma populations have many "forced" marriages, while low-stigma populations tend to marry after the illegitimate birth.

In low-stigma Sweden and Denmark, where this explanation of illegitimacy is popular, the higher risk of death to the illegitimate compared to the legitimate child is similar to the higher risk of death to illegitimate than to legitimate children in nations alleged to have high stigma. This should not be the case if it were true that the illegitimate child in Sweden or Denmark were really just a case of delayed marriage—if that were true, they should be protected by the kin group and have life chances equal to those of legitimate children. The higher risk of an illegitimate than legitimate death has been constant for 100 years in Sweden.

In the United States, comparison of Whites and non-Whites reveals no evidence to support the theory so often used to explain White and non-White differences. In theory, low-stigma non-Whites are more likely to have illegitimate children than are Whites because the norm about legitimacy is weak, informal social sanctions on the non-White unwed mother are weak, and non-White women believe illegitimacy will not affect their chances for a normal family life. Therefore, marriage is more likely to occur for the non-White than the White unwed mother after the premaritally conceived birth. In fact, non-White unwed mothers appear no more or less likely than White unwed mothers to marry the alleged father after the birth. The effect of alleged low stigma on just delaying the marriage does not exist.

STIGMA AND THE TIMING OF "FORCED MARRIAGES"

Populations differ in the time between illicit conception and the date of marriage—among those women who marry in time to legitimate the pregnancy. Christensen notes that in low-stigma Denmark the modal legitimated child was conceived five months before the marriage, while in high-stigma Indiana pregnancy occurred just one to three months prior to marriage. A recent study of legitimated first births in Massachusetts compares the timing of pregnancy and marriage among Whites and non-Whites. About 42 percent of White but only 17 percent of non-White legitimated first births resulted from pregnancies occurring within 84 days of marriage. Such data provide no proof that Whites are more likely than non-Whites to be "forced" to marry, since the observed difference in the timing of pregnancy and marriage may simply be due to differences in the timing of premarital intercourse. Unmarried Whites may be more likely than non-Whites to wait for a commitment to marry before becoming sexually active with the groom-to-be. If true, their out-of-wedlock conceptions will occur closer to the date of marriage than will be the case among non-Whites. In any case, the population of pregnant brides is only one segment of the sexually active unmarried population, and differences in characteristics of pregnant brides may be of little value in understanding the role of stigma in illegitimacy.

In the Bowerman study, a number of questions were asked which may give additional support to the view that social stigma has little to do with controlling illegitimacy. For example, about 30 percent of White and 10 percent of the non-White unwed mothers were pregnant by a man who could not possibly marry them—the man was already married. Further, only 14 percent of the White mothers said that both she and the alleged father were legally able to marry and actually "wanted" to get married at the time of the pregnancy; for non-Whites, the comparable figure is only 21 percent. (Some 18 months had gone by from birth to interview, and these women still were not married.) One concludes that these unwed mothers became unwed mothers, in large part, because they were copulating and became pregnant by a man they did not intend or want to marry and/or who they knew neither wanted, intended, or was legally eligible to marry them. They copulated in spite of the knowledge that the pregnancy would not be legitimated.

Bowerman reports little difference between White and non-White unwed mothers on other measures that might relate to stigma—no difference in feeling of displeasure at the discovery that they were pregnant, no difference in change of residence due to social pressures relating to the illegitimate birth, no difference before and after the birth in residing with parents, no difference in aid by the kin group to the unwed mothers, no difference in their judgment that the illegitimate birth would not help their chances for later marriage, no difference in the perceived reaction of their girl friends, and no difference in offers of kin to adopt or care for the child.

If there is less difference than one might expect among White and non-White unwed mothers, this does not allow a conclusion that the respective populations of unmarried women have similar views about illegitimacy. All that appears clear at this point is that alleged differences in illegitimacy between these two populations are not related to stigma—at least as this hypothetical construct makes itself manifest in color differences in delayed marriage. Still, perhaps stigma is an important factor because it affects the probability that a pregnant unmarried woman will marry before the child is born.

STIGMA AS A CAUSE OF LEGITIMATION OF OUT-OF-WEDLOCK CONCEPTIONS

There is a large difference between White and non-White chances of marriage prior to the birth of a child conceived out of wedlock. For example, national data for 1964 to 1966 show that about 61 percent of all White but only 24 percent of all non-White out-of-wedlock conceptions carried to term were legitimated by marriage before birth. Is this difference evidence of higher stigma in the White that in the non-White population? Is the White chance for legitimation high because social pressures force Whites to marry and thus avoid the illegitimate birth?

By examining the chances for legitimation according to the characteristics of the pregnant unmarried woman, we can test this view. For example, the probability that an out-of-wedlock conception ending in a live birth will be legitimated is about the same for Whites and non-Whites in the higher birth orders for women 20 and older. That is, a White with one or more children already born trying (presumably) to get married and legitimate her out-of-wedlock pregnancy has no better chances than does the similar non-White woman. The stigma theory thus fails to help a sizable portion of pregnant unmarried Whites. Among girls under 20, marriage rates are higher for non-Whites than Whites—so we cannot evoke a low non-White marriage rate to explain higher teen-age illegitimacy among non-Whites. Rather, a non-White teen-ager is actually more likely than the White teen-ager to have a legitimated birth.

If it were true that the higher chances that a teen-age White pregnancy will be legitimated by marriage were due to social pressures, we would expect that the economic status of teen-age Whites pregnant at marriage would be lower than the economic status of teen-age White brides who were not "forced" to the altar. This expectation rests on the very great differences in out-of-wedlock pregnancy rates between low income and nonpoor Whites. Our research, however, found no income differences between the pregnant bride and the teen-age bride who becomes pregnant shortly after her marriage. This lack of economic status differences between alleged forced and unforced marriages allows one to further question the view that the higher chance for legitimation among White than among non-White teen-agers is due to the greater likelihood of forced marriages in the White than the non-White population.

Finally, even if the White chances for legitimation were equal to those of non-Whites (24 percent), the White illegitimacy rate for 1964 to 1966 would have increased from the observed 11.3 to only 21.6. These figures may be compared to the non-White rate of 88.2 and thus allow one to conclude that although color differences in the chances of legitimation are large, they do not do a great deal to explain color differences in illegitimacy rates.

What does explain differences in the chances for legitimation between Whites and non-Whites? First, we noted earlier that these differences are quite small for ever-pregnant women 20 and older, and are small for women 25 and older regardless of previous fertility. Since many more non-Whites than Whites are in the higher birth orders, this is one factor to consider.

Second, within the same population over time, and among different populations measured at the same period, our cross-national comparisons have found that the chances for legitimation are a function of the level and change in the level of the out-of-wedlock conceived birth rate (OWCBR). Populations with high out-of-wedlock conceived birth rates will have low legitimation chances, while populations with lower levels of out-of-wedlock pregnancies will have higher chances for legitimation. For unmarried women 15 to 44, the out-of-wedlock conceived birth rate in 1964 to 1966 was 28 and 116 per 1,000 for Whites and non-Whites. When compared with other populations with different levels of OWCBR, the lower level of non-White than White chances for legitimation in the United States is to be expected.

The question, then, is not why the probability of legitimation is high or low; rather, the question is why the out-of-wedlock conceived birth rate is high or low, for it is the out-of-wedlock conceived birth rate that will determine not only the chances for legitimation but the illegitimacy rate as well. It has this effect because the OWCBR will be high when many unmarried women are copulating with men they will not or cannot marry; the OWCBR will be low when only couples planning marriage are sexually active—and these sexually active unmarried women will get married whether they become pregnant or not.

Since this review indicates that illegitimacy rates are not substantially affected by factors alleged to "force" couples to marry, and other evidence failed to support stigma explanations of illegitimacy, it may be time to discard the stigma theory. In the meantime, it is possible to move from a theoretical debate to an examination of the immediate causes of fertility in order to understand how illegitimacy rates change. The following example is taken from an analysis of changes in U.S. illegitimacy rates over recent decades.

FACTORS THAT EXPLAIN CHANGES IN U.S. ILLEGITIMACY RATES

I have recomputed U.S. illegitimacy rates to take into account underenumeration of unmarried women by census and underregistration of births. Census undercount tends to inflate illegitimacy rates, especially among non-Whites, while underregistration of births in earlier years tended to deflate the count of illegitimate births and hence deflated the rate. With these corrected rates, we can look at trends since 1920.

Between 1920 and 1940, the rate declined slightly among Whites. Among non-Whites, it declined between 1920 and 1930 and then increased. By 1940, it was above the 1930 level but still below the rate for 1920. After 1940, illegitimacy rates in both populations increased through 1965. Between 1965 and 1968 (the last year for which information is available) teenage illegitimacy continued to increase among Whites and non-Whites; among Whites 20 and older, the rates stabilized; among non-Whites 20 and older, the rates in the various age groups declined by 23 to 42 percent between 1965 and 1968! Now, what explains these trends?

Since I have eliminated chances for legitimation as an immediate cause of the illegitimacy rate, we have only the following factors to consider:

1. Changes in nonmarital sexual activity.
2. Changes in involuntary controls over conception—fecundity and sterility.
3. Changes in involuntary controls over gestation—spontaneous abortion.
4. Changes in voluntary control over conception by the sexually active—contraception.
5. Changes in voluntary control over gestation by the pregnant—induced abortion.

Comparison of 1930 and 1960 studies of contraceptive use by unwed mothers indicates that, if anything, some kind of effort to contracept was more likely in 1960 than in 1940. This is certainly the case among non-Whites, since virtually any level of use in 1960 will be higher than it was in 1940, because effective contraception was not used by the non-White population in earlier years. Among Whites, it is unlikely that the rise of illegitimacy was due to a decline in contraceptive use. When used, contraception to protect illicit coitus is wholly a male affair —the male will or will not use condom, or he will or will not withdraw. We have no reason to believe that White male use changed between 1940 and 1960, since the level of condom use by White married couples did not change in the White population over those years. Female methods only increased after the Pill—and this change may soon cause problems if young males begin to think that responsibility for contraception is wholly a female responsibility. In any case, one cannot say that illegitimacy increased between 1940 and 1968 because contraception declined.

I have estimated trends in induced abortion from trends in abortion death ratios— the ratio of maternal deaths from abortion to maternal death from nonabortion causes. Both the White and the non-White abortion death ratio declined from high levels in 1940 to low points in 1950, remained low during the early 1950s, and then started to rise again. These inferred trends in induced abortion follow the trends in White and non-White fertility, as well as other reports on induced abortion trends during the 1950s and 1960s.

By 1964, the abortion death ratios were about equal to the 1940 ratios. Thus a pregnancy was about as likely to be aborted in 1964 as in 1940. If so, the 1964 illegitimacy rate was not higher than the 1940 rate because abortion use had declined.

Although frequently ignored, involuntary controls over conception and gestation are crucial determinants of fertility rates for some populations during some periods of time. Such is the case for the non-White population from sometime before 1920 to around 1960. To a lesser extent, this is also true for Whites.

Public health programs relating to the control of venereal and other diseases and to maternal and child health were fragmentary and ineffective prior to World War II. No mass treatment for venereal disease was available, and little effort to apply knowledge that existed was made for the poor population. Virtually the entire non-White population in those years was poor.

When we look at registered late fetal deaths among unmarried mothers over time, we can take this information, combine it with recent studies of spontaneous fetal loss at all gestations, and emerge with adjusted trends in spontaneous fetal loss for unmarried Whites and non-Whites. We then add to this change the decline in sterility—the percent of ever-married women who remained childless after years of exposure during marriage. A final adjustment for increasing fecundity at very early years due to declining age at menarche allows us to compute the effect of changing health conditions on illegitimacy rates after 1940. The technique simply is to ask what would the 1940 illegitimacy rate have been had women in 1940 been as healthy as women were in, say, 1960? When this is done, we find that 75 percent of the change in non-White illegitimacy to women 15 to 44 and 31 percent of the change in the White 15 to 44 rate are due to improved health conditions. That is, higher levels of fecundity and lower levels of sterility and spontaneous fetal loss (with the last factor being the most important) may explain 75 percent of the rise in non-White and 31 percent of the increase in White illegitimacy from 1940 to 1960. One effect of the public health program and improved diet was to increase the illegitimacy rate among women 15 to 44.

Given these levels of explained change in the rates with involuntary controls over gestation and conception, and the likelihood that changes in contraception and induced abortion can be ruled out, we can now ask how much sexual activity among unmarried women increased from, say, 1940 through 1968. The following analysis focuses on teen-age girls because comment on "the sexual revolution" and the "problem of teen-age pregnancy" is focused on this age group.

A TEEN-AGE SEXUAL REVOLUTION?

To estimate the change in sexual activity among unmarried girls after 1940, it is important to distinguish two types of young unmarried girls whose behavior may have changed. The first type is those girls who are involved with a male who will become their husband. These girls, if they have premarital sex, may become pregnant brides. The second group is those girls involved with a male who will not become their husband; these girls, if they have nonmarital sex, may become unwed mothers.

Using live birth data for unwed mothers and pregnant brides, we can estimate changes in sexual activity among each of these two types of unmarried women. The major assumption underlying this method is that voluntary controls over conception and gestation have changed very little over the time period. If, as we believe, this is true, then any difference in out-of-wedlock conceived births not explained by changes in health conditions must be due to increasing premarital or nonmarital sexual activity.

When the impact of improved health conditions is taken into account, the 1940 to 1968 change in the teen-age non-White illegitimacy rate is 3.7 births per 1,000; among Whites, the comparable figure is 4.8 births per 1,000. Thus, among those unmarried teen-age girls who do not become brides, about 0.5 percent were more likely to give birth to an illegitimate child in 1968 as compared to 1940 because of increasing coital activity. To this initial estimate of rising sexual activity we must add a multiplier to account for the happy fact that some sexually active girls do not become pregnant. Elsewhere we have estimated that between one in three and one in five girls sexually active at some time during a year will become pregnant and deliver an illegitimate child. Thus an estimate of rising sexual activity might conclude that between 2 and 3 percent more girls 15 to 19 who will not marry the sexual partner were sexually active in 1968 as compared to 1940. This indicates that the image of an abstinent past and a promiscuous present is exaggerated.

However, when we turn to changes in sexual activity among unmarried girls who will become brides (whether pregnant or not), we find much greater changes. Using census reports, we find that 26 percent of young (under 22 at age of marriage) White brides were pregnant in the 1960 to 1964 period compared to only 11 percent in the 1940 to 1944 period. Of this net gain of 15 percent, 11.5 cannot be explained by improved health among teen-age Whites. From a recent study of White Pennsylvania brides married in 1967, we find that perhaps one in every two sexually active teenage brides was pregnant at marriage. Therefore, we would multiply 11.5 times 2 and thus estimate a rise of 23 percent in premarital sex among young White brides. Among young non-Whites, bridal pregnancy increased by some 7 percent, but nearly 90 percent of change in teen-age non-White fertility rates between 1940 and 1968 (compared to "only" 23 percent for Whites) can be allocated to improved health. Therefore, little change in premarital sex among non-White teenage brides is possible.

With the exception of teen-age White girls involved in a relationship that will end in marriage, our method of detecting changes in sexual behavior indicated only small changes among other types of young unmarried teen-agers. We also note that during periods of stable bridal pregnancy (1920 to 1939) illegitimacy rates also were stable or changed only slightly. Periods of rising bridal pregnancy appear to be accompanied by rising illegitimacy in the United States. As premarital sex among couples committed to marriage increases, so does nonmarital sex among couples not planning marriage.

Finally, small increases in sexual activity among those not committed to marry can be seen as have "large" effects on illegitimacy rates. For example, among Whites whose sexual activity results in illegitimate births, the 15 to 19 illegitimacy increased from 4 to 10 per 1,000 between 1940 and 1968. About 5 points of this 6-point gain are independent of changes we would expect due to improved health. Some writers in looking at this change will note that the rates have doubled—which is true. But this doubling of the rate affected only about 0.5 percent of White teen-agers and was apparently caused by a change in sexual activity among only 2 or 3 percent.

DELIBERATE CHANGE IN U.S. ILLEGITIMACY RATES

Whatever one's theory of illegitimacy, the only policies that have program implications for deliberate change are those dealing with birth control. There is nothing government can do about sexual activity, and there is nothing government can or should do about legitimation of out-of-wedlock conceptions by forcing unwilling couples to marry. Of course, an increase in involuntary controls over conception or gestation through a decline in public health services is unthinkable. The only action left that we now seriously consider as possible public programs revolves around the provision of subsidized physician-prescribed contraception for indigent women, to be delivered as part of the so-called family planning program. What is the likely effect of this effort on illicit pregnancies and births?

I have written at length on the problem of increasing use of effective contraception by unmarried women. At the present time, the subsidized program in the U.S. is solely concerned with providing female contraception to indigent women. Such a program, however much it spreads to counties, cities, and hospitals that presently offer no aid, can have only a limited impact on illegitimacy. The reasons for this dismal assessment follow. First, some intuitive reasons.

The characteristics of unmarried women who are most likely to become unmarried mothers that depress their potential use of effective physician-controlled female methods of contraception are these.

1. Low frequency of sexual intercourse. Sex is usually irregular and often unpredictable.

2. Youthful age. In 1968, nearly half of all unwed mothers were pregnant at age 18 or less and nearly 25 percent—1 in 4—were pregnant at age 16 or less.

3. Low parity. Seventy-three percent of White and 54 percent of non-White illegitimate births in 1968 were first births—63 percent of all illegitimate births were first births. None of these births can be prevented by postpartum contraception programs—the programs that most efficiently reach indigent married women.

4. Poverty status. As noted above, about 80 percent of non-White and 60 percent of White illegitimate births are to poor women.

For a variety of reasons, poor people, even when married, are less likely than are the nonpoor to practice effective contraception.

To these four characteristics associated with ineffective contraception we must add a multiplier effect for marital status. That is, each of the above characteristics is less a deterrent to effective contraception for married than for unmarried couples. Perhaps the major reason sexually active women are not protected from the risk of pregnancy is because they are unmarried. Unlike the married woman, the unmarried woman who will become an unwed mother is wholly dependent on the male for protection—she herself does not contracept. (Unfortunately, we have few available means to make the male responsible.) Although the unmarried woman risking illegitimacy does not practice contraception while she is unmarried, she will, after marriage, contracept. Apparently, then, one must be married before female contraception can be defined as proper in the United States —especially among teen-age girls.

Adding together sexual inexperience, low birth order, youthful age, irregular coital activity, poverty, and the status of being unmarried rather than married, one has a package of the "hard to reach" that is hard to beat. Still, intuition is often refuted by experience, and I now turn to evaluation of the actual impact of subsidized contraception programs on illegitimacy.

A recent study of trends in illegitimate births in various counties within the states of Georgia and Tennessee—some with large contraception programs and some with no programs at all—discovered no difference in illegitimate birth trends between counties with and counties without programs.

There are two reasons the programs do not work. First, many potential unwed mothers are excluded, and among those not excluded many women are not in the program. But perhaps as important are the contraceptive failure rates to patients who are in the program. A recent study of three public and private programs, for example, reported that 27 percent of young Pill patients in these programs were pregnant within a year's time —in the same programs, 13 percent of young IUD patients were pregnant within 12 months. Still, that is a high IUD failure rate when contrasted with the much lower rates for older women. If we take an annual contraception failure rate to unmarried patients of only 10 percent, we can get a mathematical answer to this question: What is the maximum effect a contraception program can have on reducing illicit pregnancies that end in live births?

The size of this effect is dependent only on two factors—first, the percent of the sexually active population that is in the contraception program and, second, their failure rate before and after they become patients.

For the sexually active, unmarried, low income population (the population that is the target group of subsidized programs), I estimate a contraceptive failure rate of 30 percent per year. This estimate, in turn, relies on estimates of the 1964 to 1966 pregnancy rates to unmarried low income Whites and non-Whites. These rates are about 145 per 1,000 for Whites and 208 per 1,000 for non-Whites and include brides as well as unwed mothers. Apply a contraceptive failure rate that appears reasonable to these pregnancy rates gives us the number of 30 per 100. These failure and pregnancy rates also suggest that about 48 percent and 69 percent of unmarried poverty-level Whites and non-Whites aged 15 to 44 have intercourse at least once during that year. The mean number of coital acts is probably around 16—a number that may be compared to 80 among married couples.

If the failure rate is 30 before the population enters a contraception program, the patient failure rate must be less than 30 if the program is to have any effect. The patient failure rate of 27 percent cited above is not much below 30. But assume the program gets the rate down to 10—a rate about equal to IUD failure rates among married couples in the 1960 to 1965 period. If as many as 40 percent of sexually active low income women were in the program, illicit pregnancies would be reduced 27 percent. I doubt that more than 40 percent of unmarried women who are sexually active at any time during the year will ever be enrolled in a contraception program. Even if 70 percent get in the program, less than half of unwanted illicit pregnancies will be avoided—again assuming the low level of patient failure at 10 percent. Moreover, the 10 percent failure rate is just for 1 year —it has now been demonstrated that IUD and Pill dropout rates after 1 or 2 years in various public programs or patients under private care are often such that the majority of married women are left without either method after trying them for a while. If the married do not stay on IUD or Pill year after year, why would we expect the unmarried to do any better? The extended use effectiveness of all present contraceptive methods is exceedingly low—a fact that is recognized by only a few biomedical and demographic researchers.

So what safe and proven method do we have that will reduce illegitimacy or unwanted bridal pregnancy among the poor and the nonpoor, the young and the old, the never-pregnant and the ever-pregnant, the White and the non-White, the woman with and the woman without frequent sexual activity? We have very little in the contraception line. However, if the goal is extended to prevention of unwanted births, rather than the more limited task of preventing unwanted pregnancy, we can take a more hopeful view. Let's look at abortion.

WILL ABORTION WORK?

Under legal abortion in New York City, we now have a report from the New York City Department of Health covering the first nine months of the program. There were 448 legal abortions per 1,000 live births to New York City residents in this period. For first births, the abortion ratio was higher—about 590 per 1,000 first births; for women under 20, the ratio was 527 per 1,000 live births—again higher than the total ratio; for non-Whites, the figure was 595—well above the 422 ratio for Whites; in municipal hospitals which

serve the poor, the ratio was 775 legal abortions per 1,000 live births. These figures for residents of New York City indicate that the poor, the non-White, the young, and the never-pregnant are more likely to be aborted than are the other women. The reason for this is quite simple—these are the same women most likely to be pregnant but unmarried, or to be married but pregnant due to contraceptive failure. The very groups least likely to practice effective contraception are those most likely to use legal abortion when it is made available to them.

How much will abortion-on-demand reduce U.S. illegitimacy? The answer still awaits development of the New York program. However, illegitimate births during the third to ninth month following legal abortion ran 3 percent below the number in the same months of the preceding year. This small percentage decline should be seen in the perspective of an 11 percent annual rate of increase prior to the introduction of legal abortion. It is noteworthy that the 11 percent annual increase in the number of illegitimate births in New York City during the 1960s occurred during a period when the percent of the indigent population enrolled in a contraception program increased from about 0 to nearly 50 percent. Contraception did not work.

The experiences of nations that have legalized abortion-on-demand all show that the impact of legal abortion on illegitimacy rates increases with time. After 6 to 8 years with legal abortion, the national illegitimacy rate in nations such as Hungary, Poland, Czechoslovakia, and Japan declined by 30 percent. There is no evidence that any contraception program anywhere has ever done as much. . . .

CONCLUSION

This review of trends in illegitimacy rates tested various traditional theories of illegitimacy. In general, popular explanations of illegitimacy which claim religious and economic sanctions as important sources of control were not supported by the evidence. Social scientific theories relying on vague notions of social stigma or social disorganization also failed to account for high or low rates in different populations or for changes in the rates over time.

We focused on the immediate causes of illegitimacy (sexual activity, voluntary and involuntary controls over conception and gestation) rather than on those factors more remote in a causal chain of events. It seems clear that an increase in nonmarital sex resulted in increasing illegitimacy rates in most European nations from around 1750 through 1880, but the question of why nonmarital sex increased may still be open to further study. We do not know why married and unmarried couples in Europe began a "demographic transition" from high to low fertility around 1880—we only know that the fertility rates declined because voluntary controls over conception and gestation increased. In the post-World War II years, we do not know why marital fertility and the age at legitimate childbearing differed among nations—we only know that these changes in fertility behavior account for most of the national differences in changing post-World War II illegitimacy rates.

Our analysis of illegitimacy trends in the United States distinguished between that portion of the increase in illegitimacy rates that could be ascribed to rising sexual activity and that which could be explained in physiological terms. Since unmarried women who are sexually active are divided between those who can and will marry the sexual partner and those who cannot or will not marry the partner, estimates of sexual activity among the "unmarried" should distinguish between these two types of women. When that was done, we found the larger increases in sex among the unmarried to be concentrated among White girls involved with a male who will become their husband. Although the changing level of nonmarital sex among the other types of unmarried girls involves only a small percent of the total population of unmarried women, these changes have effects on illegitimacy rates which tend to be exaggerated and used as evidence of a dramatic increase in nonmarital sex. The available evidence does not support the view that a change of revolutionary magnitude has occurred.

When the results of this research are applied to the problem of devising a program to reduce illegitimacy, we find that answers to traditional questions such as "Who is the unwed mother?" or "Why is she pregnant?" are unnecessary. A continuing effort over several decades to answer the question of what differentiates (in psychological terms) the pregnant from the nonpregnant unmarried woman has yet to deliver an answer. Such questions are not asked of married women having unwanted legitimate children. Instead, the design of realistic programs to reduce unwanted legitimate births is based on improving the methods of controlling conception and gestation and reducing barriers that presently inhibit maximum use of the most effective methods available. The development of a program to reduce illegitimate births can proceed along similar lines.

11. PROSTITUTION AND POLITICS

PAMELA A. ROBY

Reprinted with permission from Pamela A. Roby, "Politics and Criminal Law: Revision of the New York State Penal Law on Prostitution," Social Problems 1 (Summer 1969): 83-109. Copyright 1969 by The Society for the Study of Social Problems. Pamela A. Roby is Associate Professor of Sociology and Community Studies at the University of California at Santa Cruz. In addition to this work on criminal law revision she has written on inequality and social stratification, as coauthor (with S. M. Miller) of The Future of Inequality *(Basic Books, 1970), and on day care.*

■ Prostitution as the "oldest profession" has been a subject of considerable interest in sociology, though perhaps more so in earlier years than recently. Most sociological interest has been directed at studying the prostitute or the system of vice of which prostitution is a part. Here, in keeping with the labeling or social policy model for studying deviant behavior, Roby focuses instead on the law that makes prostitution a crime and on the various interest groups that feel they have a stake in how that law is defined and applied. She shows how many different kinds of individuals and groups were able to assert themselves in determining the legal definition of the transaction between customer and prostitute.

The milieu and experiences of the small-time prostitute in New York City have been described by John Murtagh and Sara Harris, *Cast the First Stone* (McGraw-Hill, 1957). Harold Greenwald has studied prostitutes at a higher status level in *The Call Girls* (Ballantine, 1958). The classic sociological analysis of the functions of prostitution is Kingsley Davis, "The Sociology of Prostitution," *American Sociological Review,* October 1937, pp. 746-55. A collection of historical information about prostitution is in Harry Benjamin and R. E. L. Masters, *Prostitution and Morality* (Julian Press, 1964). A more recent survey of prostitution in the United States is Charles Winick and Paul M. Kinsie, *The Lively Commerce* (Quadrangle Books, 1971). ■

PERSONS ARE NOT "CRIMINALS" unless a law defines their behavior as "crime." The purpose of this paper is to examine the political process through which certain behavior is defined as criminal and other behavior as noncriminal. What groups and persons influence the decisions through which penal laws are created? When groups have conflicting interests, which interests are written into law? Under what conditions are groups or individuals able to shape the law in the manner they intend?

Durkheim early in his career stressed the apolitical nature of law, ". . . once we grant that there is a determinate order in social existence, we necessarily reduce the role of the lawgiver. For if social institutions follow from the nature of things, they do not depend upon the will of any citizen or citizens." Marx, on the other hand, maintained that lawmakers along with the state were the "arm of the bourgeois class" and that although the groups which ruled changed over time, they always belonged to the bourgeoisie. Domestic legislation was for the ruling class and against the proletariat.

More recently, Schur in discussing the relationship between law and the social order has argued that a legal system "represents an institutionalization of conflict, for it provides social means of resolving the specified disputes and in some sense reconciling the more general conflicts of interests and values within a society." In this view, the formulation of law is a political process—i.e., a process in which individuals and groups attempt "to gain, limit, escape, or resist power."

The essence or definition of power has been the source of considerable debate within the social sciences. Gerth and Mills and Blau stress the asymmetry of power relations. Wrong has maintained that power is *not* completely asymmetrical, for intercursive power is

116

characterized by a division of scopes between parties. Thus "one actor controls the other with respect to particular situations or scopes . . . while the other is dominant in other areas of situated activity."

Over the sum of scopes some are "less equal than others," but except in those cases of physical violence when the person is no longer treated as a human being, all exercise some degree of power or reciprocal influence. In the formulation of law, one group may obtain its interests in the writing of a particular article while another may do so with respect to another section of the law. Groups which are unable to shape the enacted law according to their interests may be able to affect the enforcement of the law or to amend the law at a later date.

Given these diverse characterizations of the nature of law and of power, we turned to the Revised Penal Law of New York State in an effort to gain a clearer understanding of the relationship between law and the exercise of power within society. The recent revision of the Penal Law which became effective September 1, 1967, and the efforts of various groups to amend certain of the revised articles provide sociologists with a unique opportunity to study the social processes through which behaviors come to be defined as criminal or noncriminal. The 1965 Penal Law represents a complete reorganization of the 1864 New York State Field Commission Revised Code of Criminal Procedure, which became effective in 1881 and was amnded in 1909. The recent revision redefined certain previously noncriminal acts as criminal and previously criminal acts as noncriminal, placed related crimes together under logically related titles, transferred many provisions from the 1909 Code of Criminal Procedure and Penal Law to other more appropriate state laws, clarified previously ambiguous definitions and provisions, and prescribed new sentencing schemes.

METHOD

Of the approximately 520 sections in the 1965 New York State Penal Law, we will examine article 230, which represents a "deviant" case. Most articles of the Law were not debated outside of the Penal Law and Criminal Code Revision (PLCCR) Commission either before or after their enactment. Article 230 was one of a small number of articles debated during the Public Hearings held in November 1964 on the Proposed Revised Penal Law and one of the very few articles which was revised by the commission in accordance with sentiments expressed in the public hearings. The article was not debated by the legislature before its passage, but it was the center of much controversy after it became effective September 1, 1967.

Sections 230.00, 230.05, and 230.10 of the 1965 New York State Penal Law read as follows.

§ 230.00 Prostitution

A person is guilty of prostitution when such person engages or agrees or offers to engage in sexual conduct with another person in return for a fee.

Prostitution is a violation. L. 1965, c. 1030, eff. Sept. 1, 1967.

§ 230.05 Patronizing a prostitute

A person is guilty of patronizing a prostitute when:

1. Pursuant to a prior understanding, he pays a fee to another person as compensation for such person or a third person having engaged in sexual conduct with him; or

2. He pays or agrees to pay a fee to another person pursuant to an understanding that in return therefor such person or a third person will engage in sexual conduct with him; or

3. He solicits or requests another person to engage in sexual conduct with him in return for a fee.

Patronizing a prostitute is a violation. L. 1965, c. 1030, eff. September 1, 1967. §230.10 Prostitution and patronizing a prostitute; no defense

In any prosecution for prostitution or patronizing a prostitute, the sex of the two parties or prospective parties to the sexual conduct engaged in, contemplated, or solicited is immaterial, and it is no defense that:

1. Such persons were of the same sex; or

2. The person who received, agreed to receive or solicited a fee was a male and the person who paid or agreed or offered to pay such fee was a female. L. 1965, c. 1030, eff. Sept. 1, 1967.

We chose to study this "deviant"—i.e. controversial—article so that we could analyze the political processes which were a part of the formulation of the law. The choice of a controversial article was necessary because secrecy veiled most of the PLCCR Commission debates (except for supporting arguments which were published with the law). Minutes of the commission meetings were available only to commission members and commission staff. The assistant counsel to the commission explained that what went on in the commission was "confidential so that it wouldn't become political." By analysing an article which was publicly debated, we were able to infer many of the factors influencing the commission's decisions. In making generalizations from the history of article 230, we must remember, however, that most articles were passed without public notice and that the politics involved in their formulation were confined to the room of the Penal Law Revision Commission.

Data were collected for the study by means of interviews, summary analyses of the prostitution cases reported in the "Docket Sheets" of the Criminal Court of New York City and of data on arraignments and dispositions of prostitution, disorderly conduct, and loitering cases contained in the Statistics Office of the Criminal Court; and examination of the transcript of the Public Hearings held by the PLCCR Commission on the Proposed Penal Law, law review articles and books which suggested means of dealing with prostitution in New York state, and clippings gathered by the Albany New Clipping Service which were contained in the Chief Assistant Counsel of the PLCCR Commission's file on "Prostitution and Article 230."

FINDINGS

The development of article 230 may be divided into five phases: (1) the Penal Law and Criminal Code Revision Commission's writing of the "Proposed New York Penal Law," article 235 (1962-1964); (2) introduction of the "Proposed Penal Law" as a study bill in the New York State Assembly and Senate (1964), public hearings on the proposed law (November 1964), and the com-

mission's subsequent rewriting of the law relating to prostitution (retitled article 230); (3) enactment of the 1965 Penal Law by the New York State Senate and Assembly (March 1965); (4) enforcement of and public reactions to the 1965 Penal Law following September 1, 1967, the date it became effective; (5) proposed amendments to article 230, *1965 New York Penal Law.* . . .

After nearly four years of work, the commission published the *Proposed Penal Law.* This was introduced as a study bill at the 1964 legislative session. The bill was not to be voted upon, but was a means of eliciting the senators' and assemblymen's as well as the general public's opinions regarding the commission's proposals. This was the law's first large preview. The only section pertaining directly to the 1965 P.L., SS 230.00, 230.05, 230.10 read as follows.

§§ 235.00 Prostitution
A person is guilty of prostitution when he or she commits or submits to, or offers to commit or to submit to, any sexual act with or upon another person, whether of a different or of the same sex, in return for a fee or compensation.
Prostitution is a violation.

The proposed article, unlike the 1959 Model Penal Code and the 1961 Illinois Criminal Code, did not make patrons guilty. According to staff members, the New York PLCCR Commission's first inclination was to leave the law concerning prostitutes' customers unclear. Later the commission decided it was best to strive for clarity and to follow existing practice by excluding any reference to prostitutes' patrons from the Proposed Penal Law.

By stating in the proposed article that "a person is guilty of prostitution when *he or she* . . . " the commission eliminated any question as to the generality of prostitution. This decision was in keeping with the 1960 decision of *People* v. *Hale,* where prostitution was held to include homosexual as well as heterosexual situations. It was also in accord with the United Nations Declaration on the Rights of Women and expressed the same intent as the terminology used in the Model

Penal Code (1959 Draft) and in the statutes of Illinois, New Jersey, and Hawaii.

The proposed article also made prostitution a "violation" rather than a crime, the maximum sentence for a violation being 15 days rather than a year in jail or 3 years in a reformatory.

Arnold Hechtman, assistant counsel to the commission, explained the commission's decision to make prostitution a violation by saying that since there is no health program in New York for prostitutes, the commission could not write a law to treat prostitutes clinically. Because of sentiment in New York State, the commission members felt that they had to keep prostitution "on the books." Therefore, they resorted to "the next best action and whittled the punishment for prostitution down as far as they felt they could —down to a 'violation'." Hechtman defended this change as in keeping with existing practice by adding that even under the old law, in New York City prostitutes were generally given only 5 to 30 days, and the latter only when they were uncooperative. In upstate New York, however, prostitutes were generally given longer sentences.

PUBLIC HEARINGS AND REVISION OF THE
PROPOSED PENAL LAW

In November 1964 the commission held public hearings throughout the state on the Proposed Penal Law. What was the purpose of these hearings? One commission staff member remarked, "Public hearings are hogwash." He explained the meaning of his statement by saying that the public seldom knows what goes on in the legislature. Therefore, only organized interest groups, which have generally already made their wishes known to the commission at the commission's closed meetings or by letters, appear at the public hearings. A few of the same groups, such as the societies concerned with humanity to animals, spoke at the public hearings in all four cities. He added that the public hearings are politically useful because they satisfy the public's wish to be heard. If the commission makes changes following the hearings,

he claimed, it is generally not because of the public's statements but because the commission is continually rethinking the law. If the commission rejects groups' opinions, the groups can go to their legislatures, he added. In summary, this staff member believed that interested, organized groups possessing sufficient power would eventually obtain their wishes with or without public hearings and that the general public would remain ignorant of the legal changes.

Article 235 of the Proposed Penal Law was one of the few articles which was rewritten, prior to being presented to the legislature, in accordance with the wishes which groups expressed at the public hearings. In its final form, the article was numbered 230, and the section defining prostitution finally read as given above.

Few changes were made in the definition of prostitution. Only the words "or compensation" were deleted from the clause of the Proposed Penal Law which defined prostitution as sexual conduct "in return for a fee *or compensation.*" The clause defining the generality of the act was placed in a separate section, 230.10, as noted above.

The main issue in the development of the law on prostitution offenses and the main source of controversy after the law's enactment was whether "patronizing a prostitute" should be classified as an "offense." It will be remembered that in the Proposed Penal Law "patronizing a prostitute" was not classified as an offense.

During the public hearings, three persons forcefully expressed their views on the act of "patronizing a prostitute." Mr. Furst, president of the American Social Health Association, appeared first, and his statement attracted the most news coverage. Mr. Furst submitted an amendment to the Proposed Penal Law which would make "Patronizing Prostitutes" a violation. Arguing that both the patron and the prostitute are "culpable in the spreading of disease," the ASHA representative disagreed with the position debated by the American Law Institute and held by Judge Murtagh that prostitution is a private matter. The association therefore recommended that both patrons and prostitutes be guilty of commiting a violation.

Others in New York City argued against including a "patron" clause on the basis that doing so would make prostitution convictions more difficult. Traditionally, New York City police used customers to testify against prostitutes. Furst contended that this argument was invalid because difficulty in conviction should not override "customer guilt," and because this situation was peculiar to New York City. In smaller towns without the anonymity of New York City, he argued, customers would not consider testifying because their doing so would make their activities with prostitutes general knowledge.

In her written testimony, Dorris Clarke, attorney and retired chief probation officer of the N.Y.C. Magistrates Court, also concluded that "patronizing a prostitute" as well as "prostitution" should be classified as a violation. However, her arguments for this reform differed from those of Furst. Clarke maintained that prostitution should be dealt with under the Public Health Law rather than under the Penal Law, but that as long as prostitution was included under the Penal Law, the exclusion of "patronizing a prostitute" from the Penal Law represented unequal treatment, "a fantastically unbelievable piece of legal hocus-pocus and philosophical hairsplitting." In her testimony she stressed:

. . . few jurisdictions place any blame upon the customer; and where there *are* such laws, *enforcement* is sporadic or non-existent. YET, WITHOUT CUSTOMERS, THERE WOULD BE NO PROSTITUTES.

She pointed out further that although judges and police were careful to preserve the anonymity of customers, distinguished or otherwise, the same kindness had never been extended to the prostitute. Citing examples from the sixties, she observed:

. . . the papers are having a heyday with exposés of "suburban housewives" offering "sex for sale." . . . When arrests are made, there is no hesitancy in publishing the names and addresses of the females. Even their husbands are not immune from publicity, but the "customers," while usually referred to as "well-to-do businessmen," or "upper class" remain cloaked in anonymity.

In debating Mr. Atlas of the commission who suggested that sending "customers" to prison would hurt their families, Miss Clarke suggested that only some customers—perhaps those who had brutally treated a prostitute —might be sentenced to prison; others would be given other treatments. . . .

Dr. Grabinska, the third person to testify, presented a lengthy written statement in which she argued that because the "customer" and the "prostitute" are equally guilty, they should be given equal treatment. Dr. Grabinska, who had a Polish law degree and who had long followed cases concerning women's rights, represented no organization but spoke as an "interested citizen."

Following the public hearings, the PLCCR Commission added § 230.05 concerning patrons. The section as passed by the legislature is given above. In its comments on article 230., the commission termed the addition of the new offense, "Patronizing a Prostitute," the most important change in the article. In explaining the change, the commission wrote:

Though not presently an offense in New York, such "patronizing" conduct is proscribed in various forms by the penal codes of several other jurisdictions, including the recently revised codes of Illinois and Wisconsin and it is included as an offense in the American Law Institute's Model Penal Code.

At the public hearings held by the Commission with respect to the proposed Penal Law, and in conferences and correspondence with the Commission and its staff, a number of persons and organizations have strongly urged the inclusion of a "patronizing" offense. The reasons most vigorously advanced are: (1) that criminal sanctions against the patron as well as the prostitute should aid in the curtailment of prostitution; and (2) that to penalize the prostitute and exempt the equally culpable patron is inherently unjust.

After consideration of these contentions, the Commission decided to include the indicated patronizing offense in the new bill as a proper corollary to prostitution.

ENACTMENT AND ENFORCEMENT OF THE LAW

In 1965, the new sections passed the legislature without comment. The *New York Times* merely noted the following.

In another revision the commission recommended that the customer of a prostitute, as well as the prostitute herself, be made subject to prosecution. Mr. Bartlett (chairman) said he was "persuaded that there is no moral or ethical reason to exclude the customer from criminal liability in a sex-for-hire situation."

The new law radically changed the legal status of prostitutes' patrons and modified the status of prostitutes. In addition, the law prevented police from using customers as witnesses in prosecutions, and *technically* prohibited plainclothesmen from obtaining solicitations from and subsequently testifying against prostitutes. The one legal basis for arresting prostitutes and patrons was for plainclothesmen to observe a couple while the patron offered and the prostitute accepted a fee for sexual conduct. As the time for the new law to become effective approached, one wondered whether the police would attempt to enforce the legal changes, follow traditional practice, or attempt to amend the law.

In May 1967 the police ended their practice of having patrolmen who made arrests act as prosecutors in Women's Court. During the early summer months, the police relaxed their prostitution pickups. This relaxation may have been in anticipation of the Revised Penal Law or a consequence of the Police Department's energies being diverted by racial unrest. Whatever the cause, an alleged influx of prostitutes began to descend upon Manhattan and the Times Square area. Some persons say that a rumor went around among prostitutes that prostitution was legal. According to these sources, prostitutes came to New York from around the nation and around the world; others came out of retirement; and some women entered the business for the first time.

The dimensions of the "invasion," and whether the invasion actually took place, are unknown. The amount of prostitution which exists at any one time cannot, as many sociologists and other writers have pointetd out, be measured by arrest rates. Arrest rates, particularly for prostitution, go up and down more as a result of pressures from the political and police system than as a consequence of the actual rate of prostitution.

New York politicians, businessmen, and police may have begun to talk about an influx of prostitutes and the need for a "cleanup" because they were dissatisfied with the law's becoming "soft" on prostitutes. Also representatives of the Police Department appeared to speak periodically to newsmen about "increases in prostitution." Only a year before the alleged '67 influx, S. V. Killorin, Commander of the Third Division, had stated, "For some reason, many prostitutes seem to be coming from out of town."

Members of the PLCCR Commission staff who naturally felt some need to protect the new law, questioned whether the actual rate of prostitution had risen at all. Whatever the dimensions of the alleged "influx," in August the police reportedly were pressured by politicians, Midtown businessmen, and City Hall to "cleanup" the Times Square area. The New York Hotel Association complained especially bitterly about the influx.

August 20th, the first day of the Times Square "cleanup," marked the start of a fiery checkboard game between the police and the district attorney's office on the one hand, and the Civil Liberties Union, the Legal Aid Society, and certain judges on the other. Because of the speed and political complexity of the moves, we will outline them chronologically.

August 20, 1967:
  The New York City police began their drive against prostitution by arresting 121 alleged prostitutes. Deputy Police Commissioner Nevard said that the drive had been planned for some time but that it had been held up until this date because of manpower needs in areas of racial tensions. He added, "We hope to keep the Times Square area clean."

August 22, 1967:
  On the nights of August 20 and 21 the police "successfully pulled in" many prostitutes. Then the prostitutes "got smart" and left the streets. The police continued to be told to bring prostitutes in, and, being unable to arrest streetwalkers, "they started bringing in legitimate women who

were standing on the street." According to Judge Basel, "The police also began to make deals with the "Johns" so as to get the prostitutes."

September 1, 1967:

The Revised Penal Law became effective.

September 8, 1967:

The cases of the defendants who had been arrested on "loitering" charges began to come before the court. The women had been arrested by plainclothesmen who had simply seen them standing in hotel doorways nodding to men who entered. The plainclothesmen testified that they knew the women were prostitutes because they knew they had been arrested before. After dismissing the cases because there was not enough evidence to hold the defendants, Judge Basel said the arrests had been made to "harass" the women and get them off the streets. He said he felt the patrolmen knew there could not be convictions in these cases.

September 22, 1967:

In a press release, the New York Civil Liberties Union protested police practices in the "Times Square cleanup campaign." The NYCLU reported, "Literally hundreds of women have been arrested and charged with disorderly conduct during the summer months, and the situation still continues." ". . . there is a conspiracy on the part of the police to deprive these women of their civil rights by arresting them on insubstantial charges." ". . . women are being arrested in a dragnet and charged with disorderly conduct and loitering in order to raise the number of arrests." ". . . many innocent girls are undoubtedly being caught in the net and the entire practice is an outrageous perversion of the judicial process. Furthermore, women who refuse to submit to the unlawful practices of the police have been manhandled."

The union reported Judge Basel saying, "I don't doubt that most of them are prostitutes, but it is a violation of the civil liberties of these girls. Even streetwalkers are entitled to their Constitutional rights. The District Attorney moved in all these cases to have the charges thrown out, but in every case the girls were arrested after it was too late for night court, so they were kept over night with no substantial charges pending against them."

August 20-September 23, 1967:

1,300 prostitution arrests made: most were on charges of disorderly conduct or loitering rather than prostitution. In explaining the move to arrest prostitutes under disorderly conduct or loitering rather than under prostitution, Jacques Nevard, press spokesman for the police department, said: "It's unprofitable and uneconomical to make solicitation arrests required to substantiate a prostitution charge." Throughout this period, the district attorney's office had dismissed nearly all of the complaints of disorderly conduct and loitering.

September 23, 1967:

The police department appeared to be embarrassed by the district attorney's repeated dismissals of the cases, by the NYCLU's protests, and by Judge Basel's denunciation of its activities. Therefore, the *New York Times* reported "informed legal sources" as revealing the police department prevailed upon DA Frank S. Hogan's office to begin prosecuting the cases. Hogan's office suggested that the police arrest the women on loitering charges.

September 25, 1967:

The district attorney's office requested Judge Basel to hold the next cases over for trial. Basel reluctantly held 30 women over for trial for loitering, most of them being released on low bail—around $25; and described the dragnet as a "disgrace." The DA's office spiritedly defended the legality of arrests of *suspected* prostitutes for loitering.

September 26, 1967:

Gerald Kearney, an attorney for the Legal Aid Society, according to the *New York Times*, moved to dismiss the loitering cases "on the ground that the loitering statute requires that the person arrested be suspected of committing a crime." Since prostitution is a violation and not a misdemeanor or a felony, Mr. Kearney argued that it was not a crime under the penal law. Kearney, in an interview, later said that he had moved to dismiss the cases on the ground that 1967 NYPL § 240. 35 was in violation of the Fourth and Fourteenth Amendments of the Constitution of the United States. Kearney also claimed that approximately half of his cases were innocent, had never before been arrested for prostitution, and were shocked to find themselves inside a courtroom.

Following Kearney's move, Peter Schweitzer, an assistant district attorney, argued argued that the complaint was legal. When Judge Basel said that prostitution was not a crime, Schweitzer said, "Maybe the law has been amended." "I think I have the latest edition of the penal law," Judge Basel countered. After a short recess, Schweitzer moved to dismiss each of the remaining loitering cases saying, "The people move to dismiss on the grounds that the case cannot be proved beyond a reasonable doubt." Judge Basel later said that he had intended to dismiss the case anyway. The judge also dismissed disorderly conduct charges against two defendants, but he did not dismiss any of the straight prostitution cases.

That day, the *New York Times* reported, Police Chief Leary also met with his top commanders concerning the strategy which the department should pursue with regard to prostitution. Their decisions, Leary said would not be made public. However, there was a change in the arrest pattern: 30 out of 43 defendants were charged with prostitution as a result of solicitation of policemen.

September 27, 1967:
The police department presumably put new pressure on the district attorney's office.

The NYCLU indicated that it would file a suit in the federal court the following week seeking an injunction against the arrests. Aryeh Neier, executive director of the CLU criticized the "rapid-fire switches" of the DA's office, saying: "When

the law enforcement agencies adapt their procedures to the political order of the day, they are not only in derogation of the Constitution, but they make a burlesque of it." During the following days, the NYCLU did draw up a complaint seeking action for "an injunction to prevent the further deliberate deprivation of the defendants of rights, privileges and immunities secured by New York State law, and the Constitution of the U.S. and the State of New York." The union was unable to pursue the complaint because the plaintiffs, three alleged prostitutes, ran away.

September 28, 1967:
Assistant DA L. Goldman asked Judge Basel to uphold the legality of the loitering charges. Basel paroled four women charged with loitering until he reached a decision on the legality of the practice. Legal briefs were to be submitted by the district attorney's office and the Legal Aid Society by November 9th.

August 20-September 30, 1967:
Police made 2,400 arrests in the prostitution "cleanup." This was only 200 less in 6 *weeks* than the number of prostitution arrests during the first 6 *months* of the year.

October 1, 1967:
The *New York Times* stated, "unless and until an injunction is granted, the police will be under no serious pressure to stop (the unconstitutional arrests) and indeed the pressure will more than likely be in the other direction."

November 9, 1967:
Judge Basel dismissed loitering charges against 41 women. "The arrests," he said, "were illegal and made in violation of the clear mandate of the loitering statute and in violation of the rights of all the defendants." The ruling, made in a test case with the consent of District Attorney Hogan, will "terminate" the crackdown, Basel said. Mr. Hogan agreed that "crime" means "a misdemeanor or a felony" and therefore the charges could not stand.

During the rapid changes in prostitution

cleanup procedures, how was the new "patron" law being enforced? We observed that the newspapers contained no reports or stories on arrests of "Johns." Because the papers generally contain monthly or bi-monthly reports on prostitution arrests, and frequently include public interest stories about prostitutes, we asked the Criminal Court Statistics Office to show us their record on the arraignments and dispositions of persons charged with "patronizing prostitutes." In comparing the figures for "prostitution" and "patronizing a prostitute," we should remember that in addition to the 1,159 prostitution arrests under § 230.00 during the months of September and October, over 2,000 women were arrested for loitering or disorderly conduct.

Of the *new* prostitution and patronizing cases, only 6 percent were for patronizing a prostitute during the months of September and October. Of the 508 *convicted* dispositions, only 0.8 percent were for patronizing a prostitute. Between November and February an average of 14 patrons were arrested monthly as compared with an average of 35 during September and October; only one of these cases was convicted. The high number of prostitution arrests during October and November (monthly average 738) returned to normal (400-500 a month) between December and February.

Three observations may be made from these statistics. First, since the only legal basis for arresting prostitutes was for plainclothesmen to observe a couple while the patron offered and the prostitute accepted a fee for sexual conduct, the enforcement of the law was not consistent with the provisions of the new law. Second, since 72 persons had been arrested on patronizing charges during September and October, the newspapers by not reporting on any of the patronizing cases were obviously extending a courtesy to patrons which they do not extend to prostitutes. Third, the decline in the number of prostitution arrests between December and February indicates either that the prostitutes who "swarmed to New York City" during October left quickly after the police

clampdown, or that the increase in prostitution arrests was an artifact of political pressures.

Not only patrons but high priced call-girls were ignored by the police during the "cleanup" period. The large number of arrests of Times Square "streetwalkers" and the small number of arrests of call-girls may be interpreted in two ways: First, in enforcement practices, there may be decreasing moralistic concern with the private actions of individuals. Second, streetwalkers and their customers rank lowest in prestige among those who participate in prostitution or patronizing prostitutes. Call-girls serve "upper class," sometimes famous, patrons for high fees. One madame, described as well known among New York's upper classes, publishes a book on her girls. The "class A" girls frequently accompany corporation customers to dinner and the theatre as well as engage in sexual conduct with them. Because such behavior is generally not regarded as offensive, political groups do not exert pressure upon the police and City Hall to "clean it up."

We have seen that in its enforcement practice, the police department reacted initially to § 230.00 and prostitution by unconstitutionally "sweeping" the streets of prostitutes under the cloak of legality provided by the sections on loitering and disorderly conduct. The department reacted to the new "violation" of patronizing prostitutes by making a small number of token arrests of patrons and by letting most "Johns" go. In turn, the New York Civil Liberties Union, the Legal Aid Society and certain judges reacted to the police actions by defending the women's rights.

In what other ways did the community react to the new provisions? The Hotel Association and businessmen in the Times Square area vociferously complained to the police and City Hall about the influx of prostitutes. The New York Commission on the United Nations Secretariat allegedly complained about the arrest of businessmen and other visitors from foreign countries who did not realize that "patronizing prostitutes" was an offense. The hotel managers felt that not only did the prostitutes inconvenience persons staying at their hotels but that sex was used as a come-on for many ancillary crimes such as muggings, petty larceny, extortion, and breaking and entering.

In addition to the "cleanup," City Hall reacted to the political pressure exerted by the hotels and businessmen by creating the Mayor's Committee on Prostitution. Daniel C. Hickey, president of the New York City Hotel Association, was appointed to the 15-man committee. In November, Mayor Lindsay sat in on the committee's first session and was reported by the press as "deeply concerned" with the problem.

At its first meeting, the committee set up three subcommittees, which, in effect, represented the various interests in the controversy: (1) Penal Law Revision—Chairman, Judge Amos Basel, Criminal Court; (2) Rehabilitation of Prostitutes in Correction Facilities—Chairman, Mary K. Lindsay, Former Superintendent of the Women's House of Detention; (3) Study Group to Determine Non-Criminal Approaches to the Problem of Prostitution—Chairman, Dr. Alfred Freedman, Department of Psychiatry, New York Medical College.

Queens District Attorney Thomas Mackell was appointed chairman of the overall committee. In May 1967 Mackell had written to Governor Rockefeller "repeating a suggestion that he said he made 'long ago' that 'prostitution be dealt with by a specially qualified social agency rather than an already overburdened criminal justice machinery." Mackell had made similar proposals to Mayor Lindsay and legislative leaders as well as expressing them publicly in the *New York Law Journal*.

Joan Cox, an attorney for the Legal Aid Society who worked in the Women's Court for seven years, also served on the committee. She agreed with Mackell that prostitution should not be punished except as a public nuisance. However, she said she was not opposed to fines, because, "after all, prostitutes pay no income taxes!" The Vera Institute of Justice has also recommended a "halfway house" in which prostitutes would be offered a full battery of services from psychiatrists, psychologists, social workers, and vocational guidance experts.

In a formal statement, Judge Basel, Chairman of the Subcommittee on Penal Law, said he feared that the state penal code would make "Fun City" the vice capital of the world. He added, "I think that until a method is devised for effectively treating them as social problems—and such a method has not yet been found—we should leave the old law on the books." In an interview, Basel said that he thought it would be very worthwhile for a foundation to give a group of psychiatrists and other professionals money to devise an experimental demonstration center or clinic for rehabilitating prostitutes. He pointed out that to his knowledge no such experiment had been tried.

PROPOSED AMENDMENTS

The police department, along with the hotel association, most vigorously opposed the law. In September 1967 the department prefiled draft amendments to the Penal Law for the 1968 legislature. One amendment if passed would have extended the loitering section (240.35.3) to include "loitering for the purpose of . . . prostitution." In support of this proposed amendment, the department wrote:

The inclusion of this provision within the "loitering" section of the Penal Law would be of great assistance to law enforcement officials in combating prostitution. The actions of these individuals have always had a deleterious effect on the business and social life of the community. This proposal should prove instrumental in eradicating or substantially decreasing the problem of streetwalkers.

Furthermore, it is the opinion that such amendment would result in a decrease in the incidence of venereal disease and in the number of muggings, assaults, and robberies which are often a by-product of this type of activity.

Two other proposed amendments prefiled by the department would: (1) extend the loitering provisions to include loitering for the purpose of engaging in an offense (rather than only loitering for the purpose of engaging in a crime—§ 240.35(6)); and (2) make prostitution a class B misdemeanor (a crime) rather than a violation (230.00.). If prostitution were made a class B misdemeanor, prostitutes could be sentenced to a maximum of 91 days, still considerably less than the 3-year maximum reformatory sentence provided under 1909 § 891 (a). In support of the first provision, the department stated:

This additional authority would be of great assistance to law enforcement officials in combating prostitution as the prostitutes who are observed approaching different people at various intervals would have to give a reasonably credible account of such actions.

The police department argued that prostitution should be made a class B misdemeanor on the basis that:

Though other provisions of Article 230 (i.e. those for the promotion of prostitution) of the Revised Penal Law are directed primarily at organized vice and those who knowingly advance or profit from prostitution such activities are impossible in the main without the prostitute and her services. To designate 'prostitution' as a violation with a penalty of a term not to exceed 15 days is highly unrealistic. Such a penalty is tantamount to 'licensing' prostitutes and results in turnstile justice and an increase in such activities.

To the writer's knowledge, the police department prefiled no amendment to eliminate the "patronizing" clause from the Penal Law. Perhaps the department did not do so because it could effectively evade enforcing the law or because it believed it could not defeat the political pressure which was shown to support the "patronizing provision" during the Penal Law public hearings.

The Buffalo area police and legislators were also against the new law's provisions pertaining to prostitution. Assemblyman Albert J. Hausbeck of Buffalo's 114th District said that the new Penal Law was too lenient on convicted prostitutes and that he intended to prefile three amendments to the new State Penal Code. Captain Kenneth Kennedy, commander of the Buffalo Vice Enforcement Bureau, speaking before the Rotary Club, asked, "If the legislators want open prostitution, why don't they just say so?" He predicted that disease, broken homes, and in-

volvement of organized crime in prostitution would follow the "condonation" of it under the new law, and he blamed "do-gooders" for the changes in the law, saying they have perpetrated "frauds" on legislators and the public to support unfounded theories that prostitution does not harm.

In January the Mayor's Committee on Prostitution recommended that the offense of prostitution be reclassified from a violation to a class A misdemeanor, effective September 1, 1968. The recommendation was submitted to the state Senate in the form of an amendment to the Penal Law. The amendment, if passed, would have increased the maximum penalty for the offense from 15 days to 1 year imprisonment.

At the same meeting, the committee disapproved several pending bills, including that submitted by the police department, on prostitution. One would have made prostitution a Class B misdemeanor. It was disapproved on the ground that the three-month sentence would not allow sufficient time for rehabilitation. Several bills extending the loitering statutes to include "offenses" (i.e., prostitution under the Revised Penal Law) were disapproved on the grounds of doubtful constitutionality. . . .

In April the Senate committed the bill to amend the Penal Law to the Committee on Codes. The committee debated the bill and voted *not* to send it back to the Senate for a vote. This action meant that the sections of the Penal Law concerning prostitution would remain unchanged for at least another year.

Why, when so many seemingly politically influential groups were pressuring for a higher prostitution penalty, did the committee vote no? In an interview, Martin Schaum, counsel to the Committee on Codes, gave three reasons for the no vote. First, the committee believed that the Penal Law Commission's decision to make prostitution a violation had been well considered and that the law had been in effect too short a time for any group to be able to evaluate its effectiveness. Second, the committee feared that giving prostitutes one-year sentences would overcrowd the jails. Third, the senators on the committee did not believe that the act of prostitution warranted a one-year jail sentence.

Scanning the occupations and affiliations of the committee members, we noted two additional factors which may have influenced the committee's decision. First, all of the 16 committee members were lawyers. The New York Bar Association, and lawyers generally, respected and supported the Penal Law Commission (which is also composed entirely of lawyers) and its decisions. Had businessmen or the police, particularly those of New York City or Buffalo, been represented on the committee, the decision might well have been in support of the amendment. At least vigorous opposition would have been expressed toward voting down the amendment. Second, John Dunne, a member of the committee, was also a member of the PLCCR Commission. Although we cannot be certain of Dunne's position since the committee did not release minutes of its meetings, we imagine that he supported leaving the Penal Law unchanged.

SUMMARY AND CONCLUSIONS

This study suggests that lawmaking and law enforcement cannot be understood as apolitical, technical, value-free processes. Theories of law must include a knowledge of the political processes. Further study will be required to adequately characterize the relationship between law and the exercise of power in society. The findings of this study could provide a framework for such research.

Throughout the development of the New York State Penal Law, Section 230, numerous interest groups and individuals worked diligently in an effort to have the law written or enforced in the manner they desired. The results of their efforts clearly illustrate the limited comprehensiveness of power suggested by Wrong. During the five stages in the formulation and enforcement of the Penal Law concerning prostitution, power shifted from first one interested group to another. One group frequently exercised power with respect to one section of the law, while another did so with respect to another section. In the final stage of the law's history, civil liberties and welfare groups dominated over businessmen and the police with respect to the clause making prostitution a violation subject to a maximum 15-day sentence, while the police and businessmen dominated over the civil liberties and welfare groups with respect to the nonenforcement of the "patron" clause.

Under what conditions were certain individuals or groups able to shape the law in the manner in which they intended? A small number of organizations and individuals, represented by the president of the American Social Health Association and a retired chief probation officer of the N.Y.C. Magistrates Court, were able to insert the "patron" clause into the Law. These groups possessed legal knowledge, were aware of the PLCCR Commission's pending actions and that their own interests would be affected by these actions, and recognized that by acting they could probably affect the law. Because of these factors and because groups with opposing views slept, the groups favoring the patron clause were able to make the clause part of the law. The groups opposing the patron clause, however, appeared to represent a larger proportion of the public and were able to later resist enforcing the new law. Consequently, the only lasting effect of the "patron clause" was to prohibit the police from using patrons as witnesses against prostitutes.

The formulation and enforcement of the law for arresting and penalizing prostitutes was more complex than that for patrons. Power shifted rapidly from group to group. Largely under the influence of Judge Murtagh who had actively campaigned for reform in moralistic laws and was widely respected, the PLCCR Commission reduced the penalty for prostitution from a maximum of 1 year to 15 days imprisonment. After this change was enacted into law, it was assailed by hotel owners, businessmen, the police, and a few legislators. Their pressure led to a police "cleanup" of prostitution in Manhattan. Civil liberties and welfare groups condemned the "cleanup," and after much controversy the legal bases for many of the arrests were held to be unconstitutional. Once it was no longer possible to arrest prostitutes in mass, the police and other groups submitted amendments to the New York State Legislature to make prostitution a Class A misdemeanor subject to a maximum penalty of one year imprisonment and to extend the loitering section to include "loitering for the purpose of prostitution." Nearly 10 months after the 1965 NYS Penal Law became effective, the NYS Senate Committee on Codes killed these amendments, leaving the new law concerning prostitution at least temporarily unchanged.

The conditions for groups' power also varied from stage to stage in the history of the controversy. The primary bases for groups obtaining power appeared to be (1) their awareness of the various actions taken and to be taken in the formulation or enforcement of the law; (2) their recognition of the importance of these actions to their interests; (3) their professional (especially legal) knowledge or expertise; (4) their public (scattered and unorganized) support gained through their expertise and conscious appeals to the community; (5) their political and financial support by organized groups; (6) their personal charisma; and (7) their means to informally withhold needed support or cooperation from the significant actor.

In summary, this study suggests that behaviors are not "automatically" defined as criminal. The formulation and enforcement of the 1965 NYS Penal Law on prostitution were *political* processes, processes involving numerous efforts on the part of a relatively small number of interested groups to obtain the means to affect the behavior of other men. During these processes, the groups which exercised power with respect to any particular section of the law changed over time, and at most instances in time different groups exercised power over different sections of the law.

12. HOMOSEXUAL EXCHANGES IN PUBLIC PLACES

LAUD HUMPHREYS

Reprinted from "Impersonal Sex and Perceived Satisfaction," in James N. Heslin (ed.), Studies in the Sociology of Sex. Copyright © 1971 by Meredith Corporation. By permission of Appleton-Century-Crofts, Educational Division, Meredith Corporation. Laud Humphreys is Associate Professor of Sociology at Pitzer College. He has taught and done research in medical sociology and the sociology of deviance, crime, and legal institutions. He has carried out two classic studies of the situation of homosexuals in American society, the first, Tearoom Trade (Aldine Publishing Company, 1970), dealing with participants in homosexual behavior in public restrooms, and a second, Out of the Closet, describing the growth of the homosexual liberation movement during the latter part of the 1960s and the early 1970s. The first book was the winner of the C. Wright Mills Award of the Society for the Study of Social Problems.

■ The situation of participants in homosexual encounters provides particularly useful examples of the social and interpersonal forces at work in deviant exchanges. These participants persist in their sexual behavior against tremendous pressure by society and must either suffer or devote a great deal of energy to protecting themselves from highly damaging labels and stigmatization by those around them—often including family and friends as well as various officials who are authorized to treat these exchanges as unlawful or immoral.

In this article, Humphreys analyzes how one segment of the homosexual market operates and shows some of the ways in which the structure of that market can be understood as the result of the preferences of participants and of adaptation to the dangers of detection and stigmatization. His analysis is particularly useful because it demonstrates the pitfalls of assuming that people fall neatly into sexual types—hetrosexual or homosexual, "active" or "passive" homosexuals, etc. He shows instead that highly diverse sexual orientations bring individuals to the public restroom for a transitory sexual encounter. The principal characteristic they have in common is a desire for a brief and impersonal sexual experience.

There is, of course, a vast literature on homosexuality, but there is little in the way of systematic social science dealing with homosexual behavior. Among the more useful studies are Evelyn Hooker, "The Adjustment of the Male Overt Homosexual," in *The Problem of Homosexuality in Modern Society*, Hendrik M. Ruitenbeek, ed., New York: Dutton, 1963, and John

I. Kitsuse, "Societal Reaction to Deviant Behavior Problems of Theory and Method" and Albert J. Reiss, Jr., "The Social Integration of Queers and Peers," both in *The Other Side*, Howard S. Becker, ed., New York: The Free Press, 1964. A useful integration of a wide range of social, psychological, historical, and legal studies of homosexuality is D. J. West, *Homosexuality*, Chicago: Aldine, 1968. For a very interesting study of some of the costs of the public preoccupation with private homosexual behavior, see John Gerassi, *The Boys of Boise: Furor, Vice and Folly in an American City*, New York: Macmillan, 1966. The study of police enforcement against homosexuals to which Humphreys refers is found in Jon J. Gallo *et al.*, "The Consenting Adult Homosexual and the Law: An Empirical Study of Enforcement and Administration in Los Angeles Country," *U.C.L.A. Law Review* 13 (March: 643-832, 1966). See also Martin Hoffman, *The Gay World: Male Homosexuality and the Social Creation of Evil*, New York: Basic Books, 1968, pp. 73-74. In addition to Humphreys' *Out of the Closet* (Prentice-Hall, 1972), see the analysis of gay liberation in Dennis Altman, *Homosexual Oppression and Liberation*, New York: Outerbridge and Dienstfrey, 1971; and John Murphey, *Homosexual Liberation: A Personal View*, New York: Praeger Publishing Company, 1971. ■

IN A PREVIOUS study of sexual activity in public restrooms, I have indicated that many American males—perhaps millions of them—resort to these facilities because of the opportunity they afford for fast, economical, and impersonal sexual relationships: "What the covert deviant needs is a sexual machine —collapsible to hip-pocket size, silent in operation—plus the excitement of a risk-taking encounter. In tearoom sex he has the closest thing to such a device. This encounter functions, for the sex market, as does the automat for the culinary, providing a low-cost, impersonal, democratic means of commodity distribution."[1]

It is the fleeting nature of the activity they shelter that makes tearooms popular for most participants. Recently, in the course of research in an Eastern seaboard city, I discovered that the closing of park restrooms merely results in the relocation of impersonal homosexual activity. For reasons unknown, officials of that large metropolitan center closed every rest facility in its public parks. The locks are now rusty and the doors nailed shut; nevertheless, impersonal sex still flourishes. Such encounters now occur in the restrooms of subway stations and parking facilities, among reeds that line the rivers, behind the bushes along freeways, or in the shadowy environs of truckstops. In other words, the marketing of impersonal sex appears to be highly adaptable to pressures from social control forces. "I want the quick thing," says one respondent, "and there's always someplace to get it . . . I'm just too damned busy and involved to look for anything else!"

In *Tearoom Trade: Impersonal Sex in Public Places,* I discuss the risks taken by participants in these "quickie" relationships. Not only do young toughs present physical dangers, but there is the constant threat of blackmail, assault, and arrest by the police. During a recent year, for example, the Sheriff's Department of Los Angeles County arrested seventy men in one public restroom.[2] From available arrest data, it appears that the majority of criminal charges involving homosexual activity in this country have their source in police surveillance of public restrooms.

The fear of exposure for tearoom activity has resulted in the creation of a lookout role, one well suited for sociological observation

of these sexual encounters. I played this role while observing some 200 acts of fellatio between men, for fifty of which I made careful and systematic notes. In connection with such participant observation, I also collected a sample of participants (representative on the bases of both time and place) by tracing license plate numbers. Later, I interviewed the sample of fifty participants, under the pretext of a public health survey. A control sample of men, randomly selected from the population but matched with the participants on the bases of race, occupational level, area of residence, and marital status, was also interviewed.

Social factors, primarily occupation and marital status, influence the amount of "drive" behind the search for impersonal sex. Tearoom encounters are not only games of chance, risk-taking adventures but also sexual outlets for those who require them. The overall task of this paper is to assess the sexual needs and performances of those who seek impersonal sex and to relate those needs and activities to their social characteristics.

RESEARCHING SEXUAL NEEDS AND PERFORMANCE

When a mate, lover, or friend knows that a person engages in a particular type of sexual act, he or she commonly identifies the performer with that act or set of acts. One's sexual identity is formed, in no small part, around such reports or observations of one's erotic activity. Thus, among adolescents, a boy who has exhibited his prowess at masturbation on a Scout outing may find himself shackled with a nickname like "J.O." Another may build a reputation as a stud with the girls. As Kitsuse[3] has noted, such labeling may result from an isolated instance that gives rise to a process of retrospective reinterpretation of past interaction with the subject.

The problem, of course, is not only that such labels are adhesive but that they also tend to subsume other characteristics of the individual. Hughes has discussed this phenomenon as "master status-determining traits." [4] An unfortunate choice of time, place, or sexual partner frequently converts the "weak moment" of an experimenter into a permanent social identity. A girl with little (or no) coital experience may be stigmatized as a "slut," or an otherwise faithful husband may become an adulterer or a "queer."

This is the stuff of which both nightmares and short stories are made. It also contains serious pitfalls for one who does research in sexual behavior. He, too, may commit the fallacy of labeling a subject on the basis of behavior once observed or reported. In the course of studying homosexual activity in public restrooms, I observed some 200 acts of fellatio. The vast majority of participants in these encounters were seen only once by the researcher in such behavior. Although I had actually observed each respondent engaging in an act of fellatio, I had no way of knowing, in most cases, whether these men engaged in repeat performances of homosexual acts, much less of gauging the degree to which this behavior may have been habitual for them. The extent of my observations did enable me to identify a few as "habitual insertees," those who frequently occupied stalls to receive the penises of others into their mouths. Others became known to me as tearoom habitues. It is, nevertheless, possible that some men may have become data upon the occasion of their single, experimental venture into that stigmatized activity.

Apart from theoretical considerations, that is why it is unwise for a sex researcher to refer to any person as "a homosexual." Evelyn Hooker's research indicates that standard psychological tests fail as indices of sexual orientation. But even a method as empirical as direct observation tells us little of such matters as the individual's overall orientation or self-image.

For this reason, I refer to research subjects only as participants in homosexual encounters. In a particular instance, one may have played the role of insertor, another the insertee part. But, even when observed once in a particular role, they cannot properly be characterized as "insertees" or "insertors" for purposes

beyond the description of the interaction itself. Such categorization is prohibited by the tendency of those observed to switch parts in subsequent sexual games.

If it is our purpose to enter into a scientific analysis of sexual activity, then it is essential to acquire longitudinal data on the sexual actors. We must know not only what we saw them do (important as that may be) but what they did, by way of sex, during the days and weeks and years before they were "caught in the act." Such long-term observation is impractical, if not impossible. We are driven back, then, to methods that are only secondarily empirical. For much of his data, the sex researcher must rely on interview material.

At best, such interview data—subject as they are to both intentional and unintentional distortion—consist of accurate reports of the respondent's own perception of his sex life. He may believe (as, indeed, many who think of themselves as being homosexual do believe) that his sexual fantasies have always been homoerotic. The researcher may doubt it, cannot prove otherwise, and must record it thusly.

The man whose average rate of intercourse is 2.5 coital acts per month may think he enjoys such relations "about once a week." On an annual basis, the difference is that between 30 and 52 acts. The researcher can only report the latter rate (although, if an ethnographer, he may add a footnote to read: "Subject also goes to tearooms from time to time for a blow job.")

Any distortion of data resulting from such reports, however need not be seen as a deterrent to knowledge. Apart from a strictly biological orientation to the question, the important information to be gained from interviews concerns the subject's *perception* of his performance, needs, and satisfaction.

The interview schedules used in my study of tearoom participants contain questions concerning the frequency of intercourse (frequency of orgasm for single men). They also cover the respondents' perceptions of sexual needs in relation to others, of the importance of having his sexual needs satisfied, as well as his assessment of whether these needs are currently being met. These questions were asked of the fifty men in my participant sample and of fifty who were randomly selected from the general population of the metropolitan area. Additional data were gained from numerous open-ended interviews with cooperating respondents.

PERCEIVED DRIVE AND PROFESSED NORMALCY

The questions on need and relative importance were intended to serve as checks one on the other and were effective for that purpose. Among the married and single men of both samples, most of those who perceived their sexual needs as being "greater than most other men" also felt it "extremely important" that those needs be met. Conversely, all those who judged their needs as being less than those of others perceived their fulfillment as being "not at all important."

A strong majority of both samples reported that it is "very important" for their sexual needs to be met—but there the similarities end. Perceptions of the importance of sexual need-satisfaction (which, for the sake of brevity, I shall call "drive") differ along the lines of the social characteristics of age, marital status, and occupation.

One variance in perceived drive between the participant and control samples is in the tendency of participants to profess ignorance of what other men's sexual needs may be. Forty-two percent of those observed in tearooms answered with a variation of "How should I know?" when asked to compare their sexual needs with those of other men. Only 16 percent of those in the control sample failed to make some estimate of comparison.

Presuming that those who engage in sex with other men have at least as much knowledge of the sexual needs of other males as do their nondeviant counterparts, we can only conclude that this professed ignorance is an instance of deviance disavowal. This manner of professing normalcy is more pronounced among the married participants than the unmarried; however, this is clearly a function of the age differential between married and single respondents of both samples. (Although the median age of the controls is five years above that of the participants, that of the combined married men is fourteen years above the median age of the single men of both samples.) Nearly all of those in both groups who professed ignorance of the needs of others were age thirty or older.

There is also evidence that the impact of aging differs somewhat between participants and controls. Those over age fifty-five in the nondeviant sample consistently reported a low level of both drive and frequency of intercourse. In spite of declining conjugal activity, however, the older participants claimed a normal level of sexual drive. The following examples illustrate the differences in these perceptions of drive between the participants and controls.

A member of the randomly selected control sample, Gus, is sixty-one. He has been on his job as a machinist for thirty-six years and professes being happily married. Never having suffered a major illness, Gus has missed one day of work in the last five years. "I had the flu," he says. He has intercourse with his wife, "once in a while"; but, when questioned about his sexual needs, he reports: "Son, when you start getting my age, you don't have too many needs anymore."

Arthur was observed in the insertee role in a tearoom. At sixty-seven, he is retired. In the last five years, he has suffered a coronary occlusion among other ailments. He blames his lack of intercourse on his invalid wife, claiming that his marriage does not meet his "average" sexual needs.

Bill is manager of a small store. At sixty-one, he has two grown children. He thinks it is unimportant to have sexual satisfaction. "I don't have sex anymore," he says. "I'm too old." This member of the control sample has no sex life to report. He is matched with Frank, a sixty-seven-year-old tearoom participant. Frank's son is also grown and in

Vietnam. Like Bill, this salesman has had no serious illness in more than five years. His weekly intercourse with his wife is, he feels, very important. We did not discuss his extramarital sexual activity.

A similar pattern holds for older single men in the two samples. A fifty-nine-year-old accountant, whom I shall call Mike, is unmarried and in good health. This member of the control sample reports sex needs that are less than those of other men he knows. How often does he have an orgasm? "Nowadays, almost never." His counterpart among the tearoom participants is Al, a salesman, age fifty-eight. This single man has an orgasm "four times a week." He thinks his sexual needs are "about the same as those of other men" and "very important."

The staff of the Institute for Sex Research, in their study of sexual offenders, conclude that homosexual offenders vs. adults appeared to have the strongest sex drive of the groups studied, if frequency of activity is taken as a measure. The tearoom research provides no evidence of greater *activity* on the part of participants that might support this finding; but it does indicate that, at least for the older men, the *perception* of sex drive is stronger among those who engage in homosexual behavior.

On the basis of social scientific evidence, it is difficult to explain these differences in sex drive and performance among the older respondents. In his original study, Kinsey found that "the boys who are earliest adolescent, by age twelve at the latest, are the ones who most often have the highest rate of outlet in the later years of their lives." [5] He also reported that "homosexual activities occur in a much higher percentage of the males who became adolescent at an early age." [6] Might this correlation between earlier puberty and higher rates of outlet in later years account for my findings? If so, my data do not support it. There is no difference between the two samples in the tearoom study, at least in so far as my respondents were able to recall the ages at which their puberty began. As regards the older men, the median age for onset of puberty among the par-

ticipants was fourteen, compared with thirteen for the median age of the controls.

Certainly, as evidenced by the case histories reported above, health was not a factor in declining sexual interest and activity, that group of participants with somewhat poorer health reporting greater drive and intercourse than the healthier controls. Perhaps, then, those who engage in homosexual activity may be "oversexed." If that were true, however, the younger participants would also report greater sexual activity and drive. As we shall see, this is not true for the younger men. Those interested in the sociology of sex should beware of imposing an interpretation of abnormality (in the sense of "unhealthiness" or "unnaturalness") upon these indications of greater sexual interest and activity on the part of the aging tearoom participants. Perhaps, being less discriminating in their choices of sexual outlet, the tearoom patrons are leading more "natural" sex lives than do the "straights."

TEAROOM SEX AS AN ALTERNATIVE TO MASTURBATION

The interviewer asked Sam, a young grocery clerk: "How often do you have an orgasm by any means?" "Almost every day," this member of the control sample answered. "But that's almost totally by masturbation." Another single man from the same sample answered: "I masturbate every day, if that's what you mean."

These examples illustrate one side of a dichotomy within the control sample of unmarried men that differentiates them from the single deviants. Half the men in the control sample were quick to mention masturbation as their primary sexual outlet, and those were the single straights who perceived their sexual needs as the same or greater than those of other men. Men of their type who did not mention masturbation generally rated their sexual needs as less than others they knew.

Typical of the latter group is Jeff, a handsome university student, who says that having sex is only "somewhat important" and who reports his sexual needs as being less than most. "I have an orgasm very infrequently," he reports. "I can't remember the last time." This asexual sort of response was provided by nearly a third of the single men in the control sample, compared with only two among the unmarried participants.

Although a number of unmarried participants were quite open in admitting homosexual activity, few mentioned masturbation as a sexual outlet. If their reported assessment of sexual outlet is reliable, we must conclude that the single controls rely on masturbation to a far greater extent than do their deviant counterparts—with much the same result in terms of frequency of orgasm. The mean frequency of reported orgasms for unmarried participants is 11.5 orgasms per month, compared with 9.9 per month for single members of the control sample.

From the interviews, there is no evidence of masturbaphobia on the part of tearoom participants. The most obvious explanation of the observed differences is that the alternative to masturbation for those who enjoy homosexual activity is more readily available than is the alternative acceptable to men of the control sample. In spite of the pill, willing girls are not as easy for the single man to find in our society as are the willing seekers of impersonal sex. Moreover, it takes a great deal of time to court a young lady. In terms of time outlay, the average fifteen-minute encounter in a tearoom is almost as cheap as automanipulation. Evidently, for many men, it is a viable alternative to the latter.

RELIGION AND FREQUENCY OF INTERCOURSE

In terms of frequency of outlet, if not form, there is little difference between unmarried participants and controls. They are a younger population than the married men, and a rate of orgasm slightly greater than twice a week should not be surprising. For the married men, on the other hand, there are striking differences in the reported frequency of intercourse—not only between samples but between occupational classes and religious groups within each sample.

The mean frequency of conjugal outlet for tearoom participants, 7.6 per month, is slightly more than half that reported by the controls, 12.8 per month. By eliminating those who consider themselves too old for intercourse from the calculations, the rate of the nondeviants is just double that of the men observed in tearooms. It is, of course, important to note that the range of frequency is wide within both these samples, from none to sixty acts of intercourse per month. It is also strongly correlated with the age of respondents, but median ages for the two samples of married men differ little—forty for the participants, forty-three for controls.

By projecting the mean total sexual outlet per week for men in the original Kinsey study (including all those between adolescence and eighty-five years of age) to a monthly rate, it is possible to compare the frequencies reported in this study with Kinsey's data. Kinsey's figure of 2.74 per week projects to 11.9 sexual acts per month, compared with the 12.8 reported by my married controls. Kinsey's mean includes all outlets—marital intercourse, extramarital activity, masturbation, nocturnal emissions, and homosexual and animal contact—about "85 to 89 percent" of which are accounted for by marital intercourse.[7] Since the ages of my married respondents range only from twenty-two to seventy, including neither of the less active extremes found in the Kinsey data, it should not be surprising to find a mean of marital intercourse for my control sample (median age forty-two) somewhat higher than that indicated by *Sexual Behavior in the Human Male*.

The purpose of this comparison with data from the Kinsey study is to establish the mean monthly frequency reported by the married controls as a base rate, paralleling the "American norm" of approximately twelve outlets per month. Granted this, it is possible—lacking evidence to the contrary—to infer that the sexual needs of the average married man in the control sample are being met in his relationships with his wife. With one exception, a man who reported that his wife has "warped views on sex," all of the married controls claimed that their sexual needs were met in their marital relationships.

A very different picture emerges from discussions of the conjugal relations of tearoom participants. If we recall that their perception of sexual needs and importance roughly parallels that of the controls—and that their reported frequency of intercourse is about half that of the nondeviants—we should not be surprised that they also complain of not being satisfied in the marriage bed.

When asked if he thought his sexual needs were adequately met in his relationships with his wife, a forty-two-year-old machinist answered sharply: "No! Does any man?" He hesitated in replying when questioned on the frequency of intercourse. "My wife's been sick," he said. Later, when discussing his marriage in open-ended questions, he was careful to cover the hostility revealed in earlier answers.

I have indicated elsewhere[8] that, from surface appearances, tearoom participants maintain exemplary marriages. Longer interviews with cooperating respondents, on the other hand, sometimes shatter these superficial reports. An upper-class man, who makes the tearoom scene almost daily, expressed his feelings thus: "Madge is the classic bitch! Her most striking point is her limited understanding and intelligence. Financial security is her only interest . . . We haven't had intercourse for years—and I don't want it!"

A factory foreman, age thirty-eight, says that his wife "has trouble in bearing children. Our little daughter is very important to us; but the wife had lots of trouble with a miscarriage a few months ago and we just don't want to take the risk." Devout Roman Catholics, they will not use "artificial" birth-control devices. How often does he have intercourse with his wife? "Not very often right now—once a month or so." He hesitated when asked whether his sexual needs are met in these relationships: "I guess so—no,

not really." He gave no sign of remembering the interviewer-lookout who had seen him, a year earlier, taking the insertor part in an act of fellatio.

Half the married participants are either Roman Catholics or married to Catholics, compared to 26 percent of the married controls. In both groups, the Roman Catholics report a rate of marital intercourse 40 percent below that of their Protestant, Jewish, and nonaffiliated counterparts. In spite of this lower frequency of marital intercourse, Catholic respondents have more children than those of other religious affiliations. Although these data do not justify the inference that Roman Catholics are more apt to engage in tearoom encounters than those of other religious affiliations, they do strongly indicate that those who seek sex in public restrooms are twice as likely to be Roman Catholics and dissatisfied with their conjugal relations as those in the nondeviant sample.

I asked a Roman Catholic respondent, who cooperated in lengthy interviews, about the effect of his religion on his sexual activity. He reported a great deal of drive and was a daily tearoom visitor.

"Sure, he said, "my being a Catholic has a lot to do with [my] going to the tearooms. You remember I told you that a priest was the first to put the make on me, but I'd also probably screw my wife a lot more if she'd take the pill."

"But I don't understand," I said. "You won't violate the church's teaching on birth control, yet you will engage in homosexual acts. Isn't that adultery?"

"The church says masturbation is a sin, too," he replied. "But I don't think of what I do in the park as adultery. I don't get involved with those people. It's just as sinful to beat your meat or—or take a pill. This way, at least, my wife isn't sinning."

A PARTICIPANT TYPOLOGY

From the interviews, I constructed a typology of tearoom participants, differentiated along the lines of marital and occupational

TABLE 12.1.

PERCEPTIONS OF SEXUAL NEED, SATISFACTION, AND OUTLET OF TEAROOM PARTICIPANTS
BY TYPE, COMPARED WITH MATCHED PAIRS FROM THE CONTROL SAMPLE

	Participants	*Controls*

Type I:
 	
Dependent
  occupations,
Married men
	("Trade")
	Drive: "normal"
	Opportunity: "inadequate"
	Frequency
	  of intercourse: 8.7*
	Median age: 38
	N = 17
		("Straights")
		Drive: "normal"
		Opportunity: "adequate"
		Frequency
		  of intercourse: 16.3*
		Median age: 42
		N = 17

Type II:
 	
Independent
  occupations,
Married men
	("Ambisexuals")
	Drive: "high"
	Opportunity: "inadequate"
	Frequency
	  of intercourse: 5.7*
	Median age: 43
	N = 10
		("Straights")
		Drive: "normal"
		Opportunity: "adequate"
		Frequency
		  of intercourse: 9.1*
		Median age: 43
		N = 10

Totals: Married men	Mean frequency: 7.6* Median age: 40 N = 27	Mean frequency: 12.8* Median age: 43 N = 27

Type III:
 	
Independent
  occupations,
Single men
	("Gay")
	Drive: "high"
	Opportunity: "adequate"
	
	Frequency
	  of orgasm: 15.0*
	Median age: 28
	N = 9
		("Straights")
		Drive: "normal"
		Opportunity: "inadequate"
		  plus masturbation
		Frequency
		  of orgasm: 11.6*
		Median age: 21
		N = 9

Type IV:
 	
Dependent
  occupations,
Single men
	("Closet Queens")
	Drive: "normal"
	Opportunity: "inadequate"
	
	Frequency
	  of orgasm: 8.0*
	Median age: 34
	N = 14
		("Straights")
		Drive: "low"
		Opportunity: "inadequate"
		  plus masturbation
		Frequency
		  of orgasm: 8.7*
		Median age: 34
		N = 14

Totals: Single men	Mean frequency: 11.5* Median age: 30 N = 23	Mean frequency: 9.9* Median age: 25 N = 23

* Mean reported frequency per month.

autonomy (see Table 12.1). The question of marital autonomy was determined by the characteristics of marital status. For the purpose of this paper, however, it should be noted that the three men in each sample who were divorced or separated must be classified as "single" for the purposes of analyzing

sexual behavior. In earlier analyses of the data, where the emphasis was on the respondents' life styles, these individuals were grouped with the married men.

Because the impersonal sexual activity found in restrooms is furtive and fear-laden, the relative resources of participants for controlling information and avoiding exposure are of crucial importance. Along with marital status, then, occupational status must be seen as a decisive variable. Men who work for large industries or the government, who work as truck drivers, salesmen, school-teachers, or in clerical capacities, have little autonomy. Stigmatization would almost certainly result in the loss of employment. These men are generally of lower-middle or upper-lower socioeconomic status, possessing little capital with which to pay off policemen or otherwise defend their moral histories. If married, they have been classified as Type I participants. I refer to them as "trade" because that term is applied by the homosexual community to men like these whose self-identity is heterosexual and who generally take only the insertor (penetrating) role in homosexual activity. To avoid jeopardizing their family relationships, the trade are isolated from the sexual market provided by both homosexual and prostitute subcultures. In their furtive search for an inexpensive, expedient form of sexual activity, they turn to public restrooms.

Single men with little occupational independence (Type IV participants) I have labeled as "closet queens." In the homosexual vocabulary, closet queens are men who recognize their own homosexuality but are afraid to admit it to other than a few close friends. Neither trade nor closet queens are active in the homosexual subculture. They avoid the gay bars and public baths, those "gay" (homosexual) marketplaces providing too much danger of exposure for covert deviants. Together, these groups comprise 62 percent of my sample of tearoom participants.

Married men who are self-employed or who fill a managerial capacity were classified as Type II participants or "ambisexuals." Although most men involved in tearoom sex have had both heterosexual and homosexual experiences, and thus might be called ambisexual, this group from the upper-middle and upper classes are most apt to identify themselves as such. As might be expected, income, educational level, and other indicators of social class increase with occupational in-

dependence. The ambisexuals, like respondents of Types I and IV, avoid the meeting places of the homosexual society. In their case, however, there are strong friendship networks binding these prosperous men together and providing them with the advantages of increased communication and mutual protection.

Type III respondents, the smallest group in the participant sample, are called "gay" because of their approximation to the homosexual stereotype. (Men with dependent occupations are sometimes called "gay," as those with greater autonomy may be labeled "closet queens"; however, for the purposes of this typology, I use these terms as tags of my marital-occupational subgroups.) They are single men with relatively high occupational autonomy: students, artists, hair dressers, and merchants. Because they are likely to patronize gay bars, they resort to tearooms for sex only for an occasional "change of scene" or because a lover is out of town.

The less vulnerable participants, ambisexuals and the gay, have less to fear in the tearooms because their resources decrease the threat of exposure. They are attracted to the tearooms both because of the wide variety of sexual objects provided by the influx of nonsubcultural working men to these settings and because this is adventurous activity, a source of "kicks."

OCCUPATION AND FREQUENCY OF INTERCOURSE

Upon dividing the participant and control samples of married men into these classifications, strong differences appear between the Type I and Type II respondents within each sample. The trade report a mean monthly frequency of marital intercourse of 8.7. Ambisexuals claim a much lower average of 5.7 per month. Members of the control sample, matched on an occupational basis with participants, evidence means of 16.3 conjugal relations a month for those in Type I, contrasted with 9.1 for Type II. Although the frequencies for both types of nondeviants are higher than those reported by the matching groups of tearoom respondents, it is evident that the upper class men of both samples engage in much less intercourse with their wives than do those of the lower classes.

Of these four groups, the ambisexuals (upper-class participants) report the strongest perceptions of sexual drive, along with the lowest frequency of marital intercourse. Thus, those who engage in the least conjugal activity perceive the importance of their sexual needs as being the greatest! They suffer, then, from a *sexual bind*—the discrepancy between perceived and fulfilled sexual needs.

Nondeviants with high occupational autonomy may also be seen as victims of the sexual bind; however such interpretation is doubtful in their case. In the first place, their conjugal relations are 40 percent more frequent than those of the participants matched with them; moreover, their perception of sexual drive is less. During the interviews, not one of the upper-class controls complained of lacking sexual fulfillment in marriage. Thirty percent of the participants in this class reported that their marital relationships were inadequate, compared with none of the controls.

Apparently, the sexual needs that most upper-class men perceive as normal, "about the same as those of other men," are not as great as the perceived needs of men in the working class. If we are to trust their claims of satisfaction—and lacking evidence of extramarital relations other than those observed on the part of participants—we must conclude that they are satisfied with a rate of intercourse that is about 60 percent of that enjoyed by men of the lower classes.

As there are no bases, including age differences, on which a biological difference can be postulated for men of the two occupational groups, it may be assumed that this contrast in perceptions of sexual drive is socially determined. Not only do men of a like occupational level communicate norms to each other, but the nature of their work and life style may result in satisfaction with less in the way of sex.

The Swedish economist, Staffan Linder, has suggested one such determining factor in his study of "the harried leisure class": in writing of the "increasing scarcity of time" in our age of affluence, he quotes Warner and Abegglen [9] who find that an executive's wife "must not demand too much of her husband's time or interest. Because of his single-minded concentration on the job, even his sexual activity is relegated to a secondary place." Linder's point is one that busy executives in my samples affirm: they are often too tired to engage in sex at the end of a day.

It is questionable whether the sexual effects of time's increasing scarcity are equally felt by all members of highly industrialized, consumption-oriented societies. Linder notes that affairs are becoming "less attractive; the time spent on each occasion of lovemaking is being reduced; the total number of sexual encounters is declining." [10] Data from this study support his latter point only as regards those with greater occupational autonomy (and then only in rough comparison with data from the Kinsey study). What is certain is that the time spent on each occasion of lovemaking is being reduced, at least for those men who choose impersonal action in the tearooms.

The trade (Type I, or working class, participants) suffer from a sexual bind without the distraction or excuse of executive pressures. Their perceived need being slightly higher, their frequency of marital sex is little more than half of the control counterparts. If it were not for one, newly married, black soldier in this group who reported "at least twice a day, when I'm home," as his frequency of intercourse, the mean frequency of this group would drop sharply. This man's wife was giving birth to their child at about the time I observed him as an insertor in a tearoom. Had I not seen him, the mean frequency for the lower-class sample of participants would drop to less than five acts of marital intercourse per month or less than a third that of the matched controls.

The reported frequency for the control group from the lower classes is about four acts per week. Again, three individuals report intercourse with their wives at least once a day. In spite of these exceptional performers, these men evidence no sexual bind and are in general agreement that their conjugal relations meet their sexual needs. They do not appear to be more masculine than the participants matched with them. Their perceived needs are somewhat lower. By every indication, these two groups differ most in terms of their frequency of sexual outlet in marriage. Only religious differences are so strong between the two samples.

THE QUESTION OF CAUSALITY

These data, then, confront the student of sexual behavior with a choice: does the sexual bind serve as a causal factor of the inverse correlation between observed sexual deviance and reported satisfaction in conjugal relations, or is it merely a phantom explanation? Are some men, at least, driven from a sexless marriage bed to the impersonal sex of public restrooms; or do other factors, perhaps psychological, produce a desire for furtive homosexual activity which, in turn, decreases their performance at home?

Longitudinal data from interviews with cooperating respondents support both directions of causation. Married men of the upper classes indicate a great deal of premarital reinforcement in homosexual activity, beginning in preparatory school or at summer camp. After marrying (largely as a concession to social pressures), they tend to remain sexually faithful to their wives for as long as three or four years. Then the sexual bind appears: the Roman Catholic wife will not use birth control measures, in spite of their wish to have no more children; or the man is stationed overseas in wartime. He then returns to homoerotic experiences—activities that, although generally of a one-night-stand variety, may involve long-term relationships. This, in turn, tends to decrease the need for conjugal activity. The ensuing chain reaction, combined with the pressure on time in their professional careers, results in a portrait of the ambisexual.

With the trade, the pattern is somewhat simpler and more unidirectional: there is little evidence of early homosexual activity. From cooperating respondents, I concluded that there may have been isolated experiences of a homoerotic nature: some hustling in the milieu of a teenage gang; instances of serving as insertor in an act of fellatio with an old man or army buddy, accompanied by financial reward in the former case or by heavy drinking in the latter. Few of these men have had extensive reinforcement in homosexual behavior, nor is there any evidence that they think of themselves as being "gay" or ambisexual.

"At lower (educational and social) levels," writes Kinsey, "there are definite taboos against masturbation . . . Most males of this level find it difficult to understand how a grown man could think of masturbating, particularly if he is married and living with his wife." [11] We have seen, however, that single males of the working class control sample resort to masturbation at least often enough to bring their mean frequency of orgasm up to 8.7 per month. To many married men of the same socioeconomic level, however, masturbation is unthinkable as a sexual outlet. When caught in the sexual bind, therefore, they turn to other interpersonal outlets. Half a century ago, they would have been customers in two-bit bordellos, where madams carefully timed the encounters to maintain a profit-making volume. Like modern tearooms, these facilities provided a relatively inexpensive, expedient noninvolving outlet for men of the working classes who want to supplement (but not supplant) their conjugal outlet. As I have stated previously, "Men with heavy emotional commitments to families and jobs . . . may not be able to afford investment in other than the most transient and impersonal types of extramarital sex."

At least as regards the trade, the largest group in my sample of participants, the sexual bind appears to have a causal relationship to tearoom activity. This conclusion is further strengthened by the observation that at least one variable causing the sexual bind, religious affiliation, is prior in time to the deviant activity. The interviews provide strong evidence of a cause-effect sequence: the prohibition of artificial birth control devices are seen to produce a decline of sexual satisfaction in marriage that, in turn, drives some victims of that sexual bind to the tearooms for satisfaction.

SEXUAL BIND AND THE SINGLE MAN

It might be assumed that all single men suffer from the sexual bind between perceived needs and available outlet. For most of the unmarried men in the samples, this appears to be true. In the case of those participants active in the homosexual subculture (the "gay" men), however, this generalization does not hold. They report a perceived adequacy of outlet that compares only with the married controls. With little mention of masturbation as an outlet, they maintain a frequency of orgasms of 15.0 per month, greater than the mean reported by the controls matched with them, 11.6. With the sexual markets open to them in the gay world, it should not be surprising that they manage to exceed the base frequency for the married controls without resorting to either marital sex or masturbation.

The control sample of single men and the working class participants are less satisfied with their sexual lives. Whereas none of the controls who lack college education mention masturbation as an outlet, two-thirds of those who had completed at least one year of higher education give masturbation as their primary source of orgasm. Automanipulation, then, relieves the sexual bind of the unmarried, better educated nondeviants, providing them with a frequency of outlet second only to that achieved by the working class, married controls through marital sex.

Two-thirds of the single controls with less occupational autonomy complain of the inadequacy of their mean 8.7 orgasms per month to meet their sexual requirements. Although some of these men have premarital heterosexual partners, the majority will probably get married in order to ease the sexual bind. In their interviews, at least the younger men indicated their intentions of future matrimony.

Finally, the sexual bind is strongly felt by the closet queens. Their frequency of orgasm (8.0 per month) is lower than any other group of unmarried men reported. Although their needs are perceived as being "about average," masturbation is not thought to be a viable alternative outlet. Few of these men have any intention of marrying or of taking part in the sexual markets of subcultural homosexuality, which they fear and despise. Their tendency is to engage in what may best be described as "lone wolf" activity: furtive excursions to the tearooms, picking up teenage hustlers, even the seduction of boys with whom they work. Unlike the gay men, their acceptance of the homosexual self-image is a begrudging one. Unless they find a "permanent lover," their sexual lives are apt to continue to be inadequate and marked by guilt and self-hatred.

RECIPROCAL TRADE

Tearoom activity constitutes a free market in the sexual economy. There is no exchange of money between the participants in restroom fellatio; rather, certain "goods" are traded for certain "services." In summarizing the above data, it may help for us to think of the male sex organ as the essential "goods" for this exchange. My respondents assure me that these goods must be supplied in sufficient quantity and variety for the market to be viable.

In return for the erect penis the insertee supplies a needed service, the sucking action that produces orgasm. It should be made clear that it is equally possible to view the mouths of insertees as the "goods" and the insertion of the penises as the "services." Regardless of of the viewpoint taken, it should also be remembered that the man who provides the goods in one encounter may provide the service in another. From the tearoom observations, however, it is evident that there is a central tendency for certain men, generally those of the lower classes, to serve as insertors while others prefer the insertee role.

What emerges from this analysis is that the two groups most caught in the sexual bind, most dissatisfied by the discrepancies between perceived sexual needs and actual frequency of outlet, are those who provide the essential supply of goods for the tearoom market. Together, the trade and closet queens constitute 62 percent of the participant sample; but these types were observed providing 75 percent of the desired goods. Three of every four insertors in the encounters from which my sample was collected were men of lower occupational autonomy.

Ambisexuals, the gay, a minority of the closet queens, would not venture into tearooms if there were not a variety of men to be found there who are unavailable in other one-night-stand marketplaces. The most crucial group of participants in this exchange are aptly called "the trade." Masculine in appearance and heterosexual in self-concept, they enter the public restrooms in search of a service they seldom find at home and cannot afford to acquire in any other place. Without this abundant supply of goods—or lacking the services offered by those who share a more homosexual identity—the tearoom market would atrophy.

Some men choose impersonal sex over the alternative of masturbation. Others find satisfaction in their marital or premarital heterosexual relationships. All act in response to the pressure of certain social factors: their religious beliefs, occupational or educational restrictions, the increasing scarcity of time in an affluent society. Those caught in the sexual bind produced by these characteristics will seek that form of reciprocal trade relationship that provides the lowest costs in terms of personal involvement, money, and time expended. At present, the social control forces can only determine whether such markets will be located in bordellos, roadside bushes, or restrooms. The lack of perceived sexual satisfaction will, no doubt, continue to provide ample customers in the foreseeable future.

SUMMARY OF FINDINGS

By comparing participants in tearoom encounters with a randomly selected control sample, I found that those who seek the impersonal sex of public restrooms are caught in a sexual bind between their perceived sexual needs and the satisfaction of those needs by socially prescribed means. The largest group of participants (34 percent) are married men with little occupational autonomy. Due, in part, to the Roman Catholic proscription of artificial contraceptives, these men seek relief from a frequency of marital intercourse that is half that reported by their counterparts in the control sample.

The more suffluent married men, ambisexuals, present a more complex portrait. In their case, a higher perception of sexual drive combines with religious, occupational, and other marital factors to cause inadequate opportunity for sexual outlet in their conjugal relationships. Although married men with independent occupations from both samples evidence less marital intercourse than do the working class men (perhaps a result of "the increasing scarcity of time" in our consuming society), the ambisexuals report both the lowest frequency of marital outlet and the highest perception of sexual drive.

Those who are least apt to be encountered in tearooms, the overtly gay respondents who are unmarried and enjoy relative occupational autonomy, report greater satisfaction in their sexual lives than any other group of participants. The "straight" single men, while complaining of "inadequate" sexual opportunity, employ masturbation as a major form of outlet.

Finally, the working class, unmarried tearoom participants (largely due to a lower educational level and other factors that make masturbation unacceptable) seek impersonal and furtive encounters to relieve the sexual bind. The chief difference between participants and controls who are single is in their acceptance of masturbation as a viable sexual outlet.

Such social characteristics as religious affiliation, occupational demands, and level of education are seen as explaining the drive behind the search for tearoom sex. If combined with the normative push for expedient, impersonal relations that our consumption-oriented, market economy provides, these social factors alone are strong enough to explain the sexual activity in public restrooms. It is unnecessary to look for interior, psychological factors behind such behavior.

NOTES

1. Humphreys, Laud. *Tearoom Trade: Impersonal Sex in Public Places*. Chicago: Aldine Publishing Co., 1970.

2. Gallo, Jon J. *et al.* "The Consenting Adult Homosexual and the Law: An Empirical Study of Enforcement and Administration in Los Angeles County." *UCLA Law Review 13* (March): 643-832, 1966.

3. Kitsuse, John I. "Societal Reaction to Deviant Behavior: Problems of Theory and Method." In *The Other Side,* edited by Howard S. Becker. New York: The Free Press, 1964, pp. 87-102.

4. Hughes, Everett C. *Men and Their Work.* Glencoe, Ill.: The Free Press, 1958, p. 111.

5. Kinsey, Alfred C.; Pomeroy, Wardell B.; and Martin, Clyde E. *Sexual Behavior in the Human Male.* Philadelphia: W. B. Saunders Co., 1948, p. 213.

6. Ibid., p. 630.

7. Ibid., p. 257.

8. Humphreys, 1970, p. 105.

9. Warner, W. Lloyd, and Abegglen, James C. "Successful Wives of Successful Executives," *Harvard Business Review,* March-April, 1956, pp. 64-70, as cited in Staffan B. Linder, *op. cit.*

10. Linder, Staffan B. *The Harried Leisure Class.* New York: Columbia University Press, 1970, p. 84.

11. Kinsey, 1948, p. 508.

12. Humphreys, 1970, p. 154.

13. THE EFFECTS OF PORNOGRAPHY

THE COMMISSION ON OBSCENITY AND PORNOGRAPHY

Abridged from The Report of the Commission on Obscenity and Pornography *(Bantam, 1970).*

■ The Commission on Obscenity and Pornography was established at the direction of Congress to study and report on (a) constitutional and definitional problems related to obscenity controls, (b) traffic in and distribution of obscene and pornographic materials, and (c) the effects of such material, particularly on youth, and their relationship to crime and other antisocial conduct. Beginning in 1968 the Commission conducted the most wide-ranging and systematic investigation ever undertaken of the kind of behavior and communications labeled as obscenity and poronography. Its technical reports provide an exhaustive review of the state of knowledge up to its creation and a large variety of original studies dealing with legal, organizational, public attitudinal and social psychological aspects of pornography.

This selection is a summary of the report of the "effects panel," which was concerned with the effect of erotic material on those exposed to it. The Commission supported a number of innovative and well-controlled social psychological studies designed to test commonly held notions about the effects of erotica. In addition, the effects panel critically assessed other work on the subject and formulated in a concise way the most plausible conclusions to be made from the current state of research on it.

It is perhaps not surprising to learn that from the White House to Congress the reaction of traditional politicians to the Commission findings was hardly positive. On balance the Commission's work suggested that obscenity and pornography were not important social problems, that no evidence indicated that exposure to such materials was damaging to individuals, and that in general legal and policy initiatives in this area were more likely to create than to solve problems.

A recent book collecting various anti-pornography views is David Holbrook (ed.) *The Case Against Pornography* (Library Press, 1973). For an interesting study of Victorian pornography, see Stephen Marcus, *The Other Victorians* (Basic Books, 1966). The most complete selection of materials analyzing the sociology, economics, and social psychology of obscenity and pornography as social activities is found in the technical reports of the Commission. ■

IF A CASE is to be made against "pornography" in 1970, it will have to be made on grounds other than demonstrated effects of a damaging personal or social nature. Empirical research designed to clarify the question has found no reliable evidence to date that exposure to explicit sexual materials plays a significant role in the causation of delinquent or criminal sexual behavior among youth or adults.

Existing legislation and judicial decisions are based upon considerations other than demonstrable effects of this nature, although the possibility of such effects seems to underlie this body of law. Legal judgments and social policy established without consideration of effects would seem to be inherently limited. The Effects Panel has examined existing popular and scientific literature and has initiated new empirical research. In drawing conclusions, we have been sensitive to both the quantity and quality of the research. The conclusion to be drawn from the totality of these research findings is that no dangerous effects have been demonstrated on any of the populations which were studied. . . .

ORIENTATION TO THE STUDY OF EFFECTS

In July of 1968, the Commission established an Effects Panel, as one of four working panels, and charged it with principal responsibility for three activities: *(a)* to review and evaluate existing research bearing on the effects of exposure to sexual stimuli; *(b)* to design a program of new research in the area; *(c)* to summarize, evaluate, and report the findings of these studies to the full Commission.

The first task facing the Panel was to identify presumed effects of erotic materials and refine these for purposes of research. Two sources were consulted for guidance: (a) previous research in this area, and (b) the claims which had been made about the consequences of reading and viewing erotic material. Reviews of this literature generated several basic questions. If exposure to erotic materials does, in fact, have harmful effects, what kinds of effects are these and who experiences them? Distinctions can be made, for example, between "short-term" effects and "long-term" effects, between "direct" and "indirect" effects, and between effects upon conduct and effects upon emotions, attitudes, opinions, and moral character. Are these effects experienced by adequately socialized "normal" individuals or only by persons who have already experienced some form of psychopathic or sociopathic condition? Are adults affected, or only children, or both? Various other questions can be asked, but these will perhaps suffice as examples.

A review of empirical studies published prior to 1968 revealed little research directly relevant to the total assessment of effects.

The Panel learned that existing empirical knowledge pertained generally to sexual arousals, responses, and it could be summarized briefly: (a) pictures and words depicting various aspects of human sexuality produce sexual arousal in a considerable proportion of the adult population; (b) materials which elicit arousal differ according to the sex of the viewer; (c) persons differ in their preference for, and response to, sexual stimuli; and (d) the context in which the viewing occurs is a significant determinant of the extent to which persons will be aroused by the materials. The reviewers found no research indicating the duration of arousal or how this stimulation might affect overt behavior, attitudes governing behavior, or mental health. A later Commission-sponsored review of the literature concluded that "we still have precious little information from studies of humans on the questions of primary import to the law . . . the data 'stop short at

the critical point.' Definitive answers on the determinants and effects of pornography are not yet available." . . .

PUBLIC OPINION ABOUT SEXUAL MATERIALS

The relative absence of research on the effects of erotica has not deterred the formation of strong opinions about (a) the extent to which available pornography constitutes a social problem and (b) the possible effects of exposure to sexually explicit depictions. Prior to 1970, however, opinion surveys had not attempted to assess in any depth the state of general public opinion in this sensitive area.

Systematic assessment of opinion is especially important in policy-related areas where community judgments may provide a basis for government action. In areas which lend themselves to empirical investigation, but where research is absent or available research is inadequate, the role of public opinion in the formulation of policy and legal statutes can be of critical importance. Although the issues of obscenity and pornography have been pronounced upon by the courts and the Congress, as well as by innumerable experts from various fields, these judgments could not have been illuminated by knowledge of public opinion until very recently.

Results of a Commission-sponsored survey are reported in the following pages. The findings show that in 1970, American public opinion on the effects of erotica is more varied than critics may have anticipated.

In 1970, a survey involving face-to-face interviews with a random sample of 2,486 adults and 769 young persons (ages 15 to 20) was conducted at the Commission's request. One of the purposes of the survey was to determine whether Americans regard and define the area of erotic materials as a significant or important social problem. Adult respondents in the survey were asked: "Would you please tell me what you think are the two or three most serious problems facing the country today?" Only 2 percent of the population referred to erotic materials, and many of these comments alluded to erotica through criticism of mass media or contemporary sexual standards. The most frequently mentioned problems were: war (54 percent), race (36 percent), the national economy (32 percent), youth rebellion (23 percent), breakdown of law and order (20 percent), drugs (20 percent), pollution and misuse of resources (19 percent), poverty and poverty programs (12 percent), moral breakdown (9 percent), and dissatisfaction with government (9 percent). About 4 percent of the population mentioned education, overpopulation, and foreign policy as serious problems, and only 2 percent mentioned erotic materials. . . .

Neither the substance of these statements [about erotic materials] nor the frequency with which they were mentioned constitutes a strong indictment of sexual materials or establishes erotica as a major concern.

Opinion surveys sometimes appear to report contradictory findings, and the findings of the Commission study may appear to be inconsistent with reports that 85 percent of the American adults "favor stricter laws on pornography" and that "76 percent want pornographic literature outlawed and 72 percent believe smut is taking the beauty out of sex." Certain complexities of the issues appear to be responsible for these inconsistencies. Actually, Abelson's first, and extremely generic question on the topic revealed that 68 percent of the sample felt that "some people should not be allowed to read or see some" sexual materials (32 percent felt that "people should be allowed to read or see anything they want to"). Further questioning revealed, however, that many opinions on both sides of the issue are actually conditional or qualified. Careful analysis showed that, although substantial proportions of the population endorse some form of restriction on the availability of erotic materials, nearly half (44 percent) qualify their response in terms of knowledge about the effects of such materials. For example, it was found that 51 percent of the population would be inclined to sanction availability of erotic materials if it were clearly demonstrated that

such materials had no harmful effects on the user. About 8 persons in 10 (79 percent) would oppose the availability of such materials if they were convinced that such materials were harmful. At the polar positions, about a third (35 percent) of the population would oppose availability even if it were shown that such materials were not harmful, and 7 percent would favor availability even if it were shown that there were harmful effects.

These findings underline the degree to which public opinion regarding the availability of erotica is contingent upon whether such material is shown to have, or not to have, harmful effects. . . .

BEHAVIORAL RESPONSES TO EROTICA

There are two elementary, but fundamental, questions about erotic materials upon which nearly all concerns with the subject are based. First, does exposure to erotic stimuli sexually excite and arouse the viewer? Second, does such exposure affect the subsequent sexual behavior of the user? An adequate answer to the first requires carefully designed experimental studies. The second question can best be answered by research which extends beyond the laboratory, longitudinally, into the natural environment, where sexuality is expressed in a context of established attitudes, individual interests, needs, and social relationships.

Studies in this area were not undertaken until recently, and there is not yet a large research literature. Substantial beginnings have been made, however, in both the measurement of sexual arousal and sexual behavior and in identifying the important variables which affect sexuality.

What follows is a review and discussion of contemporary knowledge about the relationship between exposure to erotic stimuli and (a) psychosexual stimulation (sexual arousal), and (b) sexual behavior.

Of all the presumed consequences of exposure to erotic stimuli, the effect of sexual excitement is probably the most widely held and commonly mentioned. In the national survey conducted for the Commission 72 percent of adult males and 63 percent of adult females indicated that they believed that "sexual materials excite people sexually," although considerably fewer reported experiencing this effect themselves. The growing body of research which bears on this question shows, in general, that photographs, stories, and films which depict various aspects of human sexuality produce excitement in a large proportion of the population.

Available knowledge in this area, however, continues to be complicated by certain technical problems in the measurement and interpretation of physiological and psychological responses to sexual stimulation. . . .

It has been hypothesized (a) that repeated exposure to sex stimuli "results not in continued excitement, but in boredom"; and (b) that the capacity of erotic stimuli to excite the viewer or user diminishes after a few hours of exposure, that "the half-life of pornography is approximately two to three hours in one's total life time." A systematic study of the sexual behaviors and habits of nearly 3,000 American males, including sex offenders, concluded that: "We have often found that men with large collections [of erotic materials] of longstanding lose much of their sexual response to the materials, and while their interest in collecting may continue unabated, their motivation is no longer primarily sexual."

A recent experimental study appears to confirm the hypothesized satiation effect. Subjects consisted of 23 volunteers, all of them male university students, aged 21 to 23. Each weekday for 3 weeks, each subject spent 90 minutes a day alone in a room containing a large collection of erotic material (films and textual) as well as generally nonerotic materials such as Readers' Digest. Subjects were free to view or read whatever interested them, or, if they chose, to ignore these materials. Psychosexual stimulation was assessed by introspective self reports and by monitoring selected cardiovascular and physiological functions: penile volume, urinary acid phosphatase, and heart rate. Interest in these materials was assessed by recording the proportion of time subjects spent in each session reading or viewing erotic materials. A variety of psychological tests and inventories were employed in addition to three psychiatric interviews with each subject.

During the first few sessions of the experiment, subjects spent most of the experimental time reading or looking at erotic material. During those days, subjects reported substantially more time thinking about sexual matters and reported increased levels of general sexual arousal. All subjects reported being initially stimulated by the erotic materials, and physiological measurements confirmed high levels of reported psychosexual stimulation.

During the second week of experimental sessions, sexual feelings and both physiologically measured and reported arousal continued, generally, to decline. After the first 90-minute session, subjects' sexual arousal dropped significantly.

Concomitant with increasingly attenuated levels of sexual arousal, all subjects reported and showed a marked decline of interest in viewing or reading the materials. Subjects' interest in continued participation in the experiment showed a steady and significant decrease over the three weeks. The proportion of time actually spent with erotic stimuli during each exposure session dropped to approximately 30 percent by the 11th session. At this point, novel sexual materials were introduced, and both reported and observed sexual arousal increased to the initially high level obtained during the first session but returned to a declining level immediately. It is also of interest to note that at the beginning of the experiment all subjects reported interest in viewing erotic material, including a willingness to pay for the opportunity to participate. Nine weeks after the daily exposure sessions ended, however, all subjects reported boredom, and a number reported refused private opportunities to view erotica.

The experiment was designed in such a way that prior to, and twice after, the series of 90-minute exposure sessions, the subjects and a group of control subjects, who did not participate in the exposure sessions, viewed an erotic film. Comparison showed that before the 90-minute exposure sessions, both experimental and control subjects reported equally high levels of sexual arousal. Physiological measurement confirmed these reports. In reference to the second film, viewed after the end of 3 weeks of 90-minute exposure sessions, the observed and reported arousal levels of the two groups differed substantially: subjects who had participated in the daily exposure sessions showed about 60 percent as much psychosexual stimulation as they did for the first film and were significantly less aroused than the controls. Two months after the daily exposure sessions, subjects who participated in the daily sessions viewed a third erotic film. Level of arousal for these subjects increased slightly from that observed during the second film, and was no longer significantly below the level observed during the first film.

The results obtained from both physiological measures and reported levels of psychosexual stimulation support the hypothesis that repeated exposure to sexual stimuli results in decreased responsiveness. In addition, degree of interest in both the study and the stimulus materials declined predictably among the subjects. Although complete satiation in the sense of total inhibition of response did not occur, the physiological data and reported levels of arousal and interest point toward satiation in terms of diminished response. At no time during the course of the experiment did the subjects report detrimental effects of the experiment upon sleep, mood, study or work habits, or any other aspect of their personal or social behavior. Satiation was specific to erotic material and did not extend to their personal sexual activities.

This particular experiment marks the first attempt to study the effects of repeated and prolonged exposure to sexual stimuli. Additional studies with a broader range of subjects and different intervals of exposure under different social conditions will be necessary before these results can be generalized, although the observation of short-term psycho-sexual stimulation is certainly consistent with several other studies.

Accumulated research on psychosexual stimulation shows that exposure to erotic photographs, narratives, and film produces sexual arousal in substantial proportions of both males and females. Studies in this area also demonstrate that differences among individuals in psychosexual response are largely a function of sexual orientation and preferences. Regardless of the medium of presentation, however, depictions of heterosexual coitus and petting elicit more frequent and stronger arousal responses than depictions of homosexuality, sadistic and masochistic sexuality. One study found that erotic fantasies or imagined sexual depictions were reported to be considerably more sexually stimulating than explicit textual or visual presentations.

Several recent studies suggest that traditional hypotheses of gender differences in psychosexual responses may require revision. These studies indicate that while males tend to judge erotic stimuli as more arousing than females, the sexes do not differ substantially in physiological sexual response to these stimuli. Not surprisingly, research indicates that females are less responsive to male-oriented erotica, but about equally responsive to heterosexual action themes. Differences in psychosexual response between the sexes appear to be essentially qualitative rather than quantitative.

A systematic analysis of the consequences of repeated exposure of young males to erotic stimuli found that continued exposure results in satiation of both sexual arousal and interest in erotic material. After 15 viewing sessions, these males showed substantial reductions in stimulation and reported increased boredom and indifference to sex stimuli; diminished responsiveness was observed as long as eight weeks after the study.

ATTITUDINAL, EMOTIONAL, AND JUDGMENTAL RESPONSES TO EROTICA

Inappropriate or undesirable attitudes, values, moral standards, thoughts, feelings, and emotions are often mentioned as consequences of exposure to sexual stimuli. Some have argued that studies which look for effects in crime and antisocial behavior will not uncover the real effects of erotica—i.e., the effects upon moral character and sexual orientation. These alleged effects are particularly difficult to investigate empirically because they do not lend themselves to precise formulation and because their occurrence would not necessarily be manifested in overt, physical behavior. In the past two years, however, several studies have been undertaken to investigate attitudinal, emotional, and judgmental responses of users and viewers of erotica. . . .

The argument that exposure to sexual stimuli results in unconventional sexual attitudes and orientations may be investigated by (a) determining whether persons with differing amounts and frequencies of exposure differ attitudinally, and (b) measuring attitudes and orientations before and after exposure. . . .

Persons who are more experienced with erotica are more liberal or tolerant than those with less experience in reference to other people's behavior. They are, for example, more likely to feel that, "when it comes to sex, there is a great difference between what most people do and what they would like to do" and less likely to agree that "a girl who goes to bed with a boy before marriage will lose his respect." They are also more tolerant of masturbation in their children.

Experimental studies to date indicate that exposure to erotic stimuli have little or no effect on established attitudinal commitments regarding either sexuality or sexual morality. Comparison of attitudes before and after single or repeated exposure reveal almost no significant differences. Such isolated differences as were observed principally involve somewhat increased tolerance for other peoples' activities and are in some respects contradictory. The overall picture is almost uniformly one of no significant change. A study of 300 young males indicates that exposure to erotica has no direct relationship to "moral character."

Available research indicates that exposure to pornography does tend to liberalize attitudes, regarding whether such material is itself harmful or whether it should be restricted. Such attitudes are also apparently related to feelings of guilt, politicosocial attitudes, and other personality characteristics.

Several attempts have been made to identify the social and psychological variables which determine judgments such as "obscene" and "pornographic" in response to sex stimuli. Available research indicates that characteristics of both the stimulus and the rater influence such evaluations. One factor which has been found to be highly associated with "obscenity" judgments is the degree of nudity thought to be acceptable to most people. Research in this area also shows that individual sexual preferences, sexual experience, tolerant attitudes, and educational backgrounds are important determinants of the judgments made about erotic stimuli. Finally, the data suggest that familiarity with erotica is an important determinant of evaluative reactions.

A set of experimental studies indicates that exposure to erotic material activates a variety of general emotional responses, including agitation and malaise among both males and females. A study of repeated exposure suggests that these effects are transitory (less than 24 hours).

Affective responses are varied, and differ with sociopsychological characteristics of the subjects. Erotic stimuli are variously regarded as both arousing and repelling, arousing but not repelling, and repelling but not arousing.

EROTICA AND ANTISOCIAL AND CRIMINAL BEHAVIOR

In its assignment to the Commission "to study the effect of obscenity and pornography upon the public," Congress added for emphasis "and particularly minors, and its relationship to crime and other antisocial behavior." This emphasis reflects: (a) a long-standing concern that has been voiced by many officials and (b) the state of scientific knowledge at the time the Commission was established.

The paucity of research information regarding the effects of pornography on the antisocial behavior of adults and youth is partly a function of a general sensitivity about the scientific study of private behavior—especially sexual behavior and specifically as it concerns children. The Commission was not immune to social forces restricting research in this area nor to the logistical and methodological difficulties inherent in pioneering efforts. Research that the Commission initiated is, therefore, somewhat more restricted in quantity and in the quality of rigor than that required for unequivocal conclusions. Nevertheless, many more empirical observations were accumulated during the past two years than had been brought to bear on the issue previously. Sufficient information is now available to discuss these issues within the framework of scientific knowledge.

The following discussion is organized around two general research problems: (*a*) the relationship between availability of erotic material and the incidence of antisocial behavior, and (*b*) the experience of convicted offenders with sexual materials. . . .

Analyses of the United States crime rates do not support the thesis of a causal connection between the availability of erotica and sex crimes among either juveniles or adults. Because of limitations in both the data and inferences which can validly be drawn from them, the data cannot, however, be said absolutely to disprove such a connection. Similar analyses for Denmark show that in that country the increased availability of erotica has been accompanied by a decrease in sex crimes.

Studies of juvenile delinquents indicate that their experience with erotica is generally similar to that of nondelinquents in reference to extent and amount of experience, age of first exposure, and arousal. Such small differences as exist appear to be products of age and subculture variables. Research does suggest that exposure to erotic materials may sometimes be part of a deviant life-style and may reflect, rather than affect, the character, attitudes, and conduct of delinquent youth. There is no basis in the available data, how-ever, for supposing that there is any independent relationship between exposure to erotica and delinquency.

Studies show that in comparison with other adults, sex offenders and sexual deviants are significantly less experienced with erotica during adolescence. As adults, sex offenders are not significantly different from other adults in exposure or in reported arousal or reported likelihood of engaging in sociosexual behavior following exposure to erotica.

Various studies revealed no significant differences between sex offenders and other groups in reference to whether erotica had affected their morals or produced preoccupation with sexual materials. When explicitly given the opportunity to do so, a small minority of sex offenders say that erotica or pornography had some relationship to their committing sex crimes, but for reasons detailed above, these data cannot be regarded as reliable evidence of such a relationship.

Sex offenders generally report sexually repressive family backgrounds, immature and inadequate sexual histories, and rigid and conservative attitudes concerning sexuality. Research suggests that childhood experiences which encourage sexual repression and inhibition of sexual curiosity are associated with psychosexual maladjustment and antisocial sexual behavior.

Research to date thus provides no substantial basis for the belief that erotic materials constitute a primary or significant cause of the development of character deficits or that they operate as a significant determinative factor in causing crime and delinquency.

This conclusion is stated with due and perhaps excessive caution, since it is obviously not possible, and never would be possible, to state that never on any occasion, under any conditions, did any erotic material ever contribute in any way to the likelihood of any individual's committing a sex crime. Indeed, no such statement could be made about any kind of nonerotic material. On the basis of the available data, however, it is not possible to conclude that erotic material is a significant cause of sex crime.

III.
DEVIANT PERSONAL CONTROL: ILLNESS, VIOLENCE, AND CRIME

IN PART II we examined several analyses of deviant behavior that in one way or another emphasized the deviant label for particular voluntary transactions between people. In this part the focus shifts from the transactional character of behavior labeled as deviant to deviant forms of personal control. Obviously these are simply two different perspectives that overlap considerably. In some kinds of deviant behavior, however, the social definitions clearly go directly to the issue of personal control. That is, what is "wrong" is that individuals do not control themselves as they are expected to do, and this behavior is labeled as deviant.

The matter of personal control is quite clear when we discuss mental illness or when we consider personal violence. But we see the same concerns at work when we look at some of the subtler issues of physical illness; it appears that deviance may also lie in the inability of the sick or disabled person to present himself convincingly as "normal."

Some of the forms of deviant behavior examined here have undoubted victims, unlike the crimes without victims discussed earlier. Murder or such less dramatic crimes as vandalism, petty theft, and the like have unambiguous victims; so this part concludes with a selection that presents data on the extent of criminal victimization in the United States.

The central issue in the labeling process here is the definition of behavior as failing to reflect a proper degree of personal control. The causes imputed for this lack of control vary considerably, but most commonly behavior deemed wanting in restraint is judged to be a result of immorality, of an unwillingness to follow proper moral guides. In a more "modern" view failures of personal control are often seen as the product of illness rather than of immorality, and in a still more modern view such behavior may be regarded as reflecting not so much a disordered mental condition as a failure in society's socialization processes, because of the inadequacy of family environment or other and larger institutions. In any case, the societal view of the end result is that the individual is not capable of bringing to bear on himself the necessary degree of personal control and so displays behavior that is objectionable, thereby exposing himself to legitimate processing as deviant.

As we will see, the processes that result in this kind of labeling are rich in possibilities for the creation of social problems, both through their failure to limit or reduce the incidence of crimes with victims and in the opportunities they provide for zealous infringement of the liberties of individuals labeled as deviant.

14. MENTAL ILLNESS AS RESIDUAL DEVIANCE

*Reprinted from "The Role of the Mentally Ill and the Dynamics of Mental Disorder,"
Sociometry 26 (December 1963): 436-53. Thomas J. Scheff is Professor of Sociology at
the University of California, Santa Barbara. He has written extensively on the sociology
of mental illness, societal reactions to deviant behavior, and the social processes by which
groups define reality. His best-known book is* Being Mentally Ill *(Aldine, 1966).*

■ The phenomenon of mental illness clearly poses many problems for modern societies—problems ranging from the disruption of important social relations within the personal networks of mentally ill individuals, to the cost of maintaining large establishments for the care and control of disabled people, to the cost to liberty involved in the forced confinement of individuals on the sometimes shaky grounds that it is to protect them and others. As with other departures from the normal, though, the human sciences have not provided us with unambiguous knowledge about the causes of mental disorders. During the 19th century it was assumed that mental illness had biological causes. In the early part of the 20th century psychological explanations gained ground, particularly those associated with the theories of Sigmund Freud and his psychoanalytic followers. More recently biological theories have again come into fashion.

The sociologists' contributions to this discussion have tended to be peripheral to the main issues of the nature of mental illness. Sociologists have shown how the incidence of different kinds of mental illness varies from one social group to another and how different social classes avail themselves of treatment to differing extents. Taking another tack, Scheff concentrates on the central issue of how behavior that eventually is labeled as mentally ill comes to be perceived in that way. He observes that the diagnosis of illness proceeds from the observation of a person's behavior. He uses the concept of residual deviance as a general rubric to include the diverse kinds of behavior that are likely to be regarded as indicating mental disorder. He then shows how individuals can be led to assume the role of a mentally ill person, based on common views about what such a person is like.

Erving Goffman first developed this approach to the study of mental illness in *Asylums* (Aldine 1961) and later in "Mental Symptoms and Public Order," reprinted in his *Interaction Ritual* (Doubleday-Anchor, 1967). A psychiatrist, Thomas S. Szasz, developed much the same view in *The Myth of Mental Illness* (Harper & Row, 1971); as did Ernest Becker in *The Birth and Death of Meaning: A Perspective in Psychiatry and Anthropology* (Free Press, 1962). Other sociological contributions to the study of mental illness include A. B. Hollingshead and R. C. Redlich, *Social Class and Mental Illness: A Community Study* (Wiley, 1958); Jerome K. Meyers and Bertram H. Roberts, *Family and Class Dynamics in Mental Illness* (Wiley, 1959); Charles E. Hughes, Marc-Adelard Tremblay, Robert N. Rapoport, and Alexander H. Leighton, *People of Cove and Woodlot: Community Studies From the Viewpoint of Social Psychiatry* (Basic Books, 1960); and Leo Srole, Thomas S. Langner, Stanley T. Michael, Marvin K. Opler, and Thomas A. C. Rennie, *Mental Health in the Metropolis: The Mid-Town Manhattan Study* (McGraw-Hill, 1962). For an extraordinarily precise analysis of the reciprocal relationship of the mentally ill person with those around him see Edwin M. Lemert, "Paranoia and the Dynamics of Exclusion," in *Human Deviance, Social Problems and Social Control* (Prentice-Hall, 1967). ■

ALTHOUGH THE LAST TWO DECADES have seen a vast increase in the number of studies of functional mental disorder, there is as yet no substantial, verified body of knowledge in this area. A quotation from a recent symposium on schizophrenia summarizes the present situation.

During the past decade, the problem of chronic schizophrenia have claimed the energy of workers in many fields. Despite significant contributions which reflect continuing progress, *we have yet to learn to ask ourselves the right questions.*

Many investigators apparently agree; systematic studies have not only failed to provide answers to the problem of causation, but there is considerable feeling that the problem itself has not been formulated correctly.

One frequently noted deficiency in psychiatric formulations of the problem is the failure to incorporate social processes into the dynamics of mental disorder. Although the importance of these processes is increasingly recognized by psychiatrists, the conceptual models used in formulating research questions are basically concerned with individual rather than social systems. Genetic, biochemical, and psychological investigations seek different causal agents but utilize similar models: dynamic systems which are located within the individual. In these investigations, social processes tend to be relegated to a subsidiary role, because the model focuses attention on individual differences, rather than on the social system in which the individuals are involved.

Recently a number of writers have sought to develop an approach which would give more emphasis to social processes. Lemert, Erikson, Goffman, and Szasz have notably contributed to this approach. Lemert, particularly, by rejecting the more conventional concern with the origins of mental deviance, and stressing instead the potential importance of the societal reaction in stabilizing deviance, focuses primarily on mechanisms of social control. The work of all of these authors suggests research avenues which are analytically separable from questions of individual systems and point, therefore, to a theory which would incorporate social processes.

The purpose of the present paper is to contribute to the formulation of such a theory by stating a set of nine propositions which make up basic assumptions for a social system model of mental disorder. This set is largely derived from the work of the authors listed above, all but two of the propositions (4 and 5) being suggested, with varying degrees of explicitness, in the cited references. By stating these propositions explicitly, this paper attempts to facilitate testing of basic assumpions, all of which are empirically unverified, or only partly verified. By stating these assumptions in terms of standard sociological concepts, this paper attempts to show the relevance to studies of mental disorder of findings from diverse areas of social science, such as race relations and prestige suggestion. This paper also delineates three problems which are crucial for a sociological theory of mental disorder: what are the conditions in a culture under which diverse kinds of deviance become stable and uniform; to what extent, in different phases of careers of mental patients, are symptoms of mental illness the result of conforming behavior; is there a general set of contingencies which lead to the definition of deviant behavior as a manifestation of mental illness? Finally, this paper attempts to formulate special conceptual tools to deal with these problems, which are directly linked to sociological theory. The social institution of insanity, residual deviance, the social role of the mentally ill, and the bifurcation of the societal reaction into the alternative reactions of denial and labeling are examples of such conceptual tools.

These conceptual tools are utilized to construct a theory of mental disorder in which psychiatric symptoms are considered to be violations of social norms, and stable "mental illness" to be a social role. The validity of this theory depends upon verification of the nine propositions listed below in future studies and should, therefore, be applied with caution and with appreciation for its limitations. One such limitation is that the theory attempts to account for a much narrower class of phenomena than is usually found under the rubric of mental disorder; the discussion that follows will be focused exclusively on stable or recurring mental disorder and does not explain the causes of single deviant episodes. A second major limitation is that the theory probably distorts the phenomena under discussion. Just as the individual system models under-stress social processes, the model presented here probably exaggerates their importance. The social system model "holds constant" individual differences in order to articulate the relationship between society and mental disorder. Ultimately, a framework which encompassed both individual and social systems would be desirable. Given the present state of knowledge, however, this framework may prove useful by providing an explicit contrast to the more conventional medical and psychological approaches and thus assisting in the formulation of sociological studies of mental disorder.

THE SYMPTOMS OF "MENTAL ILLNESS" AS RESIDUALLY DEVIANT BEHAVIOR

One source of immediate embarrassment to any social theory of "mental illness" is that the terms used in referring to these phenomena in our society prejudge the issue. The medical metaphor "mental illness" suggests a determinate process which occurs within the individual: the unfolding and development of disease. It is convenient, therefore, to drop terms derived from the disease metaphor in favor of a standard sociological concept, deviant behavior, which signifies behavior that violates a social norm in a given society.

If the symptoms of mental illness are to be construed as violations of social norms, it is necessary to specify the type of norms involved. Most norm violations do not cause the violator to be labeled as mentally ill but as ill-mannered, ignorant, sinful, criminal, or perhaps just harried, depending on the type of norm involved. There are innumerable norms, however, over which consensus is so complete that the members of a group appear to take them for granted. A host of such norms surround even the simplest conversation: a person engaged in conversation is expected to face toward his partner, rather than directly away from him; if his gaze is toward the partner, he is expected to look toward his eyes, rather than, say, toward his forehead; to stand at a proper conversational

distance, neither one inch away nor across the room, and so on. A person who regularly violated these expectations probably would not be thought to be merely ill-bred but strange, bizarre, and frightening, because his behavior violates the assumptive world of the group, the world that is construed to be the only one that is natural, decent, and possible.

The culture of the group provides a vocabularly of terms for categorizing many norm violations: crime, perversion, drunkenness, and bad manners are familiar examples. Each of these terms is derived from the type of norm broken, and ultimately from the type of behavior involved. After exhausting these categories, however, there is always a residue of the most diverse kinds of violations, for which the culture provides no explicit label. For example, although there is great cultural variation in what is defined as decent or real, each culture tends to reify its definition of decency and reality, and so provide no way of handling violations of its expectations in these areas. The typical norm governing decency or reality, therefore, literally "goes without saying," and its violation is unthinkable for most of its members. For the convenience of the society in construing those instances of unnamable deviance which are called to its attention, these violations may be lumped together into a residual category: witchcraft, spirit possession, or, in our own society, mental illness. In this paper, the diverse kinds of deviation for which our society provides no explicit label, and which, therefore, sometimes lead to the labeling of the violator as mentally ill, will be considered to be technically *residual deviance.*

THE ORIGINS, PREVALENCE, AND COURSE OF RESIDUAL DEVIANCE

The first proposition concerns the origins of residual deviance. *1. Residual deviance arises from fundamentally diverse sources.* It has been demonstrated that some types of mental disorder are the result of organic causes. It appears likely, therefore, that there are genetic, biochemical, or physiological origins for residual deviance. It also appears that residual deviance can arise from individual psychological peculiarities and from differences in upbringing and training. Residual deviance can also probably be produced by various kinds of external stress: the sustained fear and hardship of combat, and deprivation of food, sleep, and even sensory experience. Residual deviance, finally, can be a volitional act of innovation or defiance. The kinds of behavior deemed typical of mental illness, such as hallucinations, delusions, depression, and mania, can all arise from these diverse sources.

The second proposition concerns the prevalence of residual deviance which is analogous to the "total" or "true" prevalence of mental disorder (in contrast to the "treated" prevalence). *2. Relative to the rate of treated mental illness, the rate of unrecorded residual deviance is extremely high.* There is evidence that grossly deviant behavior is often not noticed or, if it is noticed, it is rationalized as eccentricity. Apparently, many persons who are extremely withdrawn, or who "fly off the handle" for extended periods of time, who imagine fantastic events, or who hear voices or see visions, are not labeled as insane either by themselves or others. Their deviance, rather, is unrecognized, ignored, or rationalized. This pattern of inattention and rationalization will be called "denial."

In addition to the kind of evidence cited above there are a number of epidemiological studies of total prevalence. There are numerous problems in interpreting the results of these studies; the major difficulty is that the definition of mental disorder is different in each study, as are the methods used to screen cases. These studies represent, however, the best available information and can be used to estimate total prevalence.

A convenient summary of findings is presented in Plunkett and Gordon (*Epidemiology and Mental Illness* [New York: Basic Books, 1960]). This source compares the methods and populations used in 11 field studies, and lists rates of total prevalence (in percentages)

as 1.7, 3.6, 4.5, 4.7, 5.3, 6.1, 10.9, 13.8, 23.2, 23.3, and 33.3.

How do these total rates compare with the rates of treated mental disorder? One of the studies cited by Plunkett and Gordon, the Baltimore study reported by Pasamanick, is useful in this regard since it includes both treated and untreated rates. As compared with the untreated rate of 10.9 percent, the rate of treatment in state, VA, and private hospitals of Baltimore residents was .5 percent. That is, for every mental patient there were approximately 20 untreated cases located by the survey. It is possible that the treated rate is too low, however, since patients treated by private physicians were not included. Judging from another study, the New Haven study of treated prevalence, the number of patients treated in private practice is small compared to those hospitalized: over 70 percent of the patients located in that study were hospitalized even though extensive case-finding techniques were employed. The overall treated prevalence in the New Haven study was reported at .8 percent, which is in good agreement with my estimate of .7 percent for the Baltimore study. If we accept .8 percent as an estimate of the upper limit of treated prevalence for the Pasamanick study, the ratio of treated to untreated cases is 1/14. That is, for every treated patient we should expect to find 14 untreated cases in the community.

One interpretation of this finding is that the untreated patients in the community represent those cases with less severe disorders, while those patients with severe impairments all fall into the treated group. Some of the findings in the Pasamanick study point in this direction. Of the untreated patients, about half are classified as psychoneurotic. Of the psychoneurotics, in turn, about half again are classified as suffering from minimal impairment. At least a fourth of the untreated group, then, involved very mild disorders.

The evidence from the group diagnosed as psychotic does not support this interpretation, however. Almost all of the cases diagnosed as psychotic were judged to involve severe impairment; yet half of the diagnoses of psychosis occurred in the untreated group. In other words, according to this study there were as many untreated as treated cases of psychoses.

On the basis of the high total prevalence rates cited above and other evidence, it seems plausible that residual deviant behavior is usually transitory, which is the substance of the third proposition. *3. Most residual deviance is "denied" and is transitory.* The high rates of total prevalence suggest that most residual deviancy is unrecognized or rationalized away. For this type of deviance, which is amorphous and uncrystallized, Lemert uses the term *primary deviation.* Balint describes similar behavior as "the unorganized phase of illness." Although Balint assumes that patients in this phase ultimately "settle down" to an "organized illness," other outcomes are possible. A person in this stage may "organize" his deviance in other than illness terms—e.g., as eccentricity or genius, or the deviant acts may terminate when situational stress is removed.

The experience of battlefield psychiatrists can be interpreted to support the hypothesis that residual deviance is usually transistory. Glass reports that combat neurosis is often self-terminating if the soldier is kept with his unit and given only the most superficial medical attention. Descriptions of child behavior can be interpreted in the same way. According to these reports, most children go through periods in which at least several of the following kinds of deviance may occur: temper tantrums, head banging, scratching, pinching, biting, fantasy playmates or pets, illusory physical complaints, and fears of sounds, shapes, colors, persons, animals, darkness, weather, ghosts, and so on. In the vast majority of instances, however, these behavior patterns do not become stable.

If residual deviance is highly prevalent among ostensibly "normal" persons and is usually transitory, as suggested by the last two propositions, what accounts for the small percentage of residual deviants who go on to deviant careers? To put the question another way, under what conditions is residual deviance stabilized? The conventional hypothesis is that the answer lies in the deviant himself. The hypothesis suggested here is that the most important single factor (but not the only factor) in the stabilization of residual deviance is the societal reaction. Residual deviance may be stabilized if it is defined to be evidence of mental illness, and/or the deviant is placed in a deviant status, and begins to play the role of the mentally ill. In order to avoid the implication that mental disorder is merely role-playing and pretense, it is first necessary to discuss the social institution of insanity.

SOCIAL CONTROL: INDIVIDUAL AND SOCIAL SYSTEMS OF BEHAVIOR

In *The Myth of Mental Illness*, Szasz proposes that mental disorder be viewed within the framework of "the game-playing model of human behavior." He then describes hysteria, schizophrenia, and other mental disorders as the "impersonation" of sick persons by those whose "real" problem concerns "problems of living." Although Szasz states that role-playing by mental patients may not be completely or even mostly voluntary, the implication is that mental disorder be viewed as a strategy chosen by the individual as a way of obtaining help from others. Thus, the term *impersonation* suggests calculated and deliberate shamming by the patient. In his comparisons of hysteria, malingering, and cheating, although he notes differences between these behavior patterns, he suggests that these differences may be mostly a matter of whose point of view is taken in describing the behavior.

The present paper also uses the role-playing model to analyze mental disorder, but places more emphasis on the involuntary aspects of role-playing than Szasz, who tends to treat role-playing as an individual system of behavior. In many social psychological discussions, however, role-playing is considered as a part of a social system. The individual plays his role by articulating his behavior with the cues and actions of other persons involved in the transaction. The proper performance of a role is dependent on having a cooperative audience. This proposition may also be reversed: having an audience which acts toward the individual in a uniform way may lead the actor to play the expected role even if he is not particularly interested in doing so. The "baby of the family" may come to find this role obnoxious, but the uniform pattern of cues and actions which confronts him in the family may lock in with his own vocabulary of responses so that it is inconvenient and difficult for him not to play the part expected of him. To the degree that alternative roles are closed off, the proffered role may come to be the only way the individual can cope with the situation.

One of Szasz's very apt formulations touches upon the social systemic aspects of role-playing. He draws an analogy between the role of the mentally ill and the "typecasting" of actors. Some actors get a reputation for playing one type of role, and find it difficult to obtain other roles. Although they may be displeased, they may also come to incorporate aspects of the type-cast role into their self-conceptions, and ultimately into their behavior. Findings in several social psychological studies suggest that an individual's role behavior may be shaped by the kinds of "deference" that he regularly receives from others.

One aspect of the voluntariness of role-playing is the extent to which the actor believes in the part he is playing. Although a role may be played cynically, with no belief, or completely sincerely, with wholehearted belief, many roles are played on the basis of an intricate mixture of belief and disbelief. During the course of a study of a large public mental hospital, several patients told the author in confidence about their cynical use of their symptoms—to frighten new personnel, to escape from unpleasant work details, and so on. Yet these *same* patients, at other times, appear to have been sincere in their symptomatic behavior. Apparently it was sometimes difficult for them to tell whether they were playing the role or the role

was playing them. Certain types of symptomatology are quite interesting in this connection. In simulation of previous psychotic states, and in the behavior pattern known to psychiatrists as the Ganser syndrome, it is apparently almost impossible for the observer to separate feigning of symptoms from involuntary acts with any degree of certainty. In accordance with what has been said so far, the difficulty is probably that the patient is just as confused by his own behavior as is the observer.

This discussion suggests that a stable role performance may arise when the actor's role imagery locks in with the type of "deference" which he regularly receives. An extreme example of this process may be taken from anthropological and medical reports concerning the "dead role," as in deaths attributed to "bone-pointing." Death from bone-pointing appears to arise from the conjunction of two fundamental processes which characterize all social behavior. First, all individuals continually orient themselves by means of responses which are perceived in social interaction: the individual's identity and continuity of experience are dependent on these cues. Second, the individual has his own vocabulary of expectations, which may in a particular situation either agree with or be in conflict with the sanctions to which he is exposed. Entry into a role may be complete when this role is part of the individual's expectations, and when these expectations are reaffirmed in social interaction. In the following pages this principle will be applied to the problem of the causation of mental disorder.

What are the beliefs and practices that constitute the social institution of insanity? And how do they figure in the development of mental disorder? Two propositions concerning beliefs about mental disorder in the general public will now be considered.

4. Stereotyped imagery of mental disorder is learned in early childhood. Although there are no substantiating studies in this area, scattered observations lead the author to conclude that children learn a considerable amount of imagery concerning deviance very early, and that much of the imagery comes from their peers rather than from adults. The literal meaning of "crazy," a term now used in a wide variety of contexts, is probably grasped by children during the first years of elementary school. Since adults are often vague and evasive in their responses to questions in this area, an aura of mystery surrounds it. In this socialization the grossest stereotypes which are heir to childhood fears—e.g., of the "boogie man"—survive. These conclusions are quite speculative, of course, and need to be investigated systematically, possibly with techniques similar to those used in studies of the early learning of racial stereotypes.

Assuming, however, that this hypothesis is sound, what effect does early learning have on the shared conceptions of insanity held in the community? There is much fallacious material learned in early childhood which is later discarded when more adequate information repplaces it. This question leads hypothesis 5.

5. *The stereotypes of insanity are continually reaffirmed, inadvertently, in ordinary social interaction.* Although many adults become acquainted with medical concepts of mental illness, the traditional stereotypes are not discarded, but continue to exist alongside the medical conceptions, because the stereotypes receive almost continual support from the mass media and in ordinary social discourse. In newspapers, it is a common practice to mention that a rapist or a murderer was once a mental patient. This negative information, however, is seldom offset by positive reports. An item like the following is almost inconceivable. "Mrs. Ralph Jones, an ex-mental patient, was elected president of the Fairview Home and Garden Society in their meeting last Thursday." Because of highly biased reporting, the reader is free to make the unwarranted inference that murder and rape occur more frequently among ex-mental patients than among the population at large. Actually, it has been demonstrated that the incidence of crimes of violence, or of any crime, is much lower among ex-mental patients than among the general popu-

lation. Yet, this is not the picture presented to the public.

Reaffirmation of the stereotype of insanity occurs not only in the mass media but also in ordinary conversation, in jokes, anecdotes, and even in conventional phrases. Such phrases as "Are you crazy?" or "It would be a madhouse" or "It's driving me out of my mind" or "It's driving me distracted" and hundreds of others occur frequently in informal conversations. In this usage insanity itself is seldom the topic of conversation; the phrases are so much a part of ordinary language that only the person who considers each word carefully can eliminate them from his speech. Through verbal usages the stereotypes of insanity are a relatively permanent part of the social structure.

In a recent study Nunnally demonstrated that reaffirmation of stereotypes occurs in the mass media. In a systematic and extensive content analysis of television, radio, newspapers, and magazines, including "confession" magazines, they found an image of mental disorder presented which was overwhelmingly stereotyped.

. . . media presentations emphasized the bizarre symptoms of the mentally ill. For example, information relating to Factor I (the conception that mentally ill persons look and act different from "normal" people) was recorded 89 times. Of these, 88 affirmed the factor—that is, indicated or suggested that people with mental-health problems "look and act different"; only one item denied Factor I. In television dramas, for example, the afflicted person often enters the scene staring glassy-eyed, with his mouth widely ajar, mumbling incoherent phrases or laughing uncontrollably. Even in what would be considered the milder disorders, neurotic phobias and obsessions, the afflicted person is presented as having bizarre facial expressions and actions.

DENIAL AND LABELING

According to the analysis presented here, the traditional stereotypes of mental disorder are solidly entrenched in the population because they are learned early in childhood and are continuously reaffirmed in the mass media and in everyday conversation. How do these beliefs function in the processes leading to mental disorder? This question will be considered by first referring to the earlier discussion of the societal reaction to residual deviance.

It was stated that the usual reaction to residual deviance is denial, and that in these cases most residual deviance is transitory. The societal reaction to deviance is not always denial, however. In a small proportion of cases the reaction goes the other way, exaggerating and at times distorting the extent and degree of deviation. This pattern of exaggeration, which we will call labeling, has been noted by Garfinkel in his discussion of the "degradation" of socially recognized criminals. Goffman makes a similar point in his description of the "discrediting" of mental patients. Apparently under some conditions the societal reaction to deviance is to seek out signs of abnormality in the deviant's history to show that he was always essentially a deviant.

The contrasting social reactions of denial and labeling provide a means of answering two fundamental questions. If deviance arises from diverse sources—physical, psychological, and situational—how does the uniformity of behavior that is associated with insanity develop? Second, if deviance is usually transitory, how does it become stabilized in those patients who become chronically deviant? To summarize, what are the sources of uniformity and stability of deviant behavior?

In the approach taken here the answer to this question is based on hypotheses 4 and 5, that the role imagery of insanity is learned early in childhood and is reaffirmed in social interaction. In a crisis, when the deviance of an individual becomes a public issue, the traditional stereotype of insanity becomes the guiding imagery for action, both for those reacting to the deviant and, at times, for the deviant himself. When societal agents and persons around the deviant react to him uniformly in terms of the traditional stereotypes of insanity, his amorphous and unstructured deviant behavior tends to crystallize in conformity to these expectations, thus becoming similar to the behavior of other de-

viants classified as mentally ill, and stable over time. The process of becoming uniform and stable is completed when the traditional imagery becomes a part of the deviant's orientation for guiding his own behavior.

The idea that cultural stereotypes may stabilize primary deviance and tend to produce uniformity in symptoms is supported by cross-cultural studies of mental disorder. Although some observers insist there are underlying similarities, most agree that there are enormous differences in the manifest symptoms of stable mental disorder *between* societies, and great similarity *within* societies.

These considerations suggest that the labeling process is a crucial contingency in most careers of residual deviance. Thus Glass, who observed that neuropsychiatric casualties may not become mentally ill if they are kept with their units, goes on to say that military experience with psychotherapy has been disappointing. Soldiers who are removed from their units to a hospital he states, often go on to become chronically impaired. That is, their deviance is stabilized by the labeling process, which is implicit in their removal and hospitalization. A similar interpretation can be made by comparing the observations of childhood disorders among Mexican-Americans with those of "Anglo" children. Childhood disorders such as *susto* (an illness believed to result from fright) sometimes have damaging outcomes in Mexican-American children. Yet the deviant behavior involved is very similar to that which seems to have high incidence among Anglo children, with permanent impairment virtually never occurring. Apparently through cues from his elders the Mexican-American child, behaving initially much like his Anglo counterpart, learns to enter the sick role, at times with serious consequences.

ACCEPTANCE OF THE DEVIANT ROLE

From this point of view, then, most mental disorder can be considered to be a social role. This social role complements and reflects the status of the insane in the social structure. It is through the social processes which maintain the status of the insane that the varied deviancies from which mental disorder arises are made uniform and stable. The stabilization and uniformization of residual deviance are completed when the deviant accepts the role of the insane as the framework within which he organizes his own behavior. Three hypotheses are stated below which suggest some of the processes which cause the deviant to accept such a stigmatized role.

6. Labeled deviants may be rewarded for playing the stereotyped deviant role. Ordinarily patients who display "insight" are rewarded by psychiatrists and other personnel. That is, patients who manage to find evidence of "their illness" in their past and present behavior, confirming the medical and societal diagnosis, receive benefits. This pattern of behavior is a special case of a more general pattern that has been called the "apostolic function" by Balint, in which the physician and others inadvertently cause the patient to display symptoms of the illness the physician thinks the patient has. Not only physicians but other hospital personnel and even other patients reward the deviant for conforming to the stereotypes.

7. Labeled deviants are punished when they attempt the return to conventional roles The second process operative is the systematic blockage of entry to nondeviant roles once the label has been publicly applied. Thus the ex-mental patient, although he is urged to rehabilitate himself in the community, usually finds himself discriminated against in seeking to return to his old status and on trying to find a new one in the occupational, marital, social, and other spheres. Thus, to a degree, the labeled deviant is rewarded for deviating and punished for attempting to conform.

8. In the crisis occurring when a primary deviant is publicly labeled, the deviant is highly suggestible, and may accept the proffered role of the insane as the only alternative. When gross deviancy is publicly recognized and made an issue, the primary deviant may be profoundly confused, anxious, and ashamed. In this crisis it seems reasonable to assume

that the deviant will be suggestible to the cues that he gets from the reactions of others toward him. But those around him are also in a crisis; the incomprehensible nature of the deviance and the seeming need for immediate action lead them to take collective action against the deviant on the basis of the attitude which all share—the traditional stereotypes of insanity. The deviant is sensitive to the cues provided by these others and begins to think of himself in terms of the stereotyped role of insanity, which is part of his own role vocabularly also, since he, like those reacting to him, learned it early in childhood. In this situation his behavior may begin to follow the pattern suggested by his own stereotypes and the reactions of others. That is, when a primary deviant organizes his behavior within the framework of mental disorder, and when his organization is validated by others, particularly prestigeful others such as physicians, he is "hooked" and will proceed on a career of chronic deviance.

The role of suggestion is noted by Warner in his description of bone-pointing magic:

The effect of (the suggestion of the entire community on the victim) is obviously drastic. An analogous situation in our society is hard to imagine. If all a man's near kin, his father, mother, brothers and sisters, wife, children, business associates, friends and all the other members of the society, should suddenly withdraw themselves because of some dramatic circumstance, refusing to take any attitude but one of taboo . . . and then perform over him a sacred ceremony . . . the enormous suggestive power of this movement . . . of the community after it has had its attitudes (toward the victim) crystallized can be somewhat understood by ourselves.

If we substitute for black magic the taboo that usually accompanies mental disorder, and consider a commitment proceeding or even mental hospital admission as a sacred ceremony, the similarity between Warner's description and the typical events in the development of mental disorder is considerable.

The last three propositions suggest that once a person has been placed in a deviant status there are rewards for conforming to the deviant role, and punishments for not conforming to the deviant role. This is not to imply, however, that the symptomatic behavior of persons occupying a deviant status is always a manifestation of conforming behavior. To explain this point, some discussion of the process of self-control in "normals" is necessary.

In a recent discussion of the process of self-control, Shibutani notes that self-control is not automatic, but is an intricate and delicately balanced process, sustainable only under propitious circumstances. He points out that fatigue, the reaction to narcotics, excessive excitement or tension (such as is generated in mobs), or a number of other conditions interfere with self-variety of contingencies which lead to labeling rather than denial, these contingencies can be usefully classified in terms of the nature of the deviant behavior, the person who commits the deviant acts, and the community in which the deviance occurs. Other things being equal, the severity of the societal reaction to deviance is a function of, first, the degree, amount, and visibility of the deviant behavior; second, the power of the deviant, and the social distance between the deviant and the agents of social control; and finally, the tolerance level of the community, and the availability in the culture of the community of alternative nondeviant roles. Particularly crucial for future research is the importance of the first two contingencies (the amount and degree of deviance), which are characteristics of the deviant, relative to the remaining five contingencies, which are characteristics of the social system. To the extent that these five factors are found empirically to be independent determinants of labeling and

denial, the status of the mental patient can be considered a partly ascribed rather than a completely achieved status. The dynamics of treated mental illness could then be profitably studied quite apart from the individual dynamics of mental disorder.

CONCLUSION

This paper has presented a sociological theory of the causation of stable mental disorder. Since the evidence advanced in support of the theory was scattered and fragmentary, it can only be suggested as a stimulus to further discussion and research. Among the areas pointed out for further investigation are field studies of the prevalence and duration of residual deviance; investigations of stereotypes of mental disorder in children, the mass media, and adult conversations; studies of the rewarding of stereotyped deviation, blockage of return to conventional roles, and of the suggestibility of primary deviants in crises. The final causal hypothesis suggests studies of the conditions under which denial and labeling of residual deviation occur. The variables which might effect the societal reaction concern the nature of the deviance, the deviant himself, and the community in which the deviation occurs. Although many of the hypotheses suggested are largely unverified, they suggest avenues for investigating mental disorder different than those that are usually followed, and the rudiments of a general theory of deviant behavior.

15. DEVIANCE DISAVOWAL AND THE VISIBLY HANDICAPPED

FRED DAVIS

Reprinted with permission from "Deviance Disavowal: The Management of Strained Interaction by the Visibly Handicapped," Social Problems 9 (Fall 1961): 120-32. Copyright 1961 by The Society for the Study of Social Problems. Fred Davis is Professor of Sociology at the University of California Medical Center, San Francisco. His work has been described in the introduction to Selection 8.

■ The visibly handicapped, as Goffman observes in Section 2, often are subject to labeling as deviant, a particularly nasty reaction on the part of society since the handicapped are so clearly not responsible for their situation. Yet this response seems deeply rooted and persistent despite much exhortation to the contrary. In this selection Fred Davis analyzes how visibly handicapped persons cope with the strained face-to-face interaction that results. He shows that despite the tenacity of the deviant label both the handicapped person and others have an interest in carrying out "normal" interaction and that both are likely to try to disavow their initial perceptions of the situation.

Useful reviews of sociological and social psychological research on the physically handicapped can be found in R. G. Barker et al., *Adjustment to Physical Handicap and Illness: A Survey of the Social Psychology of Physique and Disability* (Social Science Research Council, 1953); and Frances C. MacGregor et al., *Facial Deformities and Plastic Surgery: A Psycho-Social Study* (Charles C. Thomas, 1953). See also Marvin B. Sussman, et al., *Walking Patient: A Study in Outpatient Care* (Case Western Reserve Press, 1967). ■

A RECURRING ISSUE in social relations is the refusal of those who are viewed as deviant to concur in the verdict. Or, if in some sense it can be said that they do concur, they usually place a very different interpretation on the fact or allegation than do their judges. In our society this is especially true of deviance which partakes to ascription (e.g., the Negro) as against that which partakes to some significant degree of election (e.g., the homosexual). And while it may be conjectured

that ultimately neither the Negro nor the homosexual would be cast in a deviant role were it not for society's devaluation of these attributes in the first place, barring such a hypothetical contingency it remains the more persuasive argument in a democracy to be able to claim that the social injury from which one suffers was in no way self-inflicted.

In these pages I wish to discuss another kind of non-self-inflicted social injury, the visible physical handicap. My aim, though, is not to survey and describe the many hardships of the visibly handicapped but to analyze certain facets of their coping behavior as it relates to the generalized imputations of deviance they elicit from society, imputations which many of them feel it necessary to resist and reject.

There are, of course, many areas in which such imputations bear heavily upon them: employment, friendship, courtship, sex, travel, recreation, residence, education. But the area I treat here is enmeshed to some extent in all of these without being as categorically specific as any. I refer to situations of sociability, and more specifically to that genre of everyday intercourse which has the characteristics of being: (1) face-to-face; (2) prolonged enough to permit more than a fleeting glimpse or exchange, but not so prolonged that close familiarity immediately ensues; (3) intimate to the extent that the parties must pay more than perfunctory attention to one another, but not so intimate that the customary social graces can be dispensed with; and (4) ritualized to the extent that all know in general what to expect, but not so ritualized as to preclude spontaneity and the slightly novel turn of events. A party or other social affair, a business introduction, getting to know a person at work, meeting neighbors, dealing with a salesman, conversing with a fellow passenger, staying at a resort hotel—these are but a few of the everyday social situations which fall within this portion of the spectrum of sociability, a range of involvement which can also be thought of as the zone of first impressions.

In interviews I conducted with a small number of very articulate and socially skilled informants who were visibly handicapped I inquired into their handling of the imputation that they were not "normal, like everyone else." This imputation usually expresses itself in a pronounced stickiness of interactional flow and in the embarrassment of the normal by which he conveys the all too obvious message that he is having difficulty in relating to the handicapped person as he would to "just an ordinary man or woman." Frequently he will make *faux pas,* slips of the tongue, revealing gestures and inadvertent remarks which overtly betray this attitude and place the handicapped person in an even more delicate situation. The triggering of such a chain of interpersonal incidents is more likely with new persons than with those with whom the handicapped have well-established and continuing relations. Hence the focus here on more or less sociable occasions, it being these in which interactional discomfort is felt most acutely and coping behavior is brought into relief most sharply.

Because the visibly handicapped do not comprise a distinct minority group or subculture, the imputations of generalized deviance that they elicit from many normals are more nearly genuine interactional emergents than conventionalized sequels to intergroup stereotyping as, for example, might obtain between a Negro and White. A sociable encounter between a visibly handicapped person and a normal is usually more subject to ambiguity and experimentation in role postures than would be the case were the parties perceived by each other primarily in terms of member group characteristics. The visibly handicapped person must with each

new acquaintance explore the *possibilities* of a relationship. As a rule there is no ready-made symbolic shorthand (e.g., "a southerner can't treat a Negro as a social equal," "the Irish are anti-Semitic," "working class people think intellectuals are effeminate") for anticipating the quality and degree of acceptance to be accorded him. The exchange must be struck before its dangers and potentialities can be seen and before appropriate corrective maneuvers can be fed into the interaction.

THE HANDICAP AS THREAT TO SOCIABLE INTERACTION

Before discussing how the visibly handicapped cope with difficult interaction, it is appropriate to first consider the general nature of the threat posed to the interactional situation per se as a result of their being perceived routinely (if not necessarily according to some prevalent stereotype) as "different," "odd," "estranged from the common run of humanity," etc.; in short, other than normal. (Achieving ease and naturalness of interaction with normals serves naturally as an important index to the handicapped person of the extent to which his preferred definition of self—i.e., that of someone who is merely different physically but not socially deviant—has been accepted. Symbolically, as long as the interaction remains stiff, strained, or otherwise mired in inhibition, he has good reason to believe that he is in effect being denied the status of social normalcy he aspires to or regards as his due.) The threat posed by the handicap to sociability is, at minimum, fourfold: its tendency to become an exclusive focal point of the interaction, its potential for inundating expressive boundaries, its discordance with other attributes of the person and, finally, its ambiguity as a predicator of joint activity. These are not discrete entities in themselves as much as varying contextual emergents which, depending on the particular situation, serve singly or in combination to strain the framework of normative rules and assumptions in which sociability develops. Let us briefly consider each in turn.

A FOCAL POINT OF INTERACTION

The rules of sociable interaction stipulate a certain generality and diffuseness in the attentions that parties are expected to direct to each other. Even if only superficially, one is expected to remain oriented to the whole person and to avoid the expression of a precipitous or fixed concern with any single attribute of his, however noteworthy or laudable it may be. When meeting someone with a visible handicap, a number of perceptual and interpretative responses occur which make adherence to this rule tenuous for many. First, there is the matter of visibility as such. By definition, the visibly handicapped person cannot control his appearance sufficiently so that its striking particularity will not call a certain amount of concentrated attention to itself. Second, the normal, while having his attention so narrowly channeled, is immediately constrained by the requirements of sociability to act as if he were oriented to the totality of the other rather than to that which is uppermost in his awareness—i.e., the handicap. Although the art of sociability may be said to thrive on a certain playful discrepancy between felt and expressed interests, it is perhaps equally true that when these are too discrepant strain and tension begin to undermine the interaction. (Conversely, when not discrepant enough, flatness and boredom frequently ensue.) Whether the handicap is overtly and tactlessly responded to as such or, as is more commonly the case, no explicit reference is made to it, the underlying condition of heightened, narrowed awareness causes the interaction to be articulated too exclusively in terms of it. This, as my informants described it, is usually accompanied by one or more of the familiar signs of discomfort and stickiness: the guarded references, the common everyday words suddenly made taboo, the fixed stare elsewhere, the artificial levity, the compulsive loquaciousness, the awkward solemnity.

Second-order interactional elaborations of the underlying impedance are also not uncommon. Thus, for example, the normal may take great pains to disguise his awareness, an exertion that is usually so effortful and transparent that the handicapped person is then enjoined to disguise his awareness of the normal's disguise. In turn, the normal sensing the disguise erected in response to his disguise . . . and so forth. But unlike the infinitely multiplying reflections of an object located between opposing mirrors, this process cannot sustain itself for long without the pretense of unawareness collapsing, as witness the following report by a young woman.

> I get suspicious when somebody says, "Let's go for a uh, ah [imitates confused and halting speech] push with me down the hall," or something like that. This to me is suspicious because it means that they're aware, really aware, that there's a wheelchair here, and that this is probably uppermost with them. . . . A lot of people in trying to show you that they don't care that you're in a chair will do crazy things. Oh, there's one person I know who constantly kicks my chair, as if to say, "I don't care that you're in a wheelchair. I don't even know that it's there." But that is just an indication that he *really* knows it's there.

INUNDATING POTENTIAL

The expressive requirements of sociability are such that rather strict limits obtain with respect to the types and amount of emotional display that are deemed appropriate. Even such fitting expressions as gaiety and laughter can, we know, reach excess and lessen satisfaction with the occasion. For many normals, the problem of sustaining sociable relations with someone who is visibly handicapped is not wholly that of the discrepancy of the inner feeling evoked—e.g., pity, fear, repugnance, avoidance. As with much else in sociability, a mere discrepancy of the actor's inner state with the social expectation need not result in a disturbance of interaction. In this instance it is specifically the marked dissonance of such emotions with those outward expressions deemed most salient for the occasion (e.g., pleasure, identification, warm interest) that seems to result frequently in an inundation and enfeeblement of the expressive controls of the individual. With some persons, the felt intrusion of this kind of situationally inappropriate emotion is so swift and overwhelming as to approximate a state of shock, leaving them expressively naked, so to speak. A pointed incident is told by a young blind girl.

One night when I was going to visit a friend two of the people from my office put me into a taxi. I could tell that at first the taxi driver didn't know I was blind because for a while there he was quite a conversationalist. Then he asked me what these sticks were for [a collapsible cane]. I told him it was a cane, and then he got so different. . . . He didn't talk about the same things that he did at first. Before this happened he joked and said, "Oh, you're a very quiet person. I don't like quiet people, they think too much." And he probably wouldn't have said that to me had he known I was blind because he'd be afraid of hurting my feelings. He didn't say anything like that afterwards.

The visibly handicapped are, of course, aware of this potential for inundating the expressive boundaries of situations, and many take precautions to minimize such occurrences as much as possible. Thus, an interior decorator with a facial deformity would when admitted to a client's house by the maid station himself whenever he could so that the client's entrance would find him in a distantly direct line of vision from her. This, he stated, gave the client an opportunity to compose herself, as she might not be able to were she to come upon him at short range.

CONTRADICTION OF ATTRIBUTES

Even when the inundating potential is well contained by the parties and the normal proves fully capable of responding in a more differentiated fashion to the variety of attributes presented by the handicapped person (e.g., his occupational identity, clothes, speech, intelligence, interests, etc.), there is frequently felt to be an unsettling discordance between these and the handicap. Sociable interaction is made more difficult as a result because many normals can resolve the seeming incongruence only by assimilating or subsuming (often in a patronizing or condescending way) the other attributes to that of the handicap, a phenomenon which in analogous connections has been well described by Hughes. Thus, one informant, a strikingly attractive girl, reports that she frequently elicits from new acquaintances the comment, "How strange that someone so pretty should be in a wheelchair." Another informant, a professional worker for a government agency, tells of the fashionable female client who after having inquired on how long the informant had been in her job remarked, "How nice that you have something to do." Because the art of sociability deigns this kind of reductionism of the person, expressions of this type, even when much less blatant, almost invariably cast a pall on the interaction and embarrass the recovery of smooth social posture. The general threat inherent in the perceived discordance of personal attributes is given pointed expression by still another informant, a paraplegic of upper middle class background who comments on the attitude of many persons in his class.

Now, where this affects them, where this brace and a crutch would affect them, is if they are going someplace or if they are doing something, they feel that, first, you would call attention and, second—you wouldn't believe this but it's true; I'll use the cruelest words I can—no cripple could possibly be in their social stratum.

AMBIGUOUS PREDICATOR

Finally, to the extent to which sociability is furthered by the free and spontaneous initiation of joint activity (e.g., dancing, games, going out to eat—in short, "doing things") there is frequently considerable ambiguity as regards the ability of the handicapped person to so participate and as regards the propriety of efforts which seek to ascertain whether he wants to. For the normal who has had limited experience with the handicapped it is by no means always clear whether, for example, a blind person can be included in a theater party or a crippled person in a bowling game. Even if not able to engage in the projected activity as such, will he want to come along mainly for the sake of company? How may his preferences be gauged without, on the one hand, appearing to "make a thing" out of the proposal or, on the other, conveying the impression that his needs and limitations are not being sufficiently considered? Should he refuse, is it genuine or is he merely offering his hosts a polite, though halfhearted, out? And, for each enigma thus posed for the normal, a counterenigma is posed for the handicapped person. Do they really want him? Are they merely being polite? In spite of the open invitation, will his acceptance and presence lessen somehow their enjoyment of the activity? It is easy to see how a profusion of anticipatory ambiguities of this kind can strain the operative assumptions underlying sociable relations.

PROCESS OF DEVIANCE DISAVOWAL AND NORMALIZATION

The above features, then, may be said to comprise the threat that a visible handicap poses to the framework of rules and assumptions that guide sociability. We may now ask how socially adept handicapped persons cope with it so as to keep it at bay, dissipate it, or lessen its impact upon the interaction. In answering this question we will not consider those broad personality adjustments of the person (e.g., aggression, denial, compensation, dissociation) which at a level once removed, so to speak, can be thought of as adaptive or maladaptive for, among other things, sociability. Nor, at the other extreme, is it possible in the allotted space to review the tremendous variety of specific approaches, ploys, and stratagems that the visibly handicapped employ in social situations. Instead, the analysis will attempt to delineate in transactional terms the stages through which a sociable relationship with a normal typically passes, assuming, of course, that the confrontation takes place and that both parties possess sufficient social skill to sustain a more than momentary engagement.

For present purposes we shall designate these stages as: (1) fictional acceptance, (2) the facilitation of reciprocal role-taking around a normalized projection of self and

(3) the institutionalization in the relationship of a definition of self that is normal in its moral dimension, however qualified it may be with respect to its situational contexts. As we shall indicate, the unfolding of these stages comprises what may be thought of as a process of deviance disavowal or normalization, depending on whether one views the process from the vantage point of the "deviant" actor or his alters.

FICTIONAL ACCEPTANCE

In Western society the overture phases of a sociable encounter are to a pronounced degree regulated by highly elastic fictions of equality and normalcy. In meeting those with whom we are neither close nor familiar, manners dictate that we refrain from remarking on or otherwise reacting too obviously to those aspects of their persons which in the privacy of our thoughts betoken important differences between ourselves. In America at least, these fictions tend to encompass sometimes marked divergencies in social status as well as a great variety of expressive styles; and it is perhaps the extreme flexibility of such fictions in our culture rather than, as is mistakenly assumed by many foreign observers, their absence that accounts for the seeming lack of punctiliousness in American manners. The point is nicely illustrated in the following new item.

NUDE TAKES A STROLL IN MIAMI
MIAMI, Fla., Nov. 13 (UPI)—A shapely brunette slowed traffic to a snail's pace here yesterday with a 20-minute nude stroll through downtown Miami. . . .
"The first thing I knew something was wrong," said Biscayne Bay bridge-tender E. E. Currey, who was working at his post about one block away, "was when I saw traffic was going unusually slow."
Currey said he looked out and called police. They told him to stop the woman, he said.
Currey said he walked out of his little bridge house, approached the woman nervously, and asked, "Say, girl, are you lost?"
"Yes," she replied. "I'm looking for my hotel."
Currey offered help and asked, "Say, did you lose your clothes?"
"No," he said the woman replied, "Why?"
Currey said that he had to step away for a

moment to raise the bridge for a ship and the woman walked away. . . .

Unlike earlier societies and some present-day ones in which a visible handicap automatically relegates the person to a castelike, inferior status like that of mendicant, clown, or thief—or more rarely to an elevated one like that of oracle or healer—in our society the visibly handicapped are customarily accorded, save by children, the surface acceptance that democratic manners guarantee to nearly all. But, as regards sociability, this proves a mixed blessing for many. Although the polite fictions do afford certain entrée rights, as fictions they can too easily come to serve as substitutes for "the real thing" in the minds of their perpetrators. The interaction is kept starved at a bare subsistence level of sociability. As with the poor relation at the wedding party, so the reception given the handicapped person in many social situations: sufficient that he is here, he should not expect to dance with the bride.

At this stage of the encounter, the interactional problem confronting the visibly handicapped person is the delicate one of not permitting his identity to be circumscribed by the fiction while at the same time playing along with it and showing appropriate regard for its social legitimacy. For, as transparent and confining as the fiction is, it frequently is the only basis upon which the contact can develop into something more genuinely sociable. In those instances in which the normal fails or refuses to render even so small a gesture toward normalizing the situation, there exists almost no basis for the handicapped person to successfully disavow his deviance. The following occurrence related by a young female informant is an apt, if somewhat extreme, illustration.

I was visiting my girl friend's house and I was sitting in the lobby waiting for her when this woman comes out of her apartment and starts asking me questions. She just walked right up. I didn't know her from Adam; I never saw her before in my life. "Gee, what do you have? How long have you been that way? Oh gee, that's terrible." And so I answered her questions, but I got very annoyed and wanted to say, "Lady, mind your own business."

"BREAKING THROUGH"—FACILITATING NORMALIZED ROLE-TAKING

In moving beyond fictional acceptance what takes place essentially is a redefinitional process in which the handicapped person projects images, attitudes, and concepts of self which encourage the normal to identify with him (i.e., "take his role") in terms other than those associated with imputations of deviance. Coincidentally, in broadening the area of minor verbal involvements, this also functions to drain away some of the stifling burden of unspoken awareness that, as we have seen, so taxes ease of interaction. The normal is cued into a larger repertoire of appropriate responses, and even when making what he, perhaps mistakenly, regards as an inappropriate response (for example, catching himself in the use of such a word as cripple or blind) the handicapped person can by his response relieve him of his embarrassment. One young informant insightfully termed the process "breaking through."

The first reaction a normal individual or good-legger has is, "Oh gee, there's a fellow in a wheelchair," or "there's a fellow with a brace." And they don't say, "Oh gee, there is so-and-so, he's handsome" or "he's intelligent," or "he's a boor," or what have you. And then as the relationship develops they don't see the handicap. It doesn't exist any more. And that's the point that you as a handicapped individual become sensitive to. You know after talking with someone for awhile when they don't see the handicap any more. That's when you've broken through.

What this process signifies from a social psychological standpoint is that as the handicapped person expands the interactional nexus he simultaneously disavows the deviancy latent in his status; concurrently, to the degree to which the normal is led to reciprocally assume the redefining (and perhaps unanticipated) self-attitudes proffered by the handicapped person, he comes to normalize (i.e., view as more like himself) those aspects of the other which at first connoted deviance for him. (Sometimes, as we shall see, the normal's normalizing is so complete that it is unwittingly applied to situations in which the handicapped person cannot possibly function "normally" due to sheer physical limitations.) These dynamics might also be termed a process of identification. The term is immaterial, except that in "identifying" or "taking the role of the other" much more is implicated sociologically than a mere subjective congruence of responses. The fashioning of shared perspectives also implies a progressively more binding legitimation of the altered self-representations enacted in the encounter; that is, having once normalized his perception of the handicapped person, it becomes increasingly more compromising—self-discrediting, as it were—for the normal to revert to treating him as a deviant again.

The ways in which the visibly handicapped person can go about disavowing deviance are, as we have stated, many and varied. These range from relatively straightforward conversational offerings, in which he alludes in passing to his involvement in a normal round of activities, to such forms of indirection as interjecting taboo or privatized references by way of letting the normal know that he does not take offense at the latter's uneasiness or regard it as a fixed obstacle toward achieving rapport. In the above quote, for example, the informant speaks of "good-leggers," an in-group term from his rehabilitation hospital days, which along with "dirty normals" he sometimes uses with new acquaintances "because it has a humorous connotation . . . and lots of times it puts people at their ease."

Still other approaches to disavowing deviance and bridging fictional acceptance include: an especially attentive and sympathetic stance with respect to topics introduced by the normal; showing oneself to be a comic, wit or other kind of gifted participant; and, for some, utilizing the normalization potential inherent in being seen in the company of a highly presentable normal companion. These, and others too numerous to mention, are not, of course, invariably or equally successful in all cases; neither are such resources equally available to all handicapped persons, nor are the handicapped equally adept at exploiting them. As a class of corrective strategies,

however, they have the common aim of overcoming the interactional barrier that lies between narrow fictional acceptance and more spontaneous forms of relatedness.

Inextricably tied in with the matter of approach are considerations of setting, activity, and social category of participants, certain constellations of which are generally regarded as favorable for successful deviance disavowal and normalization while others are thought unfavorable. Again, the ruling contingencies appear to be the extent to which the situation is seen as containing elements in it which: (1) contextually reduce the threat posed by the visible handicap to the rules and assumptions of the particular sociable occasion; and (2) afford the handicapped person opportunities for "breaking through" beyond fictional acceptance.

The relevance of one or both of these is apparent in the following social situations and settings about which my informants expressed considerable agreement as regards their preferences, aversions, and inner reactions. To begin with, mention might again be made of the interactional rule violations frequently experienced at the hands of small children. Many of the informants were quite open in stating that a small child at a social occasion caused them much uneasiness and cramped their style because they were concerned with how, with other adults present, they would handle some barefaced question from the child. Another category of persons with whom many claimed to have difficulty is the elderly. Here the problem was felt to be the tendency of old people to indulge in patronizing sympathy, an attitude which peculiarly resists redefinition because of the fulsome virtue it attributes to itself. In another context several of the informants laid great stress on the importance of maintaining a calm exterior whenever the physical setting unavoidably exposed them to considerable bodily awkwardness. (At the same time, of course, they spoke of the wisdom of avoiding, whenever possible, such occasions altogether.) Their attitude was that to expressively reflect gracelessness and a loss of control would result in further interactional obstacles toward assimilating the handicapped person to a normal status.

It makes me uncomfortable to watch anyone struggling, so I try to do what I must as inconspicuously as possible. In new situations or in strange places, even though I may be very anxious, I will maintain a deadly calm. For example, if people have to lift the chair and I'm scared that they are going to do it wrong, I remain perfectly calm and am very direct in the instructions I give.

As a final example, there is the unanimity with which the informants expressed a strong preference for the small as against the large or semipublic social gathering. They believe not only that, as one handicapped person among the nonhandicapped, they stand out more at large social gatherings but also that in the anonymity which numbers further there resides a heightened structural tendency for normals to practice avoidance relations with them. The easy assumption on such occasions is that "some other good soul" will take responsibility for socializing with the handicapped person. Even in the case of the handicapped person who is forward and quite prepared to take the initiative in talking to others, the organization and ecology of the large social gathering is usually such as to frustrate his attempts to achieve a natural, nondeviant, place for himself in the group. As one young man, a paraplegic, explained:

The large social gathering presents a special problem. It's a matter of repetition. When you're in a very large group of people whom you don't know, you don't have an opportunity of talking to three, four or five at a time. Maybe you'll talk to one or two usually. After you've gone through a whole basic breakdown in making a relationship with one—after all, it's only a cocktail party—to do it again, and again, and again, it's wearing and it's no good. You don't get the opportunity to really develop something.

INSTITUTIONALIZATION OF THE NORMALIZED RELATIONSHIP

In "breaking through" many of the handicapped are confronted by a delicate paradox, particularly in those of their relationships which continue beyond the immediate occasion. Having disavowed deviance and induced the other to respond to him as he would to a normal, the problem then becomes one of sustaining the normalized definition in the face of many small amendments and qualifications that must frequently be made to it. The person confined to a wheelchair, for example, must brief new acquaintances on what to do and how to help when they come to stairs, doorways, vehicle entrances, etc. Further briefings and rehearsals may be required for social obstructions as well: for example, how to act in an encounter with—to cite some typical situations at random—an overly helpful person, a waitress who communicates to the handicapped person only through his companion, a person who stares in morbid fascination.

Generally, such amendments and special considerations are as much as possible underplayed in the early stages of the relationship because, as in the case of much minority group protest, the fundamental demand of the handicapped is that they first be granted an irreducibly equal and normal status, it being only then regarded as fitting and safe to admit to certain incidental incapacities, limitations, and needs. At some point however, the latter must be broached if the relationship to the normal is to endure in viable form. But to integrate effectively a major claim to "normalcy" with numerous minor waivers of the same claim is a tricky feat and one which exposes the relationship to the many situational and psychic hazards of apparent duplicity: the tension of transferring the special arrangements and understandings worked out between the two to situations and settings in which everyone else is "behaving normally"; the sometimes lurking suspicion of the one that it is only guilt or pity that cements the relationship, of the other that the infirmity is being used exploitatively, and of onlookers that there is something "neurotic" and "unhealthy" about it all.

From my informants' descriptions it appears that this third, "normal, but . . ." stage of the relationship, if it endures, is institutionalized mainly in either one of two ways. In the first, the normal normalizes his perceptions to such an extent as to suppress his effective awareness of many of the areas in which the handicapped person's behavior unavoidably deviates from the normal standard. In this connection several of the informants complained that a recurring problem they have with close friends is that the latter frequently overlook the fact of the handicap and the restrictions it imposes on them. The friends thoughtlessly make arrangements and involve them in activities in which they, the handicapped, cannot participate conveniently or comfortably.

The other major direction in which the relationship is sometimes institutionalized is for the normal to surrender some of his normalcy by joining the handicapped person in a marginal, half-alienated, half-tolerant, outsider's orientation to "the Philistine world of normals." Gowman nicely describes the tenor and style of this relationship and its possibilities for sharply disabusing normals of their stereotyped approaches to the handicapped. *Epater le bourgeois* behavior is often prominently associated with it, as is a certain strictly in-group license to lampoon and mock the handicap in a way which would be regarded as highly offensive were it to come from an uninitiated normal. Thus, a blind girl relates how a sighted friend sometimes chides her by calling her "a silly blink." A paraplegic tells of the old friend who tries to revive his flagging spirits by telling him not to act "like a helpless cripple." Unlike that based on overnormalization, the peculiar strength of this relationship is perhaps its very capacity to give expressive scope to the negative reality of the larger world of which it is inescapably a part while simultaneously removing itself from a primary identification with it.

IMPLICATIONS

Two, more general, implications seem worth drawing from this analysis.

First, in studies which trace the process wherein an actor who deviates comes to be increasingly defined as a deviant (e.g., the premental patient, the prealcoholic, the pre-juvenile delinquent), unusual prominence is given to the normalizing behavior of those close to him (spouse, parents, friends, etc.). The picture that emerges is one of these persons assuming nearly the whole burden— by rationalizing, denying, and overlooking his offensive acts—of attempting to reestablish a socially acceptable relationship with him. He is depicted typically as compulsively wedded to his deviance and incapable or uninterested in making restitutive efforts of his own. Finally, following some critical act of his, normalization fails *in toto* and community agencies are called in to relieve the primary group of its unmanageable burden.

There is much about this picture that is doubtlessly true and consonant with the ascertainable facts as we later come to learn of them from family, friends, police, courts, and social agencies. We may question, however, whether it is a wholly balanced picture and whether, given the situational biases of these informational sources, all of the relevant facts have had an equal chance to surface. The perspective developed here suggests that it may be useful to consider whether, and to what extent, the deviator himself is not also engaged, albeit ineffectively, in somehow trying to sustain a normal definition of his person. Were research to indicate that such is the case, we might then ask what it is about his reparative efforts and the situations in which they occur that, as contrasted with the subjects of this study, so often lead to failure and an exacerbation of the troublesome behavior. (We probably will never know, except inferentially by gross extrapolation, of the possibly many cases in which some such interactive process succeeds in favorably resolving the deviating behavior.). In other words, as against the simplistic model of a compulsive deviant and a futile normalizer we would propose one in which it is postulated that both are likely to become engaged in making corrective interactional efforts toward healing the breach. And when such efforts fail, as they frequently do, it is as important in accounting for the failure to weigh the interactional dynamics and situational contexts of these efforts as it is the nature of the deviant acts and the actor.

Second, we would note that the interactional problems of the visibly handicapped are not so dissimilar from those which all of us confront, if only now and then and to a lesser degree. We, too, on occasion find ourselves in situations in which some uncamouflagable attribute of ours jars the activity and the expectations of our company. We, too, if we wish to sustain—and, as is typically the case, our company wishes us to sustain—a fitting and valued representation of ourselves, will tacitly begin to explore with them ways of redressing, insulating, and separating the discrepant attribute from ourselves. Our predicament, though, is much less charged with awareness, more easily set to rights, than that of the visibly handicapped person and his company. But it is precisely this exaggeration of a common interactional predicament that affords us an added insight into the prerequisites and unwitting assumptions of sociable behavior in general. Put differently, it can be said that our understanding of a mechanism is often crude and incomplete until it breaks down and we try to repair it. Breakdown and repair of interaction is what many of the visibly handicapped experience constantly in their lives. In studying this with them we are also studying much about ourselves of which we were heretofore unaware.

16. THE DRUNK'S MORAL PASSAGE

JOSEPH R. GUSFIELD

*Reprinted from "Moral Passage: The Symbolic Process in Public Designations of Deviance,"
Social Problems 15 (Fall 1967): 175-88 with permission of The Society for the Study of
Social Problems and the author. Joseph R. Gusfield is Professor and Chairman of the
Department of Sociology, University of California at San Diego. This article is one product
of his continuing interest in the sociological study of societal reactions to drinking and of
the temperance movement in particular. He also has made contributions to the fields of
social stratification, political sociology, social movements, higher education, and com-
parative sociology. His books include* Symbolic Crusade: Status, Politics and the American
Temperance Movement; Protest, Reform and Revolt: A Reader in Social Movements and
Collective Action; *and, with David Riesman and Zelda Gamson,* Academic Values and
Mass Education.

■ Beverages that contain alcohol have been an important part of the material culture of most human societies. In many of them alcoholic beverages have been central to the definition of acceptable and unacceptable behavior. David J. Pittman has described four cultural attitudes that can be identified from cross-cultural study: an abstinence culture, in which prohibitive attitudes toward alcohol dominate; a permissive culture, in which the attitudes generally favor drinking but not drunkeness; an ambivalent culture, which has strongly conflicting values about drinking; and overpermissive culture which permits not only drinking in general but also behavior that occurs when people are intoxicated, and which displays little concern about the pathologies that can result from heavy drinking. Pittman considers American society to represent clearly an ambivalent culture, and many analysts of drinking behavior have suggested that the problems and pathologies associated with overindulgence in alcohol are in some measure a product of this strong ambivalence.

In this selection Gusfield shows some of the ways in which negative views of drinking vary from one time to another in terms of the popular diagnosis of what is wrong with the drinker. He also links the ways in which society controls or seeks to control drinking behavior and the larger sociopolitical issues that are brought into play as efforts at control are seen to impinge on the interests of social groups other than those who drink and those who supply them. He shows how the particular definition of a problem—in this case, alcohol abuse—reflects broader cultural currents and conflicts and has important effects in determining the segments of society that are mobilized to do something about what is defined as a problem. If drinking is defined as a moral problem, then preachers and other functionaries have a right to define treatment; if drinking is defined as a sickness, then those in the business of moral treatment lose power and those with professional medical expertise are in the ascendancy.

During the Prohibition era when the sale of alcoholic beverages was illegal, the use of alcohol involved a deviant exchange like the transactions discussed in Part II. The legal ambivalence of this transaction is still an important part of socially problematic aspects of alcohol use, but societal concern now lies mainly in the effects of drinking on personal control—violations of etiquette and decorum, the dangers of a reduced ability to control automobiles, and similar problems.

Two useful collections of articles that deal with drinking behavior are David J. Pittman and Charles Snyder, eds., *Society, Culture, and Drinking Patterns* (Wiley, 1962); and David J. Pittman, *Alcoholism* (Harper & Row, 1967). See also Craig MacAndrew and Robert B. Edgerton, *Drunken Comportment: A Social Explanation* (Aldine, 1969), and Edwin Lemert's papers on alcohol behavior, several of which are included in his *Human Deviance, Social Problems, and Social Control* (Prentice-Hall, 1967). For a thorough portrait of a skid row bum see James P. Spradley, *You Owe Yourself a Drunk: An Ethnography of Urban Nomads* (Little Brown, 1970). ■

RECENT PERSPECTIVES on deviant behavior have focused attention away from the actor and his acts and placed it on the analysis of public reactions in labeling deviants as "outsiders." This perspective forms the background for the present paper. In it I will analyze the implications which defining behavior as deviant has for the public designators. Several forms of deviance will be distinguished, each of which has a different kind of significance for the designators. The symbolic import of each type, I argue, leads to different public responses toward the deviant and helps account for the historical changes often found in treatment of such delinquents as alcoholics, drug addicts, and other "criminals"—changes which involve a passage from one moral status to another.

INSTRUMENTAL AND SYMBOLIC FUNCTIONS OF LAW

Agents of government are the only persons in modern societies who can legitimately claim to represent the total society. In support of their acts, limited and specific group interests are denied while a public and societal interest is claimed. Acts of government "commit the group to action or to perform coordinated acts for general welfare." This representational character of governmental officials and their acts makes it possible for them not only to influence the allocation of resources but also to define the public norms of morality and to designate which acts violate them. In a pluralistic society these defining and designating acts can become matters of political issue because they support or reject one or another of the competing and conflicting cultural groups in the society.

Let us begin with a distinction between *instrumental* and *symbolic* functions of legal and governmental acts. We readily perceive that acts of officials, legislative enactments, and court decisions often affect behavior in an instrumental manner through a direct influence on the actions of people. The Wagner Labor Relations Act and the Taft-Hartley Act have had considerable impact on the conditions of collective bargaining in the United States. Tariff legislation directly affects the prices of import commodities. The instrumental function of such laws lies in their enforcement; unenforced they have little effect.

Symbolic aspects of law and government do not depend on enforcement for their effect. They are symbolic in a sense close to that used in literary analysis. The symbolic act "invites consideration rather than overt reaction." There is a dimension of meaning in symbolic behavior which is not given in its immediate and manifest significance but in what the action connotes for the audience that views it. The symbol "has acquired a meaning which is added to its immediate intrinsic significance." The use of the wine and wafer in the Mass or the importance of the national flag cannot be appreciated without knowing their symbolic meaning for the users. In analyzing law as symbolic we are oriented less to behavioral consequences as a means to a fixed end, more to meaning as an act, a decision, a gesture important in itself.

An action of a governmental agent takes on symbolic import as it affects the designation of public norms. A courtroom decision or a legislative act is a gesture which often glorifies the values of one group and demeans those of another. In their representational character, governmental actions can be seen as ceremonial and ritual performances, designating the content of public morality. They are the statement of what is acceptable in the public interest. Law can thus be seen as symbolizing the public affirmation of social ideals and norms as well as a means of direct social control. This symbolic dimension is given in the statement, promulgation, or announcement of law unrelated to its function in influencing behavior through enforcement.

It has long been evident to students of government and law that these two functions, instrumental and symbolic, may often be separated in more than an analytical sense. Many laws are honored as much in the breach as in performance. Robin Williams has labeled such institutionalized yet illegal and deviant behavior the "patterned evasion of norms." Such evasion occurs when law proscribes behavior which nevertheless occurs in a recurrent socially organized manner and is seldom punished. The kinds of crimes we are concerned with here quite clearly fall into this category. Gambling, prostitution, abortion, and public drunkenness are all common modes of behavior although laws exist designating them as prohibited. It is possible to see such systematic evasion as functioning to minimize conflicts between cultures by utilizing law to proclaim one set of norms as public morality and to use another set of norms in actually controlling that behavior.

While patterned evasion may perform such harmonizing functions, the passage of legislation, the acts of officials, and decisions of judges nevertheless have a significance as gestures of public affirmation. First, the act of public affirmation of a norm often persuades listeners that behavior and norm are consistent. The existence of law quiets and comforts those whose interests and sentiments are embodied in it. Second, public affirmation of a moral norm directs the major institutions of the society to its support. Despite patterned practices of abortion in the United States, obtaining abortions does require access to a subterranean social structure and is much more difficult than obtaining an appendectomy. There are instrumental functions to law even where there is patterned evasion.

A third impact of public affirmation is the one that most interests us here. The fact of affirmation through acts of law and government expresses the public worth of one set of norms, of one subculture vis-a-vis those of others. It demonstrates which cultures have legitimacy and public domination, and which do not. Accordingly it enhances the social status of groups carrying the affirmed culture and degrades groups carrying that which is condemned as deviant. We have argued elsewhere that the significance of Prohibition in the United States lay less in its enforcement than in the fact that it occurred. Analysis of the enforcement of Prohibition law indicates that it was often limited by the unwillingness of Dry forces to utilize all their political strength for fear of stirring intensive opposition. Great satisfaction was gained from the passage and maintenance of the legislation itself.

Irrespective of its instrumental effects, public designation of morality is itself an issue generative of deep conflict. The designating gestures are dramatistic events, "since it invites one to consider the matter of motives in a perspective that, being developed in the analysis of drama, treats language and thought primarily as modes of action." For this reason the designation of a way of behavior as violating public norms confers status and honor on those groups whose cultures are followed as the standard of conventionality, and derogates those whose cultures are considered deviant. My analysis of the American Temperance movement has shown how the issue of drinking and abstinence became a politically significant focus for the conflicts between Protestant and Catholic, rural and urban, native and immigrant, middle class and lower class in American society. The political conflict lay in the efforts of an abstinent Protestant middle class to control the public affirmation of morality in drinking. Victory or defeat were consequently symbolic of the status and power of the cultures opposing each other. Legal affirmation or rejection is thus important in what it symbolizes as well or instead of what it controls. Even if the law was broken, it was clear whose law it was.

DEVIANT NONCONFORMITY AND DESIGNATOR REACTION

In Durkheim's analysis of the indignant and hostile response to norm violation, all proscribed actions are threats to the existence of the norm. Once we separate the instrumental from the symbolic functions of legal and governmental designation of deviants, however, we can question this assumption. We can look at norm violation from the standpoint of its effects on the symbolic rather than the instrumental character of the norm.

Our analysis of patterned evasion of norms has suggested that a law weak in its instrumental functions may nevertheless perform significant symbolic functions. Unlike human limbs, norms do not necessarily atrophy through disuse. Standards of charity, mercy, and justice may be dishonored every day yet remain important statements of what is publicly approved as virtue. The sexual behavior of the human male and the human female need not be a copy of the socially sanctioned rules. Those rules remain as important affirmations of an acceptable code, even though they are regularly breached. Their roles as ideals are not threatened by daily behavior. In analyzing the violation of norms we will look at the implications of different forms of deviance on the symbolic character of the norm itself. *The point here is that the designators of deviant behavior react differently to different norm-sustaining implications of an act.* We can classify deviant behavior from this standpoint.

THE REPENTANT DEVIANT

The reckless motorist often admits the legitimacy of traffic laws, even though he has broken them. The chronic alcoholic may well agree that both he and his society would be better if he could stay sober. In both cases the norm they have violated is itself unquestioned. Their deviation is a moral lapse, a fall from a grace to which they aspire. The homosexual who seeks a psychiatrist to rid himself of his habit has defined his actions similarly to those who have designated him as a deviant. There is a consensus between the designator and the deviant; his repentance confirms the norm.

Repentance and redemption seem to go hand-in-hand in court and church. Sykes and Matza have described techniques of neutralization which juvenile delinquents often use with enforcement agencies.

The juvenile delinquent would appear to be at least partially committed to the dominant social order in that he frequently exhibits guilt or shame when he violates its proscriptions, accords approval to certain conforming figures

and distinguishes between appropriate and inappropriate targets for his deviance.

A show of repentance is also used, say Sykes and Matza, to soften the indignation of law enforcement agents. A recent study of police behavior lends support to this. Juveniles apprehended by the police received more lenient treatment, including dismissal, if they appeared contrite and remorseful about their violations than if they did not. This difference in the posture of the deviant accounted for much of the differential treatment favoring middle class "youngsters" as against lower class "delinquents."

THE SICK DEVIANT

Acts which represent an attack upon a norm are neutralized by repentance. The open admission of repentance confirms the sinner's belief in the sin. His threat to the norm is removed and his violation has left the norm intact. Acts which we can perceive as those of sick and diseased people are irrelevant to the norm; they neither attack nor defend it. The use of morphine by hospital patients in severe pain is not designated as deviant behavior. Sentiments of public hostility and the apparatus of enforcement agencies are not mobilized toward the morphine user. His use is not perceived as a violation of the norm against drug use but as an uncontrolled act, not likely to be recurrent.

While designations of action resulting from sickness do not threaten the norm, significant consequences flow from such definitions. Talcott Parsons has pointed out that the designation of a person as ill changes the obligations which others have toward the person and his obligations toward them. Parsons' description sensitizes us to the way in which the sick person is a different social object than the healthy one. He has now become an object of welfare, a person to be helped rather than punished. Hostile sentiments toward sick people are not legitimate. The sick person is not responsible for his acts. He is excused from the consequences which attend the healthy who act the same way.

Deviance designations, as we shall show

below, are not fixed. They may shift from one form to another over time. Defining a behavior pattern as one caused by illness makes a hostile response toward the actor illegitimate and inappropriate. "Illness" is a social designation, by no means given in the nature of medical fact. Even lefthandedness is still seen as morally deviant in many countries. Hence the effort to define a practice as a consequence of illness is itself a matter of conflict and a political issue.

THE ENEMY DEVIANT

Writing about a Boston slum in the 1930s, William F. Whyte remarks:

> The policeman is subject to sharply conflicting pressures. On one side are the "good people" of Eastern City, who have written their moral judgments into law and demand through their newspapers that the law be enforced. On the other side are the people of Cornerville, who have different standards and have built up an organization whose perpetuation depends upon the freedom to violate the law.

Whyte's is one of several studies that have pointed out the discrepancies between middle class moralities embodied in law and lower class moralities which differ sharply from them. In Cornerville, gambling was seen as a "respectable" crime, just as antitrust behavior may be in other levels of the social structure. In American society, conflicts between social classes are often also cultural conflicts reflecting moral differences. Coincidence of ethnic and religious distinctions with class differences accentuates such conflicts between group values.

In these cases, the validity of the public designation is itself at issue. The publicly defined deviant is neither repentant nor sick but is instead an upholder of an opposite norm. He accepts his behavior as proper and derogates the public norm as illegitimate. He refuses to internalize the public norm into his self-definition. This is especially likely to occur in instances of "business crimes." The buyer sees his action as legitimate economic behavior and resists a definition of it as immoral and thus prohibitable. The issue of off-track betting illustrates one area in which clashes of culture have been salient.

The designation of culturally legitimate behavior as deviant depends upon the superior power and organization of the designators. The concept of convention in this area, as Thrasymachus defined Justice for Socrates, is the will of the stronger. If the deviant is the politically weaker group, then the designation is open to the changes and contingencies of political fortunes. It becomes an issue of political conflict, ranging group against group and culture against culture, in the effort to determine whose morals are to be designated as deserving of public affirmation.

It is when the deviant is also an enemy and his deviance is an aspect of group culture that the conventional norm is most explicitly and energetically attacked. When those once designated as deviant have achieved enough political power they may shift from disobedience to an effort to change the designation itself. This has certainly happened in the civil rights movement. Behavior viewed as deviant in the segregationist society has in many instances been moved into the realm of the problematic, now subject to political processes of conflict and compromise.

When the deviant and the designator perceive each other as enemies, and the designator's power is superior to that of the deviant, we have domination without a corresponding legitimacy. Anything which increases the power of the deviant to organize and attack the norm is thus a threat to the social dominance symbolized in the affirmation of the norm. Under such conditions the need of the designators to strengthen and enforce the norms is great. The struggle over the symbol of social power and status is focused on the question of the maintenance or change of the legal norm. The threat to the middle class in the increased political power of Cornerville is not that the Cornerville resident will gamble more; he already does gamble with great frequency. The threat is that the law will come to accept the morality of gambling and treat it as a legitimate business. If this happens, Boston is no longer a city dominated by middle class Yankees but becomes one dominated by lower class immigrants, as many think has actually happened in Boston. The maintenance of a norm which defines gambling as deviant behavior thus symbolizes the maintenance of Yankee social and political superiority. Its disappearance as a public commitment would symbolize the loss of that superiority.

THE CYNICAL DEVIANT

The professional criminal commits acts whose designation as deviant is supported by the wide social consensus. The burglar, the hired murderer, the arsonist, the kidnapper all prey on victims. While they may use repentance or illness as strategies to manage the impressions of enforcers, their basic orientation is self-seeking, to get around the rules. It is for this reason that their behavior is not a great threat to the norms although it calls for social management and repression. It does not threaten the legitimacy of the normative order.

DRINKING AS A CHANGING FORM OF DEVIANCE

Analysis of efforts to define drinking as deviant in the United States will illustrate the process by which designations shift. The legal embodiment of attitudes toward drinking shows how cultural conflicts find their expression in the symbolic functions of law. In the 160 years since 1800, we see all our suggested types of nonconforming behavior and all the forms of reaction among the conventional segments of the society.

The movement to limit and control personal consumption of alcohol began in the early 19th century, although some scattered attempts were made earlier. Colonial legislation was aimed mainly at controlling the inn through licensing systems. While drunkenness occurred, and drinking was frequent, the rigid nature of the colonial society, in both North and South, kept drinking from becoming an important social issue.

THE REPENTANT DRINKER

The definition of the drinker as an object of social shame begins in the early 19th century and reaches full development in the late 1820s and early 1830s. A wave of growth in temperance organizations in this period was sparked by the conversion of drinking men to abstinence under the stimulus of evangelical revivalism. Through drinking men joining together to take the pledge, a norm of abstinence and sobriety emerged as a definition of conventional respectability. They sought to control themselves and their neighbors.

The norm of abstinence and sobriety replaced the accepted patterns of heavy drinking countenanced in the late 18th and early 19th centuries. By the 1870s rural and small-town America had defined middle class morals to include the Dry attitude. This definition had little need for legal embodiment. It could be enunciated in attacks on the drunkard which assumed that he shared the normative pattern of those who exhorted him to be better and to do better. He was a repentant deviant, someone to be brought back into the fold by moral persuasion and the techniques of religious revivalism. His error was the sin of lapse from a shared standard of virtue. "The Holy Spirit will not visit, much less will He dwell within he who is under the polluting, debasing effects of intoxicating drink. The state of heart and mind which this occasions to him is loathsome and an abomination."

Moral persuasion thus rests on the conviction of a consensus between the deviant and the designators. As long as the object of attack and conversion is isolated in individual terms, rather than perceived as a group, there is no sense of his deviant act as part of a shared culture. What is shared is the norm of conventionality; the appeal to the drinker and the chronic alcoholic is to repent. When the Woman's Anti-Whiskey Crusade of 1873-1874 broke out in Ohio, churchwomen placed their attention on the taverns. In many Ohio towns these respectable ladies set up vigils in front of the tavern and attempted to prevent men from entering just by the fear that they would be observed. In keeping with the evangelical motif in the temperance movement the Washingtonians, founded in 1848, appealed to drinkers and chronic alcoholics with the emotional trappings and oratory of religious meetings, even though devoid of pastors.

Moral persuasion, rather than legislation, has been one persistent theme in the designation of the drinker as deviant and the alcoholic as depraved. Even in the depictions of the miseries and poverty of the chronic alcoholic, there is a decided moral condemnation which has been the hallmark of the American temperance movement. Moral persuasion was ineffective as a device to wipe out drinking and drunkenness. Heavy drinking persisted through the 19th century and the organized attempts to convert the drunkard experienced much backsliding. Nevertheless, defections from the standard did not threaten the standard. The public definition of respectability matched the ideals of the sober and abstaining people who dominated those parts of the society where moral suasion was effective. In the late 19th century those areas in which temperance sentiment was strongest were also those in which legislation was most easily enforceable.

THE ENEMY DRINKER

The demand for laws to limit alcoholic consumption appears to arise from situations in which the drinkers possess power as a definitive social and political group and, in their customary habits and beliefs, deny the validity of abstinence norms. The persistence of areas in which temperance norms were least controlling led to the emergence of attempts to embody control in legal measures. The drinker as enemy seems to be the greatest stimulus to efforts to designate his act as publicly defined deviance.

In its early phase the American temperance movement was committed chiefly to moral persuasion. Efforts to achieve legislation governing the sale and use of alcohol do not appear until the 1840s. This legislative movement had a close relationship to the immigration of Irish Catholics and German Lutherans into the United States in this period. These nonevangelical and/or non-Protestant peoples made up a large proportion of the urban poor in the 1840s and 1850s. They brought with them a far more accepting evaluation of drinking than had yet existed in the United States. The tavern and the beer parlor had a distinct place in the leisure of the Germans and the Irish. The prominence of this place was intensified by the stark character of the developing American slum. These immigrant cultures did not contain a strong tradition of temperance norms which might have made an effective appeal to a sense of sin. To be sure, excessive drunkenness was scorned, but neither abstinence nor constant sobriety were supported by the cultural codes.

Between these two groups—the native American, middle class evangelical Protestant and the immigrant European Catholic or Lutheran occupying the urban lower class—there was little room for repentance. By the 1850s the issue of drinking reflected a general clash over cultural values. The temperance movement found allies in its political efforts among the nativist movements. The force and power of the antialcohol movements, however, were limited greatly by the political composition of the urban electorate, with its high proportion of immigrants. Thus the movement to develop legislation emerged in reaction to the appearance of cultural groups least responsive to the norms of abstinence and sobriety. The very effort to turn such informal norms into legal standards polarized the opposing forces and accentuated the symbolic import of the movement. Now that the issue had been joined, defeat or victory was a clear-cut statement of public dominance.

It is a paradox that the most successful move to eradicate alcohol emerged in a period when America was shifting from a heavy-drinking society, in which whiskey was the leading form of alcohol, to a moderate one, in which beer was replacing whiskey. Prohibition came as the culmination of the movement to reform the immigrant cultures and at the height of the immigrant influx into the United States.

Following the Civil War, moral persuasion and legislative goals were both parts of the movement against alcohol. By the 1880s an appeal was made to the urban, immigrant lower classes to repent and to imitate the habits of the American middle class as a route to economic and social mobility. Norms of abstinence were presented to the non-abstainer both as virtue and as expedience. This effort failed. The new, and larger, immigration of 1890-1915 increased still further the threat of the urban lower class to the native American.

The symbolic effect of prohibition legislation must be kept analytically separate from its instrumental, enforcement side. While the urban middle class did provide much of the organizational leadership to the temperance and prohibition movements, the political strength of the movement in its legislative drives was in the rural areas of the United States. Here, where the problems of drinking were most under control, where the norm was relatively intact, the appeal to a struggle against foreign invasion was the most potent. In these areas, passage of legislation was likely to make small difference in behavior. The continuing polarization of political forces into those of cultural opposition and cultural acceptance during the prohibition campaigns (1906-1919), and during the drive for Repeal (1926-1933), greatly intensified the symbolic significance of victory and defeat. Even if the prohibition measures were limited in their enforceability in the metropolis there was no doubt about whose law was public and what way of life was being labeled as opprobrious.

After Repeal, as Dry power in American politics subsided, the designation of the drinker as deviant also receded. Public affirmation of the temperance norm had changed, and with it the definition of the deviant had changed. Abstinence was itself less acceptable. In the 1950s the temperance movement, faced with this change in public norms, even introduced a series of placards with the slogan, "It's Smart *Not* to Drink."

Despite this normative change in the public designation of drinking deviance, there has not been much change in American drinking patterns. Following the Prohibition period the consumption of alcohol has not returned to its pre-1915 high. Beer has continued to occupy a more important place as a source of alcohol consumption. "Hard drinkers" are not so common in America today as they were in the 19th century. While there has been some increase in moderate drinking, the percentage of adults who are abstainers has remained approximately the same (one-third) for the past 30 years. Similarly, Dry sentiment has remained stable, as measured by local opinion results. In short, the argument over deviance designation has been largely one of normative dominance, not of instrumental social control. The process of deviance designation in drinking needs to be understood in terms of symbols of cultural dominance rather than in the activities of social control.

THE SICK DRINKER

For most of the 19th century the chronic alcoholic as well as the less compulsive drinker was viewed as a sinner. It was not until after Repeal (1933) that chronic alcoholism became defined as illness in the United States. Earlier actions taken toward promotion of the welfare of drinkers and alcoholics through temperance measures rested on the moral supremacy of abstinence and the demand for repentance. The user of alcohol could be an object of sympathy, but his social salvation depended on a willingness to embrace the norm of his exhorters. The designation of alcoholism as sickness has a different bearing on the question of normative superiority. It renders the behavior of the deviant indifferent to the status of norms enforcing abstinence.

This realization appears to have made supporters of temperance and prohibition hostile to efforts to redefine the deviant character of alcoholism. They deeply opposed the reports of the Committee of Fifty in the late 19th century. These volumes of reports by scholars and prominent men took a less moralistic and a more sociological and functional view of the saloon and drinking than did the temperance movement.

The soundness of these fears is shown by what did happen to the temperance movement with the rise of the view that alcoholism is illness. It led to new agencies concerned with drinking problems. These excluded temperance people from the circle of those who now define what is deviant in drinking habits. The National Commission on Alcoholism was formed in 1941 and the Yale School of Alcoholic Studies formed in 1940. They were manned by medical personnel, social workers, and social scientists, people now alien to the spirit of the abstainer. Problems of drinking were removed from the church and placed in the hands of the universities and the medical clinics. The tendency to handle drinkers through protective and welfare agencies rather than through police or clergy has become more frequent.

"The bare statement that 'alcoholism is a disease' is most misleading since . . . it conceals what is essential—that a step in public policy is being recommended, not a scientific discovery announced." John Seeley's remark is an apt one. Replacement of the norm of sin and repentance by that of illness and therapy removes the onus of guilt and immorality from the act of drinking and the state of chronic alcoholism. It replaces the image of the sinner with that of a patient, a person to be helped rather than to be exhorted. No wonder that the temperance movement has found the work of the Yale School, and often even the work of Alcoholics Anonymous, a threat to its own movement. It has been most limited in its cooperation with these organizations and has attempted to set up other organizations which might provide the face of science in league with the tone of the movement.

The redefinition of the alcoholic as sick thus brought into power both ideas and organizations antithetical to the temperance movement. The norm protected by law and government was no longer the one held by the people who had supported temperance and prohibition. The hostility of temperance people is readily understandable; their relative political unimportance is crucial to their present inability to make that hostility effective.

MOVEMENTS OF MORAL PASSAGE

In this paper we have called attention to the fact that deviance designations have histories; the public definition of behavior as deviant is itself changeable. It is open to reversals of political power, twists of public opinion, and the development of social movements and moral crusades. What is attacked as criminal today may be seen as sick next year and fought over as possibly legitimate by the next generation.

Movements to redefine behavior may eventuate in a moral passage, a transition of the behavior from one moral status to another. In analyzing movements toward the redefinition of alcohol use, we have dealt with moral crusades which were restrictive and others which were permissive toward drinking and toward "drunkards." (We might have also used the word "alcoholics," suggesting a less disapproving and more medical perspective.) In both cases, however, the movements sought to change the public designation. While we are familiar with the restrictive or enforcing movements, the permissive or legitimizing movement must also be seen as a prevalent way in which deviants throw off the onus of their actions and avoid the sanctions associated with immoral activities.

Even where the deviants are a small and politically powerless group they may nevertheless attempt to protect themselves by influence over the process of designation. The effort to define themselves as ill is one plausible means to this end. Drug addiction as well as drunkenness is partially undergoing a change toward such redefinition. This occurs in league with powerful groups in society, such as social workers, medical professionals, or university professors. The moral passage achieved here reduces the sanctions imposed by criminal law and the public acceptance of the deviant designation.

The "lifting" of a deviant activity to the level of a political, public issue is thus a sign that its moral status is at stake, that legitimacy is a possibility. Today the moral acceptance of drinking, marijuana and LSD use, homosexuality, abortion, and other "vices" is being publicly discussed, and movements championing them have emerged. Such movements draw into them far more than the deviants themselves. Because they become symbols of general cultural attitudes they call out partisans for both repression and permission. The present debate over drug addiction laws in the United States, for example, is carried out between defenders and opposers of the norm rather than between users and nonusers of the drugs involved.

As the movement for redefinition of the addict as sick has grown, the movement to strengthen the definition of addiction as criminal has responded with increased legal severity. To classify drug users as sick and the victims or clients as suffering from "disease" would mean a change in the agencies responsible for reaction from police enforcement to medical authorities. Further, it might diminish the moral disapproval with which drug use, and the reputed euphoric effects connected with it, are viewed by supporters of present legislation. Commenting on the clinic plan to permit medical dispensing of narcotics to licensed addicts, U.S. Commissioner of Narcotics Anslinger wrote:

This plan would elevate a most despicable trade to the avowed status of an honorable business, nay, to the status of practice of a time-honored profession; and drug addicts would multiply unrestrained, to the irrevocable impairment of the moral fiber and physical welfare of the American people.

In this paper we have seen that redefining moral crusades tends to generate strong countermovements. The deviant as a cultural opponent is a more potent threat to the norm than is the repentant, or even the sick deviant. The threat to the legitimacy of the norm is a spur to the end for symbolic restatement in legal terms. In these instances of "crimes without victims" the legal norm is *not* the enunciator of a consensus within the community. On the contrary, it is when consensus is least attainable that the pressure to establish legal norms appears to be greatest.

17. OPIATE ADDICTION IN A SLUM AREA

DANIEL GLASER, BERNARD LANDER, AND WILLIAM ABBOTT

Reprinted with permission from "Opiate Addicted and Non-Addicted Siblings in a Slum Area,"
Social Problems *18, no. 4 (Spring 1971): 510-20. Copyright 1971 by The Society for the*
Study of Social Problems. Daniel Glaser is Professor of Sociology at the University of
Southern California and a prolific contributor to the sociology of crime and correction.
Bernard Lander is Associate Professor of Sociology at Hunter College, and William Abbott
is with the New York State Narcotics Addiction Control Commission.

■ We have already looked at drug use and the deviant exchanges it involves. In this selection our concern is with the lower degree of self-control presumed to characterize persons with opiate addiction and with the etiology of this particular form of deviant behavior.

Under the influence of the labeling theorists, in particular Lemert and Becker, the general thrust of sociological research has been against the traditional psychiatric and psychological concern with etiology. This point of view served a useful purpose, but interesting and important questions still arise in the issue of how some people come to adopt deviant behaviors and others do not. In this selection the authors go to the heart of the puzzle by comparing addicted and nonaddicted siblings of the same sex. They are able to systematically compare patterns of socialization from childhood into late adolescence; so the article exemplifies some of the issues Cohen raised in his discussion (Selection 4) of the development of deviant commitments and identity.

Other studies relevant to the etiology and distribution of drug addiction include John C. Ball and Carl D. Chambers, *The Epidemiology of Opiate Addiction in the United States* (Charles C. Thomas, 1970); Daniel M. Wilner and Gene J. Kassebaum, eds., *Narcotics* (McGraw-Hill, 1965); and Alfred R. Lindesmith, *Addiction and Opiates* (Aldine, 1968). For interesting case studies of drug use, see Helen McGill Hughes, *Fantastic Lodge* (Fawcett World, 1971), James Mills, *The Panic in Needle Park* (Signet Books, 1971), and Jeremy Larner and Ralph Tefferteller, *The Addict in the Street* (Grove Press, 1965). For an analysis of drug laws, see Troy Duster, *The Legislation of Morality* (The Free Press, 1972). ■

THIS STUDY explores an age-old question that has repeatedly perturbed parents and social scientists: why does one child in a family become deviant and another not? It also identifies and provides some test for a recently emergent theory to explain the post-World War II increase of opiate addiction among minority group youth in slum communities of the United States.

THEORY TESTED

The theory which this research was designed to test is implied by Finestone and by Abrams, Gagnon, and Levin. It might be designated the "relative deprivation-differential anticipation" theory of opiate addiction.

It should be stressed that this theory applies only to opiate usage in urban slum communities in the United States during the third quarter of the 20th century. In the first quarter of this century, the pattern of opiate use predominant in the United States involved mostly middle-aged women in rural areas. There were also medical and related profession and artist colony drug use patterns. These older patterns survive, but since World War II, opiate use in the United States appears to predominate in slum areas, with about 95 percent of the participants aged 15 to 44, most of them minority group members, and a large proportion engaging in delinquency or crime before their addiction.

We are implying that an explanation of the aspects of drug usage with which we are concerned must be ideographic, in that it is applicable only to a particular historical and cultural setting. This contrasts with an explanation that is nomothetic in being applicable to aspects of drug addiction anywhere, at any time, or involving anyone. Such a nomothetic "culture free" explanation was provided by Lindsmith for the already addicted person's dependence on drugs. For over three decades he has explained this dependence primarily as a consequence of a process that must include both use of opiate dosages sufficient to create withdrawal effects and the user's learning that these effects are relieved by taking more drugs, so that drug use thereafter is due to a continued fear of withdrawal effects. However, as he has in part pointed out, this explanation is irrelevant to such aspects of opiate use as its initiation, its persistence when dosage is too light for withdrawal effects, and its resumption after prolonged abstinence and the disappearance of withdrawal symptoms. It is these phenomena, particularly initiation, which we assume are culture-bound and may merit ideographic explanation based on analysis of the setting of drug use. Of course, this does not deny that ideographic causal processes may in turn be explained nomothetically as instances of more general learning mechanisms; ideographic theory is concerned with identifying and explaining the specific stimulus and reinforcement components in a particular social and cultural environment. We shall first set forth and justify the "relative deprivation-differential anticipation" theory in terms of a few gross dimensions and ethnographic impressions, then describe our efforts to test this view by sibling comparisons.

Some statistical clues in the literature suggest that the typical addict today was before addiction a person of greater aspiration than others of his background. For example, drug addicts in Chicago and Puerto Rico had higher educational achievement than nonaddicts of similar ethnic descent. Another clue is that Negro drug addicts in Chicago and New York are more often Catholic than most Negroes there, which can be interpreted in these communities as an index of their families' status mobility striving. What is inferred from these scattered clues is that today's slum addicts have been more frustrated than other slum residents not because they have been deprived more but because they have aspired to more.

For a slum youth or unskilled adult to have a narcotic habit, he must also have a "hustle." Most require $20 to $50 per day for drugs, the latter sum being far more than they can earn legitimately; and occasionally they spend much more. Hustling varies tremendously. For women addicts it is predominantly prostitution, but both statistics on officially known cases and the list of addicts in this area known to our interviewers indicate that there are four or five male addicts to one female, perhaps because females have more attractive job and marital opportunities than unskilled males find in the city.

Some male addicts support their habit by pimping and some by pushing drugs, but the most common hustle is stealing. This includes burglary, shoplifting, theft from automobiles, and robbery. They usually have to steal goods worth several times as much in retail value as the cash that they require, for they must sell cheaply. As Lewis shows in detail, hustling requires hard work, ingenuity, and organizing skill, not just to procure but also to find and maintain a market for stolen goods; it requires many values identical with those motivating legitimate business entrepreneurs. Many addicts seem to mix a variety of illegal hustles with some legitimate work or business. Many are also on welfare.

When the habit becomes too expensive, addicts seek admission to hospital detoxification centers, apparently more for respite than for cure. They depart against medical advice when their withdrawal discomfort diminishes and, en masse, when welfare checks are due. It is notable that they return quickly to opiate use even after long incarceration, when their withdrawal effects presumably are completely gone. Also, many persist for years in the intake of opiates at such a low dosage that acute physiological withdrawal effects are reported to be much less frequent in the past dozen years than formerly.

Even more preoccupying than the hustle is the narcotic addict's concern with his habit. His life is organized from one fix to the next, and he must have extensive contacts with others in the drug world in order to know sources of supply and the reputation of dealers and of their goods. We note that when addicts congregate there is much talk of various mixtures and sequences in drug-taking, of alleged "good" or "bad" batches of drugs, and boasting or complaining about various drug use and hustling experiences. In being a heroic adventurer of the hustle and a connoisseur of the habit there is an opportunity structure, a chance to feel successful or that success is accessible, which these persons do not experience in the legitimate world. Alternating with the excitement, of course, is the relaxation and indifference to problems and pressures while "nodding" under the peak influence of heroin. In summary, the "relative deprivation-differential anticipation" theory explains today's slum drug usage primarily by the fact that this usage gives addicts a sense of belonging and achievement, even many periods of hope, in sharp contrast to the "atonie," or "tonelessness" for them of the "square scene."

PROCEDURE

This study compared addicted and nonaddicted siblings of families residing in and around a slum block in New York. Our interviewers were long-time residents of the block, one a former addict and the other a former gang leader, and both previously employed in research and social service in the neighborhood. . . .

From an inventory of 138 families in the area whom our interviewers knew had one or more addicts, exaddicts or occasional users of heroin, 40 pairs of addict and nonaddict siblings of the same sex, 18 years of age or older, were identified in 38 families. The nonaddicts never used heroin. In late 1969 and early 1970 37 pairs were interviewed (3 had 1 member inaccessible). Each subject was paid $5 to be interviewed, the traditional fee in this area where for various other studies

many residents had completed questionnaires, interviews, or psychological tests for this sum. The interviews were conducted privately with each sibling, in various neighborhood settings, including a corner of a hospital's large waiting room, a room in a family clinic, or the subject's home.

The subjects ranged in age from 18 to 42 when interviewed, with a mean age of 26.0 for addicts and 26.7 for nonaddicts. When several sibling pairings were possible, those closest in age were sought. The mean difference between the siblings was 3.7 years, but 3 were only 1 year and 14 were only 2 years apart in age. Three pairs were female and the rest male. Ethnically, 27 pairs were of Puerto Rican, 3 of other West Indies, and 7 of U.S. mainland descent, with the latter all Black but the others racially diverse (and from cultures rational enough not to make absolute racial classifications). Two of the addicts were off heroin when interviewed, one being in a methadone program and the other still abstinent since release from jail; they were interviewed in terms of their condition as of their last drug usage.

On most questions each subject was asked both about himself and about his sibling, to provide a validity check. If there was disagreement, the divergence of opinion was simply recorded as a datum, but discrepancies on factual matters were checked by our two interviewers, who as co-residents of the central block in the neighborhood were personally acquainted with many of the subjects and their families and friends. This familiarity facilitated interpretation of the indexical expressions of respondents in the few instances where their meanings might otherwise have been unclear.

FINDINGS ON THE SIBLINGS

Our findings in comparisons of the siblings are summarized in Table 17.1 and in greater detail in the following discussion.

HOME ENVIRONMENT

The average time of residence in the neigh-

TABLE 17.1
SUMMARY OF DATA ON 37 ADDICT AND NONADDICT SIBLING PAIRS FROM A
NEW YORK CITY SLUM

Variable	Addicts	Nonaddicts
Mean age when interviewed	26.0	26.7
Home Background		
Mean age on move to N.Y.C. for 23 of each (63%) born elsewhere	8.3	10.4
Never left parental home for 3 months or more	11 (30%)	17 (46%)
For remainder: Mean age when first left	17.4	18.0
First 3 months or more departure was to institution	26 (70%)	3 (8%)
One whom both agree:		
Stayed home most as a teen-ager	7 (19%)	16 (43%)
Got along best with mother	8 (22%)	8 (22%)
Got along best with father	12 (32%)	13 (35%)
Parents expected to be most successful	13 (35%)	16 (43%)
Education		
Left school earliest (9 pairs tied)	22 (59%)	6 (16%)
Graduated from high school	12 (32%)	23 (62%)
One whom pair agree did best in school	10 (27%)	25 (68%)
Drug Use		
Used marihuana	37 (100%)	11 (30%)
Mean age at first marihuana use	14.8	16.4
Used opiates	37 (100%)	none
Mean age at first opiate use	17.8	none
Delinquent and Criminal Experience Indicator		
Member of gang "as kid"	22 (59%)	7 (19%)
Arrested	30 (81%)	2 (5%)
Served prison sentence	18 (49%)	1 (3%)
Sexual Pursuits		
Youngest when started "steady"	23 (62%)	8 (22%)
Reported homosexual experience	8 (22%)	none
Work		
Teenage occupational expectations:		
Unskilled	3 (8%)	2 (5%)
Skilled	9 (24%)	16 (43%)
Artistic, athletic, adventurous, or criminal	11 (30%)	5 (14%)
Professional or business	5 (14%)	9 (24%)
Don't know	9 (24%)	5 (14%)
Currently employed full-time	3 (8%)	31 (84%)
Curently employed part-time	4 (11%)	4 (11%)
Mean duration of longest job, in years	1.1	3.0
Longest job is at skilled trade	2 (5%)	14 (38%)

TABLE 17.1 (*Continued*)

Variable	Addicts	Nonaddicts
Personality (for 34 pairs only)		
Anomia scale: Mean score	2.9	1.5
Higher score than sib (6 pairs tied)	21 (62%)	7 (21%)
Alienation scale: Mean score	4.1	3.0
Higher score than sib (3 pairs tied)	19 (56%)	12 (35%)
Own Explanation for Sibling Difference on Addiction*		
Different peer associates, "crowds"	12 (32%)	16 (43%)
Difference of tastes or values	10 (27%)	8 (22%)
Addict's stupidity or ignorance	14 (38%)	4 (11%)
Other	1 (3%)	1 (3%)
Don't know	2 (5%)	9 (24%)

* Includes dual-category responses.

borhood was 18.6 years for the 37 addicts and 18.1 years for their nonaddict siblings. Both members of 21 of the sibling pairs were born in Puerto Rico, the West Indies, or the southern United States, as were 2 addicts and 2 nonaddicts whose siblings were born in New York; these comprise 63 percent of our sample. The addicts born elsewhere averaged 8.3 years old on coming to New York, the nonaddicts 10.4 years.

Of those who never left the parental home for 3 months or more; 11 were addicts and 17 nonaddicts; for the remainder, the average age at first leaving was 17.4 for the addicts and 18.0 for the nonaddicts, with the addicts also leaving more frequently. The place to which they went on first leaving was a jail or other place of confinement for all 26 of the departing addicts but for only 3 of the nonaddicts. The nonaddicts more often left the parental home for the armed forces or their own home on marriage. In response to the question, "Which kid stayed at home most when he was a teenager?" 7 pairs agreed in naming the addict, 16 the nonaddict and 7 that there was no clear difference; there was disagreement in 7 pairs. At the time of the interviews 19 of the addicts and 23 of the nonaddicts were living in the home of their parents.

With regard to the subjective aspects of home relationships, differences were small.

Responding to the question, "Which kid got along best with your mother?" both agreed it was the addict in eight pairs and the nonaddict in eight others, and that no distinction was possible in six cases. They disagreed in 15 cases: in 5 the addict said it was he but the other said there was no difference between them; in 4 each named himself; in 2 each named the other; in 1 the nonaddict named himself and the addict said there was no difference. To the question, "Which kid got along best with your father?" both siblings agreed on the addict in 13 cases, the nonaddict in 12 cases, and in 6 cases that there was no difference; they disagreed in 6 cases, in diverse ways.

We also asked, "Which kid did your parents expect would be the most successful in life?" and "Why?" Both agreed in 13 pairs that it was the addict, in 16 that it was the nonaddict, and in 4 that no differentiation was evident. In only one pair did each name himself; in three others one saw a parental distinction but the other thought their parents expected the same for both. In 7 of the 13 cases where they agreed that most was expected of the addict, the reason the addict gave was primarily that he was considered the "smarter" of the two, and the nonaddict agreed in three of these cases. Contrastingly, in only 2 of the 16 cases where they agreed most was expected of the nonaddict did they say that this was because he was "smarter." In other cases high parental expectations were ascribed to one's being older, working harder, staying in school longer, or being the parental favorite, but no reason was so frequent or so patterned as "smartness." The addict's somewhat more frequent self-perceived reputation for being bright seems consistent with the explanation of addiction by relative deprivation; he would presumably have higher norms of achievement for himself than for a sibling regarded as less clever.

In summary, the kinds of home environment data we were able to collect show only slight distinctions between the addict and the nonaddict siblings. The typical addict was two years younger than his nonaddict sibling on moving to the neighborhood, and spent appreciably less of his teen-age and adult life at home, with his first long departure from home due to jailing. There was no clear indication that either addict or nonaddict got along better with either parent. The only somewhat marked subjective difference was the extent to which the addict considered himself the brighter of the pair in explaining why he thought his parents viewed him as more likely to succeed in life than his sibling. While none of these differences was pronounced or consistent enough to be conclusive, what is clear is that their opposites were also not true: before addiction the addicts were neither the outcasts of their families, the children most in conflict with the parents, nor in any sense predominantly more rejected or alienated from the family than their nonaddicted siblings.

EDUCATION, RECREATION, AND WORK

The impressions of some addicts that their parents regarded them as bright was not reflected in duration of schooling; 22 left school at an earlier age than their nonaddicted sibling, 9 left in the same year of age, and in only 6 pairs did the nonaddict leave earlier. Of the nonaddicts 23 graduated from high school as compared with only 12 of the addicts. One of the latter graduated in prison. When asked their favorite subject in school,

14 of the nonaddicts and only 5 of the addicts mentioned a vocational shop or craft course, while 4 of the addicts and none of the nonaddicts mentioned music or art. Other subjects—English, science, and history—were selected with more nearly identical frequencies by both groups. The pairs agreed in 25 cases that the nonaddict was better than the addict in school and in 10 that the addict was better, only 2 pairs disagreeing on this. All of our educational achievement data contradict the Chicago and Puerto Rico statistics cited earlier on addicts' educational superiority, but as noted earlier, failure to control for age may make those statistics misleading.

What seems to have produced these school performance differences was that the addict's recreation interests interfered with his education. All of the addicts had used marihuana, and all but one started using it while still in school. Also, 14 started their heroin use while still in school. Indeed, average age at first marihuana use was 14.8, with 4 starting at 12 and all but one using it before their 18th birthday. Their average age at first heroin use was 17.8, with 1 starting at 13 and 2 at 14; the oldest age at first heroin use was 24. None of the nonaddict siblings ever tried heroin, and only 11 ever used marihuana. These 11 did not persist in its use and most of the remaining 26 volunteered rather proudly that they never wanted to try it.

Even more indicative of recreation that competed with schooling were answers to the questions, "Were you or any other kids in your family in gangs?" If "yes," then Which kids? At which ages? Which kids spent the most time with their gang? Which kids were leaders or 'big shots' in their gangs?" Gang involvement was reported for 22 addicts, and for their nonaddict sibling also in 7 of these pairs. In 5 of the 7 the separate responses of each sibling were in agreement in designating the addict as the one who spent the most time with the gang. In three pairs both said the addict was a gang leader, in three both said this of the nonaddict, and in one pair the addict claimed leadership while in another the nonaddict claimed it, but in both these pairs the sibling disagreed. Mean age at gang entrance for the addicts was 14.5, with a range from 10 to 17, for the 17 cases on which we had this age information. Nine of these started marihuana use before gang entrance, 6 after gang entrance, and 2 during the same year.

Thirty of the addicts but only 2 of the nonaddicts reported ever being arrested. The median age at first arrest for the arrested addicts was 18.4, with a range from 13 to 28. Their median number of arrests was 3. Contrastingly, one nonaddict was arrested once when 21 and the other 4 times when 18 and 19 years old, which was a decade prior to our interviews. The median total time confined was 2.3 years for the incarcerated addicts. Eighteen of the addicts but only 1 nonaddict had served a prison sentence.

The average age when our subjects began "going steady" with a member of the opposite sex was 15.1 for the addicts and 15.8 for the nonaddicts. In 23 pairs the addict was younger in this, in 8 pairs the nonaddict was younger and in 6 pairs they started at about the same age. Seven of the addict and 13 of the nonaddicts had been married, with three addicts and one nonaddict divorced or separated. Eight of the addicts and none of the nonaddicts admitted having engaged in homosexuality, four of these saying that they did it only for money. Three, including one who denied it, are reported by our interviewers to be predominantly homosexual now (two of these three are female).

We asked our subjects, "When you were a teen-ager, what did you think you would be when you grew up?" Nine of the addicts and 16 of the nonaddicts specified a skilled tradesman, such as butcher, baker, printer, barber, or beautician, while three addicts and two nonaddicts described unskilled work. On the other hand, nine of the addicts and five of the nonaddicts gave what might be called artistic or masculine hero occupations (musician, boxer, pilot, policeman, fireman), one addict said "a racketeer," and another said "a hustler." Five of the addicts but nine of the nonaddicts specified a profession or being a business owner. Nine addicts and five nonaddicts said they did not know.

Three of the addicts and all but six of the nonaddicts had full-time employment at the time of the interview, with four in each group working part-time. Both of the nonworking nonaddicts were receiving welfare payments, 1 a female on ADC, as were 10 of the 29 nonworking addicts. The working addicts included one of the seven who never had been arrested; he worked in all but the worst weather as a helper on a produce truck, picking up jobs in the predawn hours at the wholesale market. One worked as a doorman in an apartment building and one as a watchman. Three of the working nonaddicts were in the US Army and were interviewed when they were on home visits. Several of the working addicts were known to our interviewers to be thieves also, but it is well established in the neighborhood that work is compatible with taking four to eight bags of heroin daily, and many can keep their dosage this low for long periods, partly because street heroin is usually highly diluted with inert substances. Heroin was sold for $2 per bag most of the time, in this area. Thirty-two of the nonaddicts and only sixteen of the addicts had at one time or another worked for one employer for a year or more, with the longest job averaging 5.0 years for the nonaddicts and 1.1 years for the addicts. Work that could be classified as skilled was involved in the longest job for only 2 of the addicts but for 14 of the nonaddicts.

PERSONALITY

Only a limited personality measurement effort was made in this study. At the conclusion of our interview, each sibling was given orally the 5 item Srole Anomia Scale and a 10-item alienation scale. For three pairs, time pressures prevented completion of scales.

On the Anomia scale the mean score for 34 addicts was 2.9, almost twice the 1.5 mean for their nonaddict siblings. In 21 pairs, the addict had the higher score of the two siblings, and in 7 pairs the nonaddict was higher, with 6 pairs tied. Each of the five statements in this scale was endorsed by more of the addicts than the nonaddicts. The most differentiating items were "In spite of what some people say the life of the average man is getting worse, not better," to which 16 addicts but only 4 nonaddicts agreed; and "It's hardly fair to bring people into this world the way things look for the future," to which 14 addicts and only 5 nonaddicts agreed. Of course, such differences may well reflect consequences rather than causes of addiction in the thinking patterns of the subjects.

A similar interpretation may be appropriate for the somewhat less contrasting responses of these subjects on the alienation scale. Mean score was 4.1 for addicts and 3.0 for nonaddicts, with the addict having a higher score than his nonaddict sibling in 19 pairs, the reverse occurring in 12 pairs, and ties occurring in only 3 cases. One discriminating item in this forced-choice paired-statements scale was "It's not always wise to plan far ahead because many things turn out to be a matter of good or bad luck anyhow," which 14 addicts but only 4 nonaddicts chose as more accurately reflecting their views than "When I make plans, I am almost certain that I can make them work." Also contributing much to the contrast in total score was "It is hard to know whether or not a person really likes you," which 23 addicts but only 10 nonaddicts chose as more accurately reflecting their views than "How many friends you have depends upon how nice a person you are." Most of the other 8 items contributed little or nothing to the difference in addict and nonaddict mean scores, with one item yielding results in a direction opposite to the others; 30 nonaddicts but only 24 addicts endorsed "The trouble with most children nowadays is that their parents are too easy with them" as preferable to "Children get into trouble because their parents punish them too much." One might infer, however, that both statements are alienation indicators.

In concluding the interviews we asked the subjects why, in their families, one of the children became addicted and one did not. While their answers are interesting, their involvement clearly was not a guarantee of insight and certainty. Twelve of the addicts

and sixteen of the nonaddicts emphasized companions. "I just wanted to be one of the boys"; "He never hung with the same crowd I did"; "He always wanted to be slick, smart, so he hung with the older guys that were hooked"; "She always wanted to be down, and be one of the gang, so she married an addict and they use it together." Ten of the addicts and eight of the nonaddicts stressed a difference in taste or values. "I have always looked for new kicks. I was never clean except when I was in jail"; "I liked drugs and he didn't"; "He never wanted to try them and I did"; "He always worked, but I wanted to be down"; "I never wanted to be strung out. I can't stand junkies"; "He didn't want anything out of life but I did." Fourteen of the addicts and four of the nonaddicts ascribed the difference to the addict's stupidity or ignorance. "I didn't realize what I was doing and I got hooked"; "I was stupid"; "My brother saw what happened to me"; "Some of us were smarter than the others." One addict ascribed his habit to marital troubles and one nonaddict blamed his brother's addiction on their parents' permissiveness with his brother after strictness with him. Nine nonaddicts but only two addicts gave "don't know" responses.

SUMMARY AND CONCLUSIONS

We interpret these data as supporting the "relative deprivation-differential anticipation" theory, since the typical addict differed most from his nonaddict sibling in the extent of his involvement in delinquency and marihuana use at an early age, and in consequent arrest, incarceration, deficiencies of schooling, and limited employment. There was a less marked difference in home situation, but of a type conducive to the addict's earlier involvement in an illegitimate opportunity structure; he came to the slum at an earlier age and stayed at home less. No appreciable differences were revealed by our probes on relationships with parents. There was some tendency for the addicts to have more unrealistic career aspirations than the nonaddicts at an early age, perhaps implying that they would be more dissatisfied with the ordinary jobs available to them. The addicts scored higher on anomie and alienation scales than the nonaddicts, which may be more consequence than cause of the difference in their life styles.

What was most clearly indicated is the difference in early reference group orientation in these sibling pairs. The addicts were highly involved in the illegitimate opportunity structure of the street at an early age, with arrest and incarceration consequences that would be long-run barriers to mobility in legitimate careers. Contrastingly, the nonaddicts early eschewed the illegitimate world and sought conventional employment. This contrast is similar to the early and subsequently stable differences in self-conceptions which Reckless and his associates found in long-term studies of delinquents and nondelinquents in slum schools. The contrast of behavior we repeatedly found within families suggests the validity of Parsons' deviance polarization paradigm, that motivational stress from ambivalence about norms is relieved by either compulsive conformity or compulsive alienation.

Such a persistent disjunction between the "good boy" and the "bad boy," becoming later in high drug use areas a contrast of addict with nonaddict, is understandable on both psychological and sociological grounds. Psychological law, from Thorndike to Skinner, points to the persistence of men in that behavior which is most gratifying to them. Sociological studies stress the rejection in conforming social circles of those who have been publicly labeled deviant, and the mutual support through deviant subcultures which those thus rejected give each other. Thus social consequences of early deviance, making later efforts at conformity less gratifying, and further deviance more immediately reinforced by peers, easily explain psychologically the persistence or even amplifiication of deviance with age.

Our theory and data imply that delinquency creates for slum youth something analogous to what Wiley called a "mobility trap"; while it enables them to feel like "big shots" in childhood and early adolescence, the delinquency record and the school retardation that is its usual consequence reduce status opportunities later, regardless of ability. Eventually, of course, the deviance may also be a trap, partly because the state ultimately sanctions severely most of those who persistently violate felony laws, and partly because persistent heavy opiate usage and desperate hustling create eventual physical debilitation in many cases.

Our data suggest the tendency for a progressive differentiation of deviant from nondeviant careers but some bridging of the two life-styles. Furthermore, these contrasting moral orders are not segregated from each other. In slum areas of New York City where 10 to 20 percent of the 15 to 44-year-old population are regular users of opiates, extreme segregation is impossible. Indeed, what our data highlight most dramatically is the error in conceptions of slum life, family life, or lower class culture as monolithic and uniform; they are diverse and mixed, with sharp contrasts even within single households.

18. AMERICAN MEN'S ATTITUDES TOWARDS VIOLENCE

MONICA D. BLUMENTHAL, ROBERT L. KAHN,
FRANK M. ANDREWS, AND KINDRA B. HEAD

Excerpted from a paper presented at the Fourth Annual Briefing on the Social and Behavioral Sciences, Council for the Advancement of Science Writing, Inc., New York City, May 24-25, 1971; this selection is essentially a summary of the work reported in M. D. Blumenthal, R. L. Kahn, F. M. Andrews, and K. B. Head, Justifying Violence: Attitudes of American Men (Ann Arbor, Mich.: Institute for Social Research, 1972). Monica D. Blumenthal is Associate Professor of Psychiatry at the University of Michigan and a program director at the Survey Research Center of the Institute for Social Research. Robert L. Kahn is Professor of Psychology and director of the Survey Research Center. Frank M. Andrews is Associate Professor of Psychology and a program director at the Center. Kindra B. Head is a graduate student in the Department of Psychology at the University of Michigan.

■ Private violence, except in self-defense, is heavily disapproved of in American society, yet the incidence of private violence in this country is considerably higher than in European countries. Pittman's characterization of the United States as having an ambivalent culture with respect to alcohol applies equally to the society's stance toward violence. The rates of personal crimes are very high in the United States, as we will see, but we condemn violence and expend great efforts in child socialization and adult exhortation to limit violence to the actions of police and other official agencies. Americans have traditionally taken the law into their own hands and have used violence to settle personal disputes, particularly in the regional cultures of the South and West. The acceptability of private violence is thought to be conducive to high rates of this kind of deviance as well as to excessive official violence on the part of policemen, prison guards, and others with authority to use force.

The combinations of ghetto riots, political assassinations, and "police riots" in the late 1960s centered considerable attention on the question of the attitudinal support in American culture for the level of violence the country was experiencing. In this selection the authors examine the basic question of how American men feel about personal violence and the extent to which different kinds of actions by private citizens and officials are defined as violent. The study considers the role of feelings of retribution, belief in self-defense, and the valuation of property as elements in the attitudes shown among a representative sample of American men.

An extensive review of historical and contemporary sociological material on violence in American society can be found in the various reports of the U.S. National Commission on the Causes and Prevention of Violence, which President Johnson appointed in the aftermath of the assassinations of Robert Kennedy and Martin Luther King. They include several task force reports as well as an overall report that summarizes the whole: *To Establish Justice, To Insure Domestic Tranquility,* Final Report of the U.S. National Commission on the Causes and Prevention of Violence (Government Printing Office, 1969). One report that the government refused to publish, dealing with the police riot against demonstrators during the Democratic National Convention in 1968, is *Rights in Conflict* (Bantam Books, 1969). For a study of regional attitudes toward violence see John Shelton Reed, "To Live—and Die— in Dixie: A Contribution to the Study of Violence," *Political Science Quarterly* 86, No. 3 (September 1971): 429 ff.; and for an analysis of homicide rates as a function of regional differences see Thomas F. Pettigrew and Rosalyn Barclay Spier, "The Ecological Structure of Negro Homicide," *American Journal of Sociology* 67, No. 6 (May 1962): 21 ff. ■

IN THE SUMMER OF 1969 the Survey Research Center of the University of Michigan in a national survey on attitudes toward violence interviewed 1,374 men between the ages of 16 and 64. Of those who had been originally selected for the study, 80 percent finally participated. Because of the scientific way in which these men were selected, the opinions of this group may be taken to represent the opinions of American men as a whole at that time. This survey is the first in an expected series of studies which will periodically assess attitudes toward violence in the United States. . . .

American men are deeply concerned about violence; 65 percent of them spontaneously mentioned violence or violence-related events when asked what things going on in the United States concerned them. Moreover, the major concern was with civil disturbances; 68 percent of American men cited these as opposed to 27 percent who cited crime as the type of violence which most concerned them.

The vast majority of American men felt that the roots of violence lie in the social problems of our times. When questioned as to their beliefs about what causes violence, the largest proportion cited lack of understanding, communication, and mutual respect. Over 70 percent of all men agreed that poverty, lack of good jobs, poor education, and discrimination contribute to causing violence. However, although the vast majority of Americans agreed that violence has its roots in the social problems of our times, many looked to more punitive legislation and bolstered police forces as a means of preventing violence.

MEASURING ATTITUDES
TOWARD VIOLENCE

The survey specifically measured attitudes toward how much police force should be used in the control of a variety of disturbances, including campus disturbances, ghetto disturbances and disturbances caused by hoodlum gangs. For each of these situations the respondent was asked whether the police should let it go, make arrests without using clubs or guns, use clubs but not guns, shoot but not to kill, or shoot to kill. In each case the recommendation could be made to use each method "almost always," "sometimes," "hardly ever," or "never."

There is widespread agreement among American men that the less forceful police methods be used. From 76 to 87 percent of American men agreed that such methods should be used "almost always" or "sometimes," depending on the specific situation. There is more disagreement among Americans on the use of more forceful methods; however, many American men were willing to recommend high levels of police force. From 48 to 64 percent of American men felt the "police should shoot but not to kill" "almost always" or "sometimes" to control disturbances, depending on the specific situations; 19 to 32 percent of American men felt "the police should shoot to kill" "almost always" or "sometimes" in control of such disturbances. The opinions referring to how much force the police should use were combined in a scale which will be referred to as Violence for Social Control.

The survey also measured attitudes toward how much property damage and personal injury the respondents felt necessary to bring about social change fast enough. Specifically, the respondent was asked how much violence was necessary to bring about changes of the type needed by students, by Blacks, and in general. The amount of violence thought necessary varied only slightly with the three situations. While 82 percent of Americans agreed that changes can be made fast enough without property damage or injury, about 25 percent of Americans thought protest involving some personal injury or some property damage is necessary to bring about changes fast enough, and 10 percent of American men agreed protest involving much property damage or some deaths is necessary to bring about change fast enough. It should be noted that the phrasing of the question is such that agreement with the statement does not necessarily mean that the respondent himself endorsed or would participate in violence to bring about social change, merely that the respondent felt changes would not occur at a reasonably rapid rate without violence. One interpretation of this measure is as a measure of the cynicism with which American men regard the ability of the system to remedy social problems. Responses to the questions about how much property damage and personal injury is required to bring about social changes fast enough were scaled and will be referred to as Violence for Social Change from here on.

DEMOGRAPHIC CHARACTERISTICS AND ATTITUDES TOWARD VIOLENCE

Attitudes toward Violence for Social Control and Violence for Social Change are related to age. Older people were more likely to recommend higher levels of Violence for Social Control and less likely to feel high levels of Violence for Social Change necessary. However, the association is small. Education seems to ameliorate attitudes toward both Violence for Social Control and Violence for Social Change. More educated individuals were less likely to recommend high levels of violence of either type. Income is associated with attitudes for Violence for Social Change; the lower the income, the more likely the respondent was to feel violence necessary to produce change. There are some small differences in attitudes toward violence associated with where the respondent lived and his religious preference. People living in the South or border states were more likely to recommend high levels of Violence for Social Control as were fundamentalist Protestants, while Jews were likely to score low on Violence for Social Control. The larger the size of the town in which the respondent lived, the more likely he was to score low on Violence for Social Control, but those living in big cities were more likely to score high on Violence for Social Change than were any others.

The largest difference in attitudes toward violence which could be attributed to a background characteristic is associated with race.

Black men were less likely to advocate high levels of Violence for Social Control than were others and more likely to recommend high levels of Violence for Social Change.

In terms of responses to specific items, these differences in attitudes between the races meant that 41 percent of Blacks as compared to 50 percent of Whites felt that the police should handle campus disturbances by shooting (but not to kill) "almost always" or "sometimes," and 50 percent of Blacks as compared to 62 percent of Whites felt shooting is the way to handle ghetto disturbances. On the other hand, in relation to how much violence was thought to be necessary to produce social change, over 25 percent of Black men felt that protest involving some deaths and much property damage would be necessary to bring about change fast enough in contrast to 6 or 7 percent of Whites. Almost 50 percent of all Black men thought protest involving some property damage or personal injury would be necessary as compared to slightly less than 20 percent of Whites.

American men show a marked cynicism about the court system; 79 percent of all men felt the rich are treated better in court than are the poor, and 40 percent felt that Whites are treated better than Blacks. Among Black men, 66 percent felt Blacks are likely to be treated worse by the courts and, in addition, 34 percent of Blacks as opposed to only 6 percent of Whites felt that they themselves personally would be treated worse than others in court. The more the individual felt that courts are unfair, the more likely he was to feel violence is necessary to produce social change.

WHAT AMERICAN MEN CALL VIOLENCE

To find out what acts American men regarded as violence, the respondents were asked: "Here is a list of nine things that have been in the news. Tell me if you think about these as violence. I don't mean if they lead to violence, but if you think about them *as violence in themselves*." (See Table 18.1).

TABLE 18.1

RESPONDENTS DEFINING CERTAIN ACTS AS VIOLENCE

(percent)

	Yes	Both	No	Total
Do you think of looting as violence?	85%	3%	12%	100%
Do you think of burglary as violence?	65	5	30	100
Do you think of draft card burning as violence?	58	4	38	100
Do you think of police beating students as violence?	56	14	30	100
Do you think of not letting people have their civil rights as violence?	49	8	43	100
Do you think of student protest as violence?	38	15	47	100
Do you think of police shooting looters as violence?	35	8	57	100
Do you think of sit-ins as violence?	22	9	69	100
Do you think of police stopping to frisk people as violence?	16	10	74	100

American men were more agreed that acts against property, such as burglary and looting, constitute violence more than acts involving personal injury, such as the police shooting looters or beating students. Of all the men 85 percent thought that looting is violence but only 35 percent felt that police shooting looters is violence; 59 percent of Blacks and 50 percent of men with a college degree felt that such shooting is violence but only 23 percent of White union members thought so. Similarly, 18 percent of college students and 23 percent of Blacks considered student protest violence, but more than twice as many White union members considered such protest violence. More American men felt that burning a draft card was violence than thought that beating students violence, although there was wide disagreement between subgroups in the population on this matter. (See Table 18.2).

Whether or not the individual called acts of protest violence strongly relates to the level of police force he recommended for the control of disturbances. The more a person thought protest violence, the higher the levels of police force recommended. Moreover, the less the individual considered police acts such as shooting looters, beating students, and frisking people violence, the higher the levels of police force he was likely to recommend.

AMERICAN VALUES AND ATTITUDES TOWARD VIOLENCE

American men express high levels of agreement with the notion of retributive justice, 71 percent agreeing that people who murder deserve capital punishment, 67 percent that people should be paid back for wrongs they commit, 44 percent that violence deserves violence. The only item measuring retributiveness with which American men generally disagreed was "an eye for an eye, a tooth for a tooth is a good rule for living." However, 64 percent felt it is often necessary to use violence to prevent violence. Such attitudes are related to how much force an individual feels the police should use. Among Black men, attitudes toward retributiveness are related to opinions about how much property damage and personal injury is necessary to bring about social change fast enough.

A second value which strongly relates to attitudes of American men toward violence is the degree to which they believed in self-defense. This belief was strongly endorsed by American men as 60 percent believed strong-

TABLE 18.2

WHO CALLS WHAT VIOLENCE

(percent)

	College Students	College Degree and Over	White Union Member	Blacks
Police				
Police beating students is violence	79%	66%	45%	82%
Police shooting looters is violence	43	50	23	59
Police frisking is violence	16	16	10	34
Burglary				
Looting is violence	76	79	91	74
Burglary is violence	47	54	67	70
Dissent				
Student protest is violence	18	22	43	23
Sit-ins are violence	4	13	24	15
Draft card burning is violence	26	35	63	51
Denial of civil rights is violence	54	45	40	70
N	(63)	(172)	(279)	(303)

ly that a man has the right to kill another man in self-defense, 69 percent agreed strongly he has a right to kill to defend his family, and 58 percent agreed either "strongly" or "somewhat" he has a right to kill to defend his house. The more a person agreed with these concepts, the higher the levels of police force recommended in the control of disturbances. Among Black men, the more the individual believed in self-defense, the more he was apt to believe that high levels of violence are necessary to produce social change.

Interestingly enough, the extent to which an individual believed in the golden rule or kindness did not relate to his attitudes toward violence.

ATTITUDES TOWARD DISSENTERS AND ATTITUDES TOWARD VIOLENCE

Another important factor relating to attitudes of American men toward violence was the extent to which they held positive or negative beliefs about individuals participating in the disturbances—that is, White student demonstrators, Black protesters, or the police. Whether or not the individual believed that White student demonstrators or Black protesters were looking for trouble, hostile, untrustworthy, and likely to make life change for the worse was related to the levels of police force recommended in the control of disturbances. The more the respondent thought student demonstrators or Black protesters hostile, looking for trouble, untrustworthy, and likely to change life for the worse, the higher the levels of police force recommended. On the other hand, the more the respondents thought Black protesters trustworthy, helpful, likely to change life for the better and unlikely to dislike the respondent, the more likely the respondent was to score high on the Violence for Social Change measure. In addition, the more the respondent thought the police untrustworthy, looking for trouble, hostile, and likely to change life for the worse, the more apt he was to feel that violence was necessary to produce social change.

All together, the values held by American men, their attitudes toward the contenders in the violence scenarios, how they defined violence, and what they thought of social issues explained 31 percent of the variation in attitudes toward Violence for Social Control. Among the highly educated—those with at least some college education—47 percent of the variation in such attitudes could be explained by these issues. In addition, among American men in general, values, attitudes toward the contenders, how violence was defined, beliefs about social issues, and whether or not the individual was inclined to be trusting or resentful accounted for 33 percent of the variation in attitudes toward Violence for Social Change. Among those with a college education, these same variables accounted for 54 percent of such variation.

To summarize, this study showed that a majority of Americans are willing to tolerate very high levels of violence used by police, while a minority segment of the American male population believes that violence is necessary to produce social change. The most important factors in explaining violence are not such factors as age or education but, rather, the basic values held by American men, including attitudes toward retributiveness, self-defense, and how property is valued relative to persons. In addition, attitudes toward the contenders involved in disturbances are an important determinant of attitudes toward violence. That is, individuals who see White student demonstrators and Black protesters as untrustworthy, looking for trouble, and likely to change life for the worse are apt to recommend higher levels of police force than those who do not hold such opinions about Black protesters and student demonstrators. On the other hand, those who hold such opinions about the police are likely to feel that higher levels of violence will be necessary to produce social change fast enough. Attitudes toward social issues are also related to attitudes toward violence. The data also show that rhetoric influences attitudes toward violence; the more often nonviolent forms of protest are labeled violence, the more often violent police tactics are labeled nonviolence, the more police force is condoned by the public. It appears that among American men attitudes toward violence are determined more by the extent to which they believe violence will achieve desired goals than by other considerations.

The data suggest that the reduction of domestic violence in the United States requires that mechanisms be developed through which real social changes can be brought about by nonviolent means. Such mechanisms would require that minority groups of all kinds be given real opportunities to speak for their goals, and that appropriate governmental branches and agencies begin a serious consideration of how all the needs of the many varying segments of the population can be met, irrespective of whether or not the segment whose needs are being considered forms a majority. The data suggest that it is not in the interest of domestic tranquility for the government to respond to protest by refusing to listen. It also suggests that it is dangerous for influential persons to label nonviolent protest "violent" since doing so will increase the willingness of the public to sanction inappropriately violent police methods, which in turn probably increase the willingness of other segments of the public to turn toward violence as a means of producing social change.

19. HOMICIDE IN CHICAGO: 1965-1970

RICHARD BLOCK AND FRANKLIN E. ZIMRING

Reprinted, with permission of the National Council on Crime and Delinquency, from the Journal of Research in Crime and Delinquency *10, no. 1 (January 1973): 1-12. Richard Block and Franklin E. Zimring are associated with the Center for Studies in Criminal Justice at the University of Chicago.*

■ Among violent crimes murder provides the sharpest contrast between the United States and Western European countries. Murder rates in the United States have always been high and have risen dramatically over the past decade. Fewer homicides were reported in England in the first half of the century than occurred on the average in any one year in the United States.

Much useful sociological research helps to illuminate the question of who kills whom and in what circumstances. It has been discovered that most often the victim and his killer are known to each other—indeed, that more often than not they are friends, lovers, or kinsmen. Most homicides take place in private places, not on the street. Nevertheless, much public anxiety about homicidal assault is addressed to the risk of becoming a victim of a stranger's attack.

Most sociological research on the cast of characters for this crime has been cross-sectional. In this selection Block and Zimring analyze changes in one city, Chicago, over a five-year period during which the homicide rate more than doubled. They analyze the changing characteristics of victims and offenders and the relationship between the two.

A set of careful studies dealing with homicide is in Marvin E. Wolfgang, *Studies in Homicide* (Harper & Row, 1967); see also Marvin E. Wolfgang and Franco Ferracuti, *The Subculture of Violence: Towards an Integrated Theory of Criminology* (Barnes & Noble Social Science Paperback, 1957). An early, now classic, examination of variation in homicide rates is Andrew F. Henry and James F. Short, Jr., *Suicide and Homicide: Some Economic, Sociological, and Psychological Aspects of Aggression* (Free Press, 1954). See also the staff report to the National Commission on the Causes and Prevention of Violence, *Crimes of Violence,* by Donald Mulvahill, Melvin Tumin,

and Lynn Curtis (Government Printing Office, 1970). ■

THE MOST RECENT GENERATION of studies in patterns of criminal homicide has emphasized the static analysis of police-reported data in major American metropolitan areas. Information is gathered on the number of homicides that took place in a given period—either a year or a series of years compressed into a single sample—and analysis of the data treats the different killings in different periods of time as part of a single observation of what is implicitly assumed to be a stable phenomenon. Yet, if rates of criminal homicide are used as a measure, violent killing in the major metropolitan areas of the United States is anything but a stable phenomenon. In 1965 Chicago police reported 395 criminal homicides, or a general victimization rate of 11.4 per 100,000. The homicide rate and number of killings in that year are representative of the Chicago experience during the prior decade. But over the six-year span from 1965 to 1970, the homicide rate in Chicago more than doubled, to 24.3 per 100,000. This great increase in rate is not unique to Chicago and suggests that analysis in patterns of homicide over time might add a useful dimension to the data base provided by earlier studies.

This note reports on a preliminary attempt to deal with police-recorded information about Chicago killings during the six-year period from 1965 through 1970 as a series of six separate observations. In pursuing this analysis we are looking for indications of either constancy or change in patterns of criminal homicide that may produce clues to the origin of the frightening increase in rate. The technique we use is promising but limited: after-the-fact analyses of changes in factors associated with homicide are more suitable to the generation of hypotheses than to answering important policy questions about the causation of violent death. However, the hypotheses generated by our preliminary analysis are interesting and, in one or two cases, potentially important.

PATTERNS OF HOMICIDE— A FIRST LOOK

In the aggregate, the analysis of any single year of Chicago's homicide experience or of all the years we have studied in combination would paint a picture that is unremarkably similar to those of other similar studies in other cities and for other years (the offense is basically intraracial; Black rates of offense and victimization far outstrip White rates; the majority of killings are associated with some prior relationship between offender and victim).

When the years covered in our study are considered as a progressive sequence, the pattern is fairly even (see Table 19.1).

A quick glance across the columns of Table 19.1 gives a picture of stability. Homicide remains about 90 percent intraracial. It remains an event involving Black offenders about 80 percent of the time and a nearly equal number of Black victims. The mean age for victims is more remarkable for its lack of change than for any apparent change in pattern. Even the difference in mean age of the offender shows a less-than-astounding four-year variation over the period of the study. The only apparently important changes are the shift from three out of four cases involving prior acquaintance between victim and offender to three out of five cases and the change in the gun share of homicides from 50 to 65 percent.

There are major qualifications that should be set out about treating this kind of data in this way. Table 19.1 uses percentage figures based on a rate that doubled during the period studied. The use of the percentage thus tends to understate differences in the relative magnitude of variables. These would look far more impressive if we were using percentage change from 1965 as an index. Take, for example, the shift from 76 percent to 62 percent in victim's prior acquaintance with offender, expressed as the percentage change

TABLE 19.1
CRIMINAL HOMICIDE IN CHICAGO—1965-70

	1965	1966	1967	1968	1969	1970
Percentage of homicides with Black victims	72%	71%	71%	73%	73%	74%
Percentage of homicides attributed to Black offenders	78%	77%	78%	79%	78%	83%
Percentage of homicide victims and offenders same race	90%	90%	86%	89%	89%	86%
Mean age of victim	35.4	35.1	34.9	33.8	33.4	34.4
Mean age of offender	33.2	31.9	31.6	31.9	30.4	29.2
Percentage of homicides where victim and offender had been acquainted	76%	73%	73%	73%	63%	62%
Percentage of homicides by gun	50%	52%	57%	58%	61%	65%

from 1965. This means that acquaintance homicide increased 59 percent while stranger homicide increased 290 percent. That the increase looks more dramatic does not, of course, mean that percentage change is the correct way to express increase. Yet, there is reason to believe that percentage change is the most appropriate measure for our study. Our search in this note is for clues to the origin of the extra number of homicides in Chicago, for the unstable element in the equation. Using rate change comparisons is thus appropriate; comparing total rates for any given year obscures differences. Using the percentage as a variable of each year's total homicide is like investigating the difference between blondes and redheads by comparing the divorce rate of blondes to the divorce rate

TABLE 19.2

HOMICIDE OFFENSE RATES PER 100,000 BY RACE, SEX, AND AGE OF OFFENDER
CHICAGO, 1965 THROUGH 1970

Offender	1965	1966	1967	1968	1969	1970
Black males						
5-14	—	9.4	4.9	3.9	4.5	5.7
15-24	107.8	157.1	172.8	218.8	264.0	298.1
25-34	107.4	115.5	131.3	135.8	158.6	164.0
35-44	97.0	72.6	83.9	98.4	95.5	104.0
45-54	50.8	92.7	95.3	78.1	78.8	54.3
55-64	65.1	33.7	36.6	36.1	64.7	76.5
65 and over	28.0	53.7	38.8	49.9	36.2	35.0
All ages	53.1	64.1	68.9	78.1	92.8	100.4
White and other males						
5-14	—	.5	0	.5	0	0
15-24	10.1	13.6	12.9	11.6	4.6	10.9
25-34	6.9	14.8	11.8	13.3	13.6	13.8
35-44	9.2	9.7	10.1	11.3	23.8	7.5
45-54	6.8	3.8	4.6	8.1	18.0	3.6
55-64	1.4	3.6	5.1	4.5	6.1	2.3
65 and over	0	4.0	2.4	2.4	1.6	.8
All ages	4.6	6.5	6.3	7.0	8.6	5.3
Black females						
5-14	0	0	.8	0	0	.7
15-24	13.4	23.0	22.9	25.0	28.8	24.6
25-34	23.6	34.7	21.4	38.3	25.4	43.9
35-44	29.1	31.6	29.5	30.5	27.1	30.8
45-54	21.2	10.3	20.0	31.1	15.1	25.9
55-64	3.1	9.0	2.9	5.7	13.9	8.2
65 and over	0	3.5	0	6.4	6.1	0
All ages	11.7	14.7	13.2	17.3	14.7	17.6
White and other females						
5-14	0	0	0	0	0	0
15-24	1.1	.5	0	2.7	.5	.7
25-34	2.0	.7	3.5	2.1	0	2.5
35-44	.6	1.3	3.0	1.2	4.0	1.3
45-54	.5	0	1.1	0	.6	2.0
55-64	0	0	.6	6.8	0	.6
65 and over	.6	0	0	0	0	0
All ages	.6	.3	1.0	1.2	.6	.7

of blondes and redheads. We will reexamine the data by using percentage change of particular events from 1965 as one major index and the importance of a factor's increase to the total increase in homicide as a second index.

A SECOND LOOK

A detailed analysis of the six-year sequence does produce more important indications of change. To begin with, the four-year decrease in the mean age of police-identified homicide offenders becomes more impressive when homicide offenders are considered separately in specific age groups. Table 19.2 gives rate data for each race and sex category by age groups.

Table 19.2 shows important differences over the period 1965 through 1970 with respect to sex, race, and age changes. As to race, it is notable that while White rates rose somewhat during the middle of the period, comparison of 1970 with 1965 shows they have remained relatively stable. White female rates remained stable, homicides by Black females increased by 50 percent, and the rate per 100,000 of homicides by Black males increased by an aggregate total of 89 percent. The Black male rate increase is not spread uniformly across all age groups. Table 19.3 sets out the homicide rate attributable to offenders within the age group 15 to 24 and the homicide rate attributable to other age groups for Black males for each of the six years.

The offender rate for Black males not in the 15 to 24 age bracket increased from 42.6 to 55.2, or 34 percent. Offender rates for Black males aged 15 to 24 increased from 107.8 to 298.1, or 178 percent. The increase in offense rates for Black males aged 15-24 accounts for about 40 percent of the increase in Chicago's aggregate homicide rate.

Trends in victimization are similar to the change in offender pattern. . . .

Again, the most dramatic single statistic is the increase in victimization rates for Black males aged 15 to 24 from 54.0 in 1965 to 192.9 in 1970. On a percentage change basis, the change in victimization is greater than the change in offense rate. Still, the 1970 rate of killings by this age group exceeds the rate of deaths in the group by 100 per 100,000—or twice the 1965 margin.

Two other trends are worthy of note. The first is that the most dramatic increases in victimization occur in the same race and sex categories that account for the most important increases in offender rates. Black male victims account for 60 percent of all homicide victims in 1970, and the increase in Black male victimization accounts for 68 percent of the total increase in homicide victimization between 1965 and 1970. There is some unevenness to this general tendency, however. The rate of victimization of older White males increases sharply, even though the number of older White male offenders does not.

The second trend worth noting is that while the mean age of homicide victims changes very little between 1965 and 1970, their age distribution changes substantially. The most important numerical and rate increase is in the Black group aged 15 to 24. This is balanced, because of the peculiar nature of a mean age statistic in this type

TABLE 19.3
HOMICIDE OFFENSE RATES PER 100,000 FOR BLACK MALES
CHICAGO, 1965 THROUGH 1970

Age	1965	1966	1967	1968	1969	1970
15-24	107.8	157.1	172.8	218.8	264.0	298.1
All others	42.6	47.0	48.9	50.5	54.5	55.2
Total	53.1	64.1	68.9	78.1	92.8	100.4

of situation, by the much smaller increase in the number of victims over the age of 35.

CHANGES IN TYPE OF HOMICIDE

As attention shifts to the situation associated with homicide, it becomes proper for the presentation to use trends in numbers of killings rather than rates of killings. Between 1965 and 1970, the rate of homicides associated with domestic and romantic altercations increased, but not so much as the total rate. . . . A necessary implication of the large increase in the total rate combined with the relative stability of this group is that other types of homicide have been increasing even more dramatically than the general rate. This is particularly the case for homicides where the police-nominated motive was robbery and for multiple-offender killings.

Table 19.4 sets out the number of robbery killllings by year for the period 1965 through 1970. The percentage increase is 345 percent. The numerical increase is 114. And the increase in robbery victimization rates alone accounts for 27 percent of the total homicide increase. When the data on robbery killings are cross-tabulated by age of victim and offender, a more detailed pattern emerges. In the first instance, robbery killings by males between 15 and 24 increased at a much faster rate than robbery killings by other age groups. . . . At the same time, robbery killings involve a greater age spread between victim and offender than other homicides do. . . .

One other factor growing out of the increase in the rate of robbery killings, both absolutely and as a proportion of all killings, is the increase in interracial homicides. The vast majority of all homicides were still in-

TABLE 19.5
RACE OF OFFENDER BY TYPE OF KILLING FOR WHITE VICTIMS, 1970

Offender's Race	Robbery Killings	Other Killings	Total
White	17%	70%	48%
Black	83%	30%	52%
Total killings of White victims	48	67	115

traracial in 1970, with the percentage of interracial homicides increasing from 10 to 14 percent. But the increase in robbery killings has a more telling effect on interracial homicide proportions in the White male victim group. Even though 64 percent of all robbery killings committed by Blacks have Black victims, the residual 36 percent of these robbery killings, coupled with the great increase in rate, results in the fact that only 48 percent of the White male homicide victims killed in 1970 were killed by White offenders. Table 19.5 shows this pattern and its origins. While this is a significant change in situation, it is still the case that the risk of a White male's being killed in Chicago is quite small compared to Black male and Black female victimization rates. Moreover, during the six years total homicide victimization for White males moved from 5.9 to 10.3 per 100,000, or less than the total percentage increase in homicide. There is also no reason to believe that robbery killings result from any distinctly racial motive. While the number of interracial robbery killings increased substantially, the number of robbery killings involving a Black victim and a Black offender increased even more substantially, so that the percentage of all robbery killings that were interracial decreased from 50 percent

TABLE 19.4
ROBBERY KILLINGS IN CHICAGO, 1965-70

	1965	1966	1967	1968	1969	1970
Number of robbery killings	33	52	63	68	113	147
Percentage of total killings	8%	10%	11%	11%	15%	18%

in 1965 to 34 percent in 1970. What *has* changed is the importance of this type of crime in relation to the other homicide risks a White male confronts.

Killings involving more than one police-nominated offender are much more common among younger age groups than among older age groups. . . . Thus, it is not surprising that the number of killings involving multiple offenders has increased dramatically along with the downward drift in the age of homicide offenders and the emerging role of the 15-to-24 group. Moreover, the tendency for younger offenders to be involved in multiple-offender homicide is somewhat more pronounced in Black offender groups than in White offender groups. Therefore, an increase in the multiple-offender category could be expected (even if there is no shift in relative emphasis to multiple-offender homicides), simply as a function of the increasing role of the Black male offender between ages 15 and 24. [The data show], however, that the actual increase in multiple-offender homicide is somewhat greater than one would expect given the change in rates attributable to young Black males. . . .

During the period from 1965 to 1970, single-offender homicides by Black males aged 15 to 24 increased from 59 to 139, while multiple-offender homicides increased from 13 to 119. This suggests that group violence among young Blacks is making an independent contribution to the increase in the homicide rate. On the other hand, these data fail to point unambiguously to gang or even group activity as the dominant cause of the increase in the homicide rate, either among this young offender group or in Chicago generally. The increase in multiple-offender killings is one-fourth of the total increase in killings and slightly more than half the total increases in offenses attributable to Blacks between the ages of 15 and 24. To the extent that multiple-offender homicide is taken as the single index of gang activity, this activity seems a very important factor but not a dominant one. Yet there is no reason that group-related or gang-related shooting must necessarily result in the police notation that more than one offender was involved, nor is there any reason to suppose that every killing by more than one young Black is a "gang killing" unless the term "gang" is defined very loosely. To the extent that one views the *total* increase in homicides attributable to young Blacks as a function of gang activity, the increase is far more substantial than the multiple-offender statistics would indicate. Unfortunately, there is no ready method of validating the assumption that most violence by young Blacks is related to organized street gangs. One can suspect that gang activity has played a substantial role in increasing homicide in this age group. But data on group involvement in homicide or on the sharp increase in homicide by this age group are not sufficient to prove the suspicion.

Another important change in Chicago homicides between 1965 and 1970 is the steadily increasing role of firearms. Guns were involved in 50 percent of all 1965 killings and in 65 percent of all 1970 killings. A more pronounced pattern is evident if gun and nongun killings are treated separately for the period from 1965 to 1970, as is done in Table 19.6.

Firearms homicide increased 169 percent, while homicide by other means increased by 47 percent. Of equal importance is the fact that firearms homicide increased most dramatically for Black male offenders between

TABLE 19.6
HOMICIDE BY WEAPON, 1965-70

Weapon	1965	1966	1967	1968	1969	1970	Change 1965-1970
Firearms	196	264	314	370	462	528	169%
All other means	197	246	237	265	286	289	47%
Total	393	510	551	635	748	817	113%

the ages of 15 and 24, the age group where homicide increased most dramatically. For those offenders, 76.3 percent of all homicides committed in 1970 were committed by gun. The rate of gun homicide by Black males between the ages of 15 and 24 increases 444 percent between 1965 and 1970, compared to 69 percent for homicide by all other means. Earlier data from this project support the proposition that the increasing use of firearms will increase the death rate from attacks, all other things being constant.

SUMMARY OF CHANGES

In the summary picture that emerges from the preceding data, robbery killings and more common and less specifically motivated altercation killings increase substantially. Young and very young offenders account for half the general increase and are rapidly bringing the age distribution of known homicide offenders in Chicago closer to age distributions noted for other crimes. In general, and with the robbery killing trends as an exception, changes in age distribution and race of victims are similar to the changes in the age distribution and race of offenders. A conservative treatment of the data on multiple offenders between ages 15 and 24 still suggests that an increase in group-related violence is making an independent contribution to the increase in Chicago's homicide rate. The data on the dramatic increase in gun homicide, and particularly the very substantial rise in gun use among Blacks aged 15 to 24, suggest that increased use and, probably, carrying of firearms are of additional and substantial importance in explaining the rise in the homicide rate.

One other conclusion seems inescapable given the present data: the six-year period witnessed a real increase in homicide rates, apart from differences in the age distribution of the population, and apart from patterns of immigration or change in racial composition. Overwhelmingly, the victims of this very real increase are similar to the groups among whom the offense rate increases most sub-

stantially. One exception to this pattern is the increase in robbery killings. This robbery-murder increase is an issue for public concern. Yet it would be unfortunate if that single increase were perceived as the only issue for concern. The increasing number of robbery killings, like the general statistics, also shows increases in multiple-offender killings, increases in gun use, a downward migration in the age structure of homicide offenders and downward age migration in gun use. The robbery killings appear to be part of a much larger set of changes in the context of violence in Chicago.

Reversing this six-year trend will prove difficult. Identification of problems is always easier than the prescription of solutions and, one might add, a good deal cheaper. Yet it bears repetition that Chicago's experience is not unique; the problem seems substantial enough to merit constructive public and governmental concern.

THE LIMITS OF HOMICIDE STUDIES

One of the more important limitations on the present study is that, in dealing with homicide data alone, we are probably dealing with one manifestation of a group of much larger behavior systems. It is thus difficult, on the basis of a body count, to do more than speculate to what extent the difference in the death rate from one particular activity represents a difference in the *quality* of that activity in Chicago or a difference in the *quality* of the activity. Two examples of the problem will suffice.

Is the alarming increase in the robbery-murder rate an indication that (*a*) the base robbery rate is going up (perhaps faster than crime statistics indicate); (*b*) new groups are committing robberies in different ways; (*c*) mechanisms, principally guns, are being used at a greater rate; or (*d*) Chicago is experiencing a more lethally motivated robber?

All of these are possible explanations of the dramatic rise in the robbery-homicide rate, and all are probably partially true. But to get a firm grasp on the importance of each factor in explaining the great rate increase, we have to study trends in the larger category of robbery as well as those in robbery-murder. Such a study could also address the question of whether and where there are important similarities as well as differences between fatal and nonfatal robbery episodes in Chicago.

With respect to nonrobbery killings, information on the quantity and quality of nonfatal attacks with deadly weapons would add a valuable dimension to the information developed on homicide in the preceding pages. Two other reports from this research project have attempted to add that dimension with varying degrees of success.

There are a number of other promising uses for data on patterns of homicide compared with homicide-related offenses. The Task Force on Individual Acts of Violence of the Eisenhower Commission did a comparative study of patterns of a wide spectrum of violent offenses in 17 cities. Where rates of behavior are changing, it would be appropriate to add a time dimension to analyses like that done by the task force. The analysis of data on a number of violence-related offenses over a series of discrete time observations promises to make the statistical study of patterns of violence a more powerful tool than it has been and a useful source of data in an area of social concern where insights into causation and prevention are scarce.

20. THE RIOT THAT DIDN'T HAPPEN

ROBERT SHELLOW AND DEREK VON ROEMER

Reprinted from Social Problems *14, No. 2 (Fall 1966): 221-33 with permission of The Society for the Study of Social Problems and the authors. Both authors have been associated with the Adolescent Process Section, Mental Health Study Center of the National Institutes of Mental Health. Robert Shellow is Professor of Urban Affairs at Carnegie-Mellon University in Pittsburgh. Derek Von Roemer is Chief of the Division of Drug Abuse, Baltimore County Department of Health, Towson, Maryland.*

■ This selection deals with a peace-keeping problem that from time to time receives considerable public and political attention—the holiday riot. Rioting activities in which much property damage and occasional injury or death occur have been a somewhat rare but always dramatic accompaniment to holiday weekends (such as Labor Day and the 4th of July) and occasionally to student spring vacations in Florida. These riots play a significant part in establishing images of various kinds of youth deviance—irresponsible college students, violence-crazed lower class hoodlums, and the like. No group has more fully captured public attention as a symbol of "modern youth's" tendency to the loss of personal control than have the motorcycle gangs, first portrayed on film by Marlon Brando in *The Wild Ones* and later popularized by the Hell's Angels of California (with the enthusiastic if somewhat inadvertent cooperation of local police and prosecuting attorneys in that state).

Shellow and Romer deal with a police effort to avoid a riot in a situation when one seemed highly likely—a national motorcycle race in a rural area not far from Washington, D.C. They show how two social scientists, working with local police and other officials tried to manage the situation so as to minimize the instigations to rioting so often set up in the interaction between the young participants and the local officials and citizens.

A general theory of the kind of collective behavior that riots exemplify is in Neil J. Smelser, *A Theory of Collective Behavior* (Free Press, 1963). Another approach to collective behavior is Ralph H. Turner and L. M. Killian, *Collective Behavior* (Prentice-Hall, 1957). Orrin B. Klapp analyzes the role of the mass media in propagating new folk heroes, such as the

Hell's Angels, in two books: *Heroes, Villains, and Fools* (Prentice-Hall, 1962); and *Symbolic Leaders* (Aldine, 1964). For an excellent description of the life style of the Hell's Angels see Hunter S. Thompson, *Hell's Angels: The Strange and Terrible Saga of the Motorcycle Gangs* (Random House, 1967). For an autobiography of one of the Hell's Angels see Frank Reynolds, *Freewheeling Frank: Secretary of the Angels* (Grove Press, 1967). The most comprehensive comparative and interdisciplinary review of the general subject is in James F. Short, Jr. and Marvin F. Wolfgang, eds., *Collective Violence* (Aldine, 1972). ■

ALTHOUGH CITIZENS traditionally rely upon police for prevention and control of civil riot, most police departments have only limited experience in coping with large crowds, much less full riot conditions. Moreover, it seems likely that police will be called to serve in this capacity with growing frequency as public streets become more and more the stage on which social protests and counter-protests are acted out.

This growing threat to civil order poses questions of specific relevance for social scientists. Can the approach and theories of social science be put to use in communities facing the threat or fact of civil disorder? Can social scientists study riot behavior as it develops, while at the same time sharing the responsibility for its prevention?

The authors of this paper were confronted by these two questions in the summer of 1965. A national motorcycle race was scheduled for the Labor Day weekend at Upper Marlboro, the County seat of Prince

George's County, Maryland. This county of 500,000 population is adjacent to Washington, D.C., and is partly suburban, partly rural. Upper Marlboro is in a rural sector but is only about 15 miles from well-populated suburbs.

Our involvement in what later turned out to be six weeks of planning for riot prevention began as a casual conversation between one of the authors and a detective lieutenant. The news media had reported all the gory details of the Weir's Beach riot, which followed the National Championship motorcycle races near Laconia, New Hampshire. The first details of the July 4th resort riots were still page-one news. The lieutenant reported that shortly after the Weir's Beach episode three motorcyclists claiming to be "Hell's Angels" were arrested and jailed for disorderly conduct by town policemen in Prince George's County. Angered by being forced to bathe for court, the cyclists threatened to return in force over Labor Day to "tear up the county."

Wishing to be kept posted on the local situation, we spoke to the inspector responsible for police action over Labor Day. He was concerned, but he wasn't sure how seriously to take the possibility of violence. We all agreed that very little was known about the Hell's Angels and how they were likely to behave among several thousand motorcyclists amassed for a big race. Our professional curiosity aroused, we offered to try to chase down the rumors and bring the results of our inquiries back to the police. But two weeks of search failed to turn up so much as one Hell's Angel, though the rumors of invasion and destruction were persistent and proliferating.

When we reviewed accounts of a number of recent riots and disturbances in connection with recreational or sporting events, we noted several factors which seemed to be significant in all of them. Though they are not based on a systematic review of the relevant sociological literature, we have found that the following generalizations fit rather well with at least one major theoretical analysis.

1. An influx of outsiders into a small town or circumscribed amusement area, where the number of outsiders was large relative to the number of local inhabitants and control personnel.
2. The outsiders were distinguished from "locals" by some common feature such as an intense interest (e.g., motorcycling), an age group (e.g., college youth), place of residence (e.g., urban areas), or race.
3. The distinction between "locals" and "outsiders" was often made more visible by differences between the two in dress, argot, and other expressive behavior.

The specific conditions under which exuberance and rowdiness exploded into rioting seemed to be the following:

1. Recreational, service, and control facilities "flooded" by overwhelming numbers of visitors, who were then left at loose ends, ready for any kind of "action."
2. Ineffectual, often provocative attempts at control and expression of authority by police or officials.
3. Development of a sense of group solidarity among members of the crowd.

Often the locals, including the authorities, contributed to the developing cohesion by perceiving the visitors as a homogeneous mass, attributing negative characteristics to them as a class, labeling them—e.g., as "hoodlums" or "young punks"—and then treating them accordingly. The effect of opposition or attack in increasing group cohesion is well documented. If the opposition is ineffectual as well, many members of the developing mob begin to sense its potential power. (Several reports of disturbances attributed careful pre-planning to a small cadre of dedicated instigators, who allegedly circulated rumors before the event and selected targets on the scene. Actual proof of "planning," however, as opposed to mere repetition of common rumors, is difficult to obtain.)

It had become obvious that in order to prepare for the Labor Day weekend much information would be needed about the organization of motorcycling, as a sport and as a way of life. Moving from one enthusiast to another and making contacts at the local Harley-Davidson dealer, we made a number of discoveries.

Motorcyclists come from all walks of life. The majority are employed, and need to be, since as much as $3,000 may be tied up in a "motor." The devotees insist that the size of the machine separates the men from the boys. Those who own enormous Harley-Davidsons and the large Triumphs or BSA's, and who engage in competitive events such as races, "field events," and "hill climbs," see themselves as a breed apart from the "candy ass" owners of Hondas and the lightweights. For the former group, the motorcycle often serves as the fulcrum of social and even family life. They enjoy being able to take off any evening at a moment's notice and ride, say, from Washington, D.C. to Atlantic City, returning as the sun rises. They travel regularly to weekend field meets and races, usually camping overnight on the scene.

Like many hobby sports, motorcycling has its formal organization, the American Motorcycle Association (AMA), and its "sanctioned" members. AMA clubs have tight rules and tolerate little deviance. There are other clubs, some of which aspire to AMA membership and some of which suit those who enjoy a more relaxed and casual organization. The latter require only that members not seriously embarrass the club in public. They tend to be more tolerant in their attitudes regarding noisy mufflers and styling, and less regimented during group expeditions. All get classified by the AMA as "outlaws."

Aside from these more or less conforming clubs, the "outlaw" class also includes groups of dedicated rowdies who pride themselves on their ability to intimidate and destroy. The *Hell's Angels Motorcycle Club of California* is such a group, as are the *Gooses*, from New York and New Jersey, and the *Pagans*, from the Washington area. Some groups and individuals trade on the established reputation of the Hell's Angels, imitating their insignia, the winged death's head and wheel.

Spokesmen for the motorcycling "Establishment" often refer to the "one percent who cause all the trouble," and give the sport a bad image. The rowdies have proudly accepted "one percenter" as an honorific epithet, and often have it emblazoned on their costumes as a badge of commitment. It is the "one percenter" who personifies the popular stereotype of the motorcycle gang member, as portrayed by Marlon Brando in *The Wild Ones*. Current styles among these individuals include long hair, beards, earrings, oily dungarees which are never washed, and an enormous variety of bizarre, highly personalized regalia. Some affect the habit, attributed to beatniks, of never bathing.

Regardless of their reference group or status within it, motorcyclists are of one voice in complaining of police persecution, and they all report victimization on the streets by ordinary motorists. Many respectable motorcyclists, like the "rowdy outlaws," see themselves as a persecuted minority.

With regard to the Labor Day weekend itself, we learned that the schedule of events was more complex than we or the police had thought. Aside from the big race on Sunday, the "Ninth Annual Tobacco Trail Classic" at the Upper Marlboro track, there were lesser races at the same track on Saturday. The main race was for the first time a National Championship event, with top riders competing for points toward the national title. At the Vista track, 14 miles away but within the same police jurisdiction, there were to be "field events" (drag races, "riding the plank," "sack races," etc.) on Saturday and Sunday and an AMA-sanctioned race meet Monday. The sponsors of the Upper Marlboro races had also scheduled a Saturday night race, at a track 30 miles away in the Baltimore suburbs, "to give people something to do and keep them out of trouble."

The Vista track had in the past operated as an "outlaw" track without AMA sanction, and most or all of the competitors and spectators had been Negroes. However, in 1965 it achieved sanctioned status, and its events were now listed in the national calendar. A dance hall, popular with Washington area

Negroes, was located in the track infield and would be operating every night of the weekend. Very likely large proportions of those attending the motorcycle events at Vista would be Negroes. The crowd at the Marlboro track was expected to be between 3,000 and 6,000; a much smaller crowd was anticipated at Vista. Most motorcyclists we spoke to thought there would be a great deal of migration during the weekend from one track to another and among the various camping areas (assuming there were more than one), the taverns, and other recreation spots. Easy mobility is the essence of motorcycling.

Concluding that our staff enjoyed a special and privileged relationship with motorcyclists, the police asked us whether or not the race should be called off. We did not feel we could take responsibility for the decision, but we joined in the deliberations. To cancel a public event on the basis of thin rumor alone was a dangerous precedent to set; yet to knowingly jeopardize the safety of innocent people was unthinkable. Finally it was decided to permit the race to be run as scheduled, with every effort being made to avert violence. Our shift in role from outside consultant to partnership with the police in this project tied us much closer to the action and events of the weekend than would have been true in the role of detached scientist-observer.

GOALS AND STRATEGIES

The decision to permit the race made, we then developed a set of major goals which we felt should guide our own planning and that of the police.

First of all we encouraged sober planning for all the events and contingencies of the long weekend. Naturally, advance planning was not foreign to a professional police department. Nonetheless we felt that the unsettled state of the Hell's Angels rumors, plus our refusal to make pseudoauthoritative pronouncements on the probable course of

events, helped maintain a degree of controlled anxiety among police officials. This limited anxiety went far to prevent a premature resolution of the planning process, either through panicky reliance on harshness or toughness on the one hand or complacent relaxation on the other. Planning, we felt, should have three major objectives: first, anticipation of the kinds, numbers, and distribution of motorcyclists and spectators, as well as the activities they would engage in and the amount of localized roving to be expected; second, the disposition of police officers and their instructions both as to general attitude and specific actions in various contingencies; third, coordination of the several police departments concerned, including the state police and the local police of nearby towns and counties to which the motorcyclists might travel in search of recreation. We relied on the county police to make contact with the other departments.

The second goal was to avoid a polarization of relations between the authorities on the one hand and motorcyclists in general on the other. We addressed our efforts to both groups. As we explored the "culture" of motorcycling, we tried to keep the police informed and interested in what we learned. We arranged a meeting between some local motorcyclists and police officials; films of sport motorcycling were shown, and afterward each group gave frank expression to its gripes concerning the other. Our educational goals with the police were: (1) to show them that motorcyclists are not essentially different from other citizens, and need not be treated as a breed apart; (2) to inform them that motorcyclists are not a homogeneous class but come in a variety of shapes and sizes, some innocuous, some potentially troublesome; (3) to impress upon them that indiscriminate harsh treatment of all motorcyclists would confirm the latter's sense of persecution, increase group solidarity among them, and go far toward creating the very polarization we wished to avoid.

In working with local motorcyclists, we had two objectives: (1) to involve the organized groups in the actual control effort, asking them not only to refrain from participating in or serving as passive audience to rowdiness but to help actively in identifying potential trouble areas, keeping police informed of large group movements, etc.; (2) to weaken the respectable motorcyclists' sense of solidarity with the "one percenters" through reinforcing their existing concern for the deteriorating "image" of motorcycling and pointing up their vested interest in a peaceful race meet.

Our third major goal was to ensure that adequate facilities were provided for the visiting motorcyclists, with an eye to both containment and entertainment. The object here was to inhibit milling behavior, a usual precursor to crowd disturbances. Specifically, we suggested that adequate and convenient camping facilities were customary and essential at motorcycle meets, and that certain informal and rather dangerous recreations (such as drag racing and stunt riding in the camp grounds), which do not impinge on the nonmotorcycling citizenry, are also customary and ought to be permitted.

Finally, our fourth major objective was to monitor the events of the weekend and keep a continuous flow of intelligence coming into command headquarters so that the senior officer could make effective decisions. Here we served in something of a combined research and undercover capacity, checking out rumors, keeping current with the temper of various groups, clubs, and gangs among the motorcyclists, and observing events such as fights or accidents as they occurred. We made a point of spending time in places where the county police could not routinely go.

EVENTS LEADING UP TO THE WEEKEND

Rumors of the arrival en masse of the Hell's Angels of California persisted through Saturday of the three-day weekend and were *never* clearly proved or disproved. However, we learned Hell's Angels were anticipated in resorts all the way from Ocean City, Maryland, 140 miles away, to the Pacific coast.

Three scattered locations (a tavern, the racetrack, and a whole town) in Prince George's County were to be wrecked. All these rumors seemed to be circulating mostly among youth and motorcyclists. We began to see that the Hell's Angels were assuming a mythical character. They had become folk heroes, functioning both as vicarious exemplars of behavior most youth could only fantasy (unless swept away in mob activity) and as legendary champions who could come to the rescue of the oppressed and persecuted. An older motorcyclist, witnessing police harassment of his fellows at a town outside Prince George's County, was heard to remark, "Just wait 'til the Angels hear about this when they come in tomorrow. They'll come down here and tear this place apart."

The police never did accept the idea of actively involving local motorcycle clubs in the control effort, even though we offered to do all the legwork in getting club representatives together for a meeting. An exception was the large club that sponsored the Marlboro races. The inspector warned them severely that any trouble this weekend would greatly reduce the likelihood of the race being permitted next year. However, he emphasized that the department would not discriminate in any way against motorcyclists, and that they by no means classified all motorcyclists with the Hell's Angels. The inspector convinced the sponsoring club of the necessity of hiring uniformed guards for the racetrack. The club also assured us that adequate camping facilities would be provided.

There was little advance coordination among the various police departments in the area. The state police initially announced a policy of "keep them moving," and said they would "get tough" with any rowdy-looking types they encountered, but later they did conform to the approach of the county police. The detailed cooperation between departments that we had envisioned, like involvement of the motorcycle clubs in police planning, was probably considered too far outside normal practice to be warranted by the situation.

Among these largely negative circumstances, one particularly positive development stood out. At each police rollcall prior to the Labor Day weekend, all the uniformed men were instructed to treat all motorcyclists just as they would any motorist visiting the county. They were told that only a very small minority of motorcyclists were troublemakers, and that only the behavior, not the style of dress, haircut or bodily cleanliness was a matter of police concern. Thus the professional police attitude of neutrality and commitment to impartial law enforcement, characteristic of the department's work in other special situations, was reinforced with respect to a new group.

On Saturday morning of the race weekend we and the police were quite disturbed to learn that the sponsoring AMA club had reneged on its promise to provide public camping facilities. Apparently they wished to avoid the expense of renting portable outhouses, which were likely to be broken up for firewood in the course of the weekend. We were further disturbed to learn that early arrivals, some of whom were pretty ragged and rough looking, had already set up camp in the large field usually rented for that purpose. This created a tricky problem for the police. They could not legitimately enter the field, which was private property, unless the owner complained or a violation of law occurred which was visible from the public highway. If the police officially notified the owner, he would be bound to ask that the trespassers be removed, because of his liability for damages incurred by people who were on his property with his implied permission. Eviction of the growing crowd of squatters would have meant removing a noisy, potentially troublesome group from a location remote from residences and businesses where the amount of property they could damage was limited. Furthermore they were not, at that time, visibly violating laws. There was no way to predict where they would go if evicted, but obviously they would not go home so early in the weekend. The problem might simply have been scattered all over the county, aggravating the difficulties of control while at the same time provoking

resentment which could have been turned against innocent citizens.

It was decided that notification of the owner of the field was not warranted and that there were tactical advantages in keeping the field open, since it seemed to be attracting and holding the rowdier element. So long as they were all in one place, surveillance would be simple and response to trouble could be quick.

The activities on the field were kept under continuous but unobtrusive observation. Police cars were continually passing the field, occasionally pausing near the entrance; the people on the field were thus kept aware of the police presence in the general area, but not so heavily as to arouse feelings of persecution. The 45-man Civil Disturbance Unit (CDU), trained in riot control but lacking experience in full riot conditions, had been mobilized and sent out on the road the night before (Friday). Only a few motorcyclists were seen in the county, and the unit was dismissed around midnight. The usual dance at the Vista track was held without incident.

From Saturday through Monday the entire force, including the CDU, was ordered on 12-hour shifts. The men were kept on the road except when responding to trouble calls, thus providing extra control for the normally heavy holiday beach traffic. We felt that the men would have been able to respond more quickly to large-scale trouble if they had been concentrated in two or three central standby locations rather than dispersed over the county's 486 square miles. However, police officials judged that the disadvantage of a possible delay in mobilization of force was offset by the double payoff from the same investment in overtime pay—more extensive traffic control as well as riot prevention.

An elaborate communications system was set up, employing the police radio (monitored by newspapers and wire services) and also a Civil Defense band which permitted more detailed discussion and open references to likely trouble spots. A special radio code was established so that squad cars using the police band could notify headquarters briefly and in confidence of the presence of groups of motorcyclists.

THE WEEKEND AS IT DEVELOPED

On Saturday, only a few hundred spectators attended the scheduled lightweight and novice races at Marlboro. Across the highway those squatters, dusty out-of-towners, and locals who preferred the role of contestant to that of passive onlooker conducted their own impromptu field games. The entire center of the squatters' field, despite its ruts and hummocks, became a drag strip. Groups, clubs, even families had set up campsites around the periphery of the field in a broken crescent.

Groups and couples who settled on the extreme ends of the crescent appeared to have expensive camping equipment and rather conventional dress. Dead center at the head of the drag strip, the most ragged troop of squatters set up headquarters in a large army tent, its center pole flying a red flag. Sullen young men and girls milled around this command post, drinking beer and making menacing noises at curiosity seekers. Clusters of jackets marked "Hell's Angels," "Pagans," or "The Gooses," were seen. Individuals sported a nose ring, a swastika, a Halloween wig, or gold cross earrings; many wore their hair in shoulder-length manes.

A group of mostly short-haired locals, more or less neat in T-shirts and jeans, tried to introduce some order into the drag races. One tried to control racing by flagging each pair of racers to a start. He was successful for several hours, but finally the enormous quantities of beer, hard liquor, and green wine consumed by participants began to undermine his authority. Racers roared past him without waiting for the flag. He shouted for order, but few responded. Nonracers crisscrossed the drag strip, narrowly escaping collision. The proximity of the self-appointed track superintendents to the encampment of long-haired outsiders and locals became abrasive. Accidents began to occur; and finally a fight broke out between a very wobbly Pagan and a helmeted short-haired local. The short-

haired hero punched the Pagan unconscious, and was then successfully protected by his associates from assault by the rest of the Pagans. The victor had the poor taste and bad judgment to sit triumphantly astride the hood of a truck, waving his beer can in bravado challenge. Now all the "one percenters" joined in a confederation and charged en masse toward the short-haired locals. Just at that moment a drunken cyclist lost his machine to a rut in the track. His mishap was noted by police on the highway, who dispatched an ambulance along with five police cruisers. The vehicles poured onto the field and fanned out in a half-circle around the casualty, thus coincidentally presenting the crowd with an array of flashing red lights. The unexpected show of power was so sudden and instantaneous that the would-be warriors at the head of the strip broke ranks and returned to the staging area. Unknowingly (since the conflict had not reached a stage when observers off the field could distinguish it as such), the police had put a stop to what might have been a bloody war, for the local motorcycle enthusiasts were far outnumbered by the combined force of Pagans, Hell's Angels, and Gooses. Quite fortuitously, those spoiling for trouble got the message that there was a large force of police nearby, ready for action on a moment's notice.

Following the withdrawal of the police, 20 Hell's Angels and Gooses set out to replenish their beer supply at the Old Tavern nearby. Just as they started to throw their weight around in the bar and threaten the owner, a police sergeant and another officer entered the room. The group quieted down and waited for the action. Three cyclists moved to the window to assess the size of the sergeant's force; four cruisers were visible. The sergeant opened with, "I hope you all are behaving yourselves." Remembering from a conversation with us that motorcycle chains worn loosely over the hips rather than through belt loops should be considered weapons, he asked, "What's that chain for?" "Hey, man, I lock up my motor with it." "Well, aren't you afraid someone'll steal your motor, not being locked up and all? You better come with me while we put that chain on right, son." The group tensed, then relaxed as the young man elected to go quietly and do as the sergeant suggested. Shortly after this low-key encounter the group roared back to the field and the Old Tavern was prematurely closed for the weekend.

At 11 P.M. about 75 cyclists were seen by one of our staff at a rock 'n' roll beach resort in a neighboring county. The chief of police there had already advised the press of his intention to lock up any rowdy motorcyclists who showed up. He arranged for the state police to back him up. Twenty state troopers in riot dress with five dogs were lined up on the main street across from the crowd of motorcycle riders, while six local policemen pushed and poked with night sticks, arresting several who took exception to their tactics. By 1:30 A.M. most of the motorcyclists had left town. Statements to the press by the chief greatly exaggerated the numbers present and arrested, thus giving an unwarranted notoriety to the evening.

By Sunday morning 300 motorcyclists had settled on the field at Marlboro. Those who had been driven from the beach resort were in a mean mood. Under the direction of the unofficial starter drag racing resumed at a more frantic tempo than on the day before. Across the highway a steady stream of spectators poured onto the track for the afternoon race. Few took notice of the accidents that were beginning to occur on the field.

At two in the afternoon a fire was set in a railroad caboose on a siding behind the field. Fire equipment and police responded quickly; no attempt was made to find the arsonists. At three o'clock a crane was started on an adjacent construction site, and tools were stolen from its cab. At four-thirty, coinciding with the Tobacco Trail Classic across the road, a young man removed the license plates from his dilapidated old car and set it afire. With another sportsman straddling the hood, the owner drove onto the drag strip and jumped free. The car rammed an accelerating motorcycle. Both hood rider and motorcyclist were thrown on impact, both suffering broken legs. A firetruck arrived to put out the fire amid jeers from spectators. A police lieutenant supervised aid to the injured, making humorous asides to cool the excited crowd and enable the ambulance to remove the casualties to the hospital.

About six o'clock the long-haired groups demanded that the locals turn over the starting flag to a Hell's Angel who appeared to be one of their leaders. Fighting broke out but subsided immediately when one squad of the CDU (10 men) drove onto the field. This time the police had riot equipment visible—helmets, clubs, shotguns, gas masks. The crowd dispersed; the squad withdrew. Since tension on the field seemed to be building, command officers set up an observation post on a cloverleaf approach overlooking the field. At six-thirty the flagman and a delegation from his club came up to plead with command officers to clear the field of hoodlums; they threatened to bring in their own weapons if police didn't protect them. Since the delegation could not agree on who should be charged with what, police action was delayed.

At seven several men broke away from the milling crowd at the center of the field and ran to their machines. From the observation post, it was clear they were returning with bars, chains, and other weapons, The entire CDU was sent onto the field where they quickly assembled in riot formation. The inspector drawled out over the bullhorn, "All right men, you've had your fun, now it's time to go home." Before he finished his sentence motorcycles began to move out of the field. Within 20 minutes the area was clear except for some peaceful campers who were allowed to finish their dinner.

Up to this time, the importance of containing troublemakers on the field was dominant in the minds of commanding officers. If the crowd were allowed to remain overnight, fighting probably would continue, but now under cover of darkness. Dispersing the squatters while it was still light would, hopefully, send them on their way home. The alternative —isolating and removing the instigators and mob leaders—was complicated by the fact that police could not remain on the field, and by the inability or unwillingness of cyclists to serve as complainants.

Fifteen minutes after the field was vacated, ten men and a girl were arrested outside the Old Tavern, where they had started to break windows. Within minutes, another 10, including the leading Hell's Angel, were arrested as trespassers at a filling station where they refused to make way for customers. There was no further trouble in the county, at the Vista track, or at the beach resort, though an anxious lookout was maintained till early the next morning. By Monday it was obvious that the danger had passed. The final races at Vista were held without incident, although some Hell's Angels and Pagans were rumored to be among the spectators.

REACTIONS TO THE WEEKEND

Both the command officers and the county commissioner responsible for police matters were satisfied that the police had conducted themselves effectively and that the control effort had been a success. They felt, however, that the situation had not warranted the extra expense and trouble. Estimates of cost ranged from $6,000 to $10,000, but certainly some of the overtime pay would have been necessary for a Labor Day weekend even without motorcyclists. The commissioner announced that he couldn't see why the county had "to put up year after year with the influx of motorcycle tramps who camp out, drink and fight among themselves."

Like the commissioner, most of the police leadership was opposed to permitting the race next year. We refrained from offering unsolicited and premature advice on the issue of future races. The club sponsoring the Marlboro races was considering cutting down the meet to a one-day event and preventing camping altogether, in the hope that this would make the event more acceptable to authorities.

Since we were unable to maintain contacts among Pagans, Gooses, or Hell's Angels, we could not ascertain *their* reactions to police policy and procedure. We did talk to our

acquaintance at the local Harley-Davidson dealership, which provides service and parts for many out-of-town motorcyclists. He reported that for the first time in nine years of race meets he had heard none of the usual atrocity stories of police mistreatment of motorcyclists in the county. The local short-haired motorcyclists who had been in the fighting on the field felt that the police had exercised entirely too much restraint in dealing with that situation. They did not know, until we told them, that the field had not been rented this year.

CONCLUSION

There was no riot in Prince George's County. The citizens and their property emerged almost unscathed. The races and field events were held. The campers drank, dragged, and scuffled undisturbed for a longer period than any of them probably expected.

Was all the concern, planning, and extra police activity justified? Would the Gooses, Pagans, and alleged Hell's Angels have been just as peaceful anyway, despite their frightening appearance? We think not, and cite the forays against the Old Tavern, the crane and the caboose, the incinerated car, and the brawling which broke out repeatedly on the field as evidence that, if unhindered and undaunted, the hoodlum element sooner or later would have left the camping area and sought glory and reputation in new arenas, before new audiences. These seem to be people who need and seek the stimulation of collective action, excitement, and violence. Without it they become depressed and demoralized. They have an affinity for the romantic role of outlaw, which is perhaps the only status in which they feel they can stand out as individuals. In it they approach the dramatic, larger-than-life identity of the mythic Hell's Angel. And only the self-justifying power of mob action could support such a heroic identity for youths such as these. We see them, then, as mob seekers and mob creators.

We consider four factors to have been critical in preventing the spread of violence to the local citizenry.

Most important was *the general police policy of strength, fairness, and neutrality,* which influenced all the tactics employed. Law violations were dealt with immediately and firmly, but motorcyclists were not harassed or deliberately antagonized. The availability of overwhelming force, literally on a moment's notice, was demonstrated but not overdramatized. Thus potential mob leaders were deprived of the rallying point of "police brutality," and potential followers never developed the sense of mob power that results from evidence of police weakness. Well-behaved motorcyclists, whatever their appearance, were not mistreated and thus were not given reason for aligning themselves with the troubleseekers and against the police.

The decision not to interfere with the motorcyclists' camping and drag racing on private property, until extreme violence impended, was also of critical importance, for several reasons. In the field the potential troublemakers were all contained in an open area where their activities, their comings and goings, could be easily observed. They were segregated by the broad highway and differentiated from the much larger mass of spectators at the track, and thus deprived of both victims and audience. The amount of property vulnerable to damage was relatively small. Finally, they were allowed to occupy their time with activities which were both customary and satisfying (drinking, dragging, showing off, etc.) while not annoying other citizens. This business of "keeping them occupied" is not trivial. Mob action, except in a catastrophe, is usually preceded by a period of "milling," wherein people whose customary lines of action are blocked or inappropriate to the situation seek new guidelines. They engage in seemingly aimless behavior, which is actually exchange of fact and rumor and movement toward consensus. It is during such periods that mob leaders can seize the initiative in directing the crowd toward specific objectives.

A third important factor was *the continu-*ous flow of intelligence, both during the weekend and over the preceding weeks. We feel that our investigations and discussions before the holiday, aside from their obvious utility in planning, helped break down police stereotypes concerning motorcyclists and reinforced an attitude of impartiality toward them.

Last but far from least was plain and simple *good luck,* which favored us on several occasions. Undoubtedly there was an element of luck in the fact that the "hoodlum element" chose to remain at the campground rather than roam the county. The factional dispute between the short-haired locals and the "one percenters" may have been fortunate, in that it kept the warlike elements busy and precluded any alliance between the two groups. It was especially fortunate that when it finally became necessary to clear the field, most of the rowdier motorcyclists left the county entirely. The Vista track, even with its nightly dances, did not attract them. The isolation of the campground from the racetrack and from settled areas was another helpful accident.

As noted above, certain policies which we considered advisable were not carried out. We believe that the trouble which did occur can be attributed in part to those omissions.

The failure of the sponsoring club to provide camping facilities at Marlboro, as promised in the race publicity, might well have had more serious consequences than it did. Depriving the visitors of the activities ordinarily organized around campsites logically means they will seek others; they become a group of potential malcontents, at loose ends, away from home, and with a grievance. Violence in such a situation need not be entirely spontaneous; norms from similar past situations (e.g., New Hampshire) exist to guide the group to it.

The fighting on the field might not have gone as far as it did if all the local motorcycle clubs had been actively involved in the control effort. The "short-hairs" who were brawling with the "one percenters" were all members of one club. In addition to avoiding trouble and reporting it when they saw it, local groups could have helped operate the camping area (if it was formally rented), directed the informal drag races with official sanction, and set up a registry of all groups entering the campground. Such a registry (including motorcycle tag numbers) might have destroyed the anonymity which allows people away from home and in a group to violate law and convention and feel safe about it.

Once coordination with the state police contingent assigned to the county was achieved, the lack of involvement of other departments in the planning was of no consequence for the county department. It might have been, had the motorcyclists chosen to roam more. Town police at the rock 'n' roll beach resort might have benefited from coordination and consultation with the county department.

As social scientists we tried to apply in this situation the specialized knowledge and theory of our field, and found it useful. The police, logically, focus on the apprehension of persons who violate laws, protection of citizens from the acts of such persons, prevention of specifically violative behavior, and the deployment of strength in accordance with those goals. As social scientists we focused on the collection of data, the analysis of differences and similarities, the understanding of group and individual behavior, and the communication and exchange of fact and opinion.

Though the events of Labor Day 1965 in Prince George's County were of little national or long-term import in themselves, we consider the principles applied and the lessons learned to have far broader relevance—a significant practice for things to come.

21. PEACE-KEEPING ON SKID ROW

EGON BITTNER

Reprinted from "The Police on Skid-Row: A Study of Peace Keeping," American Sociological Review *32, no. 5 (October 1967): 699-715. Egon Bittner is Professor of Sociology,
Brandeis University. He has made contributions to phenomenological theory in sociology
and has had a long-time interest in the social labeling and processing of marginal persons,
such as vagrants and skid-row bums, as well as in other aspects of the policing function.*

◼ Most American cities of any size have their skid rows—places where down-and-out alcoholics congregate and pursue a deviant lifestyle under the watchful eye of the police and the Salvation Army. Skid row is the principal American example of a deviant district—an area to which disapproved behavior is confined on the basis of society's understanding that in fact it cannot (or perhaps even should not) be eradicated. The job of the police in this district, as Bittner shows, is not to enforce the law but to keep the peace and to contain the deviant types within the area so that they do not bother "decent" people. It is not uncommon for the police to pick up skid-row types found outside their district and merely return them with a warning that they are to stay in their place; thus begging and panhandling activities are not allowed to intrude on other parts of the city. Bittner's study of the police on skid row is a subtle and insightful analysis of how they carry out the difficult task of keeping things under control, a responsibility for which the law provides little in the way of guidelines.

For an excellent study of a variety of policing activities see Jerome Skolnick, *Justice Without Trial* (Wiley, 1966). A useful account of police functions other than law enforcement is in Elaine Cumming and Laura Edell, "Policeman as Philosopher, Guide, and Friend," *Social Problems* 12 (1965): 276-86. Bittner has analyzed another form of police discretion in "Police Discretion in Emergency Apprehension of Mentally Ill Persons," *Social Problems* 14 (1967): 278-92. The classic study of skid row is Nels Anderson, *The Hobo* (University of Chicago Press, 1923). More recent studies include Samuel E. Wallace, *Skid Row as a Way of Life* (Bedminster Press, 1965); and Donald A. Bogue, *Skid Row in American Cities* (University of Chicago Community and Family Center, 1963). ◼

. . . SKID ROW has always occupied a special place among the various forms of urban life. While other areas are perceived as being different in many ways, skid row is seen as completely different. Though it is located in the heart of civilization, it is viewed as containing aspects of the primordial jungle, calling for missionary activities and offering opportunities for exotic adventure. While each inhabitant individually can be seen as tragically linked to the vicissitudes of "normal" life, allowing others to say "here but for the Grace of God go I," those who live there are believed to have repudiated the entire role-casting scheme of the majority and to live apart from normalcy. Accordingly, the traditional attitude of civic-mindedness toward skid row has been dominated by the desire to contain it and to salvage souls from its clutches. The specific task of containment has been left to the police. That this task pressed upon the police some rather special duties has never come under explicit consideration, either from the government that expects control or from the police departments that implement it. Instead, the prevailing method of carrying out the task is to assign patrolmen to the area on a fairly permanent basis and to allow them to work out their own ways of running things. External influence is confined largely to the supply of support and facilities on the one hand and to occasional expressions of criticism about the overall conditions on the other. Within the limits of available resources and general expectations, patrolmen are supposed to know what to do and are free to do it.

Patrolmen who are more or less permanently assigned to skid row districts tend to develop a conception of the nature of their "domain" that is surprisingly uniform. Individual officers differ in many aspects of practice, emphasize different concerns, and maintain different contacts, but they are in fundamental agreement about the structure of skid row life. This relatively uniform conception includes an implicit formulation of the problem of keeping the peace in skid row.

In the view of experienced patrolmen, life on skid row is fundamentally different from life in other parts of society. To be sure, they say, around its geographic limits the area tends to blend into the surrounding environment, and its population always encompasses some persons who are only transitionally associated with it. Basically, however, skid row is perceived as the natural habitat of people who lack the capacities and commitments to live "normal" lives on a sustained basis. The presence of these people defines the nature of social reality in the area. In general, and especially in casual encounters, the presumption of incompetence and of the disinclination to be "normal" is the leading theme for the interpretation of all actions and relations. Not only do people approach one another in this manner but presumably they also expect to be approached in this way, and they conduct themselves accordingly.

In practice, the restriction of interactional possibilities that is based on the patrolman's stereotyped conception of skid row residents is always subject to revision and modification toward particular individuals. Thus, it is entirely possible, and not unusual, for patrolmen to view certain skid row inhabitants in terms that involve non-skid row aspects of normality. Instances of such approaches and relationships invariably involve personal acquaintance and the knowledge of a good deal of individually qualifying information. Such instances are seen, despite their relative frequency, as exceptions to the rule. The awareness of the possibility of breakdown, frustration, and betrayal is ever present; basic wariness is never wholly dissipated; and undaunted trust can never be fully reconciled with presence on skid row.

What patrolmen view as normal on skid row—and what they also think is taken for granted as "life as usual" by the inhabitants—is not easily summarized. It seems to focus on the idea that the dominant consideration governing all enterprise and association is directed to the occasion of the moment. Nothing is thought of as having a background that might have led up to the present in terms of some compelling moral or practical necessity. There are some exceptions to this rule, of course: the police themselves, and those who run certain establishments, are perceived as engaged in important and necessary activities. But in order to carry them out they, too, must be geared to the overall atmosphere of fortuitousness. In this atmosphere, the range of control that persons have over one another is exceedingly narrow. Good faith, even where it is valued, is seen merely as a personal matter. Its violations are the victim's own hard luck, rather than demonstrable violations of property. There is only a private sense of irony at having been victimized. The overall air is not so much one of active distrust as it is one of irrelevance of trust; as patrolmen often emphasize, the situation does not necessarily cause all relations to be predatory, but the possibility of exploitation is not checked by the expectation that it will not happen.

Just as the past is seen by the policeman as having only the most attenuated relevance to the present, so the future implications of present situations are said to be generally devoid of prospective coherence. No venture, especially no joint venture, can be said to have a strongly predictable future in line with its initial objectives. It is a matter of adventitious circumstance whether or not matters go as anticipated. That which is not within the grasp of momentary control is outside of practical social reality.

Though patrolmen see the temporal framework of the occasion of the moment mainly as a lack of trustworthiness, they also recognize that it involves more than merely the personal motives of individuals. In addition to the fact that everybody *feels* that things matter only at the moment, irresponsibility take an *objectified* form on skid row. The places the residents occupy, the social relations they entertain, and the activities that engage them are not meaningfully connected over time. Thus, for example, address, occupation, marital status, etc., matter much less on skid row than in any other part of society. The fact that present whereabouts, activities, and affiliations imply neither continuity nor direction means that life on skid row lacks a socially structured background of accountability. Of course, everybody's life contains some sequential incongruities, but in the life of a skid row inhabitant every moment is an accident. That a man has no "address" in the future that could be in some way inferred from where he is and what he does makes him a person of *radically reduced visibility*. If he disappears from sight and one wishes to locate him, it is virtually impossible to systematize the search. All one can know with relative certainty is that he will be somewhere on some skid row, and the only thing one can do is to trace the factual contiguities of his whereabouts.

It is commonly known that the police are expert in finding people and that they have developed an exquisite technology involving special facilities and procedures of sleuthing. It is less well appreciated that all this technology builds upon those socially structured features of everyday life that render persons findable in the first place.

Under ordinary conditions, the query as to where a person is can be addressed, from the outset, to a restricted realm of possibilities that can be further narrowed by looking into certain places and asking certain persons. The map of whereabouts that normally competent persons use whenever they wish to locate someone is constituted by the basic facts of membership in society. Insofar as membership consists of status incumbencies, each of which has an adumbrated future that substantially reduces unpredictability, it is itself a guarantee of the order within which it is quite difficult to get lost. Membership is thus visible not only now but also as its own projection into the future. It is in terms of this prospective availability that the skid row

inhabitant is a person of reduced visibility. His membership is viewed as extraordinary because its extension into the future is *not* reduced to a restricted realm of possibilities. Neither his subjective dispositions nor his circumstances indicate that he is oriented to any particular long-range interests. But, as he may claim every contingent opportunity, his claims are always seen as based on slight merit or right, at least to the extent that interfering with them does not constitute a substantial denial of his freedom.

This, then, constitutes the problem of keeping the peace on skid row. Considerations of momentary expediency are seen as having unqualified priority as maxims of conduct; consequently, the controlling influences of the pursuit of sustained interests are presumed to be absent.

THE PRACTICES OF KEEPING THE PEACE IN SKID ROW

From the perspective of society as a whole, skid row inhabitants appear troublesome in a variety of ways. The uncommitted life attributed to them is perceived as inherently offensive; its very existence arouses indignation and contempt. More important, however, is the feeling that persons who have repudiated the entire role-status casting system of society, persons whose lives forever collapse into a succession of random moments, are seen as constituting a practical risk. As they have nothing to foresake, nothing is thought safe from them.

The skid row patrolman's concept of his mandate includes an awareness of this presumed risk. He is constantly attuned to the possibility of violence, and he is convinced that things to which the inhabitants have free access are as good as lost. But his concern is directed toward the continuous condition of peril *in the area* rather than *for society in general*. While he is obviously conscious of the presence of many persons who have committed crimes outside of skid row and will arrest them when they come to his attention, this is a peripheral part of his routine activities. In general, the skid row patrolman and his superiors take for granted that his main business is to keep the peace and enforce the laws *on skid row*, and that he is involved only incidentally in protecting society at large. Thus, his task is formulated basically as the protection of putative predators from one another. The maintenance of peace and safety is difficult because everyday life on skid row is viewed as an open field for reciprocal exploitation. As the lives of the inhabitants lack the prospective coherence associated with status incumbency, the realization of self-interest does not produce order. Hence, mechanisms that control risk must work primarily from without.

External containment, to be effective, must be oriented to the realities of existence. Thus, the skid row patrolman employs an approach that he views as appropriate to the ad hoc nature of skid row life. The following are the three most prominent elements of this approach. First, the seasoned patrolman seeks to acquire a richly particularized knowledge of people and places in the area. Second, he gives the consideration of strict culpability a subordinate status among grounds for remedial sanction. Third, his use and choice of coercive interventions is determined mainly by exigencies of situations and with little regard for possible long-range effects on individual persons.

THE PARTICULARIZATION OF KNOWLEDGE

The patrolman's orientation to people on skid row is structured basically by the presupposition that if he does not know a man personally there is very little that he can assume about him. This rule determines his interaction with people who live on skid row. Since the area also contains other types of persons, however, its applicability is not universal. To some such persons it does not apply at all, and it has a somewhat mitigated significance with certain others. For example, some persons encountered on skid row can be recognized immediately as outsiders. Among them are workers who are employed in commercial and industrial enterprises that

abut the area, persons who come for the purpose of adventurous "slumming," and some patrons of secondhand stores and pawnshops. Even with very little experience, it is relatively easy to identify these people by appearance, demeanor, and the time and place of their presence. The patrolman maintains an impersonal attitude toward them, and they are, under ordinary circumstances, not the objects of his attention.

Clearly set off from these outsiders are the residents and the entire corps of personnel that services skid row. It would be fair to say that one of the main routine activities of patrolmen is the establishment and maintenance of familiar relationships with individual members of these groups. Officers emphasize their interest in this, and they maintain that their grasp of and control over skid row is precisely commensurate with the extent to which they "know the people." By this they do not mean having a quasi-theoretical understanding of human nature but, rather, the common practice of individualized and reciprocal recognition. As this group encompasses both those who render services on skid row and those who are serviced, individualized interest is not always based on the desire to overcome uncertainty. Instead, relations with service personnel become absorbed into the network of particularized attention. Ties between patrolmen on the one hand and businessmen, managers, and workers on the other hand are often defined in terms of shared or similar interests. It bears mentioning that many persons live *and* work on skid row. Thus, the distinction between those who service and those who are serviced is not a clear-cut dichotomy but a spectrum of affiliations.

As a general rule, the skid row patrolman possesses an immensely detailed factual knowledge of his beat. He knows, and knows a great deal about, a large number of residents. He is likely to know every person who manages or works in the local bars, hotels, shops, stores, and missions. Moreover, he probably knows every public and private place inside and out. Finally, he ordinarily remembers countless events of the past which he can recount by citing names, dates, and places with remarkable precision. Though there are always some threads missing in the fabric of information, it is continuously woven and mended even as it is being used. New facts, however, are added to the texture, not in terms of structured categories but in terms of adjoining known realities. In other words, the content and organization of the patrolman's knowledge is primarily ideographic and only vestigially, if at all, nomothetic.

Individual patrolmen vary in the extent to which they make themselves available or actively pursue personal acquaintances. But even the most aloof are continuously greeted and engaged in conversations that indicate a background of individualistic associations. While this scarcely has the appearance of work, because of its casual character, patrolmen do not view it as an optional activity. In the course of making their rounds, patrolmen seem to have access to every place, and their entry causes no surprise or consternation. Instead, the entry tends to lead to informal exchanges of small talk. At times the rounds include entering hotels and gaining access to rooms or dormitories, often for no purpose other than asking the occupants how things are going. In all this, patrolmen address innumerable persons by name and are in turn addressed by name. The conversational style that characterizes these exchanges is casual to an extent that by non-skid row standards might suggest intimacy. Not only does the officer himself avoid all terms of deference and respect but he does not seem to expect or demand them. For example, a patrolman said to a man radiating an alcoholic glow on the street, "You've got enough of a heat on now; I'll give you ten minutes to get your ass off the street!" Without stopping, the man answered, "Oh, why don't you go and piss in your own pot!" The officer's only response was, "All right, in ten minutes you're either in bed or on your way to the can."

This kind of expressive freedom is an intricately limited privilege. Persons of acquaintance are entitled to it and appear to exercise it mainly in routinized encounters. But strangers, too, can use it with impunity. The safe way of gaining the privilege is to respond to the patrolman in ways that do not challenge his right to ask questions and issue commands. Once the concession is made that the officer is entitled to inquire into a man's background, business, and intentions, and that he is entitled to obedience, there opens a field of colloquial license. A patrolman seems to grant expressive freedom in recognition of a person's acceptance of his access to areas of life ordinarily defined as private and subject to coercive control only under special circumstances. While patrolmen accept and seemingly even cultivate the rough quid pro quo of informality, and while they do not expect sincerity, candor, or obedience in their dealings with the inhabitants, they do not allow the rejection of their approach.

The explicit refusal to answer questions of a personal nature and the demand to know why the questions are asked significantly enhances a person's chances of being arrested on some minor charge. While most patrolmen tend to be personally indignant about this kind of response and use the arrest to compose their own hurt feelings, this is merely a case of affect being in line with the method. There are other officers who proceed in the same manner without taking offense, or even with feelings of regret. Such patrolmen often maintain that their colleagues' affective involvement is a corruption of an essentially valid technique. The technique is oriented to the goal of maintaining operational control. The patrolman's conception of this goal places him hierarchically above whomever he approaches and makes him the sole judge of the propriety of the occasion. As he alone is oriented to this goal, and as he seeks to attain it by means of individualized access to persons, those who frustrate him are seen as motivated at best by the desire to "give him a hard time" and at worst by some darkly devious purpose.

Officers are quite aware that the directness of their approach and the demands they make are difficult to reconcile with the doctrines of civil liberties, but they maintain that they are in accord with the general freedom of access that persons living on skid row normally grant one another. That is, they believe that the imposition of personalized and far-reaching control is in tune with standard expectancies. In terms of these expectancies, people are not so much denied the right to privacy as they are seen as not having any privacy. Thus, officers seek to install themselves in the center of people's lives and let the consciousness of their presence play the part of conscience.

When talking about the practical necessity of an aggressively personal approach, officers do not refer merely to the need for maintaining control over lives that are open in the direction of the untoward. They also see it as the basis for the supply of certain valued services to inhabitants of skid row. The coerced or conceded access to persons often imposes on the patrolman tasks that are, in the main, in line with these persons' expressed or implied interest. In asserting this connection, patrolmen note that they frequently help people to obtain meals, lodging, employment, that they direct them to welfare and health services, and that they aid them in various other ways. Though patrolmen tend to describe such services mainly as the product of their own altruism, they also say that their colleagues who avoid them are simply doing a poor job of patrolling. The acceptance of the need to help people is based on the realization that the hungry, the sick, and the troubled are a potential source of problems. Moreover, that patrolmen will help people is part of the background expectancies of life on skid row. Hotel clerks normally call policemen when someone gets so sick as to need attention; merchants expect to be taxed, in a manner of speaking, to meet the pressing needs of certain persons; and the inhabitants do not hesitate to accept, solicit, and demand every kind of aid. The domain of the patrolman's service activity is virtually limitless, and it is no exaggeration to say that the solution of every conceivable problem has at one time or another been attempted by a police officer. In one observed instance, a patrolman unceremoniously entered the room of a man he had never seen before. The man, who gave no indication that he regarded the officer's entry and questions as anything but part of life as usual, related a story of having had his dentures stolen by his wife. In the course of the subsequent rounds, the patrolman sought to locate the woman and the dentures. This did not become the evening's project but was attended to while doing other things. In the densely matted activities of the patrolman, the questioning became one more strand, not so much to be pursued to its solution as a theme that organized the memory of one more man known individually. In all this, the officer followed the precept formulated by a somewhat more articulate patrolman: "If I want to be in control of my work and keep the street relatively peaceful, I have to know the people. To know them I must gain their trust, which means that I have to be involved in their lives. But I can't be soft like a social worker because unlike him I cannot call the cops when things go wrong. I am the cops!"

THE RESTRICTED RELEVANCE OF CULPABILITY

It is well known that policemen exercise discretionary freedom in invoking the law. It is also conceded that, in some measure, the practice is unavoidable. This being so, the outstanding problem is whether or not the decisions are in line with the intent of the law. On skid row, patrolmen often make decisions based on reasons that the law probably does not recognize as valid. The problem can best be introduced by citing an example.

A man in a relatively mild state of intoxication (by skid row standards) approached a patrolman to tell him that he had a room in a hotel, to which the officer responded by urging him to go to bed instead of getting drunk. As the man walked off, the officer related the following thoughts. Here is a completely lost soul. Though he probably is no more than 35 years old, he looks to be in his fifties. He never works and he hardly ever has a place to stay. He has been on the street for several years and is known as Dakota. During the past few days, Dakota has been seen in the company of Big Jim. The latter is an invalid living on some sort of pension with which he pays for a room in the hotel to which Dakota referred and for four weekly meal tickets in one of the restaurants on the street. Whatever is left he spends on wine and beer. Occasionally, Big Jim goes on drinking sprees in the company of someone like Dakota. Leaving aside the consideration that there is probably a homosexual background to the association, and that it is not right that Big Jim should have to support the drinking habit of someone else, there is the more important risk that if Dakota moves in with Big Jim he will very likely walk off with whatever the latter keeps in his room. Big Jim would never dream of reporting the theft; he would just beat the hell out of Dakota after he sobered up. When asked what could be done to prevent the theft and the subsequent recriminations, the patrolman proposed that in this particular case he would throw Big Jim into jail if he found him tonight and then tell the hotel clerk to throw Dakota out of the room. When asked why he did not arrest Dakota, who was, after all, drunk enough to warrant an arrest, the officer explained that this would not solve anything. While Dakota was in jail Big Jim would continue drinking and would either strike up another liaison or embrace his old buddy after he had been released. The only thing to do was to get Big Jim to sober up, and the only sure way of doing this was to arrest him.

As it turned out, Big Jim was not located that evening. But had he been located and arrested on a drunk charge, the fact that he was intoxicated would not have been the real reason for proceeding against him but merely the pretext. The point of the example is not that it illustrates the tendency of skid row patrolmen to arrest persons who would not be arrested under conditions of full respect for their legal rights. To be sure, this, too, happens. In the majority of minor arrest cases, however, the criteria the law specifies are met. But it is the rare exception that the

law is invoked merely because the specifications of the law are met. That is, compliance with the law is merely the outward appearance of an intervention that is actually based on altogether different considerations. Thus, it could be said that patrolmen do not really enforce the law, even when they do invoke it, but merely use it as a resource to solve certain pressing practical problems in keeping the peace. This observation goes beyond the conclusion that many of the lesser norms of the criminal law are treated as defeasible in police work. It is patently not the case that skid row patrolmen apply the legal norms while recognizing many exceptions to their applicability. Instead, the observation leads to the conclusion that in keeping the peace on skid row patrolmen encounter certain matters they attend to by means of coercive action—e.g., arrests. In doing this, they invoke legal norms that are available, and with some regard for substantive appropriateness. Hence, the problem patrolmen confront is not which drunks, beggars, or disturbers of the peace should be arrested and which can be let go as exceptions to the rule. Rather, the problem is whether, when someone "needs" to be arrested, he should be charged with drunkenness, begging, or disturbing the peace. Speculating further, one is almost compelled to infer that virtually any set of norms could be used in this manner, provided that they sanction relatively common forms of behavior.

The reduced relevance of culpability in peace-keeping practice on skid row is not readily visible. As mentioned, most arrested persons were actually found in the act, or in the state, alleged in the arrest record. It becomes partly visible when one views the treatment of persons who are not arrested even though all the legal grounds for an arrest are present. Whenever such persons are encountered and can be induced to leave, or taken to some shelter, or remanded to someone's care, then patrolmen feel, or at least maintain, that an arrest would serve no useful purpose. That is, whenever there exist means for controlling the troublesome aspects of some person's presence in some way alternative to an arrest, such means are preferentially employed, provided, of course, that the case at hand involves only a minor offense.

The attenuation of the relevance of culpability is most visible when the presence of legal grounds for an arrest could be questioned—i.e., in cases that sometimes are euphemistically called "preventive arrests." In one observed instance, a man who attempted to trade a pocketknife came to the attention of a patrolman. The initial encounter was attended by a good deal of levity, and the man willingly responded to the officer's inquiries about his identity and business. The man laughingly acknowledged that he needed some money to get drunk. In the course of the exchange it came to light that he had just arrived in town, traveling in his automobile. When confronted with the demand to lead the officer to the car, the man's expression became serious and he pointedly stated that he would not comply because this was none of the officer's business. After a bit more prodding, which the patrolman initially kept in the light mood, the man was arrested on a charge involving begging. In subsequent conversation the patrolman acknowledged that the charge was only speciously appropriate and mainly a pretext. Having committed himself to demanding information, he could not accept defeat. When this incident was discussed with another patrolman, the second officer found fault not with the fact that the arrest was made on a pretext but with the first officer's own contribution to the creation of conditions that made it unavoidable. "You see," he continued, "there is always the risk that the man is testing you and you must let him know what is what. The best among us can usually keep the upper hand in such situations without making arrests. But when it comes down to the wire, then you can't let them get away with it."

Finally, it must be mentioned that the reduction of the significance of culpability is built into the normal order of skid row life, as patrolmen see it. Officers almost unfailingly say, pointing to some particular person, "I know that he knows that I know that some of the things he 'owns' are stolen, and that nothing can be done about it." In saying this, they often claim to have knowledge of such a degree of certainty as would normally be sufficient for virtually any kind of action except legal proceedings. Against this background, patrolmen adopt the view that the law is not merely imperfect and difficult to implement, but that on skid row, at least, the association between delict and sanction is distinctly occasional. Thus, to implement the law naively—i.e., to arrest someone *merely* because he committed some minor offense—is perceived as containing elements of injustice.

Moreover, patrolmen often deal with situations in which questions of culpability are profoundly ambiguous. For example, an officer was called to help in settling a violent dispute in a hotel room. The object of the quarrel was a supposedly stolen pair of trousers. As the story unfolded in the conflicting versions of the participants, it was not possible to decide who was the complainant and who was alleged to be the thief, nor did it come to light who occupied the room in which the fracas took place, or whether the trousers were taken from the room or to the room. Though the officer did ask some questions, it seemed, and was confirmed in later conversation, that he was there not to solve the puzzle of the missing trousers but to keep the situation from getting out of hand. In the end, the exhausted participants dispersed, and this was the conclusion of the case. The patrolman maintained that no one could unravel mysteries of this sort because "these people take things from each other so often that no one could tell what 'belongs' to whom." In fact, he suggested, the terms *owning, stealing,* and *swindling,* in their strict sense, do not really belong on skid row, and all efforts to distribute guilt and innocence according to some rational formula of justice are doomed to failure.

It could be said that the term *curbstone justice* that is sometimes applied to the procedures of patrolmen in skid rows contains a double irony. Not only is the procedure not legally authorized, which is the intended irony in the expression, but it does not even pretend to distribute deserts. The best among the patrolmen, according to their own standards, use the law to keep skid row inhabitants from sinking deeper into the misery they already experience. The worst, in terms of these same standards, exploit the practice for personal aggrandizement or gain. Leaving motives aside, however, it is easy to see that if culpability is not the salient consideration leading to an arrest in cases where it is patently obvious, then the practical patrolman may not view it as being wholly out of line to make arrests lacking in formal legal justification. Conversely, he will come to view minor offense arrests made solely because legal standards are met as poor craftsmanship.

THE BACKGROUND OF AD HOC DECISION MAKING

When skid row patrolmen are pressed to explain their reasons for minor offense arrests, they most often mention that it is done for the protection of the arrested person. This, they maintain, is the case in virtually all drunk arrests, in the majority of arrests involving begging and other nuisance offenses, and in many cases involving acts of violence. When they are asked to explain further such arrests as the one cited earlier involving the man attempting to sell the pocketknife, who was certainly not arrested for his own protection, they cite the consideration that belligerent persons constitute a much greater menace on skid row than anyplace else in the city. The reasons for this are twofold. First, many of the inhabitants are old, feeble, and not too smart, all of which makes them relatively defenseless. Second, many of the inhabitants are involved in illegal activities and are known as persons of bad character, which does not make them credible victims or witnesses. Potential predators realize that the resources society has mobilized to minimize the risk of criminal victimization do not protect the predator himself. Thus, reciprocal exploitation consti-

tutes a preferred risk. The high vulnerability of everybody on skid row is public knowledge and causes every seemingly aggressive act to be seen as a potentially grave risk.

When, in response to all this, patrolmen are confronted with the observation that many minor offense arrests they make do not seem to involve a careful evaluation of facts before acting, they give the following explanations. First, the two reasons of protection and prevention represent a global background, and in individual cases it may sometimes not be possible to produce adequate justification on these grounds. Nor is it thought to be a problem of great moment to estimate precisely whether someone is more likely to come to grief or to cause grief when the objective is to prevent the proliferation of troubles. Second, patrolmen maintain that some of the seemingly spur-of-the-moment decisions are actually made against a background of knowledge of facts that are not readily apparent in the situations. Since experience not only contains this information but also causes it to come to mind, patrolmen claim to have developed a special sensitivity for qualities of appearances that allow an intuitive grasp of probable tendencies. In this context, little things are said to have high informational value and lead to conclusions without the intervention of explicitly reasoned chains of inferences. Third, patrolmen readily admit that they do not adhere to high standards of adequacy of justification. They do not seek to defend the adequacy of their method against some abstract criteria of merit. Instead, when questioned they assess their methods against the background of a whole system of ad hoc decision making, a system that encompasses the courts, correction facilities, the welfare establishment, and medical services. In fact, policemen generally maintain that their own procedures not only measure up to the workings of this system but exceed them in the attitude of carefulness.

In addition to these recognized reasons, there are two background factors that play a significant part in decisions to employ coercion. One has to do with the relevance of situational factors, and the other with the evaluation of coercion as relatively insignificant in the lives of the inhabitants.

There is no doubt that the nature of the circumstances often has decisive influence on what will be done. For example, the same patrolman who arrested the man trying to sell his pocketknife was observed dealing with a young couple. Though the officer was clearly angered by what he perceived as insolence and threatened the man with arrest, he merely ordered him and his companion to leave the street. He saw them walking away in a deliberately slow manner, and when he noticed them a while later, still standing only a short distance away from the place of encounter, he did not respond to their presence. The difference between the two cases was that in the first there was a crowd of amused bystanders, while the latter case was not witnessed by anyone. In another instance, the patrolman was directed to a hotel and found a father and son fighting about money. The father occupied a room in the hotel and the son occasionally shared his quarters. There were two other men present, and they made it clear that their sympathies were with the older man. The son was whisked off to jail without much study of the relative merits of the conflicting claims. In yet another case, a middle-aged woman was forcefully evacuated from a bar even after the bartender explained that her loud behavior was merely a response to goading by some foul-mouthed youth.

In all such circumstances, coercive control is exercised as a means of coming to grips with situational exigencies. Force is used against particular persons but is incidental to the task. An ideal of "economy of intervention" dictates in these and similar cases that the person whose presence is most likely to perpetuate the troublesome development be removed. Moreover, the decision as to who is to be removed is arrived at very quickly. Officers feel considerable pressure to act unhesitatingly, and many give accounts of situations that got out of hand because of desires to handle cases with careful consideration. However, even when there is no

apparent risk of rapid proliferation of trouble, the tactic of removing one or two persons is used to control an undesirable situation. Thus, when a patrolman ran into a group of four men sharing a bottle of wine in an alley, he emptied the remaining contents of the bottle into the gutter, arrested one man—who was no more and no less drunk than the others—and let the others disperse in various directions.

The exigential nature of control is also evident in the handling of isolated drunks. Men are arrested because of where they happen to be encountered. In this, it matters not only whether a man is found in a conspicuous place or not but also how far away he is from his domicile. The further away he is, the less likely it is that he will make it to his room, and the more likely the arrest. Sometimes drunk arrests are made mainly because the police van is available. In one case a patrolman summoned the van to pick up an arrested man. As the van was pulling away from the curb the officer stopped the driver because he sighted another drunk stumbling across the street. The second man protested, saying that he "wasn't even half drunk yet." The patrolman's response was "OK, I'll owe you half a drunk." In sum, the basic routine of keeping the peace on skid row involves a process of matching the resources of control with situational exigencies. The overall objective is to reduce the total amount of risk in the area. In this, practicality plays a considerably more important role than legal norms. Precisely because patrolmen see legal reasons for coercive action much more widely distributed on skid row than could ever be matched by interventions, they intervene not in the interest of law enforcement but in the interest of producing relative tranquility and order on the street.

Taking the perspective of the victim of coercive measures, one could ask why he, in particular, has to bear the cost of keeping the aggregate of troubles down while others, who are equally or perhaps even more implicated, go scot-free. Patrolmen maintain that the ad hoc selection of persons for attention must be viewed in the light of the following consideration: Arresting a person on skid row on some minor charge may save him and others a lot of trouble, but it does not work any real hardships on the arrested person. It is difficult to overestimate the skid row patrolman's feeling of certainty that his coercive and disciplinary actions toward the inhabitants have but the most passing significance in their lives. Sending a man to jail on some charge that will hold him for a couple of days is seen as a matter of such slight importance to the affected person that it could hardly give rise to scruples. Thus, every indication that a coercive measure should be taken is accompanied by the realization "I might as well, for all it matters to him." Certain realities of life on skid row furnish the context for this belief in the attenuated relevance of coercion in the lives of the inhabitants. Foremost among them is that the use of police authority is seen as totally unremarkable by everybody on skid row. Persons who live or work there are continuously exposed to it and take its existence for granted. Shopkeepers, hotel clerks, and bartenders call patrolmen to rid themselves of unwanted and troublesome patrons. Residents expect patrolmen to arbitrate their quarrels authoritatively. Men who receive orders, whether they obey them or not, treat them as part of life as usual. Moreover, patrolmen find that disciplinary and coercive actions apparently do not affect their friendly relations with the persons against whom these actions are taken. Those who greet and chat with them are the very same men who have been disciplined, arrested, and ordered around in the past, and who expect to be thus treated again in the future. From all this, officers gather that though the people on skid row seek to evade police authority they do not really object to it. Indeed, it happens quite frequently that officers encounter men who welcome being arrested and even actively ask for it. Finally, officers point out that sending someone to jail from skid row does not upset his relatives or his family life, does not cause him to miss work or lose a job, does not lead to his being reproached by friends and associates, does not lead to failure to meet commitments or protect investments, and does not conflict with any but the most passing intentions of the arrested person. Seasoned patrolmen are not oblivious to the irony of the fact that measures intended as mechanisms for distributing deserts can be used freely because these measures are relatively impotent in their effects. . . .

22. CRIMINAL VICTIMIZATION IN THE UNITED STATES

PHILIP H. ENNIS

Reprinted from Criminal Victimization in the United States: A Report of a National Survey, *The President's Commission on Law Enforcement and Administration of Justice (Government Printing Office, 1967). Philip H. Ennis is Professor and Chairman of the Department of Sociology at Wesleyan University.*

■ The prevalence of crime is of considerable concern to citizens and policymakers alike. People have strong intuitive perceptions of whether or not crime is becoming more common, and so a reliable measure of how much crime really occurs would seem to be crucial to any sensible program in the field of criminal justice. Yet the official data on crime are so riddled with methodological inadequacies and so vulnerable to arbitrary action on the part of police that little confidence can be placed in them as indicators of the amount of crime or of changes in the amount of crime over time. The NORC study excerpted here was a pioneering attempt to develop a more reliable measure.

Ennis and his colleagues judged that the best way to measure the incidence of crime was to sample a representative number of households and to question someone in each household about whether any members had been victims of crime in the recent past. Such studies periodically conducted and using the best survey research methodology would provide a much more reliable indicator than would official statistics, both because some crimes are not reported and because police recording practices differ among jurisdictions and occasionally within the same jurisdiction. The sample survey has the added advantage of providing some knowledge about the relationship between being victimized and the victim's social and economic characteristics.

The NORC study showed that very few crimes lead to the conviction of the offender. Apparently only half of all crimes are reported to the police, and an arrest is made in only about 6 percent of the cases. Only 2.5 percent of the cases come to trial, and in half of those few, the victim felt that the offender was too leniently treated (either not convicted or convicted for a lesser offense). The victim, in short, felt vindicated by the legal process in only 1 percent of all cases.

Since this NORC study many other surveys of victims have been carried out, both locally and nationally. By 1973 the National Victim Survey had become an annual affair, so that in the future we can look forward to regular and much more precise measures of the incidence of criminal victimization. Another effort to develop more systematic measurement techniques is Thorsten Sellin and Marvin E. Wolfgang, *The Measurement of Delinquency* (Wiley, 1964), in which the emphasis is on developing measures of public views about the seriousness of different kinds of crimes rather than simply about their prevalence. A review of national Gallup Poll data on criminal victimization and changes in rates from 1960 to 1972 can be found in the *Gallup Poll Index*, January 1973. ■

THE PURPOSE of this [analysis] is to provide a quantitative answer to the question of how much crime there is. Its measurement involves formidable problems, some methodological, some substantive. . . . The first major substantive problem is the choice of what kinds of crime to include and what kinds to exclude. Obviously the whole range of regulatory and sumptuary crimes is deliberately excluded. Also because of the nature of the survey method, only those crimes that have an *individual* victim are to be counted; crimes against organizations, corporations, governmental bodies, and so forth are therefore not part of the survey. The key target is criminal victimization of the individual. . . .

The crimes included in the screening interview were, first of all, the major offenses as defined by the Part I crimes in the Uniform Crime Reports, suitably translated into everyday language yet retaining the vital elements as specified in the *Uniform Crime Reporting Handbook*.

228

TABLE 22.1

ESTIMATED RATES OF PART I CRIMES: 1965-66

Crime	NORC Sample Estimated Rate per 100,000 Population	Uniform Crime Reports: 1965 Individual or Residential Rates per 100,000 Population
Homicide	3.0	5.1
Forcible rape	42.5	11.6
Robbery	94.0	61.4
Aggravated assault	218.3	106.6
Burglary	949.1	296.6
Larceny ($50+)	606.5	267.4
Vehicle theft	206.2	226.0
Total	2,119.6	974.7

A substantial number of Part II offenses were also included in the questionnaire. In addition, several crimes at the boundary of the criminal law, such as consumer fraud, landlord-tenant problems, and family problems, were also included.

How much of what kinds of crime was there during this time, and how does the distribution compare with the Uniform Crime Reports? We begin to answer these critical questions with the presentation of the data in Table 22.1. The survey results are projected up to the total population, and crime is expressed in a rate per 100,000 population in the same way as the UCR reports crime. . . .

Two facts are impressive. First, the relative rates of the various crimes found in the survey are almost identical to those reported by the UCR; that is, the rank order of frequency of the Part I crimes found in the survey is, with the exception of vehicle theft, the same as that in the UCR. This lends substantial credence that the survey and the UCR are describing the same universe of events. The second fact is the undeniably higher rate of crime indicated by the survey. Homicide and vehicle theft are the only exceptions. The increments among the other crimes vary from rape, which appears to be 4 times as frequent as police reports indicate, to robbery, which is only 50 percent as frequent. As a whole, there appears to be twice as much major crime as is known to the police. . . .

The next question is: How much minor crime is there in the nation? Since the UCR does not report national compilations of Part II crimes, the estimates from the survey have to be presented by themselves, without any national standard of comparison. . . .

The two largest crimes are both against property—larcenies under $50 in value and malicious mischief. The least frequent crime is being victimized by someone soliciting a bribe. This latter crime is probably underreported since there is an aura of victim involvement in these situations, and this will tend to diminish forthrightness in the interview.

TABLE 22.2

INCIDENCE (PER 100,000 POPULATION) OF PART II CRIME (1965-1966)

Crime	Number per 100,000
Simple assault	394.2
Larceny (—$50)	1,458.6
Auto offense	445.8
Malicious mischief or arson	1,061.3
Counterfeiting or forgery	42.5
Fraud	251.7
Consumer fraud	121.3
Other sex	142.5
Family	206.2
Soliciting a bribe	9.1
Building violations	42.5
Kidnapping	12.1
Other victimization	51.6
Total	4,239.4

Base   32,966 individuals

The third most frequent crime is auto offense—that is, some personal injury or property damage or both—caused as the result of someone else's reckless or drunken driving—driving that is criminally negligent. This crime is at the boundary of the criminal law since at the present time in most jurisdictions no crime is committed if a person is merely hurt by a negligent act, and the level of negligence has to be gross, willful, or wanton. Yet the reports of these incidents carry as strong a sense of victimization as many of the other more traditionally accepted minor crimes. . . .

We now have the answer to the question "How much crime is there in the United States at present? We have shown that at least twice as much major crime as is reported occurs, and that minor crime is about twice the amount of major crime. The policy implications of this statement are not at all clear; much more has to be known about the distribution of crime, who its victims are, and what the consequences of victimization are before policy planning can proceed.

HOW MUCH LOSS?

The cost of crime in the United States is large and probably incalculable. The reasons for not being able to give reliable estimates of these costs are many. Even within the present survey, where extensive efforts were made to identify the extent of dollar losses, the limits of recall and accuracy of reporting are such as to make the estimates only approximations.

In spite of these limitations, it is useful to attempt the accounting in order to confront the statistics of the UCR, the only other major source of such information.

First it is necessary to describe the kinds of financial loss the survey can identify. These are:

1. Property taken or damaged.
2. Medical bills for personal injury.
3. Lost income due to time away from work because of injury, court, and police processes (including lost schooling).
4. Secondary loss and damage incurred as a direct effect of victimization.
5. Subsequent costs to increase personal and property security.
6. Intangible costs due to changed habits and attitudes (loss of reputation).

In order to assess net loss, the amount and kinds of restitution, recovery, and reimbursements were also included in the survey and have to be taken into account for the calculation of the actual loss involved. Since physical injuries were so few in number (about 5 percent of total crimes reported) and the costs so diverse, they will be excluded from this analysis.

The emphasis is on property crimes. The mean losses for the relevant Part I and Part II crimes are shown in Table 22.3. The gross losses, amounts recovered, and the net losses are shown as means of the total group

TABLE 22.3
DOLLAR LOSSES FROM PROPERTY CRIMES

Crime	Gross Loss	Recovery	Net Loss	Number of Cases
Part I				
Robbery	$ 274	$ 4	$ 271	(19)
Burglary	191	20	170	(238)
Grand larceny	160	51	109	(204)
Vehicle theft	1,141	982	159	(59)
Mean for Part I Crimes			$ 149	
Part II				
Petty larceny	$ 21	$ 6	$ 15	(391)
Auto offense	376	217	159	(133)
Malicious mischief	120	18	102	(237)
Counterfeiting and forgery	[323]	[-]	[323]	(9)
Fraud	906	150	756	(69)
Consumer fraud	99	20	78	(32)
Mean for Part II Crimes			$ 123	

of cases. These losses are within the ranges suggested by the UCR, which show an average loss of $260 for burglary (residential), $254 for robbery, and $236 for grand larcenies. The differences in these figures and the survey results are due in part to the fact that many of the latter are not reported to the police and may involve much smaller sums.

The results of Table 22.3 indicate the importance of "minor" crime. These offenses involve only slightly lower mean dollar losses —$149 for Part I crimes and $123 for Part II crimes (excluding the counterfeiting and forgery cases due to their small number). Yet the Part II offenses occur about twice as frequently as the more serious Part I offenses. The total dollar loss from minor crime may therefore exceed the losses from major crime.

The implications of these facts are not clear. Are different kinds of police resources involved in protecting people from minor and major crime? If so, should there be a reallocation of these resources to attempt to hold down these minor crimes? If not, what should be done to increase the likelihood of recovering the losses or indemnifying the victims? In either case, there is an even more basic implication here. It is that the UCR extend its reporting activities to include some of these minor crimes in much the same way the index crimes are handled. Indeed, these data underscore the necessity to rethink the entire Crime Index concept. . . .

How are these property losses distributed among various social groups? The data presented here are only preliminary, since there are many complications in matching groups which have different overall rates of victimization and different rates for the various crimes. Table 22.4 therefore should be re-

garded with caution. It shows the median net property loss for Whites and Negroes at two income levels. Surprisingly, Whites have a lower median loss than Negroes, and income seems to make little difference. This reflects the dominance of the large number of small victimizations. . . .

THE DISTRIBUTION OF CRIME

The distribution of crime in different places and among various social groups is perhaps more important than its sheer amount. The policy issues here are more visible and more involved with current political problems.

To what extent is crime concentrated, as has long been thought, in the urban environment? To what extent are these regional differences in crime rates? And to what extent are the poor, and especially the Negro, more or less likely to be victims of crime? Behind these factual questions lie alternative remedial measures—measures that range from city planning and the war on poverty to the training and organization of police departments and the allocation of their resources within the communities of the nation.

The findings of the NORC survey are certainly not sufficient to give answers to these questions, but they present fresh evidence as to the location and the nature of the problems.

We begin with the most global comparisons, those between regions. Not only are differences among the four main regions perennially interesting but they also allow a confrontation with the UCR figures. . . .

In general, the overall rates are comparable with the exception of the North Central region, in which the survey shows a relatively

TABLE 22.4
MEDIAN NET PROPERTY LOSSES BY RACE AND INCOME

Property Losses	White		Negro	
	Under $6,000	$6,000 or More	Under $6,000	$6,000 or More
Median net dollar losses	$34	$30	$50	$50
N	(1,023)	(644)	(173)	(78)

higher rate than the UCR. Almost all the individual crimes, however, show peculiar variations from region to region. Aggravated assaults are highest in the South, according to the UCR, but the survey shows a much higher rate, comparatively, in the West. Robbery is high in the North Central and West regions; the survey, however, matches the robbery rates in the North Central and the South, but indicates a rate three times that of the UCR in the Northeast. . . .

The relative positions of Part II crimes in the four regions mirror the rates for Part I crimes: the West highest, North Central next, Northeast and South lowest. Yet as with major crime, there are puzzling discontinuities among the individual minor crimes. It is impossible, however, to explain these variations from this distance. It may be that the four regions contain different mixtures of community types, populations, police practices, and the omnipresent but mysterious "cultural atmospheres." A closer look at the distribution of crime is therefore necessary.

The next step is community type. The critical dimensions here are size and density, which for simplicity of presentation we condense into (1) central cities of metropolitan areas, (2) suburban communities of the metropolis, and (3) nonmetropolitan communities. The sample of 10,000 households is almost equally divided among these three types of communities. This invites their use even though they do not begin to exhaust the ways communities should or could be categorized. Table 22.5 shows the crime rates per 100,000 population in the three types of communities.

TABLE 22.5
EVALUATED CRIME RATES BY URBANIZATION
(PER 100,000 POPULATION)

Crime	Central Parts of Metropolitan Areas	Suburban Parts of Metropolitan Areas	Nonmetropolitan Areas
Part I Total	2,860	2,347	1,267
Homicide	0	0	8
Forcible rape	83	38	8
Robbery	207	95	0
Aggravated assault	293	286	110
Burglary	1,335	839	727
Larceny ($50+)	704	810	346
Vehicle theft	238	279	68
Part II Total	4,792	5,214	2,949
Simple assault	569	467	203
Larceny (— $50)	1,532	1,840	1,056
Auto offense	435	591	313
Malicious mischief or arson	1,190	1,382	684
Counterfeiting or forgery	31	48	51
Fraud	217	334	220
Consumer fraud	135	133	110
Other sex	207	133	93
Family	331	191	118
Other victimization	145	95	101
Total	7,652	7,561	4,216
N	(9,661)	(10,491)	(11,837)

TABLE 22.6
REGIONAL AND COMMUNITY DIFFERENCES IN RATES OF SERIOUS CRIMES
AGAINST THE PERSON AND CRIMES AGAINST PROPERTY
(PER 100,000 POPULATION)

Region	Metropolitan Areas				Nonmetropolitan Areas	
	central cities		*suburban environs*			
Northeast	Person:	513	Person:	293	Person:	62
	Property:	1,653	Property:	1,552	Property:	1,055
	N =	(2,166)	N =	(1,845)	N =	(1,117)
North Central	Person:	731	Person:	323	Person:	152
	Property:	2,780	Property:	1,533	Property:	1,010
	N =	(3,511)	N =	(1,856)	N =	(1,162)
South	Person:	315	Person:	536	Person:	120
	Property:	1,957	Property:	2,236	Property:	978
	N =	(2,272)	N =	(2,772)	N =	(1,098)
West	Person:	969	Person:	593	Person:	148
	Property:	3,204	Property:	2,579	Property:	2,224
	N =	(4,173)	N =	(3,172)	N =	(2,372)

There is clearly some confirmation of hallowed beliefs in the table. The central cities of the metropolitan area produce more crimes of violence than the nonmetropolitan communities. Petty theft and malicious destruction of property are reported most often in the suburbs. But it is surprising and interesting that the crimes of false pretenses—forgery, counterfeiting, frauds, and consumer frauds—do not show any differences by type of community.

The combination of region and community type is next.

To compress this mass of material, Table 22.6 shows for the regions and community types the rates for serious crimes against the person (homicide, rape, robbery, and aggravated assault) and serious property crimes (burglary, larceny over $50, and vehicle theft).

Whatever the myth of the old Wild West, its present crime rate for both property and personal crimes is higher than that in any other region of the country—almost twice the rates of the Northeast for all three types of communities. The South, surprisingly, does not appear to have the high rate of violent crime that allegedly characterizes that region.

Irrespective of region, it is clear that as one moves from the central city to the suburbs

out into smaller towns and rural areas, the crime rates decline, but much more drastically for crimes against the person than for property crimes. The metropolitan center, that is, has a violent crime rate about *five times* as high as the smaller city and rural area but a property crime rate only *twice* as high.

Do these figures validate the charge of "crime in the streets"? Yes, the city is a more dangerous place than suburbs or small towns. Yet these figures should not be taken without these qualifications: about 40 percent of the aggravated assaults and rapes (constituting most of all the serious crimes against the person) take place *within* the victim's home, and about 45 percent of *all* the serious crimes against the person are committed by someone familiar to the victim. Random street crime by strangers is clearly not the main picture that emerges from these figures.

This brings the discussion down to people, for behind the slogan "crime in the streets" is the hidden implication that the Negro is the main offender in the crime situation. What is the situation, in fact? Table 22.7 shows the crime rates for Whites and Negroes, holding income constant.

At all levels of income, Negroes have higher rates of victimization for serious crimes against the person compared to Whites. Prop-

TABLE 22.7

DISTRIBUTION OF CRIME BY RACE AND INCOME
(RATES PER 100,000 POPULATION)*

Crime	White				Non-White		
	$0-$2,999	$3,000-$5,999	$6,000-$9,999	Above $10,000	$0-$2,999	$3,000-$5,999	$6,000+ †
Part I Total	2,124	2,267	1,685	2,170	2,894	2,581	3,387
Homicide	0	0	0	0	56	0	0
Forcible rape	58	46	0	17	111	60	121
Robbery	116	91	42	34	278	240	121
Aggravated assault	146	289	147	220	389	420	121
Burglary	1,310	958	764	763	1,336	1,261	2,056
Larceny ($50+)	378	700	565	916	501	300	363
Vehicle theft	116	183	167	220	223	300	605
Part II Total	3,928	4,168	4,604	4,866	2,057	2,461	3,508
Simple assault	494	487	324	458	278	180	242
Larceny (− $50)	1,426	1,506	1,559	1,712	723	1,021	1,451
Auto offense	233	441	628	543	111	180	242
Malicious mischief or arson	728	715	1,371	1,424	389	480	605
Counterfeiting or forgery	58	30	42	51	0	0	0
Fraud	378	335	188	305	111	180	121
Consumer fraud	87	137	115	203	0	60	0
Other sex	87	182	178	102	56	60	363
Family	437	335	199	68	389	300	484
N	(3,435)	(6,573)	(9,555)	(5,897)	(1,797)	(1,665)	(827)

* Rate per 100,000 population of each specific race and income group.
† Too few cases of non-Whites above $10,000 to maintain as separate category.

TABLE 22.8

RACIAL AND INCOME DIFFERENCES IN RATES OF SERIOUS
PERSONAL AND PROPERTY CRIMES
(PER 100,000 POPULATION)

Type of Crime	Income under $6,000		Income $6,000 or More	
	White	Negro	White	Negro
Against person	402	748	244	262
Against property	1,829	1,927	1,765	3,024
N	(10,008)	(3,462)	(15,452)	(827)

erty crimes show a more complex relationship to both race and income. For Whites, as income rises, there is a general decline of burglaries but an *increase* of larcenies and car thefts. Among Negroes the trends are less clear, but they mirror the patterns for Whites with an important exception. Burglaries rise with income. Does this suggest that residential segregation increases the risk of burglaries among upper income Negroes? They are the target of residential theft, as is the case with Whites, but may lack the opportunity for the protection that sheltered middle class neighborhoods provide.

Somewhat surprising is the relatively low rates of minor crime amongst Negroes. This is especially marked for petty larcenies and simple assaults at the lowest income level. This may be the result of differential definitions of crime held by Negroes, or it might be due to the reporting technique of the study. There is strong evidence that there is considerable under-reporting of Negro victimization.

There are, in short, definite but complex relationships of crime with race and income that both confirm ordinary expectations and go beyond them. At the risk of over-simplification, Table 22.8 shows for Whites and Negroes (with income dichotomized) the rates of victimizations for serious and nonserious crimes against persons and property.

Among lower income groups (under $6,000 per year) Negroes are much more likely than Whites to be victims of serious crimes of violence, but only very slightly more likely to be victims of property crimes. The situation is exactly reversed for upper income groups. The wealthier Negro is not much

more likely than a White person to be a victim of a violent crime but considerably more likely to have property stolen—burglary being the largest component of the property crimes against more affluent Negroes. Both these facts are important; the lower income Negro is the target of violence much more than a comparably poor White person, and the better-off Negro is more in danger of property loss than his White counterpart. . . .

Before leaving the individual characteristics, it should be useful here to note a few facts about the offender. In only one-third of the cases did the victim actually know the offender, and in a slightly larger number of cases the latter was identifiable. The one important fact about the offender-victim relationship is the racial one. Table 22.9 shows the extent to which victim and offender are of the same race.

TABLE 22.9

EXTENT OF INTERRACIAL CRIME

Offender Is:	Victim Is:	
	White	Non-White
White	88%	19%
Non-white	12	81
Total	100%	100%
N	(705)	(118)

It is difficult, without some other quantitative comparison, to say if this is a high or a low rate of interracial interaction. It is easy, however, to say that Negroes are at least as likely to be victimized by Whites as Whites are by Negroes. The fear of the Negro as the major source of crime is not borne out by these data, but they are overall national figures. One would have to come closer to the immediate scene of the crime and the nature of the community to provide more complete answers.

This brings the analysis to the more microscopic spatial dimension of the neighborhood. Where is crime committed? Fully half are in or immediately around the home, and about a quarter in public places. A fuller description is given in Table 22.10. . . .

TABLE 22.10
WHERE DOES CRIME TAKE PLACE

Inside the home/apartment	23%
Near home, yard, sidewalk	29
Other private homes or places	10
Inside public buildings (stores, restaurants)	6
Outside public places (streets, parks, beaches)	18
Other	11
No specific place	3
Total	100%
N	(2,098)

PERSONAL AND NEIGHBORHOOD SECURITY

A sense of personal safety in one's own neighborhood and a sense of security about one's own home is a major American value, one that appears to be particularly fragile and problematical in these recent years. It is not entirely clear where the burden for securing that sense of security falls; certainly the police have important responsibilities but so does the citizen himself, through his own efforts and through his concerted activities in these communities. . . .

[Survey respondents said that] crime currently was the second most important domestic issue. That concern was on a national level. How much concern is there with crime on the local level, and what is its relation to thinking it an important national issue? The respondents to the attitude questionnaire were asked how they felt about going out alone at night in their own neighborhoods, how worried they were about having their houses broken into, and related topics. The answers to these questions are presented below, separately for Whites and Negroes and for males and females. Where there are significant differences in attitude and behavior by income they will be noted.

First, how safe do people feel walking outside in their neighborhoods? During the day almost everyone of both races and sexes feels quite safe; walking alone at night, however, is quite different. Table 22.11 shows, understandably, that the fear of being outside alone at night is considerably greater for females than for males, and much greater for Negroes than for Whites.

There is, incidentally, a slight decrease in concern by Whites with higher income. From data not fully shown here, about 35 percent of White respondents with less than $6,000 annual income feel very or somewhat unsafe walking alone at night in contrast to 26 percent of Whites earning more than $6,000. But

TABLE 22.11
HOW SAFE DO YOU FEEL WALKING ALONE IN YOUR NEIGHBORHOOD AFTER DARK?

Response	White		Non-White	
	Male	Female	Male	Female
Very safe	65%	35%	33%	16%
Somewhat safe	22	24	25	19
Somewhat unsafe	9	23	22	28
Very unsafe	4	18	20	37
Total	100%	100%	100%	100%
N	(4,628)	(7,495)	(646)	(1,033)

no such income difference is found among Negroes, suggesting again the consequence of enforced segregation in housing. Negroes not only are more concerned about personal safety than are Whites but also apparently have to expose themselves more often. When asked how often they walk in their neighborhoods at night, Negroes show a higher level of exposure than do Whites. Yet the fear of unsafe neighborhoods does deter people from freely walking about their communities. Women more than men, and Negroes to a greater extent than Whites, have stayed home rather than go somewhere considered unsafe.

It is important to distinguish *fear* of crime from a more objective estimate of the actual risk of crime. These may, and as will be seen, do not necessarily agree. Table 22.12 shows the extent of perceiving the neighborhood as a high or low risk area for street crime. Not surprisingly, the same results as before emerge here; Negroes more than Whites, women more than men, see themselves in a more dangerous situation. The same results obtain for burglary in terms of worrying about having their houses broken into and in terms of assessing the likelihood of such an event.

TABLE 22.12
HOW LIKELY IS IT A PERSON WILL BE ROBBED OR ATTACKED ON THE STREETS AROUND HERE?

Response	White		Non-White	
	Male	Female	Male	Female
Very likely	6%	6%	14%	21%
Somewhat likely	14	15	25	30
Somewhat unlikely	27	32	35	32
Very likely	53	47	26	17
Total	100%	100%	100%	100%
N	(4,661)	(7,443)	(642)	(1,018)

IV.

DEVIANCE, IDENTITY, AND THE LIFE CYCLE

IN PARTS II AND III our selections centered on the labeling of exchanges as deviant or the labeling of personal control as disordered or inadequate. Here the selections deal with issues in which the labeling process relates to deviant identities and careers. Sometimes these deviant careers represent commitments to lifelong choices; elsewhere the commitment is specific to a particular phase of life that is highly vulnerable to labeling as deviant.

There is good reason to believe that the social processing of individuals early in life may set up social identities and commitments that direct individuals toward careers in deviance. We have seen one analysis of such processes in Selection 17, on the differences between addicted and nonaddicted siblings in a slum area. In the first selection here, by Jane Mercer, we see how the schools can operate to label persons as mentally retarded and thus affect the direction of their future socialization.

Several selections here deal with adolescence and youth as stages in the life cycle. In our society these stages provide a particularly fertile ground for the operation of the labeling process. American culture is extremely ambivalent about adolescence and youth, on the one hand romanticizing these ages as "the best times of life," and on the other hand maintaining extensive institutional forces designed to control and limit young people's exercise of initiative. We include one selection (24) that deals with the general process by which American society seeks to delay the assumption of a fully mature status; one (25) that discusses the adolescent and youth gangs that are a standard feature of working and lower class areas in American cities; and another (26) that considers the college campus milieu that is the comparable social reference point for the great majority of middle class youth.

Commitments to deviant identities and careers provide a fertile ground for sociological understanding. Two studies deal with the vicissitudes of criminal careers—one on armed robbery (27) and another on the adaptation of ex-offenders who return to their home communities from prison (28). James Driscoll's selection on transsexuals (29) emphasizes still another aspect of career commitments. Men who choose to become women undergo the most profound change of identity and life-style in our culture. The author is concerned with the social forces that operate when individuals seek to change their social identities and to commit themselves to a radically different career.

Finally, we examine some of the stigmatizing forces that operate at the end of the life cycle, in the period of old age. Helena Lopata's article (30) shows how community forces and the social meanings attached to the aging process and widowhood combine to heighten the problem of loneliness.

23. LABELS AND REALITY: DIAGNOSING MENTAL RETARDATION

JANE R. MERCER

From a paper presented at the meetings of the American Psychological Association, September 3-7, 1971. Jane R. Mercer is Associate Professor of Sociology at the University of California, Riverside. She has directed an extensive program of research into different aspects of the sociology of education, with particular emphasis on problems of mental retardation, the role of testing in schools, and issues of racial integration in the schools.

■ Advances in the social technology used in public institutions such as schools and hospitals during the past half century have brought with them their own problems. The schools operate as a selecting and labeling system by which identities are conferred on children —as mentally retarded, gifted, hyperaggressive, withdrawn—and these labels then affect the children's self-concepts, their experiences with their peers, and perhaps their future lives. The techniques used for this labeling have many problematic aspects; for example, it is commonly observed that teachers may use as guides other and presumably irrelevant characteristics, such as race. Even when the standardized tests on which schools rely so heavily are used in a detached and "professional" way, they have many shortcomings, which psychologists in their desire for legitimation in the larger world often have tended to underemphasize.

Perhaps no form of school-based labeling is more dramatic in its consequences for the child than the label of "mentally retarded," which places children in special classes where all their classmates are similarly "defective" students. Promotion out of the ranks of the mentally retarded is extremely unlikely, since the condition is regarded as basically biological in origin. Even if in some more liberal versions it is regarded as a result of "cultural deprivation," the effects still are considered to be almost impossible to reverse.

In this selection Jane Mercer considers the implications of the use of different criteria to make the diagnosis of mental retardation. In particular, she considers the implications of three different IQ cutoff points, each of which has some currency among clinicians. Then she considers the effects of using a two-factor rather than a single-factor approach to diagnosis. What are the effects of limiting the mental retardate label to those whose IQ scores are very low and who also demonstrate failures of social adaptation in their daily behavior? To show the implications of these different criteria she examines the characteristics of a random sample of adults in the community who fall within the mentally retarded category according to one or another of these definitions.

Her most striking finding is that only with the most conservative criteria does one avoid the inclusion of many healthy, well-functioning adults under the retarded label. The clear implication of these findings is that schools that use less conservative diagnostic criteria segregate and stigmatize children who in fact are capable of functioning in quite normal ways. Furthermore, the stigmatizing effect does not fall randomly in terms of the student's ethnic background. Mercer's work shows that Blacks and Chicanos are much more likely to be mislabeled as retarded than are Anglo children.

Mercer's work is reported in comprehensive detail in *Labeling the Mentally Retarded* (Berkeley: University of California Press, 1973). One of the first sociological studies of this subject is Bernard Farber, *Mental Retardation: Its Social Context and Social Consequences* (Houghton-Mifflin, 1968). A recent essay that is especially interesting for its comparative perspective is Robert B. Edgerton, "Anthropology and Mental Retardation," in Laura Nader and Thomas W. Maretzki (eds.), *Culture, Illness, and Health* (Anthropological Studies No. 9; American Anthropological Innovation, 1973). Other useful studies of mental retardation include Richard Coch and James Dobson, eds., *The Mentally Retarded Child and His Family: A Multi-Disciplinary Handbook* (Brunner/Mazel, Inc., 1971); and H. Carl Haywood, ed., *Social Cultural Aspects of Mental Retardation: Proceedings of the Peabody NIMH Conference* (Appleton-Century-Crofts, 1970.) ■

PLURALISTIC DIAGNOSIS is a set of procedures we are developing which attempts to take sociocultural background into account in assessing the meaning of scores on standardized measures. This approach has developed as an outgrowth of findings from an epidemiology of mental retardation which we have conducted in the city of Riverside, California, over the past eight years. In order to explain clearly the rationale behind pluralistic diagnostic procedures, it is necessary to review, briefly, the conceptual model and design used in the Riverside epidemiology and to point out those findings from that study which are most relevant to our current topic.

CONCEPTUAL MODELS USED IN THE RIVERSIDE EPIDEMIOLOGY

Two contrasting conceptual perspectives were used in the Riverside epidemiology—a clinical perspective and a social system perspective.

The social system perspective treats mental retardation as an achieved social status and a social role which some individuals play in some social systems. This aspect of the study focused on the labeling process and the characteristics of persons who achieve the status of mental retardate in various social systems in the community, especially the public school.

The clinical perspective is that commonly adopted by persons in the fields of medicine, psychology, social work, and education. Within the clinical perspective there are two definitions of "normal" which tend to be used simultaneously and interchangeably—the pathological model and the statistical model. The pathological, or medical, model, developed in medicine, defines diseases or handicaps by the biological symptoms that characterize them. A person is categorized as "abnormal" when pathological symptoms are present and "normal" when there is an absence of pathological signs. The statistical model defines abnormality according to the extent to which an individual varies from the average of the population or a particular trait. Ordinarily, if an individual is more than two standard deviations above or below the mean for the population on which a measure was standardized, he is regarded as "abnormal." The clinical perspective regards mental retardation as an attribute of the individual. His symptomatology may exist as an entity regardless of whether it has been identified and labeled by significant others in his social milieu. The trained diagnostician with his clinical measures may detect abnormalities not apparent to lay persons.

This paper focuses primarily on findings from the clinical epidemiology, which was based on the assumptions of the clinical perspective.

RESEARCH DESIGN FOR THE CLINICAL EPIDEMIOLOGY

DEFINITIONS

The definition of mental retardation operationalized in the clinical epidemiology was that of the American Association for Mental Deficiency. "Mental retardation refers to subaverage general intellectual functioning which originates during the developmental period and is associated with impairment in adaptive behavior." This is a two-dimensional definition. Before a person may be diagnosed as mentally retarded he must be subnormal in both intellectual performance and adaptive behavior. Evidence of organic dysfunction or biological anomalies is not required.

In the same document "subnormal" is defined as performance on a standard measure of intellectual functioning that is greater than one standard deviation below the population mean, approximately the lowest 16 percent of the population. Educational practice generally places the dividing line somewhat lower. The highest IQ test score for placement in a class for the educable mentally retarded ranges between 75 and 79, depending on local usage. This cutoff includes approximately the lowest 9 percent of the population. The test designers suggest a cutoff that more closely conforms with traditional definitions—an IQ below 70, approximately 3 percent of the population. In the clinical epidemiology all three cutoffs were used and the results compared.

OPERATIONS

Intellectual adequacy was measured in the clinical epidemiology by using standardized measures of intelligence, primarily the Stanford-Binet LM and the Kuhlman-Binet. We conceptualized adaptive behavior as an individual's ability to play ever more complex roles in a progressively widening circle of social systems. Because there are no generally accepted measures of adaptive behavior, we developed a series of 28 age-graded scales for this purpose, drawing heavily on the work of Doll and Gesell, especially for the younger years. Questions were answered by a respondent related to the person being evaluated.

SAMPLE

The research design called for a first-stage screening of a large sample of the population of the community, using the adaptive behavior scales, and then a second-stage testing of a subsample, using standardized IQ tests. We called these samples the screened sample and the tested subsample, respectively.

The screened sample was a stratified area probability sample of 3,198 housing units in the city of Riverside, California, selected so that all geographic areas and socioeconomic levels in the city were represented in their proper proportion. The 46 interviewers were college educated; 36 were teachers. Spanish-speaking interviewers were assigned to all households with Spanish surnames, Black interviewers were assigned to interview in housing units located in predominantly non-White neighborhoods, and Anglo interviewers were randomly assigned the remainder of the households. In each household one adult member, usually the mother, served as respondent and provided information about all other members of the household to whom she was related. Interviews were completed

in 2,661 of the 2,923 occupied housing units, an overall response rate of 90.7 percent. In all, 6,907 persons under 50 years of age were screened.

There were 483 persons selected for individual intelligence testing on the basis of a disproportionate random sampling frame. Tests were completed on 423 persons for an overall response rate of 87.6 percent. Intelligence test scores were also secured from other sources for an additional 241 persons, making a total of 664 scores available. Each person in the tested subsample was assigned a weight according to the number of persons he represented in the larger, screened sample.

TYPOLOGY OF MENTAL RETARDATION

A simplified version of our working typology of mental retardation is shown in Table 23.1. The American Association on Mental Deficiency definition contains two primary symptoms—subnormality in intellectual performance and subnormality in adaptive behavior. Combinations of these two dimensions produce four major types of persons: the clinically retarded, the quasi-retarded, the behaviorally maladjusted, and the normals. The clinically retarded are those who are subnormal in both IQ and adaptive behavior. The quasi-retarded are those who are subnormal in IQ but normal in adaptive behavior. The behaviorally maladjusted are those who have normal IQs but are subnormal in adaptive behavior, while the normals are those who pass both dimensions. In this paper we are concerned primarily with two categories in this typology—the clinically retarded and the quasi-retarded.

TABLE 23.1
TYPOLOGY OF MENTAL RETARDATION

	Intellectual Performance	Adaptive Behavior
Clinically retarded	Subnormal	Subnormal
Quasi-retarded	Subnormal	Normal
Behaviorally maladjusted	Normal	Subnormal
Normals	Normal	Normal

TABLE 23.2

COMPARISON OF BEHAVIORAL CHARACTERISTICS OF ADULTS SCORED AS RETARDED
AT THE THREE CRITERIA LEVELS GROUPED IN MUTUALLY EXCLUSIVE CATEGORIES

Characteristics	Failed Traditional Criterion (Nw=59)	Failed Educational or AAMD Criterion (Borderline Retardates) (Nw=116)	Significance Level
Educational-Intellectual Roles			
% Completed 8 or more grades	25.4	83.6	<.001
% Dropped—school academic reasons	35.6	0.0	<.001
% Trouble learning in school	65.2	37.1	<.01
% Reads newspapers	27.1	67.2	<.001
% Reads magazines	6.8	72.4	<.001
% Reads books	32.2	46.5	NS
% Reads and talks about news	66.1	84.2	NS
Occupational Roles			
% Who have held a job	54.2	82.6	<.001
% Semiskilled or higher occupation status	14.3	64.9	<.001
% Financially independent or housewife or student	62.7	80.2	<.001
Family Roles			
% Head of household or spouse of head	69.5	78.4	NS
General Community Roles			
% Belongs to social clubs	11.9	33.3	<.01
% Votes in elections	6.8	48.7	<.001
% Goes to movies	35.6	89.7	<.001
% Works with little supervision	81.4	100.0	<.001
% Goes to store alone	67.8	96.3	<.001
% Travels alone	69.5	96.3	<.001
Informal Community Roles			
% Writes letters	50.8	92.6	<.001
% Attends church	67.8	81.9	NS
% Visits relatives frequently	54.8	79.5	<.001
% Visits neighbors frequently	61.0	93.1	<.001
% Visits friends frequently	35.6	81.9	<.001
% Visits co-workers frequently	45.9	76.6	<.001
% Plays parlor games	30.5	71.3	<.001
% Goes dancing	40.7	45.7	NS
% Participates in sports	13.6	58.6	<.001

FINDINGS AND CONCLUSIONS

SUGGESTED CUTOFF LEVEL FOR SUBNORMALITY

As noted earlier, three cutoff levels are currently used for defining subnormality: the Amercian Association of Mental Deficiency proposes the lowest 16 percent of the population; educational usage defines the lowest 9 percent as subnormal; and traditional practice has been to define the lowest 3 percent as subnormal. We examined the impact of using each of these cutoffs.

Table 23.2 presents some of the behavioral characteristics of the adults in our sample who failed the traditional criterion, the lowest 3 percent, and compares them with adults who failed only the educational or the AAMD criteria. We found that the majority of the adults who were failing at a 9 percent or the 16 percent criterion were, in fact, filling the usual complement of social roles for persons of their age and sex: 83.6 percent had completed 8 grades or more in school; 82.6 percent had held a job; 64.9 percent had a semi-skilled or higher occupation; 80.2 percent were financially independent or housewives; almost 100 percent were able to do their own shopping and to travel alone; and so forth. Differences between their performance and that of persons failing the traditional criterion differed at the .001 level of significance on 21 out of 26 of the comparisons made. It is clear that most adults who appeared in the borderline category were managing their own affairs and did not appear to require supervision, control, and care for their own welfare. Their role performance appeared neither subnormal nor particularly unusual.

We found that rates for subnormality using only an IQ test score ranged from 21.4 to 36.8 to 72.8 per 1,000 for the total population of the community at each successive criterion. When a two-dimensional definition was used—i.e., persons had to fail both IQ and adaptive behavior before being defined as clinically retarded—rates shrank to 9.7, 18.9, and 34.7 per 1,000 for the total population at each criterion level. As shown in Table 23.3, there were significant differences by ethnic group and socioeconomic status. We found that rates for clinical retardation, using the two-dimensional definition, increased from 4.4 to 6.1 to 9.6 per 1,000 for the Anglo population, but increased from 4.1 to 22.4 to 53.1 per 1,000 for the Black population and from 60.0 to 127.4 to 238.4 per 1,000 for the Chicano population. Similar disparities appeared for low status as compared to high status persons, regardless of ethnic group. Proportionately more low status persons and persons from minority ethnic groups are defined as clinically retarded as the cutoff level for subnormality is raised.

We compared the findings from our field survey with the actual labeling practices of clinicians in the community and found much higher rates from the field survey than from actual labeling practices when the 16 percent or the 9 percent cutoff was used. The greatest correspondence between field survey rates and rates of labeling occurred when the traditional 3 percent cutoff was used.

We concluded that the 3 percent cutoff—that is, IQ below 70 and adaptive behavior in the lowest 3 percent of the population—was the criterion most likely to identify those in need of special assistance and supervision and least likely to stigmatize as mentally retarded persons who would be filling a normal complement of social roles as adults. Persons scoring in the so-called borderline category should be regarded as low normals rather than as clinically retarded.

A ONE- OR TWO-DIMENSIONAL DEFINITION?

Although the American Association of Mental Deficiency proposes the two-dimensional definition of mental retardation, which we used in our study, in actual clinical practice most clinicians measure only intelligence in a systematic fashion when making assessments. We examined the probable consequences of clinicians using only an IQ test score rather than measuring both IQ and adaptive behavior in reaching a diagnosis of retardation.

First, we compared the social role per-

TABLE 23.3

PREVALENCE RATES FOR CLINICAL RETARDATION PER 1,000 FOR SELECTED SUBGROUPS COMPARING THE RATES USING A ONE-DIMENSIONAL WITH THOSE USING A TWO-DIMENSIONAL DEFINITION*

	Number Fail IQ	Rate per 1,000 Fail IQ	Number Fail IQ Pass A-B	% Shrinkage	Number Fail IQ Fail A-B	Rate per 1,000 Fail IQ Fail A-B
Traditional Criterion (IQ 69— and Adaptive Behavior, Lowest 3%)						
Total population	150	21.4	82	54.7	68	9.7
Anglo	25	4.4	0	0	25	4.4
Chicano	100	149.9	60	60.0	40	60.0
Black	22	44.9	20	90.9	2	4.1
Deciles 1-3 (low)	125	78.7	69	55.2	56	35.2
Deciles 4-7 (middle)	20	7.0	11	55.0	9	3.1
Deciles 8-10 (high)	5	2.0	2	40.0	3	1.2
Educational Criterion (IQ 79— and Adaptive Behavior, Lowest 9%)						
Total population	258	36.8	126	48.8	132	18.9
Anglo	48	8.4	13	27.1	35	6.1
Chicano	161	241.4	76	47.2	85	127.4
Black	49	100.0	38	77.5	11	22.4
Deciles 1-3 (low)	188	118.3	86	45.7	102	64.2
Deciles 4-7 (middle)	59	20.6	36	61.0	23	8.0
Deciles 8-10 (high)	11	4.3	4	36.4	7	2.8
AAMD Criterion (IQ 84— and Adaptive Behavior, Lowest 16%)						
Total population	510	72.8	267	52.3	243	34.7
Anglo	135	23.5	80	59.2	55	9.6
Chicano	283	424.3	124	43.8	159	238.4
Black	88	179.6	62	70.5	26	53.1
Deciles 1-3 (low)	273	171.8	125	45.8	158	99.4
Deciles 4-7 (middle)	146	50.9	76	52.1	70	24.4
Deciles 8-10 (high)	91	35.8	75	82.4	16	6.3

* The total for the ethnic groups does not add up to the total population because there were a few persons classified as "Other Ethnic Group" not reported in this table.

formance of the quasi-retarded—i.e., those who failed only the IQ test—with the clinically retarded, school-aged child—i.e., those who failed both the IQ test and the adaptive behavior scales. Among the primary differences between the two is that the clinically retarded are reported to have had more trouble learning, are more frequently behind the school grade expected for their age, have repeated more grades, and are more likely to be enrolled in special education classes. The quasi-retardate, in spite of his low IQ test score, has avoided falling behind his agemates or being placed in special programs. We found that 80 percent of the quasi-retarded adults had graduated from high school; they all read books, magazines, and newspapers; all had held jobs; 65 percent had white-collar positions; 19 percent had skilled or semiskilled positions; and 15.7 percent were unskilled laborers. All of them were able to work without supervision, participated in sports, traveled alone, went to the store by themselves, and participated in informal visiting with co-workers, friends, and neighbors. In other words, their social role performance tended to be indistinguishable from that of other adults in the community.

As shown in Table 23.3, there was a 54.7 percent shrinkage in the rate of mental retardation for the total population of the community, at the 3 percent criterion, when adaptive behavior as well as IQ was measured. However, the shrinkage varied by ethnic group and socioeconomic status. There was no shrinkage for Anglos. Everyone who had an IQ below 70 was in the lowest 3 percent in adaptive behavior. However, 60 percent of the Chicanos and 90.9 percent of the Blacks who had IQ test scores below 70 passed the adaptive behavior measure. Comparable results were found at the other two criterion levels. A similar pattern appears for socioeconomic status but is less pronounced than in the case of ethnic group.

The most important aspect of these figures is the finding that at the 3 percent cutoff the evaluation of adaptive behavior contributed little additional information to that provided by the IQ test for Anglos. However,

evaluation of adaptive behavior was important in evaluating persons from ethnic minorities and lower socioeconomic levels—persons from backgrounds that do not conform to the modal social and cultural patterns of the community. Many of them may fail intelligence tests mainly because they have not had the opportunity to learn the cognitive skills and to acquire the knowledge needed to pass such tests. They demonstrate by their ability to cope with problems in other areas of life that they are not comprehensively incompetent.

We concluded that clinicians should develop a systematic method for assessing adaptive behavior as well as intelligence in making clinical assessments of ability and should operationalize the two-dimensional screening procedure advocated by the AAMD 10 years ago.

TAKING SOCIOCULTURAL FACTORS INTO ACCOUNT IN CLINICAL ASSESSMENT

Our third major conclusion was that the IQ tests now being used by psychologists are to a large extent Anglocentric. They tend to measure the extent to which an individual's background is similar to that of the modal cultural configuration of American society. Because a significant amount of the variance in IQ test scores is related to sociocultural characteristics, we concluded that sociocultural factors must be taken into account in interpreting the meaning of any individual score.

Specifically, we studied two different samples of persons to determine the amount of variance in IQ test scores that could be accounted for by sociocultural factors. The first group included the 100 Chicanos, 47 Blacks, and 556 Anglos from 7 months through 50 years of age for whom IQs were secured in the field survey or in the agency survey and for whom we also had information on the sociocultural characteristics of their families. Eighteen sociocultural characteristics were dichotomized so that one category corresponded to the modal sociocultural configuration of the community and the other category was nonmodal. IQ was used as the dependent variable in a stepwise multiple regression in which the 18 sociocultural characteristics were used as independent variables. The multiple correlation coefficient for this large heterogeneous sample was .50 ($p < .001$), indicating that 25 percent of the variance in the IQs of the 703 culturally and ethnically heterogeneous individuals in this group could be accounted for by sociocultural differences.

In a similar analysis, 1,513 elementary schoolchildren in the public schools of Riverside were studied, using 13 sociocultural characteristics of their families as independent variables and Full Scale WISC IQ as the dependent variable. The 598 Chicanos and 339 Black children in the sample included the total school population of the 3 segregated minority elementary schools that then existed in the district. The 576 Anglo children were randomly selected from 11 predominately Anglo elementary schools in the district. The multiple correlation coefficient was .57, indicating that 32 percent of the variance in the IQs of this socioculturally heterogeneous group of elementary schoolchildren could be accounted for by differences in family background factors. Sixty-eight percent of the variance was residual—that is, unaccounted for.

Not only did sociocultural characteristics account for a large amount of the variance in IQ test scores in the large samples, which combined all three ethnic groups, but they also accounted for a large amount of the variance in IQ within each ethnic group. A series of stepwise multiple regressions were run for Chicanos and Blacks, separately, using IQ as the dependent variable and sociocultural variables as the independent variables. . . .

For the 100 Chicanos in the field survey 18 sociocultural variables were correlated .61 with IQ and accounted for 37.2 percent of the variance in the measured intelligence of this group. The five sociocultural characteristics most significant in the stepwise regression were: living in a household in which the head of household has a white-collar job; living in a family with five or fewer members; having a head of household with a skilled or higher occupation; living in a family in which the head of household was reared in an urban environment and was reared in the United States.

There were 47 Blacks in the field survey for whom we had information on all variables in the analysis. Findings on such a small number are less reliable, but the multiple correlation coefficient between IQ and sociocultural characteristics was .52, accounting for 27 percent of the variance in IQ test scores. The five best indicators were: having a mother reared in the North; having a head of household with a white-collar job; having a male head of household; living in an intact family; and living in a family that is buying its own home.

For the elementary schoolchildren, all 17 variables were correlated .39 with Full Scale IQ for Chicano children and .44 with Full Scale IQ for the Black children. This means, that sociocultural characteristics could account for 15.2 percent of the variance in the IQ test scores of Chicano children and 19.4 percent of the variance in the IQ test scores of Black children.

In brief, Chicano elementary school children with higher IQ test scores tend to come from less crowded homes and have mothers who expect them to have some education beyond high school. They have fathers who were reared in an urban environment (over 10,000 population) and who have a ninth-grade education or more. They live in a family that speaks English all or most of the time and is buying its home. Black children with the highest IQs also come from families that have characteristics similar to those of the modal configuration of the community. They come from families with less than six members; have a mother who expects them to get some college education; have parents who are married and living together in a home which they either own or are buying; and have a father who has an occupation rated 30 or higher on the Duncan Socioeconomic Index. Thus, the more the family is like the modal sociocultural configuration of the community, the higher the IQs of Black and

Chicano children on the WISC. Clearly, sociocultural factors cannot be ignored in interpreting the meaning of a standardized intelligence test when evaluating the child from a non-Anglo background. The tests are measuring, to a significant extent, sociocultural characteristics.

DEVELOPING A SOCIOCULTURAL INDEX FOR
CLASSIFYING CHILDREN BY FAMILY
BACKGROUND

The findings from the multiple regression were used to group each Black and Chicano elementary schoolchild who was given the WISC into one of five groups according to the extent to which his family background conformed to the modal configuration for the total community of Riverside. Each child was given one point for each family background characteristic that was like the dominant society on the five primary sociocultural variables related to Full Scale IQ for his ethnic group. If his family was similar to the modal configuration on all five characteristics, he received a score of five. If his background was similar to the dominant configuration on four characteristics, he received a score of four, and so forth. The average IQ test score for children in each sociocultural grouping is shown in Table 23.4. . . .

The average IQ for the entire group of Chicano children was 90.4, approximately two-thirds of a standard deviation below the mean for the standardization group. The 127 children from backgrounds least like the modal sociocultural configuration of the community, having 0 or only 1 modal characteristic, had an average IQ of 84.5, borderline mentally retarded by the American Association of Mental Deficiency criterion. The 146 children with 2 modal characteristics in their background had a mean IQ of 88.1, those with 3 modal characteristics a mean IQ of 89.0, those with 4 modal characteristics a mean IQ of 95.5, and those with all 5 modal characteristics had a mean IQ of 104.4. When social background was held constant there was no difference between the measured intelligence of Chicano and Anglo children.

The situation is just as dramatic for Black children. The total group of 339 Black children had an average IQ of 90.5 when there was no control for sociocultural factors. The 47 children who came from backgrounds least like the modal configuration of the community had an average IQ of 82.7. Those with 2 modal characteristics had an average IQ of 87.1. Those with 3 modal characteristics had an IQ of 92.8, those with 4 characteristics an average IQ of 95.9, and those with 5 characteristics an average IQ of 99.5, exactly at the national norm for the test. Thus, Black children who came from family backgrounds comparable to the modal pattern for the community did just as well on the Wechsler Intelligence Scale for Children as the children on whom the norms were based. When sociocultural differences were held constant there were no differences in measured intelligence.

PLURALISTIC DIAGNOSIS IN THE
EVALUATION OF BLACK AND
CHICANO CHILDREN

One underlying premise of our approach to assessment is that there should be convergence between social definitions and clinical definitions. Specifically, this means that, in so far as possible, clinical procedures should not be labeling as "abnormal" persons who are regarded as "normal" by other persons in their social group or persons who are filling the usual complement of social roles typical of persons of their age and sex. A second premise of our approach is that, given the large amount of variance in IQ test scores that can be accounted for by sociocultural factors, sociocultural factors should be taken into account when interpreting the meaning of a particular set of clinical measures.

A pluralistic, sociocultural perspective would evaluate each child in terms of two frameworks simultaneously—the standardized norms for the test and the norms for the sociocultural group to which he belongs. His position on the standardized norms indicates his probability of succeeding in a regular class

TABLE 23.4

MEAN IQ'S FOR SOCIOCULTURAL MODALITY GROUPS BASED ON VARIABLES
FOUND SIGNIFICANT IN TWO SAMPLES

| | | High | | | | | Low | |
		5	4	3	2	1-0	Total
Chicano Children							
Children's sample variables	Number	25	174	126	146	127	598
	Mean	104.4	95.5	89.0	88.1	84.5	90.4
	Standard deviation	10.4	12.1	11.8	11.6	11.3	12.7
Black Children							
Children's sample variables	Number	17	68	106	101	47	339
	Mean	99.5	95.5	92.8	87.1	82.7	90.5
	Standard deviation	12.1	11.3	11.0	10.5	11.4	12.0

in the American public school system as it is now constituted. His position in the distribution of scores of other children from similar sociocultural backgrounds (that is, children who have had approximately the same opportunity to acquire the knowledge and skills needed to answer questions on an intelligence test designed for an Anglo-American society) will provide a more accurate indication of his potential for learning if enrolled in appropriate educational programs. If a child scores more than 1 standard deviation above the mean for his sociocultural group, then he probably has high normal ability, even if his actual IQ is 100—average by the standard norms of the test. Conversely, a child who achieves a score of 75 on an IQ test when he comes from the least modal sociocultural background is within the normal range for persons, like himself, who have had little exposure to the cultural materials needed to pass the typical intelligence test. His educational program should be planned on the assumption that he is a person with normal learning ability who may need special help in learning the ways of the dominant society.

SUMMARY

To summarize, a pluralistic diagnostic procedure involves securing information beyond that ordinarily considered in clinical evaluation. Our findings suggest that only persons in the lowest 3 percent of the population should be labeled as subnormals. Our findings also suggest that information about adaptive behavior, an individual's ability to cope with problems in the family, neighborhood, and community, should be considered as well as his score on an intelligence test in making clinical assessments. Only persons who are subnormal *both* on the intelligence test *and* in adaptive behavior should be regarded as clinically retarded.

Finally, the meaning of a particular IQ test score or adaptive behavior score not only should be assessed within the framework of the standardized norms for the general population but also should be evaluated in relation to the sociocultural group from which the person comes.

When we reanalyzed the survey data from the field survey of the clinical epidemiology, using these pluralistic diagnostic procedures, differences between rates for mental retardation among ethnic groups disappeared. Approximately the same percentage of persons were being identified as clinically retarded from each ethnic group. When we rediagnosed 268 children who were in classes for the educable mentally retarded in two school districts in southern California using pluralistic diagnostic procedures, we found that approximately 75 percent of the children in those classes would not have been placed in special education if their adaptive behavior and sociocultural backgrounds had been systematically taken into account at the time of assessment. When they were taken into account, the proportion of children diagnosed as mentally retarded from each ethnic group was approximately the same as the proportion of children from that ethnic group in the total public school population.

24. JUVENILIZATION AND AMERICAN YOUTH

BENNETT BERGER

Reprinted from The New York Times Magazine, *November 2, 1969. Copyright © 1969 by The New York Times Company. Bennett Berger is Professor of Sociology at the University of California, Davis. He has long had an interest in youth and has written extensively on the sociology of adolescence. His most recent research has involved him in intensive studies of communal living. In addition he is the author of a classic study of suburbanization and the myths of suburbia,* Working Class Suburb *(University of California Press, 1969).*

■ Americans traditionally have been pre-occupied with their youth and with the ways in which young people differ from their elders. But the turmoil in American colleges and universities in the 1960s brought that concern to a new height. In this selection, Bennett Berger, in addition to expressing some of his personal views about the college turmoil of the 1960s, provides a set of astute observations about the way American social institutions and values operate to establish in the social life cycle a stage called "youth," which simultaneously indulges and restricts young adults and confines them to "an almost endless adolescence."

Part of the social definition of this phase of the life cycle is that individuals in it are expected to be somewhat deviant. In Berger's view, society prefers to have youthful deviants rather than to reorganize its social and economic institutions so as to incorporate very young men and women into adult roles, responsibilities, and rights. The result is a special set of definitions and customs for youth; some provide instigations to deviance and others create special forms of deviance more or less confined to persons at this stage of the life cycle.

In this selection Berger deals with juvenilization as it applies to the middle class and higher status youth who have dominated our conceptualization of "the college years." In selection 25, Walter Miller considers a different set of youth institutions—the gangs that are central to the experience of working and lower class youth.

For other discussions of youth in American Society see Richard Flacks, *Youth and Social Change* (Markham, 1971); Theodore Roszak, *The Making of the Counter Culture* (Double-

day, 1968); Thomas J. Cottle, *Time's Children: Impressions of Youth* (Boston: Little, Brown, 1971); and Thomas J. Cottle, *The Prospect of Youth: Contexts for Sociological Inquiry* (Boston: Little, Brown, 1972). ■

WHEN I WAS AN UNDERGRADUATE 20 years ago, I was chairman of one of the radical student groups at my college and an active official in the regional intercollegiate association of that group. I marched in my share of picket lines, published an article attacking my college president for anti-Semitism, was sung to by the sirens of the local Communist party, and even, in a burst of creativity, wrote what in this age of instant classics I suppose qualifies as a classic militant's love song. I called it, "You and I and the Mimeograph Machine" and dedicated it to all the youthful romances born amidst the technology of moral protest.

Later, when I got older and became a sociologist, I resisted becoming a "political sociologist," by which in this context I mean what a lot of the militants mean: a former activist who traded his credentials as a conscious moral and political agent in exchange for the rewards of *expertise* about political behavior. Though the remarks about student militance which follow may be analytic, I yield nothing to the young in the way of moral credentials.

In trying to throw some sociological light on the nature and character of student unrest, I am not going to comfort the militants by saying that students protest because this is a racist, plastic society or because the curriculum is irrelevant or because the university has sold its soul to the military-industrial complex or because the university is a machine in which students are treated as raw material—when, indeed, their uptight teachers take time from their research to treat them as anything at all. On the other hand, I am not going to comfort their critics by saying that students rebel for kicks or because their upbringing was too permissive or because they are filled with a seething self-hatred or because they are symbolically murdering their fathers in a recurrent ritual melodrama of generational conflict.

What I will try to do is show how certain conditions generic to the direction of our present societal development have helped to bring about the present situation among youth and in the universities. I will also hazard a prediction as to the effects of these conditions during the next decade. An understanding of the problem will not make the solution any easier, for knowledge is power, but it can at least arm us against panaceas.

The problem of student unrest is rooted in the prolongation of adolescence in industrialized countries. But it should be understood that "adolescence" is only minimally a biological category; there are only a very few years between the onset of puberty and the achievement of the growth and strength it takes to do a man's or woman's work. As we know, however, culture has a habit of violating nature. Protoadolescent behavior now begins even before puberty (which itself is occurring earlier) with the action—and the orientation—we call preadolescent, while at the other end technological, economic, and social developments conspire to prolong the dependence of the young, to exclude them from many of the privileges and responsibilities of adult life, and therefore to *juvenilize** them.

The casual evidence in support of this deep institutionalization of adolescence is diffuse and quite remarkable. It includes such spectacles as 6-foot, 200-pound "boys," who in

* Juvenilize: a verb I have devised to describe a process through which "childish" behavior is induced or prolonged in persons who, in terms of their organic development, are capable of participating in adult affairs. If the process exists, there ought to be a verb to describe it.

another time and place might be founders of dynasties and world conquerors (like Alexander of Macedon), cavorting on the fraternity house lawn hurling orange peels and bags of water at each other while tolerant local police, who chucklingly *approve,* direct traffic around the battlefield. It includes the preservation of childlike cadence and intonation in voices otherwise physically mature. It includes the common—and growing—practice (even in official university documents) of opposing the word *student* to the word *adult*—as if students were by definition not adults, even as the median age of university students rises with the increase of the graduate student population.

Adolescence, then, is not the relatively fleeting "transitional stage" of textbook and popular lore but a substantial segment of life which may last 15 to 20 years, and if the meaning of adolescence is extended only slightly, it can last longer than that. I have in mind the age-graded norms and restrictions in those professions which require long years of advanced training, and in which the system of sponsorship makes the advancement of one's career dependent upon being somebody's "boy" perhaps well on toward one's middle age—a fact not uncharacteristic of university faculties.

Much of the discussion of "youth culture" in recent years reflects the prolongation of adolescence, since it is not surprising that a period of life which may last from age 12 to age 35 might develop its own cultural style, it own traditions, and its own sources of motivation, satisfaction—and dissatisfaction. There is thus an enormous stratum of persons caught in the tension between their experience of peak physical strength and sexual energy on the one hand and their public definition as culturally "immature" on the other.

This tension is exacerbated by a contradictory tendency: while modern industrial conditions promote juvenilization and the prolongation of dependence, they also create an "older," more experienced youthful cohort. They have more and earlier experience with sex and drugs; they are better educated than their parents were; urban life sophisticates them more quickly; television brings into their homes worlds of experience that would otherwise remain alien to them. Young people, then, are faced not only with the ambiguity of the adolescent role itself and its prolongation but with forces and conditions that, at least in some ways, make for *earlier* maturity. The youthful population is a potentially explosive stratum because this society is ill-equipped to accommodate it within the status system.

Erik Erikson's well-known theory of the "psychosocial moratorium" of adolescence takes the facts of adolescent prolongation and transforms them into a triumph of civilization. By emphasizing the increased time provided for young persons to postpone commitments, to try on social roles, and to play the game called "the search for identity," Erikson suggests that the moratorium on lasting adult responsibilities contributes to the development and elaboration of personal individuality. I have no wish to quarrel with Erikson's general thesis here; I have done so elsewhere. Instead, I want to emphasize a fact that is seemingly contradictory to Erikson's observations about the moratorium on adult commitments. Namely, there have actually been increasing and clearly documented pressures on young people for earlier and earlier occupational planning and choice. "Benjamin," ask that famous Graduate's parents repeatedly, "what are you going to *do*?" And the question is echoed by millions of prosperous American parents who, despite their affluence, cannot assure the future economic position of their heirs.

Logically, of course, prolonged identity play and early occupational choice cannot be encouraged at the same time; the fact is, they are. And like other ambiguous values (and most moral values are ambiguous, or can be made so), this pair permit different groups of youngsters to rationalize or justify the kinds of adaptations that differing circumstances in fact constrain them to make. The public attention generated by protesting youth in recent years (hippies, the New Left, Black militants) obscures the fact that the majority of young people are still apparently able to

tolerate the tensions of prolonged adolescence, to adjust to the adolescent role (primarily student), to take some satisfaction from the gains it provides in irresponsibility (i.e., "freedom"), and to sail smoothly through high school into college where they choose the majors and get the grades and eventually the certifications for the occupations that they want, that want them, and that higher education is equipped to provide them—degrees in education, business, engineering, dentistry, and so on.

For others, however, the search for identity (quote, unquote) functions as a substitute for an occupational orientation; it gives them something "serious" to do while coping with their problems of sex, education, family, and career. In college most of these people tend to major in the humanities or social sciences (particularly sociology), where they may take 10 years or more between the time they enter as freshmen, drop out, return, graduate, and go on to pursue graduate degrees or give up on them entirely. I will return to this matter, but for the moment I want to make two general points: (1) that the contradictions create understandable tensions in the young and feed their appetite to discover "hypocrisy" in their elders; (2) that this condition is largely beyond the control of the universities; it is generated by the exigencies of a "postindustrial" society which uses institutions of higher education as warehouses for the temporary storage of a population it knows not what else to do with.

The situation has become critical over the past 10 years because the enormous numbers of the young (even small percentages of which yield formidable numbers of troops for worthy causes) and their concentration (in schools and cities) have promoted easy communication and a sense of group solidarity among them. Numbers, concentration, and communication regarding common grievances have made increasingly viable, in almost precisely the way Karl Marx described the development of class consciousness among workers, the creation and maintenance of "deviant subcultures" of youth.

This youthful population is "available" for

recruitment to moral causes because their marginal, ambiguous position in the social structure renders them sensitive to moral inconsistencies (note their talent for perceiving "hypocrisy"), because the major framework of their experience ("education") emphasizes "ideal" aspects of the culture, and because their exclusion from adult responsibilities means that they are generally unrestrained by the institutional ties and commitments which normally function as a brake upon purely moral feeling; they also have the time for it.

The two great public issues of the decade (the Vietnam war and the rights of despised minorities) have been especially suited to enlist the militant predispositions of the young precisely because these issues are clearly moral issues. To take a strong "position" on these issues requires no great expertise or familiarity with arcane facts. And the moral fervor involved in taking such a position nicely reflects our traditional age-graded culture to the extent that it identifies virtue with "idealism," unspoiledness and innocence, precisely the qualities adults like to associate with the young.

It is almost as if the young, in the unconscious division of labor which occurs in all societies, were delegated the role of "moral organ" of society—what with all the grownups being too busy running the bureaucracies of the world (with their inevitable compromises, deals, gives and takes) to concern themselves with "ideals." This even makes a sort of good structural sense because the unanchored character of the young (that is, their relative unfetteredness to family, community, and career) fits them to perform their "ideal" functions—in the same sense and for the same reason that Plato denied normal family life to his philosopher-kings and the Roman Catholic Church denies it to their priests.

It is the combination of moral sensitivity and alienation that accounts both for the extreme juvenophile postures of moral critics like Edgar Friedenberg, Paul Goodman, and John Seeley (which sometimes reach the belief that the young are simply better people than the old or middle-aged, and hence even

a belief in juvenocracy) and the fear of and hostility toward militant youth by writers epitomized by Lewis Feuer in his new book on student movements. In the latter view, the idealism of the young becomes corrupt, violent, terroristic, and destructive precisely because, alienated, detached from institutions, youth are not "responsible"—that is, not accountable for the consequences of their moral zealotry upon the groups and organizations affected by it.

So one is tempted to say that society may just have to accept youth's irresponsibility if it values their moral contributions. But evidence suggests that adult society is in general sympathetic neither to their moral proddings nor toward granting the young any greater responsibility in public affairs. Research by English sociologist Frank Musgrove clearly documents that adults are unwilling to grant real responsibilities any earlier to the young, and there is good reason to believe the same is true in the United States, as is suggested by the repeated failures of the movement to lower the voting age to 18. And as for the "idealism" of youth, when it goes beyond the innocent virtues of praising honesty, being loyal, true, and brave, and helping old ladies across the street, to serious moral involvements promoting their own group interest ("student power") or those of the domestic or "third world" dispossessed, the shine of their "idealism" is likely to tarnish rather quickly.

Moreover, the moral activism of youth *is* sometimes vulnerable to attack on several counts. The "morality" of a political action, for example, is weakened when it has a self-congratulatory character (and the tendency to produce a holier-than-thou vanity in the actor). It also loses something when it does not involve substantial risk of personal interests of freedom (as it unambiguously *does* with the young only in the case of draft resisters). In the end, along with the society's prolongation of adolescence and encouragement of "the search for identity," continuing praise of the young for their "idealism" (except when it becomes serious) and continuing appeals to them to behave responsibly

—in the face of repeated refusal to grant them real responsibilities (except in war)— are understandable as parts of the cultural armory supporting the process of juvenilization.

Colleges, universities, and their environs are the places apparently designated by society as the primary locations where this armory is to be expended. It is clear that the schools, particularly institutions of higher learning, are increasingly being asked by society to perform a kind of holding operation for it. The major propaganda campaign to encourage students not to drop out of high school is significant less for the jobs which staying that last year or two in high school will qualify one for than it is for the reduced pressure it creates on labor markets unable to absorb unskilled 16- and 17-year-olds. The military institutions, through the draft, help store (and train) much of the working-class young, and the colleges and universities prepare many of the heirs of the middle classes for careers in business, the professions, and the semiprofessions. But higher education also gets the lion's share of the identity seekers: those sensitive children of the affluent, less interested in preparing themselves for occupations which the universities are competent to prepare them for than in transcending or trading in the stigmata of their bourgeois backgrounds (work ethic, money-grubbing, status-seeking) for a more "meaningful" life.

It is these students who are heavily represented among the student activists and among whom the cry for "relevance" is heard most insistently. Does it seem odd that this cry should be coming from those students who are *least* interested in the curricula whose relevance is palpable, at least with respect to occupations? Not if one observes that many of these students are, in a sense, classically "intellectuals"—that is, oriented toward statuses or positions for which the universities (as well as other major institutions) have seldom been able or competent to provide certification.

The statuses such students want are those to which one appoints oneself or which one drifts into: artist, critic, writer, intellectual, journalist, revolutionist, philosopher. And these statuses have been undermined for two generations or more by technical and bureaucratic élites whose training has become increasingly specialized and "scientific." In this context the cry for relevance is a protest against technical, value-neutral education whose product (salable skills or the posture of uncommitment) contributes nothing to the search by these students for "identity" and "meaningful experience."

Adding final insult to the injury of the threatened replacement of traditional humanistic intellectuals by technical élites is the ironic transformation of some of their traditional curricula (social sciences particularly) into instruments useful to the "power structure" or "the establishment" in pursuing its own ends. It makes no sense to call a curriculum "irrelevant" and then to turn right around and accuse its chief practitioners of "selling out"; the powerful do not squander their money so easily. The ironic point, then, is not that these curricula are "irrelevant" but that they are far *too* relevant to the support of interests to which the left is opposed.

The villains here are the methodological orthodoxies of the social sciences: their commitment to objectivity, detachment, and the "separation" between facts and values. In the view of radical students, these orthodoxies rationalize the official diffidence of social scientists regarding the social consequences of their research, a diffidence which (conveniently—and profitably—for social scientists, goes the argument) promotes the interests of the established and the powerful. This is far from the whole truth, of course. There is plenty of research, supported by establishments, whose results offer the establishment little comfort. But like other "nonpartisan" or value-neutral practices and procedures, the methodological orthodoxies of the social sciences do tend in general to support established interests, simply because the powerful, in command of greater resources and facilities, are better able to make use of "facts" than the weak, and because avoidance of ideological controversy tends to perpetuate the inequities of the status quo.

But the demands for a more activist and "committed" social science and for social scientists to function as advocates for oppressed and subordinated groups may not be the best way of correcting the inequities. A thorough *doctrinal* politicization of social science in the university is likely to mean the total loss of whatever little insulation remains against the ideological controversies rending the larger society; and the probable result would be that the university, instead of being more liberal than the society as a whole, would more accurately reflect the still-burgeoning reactionary mood of the country.

For students who tend to be "around" a university for a long time—the 10-year period mentioned earlier is not uncommon—the university tends to become a kind of "home territory," the place where they really live. They experience the university less as an élite training institution than as a political community in which "members" have a kind of quasi-"citizenship" which, if one believes in democratic process, means a right to a legitimate political voice in its government.*

This conception of the university is quite discrepant with the conception held by most faculty members and administrators. To most faculty members the university is the élite training institution to which students who are both willing and able come to absorb intellectual disciplines—"ologies"—taught by skilled and certified professionals whose competences are defined by and limited to those certifications. But which way one sees the university—as a political community or as an élite training institution—is not purely a matter of ideological preference.

The fact seems to be that where training and certification and performance in politically neutral skills are clearest, the more conservative view is virtually unchallenged. This is true not only for dentistry and mathematics

* Much remains to be clarified about the nature of "membership" in academic communities. So much cant has gone down in the name of "community" that I often feel about this word much like that Nazi who has gone down in history as having said, "When I hear the word 'culture,' I reach for my revolver."

but for athletics, too. Presumably many militant Blacks are not for any kind of a quota system with respect to varsity teams, and presumably football players in the huddle do not demand a voice in the decisions that shape their lives. But where what one's education confers upon one is a smattering of "high culture" or "civilized manners" or the detached sensibility and ethics of a science whose benefits, like other wealth, are not equitably distributed—in short, where the main result of liberal education is *Weltanschauung*—it indeed has "political" consequences.

These consequences were not controversial so long as the culture of the university was fairly homogeneous and so long as the "aliens" it admitted were eager to absorb that culture. They have become controversial in recent years because the democratization of higher education has revealed the "class" character of academic culture and because of the appearance on the campus of students who do not share and/or do not aspire to that culture. These newcomers have arrived in sufficiently large numbers to mount a serious challenge to the hegemony of traditional academic culture.

Despite their many differences, the new militant "ethnic" students and their supporters among "White radicals," "street people," hippies, and other young people on the Left have in common their antiacademicism, which is the campus version of the anti-establishment outlook. This is true notwithstanding that the academy has been the most liberal sector of establishment thought and the most sympathetic to at least some of the aspirations of dissident students. Partly, of course, their hostility to the academy is rooted in the fact that the university is where they're at, the institutional location in which they have to work through their prolonged adolescence and the problems associated with it. But beyond this, there is real conflict between the traditional criteria of academic performance and what dissident students demand from academic life.

Research suggests that most of the White radical students have grown up in a milieu where "intellectual" matters were discussed, where books were probably present in their homes, where middleclass manners and style were their birthright, and where, therefore, they learned how to "talk"—that is, where they developed the sort of verbal facility enabling them to do well enough in high school and to seem like promising "college material" if only because they look and sound much like college students have always looked and sounded. With the ascendence of the view that everybody has a right to a higher education (along with the fact that there's no place else to send well-born adolescents), most of them wind up in colleges and universities.

Some of them, despite their verbal facility, are not really bright; many others, despite their ability to get good college grades, strongly resist "conforming" to many of the requirements for professional certification which they demean as mere "socialization." Confronted by academic demands for rigor in their thinking, for sufficient discipline to master a systematic body of knowledge, for evidence that they can maintain a line of logical thinking beyond one or two propositions, and bring evidence systematically to bear upon a problem, many of them are found seriously wanting—some because they are not bright enough, others because they think it a point of honor to resist the intellectual demands made on them.

When their numbers are large enough to enable them to turn to each other for mutual support, it is not surprising that they should collectively turn against the system of criteria which derogates them and, in a manner not unanalogous to the "reaction formation" of slum delinquents who develop a subculture in opposition to middleclass school norms which judge them inadequate, develop an antiacademic viewpoint which defines abstraction, logical order, detachment, objectivity, and systematic thinking as the cognitive armory of a repressive society, productive of alienation, personal rigidity, and truncated capacity for feeling.

Preoccupied as most of these students are with "identity problems" and moral protest, it is again not surprising that many of them

should be less interested in the mastery of academic disciplines, even if they have the ability, than in pursuing what they are likely to call "gut-issues" or nitty-gritty. The kinds of problems they apparently are interested in studying can be inferred from the examination of almost any "Free University" brochure, and what these add up to is a sort of extension division for the underground: practical, topical "rap sessions" on Vietnam, civil rights, encounter groups, pottery, psychedelics, macrobiotics, Eastern religion, rock music, and so on.

In the conflict with the established interests of science and scholarship in the university, radical students do win significant victories. New courses do get approved; experimental curricula do get tried out; students do get appointed to important committees; greater weight is attached to teaching in the appointment and promotion of faculty members. But large numbers of these radical students, exhausted by conflict and depressed by negative criticism, drop out of school. In dropping out, however, they do not immediately disappear into the labor market. They tend to remain in the university community, employed occasionally or part-time in dead-end jobs, living in furnished rooms or communal houses near the university, and most important for my purposes here, still participating in the marginal student culture which they know so well.

Their participation in this culture is made possible to some extent by the fact that their youth protects them from the degrading consequences of being poor and having no regular or "approved" status in the community. Part of the age-grading system which postpones adulthood is the temporary protection of the young against the stigmata which, for older people, are normally attached to poverty. But over time, this group of "nonstudents" can be regarded as downward mobile, and thereby hangs an interesting prospect.

The United States has no major tradition of large-scale downward mobility. The only major image of intergenerational decline is associated with decadent aristocratic families in ruined southern mansions. Given the general tendency for downwardly mobile groups to resent the system which derogates them, and given the fact that the channels of upward mobility today are largely through higher education, the hostility to the university of these radical, middleclass "nonstudents" is probably maintained even after they leave it. The irony is that in dropping out the hippie and New Left children of the middle classes provide opportunity for the upward mobility of the new Black and other ambitious "disadvantaged" students.

The Blacks and other ethnic militants are presently using higher education in a manner different from that in which their predecessors from the lower class used it. For earlier ethnics, the university served as a channel of mobility for *individuals* from the talented poor; today, it is sought as a means of collective mobility. There are two aspects to this movement: there is the emphasis on ethnic studies programs designed to provide the members of the respective ethnic groups with a sense of pride in their history and culture, and there are the demands that the university play a more active role in ameliorating suffering in the ghettos, not merely through programs of research which exploit the cooperation of ghetto residents without helping them measurably, but by taking the university off the campus, bringing it to them, in their terms, on their turf, for their own purposes.

In the struggle to achieve the ends of the militants, Black and White, the traditional university is very vulnerable because the militants have great leverage. Just as the Blacks can conceivably turn the urban core into a guerrilla battleground, militant students can bring the universities to the proverbial grinding halt. Continual rallies, classroom disruptions, picket lines, building seizures, student intimidation and general paranoia (to say nothing of the almost continual meetings by faculty and administration committees to cope with the crises and the continual corridor and coffee room gossip by knots of faculty members) can bring the teaching and other academic functions of the university to a virtual standstill.

This prospect raises seriously for the first time the question of whether the traditional university, as we know it, is an expendable institution. And another question, as well: Is it possible that a decision has been made somewhere that it is better to risk the destruction of the university by confining the unrest to the campus than to allow it to spill over into more critical institutions? Pickets, sit-ins, building seizures, and nonnegotiable demands are one thing on the campuses. Imagine them at CBS on Madison Avenue: no TV until SDS gets equal time; at the Stock Exchange: the ticker tape does not roll until corporation X gets rid of its South African holdings; at the headquarters of the Bank of America: no depositors get through the doors until interestfree loans are made to renovate the ghettos. There would be machine guns in the streets in no time at all!

In 1969, despite the tear gas and the National Guard, it is still hard to imagine tanks and machine guns used against student radicals so long as their militance is confined to the campus. Because if they do close the universities down, exactly who would miss them? The most practical functions the university performs and its activities which are most directly relevant to the national economy (engineering, science, law, medicine, etc.) could be transferred to the private sector. The beginnings of such a transfer are apparent already in the educational functions carried on by private foundations, institutes, and industrial corporations.

And if the departments of English and history and political science and sociology and art and so on closed tight shut tomorrow, who would miss them? Aside from the implication of some social science departments in the military-industrial complex, the studies in humanities and social science departments are civilized luxuries with very few sources of government or business support. The student radicals have little sympathy for them, and there is probably even less sympathy for them among the students' severest critics. These days, even conservative legislators, in the same breath that they denounce student militance, will quickly add, "Of course, this doesn't mean that there isn't plenty wrong with the university; there is." And if the student revolution can be bought off by substituting Bob Dylan for Dylan Thomas, McLuhan for Freud, Marcuse for Plato, rock for Bach, Black culture for Greek culture, rap sessions for formal examinations, how many will care? Who needs high culture anyway? For the radicals it's an instrument of class oppression, and their oppressors, at least in America, have never been too keen on it anyway, except as a tax dodge.

Short of machine guns in the streets and outright revolution, what one can expect to see over the next decade in academic life is greater adaptation by the university to the new kinds of students it must serve and to the new publics whose anticipated support or hostility it must take into account in its planning. By the new students I mean ghetto youth, middleclass White radicals, and the identity seekers. By the new publics I mean those million of citizens whose taxes support the great state universities but who never thought of the university as "theirs" until its politicization encouraged ambitious politicians to call this fact to their attention. Having once been reminded (by Governor Reagan and others), the voters are not likely to forget it soon.

If it comes about, this adaptation is likely to occur in a manner not dissimilar to that in which the major political parties have adapted to third-party movements in the larger political community: by isolating the *most* radical through the adoption of some of their programs and demands, while at the same time adopting severe and punitive policies toward the more intransigent and violence-prone who are still unsatisfied.

For ghetto youth, then, there will be more ethnic studies programs and compensatory admissions and grading policies and practices and more energetic recruiting of ethnic students and faculty. But there will be less indecision or tolerance in the handling of sit-ins, seizures, and other disruptions. For the radicals (ethnic as well as middleclass White), there will be greater emphasis on programs granting academic credit for extension-type activities such as tutoring of ghetto children, neighborhood seminars on consumer savvy, and community organization. For the identity seekers there will be more encounter groups, more classes emphasizing "openness and honesty" in dialogue, more experiments with less structured curricular and residential communities, more "retreats," more student-initiated courses on subjects which engage their sense of "relevance" to their interests, from sex to drugs to rock. For all, there will be further loosening of the *in loco parentis* restrictions which hardly anybody in the university believes in anymore, and a little more student power (at least influence) on faculty and administrative committees. All this, combined with a more effective public relations campaign explaining the mission of the university and its problems in coping with the consequences of prolonged adolescence, may just bring about a semblance of peace on the campus. But without peace in Vietnam, it will be an uneasy peace at best.

There will be opposition. Academic conservatives will see in these new programs the prospect of the dilution or outright abandonment of traditional standards of scholarship. The legitimation of ethnicity, the amelioration of suffering by the poor, and the search for identity by the young may all be noble endeavors, they will say, but the major functions of the university are the creation and transmission of systematic bodies of abstract knowledge. Political conservatives will see in these programs harbingers of social changes which they oppose. Militant students imply more leaders and troops for restive ghettos; "the search for identity" and the self-exploratory activities the phrase suggests are redolent of the "liberalism," "permissiveness," and self-indulgence offensive to the traditional Protestant ethic which "made this country great."

Yet academic conservatives might well be reminded that the university is facing radically transformed constituencies, that academic disciplines which are well institutionalized and "traditional" today were themselves academically born in the blood of earlier periods of such transformations, and that they were initially opposed by still more "traditional" fields. Political conservatives might well be reminded that student unrest was not invented by outside agitators, that its source is in social conditions conservatives affirm and that it is not repressible short of military measures. The alternatives to the adaptable university involve blood on the quad and an expendable university.

25. AMERICAN YOUTH GANGS: FACT AND FANTASY

WALTER B. MILLER

Reprinted from "American Youth Gangs: Past and Present" in Abraham Blumberg, ed., Current Perspectives on Criminal Behavior (New York: Alfred A. Knopf, 1974). Walter B. Miller is a research fellow at the Center for Criminal Justice of the Harvard Law School. An anthropologist, he has devoted several decades to the study of working and lower class youth with particular emphasis on gang behavior and youth crime and on the police and mass media responses to it.

■ Walter Miller's opening quotation neatly demonstrates that juvenile gangs have exercised the American imagination for about as long as American cities have existed. Because of this fascination it generally has been difficult to tell the difference between fact and fiction in popular and journalistic—and sometimes social scientific—accounts of gang behavior. Drawing on an extensive comparative analysis based on his own research and a careful assessment of the work of others, Miller outlines his conclusions about the persisting features of juvenile gangs and the ways in which the gang as a social organization adapts to changing circumstances of locale, political climate, and police behavior.

In doing so Miller tells us much about what the late adolescent and early adult phases of the life cycle are like for working and lower class youth. Gang participation can be seen as an important adaptation on their part to the pressures of juvenilization which Berger described in selection 24. Selection 26, concerned with college youth, carries the discussion into the middle class milieu.

For other studies of juvenile delinquency see the classic description of juvenile groups: Frederick Thrasher, *The Gang* (University of Chicago Press, 1927). More recent works include Albert K. Cohen, *Delinquent Boys* (Free Press, 1955); Richard A. Cloward and Lloyd E. Ohlin, *Delinquency and Opportunity* (Free Press, 1960); James F. Short and Fred L. Strodbeck, *Group Process and Gang Delinquency* (University of Chicago Press, 1965); and David Matza, *Delinquency and Drift* (Wiley, 1964). ■

. . . at any and all hours of the day there are multitudes of boys wandering about and congregated on the corner of the streets, idle in their habits, dissolute in their conduct, profane and obscene in conversation and gross and vulgar in their manners. If a female passes one of these groups she is shocked by what she sees and hears . . . [Report in Brooklyn newspaper; 1865].

I'm afraid to let my daughter go out on our street. Gangs terrorize the block and drag race down the street. I'm sick with fear. Is there anything you can do? [Letter to Philadelphia newspaper; 1970].

THE YOUTH GANG, viewed as a recurrently congregating assemblage of adolescent peers, is a fundamental associational form, as old as human history and, in the United States, as old as the American city. But few social forms are subject to such extensive and persisting misrepresentation and to so much difference of opinion as to their most basic characteristics. Representations of gangs are wildly divergent. The youth gang is seen as a major instrument for the effectuation of crime and as an ingenious device for containing criminal behavior within tolerable limits; as a body forged in conflict and relentlessly dedicated to the pursuit of violence, and as a relatively peaceful group whose very structure serves to limit the exercise of violent activity; as a fleeting congeries of casual acquaintances and as the very epitome of close, loyal, and solidary mutual ties; as a rare and fragile blossom, appearing rarely and sparsely, and as a hardy perennial, ubiquitous, and enduring. The existence of such diversity with respect to a social form which is not, after all, a mysterious product of some remote and exotic tribal society calls for some sort of explanation. Why such divergency in conceptions of gangs?

A major reason relates to the propensity of gang members to engage in behavior which violates major behavioral standards—legal, moral, or both—of the adult society. Youth gangs customarily pursue a wide range of activities, always including some which are "violative" in varying degrees of frequency and seriousness. Largely because of this, many approaches to gangs focus predominantly or even exclusively on their "problematic" aspects—a procedure conducive to serious distortion. For example, although specifically illegal activities generally comprise a relatively small proportion of a gang's total activity repertoire, such activities are often represented as a dominant preoccupation or even as the major basis of the gang's existence (hence terms such as "the violent gang" or "the delinquent gang"). Uncommon or atypical forms of gang behavior are represented as customary and normal, while more common or typical forms are slighted or ignored. Similarly, those gangs whose problematic behavior is most serious and spectacular are represented as typical when in fact they may be very rare and atypical. Moreover, for some the problem perspective even determines whether or not gangs are considered to exist at all. Put in generalized terms, if youth groups in a particular community appear clearly to present a problem, they are perceived as gangs; if they do not, that community has "groups" but no "gangs." A more specific form of this perception is found in the notion that if there is no gang fighting, there are no gangs. The present paper treats illegal and problematic behavior as significant aspects of gang life but does not conceive youth gangs primarily as instruments for effecting crime nor grant the status of "gang" only to those groups whose behavior is clearly problematic.

The high degree of formal diversity of American youth gangs provides another basis for misperception and disagreement. Unlike associational units such as the nuclear family, which most observers agree takes a limited number of forms (four to six persons, two adults and two to four offspring comprising the bulk of units, youth gangs in the United States vary tremendously in such basic formal features as size, age composition, sex composition, life span, and internal differentiation. The existence of so wide a range of formal diversity provides unusual latitude for different observers to include particular groups under the label of "gang" and to exclude others on the basis of criteria which often arise out of special purposes or reflect private conceptions. For one person the only "real" gang is one which is seen as highly organized, close-knit, and autocratic in leadership; for another only those groups involved in serious criminality—particularly fighting—merit the designation of "gang." A group of adolescents which gathers recurrently at some local hangout and does not appear to pose serious problems is seen as "just a bunch of kids on the corner," and not as a "true" gang. A very substantial part of the widespread disagreement among observers as to the numbers, sizes, and activity patterns of gangs in particular communities at particular times is a simple consequence of divergent and often implicit conceptions of what a "real gang" is. For this reason it is essential that any descriptive account of youth gangs be as precise and explicit as possible in matters of definition.

A particularly pervasive basis of distortion arises from the fact that the youth gang is anything but a "neutral" phenomenon; on the contrary, it arouses strong emotions and engages deeply held values. Only a few of these can be noted. Most adults' perceptions of gangs are strongly influenced by their roles as parents. The youth gang and the family both play important parts in the socialization of youth, with the gang assuming a particularly active role during adolescence, when it provides a context for the learning and practice of essential adolescent tasks such as the achievement of independence and the assumption of adult sex roles. Most parents, however, do not perceive the gang as a benign and helpful partner in the difficult enterprise of rearing children but, rather, as a malign and dangerous competitor, with a frightening potential for sabotaging attitudes and behavioral practices which have been inculcated with considerable care and at considerable cost. Thus, insofar as their interests as parents are involved, and on the basis of values related to parenthood, many adults view the gang in a highly unfavorable light, a perspective which seriously hampers the development of a balanced and objective conception.

Representations of gangs also engage ideological and political values. Insofar as gangs are perceived as agencies for the effectuation of crime and other forms of disapproved behavior, their existence and activities evoke ideological values similar to those which apply to criminal behavior in general. Such values generally reflect partisan political positions. Those favoring a "conservative" viewpoint commonly regard gang behavior as a reprehensible and blameworthy consequence of excessive liberality or permissiveness, reflecting at once insufficient self-control and discipline by the youths themselves, insufficient control and discipline by parents, and insufficient control and discipline by official authorities. Those with more "liberal" views tend to regard gangs and their behavior more as symptoms than as phenomena in their own right. The existence of gangs is seen as incontrovertible evidence of critical deficiencies in the larger social order, reasoning from a casual theory which attributes "deviant" behavior to social ills such as poverty, racial discrimination, injustice, corruption, and the like, with the gang standing as the signal of a clear mandate to pursue urgently needed programs of social reform. Similarly, the present treatment of gangs reflects personal, professional, and political values of the author; it does, however, take as an explicit objective an attempt to present as "balanced" a view as possible—representing gangs neither as evil and self-willed authors of reprehensible behavior nor as innocent and pitiful victims of malign social forces well beyond their control. . . .

Available evidence as to gang prevalence and publicity during the present period would appear to indicate the following. Despite a surprisingly widespread impression during the 1960s that youth gangs had vanished or altered radically, recurrently congregating assemblages of adolescents remain a common and widespread phenomenon in the United States. Of the nation's large cities, youth gangs in the four largest have been pursuing a pattern of intergang conflict which has resulted in a level of gang-connected homicides high enough to bring about media attention. In other major cities gangs receive little media attention, but other sources of evidence indicate that they are present in most. Moreover, outdoor congregation by youth groups in the "new" suburbs—now containing the largest proportion of the national population—appears to be widespread and growing, with many suburban gangs approximating the features of the classic inner-city gangs of past and present. The shifting pattern of attention by the national media to so prevalent a feature of contemporary society can be explained in part as a consequence of traditional media practice with respect to coverage of "routine" events such as slum crime and family fights, and in part as a consequence of the superior news value of contemporary forms of violence whose severity exceeds that of even the most violent kinds of gang conflict.

American society, along with some others, is traditionally shortsighted about the relation of the present to the past. Americans tend to be profoundly impressed with the events of the immediate present and typically assign disproportionate weight to contemporary developments when attempting to explain social phenomena. In the case of gangs, there have always been some in each generation who attribute their very existence to the specific happenings of their own historical period. Thus, youth gangs in the late 1800s were seen as a direct product of massive waves of foreign immigration; in the 1930s as a result of a grave national economic depression; in the 1940s, and 1950s as a consequence of basic changes in the character of the family unit.

The Urban Crisis era provides no exception to the traditional predilection to see the youth gang as created anew by specific contemporary developments. There are those who feel that many of the numerous gangs of the present period represent a radical departure from past forms—that contemporary events have affected gangs so fundamentally that continuity with the past has been drastically attenuated or even lost. Of the major developments of the Urban Crisis period, . . . three in particular have been adduced to account for the emergence of the "new" gang. Two are directly related to the massive civil rights movements of the period—an increased measure of militancy and readiness to employ force by urban Blacks, and an increased involvement in political and/or ideological activism by residents of low status communities. The third is the substantial growth in the acceptibility and use of drugs among adolescents, accompanied in some instances by an ideological perspective characterized as "countercultural."

Since these developments directly involve population groups whose circumstances affect the existence and nature of gangs—youth, urbanites, and low status populations—it is scarcely conceivable that they could fail to have an impact on present-day gangs. But the issue here is not whether there has been any impact but, rather, whether that impact has been of sufficient magnitude to justify speaking of a "new" gang whose form, orientation, and customary pursuits represent a sharp break with the past rather than a contemporary version of traditional forms. Following sections will address this issue with respect to three developments: participation by gangs in the civil disorders of the 1960s, political activism by gangs, and drug use by gang members.

TRANSFORMATION THROUGH PROTEST—YOUTH GANGS AND CIVIL DISORDERS

Of all the forms of domestic violence which marked the Urban Crisis era, the form which almost certainly had the most profound impact on public consciousness was a kind of collective social event designated in more formal terms as a "civil disturbance" or "civil disorder," and less formally as "rioting." Hundreds of such events occurred in the United States during this period. The basic pattern was set in 1963 and 1964; the rioting reached a peak in 1967-68 and diminished thereafter. The kinds of events characterized as "riots" by various sources, while containing common elements, encompassed a wide variety of differing occurrences, ranging from massive outbreaks, involving scores of deaths, hundreds of injuries, and extensive property damage, to small-scale commotions scarcely distinguishable from routine slum-life disturbances. These riots were subject to voluminous reports by many writers, several governmental commissions, and scores of social analysts.

What part did youth gangs play in the disorders? Participation by youth gangs in urban rioting is nothing new; the activities of gangs during the "race riot" period of 1915-19 have been particularly well documented. But, as will be noted, the nature of gang participation during this period differed significantly from that of the more recent period. The basic and most obvious fact about gangs and riots in the Urban Crisis era is that both the locale of the major riots (urban slum areas) and the social characteristics of the most active rioters (male youth and young adults) are coterminous with those of the classic urban youth gang. The riots occurred in their own home territory; the gangs were there, the riots were there, and hundreds of groups of Black males were clearly in evidence, active, and ubiquitous.

The character of gang participation in the rioting—what gang members did as well as what they did not do—deserves attention because of the light it throws both on the nature of the gangs and the nature of the rioting. It is important to note, in the first place, that in virtually no instance did the gangs "start" the rioting—either in the sense that they agitated actively for the advent of riot conditions or that incidents involving gangs served as major trigger events. Once the riots were under way, however, gang members were among the most ardent and energetic participants.

The zeal of gang member participation in the riots should come as no surprise. As indicated elsewhere, the vital concerns of gang members revolve around such matters as excitement, risk, daring, adventure, action, defiance of authority, freedom from constraint. Gangs are attracted to situations involving "trouble" and pursue their ends in a vigorous, activistic fashion. It is hard to imagine a milieu more precisely calculated to promote the pursuit of these concerns. To the average member of the average Black gang the riot represented an extraordinary convergence of desirable conditions—a situation of unparalleled opportunity: people milling in the streets, buildings in flames, police and fire vehicles rushing to and fro, the crash of breaking glass, the hubbub of police radios, the unstilled clangor of unattended burglar alarms. Observers of gang behavior during the rioting were struck by what appeared as a current of enormous excitement—an almost ecstatic perception that all things were possible and all delights within grasp. It was the sense conveyed in those kinds of ritualized events—the bacchanalia, the mardi gras, the corroborree— when ordinary rules of conduct are suspended and one is granted special license to pursue with fervor that which is denied in ordinary times. Even in those cases where the triggering incident was most unequivocally perceived as a racial affront, the dominant emotions of most gang members appeared to be closer to elation than to anger.

The pattern of anticipation by youth gangs in the classic civil disorders of the urban crisis era may be summarized by considering the relationship between gang behavior during the riots and during ordinary times. Analyses based primarily on a careful examination of the forms and frequencies of gang member activity during the riots reveals a degree of regularity, rationality, and patterning which does not accord with a conception of youthful riot behavior as an irrational and uncontrolled outburst of long-suppressed emotions. The identity of targets of theft, assault, and property destruction reflects a process guided by orderly principles of selection. In particular, riot period gang behavior does not support the thesis that racial hatred was the dominant motive for the rioting. Racial hostility was clearly a significant factor, but it was only one of a set of coexisting motives, many of which are common to American youth of all racial and ethnic backgrounds. Moreover, to those familiar with the behavior of urban low status youth in ordinary times, the riot period behavior of gang members appeared less as a unique response to unique conditions than as a logically continuous extension of customary motives and concerns. Riot conditions, of course, provided an extraordinary climate of opportunity for the actualization of these concerns, but the fact that gang members chose to pursue more avidly during the riots the same kinds of ends they ordinarily pursue attests to the enormous influence of motives derived from their subcultural status as males, as adolescents, as citydwellers, and as residents of low status communities. Rather than serving to evoke some radically new or untapped source of motive energy, the riot experience served to illuminate with great clarity the potency of those forces which engender gang behavior during ordinary times.

TRANSFORMATION THROUGH COMMITMENT—GANGS AND POLITICAL ACTIVISM

The notion of "transforming" gangs by diverting their energies from traditional forms of gang activity—particularly illegal forms— and channeling them into "constructive" activities is probably as old, in the United States, as gangs themselves. Thus, in the 1960s when a series of social movements aimed at elevating the lot of the poor through ideologically oriented, citizen-executed political activism became widely current, it was perhaps inevitable that the idea be applied to gangs. The basic notion is simplicity itself. Once gang members can be brought to see that their energies should be devoted to a set of social reform and/or community better-ment enterprises, great amounts of potentially productive energy can be harnessed to the achievement of needed social change, at the same reducing the amount of energy available for criminal and other traditional forms of gang behavior. Two major models of activism were current; a more radical "militant" model, which saw gangs as a spearhead of a forceful attempt to undermine established sources of power (often White power), and a less radical "social betterment" model, which conceived gangs as the basis of a kind of indigenous community services delivery enterprise. The simplicity of this notion, and the perceived desirability of social/political activism by low income citizens, impelled many to predict and some to assert the prev-alence of a "new" type of gang to replace the "conflict" gang of the past—the "politi-cized" gang.

There were in fact enough developments along these lines in the middle and late 1960s to provide some substance to these predic-tions and perceptions. A small number of groups in some localities were the objects of enough publicity to create an impression of a national trend. Prominent among the groups so publicized were, on the "militant" model, the Black Panthers (Black) and the Young Lords (Hispanic), and on the "social better-ment" model the Blackstone Rangers and Devil's Disciples of Chicago, and the Real Great Society of New York. But the predicted transformation of American youth gangs never occurred. Even during the peak period of "politicization" the actual proportion of youth gangs involved, as will be shown, was small, with the great majority of gang youth remaining essentially unaffected by political/ social activism. Even among those most af-fected there is little evidence that activism *replaced* illegal and/or violent pursuits in the repertoire of gangs; rather, traditional activi-ties such as theft, assault, extortion, and various "hustles" were carried on in conjunc-tion with, and frequently as an intrinsic part of, political and social reform undertakings.

Moreover, even in those areas most affected, "politicization" appears as a relatively short-

lived development. By the early 1970s, for example, in those of Philadelphia and New York where hopes had been highest that political activism would replace gang fight-ing, levels of lethal intergang conflict were high or even increasing. Furthermore, even at its height political activism and its as-sociated ideologies had very little impact on the average "prime-age" gang member. This fact was widely misperceived. The prime age for male gang involvement in most localities runs from about 13 to 18; all but a few of the publicized politicized gangs were com-posed largely of young men in their twenties or even thirties. Often the politicized gang was not the product of a direct progression by an established prime-age gang from tradi-tional to political activities; instead, older males, generally with prime-age experience in other gangs, frequently assumed leadership in new groups after a period of separation from gang life as such.

By far the greatest amount of publicity concerning political activism by gangs cen-tered on Chicago, raising the possibility that this city may have represented an exception to the national picture. In 1966 a reporter for the *Washington Post* wrote: "[Chica-goans] believe that they are confronted with a new thing—a super gang, a gang with ideology, a gang larger and better organized than any previous juvenile gang." The gang he was referring to was called the Blackstone Rangers, and it would appear that some sub-stantial part of the general conception of the "politicized" gang in the 1960s was derived from the experience of a single gang in a single city—the Rangers of Chicago. There was more than a little substance to the *Post* writer's report. During the late 1960s and early 1970s the "Mighty Black-stone Ranger Nation"—in one or another of its changing designations (Stones; Black P. Stone, etc.)—remained a force to be reckoned with on Chicago's South Side. The Rangers claimed an extensive network of affiliates and/or subdivisions, bearing names such as the Maniac Rangers, the Conservative Rang-ers, the Imperial Pimps, the Viet Cong. They maintained an off again-on again state of "warfare" with a second "politicized" gang, the Disciples (e.g., Black, East Side, West Side), and achieved sufficient identity as an associational unit to apply for and receive a sizable grant under a federal antipoverty program. Most press sources represented the number of Rangers and affiliates at their peak at somewhere around 3,000; the Rangers themselves claimed as many as 8,000; local youth workers reckoned the number of "dependable" members and affiliates at about 500.

There can be little doubt that various of the Chicago associational units included under the designation "Rangers" as well as a few other associational complexes going under general "gang" names such as the "Disciples" and "Vice Lords" maintained some order of "lateral" or cross-neighborhood relations and devoted some part of their energies to activities which can be designated as "political" or "public service" oriented. In addition, there were a few other non-Black associational units both in Chicago and elsewhere whose activities importantly involved similar undertakings (e.g., Young Lords— Spanish-American, Chicago, New York, elsewhere; Young Patriots—Whites, Chicago). The basic issue here, however, is just how prevalent were "politicized" gangs in the city where this phenomena were best developed?

During the 1965-70 period the Chicago police estimated that there were approximately 900 "youth groups" in the city, of which about 200 were sufficiently troublesome to be designated "gangs" (on the basis of the usual police criterion for defining a "gang"), and about 20 difficult enough to be termed "hard core." While reliable prevalence estimates in a loose and rapidly changing situation of this kind are extremely difficult to derive, a rough and very generous estimate of the number of identifiable units and/or subdivisions affiliated in some manner with the major "politicized" gang names in Chicago (Rangers, Disciples, Vice Lords, a few others) would indicate something on the order of 80 units—less than 10 percent of the total number of youth gang units in the city. Thus, if during the heydey of the "politicized" gang in the city with the highest number of such gangs about 90 percent were *not* significantly involved in political activism, the politicization of the gang could hardly be said to represent a major national development. For the rest of the nation, including those Spanish-American units modeled in some degree after the adult Black Panthers, the proportion of nonpoliticized gangs was probably closer to 95 percent.

By the early 1970s it was apparent that one predicted product of the civil rights movement of the 1960s—a new, politicized gang, transformed by ideological commitment—simply had not developed. It is important to bear in mind in this connection that the majority of youth gang members in the United States are White, and even if the ideology of Black activism had importantly affected some number of Black gangs, the expected impact on Whites, and thus most gang members, could not have been significant. For most Spanish-American and other "minority" status gangs, the expected impact would be less than for Blacks. But lasting effects, even for those who might have been expected to sustain the maximum impact, were insubstantial. The media stopped heralding the politicized gang, headlining instead the rising rate of gang-connected homicide in major cities.

Rather than asking the question, "Did the civil rights movement of the 1960s "politicize" the gang?," a more relevant inquiry would be, "What *was* the impact of the movement on gangs in general and Black gangs in particular?" An examination of this issue is beyond the scope of this paper. A comprehensive analysis would have to entertain, among other results, the idea that one product of the movement was an important addition to the *language* used by some to characterize gang behavior. Many Blacks and some Spanish-Americans—both gang members and others—added an important new kind of *justificational vocabulary* to the repertoire of traditional modes for explaining gang activity. This new vocabulary incorporated basic ideological tenets of the Black rights movement and applied to customary forms of gang behavior concepts, such as exploitation by the power structure, restitution for past injustices, brutalization by the system, and the like. It is particularly important in this context to distinguish verbal behavior from actual practice. Black gang members continue by and large to do much the same kinds of things they always have, but for some there have been changes in the ways that they characterize and justify these practices. This must be seen as one effect on gangs of the civil rights movement, but it is not the kind of effect required to produce a new type of ideologically activistic gang.

TRANSFORMATION THROUGH ENHANCED EXPERIENCE— GANGS AND DRUG USE

In most recent periods in American history one particular form of youth behavior has become known as *the* paramount youth problem of the times and as such is subjected to intensive attention and concern by the media, professionals, and the public. During the Urban Crisis era the prime candidate for this role was the use of drugs, although other forms, such as student radicalism, sex mores, and rejection of authority (often seen as a related complex), competed in the minds of some for the top position. Given the widespread perception that "drug abuse" had become endemic among youth, it was perhaps inevitable that youth gangs be perceived in these terms. In fact, the prospect of increased drug use by gang members was suggested as early as the 1950s on the basis of theoretical premises similar to those which produced predictions of the "politicized" gang and which served in part to motivate researchers to search for "drug-using" or "drug-addicted" gangs. The predicted emergence of such gangs as a major new development, as was the case for predictions of politicized gangs, failed to materialize, although in both instances it has been possible to characterize a relatively small proportion of all gangs in these terms.

The issue of drug use by gangs provides a clear example of a process whereby a phenomenon perceived as a reigning social ill is granted great power to affect sundry other phenomena. During the Urban Crisis era drug use figured as a major element in a scheme used to explain both the death *and* the rebirth of "the fighting gang." This formulation, which in some quarters became part of the conventional folklore of gangs, especially in the New York area, runs as follows. The fighting gangs of the 1950s were knocked out (sometimes snuffed out) by the advent of hard drugs, particularly heroin. Gang members took to heroin primarily out of frustration engendered by the exclusionism of a discriminatory society, which afforded them only a few modes of response to their frustration—among which fighting and drug use figured prominently. Thus when gang fighting was made less practicable by police pressures, less untrammeled by social work intervention, and less modish by an ascendancy of "cool" over "heart" as a valued quality, gang members were virtually forced into drug use as one of their few remaining outlets.

Then in the 1960s the intensification of civil rights activities provided a new outlet for their frustrated energies, and they abandoned heroin for political activism. Through the civil rights movement they came to realize that one *could* take action against the system instead of retreating into drugs, that the drug traffic was another means used by the power structure to exploit the poor, and that it served the interests of the establishment to cripple potential activists by pressing them into addiction. By the late 1960s the antidrug ethic of the gang members had become so powerful that they became increasingly frustrated by the apparently deliberate ineffectiveness of officialdom in coping with the problem and were thus impelled, again in line with the new activism, to *themselves* undertake the policing functions necessary to purge their communities of drugs. However, once having re-formed their gangs for these purposes, rather than devoting their aggressive energies to driving out the pushers and exposing the corrupt policemen they began to direct them instead, for reasons **not** fully understood, toward their fellow gang members. Thus occurred a rebirth of a pattern of intergang violence much like the one that had been abandoned 10 years before—with frustration-engendered violence intensified, if anything, by the failure of the recently attempted activism to affect any really significant changes in the social order.

The need for devising this rather imaginative scenario—fighting gang to narcoticized gang to politicized gang to fighting gang in 10 years—was brought about, as shown earlier, by a prevalent impression that gangs had somehow flourished, been knocked out, and then revived—an impression not supported by available evidence. Note also that this explanation, while pivoting on drug use as its major dynamic, also works in the notion of politicization, just discussed. As is always the case for conventional wisdom explanations of this kind, there are important elements of factual accuracy interwoven throughout its fabric; but rather than attempt the difficult job of trying to disentangle them, the problem of drug use in gangs can be more profitably addressed through the question: "What *was* the impact of increasing use and availability of drugs among American adolescents?" Analysis should encompass the situation not only of Black gangs and/or the New York City area and the use of hard drugs alone, but also the use of various different types of drugs by the range of different kinds of gangs in all sections of the country.

Rather than providing the basis for the emergence of new or markedly different kinds of gangs, or of undermining the bases of gang formation itself, the increased availability of certain drugs appears instead to have fitted quite readily into an established niche. The "versatile repertoire" of gang activities noted earlier traditionally involves the use of what might be called experience-enhancing substances—a practice arising quite naturally from the "excitement" focal concern of the adolescent subculture, which serves as a major influence on gang behavior. Such substances serve largely to enhance and facilitate participation in a range of activities such as mating and recreational activities. For the average gang member the use of such substances is governed by relatively simple criteria; he wants something which is easy to get and which will provide a quick but not too potent "high" at minimum cost. Traditionally these criteria have been met primarily by alcoholic substances, principally beer. However, use of drug and/or narcotic substances, particularly those involving easier to obtain substances (pill-popping, glue-sniffing, "bennies," cough medicine containing codeine) have been familiar to gang members in many locales for quite some time. Such gangs have often employed a pragmatic "mix" of alcohol and drugs. A major consequence of the increasing acceptability of drug use among adolescents (principally marihuana) and the concomitant increased availability of certain drugs (again, primarily marihuana) has been to increase the proportion of drugs to alcohol in the drug-alcohol mix of many gangs.

Increases in the extent of drug use by both gang and nongang adolescents have been accompanied by the development of serious misconceptions on the part of many adults, and it is important to mention briefly several characteristics of the pattern of drug use by gang members. The fact that many gang members use drugs to greater or lesser degrees makes it possible to talk of "drug-using" gangs. This does not mean, however, that drug use is the central or defining activity of any significant proportion of gangs, any more than the most universal use of alcohol justifies the term "the drinking gang" as a primary designation. Moreover, outside of some inevitable experimentation the most common types of drugs used by gang members are the "soft" drugs, primarily marihuana and "pills." Heroin is rare and "psychedelic" drugs such as LSD even rarer. Furthermore, as is also the case for the adolescent population in general, alcohol remains far and away the most common form of experience-enhancing substance for gang members, with beer, the traditional staple, the most common form of alcohol. Also, contrary to one prevalent notion, most gang members do not turn to drugs as a vehicle of withdrawal, passive escape, "dropping out," or "retreatism" but, rather, use them in much the same fashion and for much the same purposes as alcohol— to enhance or heighten the quality of active involvement with music, courtship, adventure-seeking, group conversation, eating and drinking, and other traditional gang pursuits.

An additional important point concerns the relationship of gang member drug use to criminal behavior. Unlike the case of alcohol, the possession and/or use of narcotic substances for nonmedical purposes is in itself illegal in many jurisdictions. However, it is not this kind of law violation which poses a major problem for law enforcement agencies but, rather, those forms of traditional youth crime, such as robbery, burglary, and violent offenses, which may be related in some way to drug use. In practice, as in the case of youthful drinking, police seldom take action on the basis of drug "use" or "possession" alone if those using marihuana or other "soft" drugs do not at the same time engage in other more disruptive forms of behavior.

What *is* the relationship of gang member drug use to other forms of crime? Two apparently inconsistent positions are current. The first sees drug use as inhibiting crime, the second as enhancing it. The inhibition position argues that drug use serves as a surrogate for more serious forms of crime in that drug users, unlike drinkers, are generally content with legally benign activities, such as digging sounds or rapping, whereas alcohol serves to spur more "aggressive" activities, such as fighting, car theft, or dangerous driving. The enhancement position argues from a well-established "conventional wisdom" formulation, which sees the use of relatively inexpensive "soft" drugs inevitably leading to costly "hard" drugs, and the necessity for those thus addicted to engage in serious forms of nonuse crimes in order to support their habit. Neither the inhibition nor the enhancement positions, whatever their degree of validity, appear to have much application to gang member crime. Although evidence in this area is fragmentary, it would appear quite tentatively that patterns of criminal activity (theft, assault, etc.) of contemporary gangs who may use drugs in

greater or lesser measure do not differ significantly from those of analogous gangs in the predrug period. A major factor here is that the pattern of drug use among typical gang members (mostly "soft" drugs) is not very costly and thus does not provide the incentive for intensified involvement in robbery or burglary postulated by the "enhancement" position as a major element in the behavior of hard-core addicts in communities such as Harlem or Berkeley. Certainly the contemporary gangs of Philadelphia, the Bronx, and Los Angeles are not abstaining from violence as a consequence of drug use (inhibition position), and there is little evidence to link rising rates of robbery and burglary with increases in the use of drugs by gang members (enhancement position).

It is significant that two of the inaccurately predicted or perceived bases of transformation of the American youth gang—politicization and narcoticization—are consistent with, and in an important sense products of, a thesis relating to the character of contemporary adolescent subcultures. In general and simplified terms, this thesis proposes that as a consequence of certain conditions or developments in American society (some say world society), youth have become profoundly "alienated" from an unjust and obsolescent social order and have adopted a markedly (some say radically) new set of attitudes and orientations characterizable as a "counterculture." There is no doubt that various practices and outlooks consistent with the "counterculture" thesis enjoyed considerable currency among some proportion of college-level youth during the 1960s, although the size of that group and the extent of adoption of counterculture elements remains uncertain. Evidence of the present study indicating that neither the political/ideological nor the drug-use orientations represent significant developments among youth gangs recruited primarily from lower and working class populations constitutes one important kind of evidence that the influence of a "counterculture" has been of a very low order among that portion of the population represented by youth gang members. It also casts into question the validity of statements as to the present or future characteristics of youth gangs which are derived primarily from particular theoretical premises rather than careful empirical examination of the actual characteristics of existing gangs.

CYCLICAL ELABORATION AND PERCEPTIONS OF NEWNESS

Conclusions drawn from the foregoing examination of American youth gangs in the Urban Crisis era afford an unusual opportunity to address the issue of change and stability in gangs, since major developments of this period would appear, on their face, to have harbored an unusual potential for altering established societal forms. Three of these developments in particular might have been expected to have had an especially significant impact on gangs: a marked increase in the acceptability and availability of drugs, because this exerted its most direct influence on persons in those age categories from which gangs most typically recruit; a period of unusually intense activity involving race relations, since its most violent and dramatic events transpired in those locales where gangs are most typically found; and a vogue for an ideologically based rebellion against established forms—the "counterculture" movement—because it found its primary adherents among the young, depicted as "alienated" those whose behavior failed to conform to conventional middle class ideals, and aimed to erode established forms, among which the gang must be counted.

However, despite their potential for effecting change this paper has concluded that none of them, in common with other developments of this period, had very much impact on American youth gangs. At the beginning of the period youth gangs, some quite violent, flourished throughout the nation, particularly in slum areas of the largest urban centers; at the end, youth gangs, some quite violent, flourished throughout the nation, particularly in slum areas of the largest cities. The basic forms and characteristic pursuits of these

gangs, while certainly reflecting the changing fashions of the larger adolescent subculture, showed a high degree of continuity. If one grants validity to this conclusion, two additional questions at once present themselves. First, why do gangs persists, and why do their characteristic pursuits retain considerable stability in the face of changing circumstances? Second, how can one account for recurring representations that gangs have been substantially changed, radically transformed, or even extinguished entirely?

Answers to the first question can be presented here only in the most condensed form. The youth gang remains as a persisting form because it is a product of a set of conditions that lie close to the basic building blocks of our social order. These include: the necessary division of labor between the family and the peer group in the socialization of adolescents; the masculinity and collective action emphases of the male subculture; the stress on excitement, congregation, and mating in the adolescent subculture; the importance of toughness, smartness, and trouble in the subcultures of lower status populations; the density conditions and territoriality patterns which figure in the subcultures of urban and urbanized locales. It is these social conditions and their related subcultures which, taken in conjunction, generate the American youth gang, and insofar as these conditions and subcultural concerns retain continuity through time, so does the gang, their product, retain continuity.

How, then, to account for recurring perceptions that gangs come and go and that current manifestations represent "new" forms? The average youth gang, as has been shown, is a "generalized" rather than a specialized form, with a versatile rather than constricted repertoire of activities. Gangs, in common with other generalized and versatile societal forms, are sensitive to a wide variety of environmental developments which are reflected in periodic modifications in their characteristics. These modifications, however, for the most part take the form of *stylistic elaborations* of existing forms and practices rather than "inventions"—genuinely original additions to or changes in traditional features. Insofar as particular gangs devote significant portions of their energies to such elaborations, they move toward the "specialization" pole of a generalized-specialized continuum.

The fate of these elaborations varies. In some instances they remain localized; in others they spread to gangs in other areas through media publication and other means. In the 1950s some gangs in other cities in varying degrees emulated the New York fighting gang model; in the 1970s some New York gangs began to pursue the intensified patterns of homicide by firearms developed in Philadelphia some five years before. The bulk of the elaborations—especially those involving extreme manifestations of a form or practice—are relatively short-lived. Sometimes the more extreme manifestations leave a residue in the form of a more moderate version of the elaboration, as a vogue for intensive use of hard drugs in certain gangs was transmuted over time to a more moderate usage of soft drugs as a continuing component of the gangs' repertoire of experience-enhancing substances. By and large gangs do not sustain for long those elaborations whose continued practice threatens to make substantially more difficult the conduct of other components of their customary patterns of activity.

Once certain types of elaboration achieve a sufficient degree of development they begin to engage the attention of certain nongang societal agencies, who then undertake a characteristic set of responsive actions, which in turn are reacted to by gangs as part of a complex process of mutual feedback and interactive influence. Among these agencies are agencies of control (police, probation agents), social service (social workers, youth workers), and government (elected officials, bureau personnel). Agencies whose responses bear most directly on the perception-of-newness phenomena are the communications/information specialists, primarily media writers and social analysts. To professionals in these fields, "newness" is money in the bank, and "not much different than before" of negligible market value. Since the investment in newness as a saleable commodity is generally coupled with a short-time perspective, periodic elaborations of gang behavior are seized upon and marketed not as recurrent stylistic variations in a continuing pattern but as the new, the spectacular, the sensational.

Information specialists typically represent contemporary elaborations in either or both of two ways; as the emergence of previously nonexistent forms, according to the process whereby changes in the activity patterns of gangs are perceived as the appearance or disappearance of gangs themselves, or as the advent of *the* new type of gang of our times, according to the process whereby developments affecting a small proportion of gangs, often less than one-tenth, are represented as nationally prevalent. Throughout the progression of recurrent elaborations youth gangs continually scan, select from, modify and absorb available subcultural materials, and as the new gang of today's writer becomes the old gang of tomorrow's historian, they continue to thrive as a vital and adaptive form.

26. VIOLENCE AND DISRUPTION ON THE U.S. CAMPUS, 1968-1969

ALAN E. BAYER AND ALEXANDER W. ASTIN

Reprinted from The Educational Record, *Fall 1969, pp. 337-50 by permission of American Council on Education. Alan E. Bayer is Research Sociologist and Alexander Astin is Director of the Office of Research, American Council on Education. In the longitudinal study reported here, which Astin directed, the concern is with the college experiences of American youth, with particular emphasis on changing patterns of college social, political, and intellectual life.*

■ The college version of youthful aggressiveness is a centuries-old social problem. Students have rioted for academic, political, and general hell-raising reasons from time to time for as long as universities have existed. In the United States in recent times such events were regarded as merely part of the college student's recreational activity, as in the "panty raids" of the 1950s. While some social observers saw such events as marks of "moral decline," aggressiveness among college students usually was not regarded as a social problem. But the rise of political activism on campuses and the political and bureaucratic responses of university and state administrations made violence and disruption seem for a time an almost routine accompaniment of the academic year.

In this selection Bayer and Astin provide data about the extent and characteristics of campus disruptions during 1968 and 1969. While many studies deal with particular events of disruption, the Bayer and Astin material is particularly valuable because it provides a context in which the more famous (or infamous) events, such as the Columbia and Harvard disruptions and the Kent State and Jackson State tragedies, can be understood. We learn something here about the kinds of institutions most likely to experience disruption, about the events that occur during them, about the issues that inform the disruptions, and about their outcomes.

Recent writing about college student protest is, of course, extensive. Some writers have discussed the political forces that inform student protests; others have emphasized such factors as the conflict of generations or the role strains inherent in the youth period. See, for example, Shmuel N. Eisenstadt, *From Generation to Generation* (Free Press, 1956) for a general sociological statement of generation as a social force. For an analysis of the role of college attendance in American social stratification and life-styles see Christopher Jencks and David Riesman, *The Academic Revolution* (Doubleday, 1968). A useful collection of articles on student political activity is Seymour Martin Lipset, ed., *Student Politics* (Basic Books, 1967). See also Lewis Feuer, *The Conflict of Generations* (Basic Books, 1969); Irving L. Horowitz and William Friedland, *The Knowledge Factory* (Aldine, 1970); Richard Flacks, *Youth and Social Change* (Markham, 1971); and Theodore Roszak, *The Making of the Counter Culture* (Doubleday, 1968). ■

CAMPUS UNREST during the 1968-69 academic year reached a new peak of intensity and frequency. From a casual sampling of press accounts of recent protest incidents at American colleges and universities, one might conclude that many institutions are coming apart at the seams and, indeed, that higher education in general is on the brink of chaos. The great national concern with these events is reflected in many recent statements by educational groups, as well as in several bills proposed in the state legislatures and the Congress.

The high level of anxiety and tension expressed by all parties concerned with campus unrest suggests that an objective appraisal of the facts would be a useful prelude to any changes in policy that are under consideration. What is the true extent of campus unrest in the total population of colleges and universities? How does the frequency and mode of campus unrest vary from one type of institution to another? What forms has institutional response to unrest taken? Does the character of the institutional response vary with the tactics used by the protesters? What changes in institutional policy and practice have come about as a result of different types of protest?

To arrive at preliminary answers to these and related questions, the Office of Research of the American Council on Education undertook a survey of campus unrest during 1968-69, using the national sample of colleges and universities that has participated in its Cooperative Institutional Research Program. Several studies from previous years provided national estimates of the extent of campus unrest in the United States and its relation to student and institutional characteristics, but this report is the first to focus on major incidents during the most recently completed academic year and to link campus unrest with a wide variety of institutional characteristics.

DATA SOURCES

The questionnaire on campus protest was sent in June 1969 (at the close of the 1968-69 academic year) to all 427 institutional representatives in the American Council on Education's 1968 Cooperative Institutional Research Program. By July 30, responses had been received from 382 (89 percent) of the 427 institutions. The questionnaire, designed to assess factual rather than subjective data, requested information on the incidence of campus protest, the mode of the protests, the issues, and the results, consequences, and changes which occurred during the academic year 1968-69.

Survey responses were linked to the ACE master institutional file, which contains information on institutional type, control, enrollment, selectivity, and other items relating to the population of American institutions of higher education. To account for nonresponse bias and for differential sampling within strata, these data were weighted by a computer program for establishing institutional weights from a college and university

subpopulation . . . Since the initial sample of 427 was randomly selected from the original stratification design, and since the rate of response to the questionnaire was very high, these data can be regarded as closely approximating the data that would have been obtained if all institutions in the population had been surveyed and if all had responded.

The sections of the questionnaire discussed here were designed to assess the character of campus protest incidents throughout the academic year 1968-69. Inasmuch as our objective was not to document single campus incidents but to get an overall view of protest at the institution, the reader should bear in mind that the modes, issues, results, and changes as reported by a college may have involved several different protest incidents. Moreover, the data do not show what happened in previous years. Many institutions, for example, made substantial changes in their rules and policies prior to September 1968, but we are concerned here only with what took place on college campuses in the most recently completed academic year.

MODES OF PROTEST

The questionnaire asked whether the institution had experienced one or more of several different categories of protest tactics. The analyses dealt separately with the nine most severe tactics or protest modes. These nine specific modes, plus instances in which persons were either killed or injured, were also combined to form the following two general modes.

1. *Violent* protest, defined as any campus incident during the year which involved; (a) burning of building; (b) damage to building or furnishings; (c) destruction of records, files, papers; (d) campus march, picketing, or rally with physical violence; (e) one or more persons killed; or (f) some persons injured. All institutions at which such incidents took place are classified in the tabulations as having experienced violent protest.

2. *Nonviolent disruptive* protest, defined as any campus incident during the year which involved; (a) occupation of building or sec-

tion of building; *(b)* barring of entrance to building; *(c)* holding officials captive; *(d)* interruption of school function (e.g., classes, speech, or meetings); or *(e)* general campus strike or boycott of classes or of school function. All institutions at which such incidents took place and which had not also undergone incidents of violent protest are classified in the tabulations as having experienced nonviolent disruptive protest.

Other nonphysical and nondisruptive protest modes have been a traditional part of the academic milieu—even in the quiescent 1950s. Consequently, they are not generally recognized as part of the campus unrest of the 1960s and so are not treated here. Specifically excluded here are protests primarily carried out by persons acting on their own (e.g., letters to the editor, editorials, threats by individuals) or instituted through traditional democratic processes and entailing no disruption of institutional functions (e.g., circulation of petitions, presentation of list of grievances to college official, nonviolent picketing, campus march, or rally). Specifically included are those incidents which involve violence and those which are nonviolent but disruptive in the sense that they either prevent free movement of all members of the campus or interfere with administrative or institutional functions. All tabulations presented here employ these two categories as the major control variable.

PROTEST ISSUES

The questionnaire listed 23 different issues that might serve as a basis for protest. Respondents were asked to indicate whether or not a specific issue was involved in any of the protests that occurred during the academic year. As with the modes of protest, our analyses dealt with each separate issue, as well as with the following general categories.

1. *War-related* protests were defined as those concerned with opposition to *(a)* U.S. military policy (e.g., Vietnam, CBW, ABM), *(b)* Selective Service policy, *(c)* ROTC programs, *(d)* on-campus military or government research, or *(e)* on-campus recruiting by government or industry.

2. Issues involving *services to students* were defined as protests about *(a)* institutional services (e.g., food and medical service, housing and recreation facilities), *(b)* instructional procedures (e.g., class size, quality of instruction, grading system, student evaluation), or *(c)* tuition charges and fees.

3. *Minority group student* issues were defined as those which focused on *(a)* special education programs for minority groups (e.g., Black studies, compensatory programs), or *(b)* special admissions policies for minority groups.

4. *Off-campus* issues included protest concerning *(a)* war-related issues (above), *(b)* civil rights (e.g., desegregation, voter registration), *(c)* labor problems (e.g., wages, benefits, unionization), or *(d)* administrative indifference or inaction concerning local community problems.

5. *Secondary issues* were defined as protests concerning *(a)* police brutality, *(b)* requests or demands for amnesty, *(c)* administrative indifference or inaction concerning previous protest grievances, *(d)* administrative response to previous protests, or *(e)* mourning for students or others killed or wounded.

6. *Student power* issues were defined as protests concerning *(a)* institutional parietal rules (e.g., dress, dormitory regulations, drinking, sex, required attendance at school functions), *(b)* institutional student disciplinary practices, *(c)* student participation in decision making (e.g., inclusion on committees), *(d)* free expression (e.g., censorship of publications, exclusion of "controversial" speakers), or *(e)* faculty (e.g., academic freedom, hiring, tenure).

IMMEDIATE OUTCOMES

Immediate outcomes of the protests were assessed in terms of 16 different items (e.g., National Guard called in, classes suspended, formal statement issued by faculty in support of protesters. Respondents were asked to indicate whether each of these immediate outcomes had occurred during the 1968-69 academic year. The foffowing general categories of immediate outcomes were developed:

1. *Civil action,* defined as *(a)* some protesters arrested, or *(b)* some protesters indicted.

2. *Institutional discipline,* defined as *(a)* one or more students dismissed or expelled, *(b)* some students suspended or put on probation, or *(c)* financial assistance withdrawn from some protesters.

INSTITUTIONAL CHANGE

Institutional change comprised the final set of items in the questionnaire. Eleven specific changes in institutional policy and practice during the 1968-69 academic year were tabulated, as well as the foffowing three general categories:

1. *Changes in racial policies,* defined as *(a)* establishment of Black studies program or department, or *(b)* institution of special admissions policies for minority group members.

2. *Increased student power,* defined as *(a)* liberalization of parietal rules, *(b)* changes in other institutional rules and regulations governing students, or *(c)* provision to students of greater voice or representation on existing committees.

3. *Substantive institutional change,* defined as *(a)* changes in racial policy (above), *(b)* increased student power (above), *(c)* institution of curriculum changes, *(d)* termination of ROTC program, *(e)* changes in ROTC program, such as making it elective, *(f)* discontinuance of some campus research for the military, or *(g)* prohibition of on-campus recruiting for some organizations. The last general category included all but one specific institutional change, "formation of new committees or study groups on campus," which was not regarded as a substantive change.

SUMMARY OF FINDINGS

The data reported here are pertinent to all protest activities that occurred during the entire academic year of 1968-69. Since the various items are closely interrelated, most of the substantive findings are presented before any discussion or interpretation is offered.

INSTITUTIONAL CHARACTERISTICS AND
THE INCIDENCE OF MAJOR CAMPUS PROTEST

Of the more than 2,300 colleges and universities in the United States, an estimated 145, or 6.2 percent, experienced at least one incident of violent protest during the past academic year. An additional estimated 379 institutions, or 16.2 percent, experienced nonviolent disruptive protest. While these findings make clear that violence and disruption are not, as many press reports suggest, characteristic of most college campuses, they indicate also that the number of colleges that have experienced disorder is not inconsequential. A more detailed account of the characteristics of these institutions is presented below.

Control and type. At the university level, major protest incidents are about twice as likely to occur at private as at public institutions. More than one in three private universities experienced violent protests during the past academic year, whereas one in eight public universities experienced incidents of comparable severity. Approximately 70 percent of the private and 42 percent of the public universities experienced either violent or disruptive protest. In short, major campus protest incidents were more the rule than the exception in the universities, particularly in the private ones.

Among the nation's four-year colleges, incidents of violent protests were three to four times more likely in the public of the private nonsectarian institutions than in the church-related colleges. Nevertheless, only about 1 in every 14 institutions that were not church-related experienced such protests. The data also indicate that the private, nonsectarian, four-year colleges were substantially more likely than the public or sectarian colleges to have nonviolent disruptive protests.

Major protest incidents are least likely to occur in the nation's two-year colleges. Virtually none of the private two-year colleges experienced either violent or nonviolent disruptive protests. Among the public 2-year colleges, only about 1 in 20 had an incident involving violent protest; an additional 1 in 20 had a nonviolent disruptive incident.

Size. An institution's total enrollment size is highly related to the probability that it will suffer major campus disorder, but the nature of that relationship is complex and rather confusing. Very few of the institutions that enroll small numbers of students (less than 1,000) had any incidents of violent protest. None of the sample of universities or 2-year colleges enrolling less than 1,000 students reported an incident of violent protest; among the more than 500 4-year colleges in the nation with similar enrollments, less than 3 percent reported violent protests. Among institutions of intermediate size (enrollments between 1,000 and 5,000 students), 4 percent of the 2-year colleges, 5 percent of the 4-year colleges, and 14 percent of the universities experienced violent protest. Of the large institutions (enrollment over 5,000), 16 percent of the junior colleges, 14 percent of the senior colleges, and 22 percent of the universities experienced such incidents.

The results with respect to nonviolent disruptive protest incidents are similar. Of the very large junior colleges (enrollment over 5,000), more than a third experienced at least one such incident. That these larger two-year colleges tend to be public institutions is consistent with the data on institutional control. The rate of nonviolent disruptive protest among 4-year colleges of similar size is substantially less than that of the large junior colleges—about 24 percent. None of the small universities in the sample had incidents of nonviolent disruptive protest. On the other hand, such protests occurred at more than two out of three

universities of intermediate size, and at more than two-fifths of the large universities. Again, this is consistent with the earlier finding that private universities (which tend to be of moderate rather than large size) are substantially more likely than the public ones to have major protests.

In summary, the institution's size is related to the occurrence of both violent and nonviolent disruptive protest, but the nature of the relationship is confounded by type of control and by level (two-year, four-year, or university).

Selectivity. Like size, the "selectivity" of a college—defined as the average academic ability of its student body—is one of its most important attributes. Previous research has indicated that selectivity is closely related to an institution's educational environment and prestige and that it affects students' career choices and their chances of dropping out. Selectivity tends to be positively correlated with incidents of major protest, a relationship that reflects the close connection between institutional control and the quality of the student body.

Among the universities, none of the least selective had either violent or nonviolent disruptive protests. The proportion increases dramatically, however, with each higher selectivity level; about 85 percent of the most selective universities experienced either violent or nonviolent disruptive incidents.

The four-year colleges manifest a similar, though less pronounced, increase in violent or nonviolent disruptive protests as they become more selective. The trend does not occur among the two-year colleges, however: those at the lower levels of selectivity actually have a higher incidence of violent or nonviolent disruptive protest. Again, this tendency can be largely, if not wholly, attributed to the greater likelihood of major protest at the public (often less selective) than at the private two-year colleges.

SPECIFIC PROTEST INCIDENTS

The number of institutions in the sample and the estimated number in the population

TABLE 26.1

SPECIFIC INCIDENTS OCCURRING AT INSTITUTIONS EXPERIENCING VIOLENT OR NONVIOLENT DISRUPTIVE PROTEST, 1968-1969 ACADEMIC YEAR

Protest Incident	Sample Institutions at which Protest Occurred (N)	Estimated among Population of 145 Institutions Experiencing Violent Protest (N)	Percent	Estimated among Population of 379 Institutions Experiencing Nonviolent Disruptive Protest (N)	Percent	Estimated among 2,342 Institutions in the Total Population (N)	Percent
1. Burning of building	11	43	29.6			43	1.8
2. Damage to building or furnishings	18	80	55.2			80	3.4
3. Destruction of records, files, papers	5	21	14.5	No		21	0.9
4. Campus march, picketing, or rally with physical violence	18	62	42.8	Violent		62	2.6
5. One or more persons killed	2	8	5.5	incidents		8	0.3
6. Some persons injured	14	45	31.0	by		45	1.9
Total with violent protests (1-6)	61	145	100.0	definition		145	6.2
7. Occupation of building or section of building	62	50	34.5	225	59.4	275	11.7
8. Barring of entrance to building	27	38	26.2	45	11.9	83	3.5
9. Holding official captive	7	15	10.3	9	2.4	24	1.0
10. Interruption of school function (e.g., classes, speech, or meeting)	59	71	49.0	189	49.9	260	11.1
11. General campus strike or boycott of school function	20	60	41.4	81	21.4	141	6.0
Total with violent or nonviolent disruptive protests (1-11)	125	145	100.0	379	100.0	524	22.4

that have undergone each of the more severe types of incidents listed on the questionnaire are shown in Table 26.1. Among those institutions that fall into the category of having had "violent protest," the most prevalent kind of violence was damage to a campus building or its furnishings. We estimate that such an incident occurred on 3.4 percent of American college campuses, or on 80 (55 percent) of those 145 campuses where violent protest took place.

Of these same institutions, 62 (43 percent) had a campus march, picketing, or rally accompanied by physical violence; 43 (30 percent) had a building or a section of a building destroyed by fire; and 21 (15 percent) had records, files, or papers destroyed. Injuries to some persons (protesters, police, administrators, faculty, or bystanders) occurred at an estimated 45 institutions. An estimated eight institutions in the nation experienced incidents in which one or more people were killed, but this estimate is subject to considerable error because of the rarity of reported deaths in the sample (2 among the 382 institutions). These data show that while "violence," as we have defined it, is most likely to take the form of property destruction, personal injuries do occur in about one-third of such incidents.

Nonviolent disruptive protest took place at an additional 379 (16.2 percent) colleges and universities during the past academic year. The most prevalent forms of disruption were the occupation of a building (225, or 59.4 percent, of the 379 institutions); the interruption of a school function such as a class, speech, or meeting (189, or 49.9 percent); and a general campus strike or boycott of a school function (81, or 21.4 percent). Much less frequent actions were barring entrances to buildings (45 institutions) and holding administrators captive (9 institutions). At the 145 institutions experiencing violent incidents, these nonviolent disruptive forms also were employed extensively.

SPECIFIC PROTEST ISSUES

The issues raised during the past year on those campuses where there was either violent or nonviolent disruptive protest is shown in Table 26.2. The most prevalent of the specific issues on campuses that had violent protests involved (1) instituting special educational programs for disadvantaged or minority groups, (2) allowing greater student participation on committees, (3) changing institutional disciplinary practices, (4) challenging apparent administrative indifference or inaction to grievances, and (5) challenging alleged administrative indifference to local community problems. The same issues also were frequently raised on the campuses that had nonviolent disruptive protests, the two most frequent being special compensatory educational programs and student participation in decision making.

Looking at the larger categories of issues, we find that demand for increased student power was the most popular theme of major protest incidents (Table 26.2); three-fourths of the colleges that had either violent or nonviolent disruptive protests during the year also had protests on this issue. The next most frequent general category was that of off-campus problems such as the Vietnam war, civil rights, labor problems, and community problems. Issues relating to student minorities were the subject of protest on more than half of the campuses that had nonviolent disruptive incidents and on more than two-thirds of those that had violent incidents. Other major issues (raised on about half of the campuses) included institutional student services, war-related issues, and secondary issues evolving from previous protest incidents.

Is there any relationship between the protest issues and the tactics employed during the year? By comparing the relative size of the two percentages in each row of Table 26.2, we see that the use of violence is associated least with protests which concerned parietal rules or instructional procedures. The most common specific protest issue— special educational programs for minority groups—was associated more closely with violence (66 percent) than with nonviolent disruption (51 percent). Of all the specifc

TABLE 26.2

PROTEST ISSUES AT INSTITUTIONS EXPERIENCING INCIDENTS OF VIOLENT
OR NONVIOLENT DISRUPTIVE PROTEST: 1968-1969 ACADEMIC YEAR
(WEIGHTED POPULATION ESTIMATES)

Protest Issue	Among Institutions Experiencing Violent Protests (N=145)		Among Institutions Experiencing Nonviolent Disruptive Protests (N=379)	
	N	Percent	N	Percent
1. U.S. military policy (e.g., Vietnam, CBW, ABM)	56	38.6	144	38.0
2. Selective service policy	40	27.6	88	23.2
3. ROTC programs	55	37.9	65	17.1
4. On-campus military or government research	43	29.6	40	10.6
5. On-campus recruiting by government or industry	52	35.9	114	30.1
Total, war-related issues (1-5)	71	49.0	194	51.2
6. Institutional services (e.g., food and medical services, housing and recreation facilities)	45	31.0	105	27.7
7. Institutional parietal rules (e.g., dress, dormitory regulations, drinking, sex, required attendance at school functions)	20	13.8	136	35.9
8. Institutional student disciplinary practices	67	46.2	102	26.9
9. Institutional procedures (e.g., class size, quality of instruction, grading system, student evaluation)	36	24.8	125	33.0
10. Tuition charges and fees	17	11.7	36	9.5
Total, services to students issues (6, 9, 10)	64	44.1	193	50.9
11. Special educational programs for minority groups (e.g., black studies, compensatory programs)	96	66.2	194	51.2
12. Special admissions policies for minority groups	55	37.9	97	25.6
Total, minority group students issues (11-12)	101	69.1	196	51.7
13. Civil rights (e.g., desegregation, voter registration)	7	4.8	17	4.5
14. Labor problems (e.g., wages, benefits, unionization)	28	19.3	10	2.6
15. Administrative indifference or inaction concerning local community problems	61	42.1	29	7.6
Total, off-campus issues (1-5; 13-15)	102	70.3	214	56.5
16. Police brutality	37	25.5	13	3.4
17. Requests or demands for amnesty	46	31.7	50	13.2
18. Administrative indifference or inaction concerning previous protest grievances	63	43.4	106	28.0
19. Administrative response to previous protests	45	31.0	67	17.7
20. Mourning for students or others killed or wounded	22	15.2	34	9.0
Total, secondary issues (16-20)	96	66.2	157	41.4
21. Student participation in decision making (e.g., inclusion on committees)	78	53.8	147	38.8
22. Free expression (e.g., censorship of publications, exclusion of "controversial" speakers)	19	13.1	51	13.5
23. Faculty (e.g., academic freedom, hiring, tenure)	51	35.2	65	17.1
Total, student power issues (7, 8, 21-23)	113	77.9	283	74.7
24. Other	30	20.7	60	15.8
Grand total (1-24)	145	100.0	379	100.0

issues, however, opposition to ROTC, when it arose, was most likely to involve violence.

IMMEDIATE OUTCOMES OF PROTEST INCIDENTS

Table 26.3 shows some of the direct results and consequences of protest incidents, including death or injury to person, extra-institutional restraints, institutional punitive action, responses of college administrators and faculty, and national coverage by news media.

Extrainstitutional action. Temporary re-

straining orders or court injunctions were issued against demonstrators at 1 in 5 institutions in which a violent protest occurred in the past year; the comparable figure for campuses where only nonviolent disruptive protests occurred was less than 1 in 15.

Rarely was the National Guard called in, but off-campus police were employed on more than half of the campuses with violent protests and on 12 percent of those with nonviolent disruptive protests.

At more than half of the institutions which had violent protests, some protesters

TABLE 26.3

IMMEDIATE OUTCOMES OF PROTEST INCIDENTS ON CAMPUSES EXPERIENCING
VIOLENT OR NONVIOLENT DISRUPTIVE PROTEST: 1968-1969 ACADEMIC YEAR
(WEIGHTED POPULATION ESTIMATES)

Direct Results and Consequences	Among 145 Institutions Experiencing Violent Protests		Among 379 Institutions Experiencing Nonviolent Disruptive Protests	
	N	*Percent*	N	*Percent*
1. National Guard called in	2	1.4	0	0.0
2. Off-campus police called in	80	55.2	45	11.9
3. One or more persons killed	8	5.5	0	0.0
4. Some persons injured	45	31.0	0	0.0
5. Some protesters arrested	82	56.6	19	5.0
6. Some protesters indicted	37	25.5	10	2.6
Total, civil action against individual students (5-6)	87	60.0	24	6.3
7. Temporary restraining order or court injunction obtained	28	19.3	25	6.6
8. Classes suspended	60	41.4	42	11.1
9. National press or television coverage given to protest	69	47.6	143	37.7
10. Administration or faculty negotiated issues with demonstrators	90	62.1	316	83.4
11. Formal statement issued by faculty in support of protesters	43	29.6	67	17.7
12. One or more students dismissed or expelled	21	14.5	19	5.0
13. Some students suspended or put on probation	48	33.1	69	18.2
14. Formal student reprimands issued	52	35.8	41	10.8
15. Financial assistance withdrawn from some protesters	13	9.0	6	1.6
Total, major institutional discipline against individual students (12, 13, 15)	56	38.6	80	21.1
Total, either civil or institutional action against individual students (5, 6, 12, 13, 15)	109	75.2	84	22.2
16. Some faculty or administrators resigned as a result of the protest	13	9.0	2	0.5
17. Other	23	15.9	29	7.6

were arrested; at one-fourth of the institutions they were subsequently indicted. Overall, some form of civil action was taken against individual students in three-fifths of the institutions with violent protests and in less than 7 percent of those with nonviolent disruptive protests. Clearly, civil and institutional authorities distinguish between violent and nonviolent protests. Civil action is almost exclusively associated with violent protest.

Institutional punitive action. Formal student reprimands were issued to protesting students at 35 percent of the institutions with violent protests and at 11 percent of those with disruptive protests. More severe punishment (suspension or probation) was meted out at one-third of the colleges with violent protests and at almost one-fifth of those with nonviolent disruptive protests. The most severe institutional discipline— dismissal and expulsion—was incurred by some protesters at 15 percent of the campuses with violent protest and at 5 percent of those with nonviolent disruptive protest. Finally, financial assistance was withdrawn from students at few campuses.

Summary of punitive action against protesters. The figures in Table 26.3 indicate that some major civil or institutional action (arrest, indictment, dismissal, or suspension) was taken against individual students at fully three-fourths of the institutions where there were violent protests; similarly severe punitive measures were taken against individual students at more than one-fifth of the colleges that had nonviolent disruptive protests. However, since he survey was completed at many institutions prior to the end of the academic year in June, these figures are probably underestimates of the response; legal or institutional disciplinary aciton still may have been pending or prospective in a few instances. Moreover, at some college institutional actions against individual protesters may be deferred pending the result of extra-institutional proceedings so that the institutional action will not prejudice the civil action.

Response of administrators and faculty. The data indicate that college administrators and faculty often attempt to resolve the issues in a protest incident by negotiating with demonstrators. It is important to note that such procedures were even more likely to be used at institutions that had nonviolent disruptive protests (83 percent) than at those where violent incidents occurred (62 percent). This finding raises a provocative two-fold question that should be dealt with in future research: Does violence sometimes prevent the possibility of negotiation? Or does the failure to negotiate sometimes lead to violence?

At about 30 percent of the institutions with violent protest, and at 18 percent of those with nonviolent disruptive protest, some faculty issued formal statements in support of the demonstrators. Rarely did college officials or faculty members resign as a result of protest incidents, although the tendency to resign is clearly related to the use of violence. Faculty resignations stemming primarily from protests occurred at an estimated 13 institutions (10 percent) where there were violent protests and at only 2 of the 379 institutions where there were nonviolent disruptive protests.

Coverage by news media. Campus and local news media generally cover protest incidents on local campuses. About half the campuses that had violent protests and about one-third that had non-violent disruptive incidents received attention from the national news media as well. One obvious consequence of such relatively comprehensive coverage is that it creates the impression of rampant violence in the nation's colleges and universities.

INSTITUTIONAL CHANGES AS RELATED
TO MAJOR CAMPUS PROTEST

The frequency of major institutional changes is shown in Table 26.4. Although unrest and change are positively associated, the data show clearly that colleges and universities are not intransigent and that they do

TABLE 26.4

INSTITUTIONAL CHANGES AS RELATED TO MAJOR INCIDENTS OF CAMPUS PROTEST, 1968-1969 ACADEMIC YEAR

(WEIGHTED POPULATION ESTIMATES)

Changes	As a Direct Result of Protest Incident				Not as a Direct Result of Protest Incident					
	On Campuses Experiencing Violent Protests (N=145)		On Campuses Experiencing Nonviolent Disruptive Protests (N=379)		On Campuses Experiencing Violent Protests (N=145)		On Campuses Experiencing Nonviolent Disruptive Protests (N=379)		On Campuses Not Experiencing Violent or Nonviolent Disruptive Protests (N=1818)	
	N	Percent	N	Percent	N	Percent	N	Percent	N	Percent
1. Establishment of Black studies program or department	68	46.9	34	9.0	44	30.3	186	49.1	324	17.8
2. Institution of other curriculum changes	32	22.1	74	19.5	86	59.3	218	57.5	749	41.2
3. Institution of special admissions policies for minority group members	23	15.9	19	5.0	38	26.2	76	20.1	155	8.5
Total, changes in racial policies (1, 3)	80	55.2	42	11.1	61	42.1	202	53.3	424	23.3
4. Liberalization of parietal rules	8	5.5	47	12.4	78	53.8	156	41.2	448	24.6
5. Changes in institutional rules and regulations governing students	17	11.7	54	14.2	79	54.5	187	49.3	746	41.0
6. Provision to students of greater voice or representation on existing committees	33	22.8	69	18.2	81	55.9	194	51.2	823	45.3
Total, changes in student power (4-6)	37	25.5	118	31.1	104	71.7	258	68.1	1,062	58.4
7. Formation of new committees or study groups on campus	78	53.8	131	34.6	89	61.4	145	38.3	604	33.2
8. Termination of ROTC program	4	2.8	2	0.5	0	0.0	0	0.0	3	0.2
9. Changes in ROTC program, such as making it elective	16	11.0	14	3.7	4	2.8	16	4.2	19	1.0
10. Discontinuation of some campus research for the military	0	0.0	0	0.0	2	1.4	2	0.5	0	0.0
11. Prohibition of on-campus recruiting for some organizations	6	4.1	12	3.2	0	0.0	0	0.0	11	0.6
Total, substantive institutional changes (1-6, 8-11)	104	71.7	204	53.8	116	80.0	336	88.6	1,128	62.0
12. Other	13	9.0	31	8.2	5	3.4	5	1.3	36	2.0

institute changes without confrontation and crisis. Most institutions, including those where no major protest incident occurred, made major changes in institutional policy and practices during the year.

Changes resulting directly from protests. Changes that resulted directly from protest incidents on campuses where there were violent protests were most likely to take the form of new committees or study groups (53.8 percent of the 145 campuses with violent protests) or of new Black studies programs (46.9 percent of the 145 institutions). The formation of new committees, curriculum changes (including Black studies programs), and provision for greater student participation on existing committees were the changes most likely to take place as a direct result of protest on campuses that had nonviolent disruptive incidents.

Substantive institutional changes were made as a direct result of protest activities at 72 percent of the campuses where protest was violent and at 54 percent of those where it was nonviolent but disruptive. Changes in racial policies resulted from protest activities at 55 percent of the institutions with violent protests and at 11 percent of those with nonviolent disruptive protests. However, there was no major difference between colleges with violent protests and those with disruptive protests with respect to protest-induced changes which increased student power. In short, then, the use of violence appears to be associated with changes in minority group policies, but not with most other forms of substantive institutional change.

Changes not a direct result of protests. Table 26.4 also shows that many institutional changes effected during the past academic year were not the direct result of protest incidents. More than two-fifths of the institutions with violent protests, and more than half of those with nonviolent disruptive protests, changed their racial policies—but not, according to report, as a direct result of protest incidents. Of those institutions which had *not* experienced any major protest activities during the year, almost one-fourth changed

their racial policies. For all these institutions, changes in racial policies usually involved new Black studies programs rather than a relaxation in admissions requirements for minority group applicants.

Changes which increased student power were much more likely to be made independent of, rather than as a direct result of, a protest incident. The national estimates indicate that 72 percent of the colleges experiencing violent protest, 68 percent of those experiencing nonviolent disruptive protest, and 58 percent of those with no major protest gave students greater power, but not as a direct result of protest incidents. The most prevalent of these changes were those which allowed greater representation of students on committees, followed by changes in institutional rules and regulations governing students. These data raise but do not answer these questions: Do institutions which have already provided greater power to students experience more incidents of major campus protest? Or does the failure to grant such power prior to a campus protest incident give rise to violence and disruption?

In total, substantive changes that did not directly result from protest incidents were made at 80 percent of the institutions with violent protest, at 89 percent of those with nonviolent disruptive protest, and at 62 percent of those which incurred no major protest incident. Changes were usually in the direction of granting greater power to students, forming new committees or study groups, and making changes in the curriculum.

DISCUSSION AND CONCLUSIONS

One major conclusion suggested by this survey is that popular accounts of the campus "crisis" are often misleading. That is, violence and disruption are not as "rampant" on campuses as some reports would lead us to believe, nor are institutions as "irresponsible" (in attempting to curb violence) or as "unresponsive" (in instituting major changes) as many critics have claimed. While the more dramatic incidents of violence or of institutional inertia are likely to be deemed the most newsworthy, the evidence indicates that such incidents are not reflective of the "typical" American college.

It is apparent that the more severe forms of protest frequently provoke punitive response. At fully three-fourths of the institutions which had experienced violent protest, major civil or institutional action was taken against some protesters. Such institutional response has been appropriate to the protest action: the more extreme the incident, the more severe the discipline.

Frequently, civil authority has been the instrument of punitive response. In those cases where protest is violent and destructive in nature, it is frequently the courts rather than the college that deal with the matter; the institution often refrains from taking action in such cases, probably because such action would prejudice pending civil proceedings or place students in double jeopardy. In nonviolent disruptive protests, on the other hand, the college itself is more likely to institute disciplinary measures, and, correspondingly, civil authority is less apt to play a role in control and punishment.

Public alarm over campus unrest and state and federal governmental irritation over student criticism have resulted recently in the proposal or passage of bills designed to discipline and stifle protest. As our evidence suggests, however, such legislation may well be not only ineffectual but also unfair. Our findings show that major campus unrest is most prevalent in large schools, in universities, in nonsectarian four-year colleges—particularly private—and in those institutions which accept only students of high average ability and achievement levels. Consequently, state or federal legislation which inhibits institutions or deprives students in some way would have very different effects on different kinds of institutions. Junior colleges and church-related institutions would escape lightly, simply because their students are not engaging in the type of protest likely to be encom-

passed by punitive legislation or to result in the withdrawal of financial support from students. On the other hand, the nation's "centers of excellence" would suffer severely. Moreover, much of the legislation that has been enacted or proposed, particularly at the state level, would have an adverse impact on public institutions but relatively little effect on private ones—and it is a the private institutions that most major protest incidents occur.

Most colleges and universities seem to be responding in a meaningful and appropriate manner to major campus protest without a need for state or federal punitive legislation. They have employed severe disciplinary measures to curb violence. They also have made major efforts to modify curricula and racial policies and to increase the students' freedom and power. Moreover, most institutions, including those which experienced no major protest during the 1968-69 academic year, instituted substantive changes in rules or policy during that period. Undoubtedly, such changes are partly a response to earlier protests or to protests on other college campuses, partly an attempt to avert potential protest activities, and partly an effort to improve the educational environment.

Nevertheless, even though college administrators have responded significantly both to the protest tactics and to the issues, campuses will almost certainly experience more protest activity in years to come. Since dissent and protest have always been regarded as essential features of any viable and effective educational community, institutions will continue to face a major dilemma: How can they encourage the expression of protest and social criticism and, at the same time, preserve basic democratic processes and protect the rights and privileges of all members of the campus community? Our stock-taking of the responses of college administrators to campus incidents of violent or nonviolent disruptive protest indicates that substantial efforts are under way to resolve this dilemma.

27. THE SOCIAL ORGANIZATION OF ARMED ROBBERY

WERNER J. EINSTADTER

Reprinted with permission from Social Problems *17, no. 1 (Summer 1969): 65-81. Copyright 1969 by the Society for the Study of Social Problems and the author. Werner J. Einstadter is Associate Professor of Sociology at Eastern Michigan University.*

■ One of the most obvious deviant careers is that of the criminal. Although any individual may (and in one way or another most of us do) commit crimes from time to time, given the problematical nature of laws and the strains in our way of organizing social life only some individuals engage in crime in a regular and taken-for-granted way. That is, only for some individuals does crime become an occupation, a job, or a career.

For a long time sociologists have been interested in the professional criminal, but with only a few exceptions their work on this kind of career has not yielded the rich and detailed understanding that one finds in other areas of empirical sociology. It is not difficult to find reasons for this failure; beginning, perhaps, with the likelihood of quite human uneasiness among middle class sociologists approaching "criminals." Of course, in order to operate the successful criminal requires considerable secrecy and therefore is not likely to be forthcoming in responding to a request that he serve as a research subject.

The best known exception to these generalizations is the work of Edwin H. Sutherland, particularly his classic *The Professional Thief* (University of Chicago Press, 1937). Sutherland's work, though more than 30 years old, is still read and used by sociologists who want to understand professional crime; but a discipline that has to rely on only a few empirical studies is in danger of creating myths rather than providing knowledge. In this selection, Einstadter assesses Sutherland's picture of how the professional thief operates against data he has collected about how armed robbers operate. He finds, perhaps not surprisingly, that for armed robbers the social organization is not the same as that Sutherland described for professional thieves. His data are particularly rich and allow him to present a useful, empirically grounded conceptualization of the

socially patterned set of relationships involved in careers of armed robbery.

Useful general discussions of criminal careers include Edwin H. Sutherland and Donald R. Cressey, *Principles of Criminology* (Lippincott, 1966); and Marshall B. Clinard and Richard Quinney; *Criminal Behavior Systems—A Typology* (Holt, Rinehart & Winston, 1967). Several papers by Edwin M. Lemert, reprinted in *Human Deviance, Social Problems and Social Control* (Prentice-Hall, 1967), deal with variations in commitment to another kind of crime—check forgery. Mary Owen Cameron, *The Booster and the Snitch* (Free Press, 1964), reports on the social organization and careers involved in shoplifting. Donald R. Cressey reports on the predominantly white-collar crime of embezzlement in *Other People's Money* (Free Press, 1953). For a useful discussion of problems of understanding professional criminal behavior, see Ned Polsky, *Hustlers, Beats, and Others* (Chicago: Aldine, 1967). Another recent study of professional criminals designed to test the applicability of Sutherland's paradigm is Neal Shover, "The Social Organization of Burglary," *Social Problems* 20 (4): 1973, pp. 499-513. ■

IN MOST criminological studies, when the group life of adult professional criminals is discussed a single theoretical model is employed. It is usually assumed that the adult professional criminal operates within the structural context of the *mob*. The model of the mob has been variously described in the literature but was most clearly formulated by Sutherland.

A body of literature on professional crime has centered largely on an extension or modification of Sutherland's conception of the essential social characteristics of professional theft and his unifying theoretical statement of differential association. As Clinard and Quinney have pointed out, however, empirical research concerning various types of professional crime has been sparse; this is especially true with regard to the social organization of various professional criminal groups. No studies appear to have been concerned specifically with a reexamination of Sutherland's conception of the social organization of the professional criminal.

The concept of the mob implies that professional criminal collectivities operate according to a number of common understandings, rules of conduct, or working relationships which are considered binding on all its members. These modes of conduct found among groups of professional thieves are presumed to have universal applicability to all professional criminal groups.

The purpose of this paper is twofold; first, it is an attempt to relate Sutherland's conception of the mob to professional robbery and to reassess its utility and relevance as a generic explanatory model; second, it is an effort to describe a specific type of criminal behavior system.

METHODOLOGY

Twenty-five convicted robbers on parole in California were studied. In addition to interview material, data gathered over several years from an equal number of convicted robbers who were confined were used. Official records were employed as supplementary material, to check the official criminal record, prior commitments, and offense statements.

The respondents selected represent robbers who were considered to be professional or career robbers in that they all met the following criteria.

1. Each subject in company with others committed more than a single robbery prior to detection. Each subject committed either a series of robberies or several series of robberies separated by prison terms. In a number of instances there were robberies unknown to officials.

2. All were armed robbers. All employed weapons that were operative. None simulated weapons. Each instance of robbery was calculated, and the subject fully intended to carry the act to its completion.

3. Each subject considered himself a robber and for various periods had spent considerable portion of his time in the engagement of robbery.

4. In all instances the subject's sole stated interest was robbery. In no case was the robbery incidental to some other form of crime (e.g., rape, drug addiction).

The subjects, therefore, may be considered as representing more than just casual robbers but individuals who engaged in this form of criminal conduct on a purposive, rational, and sustained basis over various periods of time.

FINDINGS

Sutherland describes a number of significant features that emerge in the group life of professional thieves which he considers the binding rules of the mob. As such, these rules develop into a formal code of ethics subscribed to by the professional thief much like other codes of conduct among legitimate professional groups.

A comparison of the type of organization that develops among professional robbers with the type of organization that develops among professional thieves reveals little similarity as the following discussion will make clear. Whereas the professional thief finds his organizational counterpart in the legitimate professions, the professional or career robber may be compared more accurately with the legitimate businessman in the organizational form of the partnership.

Sutherland's thief is quite explicit in his description of the norms that develop in the mob. A review of the rules of the mob should prove revealing in highlighting the differences between the type of structure that is characteristic of groups of professional thieves and that of groups of armed robbers.

1. Gains are equally shared. A percentage is given to outsiders who assist the mob.

In general, robbers share equally with their associates whatever is taken. However, there is no sharing with outsiders as they do not exist for the robber. If someone has helpful knowledge about sites to rob or assists in some way in the robbery even if only tangentially, from the robber's point of view he is not an outsider but a member of the group and receives his share of the gain. Once robbery is discussed by a group with any amount of seriousness all become full partners and all consider themselves equally involved and have a stake in the success of the planned enterprise. Planning need not be extensive in order for this involvment to occur; there merely needs to be some discussion of robbery amongst a group that intends to carry it to completion. Hence no one is ever considered an outsider to the group after preliminary discussions have taken place. The statement of one robber is illustrative.

[If] you compare notes with somebody, you are going to join them. In other words, my crime partner and I were talking to you and another fellow, and we were comparing notes, eventually the four of us are going to do something together, whether it be tonight, tomorrow night or the next night, regardless. By openly admitting to one another our situation, I think we find a binding point, where we, you say, I know a spot over there, let's go get it. And you say let's go get it, why, the four of you go instead of one or two.

2. Expenses of the mob come off the top.

The robber's expenses are minimal and are usually paid out of pocket by the individual concerned. Such outlays are in the nature of small business expenses and are managed quite informally from one robbery to the next. One respondent stated it simply.

I paid the gas and oil on the first job, the second time around somebody else got it. Usually it was just a couple of bucks and nobody expected anything back. . . .

Large expenses, such as the purchase of an automobile or the purchase of weapons, are usually paid on a share-and-share-alike basis. Each contributes his amount to the total. In some instances, expenses are taken off the top, but this is not by any means a regular procedure. There is nothing formal about any of these arrangements; rather, like any other informal group undertaking where there are expenses, there is a tacit agreement that each member contributes his share.

3. All loans are repaid out of the first sum of stolen money.

A number of robbers who were asked about this provision seemed perplexed and had no knowledge regarding this type of arrangement. These loans refer to an organized mob that needs capital to carry out its illegal enterprises. This rarely occurs in the sense that there are financial backers for the robber. When large sums of monetary outlays are necessary that can not readily be managed by the group, other methods than seeking a backer are employed. A group that generally commits the more sophisticated variety of robbery (e.g., banks, large grocery chains) where such outlays sometimes become necessary may commit a number of small preliminary minor robberies before venturing to tackle a more formidable victim. Often such a group may rob a few smaller establishments to fund a contemplated large robbery which may require some additional equipment. Frequently such items are stolen directly.

4. A fourth rule described by Sutherland is concerned with a number of general understandings about the mob's action when a member is arrested. Basically, the understanding is that the mob helps the apprehended member by sharing the expenses of court costs if he is arrested "on business." Furthermore, a share of the *take* is saved for him, and money is regularly set aside for bail to be used by any member.

The reply of one informant when queried about this procedure is graphically illustrative and provides a good summary.

Hell, no, the guy went into this with his eyes wide open. Oh, sure, we'd feel sorry for the guy, but, hell, he'd be on his own. If he were arrested we'd split to save our own necks. He'd be expected to keep his mouth shut, but that can only last for a little while. Whatever dough there was would be split amongst the guys out; if we get caught we'd come to an understanding later, but if he ratted he'd have nothing coming.

Robbers give little thought to being arrested while actively engaging in robbery. That such occurrence is an eventuality is recognized but is given little weight. Should an arrest be made, the arrestee expects no assistance from his partners. Conversely, the group expects the member arrested to remain silent but is realistic enough to understand that this cannot be a permanent situation; nevertheless, it may apply sanctions if the arrested member gives information too readily. In view of the seriousness of the offense, robbers are rarely released on bail once arrested. When bail is set, it is usually a high amount which the arrested member has difficulty in obtaining. Were a fund established by a robbery group to meet this need it would have to be a considerable sum, something prohibitive for most groups of robbers. Both the nature of the robbery venture and the type of group that emerges precludes this kind of foresight.

Hence there is little evidence in the social organization of robbers of group cohesion during periods of stress in the manner described by Sutherland. The robber's organization is a more fluid arrangement, taking into account existing conditions; it is not conceived by those involved as a permanent group but more or less a loose confederation of individuals joined together for a specific purpose on a short-term basis. Among certain types of robbers specific role relationships do develop; however, these always are assumed to be temporary by the robbery participants even though the association is of some duration. When this type of social organization exists no provision need be made for incapacitated members; each member considers himself on his own.

5. Members of the mob are to deal honestly with each other.

This rule generally applies to armed robber groups. As was pointed out under rule 1, participants are expected to make even division of the stolen money and are required to

deal honestly in matters of robbery. But this expectation applies only to matters of the immediate present; hence robbers are not expected, for example, to reveal all their background or even be completely honest when they do. Most robbers anticipate that their partners will exaggerate about their past exploits as robbers, other criminal activities, prison experiences, dealings with women, etc., and openly tolerate a certain amount of these exaggerations when such information is supplied. Furthermore, robbers, as a rule, do not reveal too much about themselves to each other with the exception of current pressing problems, the stated reasons, which bring them into robbery. This lack of candor is respected. But there are "understandings" and cues which reveal much to the robber about his associates.

. . . And, well, I don't know it's just kind of a thing, you meet some guy and you say, I like him, and he likes you, and so you start horsing around, well, you don't know each other, really, you don't know anything about each other, but eventually, it comes out, you know. You let it slip you ask him about something—how do you like what you're doing—and he says—it's whole lot better than doing time. Then I knew, and I told him yeah, and you finally out on your backgrounds. So, we get to talking about an easy way to make money. . . . He says "I know a couple of guys, and we all got guns, and we can go out and hit a few places now and then. If we don't hit it heavy, we won't get caught." So, we started doing this stuff. . . .

. . . You are not exactly hanging around in a place for a long period of time, which we were. We were there, oh hell, six out of the seven nights a week. And, quite naturally, you learn to know somebody by their conversation, at least outwardly, you know them. And eventually the money is going to drain out; then a suggestion is going to come up, provided you feel that the person you are talking to is of your same caliber, and evidently when I met him at this particular time I felt that I could trust him, and I think it was my suggestion, if I remember correctly, that he come in with me. And between the two of us, why, we did a series of robberies.

Unless the robbers are acquaintances of long standing or are related and aware of each other's backgrounds, these understandings play a significant part in the trust relationship that becomes established.

6. Members voluntarily leaving the mob may ask to be taken back in, but it would not be proper for the leader of the mob to request they return.

This is another rule which is not applicable to armed robbers; indeed, there is serious question as to leadership in the first place. Any member is privileged to leave the group any time. He may also "sit one out" if he feels a particular robbery will be too dangerous for him, although this is not a frequent practice. Leaving robbery voluntarily is a rare occurrence; when it does occur it is temporary, and returning presents no problems. There are no particular rules of etiquette that govern robbery group conduct as the group is not a tightly knit organization with fixed personnel and standards of behavior. The needs of the moment dictate the method of operation; there are few subtleties or niceties among robbers, and in this respect also, a group of robbers bears little resemblance to the mob described by Sutherland's thief.

7. Members of the mob are not held responsible for events which they cannot control.

This is the only rule that seems relevant; robbers as well as thieves do not appreciably blame each other too severely for certain blunders that are made.

. . . We planned to get around $30,000 to $40,000 or $80,000 out of this bank; as it turned out, this one who was spending the money, he's quite a nervous fellow, anyhow, he went into the vault, had the assistant manager go into the vault, and there was a big sack. It must have been as big as a mail sack, and he picked it up and said, "What's in this?" It was locked, and the guy said it was nonnegotiable securities, so the kid let it down. Turned out it was $40,000. . . . Anyhow he went out and cleaned out two or three of the cages and he got $10,000 out of that but . . . he thought he had more . . . we found out we had missed $40,000 so we were kinda grumbling at him for overlooking it but we figured he didn't have any experience and he wouldn't know how much paper would weigh anyhow. . . .

Here a loss of $40,000 was rationalized away as insufficient experience. At a later

time this same individual again made a costly error and again he was excused.

So that time we got $16,500 and $17,000. . . . Again we passed up $80,000, I think it was, I forget the reason why they missed it. But again it was the same guy who goofed it up. . . .

The fates enter heavily into robbers' lives in general, and this is merely an instance of the common tendency among robbers to use "fate" as a rationale of life. It's the "breaks" that count; you either have them or not. Fate is deemed to control the robber's destiny; when the cards are right, when the dice are right, when the *setup* is perfect, nothing can go wrong, but if luck is against you, "you haven't got a chance." It therefore becomes easy to excuse what would under ordinary circumstances be considered an unforgivable error. Also with this rationale the occasional violence that occurs may be explained away as an accidental twist of fate. The fate motif is probably more responsible for the group attitude of not holding members responsible for uncontrollable events than any other aspect in the robber's group life. This seeming reversion to magic on the part of the robber is difficult to explain. One would expect a lessening of this motif as the robber becomes more proficient—i.e., as he has learned to reduce the hazards and is more in control of the situation; however, such is not the case. The fate motif is discernible in all levels of robbers' groups. It may be that robbery, no matter how well planned, in view of its direct personal interaction, always presents the possibility of uncontrollable hazards and hence uncertainty.

8. No member of a mob should cut in on another member. This is another etiquette rule which forbids any mob member from "cramping the style" of another. The exception being an emergency or an inexperienced member who has been given only a minor role to perform.

Robbers, when necessary, help each other out in the performance of a robbery in the event of an "emergency." The rule appears to refer to mobs of pickpockets or shoplifters, and only in a very general way would be applicable to a group of robbers.

9. The last mob maxim refers to the mob member's responsibility to do everything possible to fix a case for any other member of the mob who may have been arrested as a result of mob activities.

This raises the entire question regarding the practice of "fixing" cases, bribes, etc., as it exists today and would go beyond the confines of this paper. It is quite clear that the *fix* as described by Sutherland with reference to thieves is not practiced by contemporary armed robbers.

ARREST STRATEGY

If arrested, the strategy is to obtain the best "deal" with the prosecutor on the basis of the amount of information and evidence known to him. The "fixer" as described in the *Professional Thief* is unknown to the informants. Members of robber troupes also express no feelings of obligation to help out a member arrested; the main concern is with maintaining their own individual anonymity.

The practice of obtaining the best "bargain" possible often requires the revelation of the crime partners' identities in exchange for a more favorable disposition; knowledge of the possibility of this occurrence creates considerable anxiety on the part of a group when one of its members is arrested. The result, therefore, is for all members to "split" and attempt to "ride it out" if possible, but it is a well-known fact among robbers that the arrest of one usually spells the end for all. Hence, under present circumstances, the last thing a robber would think about is to attempt a "fix" even were it possible, for not only would he reveal his identity and suffer the likelihood of arrest but he would also defeat a possible bargaining position of his associates.

DISCUSSION

From the foregoing comparison it becomes obvious that the group of careerist robbers seems to bear only slight resemblance to the mob that Sutherland describes. How can one account for this difference? One obvious answer is simply that times have changed and so has the complexity of relationships in society. What was possible during the first quarter or more of this century is no longer feasible under present circumstances. The entire scope and function of law enforcement has changed, making certain criminal styles obsolete. One need only mention the revolutionary developments in systems of identification of criminals, modern communication, transportation methods, and methods of scientific investigation to stress the point.

The mob as an organized form of criminal activity must be related to a particular point in historical experience, a point where it served a purpose—a point where it was functional. During the first few decades of this century the "mob style" was particularly adapted to the social conditions of the day; the "fix" was possible because personal relationships were simpler and more direct. Criminals, as well as others, knew each other personally with the resultant development of congeniality and rules of behavioral etiquette which guided the criminal mob both in its relationship among its own members and with outsiders. With the increasing complexity of society, these relationships were no longer possible, and the mob was due to change. To paraphrase Bell, as the style of society changed, so did, in lagging fashion, its style of crime.

There is, however, another reason why the robber's group differs from the mob. The mob, in general, referred to the organization of professional theft, which Sutherland distinguishes from robbery on the basis of style. Whereas the thief relies chiefly on wits, front, and talking ability, Sutherland declares, ". . . robbers, kidnappers and others who engage in the 'heavy rackets' are generally not regarded as professional thieves for they depend primarily on *manual dexterity or force*." However, there are those robbers who "use their wits, 'front,' and talking ability, and these are regarded by the professional thieves as belonging to the profession." The robber's group also reflects the peculiar style of the robber; the elements of robbery require a different type of organization in order for the crime to be carried to completion. Furthermore, the robber's group reflects the life-style of persons not concerned with the etiquette of relationships nor the reciprocals inherent in group life but chiefly concerned with accomplishing a specific goal—the rapid accumulation of money.

The armed robber's entire engagement in robbery differs from the professional thief's engagement in theft, even when the former possesses "wit, front, and talking ability." Both the quality and the nature of the commitment itself differ, with the robber being more compelled in his action in the sense of feeling restricted as to the alternative courses of action open to him. He is in a "get-rich-quick enterprise" and as such needs to move quickly and strike swiftly when the opportunity presents itself. In his scheme of action, he simply does not have time for the amenities of the professional thief, nor can he appreciate the latter's moderate approach to profit. The formal relationships of the mob are not functional for his needs; more adaptable to the style necessary for the accomplishment of his goal is the social organization represented by the partnership. Much as the professional thief resembled other professionals, the careerist robber resembles the businessman who conducts his business through the tutelage of a partnership. The robber similarly works through a group of partners with whom he shares equally in what risks there are and invests his services to the total enterprise. As a partner he shares in the profits and losses of the operation. The partnership also provides opportunity for differentiation of various tasks necessary to carry out a robbery and to plan its strategy. Career robbery is conducted in and through partnerships; the lone systematic robber is rare.

Armed career robbers then develop a form of social organization that is essentially dissimilar to the model originally proposed by Sutherland for professional thieves, which by extension has been applied to all profes-

sional criminal activities. A closer examination of career armed robbery will serve to further distinguish this form of deviant action from other criminal behavior systems.

FUNCTIONAL DIFFERENTIATION AND GROUP STRUCTURE IN CAREER ROBBERY

From the beginning the strategy or engineering of a *job* is a group product and must be viewed in an interaction context. An individual may present a solid robbery plan to his associates which is eventually acted upon; however, there is always deliberation by the group. Thus, partnership consensus must be reached prior to the commission of any act of robbery.

Although there is little discernible evidence of distinctive leadership roles, previous experiences of members are given due recognition. Where leaders are recognizable, they become most apparent in adroit partnerships, in the less definitive form of what might more appropriately be titled *planning consultants*. The role behavior is one of guiding rather than directing and in this sense fully meets the role expectations of the members of the partnership. Some members may become more persuasive than others, but dicta from partners are frowned upon and do not constitute the basis of action. When there is divergence of opinion, there is majority rule of sorts, but as has been implied, there is no enforcement of majority rule on dissident members, rather, the partners make accommodations.

It may be argued that in terms of the explicit goals of the partnership these types of arrangements are functional, since to force an unwilling or dissident member to join in a robbery would only endanger the whole group. The success of the partnership depends on cooperative effort. The group then is a partnership of equals, each with a voice; what leadership arises comes out of mutual recognition of the expertise of an individual member, which serves the group's goals.

These deliberations are informally structured, vary in duration of time, and are likely to occur anywhere the potential participants happen to be congregated—an automobile, a bar, a motel room—throughout, it is a rational and deliberative, albeit at times haphazard, process of decision making. Once the decision is reached that a particular robbery or series of robberies is to be performed, there does not appear to exist a specific pattern of planning the robbery encounter. The planning of a robbery may vary from a simple drive around a neighborhood to "case a joint" to a series of complex maneuvers; the strategy employed depends on the type of robbery and the sophistication of those involved.

Prior to any robbery, however, no matter what the level of potential complexity, assignments are made as to the role each partner is to play in the encounter. In this effort the strengths and weaknesses of various members may be assessed and conclusions reached as to the roles best fitted to each participant. Again this decision is reached through group interaction; no single individual gives orders or assigns positions without group and individual consensus.

The account of one respondent who preferred not to participate directly in holdups but was a competent driver describes the process of how one such decision was reached.

For one reason, I wasn't going in, that was the first reason. I told them that, but they wanted me to go in. Then they got talking about that he (another partner) was going to drive the car because one of them couldn't see good, and the second one, he's so damn nervous he'd probably take the key out and put it in his pocket and then couldn't find the key. We didn't think he would keep his head cool enough to stay in the car listening to the radio calls come in, especially if one came in that said there was a robbery in progress. Then we didn't know how to trust the fourth guy that just came in; we didn't know whether he might run off and leave all of us, if all three of us went in. He probably wasn't going to do it, but they were considering it. Well, anyway, it all boiled down to that I should be driving the car because I don't get excited and I drive well.

At other times a more flexible arrangement is used, with assignments shifting from robbery to robbery. The functional differentiation depends chiefly on what talents are available; however, the temperament of individual partners also may enter as a determinant.

We switched around. One time I went in with——; at other times——went in. We sorta decided on the spur of the moment. All of us were pretty good, so it didn't matter. It sorta depended on how we felt at the time—you know, the mood we were in—so we usually sorta decided beforehand; we agreed on who would go in . . .

A loose type of specialization results which is flexible and adaptable according to circumstances. In this way partnerships conform to fluctuations of members' moods and the possible eccentricities of various individuals. Individuality is never completely relinquished by the careerist. He cooperates but he is never subjugated. He fits himself into the allocated roles of the partnership to accomplish certain purposes but tries whenever possible to carry them out on his own terms. In so doing, he attempts to use the partnership as a vehicle to reach his goal—nothing more.

THE MINIMUM ESSENTIALS—THE ACTOR'S ROLE

The successful completion of a robbery depends mainly on the coordination of various tasks that must be completed. Through coordination and specialization of roles of participants in the robbery, the robbery group not only assures more protection to itself but adds a measure of efficiency and shock in quickly overtaking the victim by a show of disciplined force. A well operating partnership need have only three men to successfully carry out profitable robberies. Sometimes the same results may be obtained by a dyad, but generally a group of three men appears to be the most tactically effective unit.

The typical career robbery triad consists of two men who enter the establishment armed; the third remains outside in the vicinity in an automobile and is usually armed but need not be. Of the two men who perform the actual robbery, one is considered the backup. It is his function to watch any customers in the establishment, prevent any from leaving, and cover those that might enter while his partner gathers the cash. At times he assists also in gathering the *take* if there are no customers or other conditions that need his attention. The wheel or wheelman, in addition to driving the get-away-car also acts as lookout or pointman, and at times is given added responsibilities of a variety of sorts.

An example of a wheelman's role in a series of bank robberies is informative both of his role obligation and the rather sophisticated planning that may take place in some partnerships. Not all robberies committed by the careerist robber are this well planned and executed, but the interview excerpt describes the extent to which the systematic robber may go to assure his goal.

I. So then you had the place cased and then did you commit the robbery?

S. No. we decided against it for some reason. I think we might have kept refining our plans as we went along and what we had done was decided, well we found that there were a number of characteristics the bank had to have before it was acceptable into our situation; one, it had to have a nice getaway, so we could abandon one car if a police car or some citizen chased us; we didn't want to shoot anyone, you know, or shoot at them or be shot at, so we could leave this car and either jump a fence or go through a culvert or through a walkway so no car could follow us and report it. Then we could go over and pick up another car and then take off. So not all banks would fit into this sort of category. . . . Anyhow, my job was to go up the telephone pole and cut the telephone wires so they couldn't call the cops. And then as soon as I cut the wires then these two walk in the bank and then I would go down the pole and get in the car. We had a police radio so we could tell if the cops got a signal, I could drive up to the bank and honk; otherwise I could get into the car and give them one minute exactly to go clean out the bank.

I. How did you decide on the one minute?

S. Well, we figured how long it would take, if everyone cooperated, and we decided that one minute would probably be safe. So anyway they went in. They had the stocking caps up under these men's hats, snap brim hats, and then they had masks that dropped down, I think one of them had a stocking cap that pulled over and the other one had a mask that just dropped down. So as soon as they walked in the door they just dropped it; customers walked in and noticed it; they just walked out; they didn't believe there was a bank robbery going on. So I sat there and watched all of that. I was just sitting there listening to the radio and watching my watch. So anyhow, as soon as one minute was up, I left the parking place, looking carefully to see that there were no cops, and I drove up to the bank and just as I did, the guy inside, one was holding at bay and the other was getting the money, he got nervous or something. Anyway, he gathered up all he could and ran out the door just at the very minute I got to the door, just as we had rehearsed it, and I had the doors open for him. They jumped in the car and off we went. And all the customers and people out on the sidewalk just going like this and I don't think anybody chased us, although later we heard somebody did. It was some three blocks back. So we got about $10,000 out of that. We pulled the car up near a school and went down a little ravine and jumped into another car, drove it to one of the fellow's house and drove it right into his garage, pulled the garage door down, went out the back door and went into his cottage and got in there and stayed in there listening to the police radio. . . .

Additional men may be added depending on the size of the robbery and its felt complexity; however, these men perform no different roles from the basic triad. They assist those engaged in the holdup; that is, they become extra personnel.

The wheelman does not have assistants but often has additional responsibilities such as planning the escape route, obtaining the getaway car, arranging lodging, and acting as lookout. There is general agreement among career robbers that the wheel has the greatest responsibility at the critical period of escape; as such, he is required to be the most "mature" of the group.

No matter how many robbers participate in a robbery and no matter how functionally differentiated the partnership might be, the element of surprise and momentary domination of the scene must be maximized if the robbery is to be successfully completed.

Robberies are foiled if (a) the victim is not surprised, (b) the coordination of the partnership is poor, or (c) the robbers do not completely dominate the scene. Violence is also likely to occur if any one or combinations of these conditions exist. The aim, therefore, is to so structure the situation that the victim is rendered helpless to resist and "cooperates" toward the successful completion of the crime. In the words of one robber, "It has to be a smooth operation or else someone is likely to get hurt." To accomplish this goal, robbers employ a number of tactics or styles with varying degrees of "smoothness" which reveal different levels of planning and proficiency, depending in part on the type of partnership and in part on the situation.

STYLES OF CAREER ROBBERY

These robbery tactics may for purposes of discussion be divided into three categories and labeled according to style of approach.

1. *The Ambush.* This type of robbery is the least planned of all and depends almost entirely on the element of surprise. All participants literally attack an establishment guerrilla fashion and attempt to obtain whatever might be found in cash or other items of value. There is no sophistication in this style of robbery, and it is considered the *lowest* form of robbery from the viewpoint of the careerist. There is almost randomness in the selection of the victim, with no thought as to what conditions might be present in the situation that may affect the outcome of the robbery. It is also the type of robbery where the chances of violence are high. As a rule it is a style employed by less systematic robbers.

2. *The Selective Raid.* In this form there is a minimum of planning. Sites are tentatively selected and cased, even though very briefly. Site conditions are analyzed to some degree before the robbery is attempted. There is a tentative plan of approach; however, the planning may be accomplished very casually, and several robberies may be committed in rapid succession.

3. *The Planned Operation.* Robberies that fall into this category are well-planned and well-structured crimes where all aspects are carefully delineated in the group and each

partner knows his part well. At times there may be rehearsals, or dry runs, so that all possible conditions are taken into account. Risks are held at a minimum.

It would be ideal, for purposes of analysis, if partnerships practiced one style during the life of the group. Such, however, is not the case. Each individual partnership practices different styles of robbery during its existence. Thus, for example, one partnership that is in the planning stages of a *planned operation* may commit a few *selective raids* to finance what is thought to be a more lucrative robbery. On the other hand, certain groups may practice only one style and become quite proficient in it. Generally, however, the *ambush* is a desperation measure for careerists and is resorted to only when an emergency occurs, such as the threatened capture of the group where money for flight must be raised quickly.

ROBBERY SKILLS

This raises the issue of skills required to engage in robbery. Obviously the three robbery styles require different levels of planning ability and creative potential. A *planned operation* may be a highly sophisticated crime, requiring unique creative capacities, whereas an *ambush* can be attempted by anyone. A number of skills, therefore, are necessary to plan the more resourceful types of robberies that are committed by the careerist. In order to engage in robberies other than the ambush, the robber must have a sense of organization, timing, ability to take into account unforeseen events, etc. But these are skills or capacities of planning which bring structure to the robbery; the robbery itself requires little skill or ability. The synthesizing of robbery requires talent; its commission does not. This is not the case with certain other professional crimes, the variety of which Sutherland speaks. Compare the pickpocket, who must learn intricate sets of muscular movements, learn to perfect the art of misdirection in order to become successful in his endeavor, or the booster who must learn techniques of concealment and misdirection to avoid detection as a shoplifter. The confidence man has to develop a high degree of front, wit, and talking ability, before he can carry out his swindle. All the robber needs, in the final analysis, is a revolver. This one attribute can make him the master of the situation. The skill involved in robbery pertains to the style employed and to the amount of planning of which the individual partnership is capable. These skills may be brought to robbery and need not necessarily be learned exclusively through interaction with other robbers. They may, however, be modified and shaped to meet the conditions of the robbery situation. Noncriminal learning structures may provide the necessary qualifications which may easily be converted to robbery.

Military experience of a certain variety, for example, lends itself readily to robbery.

> . . . And I thought, well, with four of us—I can start running out squad training techniques—another of those I learned in the military and that possibly we could start . . . doing some fairly large things. One thing I had sort of in mind—I thought of taking . . . the golf prizes from the . . . Lodge which usually involves a couple hundred thousand dollars—and—doing it around the point by water—and we had actually run an intelligence project on this. . . . My partner had made it a point to become acquainted with and questioned fairly thoroughly, if indirectly, a fellow that worked in the office there—the assistant to the accountant—and so we actually knew much of the scheduling around the handling of this money and the operation of the Lodge and we were going to make our approach by water—and with four of us operating as a commando unit, it would have gone quite smoothly. I approached the thing as I would approach a military problem. I ran general intelligence rather than just the sort of thing that usually in the criminal profession is called casing. I had hoped to train my men to the——disguise that didn't bear the earmarks of camouflage—whistles and so forth.

Business acumen may also be turned to robbery.

> I planned it just like I've seen businesses operate and what I did in my own "front" business. We checked out details just like anybody running a firm. I didn't want anybody getting hurt or getting too excited, so I checked to see whether anybody had heart trouble in the

bank through channels I knew about that are open to employers . . .

These planning capacities may, of course, come from previous criminal experiences or, indeed, through association with robbers, but need not be limited to these sources.

The skills of robbery, therefore, center mainly around planning ability. The greater the organization aptitudes of the members of the partnership, the greater the number of *planned operations* in the career of the partnership. The greater the number of *planned operations*, the more successful the partnership becomes, the more likely the pattern will continue.

It is as a consequence of planning ability being brought to robbery that relatively newly formed partnerships may adopt more sophisticated styles from the beginning and are thus able to prolong their careers because of their expertise. Furthermore, during the initial period they may be unknown robbers, a characteristic which tends to lessen the probability of detection. Thus one bank robber states:

> It was really a well-planned job, and we knew exactly what to do. It was perfect. . . . Now I'm known. I've been mugged and printed. I wouldn't think of trying anything. Hell, every time somebody pulls something around here and even faintly resembles me, I better have a good alibi.

PATTERNS OF ACTIVITY

Related to the particular style of the robber partnership is the choice of victim. Although among careerists there is a definite victim preference, there is much divergence among partnerships as to the type of victim preferred; hence, few generalizations can be made. Nevertheless, careerists would consider banks, loan companies, supermarkets, drugstores, bars, liquor stores, gas stations, and corner groceries a fair ranking of victims in descending order of profit but not necessarily in terms of preference. Intervening variables —i.e., the conditions sought or avoided in the robbery setting—are the important determinants in the selection of robbery victims. The victim is always viewed as part of a larger configuration; his profit potential is never the sole consideration for the armed robber. These variables, however, become different objects of concern depending on the partnership. Identical sets of conditions may be perceived in completely opposite terms by different groups of armed robbers, and distinctive, nevertheless contradictory, rationales concerning these differential perceptions develop.

Thus, for example, contrast the different victim perception of supermarkets and the antithetical rationales concerning the optimum time that robberies should be perpetrated.

There's usually quite a bit of money and there is usually quite a bit of disorganized activity. There is very little danger of being shot in the store. Many stores will have a lookout arrangement and an armed person at the lookout arrangement from, say, a walled mezzanine or something. A robber is very apt to be shot from concealment. There are enough people moving about in a supermarket that this is not very apt to happen. Your safest bet is probably a supermarket. . . .

Yes, we preferred to take an action either when there were other people in the store, which would be during operating hours, or before they would have occasion to expect anyone to be able to enter and set up a defense. . . .

We didn't ever develop any real pattern relative to that [best time of day]. We took one early in the morning when they were unloading supply trucks in the back—shortly after the time that we felt the safe would be open on its time lock. We've taken others in the late evening. Really there was—so far as we determined by operating it—no reason for taking it at one time of the day rather than at another. . . .

. . . the biggest factor was—was the place crowded? And we never did anything in the daytime. So the biggest factor was how many people would be in—that was how many people would be in that place about the time we wanted to walk in. And this is why we cruised the streets. We may just stop at a place and walk right in and rob it, because there was no one in there. . . .

Say an average of three or four people in there, which is detrimental, you can't watch all of them at the same time. Banks, well, that's like a racetrack. You've always got people. So, in my thinking the less people the better. And even the supermarket there is always too many

people in there, until absolute closing time, let them lock me in, and then I knew just where the two people were. . . .

As a consequence of these differing patterns of social perception of optimum robbery conditions and diverse interpretations as to the impact of these conditions, no unitary model of what robbers consider the ideal robbery setting is possible. Individual armed robbers all have varying opinions and rationales to such degree that the "perfect setup" may be spoken about, but there is little commonality in its explication among robbery partnerships.

The potential *take* thus never is the single criterion of victim choice, but the contingencies, as interpreted by each partnership, enter as important variables of victim selection. For this reason few careerists become bank robbers, although the lure of the vast sums to be had and the excitement involved are attractive. Generally, banks present a multiplicity of conditions to take into account; as a result they are considered only by the more accomplished partnerships as potential victims. Contrary to some accounts, banks fall prey more often to the amateur than to the committed robber. Indeed, those careerists who do specialize in bank robberies tend to fear the amateur bank robber as a potential source of difficulty.

The guy who sticks up a bank who doesn't know what he is doing makes it tough all around. He's never in control, and somebody is liable to take advantage—some hero—then there is violence. This makes it hard, for when some dude comes in who really means business they think he's just another amateur and things get out of control and somebody is liable to get hurt.

Quantitatively, careerists tend to prefer what might be termed victims of the middle range: liquor stores, drug stores, and supermarkets.

Retail liquor establishments play a peculiar role as careerists' victims; they are popular yet not necessarily preferred. Their very prevalence in urban communities and ready availability most hours of the day and night, however, make them easy if not choice victims, lending themselves readily to serial robbery. A series of liquor store holdups can yield a handsome sum, even though the single store may only give small reward.

We hit nothing but liquor stores, sometimes two or three a night. We'd make 20, 50, 100 bucks a store—that's at the most 300 split 3 ways—you'd have to hustle to make it. . . .

Although it is difficult to point to any single victim preference, among armed robbers there are a number of themes of victim choice on which there is some unanimity.

RATIONALES, MYTHS, AND VALUES

Perhaps it is imprecise to speak of a victim from the point of view of the robber, for to him a victim in the usual sense of the term is rarely present in the crime situation. Careerist partnerships make conscious efforts to choose as sites for robberies locales that are either parts of corporations or large organizations. The employee with whom the robbery encounter is made is considered to have nothing at stake, since there is no personal loss for him; at most he is conceived of as an agent-victim. It is quite clear in the career robber's rationale that for an employee to worry about a sum of money that does not belong to him in the first place is foolish. He views the actual robbery encounter as an impersonal matter, for in so doing he is not robbing a person but some amorphous mass —a bank, a supermarket, a loan company. In the actual robbery confrontation he may be dealing with a role incumbent, but the role is only in the vaguest sense representative of the impersonal company which is the object of his attack. Hence it is inconceivable to the career robber that an agent-victim should resist, since there is no cause for resistance; no one loses personally. Careerists rarely rob the patrons who happen to be in an establishment at the time of the robbery, precisely because the encounter is deemed too personal.

The careerist robber frowns on other robbers who rob individuals, considers them amateur "hot heads" and "bums who make it hot for everybody." Small neighborhood grocery stores and gas stations are the domain not of the careerist but of the latter type of robber.

No, we'd only hit big markets. They're insured anyway. Nobody is out of pocket. . . . Why should some small clerk put up a fuss? It isn't his money. They're not hurting. . . .

The careerists' ambivalence about robbing liquor stores becomes clearer when one realizes that often these businesses are owner-operated. Under such circumstances it is difficult to avoid a person who may have "something at stake," but even in these circumstances there is always the insurance rationale.

I try to make sure the owner isn't around by knocking the place over late at night, figuring he'll have somebody working for him then who wouldn't care.
I. And if the owner is around?
S. The insurance would cover him anyway, but it's riskier. The employee doesn't care; the owner does, and he might be concerned. . . .

Whenever possible, the careerist robber attempts to avoid the "human" in the situation; where it is unavoidable, he overcomes it by the rationale of recovery. Not unlike the soldier who makes a different object out of a human being by calling him the "enemy," the robber makes redefinitions in the very process of becoming a careerist. His victims are already depersonalized objects to him; robbing an impersonal business or company only makes it simpler and, as we shall see subsequently, more acceptable.

Next to the denial of the victims, the conception of honesty has an important place in the robber's rationale system. Sweeping aside the inherent paradox, the career robber views his form of acquisition as a not-too-dishonest enterprise. This appears at first glance as a peculiar stance, but becomes more intelligible when the behavioral elements that make up the robbery situation are examined. Robbery is an open, direct, face-to-face encounter coupled with a nondisguised coercive demand; there is no stealth or furtiveness, as with a thief, but a confrontation of unabashed power. It is this quality of candor that the robber equates with honesty, an apologia which in his own self-reflexive action makes the robbery career an object of worth, if not noble.

No, I never thought of committing other kinds of crime. It just never occurred to me.

I never thought about writing checks or stealing; somehow, I don't know—this will sound funny—but it just never seemed honest. It's funny. I can't really explain it. . . .

I. What do you mean, it wasn't *honest*?

S. Well I just—I couldn't steal anything. You know—behind someone's back. When I took something I'd make no bones about it. I didn't hide or make out phony papers. I don't know. I guess it's just sorta being yourself—you just take it in front of the guy; you don't pussyfoot it around and do a lot of pretending. . . .

And something else—it's a lot cleaner. You feel better about it. You're a pretty big man standing there with your gun. Makes you feel, oh—kinda important—big, somebody people don't mess with. . . .

To the robber, then, the career gives importance and is a noncontrived means of gaining a goal from a "faceless" victim in a situation in which if all "play their cards right" no one suffers.

A considerable attraction of robbery is its challenge and its call to action—qualities which are savored by the careerist and discussed in the partnership. The review and postmortem of each robbery adds further excitement and stimulation to the career. With each completed robbery a victory is achieved. In the postmortem interaction each success binds the partnership further and provides the motive for continued involvement. In this fashion, each robbery serves to stimulate the next where there is always the chance of richer rewards. Thus the career continues, and with continued success there is the ever-present proof that "nothing can go wrong." A myth of invincibility gradually develops and takes shape, and often is the precursor to the dissolution of the partnership through capture.

As already pointed out, careerists do not think in terms of capture; although they are aware of the possibility, it is always a remote awareness. As the career unfolds for the individual robber, confidence grows that no one can break his pattern—as long as he is careful. Continued interaction with his crime partners serves to reify the myth.

Yeah, we thought we'd go on indefinitely, and not get caught. I think this is everybody's feeling—that they'll never get caught. I think everything that somebody does, that they are conscious of, they think they have this feeling that they'll never get caught. I heard it time after time. "Shit, I had such a thing going for me that I thought I'd never get caught." I really don't think that the consequences are really thought about at all.

Akin to the invincibility myth is the myth of the *utopian heist*. This refers to what most careerists call the "big job," the most lucrative robbery. It is to be the final event which leads to retirement—the robbery that promises to end robbery. It is the ever-alluring pot of gold at the end of the rainbow—the solution to all the careerist's ills. In this connection, one must remember that the careerist's commitment to robbery is viewed by him as a temporary affair. To him robbery is a career escalator to more conventional endeavors. He hopes to return triumphantly where he has previously failed. The "pot of gold" could lead him there quickly. Partnerships discuss the "big job," sometimes with fervor, as a realistic possibility. In the loosely knit group of the partnership the *utopian heist* has a coalescing function. Moreover, it serves to focus the robbers' attention toward continued involvement.

When the rare "big job" is accomplished, events do not change for the rewards are dissipated only to start the cycle anew.

. . . he and I took off and got us a couple of girls, and we went down to Mexico. Well, we had a heck of a time getting across the border, because we had to cash it all into small bills. Part of it we left buried up around our homes. And we stayed down there about a week horsing around. Came back and decided we didn't want to go back to work, because it was too easy. And we started getting a little bit too rambunctious and almost every night we'd look for a place to rob. We weren't satisfied with what we had. Good clothes, the leisurely hours and the girls you could spend a lot of money on, and check into the biggest hotels, the nicest motels, all of this stuff kinda went to make us go out every night for some more.

THE CAREER ARMED ROBBER AS A TYPE

Viewed as a type, the individual careerist assumes the posture of a man whose round of life never quite seems to meet the standards of middle class convention. He need not have a delinquent background nor have committed serious crimes prior to his career, but the rhythm of his existence has never been in tune with the conventional.

Typically, the careerist represents one who lives on the fringes, more a "night" dweller than a "day" dweller. In his circle of intimate acquaintances are the hustler, the bookie, the gambler, and the pimp; the bartender, the taxidriver, and the bellhop. Involvement in robbery does not remove him from this life arena but locks him more securely in it. The career, however, promises upward social mobility; thus the robbery ostensibly to finance a legitimate business, to open a motel, to enable a trip, to start anew, but the style of life does not permit it. As the careerist reveals, he "blows it" and thus remains true to the "easy come, easy go" style of his social surroundings. Whereas the racketeer or organized criminal may achieve respectability for himself and his family, the career robber never translates his economic gain into objects of legitimate social worth or more conventional style of life. Hence, the career does not change the existing life-style; rather, it is an extreme expression of it and functions for the careerist as a transitory, if illusive, transcendent experience.

On those infrequent occasions when the careerist terminates the career on his own volition, the previous life cycle is usually resumed with reasonably appropriate accommodations as to costs and risks. The involuntary termination of the career, however, often leads to even further estrangement, for as Lemert has suggested, ". . . [when] the ex-convict advances economically to the point where better positions become open to him, he may be rejected because of inability to obtain a bond or because his past criminal record comes to light. If the man's aspirational roles are low, he may adjust successfully as, say, a laborer or casual worker; otherwise, he nearly always shows the marks of his difficult struggle."

The careerist thus eventually returns to his former milieu after the career is ended, whether he leaves it voluntarily or is forced to relinquish it by being caught and confined. In the latter instance, however, the stigmatic burden of the identified criminal makes it extremely difficult for him ever to lift himself above his circle.

I did a lot of time for a few robberies. I'm not complaining, I shoulda known better . . . when you come out you're right back where you started only worse, nobody knows you and times have changed. So you knuckle under—you can make it—but you sure have to change your way of thinking. You can't be afraid of carrying a lunch bucket—if you don't you're sunk or you go back to capering and the same old shit starts over again.

The brief triumph leads to defeat or accommodation that must ultimately involve a reorganization of the self toward acceptance of a modified role as an actor on the social stage.

28. REFORMATION AND RECIDIVISM AMONG ITALIAN AND POLISH OFFENDERS

HAROLD FINESTONE

Reprinted from the American Journal of Sociology *72, no. 6 (May 1967): 575-88. Copyright © 1967 by the University of Chicago Press. Harold Finestone is Associate Professor of Sociology at the University of Minnesota. He has made important contributions to an understanding of the sociology of criminal behavior and drug use.*

■ A crucial influence on criminal careers is the process itself whereby persons are arrested, convicted, incarcerated, and reintroduced into the community after serving a sentence. It is the presumed purpose of the correction system to "reform" criminals in such a way that they give up their life of crime. Even the most cursory examination of the histories of persons arrested from crime, however, establishes that there is considerable recidivism—that is, repeated offenses and repeated convictions and sentencing. Prisons are hardly successful in rehabilitating their inmates.

Sociologists and psychologists have engaged in many studies of recidivism, with heavy emphasis on the personal characteristics that might distinguish recidivists from nonrepeaters. In this article Finestone is concerned, instead, with the contingencies that arise in the interaction between offenders and their personal communities after they are released from prison. He indicates important differences that depend on the ethnicity of the offenders; then he shows some of the ways in which the offender's ethnic community affects community workers' efforts to assist past offenders.

For studies of the effectiveness of prison and parole systems see Daniel Glaser, *The Effectiveness of a Prison and Parole System* (Bobbs-Merrill, 1964); and Paul W. Keve, *Imaginative Programming in Probation and Parole* (University of Minnesota Press, 1967). The journal *Federal Probation* regularly contains articles on probation and parole, as does the *National Probation and Parole Journal*. A systematic study that assesses the problem of recidivism is Leslie T. Williams, *Evaluation of Penal Measures* (Random House, 1969). ■

THE PURPOSE OF THIS STUDY is to develop an "organic picture" of reformation and recidivism among Italian and Polish offenders within the setting of their ethnic communities, as constructed from interviews devoted to obtaining "detailed and intimate descriptions" of these processes.

Since there is considerable variation in the rates of recidivism associated with different categories of offenders, it was decided to limit the study to a relatively homogeneous group for whom, as judged by a comparatively high rate of recidivism, reformation and recidivism referred to real practical issues. The information available indicates that the probability of recidivism is highest among property offenders. It also reveals that the most persistent careers within this group are likely to originate during the period of youth. . . .

The interview data were ordered by constructing types of the processes of social reintegration and recidivism for the offenders of each ethnic group. The procedure was inductive and based upon a detailed search for contrasts between the experiences of offenders of both ethnic groups and within each ethnic group between reforming and recidivating offenders. A number of contrasts were observed in such facets of post-release experience as employment status, family support, marital status, saliency of the criminal stigma, etc. These separate findings were then integrated into types. Finally, the goodness of fit between the types and the empirical instances provided by the actual cases was examined. Indeed, departures from the types were to be expected, since some variability among the cases in each ethnic group had been noted from the start.

The construction of types was guided by the assumption that in each ethnic community different kinds of problems were likely to become salient within the experience of released offenders. It then followed that reformation and recidivism could be conceived of as representing alternative responses to such problems. It was hypothesized that the kinds of problems most likely to confront returning Polish offenders would be those involving the gaining of acceptance. In contrast, it was hypothesized that the problems most frequently to be encountered by the Italians would be those clustering around finding, holding, and committing themselves exclusively to legitimate employment.

A second task for analysis entailed the identification of those structural and cultural features of each ethnic community which appeared to be most intimately involved in the generation of the kinds of problems just specified. The procedure here was similar to that adopted in the construction of types—that is, the systematic search for contrasts between the two ethnic communities. The various scholarly and literary sources available in the English language dealing with these two groups was a source of information. Comparative materials were sought depicting their social heritages, their cultural values, and their development as ethnic communities in North America.

From the hypothesis that there were contrasts between the two ethnic communities in the kinds of problems with which returning offenders would be confronted, it was possible to derive a proposition which could be tested empirically. If it were true that members of the Italian ethnic community, in general, and of the offenders' families, in particular, were more accepting of released criminal offenders than were the Poles, then it was inferred that these differences should also be reflected in an earlier stage of the offenders' careers—that is, in the relative frequency of visits received by Italian and Polish prison inmates from members of their families. In order to test this inference, a matched sample of 64

pairs of inmates was selected from among those whose first prison commitment had been to Pontiac Penitentiary, an institution located approximately 100 miles from Chicago. These pairs were matched for each of the following characteristics: by Chicago as place of origin and Cook County as the jurisdiction within which the criminal trial had been held, age, period of admission to prison, type of property offense, length of sentence, IQ, presence or absence of a record of misdemeanors prior to first prison sentence, number of siblings, and presence or absence of one or both parents.

All visits received by each inmate during the first 18 months of his imprisonment were recorded. These were tabulated according to the classification of the family visitors as parents, siblings, and "other relatives," a residual category. The findings are presented in Table 28.1.

Continuing now with the presentation of the types, the offender interview data disclosed that marital status was the factor showing the greatest discrimination between Polish offenders who became reintegrated and those who recidivated, followed in second place by the factor of drunkenness, and in third place by

TABLE 28.1

TOTAL AND AVERAGE NUMBER OF VISITS RECEIVED BY A MATCHED SAMPLE OF 64 ITALIAN AND POLISH INMATES DURING 18 MONTHS OF IMPRISONMENT AT PONTIAC PENITENTIARY, FROM THEIR PARENTS, SIBLINGS, AND OTHER RELATIVES

Relationship and Number of Visits	Ethnic Group	
	Italians	Poles
Parents:		
Total	769	311
Average	12.0	4.9
Siblings:		
Total	579	310
Average	9.0	4.8
Other relatives:		
Total	341	117
Average	5.3	1.8
All relationships:		
Total	1689	738
Average	26.3	11.5

employment status. Eight out of the ten Polish one-time offenders had been married during the post-prison period, as compared with four out of the fifteen recidivists. Analysis of the Polish cultural values had suggested that, although the solidarity of the Polish extended family system with its norms of mutual assistance and control had not tended to survive in America, the nuclear family itself had continued to show unusual strength and stability. Accordingly, those released Polish offenders who married were linking themselves to the most stable social form their ethnic community afforded. By becoming attached to their roles of husband and father, they were able to escape from, and compensate for, the relative indifference they encountered in their families of orientation and in the ethnic community. Moreover, to establish and support a family through reliance upon their own efforts exemplified the Polish cultural values of individualism and personal independence.

Just as the status of being married appeared to be associated with social reintegration, a resort to drunkenness appeared to be associated with recidivism. Eleven out of the fifteen Polish recidivists had engaged in excessive drinking during the post-prison period, as contrasted with four out of ten of the one-time offenders. The case histories of the recidivists revealed, moreover, that while many of them had been drinkers prior to their first penal commitment, the onset of excessive drinking had in most cases occurred during the post-release period.

It is suggested that marriage and drinking may be viewed as two alternatives, not necessarily mutually exclusive nor exhaustive, accessible to released Polish offenders and through which they attempted to cope with the problem of gaining acceptance in nondeviant social roles. The plausibility of doing so is supported by the observation of Thomas and Znaniecki that drinking by the immigrant was always performed in company and that by heightening social emotions it produced a substitute for the primary group atmosphere. Furthermore, like the meaning of marriage itself for the Polish offenders, a pattern of immoderate drinking could be expressive of values of individualism and personal independence.

As already indicated, employment status ranked third to marital status and drunkenness as a factor discriminating between those who reformed or recidivated. Only a small proportion of both classes of offenders were not regularly employed during the post-release period: 2 out of the 10 one-time offenders and 5 out of 15 recidivists. It thus appears that the status of being legitimately employed did not in itself assure that the released Poles would thereby gain access to nondeviant social roles. Moreover, these data suggest that alternatives to working were not commonly entertained by released Polish offenders; the necessity and the desirability of legitimate employment tended to be unquestioned by one-time offenders and recidivists alike.

The cultural background for this interpretation of the meaning of employment for these offenders may be indicated. In their unskilled or semiskilled occupational statuses, they were still not far removed from the occupational outlook of the first generation. In the orientation of the latter, work was possessed of both an obligatory and a religious character; the process rather than the results of work was important.

The peer-group role also did not appear to make accessible to the released Polish offenders any alternative means through which they could attain social acceptance. For members of the ethnic community at the lowest status levels, the structuring of the communal life on a parish basis tended indirectly to reinforce the nuclear family of procreation, and simultaneously to lower the relative importance of all other groupings. Consequently, the informal peer-group associations of adult males tended to be auxiliary to either their marital or their occupational roles and to be presupposed by their adequate performance of these latter roles.

This description of the roles accessible to the released Poles has suggested the relative paucity of channels of reentry to nondeviant roles accessible to them. Nevertheless, there was nothing in their situation as so far presented which implied that their return to criminality should be inevitable. It was, however, such as to induce in them an awareness of the extremely limited nature of their prospects of becoming reinstated in nondeviant roles, and to lead to the reorientation of their behavior around a new view of themselves as disillusioned, baffled, and defeated men. Such a sense of defeat tended to initiate a process of personal demoralization, frequently accompanied by excessive drinking, and by their progressive withdrawal from their already attenuated conventional ties. They now had little choice but to consort with others of similar background. Nevertheless, it is important to recognize that they could do so without intent of reverting to criminality and solely out of a wish for acceptance. Once such ties were formed, however, contingencies were likely to arise in which they were subject to procriminal pressures. One of them described the development of his relationship with a man who had a criminal record.

I thought that maybe he could be of help to me in alleviating my condition. I used to go over to his home or go to the tavern with him and his wife. I felt more at ease around him and his wife. There never was any reference to the past. I went out with him on a robbery while I continued to work. I didn't need my portion of the take.

Unlike the typical Italian recidivists who had described their reversion to criminality as a means to attaining clearly defined goals, the typical Polish recidivists evinced a noticeable tendency to dissociate themselves from the crimes which preceded their second commitment to prison. Some illustrations follow.

We went to this tavern on the way home. It was cold out. We had a few drinks there and we got to talking to this guy and we asked him if he wanted to go to some other place. So we were walking and the next thing I know we had him in the alley and I hit him and we took his money and that was it. We didn't discuss it or anything. It just happened that way. We went into another tavern and were drinking and that's where the police caught us. The guy had told them we were both intoxicated and the cops took a chance. There were only a few places open at 2:30 a.m. and they found us. We denied it. They found his watch on us and that was it and I was on my way back

here. We had enough money to drink, but on the way somehow we got him in the alley. I was drunk, because if I knew that I had stolen anything I would have gotten away. Here I was in a tavern a few blocks away. I can't explain that. After we sobered up at the police station we said, "Holy Christ! What did we do that for?"

They handcuffed me and on the way down to 11th and State they asked me questions about the holdups. I said I didn't know, I didn't believe that I had been there on the stickups. I had been drunk and had been at a dozen or more taverns. I asked my rap partners later and they said that I had been there. They said I was in both places. I asked them if I had a gun and they said no. They wouldn't let me have a gun in the condition I was in for I might have shot somebody. Even the people who fingered me said that I didn't have a gun.

It was merely an escapade. You get a futile feeling, and you say the hell with it, and you say this is just a caper.

Unlike the Poles, the returning Italian offenders were likely to encounter tolerant attitudes from members of their families and neighbors. Consequently, they would not find it difficult to become reinstated in nondeviant social roles. With a few exceptions, the acceptance and support of their families had been extended equally to all released Italian offenders, both to those who ultimately reformed and to those who returned to criminality. Unlike the Polish offenders, the marital role among Italian offenders did not appear to exercise an influence upon the outcome of their adjustment during the post-release period, which was discernibly independent of that exerted by their family of orientation. In the group, 8 out of 10 (80 percent) of the one-time offenders and 11 out of 19 (57.9 percent) of the recidivists had married either prior to or during the post-release period.

For the released Italian offenders, it appeared to be the legitimate employment role which generated the contingencies in which alternative modes of behavior were perceived to exist. All 10 of the reformed offenders had been regularly employed during the post-release period, as compared with 8 out of 18, or 44 percent, of the recidivists. An understanding of the problem which legitimate employment status poses for released Italians requires that their occupational and peer-group roles be viewed as intimately interrelated. This interrelationship is to be accounted for by the relatively greater importance of the role played by peer-group associations in the life organization of the Italians as contrasted with their Polish counterparts; and this in turn is a reflection of the greater importance of the adult male peer group in the social structure of the Italian ethnic community.

As has already been observed, the conjugal bond tended to exert a greater moral or controlling role among released Polish offenders than it did among the Italians. Among the latter, this tie appeared to be less exclusive and less monopolizing of the life organization of the adult male. The primary allegiance of the married Polish offenders had been attached to their marital role; among the married Italian offenders, the loyalty owed to their marital role continued to be challenged by the demands of their peer-group role. In the historical development of the Italian community, the marital relationship had been more propitious toward, or at least less opposed to, the emergence of the peer group as a stable, relatively autonomous social grouping among adult males. Accordingly, Whyte in *Street Corner Society* was able to depict "The Social Structure of an Italian Slum" entirely without reference to the family or marriage institutions.

There are other historical differences between the two ethnic communities that are of even greater significance for the comparative development of the adult male peer group. The Polish immigrants had brought with them a number of unifying and integrative principles around which their community life in the new setting had been reconstituted and organized. The parish as it had existed in the homeland provided the prototype for the social structure of the new ethnic communities. Indeed, Thomas and Znaniecki observed that the parish became even more important a social unit in America than it had been in Poland.

In contrast to the Poles, the Italian immigrants brought with them no integrative principles for their new ethnic communities in America; their community life in the homeland had provided neither social prototypes nor unifying national sentiments. The only viable social institution they transplanted was the family. The deficiency of strong indigenous organizational forms in the ethnic community resulted in a kind of social vacuum, which was reinforced by the social distance and the lack of integration between the Italian community and the broader American community. Ware has depicted the unstable character of the organization of community life within the Italian ethnic community during the decade of the twenties. In describing the social structure of an Italian slum during the decade of the thirties, Whyte appears to take over where Ware left off.

The emergent organization of the Italian ethnic community was built upon the foundation provided by the corner group, the informal association of young male adults of the second generation. These street-corner groups and their leaders became the essential units in the new hierarchies of power which evolved in politics and the rackets; they provided the integrative principles for the communal life of the ethnic group which had heretofore been lacking. The informal group of adult males was relatively autonomous, auxiliary to neither the familial, marital, nor employment roles, but coordinate to these and of equal if not greater importance. Consequently, it was able to compete with these other roles for the allegiance of the adult male.

It is now possible to construct the alternatives which confronted released Italian offenders in adjusting to expectations that they fill a legitimate employment role. There appeared to be three associated problems which entered into the structuring of these alternatives: (1) level of aspiration, (2) amoral orientation, and (3) peer-group pressures.

It may be inferred that peer associations would tend to increase the pressures upon released Italian offenders to entertain a high level of aspiration. The integration of the peer group into the local hierarchies of the rackets and politics would make readily available to them, as models for emulation, the examples of other men from the same community who, starting with no more resources, education, or other advantages than they possessed, had risen to positions of prominence and affluence.

Posing the problem raised for released Italian offenders by the issue of legitimate employment—in terms of the mutually exclusive alternatives of legitimate versus illegitimate opportunities, or high versus low aspiration levels—tends to oversimplify, however, the actual alternatives confronting them. The situation of released Italian offenders presented them with a multiplicity of choices marginal to both conventionality and criminality, whose range may be at least partly encompassed by the cultural value of amorality.

There were various means short of criminality through which released offenders could apply an amoral orientation to the selection of an occupational role. In a structure such as that of the Italian ethnic community which incorporated and integrated a whole spectrum of moral orientations from the most conventional to the most criminal, released Italian offenders could initiate or join enterprises with their location in some intermediate region of the legal continuum.

In addition to the level of aspiration and the amoral orientation, the third factor which must be taken into account in determining the attitudes of released offenders toward legitimate employment is that of the possible pull of criminalistic associates. Certain peer associations or interpersonal obligations might exert a direct pressure upon released offenders to return to criminality. Such forces are distinguishable from the more indirect influences, already discussed, which peer associations might exercise as models of success in the illegal opportunity structure.

Released offenders who could moderate their levels of aspiration, place some limits upon the scope of the amoral orientation in their life organization, and insulate themselves from criminalistic group pressures, would tend to rehabilitate; those who could not or would not do so would tend to return to criminality.

CATEGORIES FOR COMPARING POST-RELEASE MILIEUS

This presentation of selected types of the processes of reformation and recidivism has related each to the setting of a particular ethnic community. Each type has been given definition by seeking to articulate the experience of released offenders with the social and cultural structures of the two ethnic communities. On the basis of this comparative study, what generic features of the post-release situation, may it be hypothesized, are most intimately connected with the mode of adjustment of the two groups of offenders? This question will be approached by briefly developing the three following categories, which are believed to constitute the most important situational forces operative in the post-prison experience of Italian and Polish offenders: (1) ethnic differences in the resources made available by the offender's family, (2) ethnic differences in the prevalent conception of human nature, and (3) ethnic differences in the degree of integration between carriers of legitimate and deviant value systems.

Among the features of the Italian and Polish ethnic communities most fateful for released offenders were the kinds of resources made available to them by their families. Both the quality and quantity of these resources appeared to vary with differences in the nature of the familial values in the two groups. Among the Poles, the sentiments of familial solidarity tended to be confined to one nuclear family—to the individual's family of orientation prior to marriage and to his family of procreation after marriage. Among the Italians, sentiments of family solidarity were not so limited by marital status; obligations transcending the nuclear family of procreation were more likely to be acknowledged. This difference was suggested earlier in the data presented on the family visits received by a sample of inmates. On the average, as compared with the Poles, the Italian inmates had received double the number of visits from parents and siblings, but triple the average number of visits—5.3 as compared with 1.8—

from "other relatives," a category inclusive of in-laws, uncles, aunts, cousins, and grandparents. The traditional familistic values had tended to persist among the Italians and to change and to become transformed among the Poles.

The Italians retain longer than many other nationalities the virtues of the primary-group organization. Their family and community life has a very affectionate and intimate character, and its ties usually remain strong enough to prevent that demoralization of the second generation which characterizes the Poles, and, to some extent, the Jews.

In marked contrast to this description are Thomas' observations about the Polish family.

The indirect aristocratic conditioning of the peasant who comes to us as immigrant is not nearly so deep as the conditioning by family and community. . . . Nevertheless the familial attitudes tend to disappear rapidly in America.

The familial life as given in the present materials is undergoing a profound disintegration along certain lines and under the influence of various factors. The main tendencies of this disintegration are: isolation of the marriage-group, and personal individualization.

When territorially isolated the marriage-group is also isolated from the traditional set of rules, valuations, and sentiments of the old community and family, and with the disappearance of these traditions the family becomes merely a natural organization based on personal connections between its members, and these connections are sufficient only to keep together a marriage-group, including perhaps occasionally a few near relatives—the parents, brothers, or sisters of husband or wife.

An important qualification of Thomas's portrayal of the Polish immigrant family is contained in the findings of a more recent study showing that the marital unit among Polish-Americans had manifested an impressive degree of stability.

The findings of a study on marriage conditions in the diocese of the Great Lakes region are very enlightening. Statistics have been gathered on about three hundred parishes, a considerable number of which are Polish. The data on separation and divorce indicate that the conjugal bond is more stable among the Polish-Americans than other American Catholics. It is difficult to reconcile this evidence with Thomas and Znaniecki's predictions.

Finally, a study of the records of the Separation Court of the Chancery Office for the Chicago Archdiocese indicates no relatively great demoralization among the Polish-American Catholics of the diocese.

It needs to be noted that such differences in familial organization as those which have just been presented do not imply that familial resources were accessible to Italian but denied to Polish offenders. They do suggest, however, that such resources differed in degree, if not in kind. Specifically, released Italian offenders would tend to have claims upon the resources of their married siblings and, to a lesser extent, upon the resources of more distantly related married relatives as well. Moreover, their claims, since they were legitimized by the values of familial solidarity, would tend to be defined with greater clarity and less ambiguity than they would be for the Poles. The claims of the latter would tend to be contingent upon the emotional ties which bound them to some and alienated them from other family members. Some of the consequences of these differences in familial sentiments for the post-release experience of offenders will now be described.

The return of the Italian offenders to their ethnic community tended to be a family occasion, accompanied by family gatherings and the presentation of gifts of money and clothing to the released offenders. The return of the Polish offenders tended to be an occasion for the reestablishment of intimate personal relationships with a few selected family members, as distinguished from a family occasion; there tended to be no family gatherings and much less emphasis upon the presentation of gifts to the offenders.

Ethnic differences in the mode of familial response to the released offenders noted at the time of their return to the community were consistently maintained throughout the post-prison period. The families of Italian offenders continued to assume collective responsibility for providing them with whatever resources were at their disposal—for example, room and board, financial assistance, etc. Family opinion operated as a source of social control over their selection of heterosexual relationships, although not in the areas of peer relationships; their families, moreover, continued to constitute an important focus for their social activities and interests.

For released Polish offenders, the amount of assistance which they received from members of their families tended to depend upon the selected personal ties which they maintained. The resources accessible to them, consequently, were likely to be those of a parent or married sibling who made a place for them in the household. These family ties were not an effective source of control over their selection of heterosexual relationships, nor did they provide much focus for their social activities and interests.

Differences in the typical responses of Italian and Polish family members to released offenders do not become intelligible solely in terms of the variations in familism just discussed. In addition, there was a seldom stated but barely concealed tendency for Polish family members to dissociate themselves from the offender. Their response to him appeared to express an uneasy compromise between two conflicting tendencies, between the bonds of affection where such existed versus a tendency to reject him on moral grounds. There was an ambivalence at the core of Polish attitudes which expressed itself in a tendency for the offender to become increasingly alienated from the members of his family, even from those to whom he had been closest. The strain to which he was exposed was particularly evident in certain of his self-regarding attitudes. Polish offenders typically experienced greater guilt about their past criminality than did the Italians and were more heavily burdened by the weight of the criminal stigma. Relevant in this connection were the differing images of rehabilitation held by each group of offenders. For the Italians, rehabilitation tended to mean maturing or "growing up." For the Poles, rehabilitation tended to refer to the means through which they could redeem themselves in their own eyes and in the eyes of others. In summary, the situation of the released Polish offenders was characterized by a rigid moralism which was relatively absent among the Italians.

It was assumed that such differences in the degree of moralism associated with each group were expressive of differences in prevailing conceptions of human nature. From the evidence gathered from various sources, the following judgments were made. The Italian ethnic group was assumed to be characterized by a dominant orientation toward human nature as a mixture of good and evil, the Polish group by a dominant orientation toward human nature as evil. A check on the reliability of these judgments was available for the Italians but not for the Poles.

In presenting their account of the conditions associated with the emergence of various delinquent subcultures, Cloward and Ohlin were particularly concerned with "crucial differences in the social organization of various slum areas." Building on the earlier work of Shaw, McKay, Kobrin, and Whyte, they developed concepts for characterizing the social structure of such local communities. One of their concepts, the degree of integration between carriers of criminal and conventional values, was found, during the course of the present study, to be especially useful in identifying crucial differences in the post-release experience of Italian and Polish offenders. It appeared that many of these differences could best be explained by assuming that a closer degree of such integration existed in the Italian as compared with the Polish community. Indeed, much of the description of the historical evolution of the two communities presented earlier could be rephrased in such terms.

Accordingly, in order to avoid the repetition of this material, the present aim is merely to discuss the relevance of this structural concept for interpreting the post-release experience of Polish offenders to whom it has not previously been applied. Returning to a milieu characterized by a lesser degree of integration between conventional and deviant values, with a correspondingly lesser ease of access to the illegitimate opportunity structure, they would tend to encounter conditions less likely to stimulate high monetary success goals than their Italian counterparts. They would, consequently, tend to be more satisfied than released Italians with the unskilled or semiskilled types of legitimate employment accessible to them. Also unlike the Italians, they would be less likely to conceive of a career on the margins of both legitimate and illegitimate opportunity structures. Furthermore, the disjunctive mutually exclusive character of the two value systems would be such as to force them to make a definite commitment to one or the other and to regard such a commitment as relatively irreversible.

The categories which have just been formulated are of assistance in interpreting additional findings of the study. As stated earlier, the analysis of the offender interview data included an examination of the goodness of fit between the types constructed for each ethnic group and the actual empirical cases. The distribution of the latter among the various types is presented in Table 28.2.

While the fit between the empirical cases of reintegrating offenders and the types constructed for each ethnic group was relatively complete, variations from the ethnic type did occur among the recidivists. Within each ethnic group, in addition to the cases which fitted the ethnic or "dominant" type, there

TABLE 28.2

DISTRIBUTION OF ITALIAN AND POLISH OFFENDERS AMONG VARIOUS TYPES OF SOCIAL REINTEGRATION AND RECIDIVISM

	Italian Offenders	Polish Offenders
Types of social reintegration:		
Collectivistic	10	
Individualistic		10
Total	10	10
Types of recidivism:		
Return to criminality as an alternative or supplement to use of legitimate means for achieving monetary goals	12	4
Return to criminality as culmination of a progressive sense of defeat in efforts to attain acceptance in conventional social roles	5	7
Residual cases	2	4
Total	19	15

were a smaller number of cases which fitted a "variant" type. Interestingly, the "dominant" type in one group corresponded to the "variant" type in the other, so that the two ethnic types previously developed were still adequate to encompass most of the empirical cases of recidivists. Thus, while the association between types of recidivism and ethnic group still prevailed, it did not assume the form of a simple dichotomy of cases fitting two ethnic types but as a different order for each group in the relative frequency with which recidivist cases were distributed among the same two types.

It appears, then, that the initial working assumptions made in order to facilitate ethnic comparisons among offenders were too restrictive. Instead of assuming that each ethnic community was to be associated with a single salient post-release problem, it would be more accurate to assume that both communities can generate both types of problems identified by the study, but can vary in the relative frequency with which each type occurs. The categories previously developed for the purpose of conceptualizing the key comparisons between Italian and Polish ethnic communities help to identify the secondary or nonsalient types of problems which arose in each ethnic community. For example, Italian recidivists who differed from the type dominant in their own ethnic group had all encountered difficulties in their familial relationships. Collectively, then, they constituted a variant type within their own group with many affinities to the type dominant among the Poles. Similarly, the Polish recidivists who were variants from the type dominant within their own ethnic group tended to be those whose prison experience had been a medium through which they gained access to illegitimate opportunities. In many important respects, their experience closely paralleled that of the dominant group of Italian recidivists.

In conclusion, some of the practical issues of rehabilitation will be approached from the perspective toward criminality adopted in this paper. It is a perspective which suggests that the goals of intervention must of necessity be modest, since the analysis has revealed how strong and insistent the pressures toward recidivism may be. However, it has also shown that post-release milieus may concurrently provide resources which contribute to reformation. That is, alternative modes of post-release adjustment were found to be consistent with the structure of both Italian and Polish communities. It follows, then, that efforts at intervention, insofar as they work within the existing structure of the community, should have the goal of seeking to increase the accessibility and attractiveness of legitimate alternatives within the experience of released offenders.

Some illumination as to the nature of such a program may be obtained by citing certain aspects of the experience of the Chicago Area Projects. It is particularly appropriate to do so since the most intensive of their pioneering efforts to work with released adult offenders, starting over a generation ago in the middle thirties, were exerted in the Italian and Polish ethnic communities. Italian community workers would tend to become involved in the case of an offender only after the latter's family had solicited their assistance. Thereafter, all work with the offender was done in cooperation with the offender's family and, as far as possible, through reliance upon its resources. Commonly, contact with the offender through visits and correspondence was initiated while he was still in prison. Either the community worker himself, or some associate, frequently the "chairman of the adult parole committee" of the local community organization, sought to establish a personal relationship with the offender as a peer. Such a bond would conform to a pattern long familiar to Italian offenders. Its novelty in this particular context lay in the purposive and controlled manner in which it was utilized so as to provide channels of reentry to conventional roles in the free community for the offender.

The goal of the program appeared to be to insulate the released offender from the pressures represented by easy accessibility to illegitimate opportunities and criminalistic associates. This was attempted through the provision of clear access to opportunities for legitimate employment and by provision of anticriminal associations. Such noncriminal associations were represented by the worker, his "indigenous" co-workers, and other members from the local community, and were given a stable group form through the organization of a community committee.

Several aspects of the program are clearly in agreement with the comparative categories developed earlier. It presupposed the centrality of the family as a key resource and exploited to the full the importance of peer-group relationships among adult males. In addition, assuming a conception of human nature as a mixture of good and evil makes it somewhat easier to comprehend how a prison inmate and a conventional stranger could form a warm, trusting relationship with a minimum of strain on both sides. Taking cognizance of the role played by familial relationships in the Italian community also contributes to an understanding of the mechanism through which an interest in reforming criminal offenders, tenuous as it was, could be generated. The selection of indigenous "volunteers," and in particular of those adult males who consented to serve in the office of "chairman of the adult parole committee," was not a random process. Some familial experience, such as a familial tie to the prisoner, or perhaps the occurrence of similar types of problems within their own families, appeared to be necessary to stimulate a reformative interest in Italian males.

In taking for granted that under appropriate conditions Italian offenders would find the work role quite attractive, the program was on solid ground. One gathers that, over the long haul, the heroes of the illegitimate opportunity structure had to compete against the glory and esteem which accrued to another type of culture hero—the workingman who was also a family man. One of the Italian informants gave the following description of such an exemplar, his brother. "When I look at it today I see it——'s way. ——, in fact, is one of the most impressive guys in the neighborhood today. He got married and settled down, he's got a trade, he drives a new car, he's got two good sons, and when he goes into the neighborhood everybody is real glad to see him. He is really respected in the sense that he is a man."

The techniques employed by the Polish community workers were perhaps ideologically similar but actually quite different in practical application. The initiative in working with a case was generally taken by the worker and only rarely by the offender's family. In all cases, the community worker would attempt to interest family members in assisting the offender. The key relationship, however, was that between the worker and the offender. Indeed, not infrequently the community worker's job was as much to protect the offender from his familial relationships as it was to use the family as a resource. Moreover, unlike the Italian worker-offender relationship, this relationship was not typically an informal peer relationship but one more formal and structured into superior and inferior status positions.

After the offender's release, the goal of the worker was to help him become established as an independent, self-reliant member of the community. For those for whom such a goal was too demanding, he sought to use whatever resources and facilities were within his grasp to forestall the demoralization of the offender. Some offenders fell into chronically marginal positions, so that they neither attained independent roles nor returned to criminality. They became "winos" and members of "bottle gangs," prematurely superannuated, but finding consolation in reliving the feats and fantasies of their youths.

The conception of human nature as evil helps in interpreting the marginal status of the Polish community workers themselves. They never attained acceptance or a role in the Polish community commensurate with that attained by Italian community workers. Part of the stigma associated with the criminal offender tended to rub off and contaminate them. Only the greatest dedication and competence, together with the personal independence so prized by the Poles, could enable workers with a reformative interest to survive and continue their work in such a milieu.

The kind of relationship between postprison milieu and the mode of adjustment of offenders dealt with in this paper also has implications for the form to be assumed by correctional programs. The mode of training and orientation appropriate to the offender who, like the Pole, must make his way largely dependent upon his own resources in the face of indifferent or hostile others is obviously different from that appropriate to the offender who, like the Italian, has access to ongoing conventional and criminally oriented groups which engage in a struggle for his loyalty. The findings further suggest that in planning a regime for the rehabilitation of the offender it is as important to take account of his post-release milieu as it is his personal and social characteristics. They point to the nature of the issues which will be raised for any thorough-going effort to coordinate the rehabilitative efforts of correctional institutions with the resources of the community.

29. IDENTITY AND THE TRANSSEXUAL ADAPTATION

JAMES P. DRISCOLL

Reprinted by permission of Transaction, Inc., from "Transsexuals, "Trans-actionSociety, Vol. 8, Nos. 5 & 6 (1971). Copyright © 1971 by Transaction, Inc. James P. Driscoll is Chairman of the Department of Sociology at Sonoma State College, Rohnert Park, California.

■ The invention of sex change surgery added a new dimensions to the kinds of deviance made possible because individuals do not always share society's conception of the sex role they should assume. For as long as male homosexuals have existed, presumably some men have regarded themselves as "a woman in man's body." The development of new surgical techniques has made possible physical confirmation of this subjective sense of identity, but at the same time, male and female identity is so basic to the way our culture regards people that the possibility of altering that identity at will seems threatening to what is "right and proper." The forces of social control therefore operate sharply to limit the availability of this operation. At one time such procedures were available only in European countries, but more recently the frequency of their performance in this country has increased.

Additional analyses of the transsexual experience can be found in Harry Benjamin, *The Transsexual Phenomenon* (Julien Press, 1966); Robert Stoler, *Sex and Gender* (Science House, 1968); and Richard Green and John Money, *Transsexualism and Sex Reassignment* (The Johns Hopkins Press, 1970). A case study appears in Harold Garfinkel, *Studies in Ethnomethodology* (Prentice-Hall, 1967). ■

THERE IS A HOTEL in the Tenderloin district of San Francisco that is inhabited almost entirely by transsexuals. It's not much of a place to look at—a tawdry three-story building. A bar occupies the first floor, apart from an outside door that leads upstairs to the hotel which consists of the top two floors of the building.

The traffic up those stairs usually begins a little after midnight. Two people enter the hotel. They climb the shabby steps and stop at a grilled window on the second floor. A flyblown sign over it reads "Manager." The middle-aged man and the young girl stop here. There is another sign that says "Positively no visitors after ten P.M." Yet another one gives the weekly rates for doubles and singles. It also announces that an additional guest may be registered for the night for three dollars.

Inside the office another girl, the manager, sits in an overstuffed chair. From here she can see her television set and still keep an eye on people from the minute they enter the ground floor. Not much escapes the manager. Outside, the girl whispers something to the man, and he hands three dollar bills through the grill. He and the girl climb the stairs to the third floor.

Not too different, one might say, from thousands of other such arrangements that go on every night. But there is a difference. The girl is not a girl. "She" is a young man of 20 dressed not only as a woman, but also in high fashion. The clothes are good and in style. Her wig is piled high on her head, on top of her own long hair. Her build, carriage, and demeanor are entirely feminine. She is a transsexual, a man who dresses as a woman and wants to undergo sex conversion surgery so that she may be a woman physically.

ENTERING THE TRANSSEXUAL WORLD

I became aware of and interested in the transsexuals about four years ago. I was working nights at the time, and our building was on the edge of the Tenderloin. My office was the only place open for several blocks. The rest of the newspaper I worked for went on all night, too, but my cubbyhole was adjacent to the street.

I had gotten used to the variety of people who dropped in there: some for a free paper, some to cadge money, some who were lonely. And some just to get out of the rain. I met my first transsexual on such a rainy night. She came in and asked if she could stand there for a while. It was all right with me. When my shift was over I told her I would have to lock up. It was five in the morning and still raining. She asked me if I could drop her off at Paul's, an after-hours coffeehouse. I said yes, and when we got there she asked me inside for a cup of coffee. I had never been inside one of these places and was curious, so I agreed. We got stools at the bar, and she introduced me to Heather, the girl serving the coffee. The place was crowded with girls and a few men. The jukebox was playing at its loudest.

She told me her name was Angie and she said hello to several of the girls at the bar. They did not respond. I was wondering what I had done wrong, when Angie told them that I was a friend and not a trick. Soon some of the other girls started talking to us, and I was quite stunned to notice, even in the dim light, that one of them needed a shave. Now I may be a little slow about some things and accustomed to take others at face value, but this was a little much. I started looking at the others closely, and sure enough, several were men. I introduced this as tactfully as possible to Angie, and she got a good laugh out of it. She admitted to being a man and was quite proud that I had not "read" her.

At this point I would like to indicate a usage that is followed in this paper. It is impossible to be associated with the transsexuals for any length of time, let alone live with them, without thinking of them as women. They always refer to themselves and each other in the feminine gender, and do all they can to reinforce a feminine identity. They call each other "girl" and refer to other transsexuals as "she" and "her." In order to

accurately reflect the feelings of the people involved, and other's perceptions of them, I will refer to the transsexuals as girls and will use feminine pronouns.

Transsexuals have a definite subculture, and it is extremely difficult to breach the walls of distrust and dislike of outsiders. There is a good reason for this. First of all, being in drag was against the law at this time. Secondly, all the girls I knew were engaged in prostitution. You may purchase any service you want at any time. But it is an entirely different matter to get one of them to sit down and talk to you. In all the conversations and interviews I had with these girls, I have given them my word that I would never do anything to harm them or put them in jeopardy. I have kept that word. The names you read are fictitious. The people, however, are real, and so are the situations. . . .

Generally I found that the girls had many things in common in their backgrounds. They had all gone through similar stages of development on their path to transsexualism. To delineate these stages and alternatives was the problem I was faced with. There was a way to make sociological sense out of the lives of these girls.

EFFEMINATE CHILDHOOD

This stage begins when the child is in infancy and continues to about the 10th or 12th year. The early years of the socialization process were disruptive ones for the girls. From infancy to puberty their gender was treated inappropriately or ambiguously by their parent or parents. Moreover, every one of the subjects came from a broken home. . . . I tried to get some other information about the childhood of these girls by asking the question: "Was your mother or father the dominant parent?" As might be expected, almost all of the subjects indicated that the mother was the dominant figure in the household. . . .

The picture that emerges of these girls in their early years is one of disorientation and confusion. The girls, of course, had no choice in this matter. The choice was made by the parents or parent. The significant other or others in the girl's life showed her how these female roles were to be performed. The child was rewarded for her behavior in various ways. She was given girls' toys and playthings; she was dressed in female clothing; she was encouraged to let her hair grow long and frequently had it set and ribbons put in it; she was taught to avoid the rough activities of boys; and in general all feminine behavior was reinforced positively.

One question put to the group was: "Did you play boy games or girl games?" None of the girls answered that they had played boys' games exclusively. Some played both. But most answers were like these.

Girl games. Dolls, doll houses, that sort of thing.

Girl games. I played jacks and jumped rope.

Both. But I preferred to play with the girls and mostly did.

In short, these children were taught to be girls. This was the role prescribed for them and was the central theme in their sexual socialization process. When they were asked if they had been raised as a boy or a girl, only 2 of the 17 subjects responded that they had been raised as a boy. One of these was ambiguous. . . .

Sociologist Howard Becker points out that the first step in the career of a deviant is usually the commission of a deviant act. In this case, however, the girls did not do anything really deviant. They obeyed their parents or guardians. They responded to the expectations of feminity by behaving like girls. Once this pattern had been established, they made feminine choices in most aspects of their lives. Eventually, they chose to identify sexually with a feminine model.

But what was seen as normal by the parent and child was perceived by others as deviant. Actual conflict began when they got to school. Here great portions of their lives were expected to be lived according to the conventional standards of normal boys. But it was impossible for them to meet these demands. They had been treated as girls and considered themselves to be so. In this way they alienated themselves from the boys in their communities.

Many of the girls recall how they hated gym class. They were forced to undress in front of others and were very self-conscious about this. Even at that age they wanted to be like girls. Besides, they were forced to play boy games, which were repugnant to them. They went to considerable trouble to develop ploys that would get them out of gym class.

One of the most important steps in the development of a deviant is that of being caught or found out and publicly labeled. This label places the deviant in a new status and in turn results in changes in his self-concept. It also changes the concepts that other people have of him. He now carries a stigma and is expected to behave in ways that people feel are consistent with the label. It is significant that the labeling process for the transsexual began in school and was brought about by the behavior of the girls and the perceptions of their peers. In response to the question "How did you get along with the other children in school?" some of the answers were:

The guys gave me a rough time for being feminine. That's why I left school. They called me a sissy and a queer.

Not very well. I was raised with my three sisters and was a sissy. I got along with the girls but not the boys.

Not too well. I liked nail polish and lipstick and makeup. I was always considered a sissy. Most of the time I was poked fun at.

Many of them recall being very lonely, as neither boys nor girls would have anything to do with them. It was a time, also, of some anguish. The girls report that they urinated sitting down and that it seemed natural for them to use the girls' restroom at school. Several of them tried this and were punished for it. They continued, however, to sneak into the girls' room whenever possible.

Even the simple process of names became a perplexing problem for the girls. They never remember being called by their given names around the house. They were called by some ambiguous abbreviation or pet name. Terrance became Terri, Gerald was Jerri, Phillip was Phyl, and James was Snooky. Even to this day one of the things that the girls hate most about a court appearance is the fact that they must stand up and reply to their male name.

It is not my contention that all children who are called sissies will grow up to be transsexuals or even homosexuals. Why some choose one form of sexual gratification and others another is not yet clear. But in my sample group it was evident that the patterning that begins in childhood was a very important variable in the lives of the girls. There is a good deal of evidence to support the notion of sexual socialization being a crucial influence on whether (or how) one defines oneself as a boy or a girl. Biology is not always destiny.

HOMOSEXUAL STAGE

The girls performed homosexual acts for some time before they perceived themselves to be homosexuals. This is hardly surprising, of course, since after all they were deeply confused as to what sex they were. This was part of the anguish, that they had to act normally while fighting an internal battle over who and what they were. It was only when they became aware that there was a gay world and that there were many others who acted as they did that they formed the self-concept of homosexual. Nevertheless, to formulate a concept of one's self as being a homosexual, a person must perform a homosexual act, and usually a series of them. . . .

Interestingly, they could recall no sexual curiosity about "real" girls. If they didn't know already, the transsexuals wanted to know how girls were built and what the differences were between themselves and the real thing. But there was none of the experimentation and "playing house" that is so common among normal children. The trans-

sexuals mainly wanted to know what was required of them so that they could be considered to be girls.

While the girls found homosexual acts pleasurable to some extent, this does not mean that they automatically had to continue them. The could have chosen the heterosexual path. But they did not. They got older and found that there were other people who performed these acts and identified themselves as homosexuals. In my study almost all the transsexuals reported that they considered themselves to be homosexuals in late adolescence.

Seventeen or eighteen. When I had accepted it and felt I couldn't be anything else.

I was eighteen. I realized that it was not a game but a way of life. I came to understand that this was the way I felt. I liked other men.

Fourteen to fifteen. I wanted to feel like a woman. I knew I was funny all my life' I wanted to go with men.

Here we see, present and at work, many of the factors that make up what has been called a career contingency—exposure to an experience, the experience itself, the desire to continue it, the response of significant others, and the eventual identification with it. But the major contingency seems to be the discovery of other homosexuals and of a gay subculture.

The gay world was a strange but pleasurable place for the girls. They began to frequent those parts of town where other homosexuals gathered. The move was an easy one; after all, they had been performing homosexual acts for some years. During that time they had felt very isolated, however; they felt that they were one of a kind and were very lonely. But now they found others who shared the same sexual preferences and that these people had their own communities. The transition to full homosexual status may even have been a relief to the girls.

But what is a homosexual? Taking a test group of 60 homosexuals, Evelyn Hooker put them through several tests, such as the Rorschach, TAT, and MAPS. On the basis of the results, it was found that homosexuality as a clinical entity does not exist. That is, it was not possible to identify the members of the test groups as homosexuals from their scores. This clearly indicates that in almost all basic areas the homosexual is not different from other men. What does set him apart is his behavior, and to explain this behavior we would do well to look closely into the sexual socialization of the homosexual. If we cannot find the cause for his behavior within the person, then we must look for patterns of interaction with other people, especially significant others, which will explain his deviation. With respect to the transsexuals I interviewed it should be plain that this socialization process was an unconventional and misleading one from the beginning.

The period when they were being socialized into the gay world was also, of course, a training in unconventionality. The girls admit to a high degree of sexuality, and their sexual encounters were many and varied. They cruised the streets looking for pickups, they frequented the Turkish baths and spent a great amount of time in homosexual bars and other hangouts. It should be pointed out that the girls came from a broad geographic area and from diverse social settings. They were raised in small towns, large cities, and the suburbs. Their origins seem to have made no difference in their activity, however, except that those from the larger cities had a greater degree of freedom and a wider range of activity. Wherever they had come from, their behavior was no different from that of many other homosexuals. And it was from these other homosexuals that the girls learned. They all report that they were swept up into the gay world. They began to associate with one another and to form friendships. In this mutual exchange they found which were the homosexual bars, where pickups could be made, what they were expected to wear and how they were expected to act. They also learned how to survive: how to recognize the police, how to approach a prospect, how to dress, how to fix their hair, how to apply a little makeup.

During this period of homosexuality, all the girls relate that they were "hair fairies." That is, they would wear their hair long and tease it. They also had what seems to be almost a uniform: a little makeup, a bulky sweater, and tight trousers—as tight as possible.

In fine, they were introduced to the gay world, liked it, and learned from it. They had entered the gay world as pretty uncertain people. Now they had a rationale for their behavior. As a result of what they learned, they emerged far more sure of themselves and far wiser. They were also far stronger in their identification of themselves.

It was at this time that most of the girls left home. For some, leaving was not voluntary; they were rousted by the police so often that they were, in effect, run out of town. Some others were simply made to feel unwelcome at home. During their early years their behavior was allowed and even encouraged by the people who raised them. But later on, usually in high school, this behavior came under public scrutiny and condemnation. Now the girls were expected to change their behavior from feminine to masculine. When they were unable to do this, many had no choice but to leave home. As one of the girls told me: "My mother wanted a little girl, but not a big one."

With their immersion in the homosexual subculture the girls became contemptuous of the rules of society. Since the homosexual finds that an important part of the moral code does not apply to him, he calls into question all parts of morality. The girls indulged in a great deal of petty theft; all admitted to male prostitution; and many reported that they had had venereal disease at this point.

I have mentioned that the desire to be feminine was very strong in the girls. In order to be as feminine as possible, they preferred the passive role in sexual activity. But even this was not enough for them. There came a time when the role of the hair fairy was no longer enough. They wanted to be more like real women, and the logical way to do this was to dress as one.

TRANSVESTITE STAGE

In general, there are two types of trans-vestites. One type finds that he gets emotional relief from dressing as a woman. Many of these men are married and lead heterosexual lives. They dress in the privacy of their homes, sometimes with the knowledge and active assistance of their wives. The wives do not see this as a healthy situation but go along for the sake of saving the marriage. Frequently the male must wear some article of female attire in order to engage in sexual intercourse, and he usually adopts the under position. This type presents no social problems as he rarely dresses in public.

The other type consists of people who are very involved with, and attached to, a femi-nine way of life. It pervades their every hour and effort. They want to wear female attire in the streets and try to wear this clothing as much as possible. These are the people with whom I am now concerned.

Transsexuals, as we have seen, usually begin cross-dressing in childhood. They were dressed in girls' attire by their mothers. Or they were given preferential treatment when they performed female roles, so that they sought these roles and wore the clothes of their sisters and mothers. They were pro-tected from the roughness of other boys and were treated as girls. Under these circum-stances it is not hard to imagine how or why the child came to prefer girls' clothes.

During their homosexual stage the girls came into frequent contact with transvestites. They both frequented the same bars, restau-rants, and coffeehouses. The girls wanted to be like the transvestites but lacked the cour-age of their convictions. There was a great deal of talk among themselves about how these other people dressed and got away with it.

The girls also talked a lot to the transves-tites and found that they had come from the same kind of background. Gradually the conviction built up that this was the life that they should be leading, and finally they decided to make the move. . . .

When the girls moved into their new status as transvestites, most of them had no idea what they were getting into or the vast changes it would make in their lives. They seem to have given little thought to what effect continual dressing would have on other aspects of their lives.

One of the first things to be affected was their jobs. Most of them simply quit and hoped somehow to make a living. But this proved to be very difficult. As has been reported, the girls had dabbled in male prostitution in their homosexual stage. Now they found that they had to hustle in earnest in order to make a living. This was an un-foreseen consequence of their change in status.

The queens frequently spent a great deal of time together. There was much for them to learn from the older queens. They had much to learn about how to dress, how to fix their hair, wear their makeup, and so forth.

In response to the question "How did you learn to dress, act, and pass as a woman?" they replied:

I watched the other kids. I wore the same hairstyles and clothes. I found out about pads and gaffs from them. Now I dress to please myself.

You get a lot of helpful hints. But you must do it yourself. You watch other queens and learn from them. People will tell you to try pads and other things.

I watched other queens. Friends showed me how to get arranged. Other girls gave me a hand with makeup and dress.

Note that the girls did not seem to pay much attention to women. When I asked them about this they told me that there was more to learn from other queens as they had similar problems. They noticed women but could not get the kind of instruction that they needed. So they turned to the queens. . . .

The girls also had other things to learn about their everyday lives. There was a tacit understanding with the police that they would not be picked up for impersonation as long as they stayed in the Tenderloin. They were also allowed on the north side of Market Street. If they strayed outside of these areas, they were liable to be, and frequently were, arrested.

They also learned a new rationale. They now considered themselves to be a cut above the homosexual and much more feminine. They now regarded the hair fairy as someone to be laughed at. This feeling is reciprocated by the homosexuals, many of whom think the queens are a bunch of nuts dressed in women's clothing. They enjoy pointing out the shortcomings of the girls, ridiculing them.

The girls have told me that at this stage they thought that they had reached the end of the rainbow. It seemed to them to be the realization of a childhood dream. They were free, they were on their own, they dressed as women, they referred to themselves in feminine terms, and they thought they had found the good life. Even prostitution did not bother them at this point. In fact, all reported that they were having a lot of fun. They did not model themselves after the middle class housewife, or even the upper class female swinger. Their dress was intended to startle and to attract attention, and it did. Frankly, they could not have looked more like whores if they tried, and they seemed to get some kinds of perverse pleasure out of this.

So this period, when the person comes out, seems to be a relatively happy one for the girls. Of course, they have their problems, especially with the police, and several of the girls were arrested for impersonation and prostitution. In San Francisco, however, this contingency was not as traumatic as it would be in other places. It is a measure of the sophistication and tolerance of that city that both the city and county jails have a special tank for the queens. In most other cities they are simply thrown in with the male prisoners and left to an uncertain fate.

The transvestite phase of the girls' life is a relatively short one. It usually lasts from three to eight months. Then something else happens. They find out about the conversion operation and discover that it is possible for them to be a woman physically. Now, however, with this new knowledge, they are ready for the next step. When they first regularly dressed as women they had wanted to get rid of some of the secondary male characteristics, especially the beard, and they had also wanted to acquire a bust. But at the transvestite stage these were merely expressed desires, and not much seems actually to have been done about them.

TRANSSEXUAL STAGE

Once they have heard of the conversion operation and know that there is such a thing as a transsexual, the self-concepts of the girls seem to change. Now they regard themselves as women in every sense of the word except one. This female identification is very strong in the transsexuals and dominates all other aspects of their lives. It is what sociologist Everett Hughes has called a master status.

An interesting and, I think, good example of this is how they regard themselves sexually. Prior to this phase they considered themselves to be homosexuals. Now they deny any such status and claim that they are normally sexed. When asked how they account for this when they admit to performing homosexual acts, the girls have told me that they think of themselves as women. This identification is so strong that to them it would be a perversion to choose a female sex partner.

Harry Benjamin has called the transsexual a psychic hermaphrodite. They have the mind of a woman in the body of a man. They can see only one way out of this dilemma: the conversion operation. They set out to attain this goal and keep after it with a tenacity that can only be referred to as fierce. It becomes the driving force in their lives.

They call it simply "the operation." The penis is excised, and the patient is castrated. Plastic reconstruction of the external genitalia is then performed. Next an artificial vagina is created. This usually consists of a pouch six to eight inches deep. The skin of the amputated penis is stripped off, inverted, and inserted into the pouch, the wound surfaces adhering to each other. This tissue from the penis contains sensory nerve ends which are partially preserved and later on may help in achieving orgasm.

There is a follow-up period of about six months during which time the vagina must be frequently dilated and a prosthetic device frequently worn so that the pouch does not seal itself. After this time the transsexual is able to perform normal sexual relations with a man.

What makes these girls want to go through such a rigorous and traumatizing operation? The only answer is that they want to be women—not just to appear as a woman and successfully pass as one but to be able to function as one. It is this drive that is characteristic of the transsexual's life. . . .

They are no longer content to imitate. They want to be. And they form a very strong conception of themselves as women. They all know that it is a long and difficult road. Many fantasize that they will meet a Sugar Daddy tomorrow and the operation will be taken care of. They think about the operation so much that several of the girls reported that from time to time they feel that they have already had it.

At the same time, however, the girls suddenly realize that it is a far cry from dressing as a woman to actually being one. Now they pay much closer attention to real women and model themselves after them rather than the queens. But they still aim at very high fashion.

The exchange of information among the girls remains free and frequent. As soon as one hears of some new tip on how to dress or make up, she will try it immediately and pass it on to the other girls. Until they go on hormones or until the hormones have a chance to effect bodily changes, the girls pad themselves. There are several makes of girdles with built-in pads, and the girls will use these as well as dancing girdles with pads in them. If the girl cannot afford these things, she is shown how to insert padded towels around her hips and buttocks under a regular girdle.

Another device is the gaff, a cradle, usually made of canvas or denim, to which elastic loops are attached. The gaff is pulled up tight at the crotch, the effect being to flatten the genitalia and to a degree force the testicles back into the body cavity. The same effect can be obtained with the use of a tight dancing girdle, and some of the girls will use both.

The masculine appearance of their legs, they have found, can be somewhat softened by wearing two pairs of dark nylon stockings. Nylons are also good for padding their bras. After much experimenting with commercial products, the girls think that wadded nylons in the bra most closely approximate the shape and feel of a breast.

The girls are all very self-conscious about the size of their hands and feet; they think people will notice them and read the boy behind the girl. They feel this way even when there is no reason for it. They frequently wear long-sleeved dresses with a ruffle at the wrist to minimize hand size. They learn to wear long fingernails with an iridescent polish. They also have what almost amounts to a fetish about shoes. The higher the heels, the better.

The dresses themselves are usually low-necked with the bosom pushed up to show as much cleavage as possible. Many of the girls apply tape across the breast from the side to the middle to create the appearance of more bosom.

These are tricks of the trade, and they learn them readily from each other, but the girls are learning from other sources as well. Some of them go to one of the doctors in San Francisco who will treat transsexual patients. Others go to the Center for Special Problems, operated by the city of San Francisco. From these people they learn about hormones, which ones to take and what can be expected from them. More than this, the medical contacts strengthen the feminine self-concept of the girls. They feel that they now have some positive medical sanction to their claims for womanhood, and this feeling commits them more firmly than ever to their career pattern as a transsexual.

The hormone treatment itself brings about some startling bodily changes in a surprisingly short period of time. After about three months of hormones, the girls begin to develop a bust, and there are visible changes in the distribution of body fat. The shoulders become thinner, and the hips and buttocks fill out. Body hair begins to fall off, and facial hair becomes lighter and sparser. Needless to say, these changes are extremely encouraging to the girls. Once they have gone this far, they begin to live almost entirely for the eventual operation. They refer to themselves exclusively as women. The drag queen is now regarded as some sort of a freak—a homosexual who dresses as a woman. The girls are now inordinately concerned with their appearance. Everything possible that can rid them of male characteristics and mannerisms is done. All the female traits are sought and coveted.

The hair becomes a hallmark of femininity, the longer the better. All the girls in my group had a collection of wigs, wiglets, and falls to supplement their natural hair. The hairdos are quite elaborate and frequently garish. But they are the pride and joy of the girls, and nothing will alter the way they wear their hair. One of the most cutting remarks that one girl can make to another is that her hair does not look natural. They have a positive horror of becoming bald.

The girls' most frequent social activity revolves around hair. They are constantly gathering in someone's room to dress a person's hair or to set a wig. They will consume a good deal of pot on these occasions, but nothing to match the consumption of hair spray; the average girl goes through five cans of hair spray in a week. One can will last my wife more than a month.

Thus a large amount of information is exchanged among the girls. They learn from each other, and the newcomer has a ready-made classroom and teacher. Moreover, there were several close friendships among the girls in La Toro, and the amount of social interchange was quite large. It is vital to note, however, that at this, the transsexual stage, the girls have come full circle in the process of socialization. Now, there is no discontinuity between childhood learning and adult learning. Much of what they are learning as

self-defined and self-accepted transsexuals is the creation of new ways of combining old response patterns. What the girls are being taught is not at variance with what they were taught as children. . . .

FEMININE STAGE

Twelve of the girls have gone on from the transsexual to what I would call a feminine stage. That is, the girls want to live the lives of normal housewives or working girls. They have given up prostitution and have found jobs of some sort or are looking for them.

A great deal of this change must be attributed to the hormones they have been taking. In the first place, the female hormones have reduced their normal male sex drive, a change that Benjamin refers to as chemical castration. They have become softer in manner and actions. I don't mean to imply that they are entirely on the side of the angels. They still smoke pot and have their one-night-stands. But there is much less drinking, and the use of speed drugs and glue has disappeared.

It is at this stage that they come out as women, as they have previously done as queens and transsexuals. They are, of course, still transsexuals. But their self-image has changed. They want to live a normal, middle class life. They no longer revel in being able to turn men's heads. They want to live and pass undetected as women, and they have modified their behavior in order to be able to do it.

This was far from easy, even with the hormones. All of the girls, as we have seen, loathed their lives as prostitutes, but few have been offered any other way of making a living. Moreover, at their level of skill and education, few of the girls could hope to earn much more than $1.35 an hour for a 32-hour week. There is not one of them who could not make this in one night of hustling. Nevertheless, when a few jobs opened up at San Francisco's Economic Opportunity Council all the vacancies were filled. Several of the girls worked on a volunteer basis at the Central City Multi-Service Center so that they would be in line for the next jobs when and if they came.

Two other girls were employed by the Neighborhood Youth Corps at the same salary. Two others were trained at the John Adams High School under the Manpower Development Retraining Act. For this they received $50 a week and transportation costs; yet the competition to get into this 36-week training course was very keen. So far two of the girls have been graduated. One works as a cashier in the box office of a theater. The other is the manager of a small hotel. Also, one of the girls from the Central City Project has been promoted to a staff position.

In the work atmosphere of the office, the girls have to learn to be in the company of normal women. At first they are quite shy about these contacts. But as time goes by, they begin to ask questions about how they can best get along and get ahead. The answers that the women give to these questions have a lasting effect on the girls. They also watch carefully what rewards and punishments are accorded to the women because of their behavior. They are especially attentive to the transsexual who has made the successful transition to the ordinary world. The girls observe to see what she does to pass successfully.

Beyond the office, too, the girls actively seek out the company of women, something they avoided in the past. Through my wife and myself they have met several of our friends. They keep in very close contact and come to visit us frequently. They are trying to find out how a normal girl lives, and their appetite for learning is very acute.

This is not to say that everything is beer and skittles for the girls, and that they have it made. At the rate they are being paid, they can just about live, to say nothing of putting anything away for the operation. But there is one big difference—hope. And with that hope comes patience and the facing up to the realities of life.

They no longer talk as if they were going to have the operation next week. They realize now that when all costs are considered—the operation itself, transportation and living expenses for the six-month follow-up period—they are talking about $8,000. So they wait in the belief that the operation will soon be openly offered here in the San Francisco Bay Area.

They act entirely differently now. They no longer have to slink along the streets, afraid of both police and customers. They now have a stronger sense of identification. They regard themselves as a minority and want the same rights other minority groups want. The girls have formed a club, COG (Correction of Gender), and have weekly meetings to discuss their problems. The girls realistically do not expect to change the world. But they would like to have some provisions made for people like themselves. And they are making some progress. At a COG meeting in 1968 there were four police captains present, as well as the police commissioner of Saint Louis, and the girls tried to get some sort of dialogue going. The succeeded, and what they also got was an agreement from the police that they wouldn't use the charge of impersonation anymore. If a criminal charge were being lodged, such as prostitution, the impersonation charge would have to be included, the police said. But at least the girls were free to walk the streets of the city, and not with the former tacit understanding with the police that they stay in the Tenderloin. Another result of this meeting was that the police captains agreed to inform their men that the girls were to be allowed to use the ladies' rooms in public places. All in all, then, the position of the girls vis-a-vis the law has greatly improved. Such a meeting would have been out of the question in any of the previous stages. It is only that the girls have matured and gained self-respect that they have the self-confidence to meet with the police. This new attitude is indicative of a similar change in their self-concepts. They now see themselves as law-abiding citizens who are entitled to their rights.

30. THE FORMS AND COMPONENTS OF LONELINESS

HELENA ZNANIECKI LOPATA

Reprinted with permission from "Loneliness: Forms and Components," Social Problems 17, no 2 (Fall 1969): 248-61. Copyright 1969 by The Society for the Study of Social Problems and the author. A sociologist, Helena Z. Lopata has conducted many studies of family life. Her books include Occupation: Housewife *(Oxford University Press, 1971), and* Widowhood in an American City *(Schenkman, 1972).*

■ In a society where the standard normality is to be a young or middle-aged married adult, old age—and in particular being old and no longer married marks off a special life situation. Here many of the dynamics of the deviance process operate much as they do in physical handicaps. Being old has been widely observed to involve a considerable amount of stigmatization in our society. Since old people are better able to defend themselves against such processes by being a partner in a functioning marriage, the older widow and widower are more fully subject to these pressures, as well as to the deprivation of intimacy and attachment that marriage involves.

In this selection, Lopata analyzes some of the variations in loneliness as widows in one large American city experienced it. For other studies of aging and loneliness see Elaine Cumming and William E. Henry, *Growing Old* (Basic Books, 1961); Donald Cowgill and Lowell Holmes, eds., *Aging in Different Societies* (Appleton-Century-Crofts, 1970); Peter Marris, *Widows and Their Families* (Routledge and Kegan Paul, Ltd., 1958); and Jeremy Tunstall, *Old and Alone* (Routledge and Kegan Paul, Ltd., 1966). ■

THE SENTIMENT of loneliness has been an object of much sociological research in spite, or maybe because, of philosophical and psychological generalizations about alienation. Anxiety raised by assumptions that modern society invariably creates loneliness may be compounded by the connection between this feeling and the death of significant others to an extent sufficient to prevent a scientific analysis of its conditions and components.

This paper is based upon descriptions of situations of loneliness and of methods used to cope with it by widows 50 years of age or older, living within an American metropolitan center. It is founded on the hypothesis that loneliness is a sentiment felt by a person when he defines his experienced level or form of interaction as inadequate. Such feelings are likely to arise when the habitual or expected depth of relations with other people is judged as temporarily or permanently unavailable, broken, or underdeveloped. Hopefully, the conclusions reached about widows in a metropolitan center of a modern industrialized society can bring insights into the forms and components of loneliness as a sentiment experienced by other people.

The women who report loneliness as a major problem of widowhood were studied through exploratory depth interviews, discussions with friends and relatives, and formalized interviews with an area probability sample of 300 respondents. The latter were conducted by the National Opinion Research Center. Attendance at meetings of NAIM, a Catholic organization for the widowed, and of a variety of clubs devoted to older persons supplied additional data, as did literature dealing with family life not only in America but in other societies.

The emerging structure of the American family and its pattern of residential settlement make the death of a spouse increasingly disorganizing for the surviving partner. In comparison to familistic groups of rural areas and past centuries, modern urban, and especially middle class, wives are usually left alone when the husband dies. Most widows are older women whose children have already left home for marriage, bachelor quarters, or residential schools. The extended family has been modified to include only limited and periodic interaction conducted from dispersed headquarters. Emphasis upon the independence of each nuclear family discourages parents from living with their married children. Not only is the older couple living alone at the time of the husband's death, but the widow, health permitting, remains in that unit, or in a similar one of smaller size, for most of her remaining years of life, which can cover more than a decade.

The decreasing functionality of the extended family and mate selection through love have placed a heavy affective, social, economic, and recreational burden upon the marital unit. Thus, the death of one of the partners cannot help but disorganize a great part of life for the other. American widowhood is made additionally difficult by the fact that this society is becoming increasingly couple-companionate in the also expanding nonwork sphere of action. Single persons, and especially single women, are simply out of place in the system, while they simultaneously lack automatic membership in a close sex-segregated network. Those who never marry build over years their own patterns of companionship and aloneness, but the widow is suddenly removed from a familiar world in which she had a comfortable position. Prior friendships were dependent upon couples doing things together evenings and weekends, and they are made awkward by the removal of one member. Sex-segregated friendship groups such as the "society of widows" found in Kansas City by Cumming and Henry are often considered less prestigeful. Many women refuse to restrict their relations to others in the same low status situation, and feel anger and loneliness when excluded from the company of prior associates whose husbands are still living. In addition, women were often socialized to be passive, particularly in past decades, and they lack tools for the development of new social roles and friendship relations.

Thus, widowhood presents for an increasingly large group of American women a break in the major forms and levels of interaction with an individual central to their role of wife, with people brought into contact with her through the husband and with former associates in couple-companionate relations. It is not, therefore, surprising that 48 percent of the random sample of widows interviewed in an urban area report loneliness as the major problem in widowhood and that an additional 22 percent refer to it in conjunction with other problems such as finances.

CHARACTERISTICS OF LONELINESS

One of the characteristics of loneliness is its infusion in all three time dimensions, past, present, and future. People often feel lonely for a person, object, event, interaction scene, or mood which had been experienced in the past. The less easily can this situation be reproduced at the time when the longing for it occurs, the more likely will there develop a sense of loneliness or "homesickness" instead of a plan of action. The homesick person reconstructs in imagination, meaningful scenes, often modifying elements to make them ideal by current standards. Many such scenes involve people or are built around them, and they are simply explained as a wish for the presence of these individuals. John is missed especially often if his memory is linked to scenes identified as pleasurable. This type of loneliness for the person is a backward-looking one; the desire is not in terms of present or future potential for the relation with the absent partner, but as a wish to repeat past scenes played with him.

The definition of loneliness as a wish for a form or level of interaction different from the one presently experienced can include references to the number of people, to forms of their behavior, or to expressed sentiments. A person may feel lonely when no one else is present, when a particular other is absent, when interaction partners treat him differently than he desires, or when aspects of the situation make him feel alienated from those with whom he could develop different relations. By such definition, loneliness may be alienation from the self when the internal dialogue is unsatisfactory, as when self-rejection is felt from an internalized specific or generalized "other." One can be poor company to oneself.

Loneliness experienced in connection with the future can be called "loneliness anxiety" when it contains a fear of losing companions and of being powerless to build satisfactory levels of new relations. It is the inability to create desired relations which seems to underlie the problem so glibly called the alienation of man in modern society. Traditional society immersed persons in multiple, automatic sets of relations varied in sentiment and depth. The automatic feature of these connecting links and their expressions in actual interaction have been removed by the mobile, large-scale social system. Not only widows, but also young people leaving schools, mobile executives, mothers suddenly removed from their circle of relations by the presence of a new-born infant, members of the "old bunch" facing its dispersal, etc.—all these people, without even considering pathological isolation, who have their relations broken by some event face at least temporary loneliness. What is significant in modern society is the gap between this reality of life and the ability of its members to build new relations. Socialization and education are still tied to a vanished village and small town world.

Some communities, groups, and individuals have evolved techniques and skills necessary in taking future relation partners through the complex of steps leading to satisfactory interaction. Generally, however, loneliness anxiety is sufficiently high in America to prevent rational plans of action which acknowledge the presence of loneliness itself in many situations of modern life, and which contain means of helping those experiencing it to build more desirable levels of interaction. The latent assumption that anyone admitting loneliness has "something wrong with him" and the anxiety that the self may end up without loved ones and friends compound the problems of the temporarily lonely person by making him the object of avoidance at the very time when he needs empathetic help.

FORMS OF LONELINESS

Widows who explain that loneliness is a major problem refer to one or a combination of the following forms of this sentiment.

1. A loneliness as a desire to carry on interaction with a particular other who is no longer available. Many, but by no means all, widows feel lonely for their deceased husband as a person whom they enjoyed, whatever the type of relation between them. They are likely to tell ancedotes pointing up the unique personality of the man they miss. Other expressions of this form of loneliness are more simply stated as, "I miss Tom," "John would have enjoyed this."

2. When a husband, parent, friend, or adult child dies or is otherwise withdrawn from interaction, the remaining partner may feel that she or he is no longer an object of love. Freud and many other analysts of human sentiments have stressed the importance to an individual of being treated by another person as something worth loving. The sentiment the recipient wants others to feel about him may be one of sexual desire, of companionate love, or understanding and respect, or a combination of all these. The death of the partner of a significant relation thus removes a major source of this identity as a love object, often leaving no other source. One widow, asked if she considers remarrying, said no, explaining that her husband had been a very kind man. "In fact, people say everybody has fights, well, we didn't—we just didn't—that's all. I think he and I, we liked each other so well—you can fall in love and maybe be disillusioned but if you like a person as well, you don't or rather you aren't let down and that's the way we always were. Here I am so big and fat and sometimes I'd be reading and would look up and he'd be sitting there looking at me— and I'd say 'what are you thinking about?', and he would say, 'Oh, I was just thinking how pretty you are.' That's the kind of person he was. Everyone liked him. . . ." This respondent's husband had been seriously ill

for 11 years, during which time she provided total care for him at home.

3. Loneliness can be felt due to the absence of anyone to care for or to be the recipient of love. Being an object of love and having one to pour one's feelings upon can be two separately felt sentiments. "You have no one to talk to, and I'm a person who needs someone to pet and care for. Maybe I spoiled my men rotten but they were good to me. I just need someone to take care of." This respondent had been married and widowed twice.

4. A loneliness can be felt for a companionate relation of the depth provided by the deceased, for the sharing of experiences with another human being. "I don't think anyone who hasn't experienced it can understand the void that is left after losing a companion for so many years—all the happy little things that come up and you think, 'Oh, I must share that'—and there isn't anyone there to share it with." "Lonesomeness, you sorta miss your partner when you was close." "We had a very close relationship and would always go places together and do everything together. You find even though there are people around —there is that great big void that's there. I don't think that the old saying 'time heals all wounds' is really true because we were so close. I find that even being around friends and relatives you can be so lonesome in a crowd; there are many a time you go places and see or do things and I find myself saying even out loud 'wait till we tell Dad'; or 'Dad should see this.' In the paper, on TV—and I can't wait to tell him."

5. A feeling of loneliness for the presence of another human being within the dwelling unit is experienced by many widows. The generalized sounds of someone moving around, or the need to organize work around another person are often missed by them; the opening of a door can herald a major shift in the day's schedule of a wife. "Now I miss my husband around 5:30 or 6:00. He'd be home from work; I'd see him coming down the side drive because he was the type of man who was always here on time and

demanded we all be home on time. He was very punctual and those are the things a person misses and it seems to be the longer he is gone, the more I miss him." "It's very lonely, when the night comes you wish someone would be there. We didn't do much but he used to just be there."

6. A feeling of loneliness as unhappiness over the absence of another person who shares the workload or carries out tasks which the remaining partner cannot or does not wish to do is expressed by several widows. Many wives feel helpless in solving problems or taking care of a home when the husband dies. They interpret this sentiment and the related frustration from trying to get the male chores performed by others as loneliness. Having become dependent upon a man who habitually met certain needs, they feel alone every time they seek replacements. "You get so disgusted when you are alone and you have to do everything yourself, especially when you are not well." "I guess everybody gets a little lonesome. I think it's just natural; now I do everything myself. I miss my husband because he used to work in the garden and do things." "I was faced immediately with all the things that happen in a home, not knowing how to manage. I'm just learning how to operate the color TV, get the colors right (her husband died one and a half years ago). My husband was an engineer and ingenious. I did not understand the operation. He would say about the car, 'now is the time to have it checked.' It's different when one must say to oneself 'you do it'."

7. Another form of loneliness is experienced as a homesickness for the style of life or some set of activities formerly carried out with the other. Many wives enjoy company parties, golf, couple-companionate dinners, and such events, and will not engage in them after the husband dies, or have them no longer available since it was his presence which formed the connecting link in the first place. "The loss of my husband is a problem; around the holidays it bothers me most. Because the holidays are the reminders of when the family was all together and now

he's not here no more and when we were together it was happiness." "We used to go to concerts, out to dinner, and now I don't go." "I stopped golfing when he was ill and I haven't gone back to it." "We went places, did things; now I sit home."

8. Many widows experiencing disengagement from a prior life-style and sets of relations express loneliness as an alienation due to a status drop. Women feel less social status in widowhood due to a lack of a male escort, because of a loss of reflected status from the positions held by the husband, or as a consequence of being a single woman in a couple-companionate world. "I feel the way, how can I put it in words, second-class citizen. Well, I think just the fact that you don't have an escort when you go places. I think that this is very pronounced and very evident if you go out to dinner. I don't like to go out to dinner alone, so consequently you try to get on the phone and call somebody else up and see if they're in the mood to go. This sets you apart—you see a couple of women—I can remember down in Miami, I hate Miami for that reason, when I was not a widow yet, you'd see groups of beautifully gowned, elegant looking elderly women, you knew they were all widows. Immediately they were an isolated segment of society, in my mind at that time, and I'm sure that other people look at us the same way." "When a woman is widowed—she's lost status, steps down—left all that behind, rejected by people," states a widow of a very wealthy and prominent Chicago businessman. "I run from big parties. For example, they arranged at a party for all widows to sit at the same table. After you dress up, get ready for a gala party, it is stunning, shattering. I will go to a cocktail party when no one knows me. Boston, New York—that is exciting, a different type of attention—but I avoid such parties at home."

9. The loss of a basic relation partner, such as a husband, can have repercussions in many interaction scenes with prior associates, which can become compounded into rifts in other social relations, thus increasing loneliness. Widows report many incidents in which they have felt unhappy with people who had been part of a previous life. There are several factors contributing to such relational strain with friends following the death of a husband:

a. According to many observers of societies sharing a Western culture, loneliness in widowhood is partially a consequence of the deinstitutionalization of the death, mourning, and bereavement sequences. Strain occurs over the form and length of "appropriate" grief reactions and over the behavior the widow expects from people defined as part of the assisting team. "No one helps you. You have to do everything yourself"; "I just had to stand on my own feet"; "I'm still grieving. My husband has been dead a little over a year, no individual has helped me at all," report some widows when asked who helped them most during the grief period. The anger produced by such a lack of cooperation comes out in many other statements they make in the interview, and women who are so oriented usually report strong feelings of alienation.

b. The gradual withering away of social relations during a husband's illness, if it lasts a long time, can leave the widow very lonely after his death. Some women mention that they had not realized how isolated they had become since the very care of the ill person filled the days, and the level of interaction had decreased gradually.

c. The traits of grief as experienced by the widow often result in an awkwardness of interaction, if not in its avoidance by both parties. Emotional outbursts or public crying go against the ethics of a society which still idealizes complete self-control. "You have to help yourself—no one else will help you. Work, if possible, to keep your mind off of your problems at least by day. And don't cry in front of your friends; you just embarrass them and they can't help you," is the advice of a widow to a woman experiencing the same event.

d. Death and loneliness anxiety, experienced consciously or camouflaged by a complex of rationalizations, contribute to the withdrawal of former friends from a widow. "I don't know what they're afraid of—that death is catching?"

e. The widow often feels that she is a "fifth wheel" or that her very presence makes social interaction awkward. The suspicion that former friends no longer wish to associate with her stops many a widow from carrying out behaviors which could increase the level of the relation. "They say 'You know we will always be there'—but when you call—'Oh, I'm sorry . . . my children . . . my husband . . .' They talk so much about how they will help you that they think they have done what they talk about." "One of my dearest friends, her husband is a judge, three or four weeks before the event she called: 'Come to the president's ball, sit at our table.' Two days before it she called: 'My husband's invited too many people . . . you understand'." "Being shunned by others— being an individual by yourself. People are afraid you're going to leech on to them. For a while, they are nice and then they forget you."

f. Some of the younger widows feel that relations have become strained because of jealousy on the part of former couple friends. Such comments are usually made unofficially after the interview or during a break, and it is hard to determine the original source of the tension and whether it concerns only the husband of the friend. Hostesses are often reported as favoring male unattached guests but as finding many reasons for not inviting their women friends who are widowed or divorced. Of course, the other situation is also likely. The widow, wishing male companionship and to be considered sexually and personally desirable, may be interpreting any action of the husband as implying advances and of the wife as based on jealousy.

g. Loneliness as a result of decreased interaction with friends is sometimes a result of prior dependency of a wife on the husband to take the initiative in arranging contact with others. His death leaves her, unless she or the friends change their behavior, increasing initiating action, unable to maintain the same round of interaction. "Financial problems and how you are going to make it, especially over a certain age, can be worrisome. A lot of people suffer from the sense of loneliness. They don't know how to take the reins themselves, they relied on their husbands so much that when they become widows they are lost." A friend of one widow explains: "She always complains about being lonely, that no one calls, that she has nothing to do. Well, Wally (the husband) was the one always on the go and he took her. Now she waits for someone to get her going . . . and we don't see much of her."

h. The inability to maintain a desired level of interaction with former friends is often a consequence of other life changes: finances, not having a car or not knowing how to drive, having to move to a less conveniently located neighborhood, etc. "I don't see my friends much any more. I don't go out alone at night and it is far to come and get me here." "I had to move to a smaller place." "I don't drive." "I try to see the Skokie friends but . . ." Twenty-one percent of the respondents found the following statement to be true: "My present income makes it impossible for me to maintain old friendships." This statement is particularly representative of the very improverished and of women whose friends have husbands who are still the labor force in well-paying jobs.

10. Loneliness in widowhood is compounded by the inability to make new friends, the lack of skills needed to build new patterns of relations when old ones become broken, strained, or not easily available. Of the widows, 71 percent feel that "old friends" cannot be replaced no matter how one tries to make new friends; 16 percent do not know anyone in their neighborhood, and 31 percent belong to no voluntary associations. They usually do not define their isolation as due to a lack in their own abilities, but women

who reengage after widowhood indicate this to be a conscious process of developing new lines of connection.

11. The feeling of loneliness may be a composite of any of the above-mentioned forms. A widow may miss her husband, find the burden of maintaining her home alone very heavy, modify her life sufficiently to make difficult contact with former friends, and feel strain in their presence, while lacking skills needed to convert casual or secondary relations into ones of greater intimacy. "Loneliness—nobody to talk; it's very important, the most really. No one to love you." (Interviewer's note: "At this point the respondent began to cry and to repeat 'no one to love you.' Finally, she got control of herself and continued.") "It's a very lonely life—you have friends, you feel happy when you're with them but you have to come home to an empty house. You can't go places because you're invited somewhere and if you are, you're the loner—everybody is there in couples. They include you but you still have the feeling they are just being polite. I went to Europe with a friend and for two weeks it was OK but the rest of the time I went to Slovakia where I knew people. Can I go to just parks and museums all alone? Perhaps if I had younger children at home it wouldn't be so bad but my mother is old and senile and that's like talking to a child. You have no one to talk to."

SOLUTIONS TO LONELINESS

Not all of the widows feel deeply lonely after the death of their husbands. Some explain this fact as a consequence of their personality. "I was an only child. I've been used to isolation, and, in fact, I enjoy my own company. I don't mean this egotistically, but I can be very happy with me and a book and something to do." "Some people cannot stand themselves, to be alone. I always had to have my own time. My husband soon learned I needed time to be alone, away from him. Even as a child, I took off certain time for myself and time to get caught up with

my thinking. So I never felt I had to be with people. I am enjoying my freedom . . . as long as I have my money I can spend on myself and on the children. An age for everything. I lived with one man for 30 years and we were congenial."

Closely knit kinship groups provide insured interaction even in urban centers and prevent many forms of loneliness. "I had so many close brothers and sisters and close friends that I didn't have the most important problem—loneliness. There were just some days of depression, when it really hit me, when I would remember all the terrible days when he was very sick. He had this disease for 24 years." This widow is not discouraged and was planning to remarry 10 days after the interview.

For some widows, the death of the husband brought little change—"he wasn't here much anyway"—or only relief, "It (widowhood) hasn't been a problem at all. My life just went on the same way. It was a relief not to have to worry about his alcoholism." A Greek respondent, whose family married her to a man 20 years her senior, stated suddenly, after some hesitation, "Free . . . that's what I am, free."

Many of those widows mention loneliness sometime during the interview, then explain the techniques they have devised to deal with this problem. Basically, the devices fall into three categories: keeping busy, developing new roles and relations, and focusing life on one social role.

The most frequently given "advice to a new widow" to to "keep busy." Busywork may consist of a simple formula for immediate action or a whole way of life. "I think we're all lonely at times. I think that's the greatest problem for me but I do something about it immediately. If I wake up at night and feel it creeping over me, I get up and make a cup of coffee, maybe walk around, maybe come out and read a chapter of a book and forget it, and go back to bed." "I find that the lonesome part of the day is at dusk. I don't have my mail delivered and I usually go out and get my mail or do some shopping at that time—just to get away from the house then. People say they call me up at 6:00 and 'you're not home'—I tell them it may be a good time for most people but it isn't a good time to get me because then I feel too lonesome, I just get out. I have a car so I drive around a little. I generally eat dinner late at night . . . I have a little TV in the kitchen, too, so I can eat out there. I think it's kind of lonely to eat alone—that's why I watch TV or read the papers."

Busywork may include, directly or indirectly, other people or it may be carried out entirely alone. "And if I haven't got anything else to do, I'll make a pie for somebody, one of the neighbors that I hear is going to have company—get busy and do something, no matter what it is—just keep busy. Even if you can't do anything else but sit down and make paper flowers—make them. If you don't know how to do it—then throw them away and make some more. Make cookies, give them away; gee, there's always places where you can take pounds of cookies— orphanages . . . Lake Bluff. I often go up there during the wintertime. I'll make cookies, then hope for a good day and take them up there, and those kids love them, you know, and it's wonderful. You come home and you think 'Gee, I did something,' you know. The space you're occupying counts for something."

Low, that is, nonimmobilizing levels of loneliness anxiety can lead to a plan of life designed to insure both activity and social contact. Such a systematic program is very much a middle and upper class phenomenon, typical of women who have had a relatively extensive educational background and prior involvement in secondary groups. "On Tuesday, I have my hair done every other week. The Card Club meets on the last Wednesday of every month. And Thursday in every other week, the Circle. Quite often on Sunday I go out to dinner with friends; we eat at different places. And then I go to Little Theater in town. They have five plays during the winter."

It is often hard to distinguish busywork from activity carried out for its own sake. The basic difference seems to be that the former is entered into for the sole purpose of avoiding loneliness rather than for its intrinsic value. It is often engaged in early in widowhood. Later, the activity acquires its own meaning apart from the original intent.

The ability to develop new relations in response to the changes in life brought about by the death of the husband is also contained primarily in the middle and upper classes of American society, and even here it is not shared by all widows. An 84-year-old pastor's wife who moved frequently during the first years of a long widowhood, staying for limited periods of time with each of her seven children, and only recently settling with one son and his wife, explains how she has handled loneliness. "One thing is—keep associating with people and do not be too choosey about one's friends. I mean sometimes people think that it isn't the person you can care too much for—and so often you can find such marvelous people that don't appear to one so much at first and they are just the people who need someone to befriend them, and they can be marvelous friends. Even these social activities, one can contribute a little. I think one shouldn't be afraid to be useful, even if one has to give themselves a little push."

Changing the role cluster to focus on a new or newly revitalized social role when that of wife is no longer available is one solution to the problems of loneliness. Many women go to work and find enjoyment in its task and relational features. One widow explained, however, that her prior shift into a focus upon the role of mother to the exclusion of other sets of relations is currently causing great unhappiness. Her sons are now getting married and changing their concern to that of their family of procreation, leaving her feeling literally deserted in a form of secondary widowhood. The role of grandmother provided a way out of loneliness for one widow who even followed her granddaughter to Denver when the latter went away to college. Remarriage is a solution to many forms of loneliness. Most respondents state that they are fearful of remarriage because "My husband was so good," "No one could love me like my husband," "I am too set in my ways," or because of stories reporting many problems in such relations. However, the flavor of quite a few interviews suggests that such statements may function as rationalizations for not having been able to remarry rather than as declarations opposing such a step.

Some solutions are not available to an individual. An older Negro widow explains that remarriage is difficult in her community: "One thing about our women—we can't get married as fast as White women who are 50 and over. The older men marry younger women . . . and, another thing . . . our women are better educated than our men. You asked me about my husband and his education—most of us came from the South. If the family was poor, they educated the girl, most of them could get a clerical job. They could teach school, or you could work in some insurance office—there weren't many clerical jobs—teaching school mostly. But the boys had to stay at home and work to help the family do all these things—and there are more educated women than men. So our women are independent today—cause they say they'd like to have a man—but where would they get one? You get so bored with what you come in contact with—so that you're not interested."

Most widows prefer living alone to moving into the homes of their married children. This attitude exists in urban centers other than those of the United States, according to studies of aging. The interviewees of this study explain that they want their independence, that each woman should be head of her own house, and that "the generation gap" makes differences in attitudes toward life and particularly toward childrearing a source of strain. "I think it's hard for people of different ages to live together. She (daughter) doesn't have the same ideas as I do. My daughter says, 'Mother, if you would just keep your mouth closed, everything would be all right.' I said, 'Well, that's the trouble, I'm not going to keep my mouth shut! What's the fun of it, if you can't open your mouth once in a while.' My daughter is very different than me, I'm slow, pokey."

However complex the reasons why older widows do not live with their married children, the fact remains that most of them choose to live alone. These respondents indicate that, although they feel the various forms of loneliness at one time or another, they have learned to live alone and 45 percent agree with the statement: "I like living alone." Very few are completely desolate. In general, they have gone through a cycle of loneliness following widowhood. After the initial stages of shock, numbness, and mourning ritual is over, the widow becomes very lonely for her husband, as a person, as a love object or provider, as a companion, as someone around whom time and work can be organized, as someone who shares the work of running a home and rearing children, or as an escort enabling wider functioning in society. These forms of loneliness often become complicated by the products of estrangement from the circle of married friends who had formed the major leisure-time interaction for the middle and upper class woman. Somewhere during the grief period these various forms of loneliness seem to combine into a very strong mood of depression. Efforts of relatives and friends, initiative behavior by the widow herself, or a combination of these two gradually lead to movement out of this depth of despair and to "grief work." This term is used by Lindemann to describe the process through which new relations are built in place of that with the deceased. The women who define life as furnishing an acceptable level of satisfaction seem to restrict their feeling of loneliness mainly to the first-mentioned form, missing the deceased as an individual who was part of a past life.

Widows differ in the lines of reengagement they develop with society, in the way they handle loneliness, and in the degree to which they build new life-styles after the period of grief is over. Three sets of factors contribute to the kinds of social roles and less integrated social relations they build into a new role complex: the social structure and culture of the society and of the segment of that society in which they are located; the family system which they have available for interaction and its cultural patterns; and the personality and life circumstances of the woman herself. Those widows who are automatically immersed in a close-knit network of family, neighborhood, and/or friends never go through some of the forms of loneliness and have therefore not been the subject of much discussion in this paper. The widows who have or develop abilities to build new social relations and social roles into a new life-style solve many of the major problems which face others in modern society. These women, most of whom have been socialized and educated into competency in dealing with current reality and urban relations, indicate that loneliness and alienation are not inevitable or irreversible. Having gone through a major disengagement from prior life and social relations, they then use emerging facilities of an individuated self and of the complex society to create new life-styles. They choose to live alone, knowing that they can find all levels of interaction when they wish and having self-confidence in their ability to convert secondary contact into new primary relations when needed. The very lonely are women socialized into passive membership in automatically encompassing groups, who now lack such relations. They are the victims of the gap between traditional ways of socializing societal members, particularly women, and the realities of modern life.

V.
MORAL ENTERPRISE AND MORAL ENFORCEMENT

"RULES ARE THE PRODUCTS of someone's initiative and we can think of the people that exhibit such enterprise as moral entrepreneurs." After making this observation, Howard S. Becker adds that there are two major kinds of moral entrepreneurship—rule creation and rule enforcement. The rule creator is concerned with the content of rules, with establishing what kind of behavior shall and shall not be judged to be in moral conformity; the rule creation process involves all those activities that go on to establish particular norms. The moral crusader who first asserts the necessity for a new rule is the most clearcut example of a rule creator, but the process has many more mundane participants, including the variety of experts who fashion the innovator's goal into practical form (e.g., lawyers). The individual who argues for the abolition of a rule— as, say, in abortion law reform—is engaged in an activity of moral enterprise as fully as the individual who proposes the rule. Both liberalization and repression are moral entrepreneurial activities.

Rule creation and demolition are aspects of social change. We seldom see major shifts in the rules, and from year to year they generally are taken as given. There is, however, an important paradox here. A rule, Erikson observes, is real only if it is enforced; therefore the process of rule enforcement is in a sense also the process of rule creation. Thus the moral entrepreneurs with the greatest impact on society may be those who enforce rules and thereby renew them.

Here we shall consider several levels of the system of moral enforcement as it operates in our society. We move from the street level, with two selections on police-citizen encounters (32 and 33); to the level of trials, with a selection that analyzes the activities of public defenders (34) and one that discusses

333

the system of justice in the juvenile court (35). Then we consider the institutions in which certain kinds of adjudicated deviants are confined. David Rothman insightfully analyzes (36) "the discovery of the asylum," the social invention of special places for rehabilitation such as mental hospitals and institutions of correction; then some of the characteristics those two kinds of institutions share as "total institutions" are discussed (38); and finally we learn (39) how the social organization of prisons develops, and why in the contemporary world there is so much unrest in prisons.

We begin this part with a selection on dirty work that is socially necessary. Sociologist Everett C. Hughes, who established the investigation of work, occupations, and professions as a major area of modern social research, here analyzes some of the German social definitions that fostered the mass murder of concentration camp victims. In the course of this analysis, however, he provides a more general model of how society gets done those kinds of work that powerful persons consider necessary but want to conceal. He is able to use an extreme and perhaps unique social event to advance our understanding of more common processes.

Moral enforcement is not a pretty business. The enforcement of norms requires the use of power and meets with resistance; so a lot of interpersonal "work" must be done and often very unpleasant emotional confrontations must be experienced. Moral enforcement thus tends to be heavily ritualized to contain the strong feelings and potentialities for violence engendered on both sides. But we know that this ritualization is not fully successful in containing and neutralizing unpleasantness. Compounding these inevitable difficulties is the knowledge that rules do not really work very well, that society is not unambiguous in providing guidelines for the moral enforcers, and that such persons often are given a fairly broad warrant to make up the law as they go along.

Hughes observes that perhaps the Germans gave the S.S. "an unconscious mandate" to go beyond anything that most citizens could have participated in. He suggests that this support represents a general process also present in our own society when some kinds of functionaries receive an unconscious mandate to do shameful work that nevertheless must be done.

31. GOOD PEOPLE AND DIRTY WORK

EVERETT C. HUGHES

Reprinted by permission of Social Problems *10 (Summer 1962). Copyright 1962 by Society for the Study of Social Problems. (Delivered as public lecture at McGill University shortly after a long visit to Western Germany in 1948). Everett C. Hughes is Professor of Sociology at Boston College and previously taught at the University of Chicago and Brandeis University. His best known book is* French Canada in Transition *(University of Chicago, 1963), in collaboration with Helen McGill; and his many important papers are collected in* The Sociological Eye *(Aldine, 1971). He is a past president of the American Socological Association, has been an honorary president of the Canadian Sociology and Anthropology Association, and is a Fellow of the American Academy of Arts and Sciences.*

■ During the 1960s school teachers, social workers, and policemen in a number of major American cities went on strike, or took sick leaves or resigned en masse where state law forbade strikes. By the early 1970s the revolt of the moral enforcers had spread to prison guards, who in various parts of the country displayed anger against what they felt to be the dangerous coddling of prisoners. In Massachusetts, for example, prison guards and their union engaged in a sustained campaign to force the resignation of the liberalizing (and Black) commissioner of corrections. Everett Hughes' article on dirty work provides one way of understanding some of this unrest and "lawlessness" on the part of those charged with enforcing society's norms.

The operation of these processes is obvious in the deeply felt American ambivalence toward the police, but they also operate more broadly. Our world, for example, has a large out-group—a separate nation of ghetto Blacks whom most White Americans feel must be controlled and confined. Yet those same White Americans are deeply ashamed of their feelings and uncertain about *how* Blacks are to be controlled and confined, and they prefer to conceal from themselves much of the detail of how the dirty work doers actually go about their assigned tasks.

As the urban ghettos have grown, so has the cohort of functionaries who receive the covert assignment to "keep the colored out of our way." In the process many institutions officially designed to further well-being and opportunity have become perverted into institutions of custody and constraint. Social workers find that their profession, designed to help, has been perverted into one designed to spy and to punish. More dramatically, the schools have become custodial institutions in which less and less learning takes place. To conceal their failure they consistently promote students who have learned less than they should. The proliferation of policemen in schools and of special schools for "incorrigible" children testify to the prisonlike functions that undergird our educational rhetoric and increasingly call into question the national ideology that education cures all ills.

The dirty workers are increasingly caught between the silent middle class, which wants them to do the work and keep quiet about it, and the objects of that work, who refuse to continue to take it lying down. Individual revolts confront teachers with "blackboard jungle" problems; welfare workers have the problem of their charges' feigned stupidity and real deception. These civilian colonial armies find their expectations of respect challenged at every turn, and often they must carry out their daily duties in fear for their physical safety. Equally ominous for the dirty workers is the organized Black challenge to their legitimacy. They must cope not only with individual resistance to their ministrations but also, more and more, with militant and insistent civil rights groups that expose their failures and tax them with their abrogation of professional responsibilities to teach, to protect, and to help. ■

THE NATIONAL SOCIALIST GOVERNMENT of Germany, with the arm of its fanatical inner sect, the S.S., commonly known as the Black Shirts or Elite Guard, perpetrated and boasted of the most colossal and dramatic piece of social dirty work the world has ever known

Perhaps there are other claimants to the title, but they could not match this one's combination of mass, speed, and perverse pride in the deed. Nearly all peoples have plenty of cruelty and death to account for. How many Negro Americans have died by the hands of lynching mobs? How many more from unnecessary disease and lack of food or of knowledge of nutrition? How many Russians died to bring about collectivization of land? And who is to blame if there be starving millions in some parts of the world while wheat molds in the fields of other parts?

I do not revive the case of the Nazi *Endloesung* (final solution) of the Jewish problem in order to condemn the Germans or make them look worse than other peoples but to recall to our attention dangers which lurk in our midst always. Most of what follows was written after my first postwar visit to Germany in 1948. The impressions were vivid. The facts have not diminished and disappeared with time, as did the stories of alleged German atrocities in Belgium in the First World War. The fuller the record, the worse it gets.

Several millions of people were delivered to the concentration camps, operated under the leadership of Heinrich Himmler with the help of Adolf Eichmann. A few hundred thousand survived in some fashion. Still fewer came out sound of mind and body. A pair of examples, well attested, will show the extreme of perverse cruelty reached by the S.S. guards in charge of the camps. Prisoners were ordered to climb trees; guards whipped them to make them climb faster. Once they were out of reach, other prisoners, also urged by the whip, were put to shaking the trees. When the victims fell, they were kicked to see whether they could rise to their feet. Those too badly injured to get up were shot to death, as useless for work. A not inconsiderable number of prisoners were drowned in pits full of human excrement. These examples are so horrible that your minds will run away from them. You will not, as when you read a slightly salacious novel, imagine the rest. I therefore thrust these examples upon you and insist that the people who thought them

up could, and did, improvise others like them, and even worse, from day to day over several years. Many of the victims of the camps gave up the ghost (this Biblical phrase is the most apt) from a combination of humiliation, starvation, fatigue, and physical abuse. In due time, a policy of mass liquidation in the gas chamber was added to individual virtuosity in cruelty.

This program—for it was a program—of cruelty and murder was carried out in the name of racial superiority and racial purity. It was directed mainly, although by no means exclusively, against Jews, Slavs and Gypsies. It was thorough. There are few Jews in the territories which were under the control of the Third German Reich—the two Germanies, Holland, Czechoslovakia, Poland, Austria, Hungary. Many Jewish Frenchmen were destroyed. There were concentration camps even in Tunisia and Algiers under the German occupation.

When, during my 1948 visit to Germany, I became more aware of the reactions of ordinary Germans to the horrors of the concentration camps, I found myself asking not the usual question, "How did racial hatred rise to such a high level?" but this one, "How could such dirty work be done among and, in a sense, *by* the millions of ordinary, civilized German people?" Along with this came related questions. How could these millions of ordinary people live in the midst of such cruelty and murder without a general uprising against it and against the people who did it? How, once freed from the regime that did it, could they be apparently so little concerned about it, so toughly silent about it, not only in talking with outsiders—which is easy to understand—but among themselves? How and where could there be found in a modern civilized country the several hundred thousand men and women capable of such work? How were these people so far released from the inhibitions of civilized life as to be able to imagine, let alone perform, the ferocious, obscene, and perverse actions which they did imagine and perform? How could they be kept at such a height of fury through years of having to see daily at close range the human wrecks they made and being often literally spattered with the filth produced and accumulated by their own actions?

You will see that there are here two orders of questions. One set concerns the good people who did not themselves do this work. The other concerns those who did do it. But the two sets are not really separate; for the crucial question concerning the good people is their relation to the people who did the dirty work, with a related one which asks under what circumstances good people let the others get away with such actions.

An easy answer concerning the Germans is that they were not so good after all. We can attribute to them some special inborn or ingrained race consciousness, combined with a penchant for sadistic cruelty and unquestioning acceptance of whatever is done by those who happen to be in authority. Pushed to its extreme, this answer simply makes us, rather than the Germans, the superior race. It is the Nazi tune, put to words of our own.

Now there are deep and stubborn differences between peoples. Their history and culture may make the Germans especially susceptible to the doctrine of their own racial superiority and especially acquiescent to the actions of whoever is in power over them. These are matters deserving of the best study that can be given them. But to say that these things could happen in Germany simply because Germans are different—from us— buttresses their own excuses and lets us off too easily from blame for what happened there and from the question whether it could happen here.

Certainly in their daily practice and expression before the Hitler regime, the Germans showed no more, if as much, hatred of other racial or cultural groups than we did and do. Residential segregation was not marked. Intermarriage was common, and the families of such marriages had an easier social existence than they generally have in America. The racially exclusive club, school, and hotel were much less in evidence than here. And I well remember an evening in 1933 when a Montreal businessman—a very nice man, too—said in our living room, "Why don't

we admit that Hitler is doing to the Jews what we ought to be doing?" That was not an uncommon sentiment, although it may be said in defense of the people who expressed it that they probably did not know and would not have believed the full truth about the Nazi program of destroying Jews. The essential underlying sentiments on racial matters in Germany were not different in kind from those prevailing throughout the Western, and especially the Anglo-Saxon, countries. But I do not wish to overemphasize this point. I only want to close one easy way out of serious consideration of the problem of good people and dirty work by demonstrating that the Germans were and are about as good and about as bad as the rest of us on this matter of racial sentiments and, let us add, their notions of decent human behavior.

But what was the reaction of ordinary Germans to the persecution of the Jews and to the concentration camp mass torture and murder? A conversation between a German schoolteacher, a German architect, and myself gives the essentials in a vivid form. It was in the studio of the architect, and the occasion was a rather casual visit, in Frankfurt am Main in 1948.

The architect: "The professor is right. Paleswhenever I think of it. But we didn't know about it. We only learned about all that later. You must remember the pressure we were under; we had to join the party. We had to keep our mouths shut and do as we were told. It was a terrible pressure. Still, I am ashamed. But you see, we had lost our colonies, and our national honor was hurt. And these Nazis exploited that feeling. And the Jews, they *were* a problem. They came from the east. You should see them in Poland; the lowest class of people, full of lice, dirty and poor, running about in their Ghettos in filthy caftans. They came here and got rich by unbelievable methods after the first war. They occupied all the good places. Why, they were in the proportion of ten to one in medicine and law and government posts!"

At this point the architect hesitated and looked confused. He continued: "Where was I? It is the poor food. You see what misery we are in here, Herr Professor. It often happens that I forget what I was talking about. Where was I now? I have completely forgotten."

(His confusion was, I believe, not at all feigned. Many Germans said they suffered losses of memory such as this, and laid it to their lack of food.)

I said firmly: "You were talking about loss of national honor and how the Jews had got hold of everything."

The architect: "Oh, yes! That was it! Well, of course that was no way to settle the Jewish problem. But there *was* a problem and it had to be settled some way."

The schoolteacher: "Of course, they have Palestine now."

I protested that Palestine would hardly hold them.

The architect: "The professor is right. Palestine can't hold all the Jews. And it was a terrible thing to murder people. But we didn't know it at the time. But I am glad I am alive now. It is an interesting time in men's history. You know, when the Americans came it was like a great release. I really want to see a new ideal in Germany. I like the freedom that lets me talk to you like this. But, unfortunately that is not the general opinion. Most of my friends really hang on to the old ideas. They can't see any hope, so they hang on to the old ideas."

This scrap of talk gives, I believe, the essential elements as well as the flavor of the German reaction. It checks well with formal studies which have been made, and it varies only in detail from other conversations which I myself recorded in 1948.

One of the most obvious points in it is unwillingness to think about the dirty work done. In this case—perhaps by chance, perhaps not—the good man suffered an actual lapse of memory in the middle of this statement. This seems a simple point. But the psychiatrists have shown that it is less simple than it looks. They have done a good deal of work on the complicated mechanisms by which the individual mind keeps unpleasant or intolerable knowledge from consciousness, and have shown how great may, in some cases, be the consequent loss of effectiveness of the personality. But we have taken collective unwillingness to know unpleasant facts more or less for granted. That people can and do keep a silence about things whose open discussion would threaten the group's conception of itself, and hence its solidarity, is common knowledge. It is a mechanism that operates in every family and in every group which has a sense of group reputation. To break such a silence is considered an attack against the group; a sort of treason, if it be a member of the group who breaks the silence. This common silence allows group fictions to grow up; such as, that grandpa was less a scoundrel and more romantic than he really was. And I think it demonstrable that it operates especially against any expression, except in ritual, of collective guilt. The remarkable thing in present-day Germany is not that there is so little reference to something about which people do feel deeply guilty, but that it is talked about at all.

In order to understand this phenomenon we would have to find out who talks about the concentration camp atrocities, in what situations, in what mood, and with what stimulus. On these points I know only my own limited experiences. One of the most moving of these was my first postwar meeting with an elderly professor whom I had known before the Nazi time; he is a heroic soul who did not bow his head during the Nazi time and who keeps it erect now. His first words, spoken with tears in his eyes, were: "How hard it is to believe that men will be as bad as they say they will. Hitler and his people said: 'Heads will roll,' but how many of us—even of his bitterest opponents —could really believe that they would do it."

This man could and did speak, in 1948, not only to the likes of me but also to his students, his colleagues and to the public which read his articles in the most natural way about the Nazi atrocities whenever there was occasion to do it in the course of his tireless effort to reorganize and to bring new life into the German universities. He had neither the compulsion to speak, so that he might excuse and defend himself, nor a conscious or unconscious need to keep silent. Such people were rare; how many there were in Germany I do not know.

Occasions of another kind in which the silence was broken were those where, in class, public lecture, or in informal meetings with students, I myself had talked frankly of race relations in other parts of the world, including the lynchings which sometimes occur in my own country and the terrible cruelty visited upon natives in South Africa. This took off the lid of defensiveness, so that a few people would talk quite easily of what happened under the Nazi regime. More common were situations like that with the architect, where I threw in some remark about the atrocities in response to Germans' complaint that the world is abusing them. In such cases, there was usually an expression of shame, accompanied by a variety of excuses (including that of having been kept in ignorance), and followed by a quick turning away from the subject.

Somewhere in consideration of this problem of discussion versus silence we must ask what the good (that is, ordinary) people in Germany did know about these things. It is clear that the S.S. kept the more gory details of the concentration camps a close secret. Even high officials of the government, the army and the Nazi party itself were in some measure held in ignorance, although, of course, they kept the camps supplied with victims. The common people of Germany knew that the camps existed; most knew people who had disappeared into them; some saw the victims, walking skeletons in rags, being transported in trucks or trains, or being herded on the road from station to camp or to work in fields or factories near the camps. Many knew people who had been released from concentration camps; such released persons kept their counsel on pain of death. But secrecy was cultivated and supported by fear and terror. In the absence of a determined and heroic will to know and publish the truth, and in the absence of all the instruments of opposition, the degree of knowledge was undoubtedly low, in spite of the fact that all knew that something both stupendous and horrible was going on; and in spite of the fact that Hitler's *Mein Kampf* and the utterances of his aides said that no fate was too horrible for the Jews and other wrongheaded or inferior people. This must make us ask under what conditions the will to know and to discuss is strong, determined, and effective; this, like most of the important questions I have raised, I leave unanswered except as answers may be contained in the statement of the case.

But to return to our moderately good man, the architect. He insisted over and over again that he did not know, and we may suppose that he knew as much and as little as most Germans. But he also made it quite clear that he wanted something done to the Jews. I have similar statements from people of whom I knew that they had had close Jewish friends before the Nazi time. This raises the whole problem of the extent to which those pariahs who do the dirty work of society are really acting as agents for the rest of us. To talk of this question one must note that, in building up his case, the architect pushed the Jews firmly into an outgroup: they were dirty, lousy, and unscrupulous (an odd statement from a resident of Frankfurt, the home of old Jewish merchants and intellectual families long identified with those aspects of culture of which Germans are most proud). Having dissociated himself clearly from these people, and having declared them a problem, he apparently was willing to let someone else do to them the dirty work which he himself would not do, and for which he expressed shame. The case is perhaps analogous to our attitude toward those convicted of crime. From time to time, we get wind of cruelty practiced upon the prisoners in penitentiaries or jails, or, it may be, merely a report that they are ill-fed or that hygienic conditions are not good. Perhaps we do not wish that the prisoners should be cruelly treated or badly fed, but our reaction is probably tempered by a notion that they deserve something, because of some dissociation of them from the in-group of good people. If what they get is worse than what we like to think about, it is a little bit too bad. It is a point on which we are ambivalent. Campaigns for reform of prisons are often followed by countercampaigns against a too-high standard of living for prisoners and against having prisons run by softies. Now the people who run prisons are our agents. Just how far they do or could carry out our wishes is hard to say. The minor prison guard, in boastful justification of some of his more questionable practices, says, in effect: "If those reformers and those big shots upstairs had to live with these birds as I do, they would soon change their fool notions about running a prison." He is suggesting that the good people are either naive or hypocritical. Furthermore, he knows quite well that the wishes of his employers, the public, are by no means unmixed. They are quite as likely to put upon him for being too nice as for being too harsh. And if, as sometimes happens, he is a man disposed to cruelty, there may be some justice in his feeling that he is only doing what others would like to do, if they were in his place.

There are plenty of examples in our own world which I might have picked for comparison with the German attitude toward the concentration camps. For instance, a newspaper in Denver made a great scandal out of the allegation that our Japanese compatriots were too well fed in the camps where they were concentrated during the war. I might have mentioned some feature of the sorry history of the people of Japanese background in Canada. Or it might have been lynching, or some aspect of racial discrimination. But I purposely chose prisoners convicted of crime. For convicts are formally set aside for special handling. They constitute an out-group in all countries. This brings the issue clearly before us, since few people cherish the illusion that the problem of treating criminals can be settled by propaganda designed to prove that there aren't any criminals. Almost everyone agrees that something has to be done about them. The question concerns what is done, who does it, and the nature of the mandate given by the rest of us to those who do it. Perhaps we give them an unconscious mandate to go beyond anything we ourselves would care to do or even to acknowledge. I venture to suggest that the higher and more expert functionaries who act in our behalf represent something of a distillation of what we may consider our public wishes, while some of the others show a sort of concentrate of those impulses of which we are or wish to be less aware.

Now the choice of convicted prisoners brings up another crucial point in intergroup relations. All societies of any great size have in-groups and out-groups; in fact, one of the best ways of describing a society is to consider it a network of smaller and larger in-groups and out-groups. And an in-group is one only because there are out-groups. When I refer to *my* children I obviously imply that they are closer to me than other people's children and that I will make greater efforts to buy oranges and cod-liver oil for them than for others' children. In fact, it may mean that I will give them cod-liver oil if I have to choke them to get it down. We do our own dirty work on those closest to us. The very injunction that I love my neighbor as myself starts with me; if I don't love myself and my nearest, the phrase has a very sour meaning.

Each of us is a center of a network of in- and out-groups. Now the distinctions between *in* and *out* may be drawn in various ways, and nothing is more important for both the student of society and the educator than to discover how these lines are made and how they may be redrawn in more just and sensible ways. But to believe that we can do away with the distinction between *in* and *out, us* and *them* in social life is complete nonsense. On the positive side, we generally feel a greater obligation to in-groups; hence less obligation to out-groups; and in the case of such groups as convicted criminals, the out-group is definitely given over to the hands of our agents for punishment. That is the extreme case. But there are other out-groups toward which we may have aggressive feelings and dislike, although we give no formal mandate to anyone to deal with them on our behalf, and although we profess to believe that they should not suffer restrictions or disadvantages. The greater their social distance from us, the more we leave in the hands of others a sort of mandate by default to deal with them on our behalf. Whatever effort we put on reconstructing the lines which divide in- and out-groups, there remains the eternal problem of our treatment, direct or delegated, of whatever groups are considered somewhat outside. And here it is that the whole matter of our professed and possible deeper unprofessed wishes comes up for consideration; and the related problem of what we know, can know, and want to know about it. In Germany, the agents got out of hand and created such terror that it was best not to know. It is also clear that it was and is easier to the conscience of many Germans not to know. It is, finally, not unjust to say that the agents were at least working in the direction of the wishes of many people, although they may have gone beyond the wishes of most. The same questions can be asked about our own society, and with reference not only to prisoners but also to many other groups upon whom there is no legal or moral stigma. Again I have not the answers. I leave you to search for them.

In considering the question of dirty work we have eventually to think about the people who do it. In Germany, these were the members of the S.S. and of that inner group of the S.S. who operated the concentration camps. Many reports have been made on the social backgrounds and the personalities of these cruel fanatics. Those who have studied them say that a large proportion were *gescheiterte Existenzen,* men or women with a history of failure, of poor adaptation to the demands of work and of the classes of society in which they had been bred. Germany between wars had large numbers of such people. Their adherence to a movement which proclaimed a doctrine of hatred was natural enough. The movement offered something more. It created an inner group which was to be superior to all others, even Germans, in their emancipation from the usual bourgeois morality; people above and beyond the ordinary morality. I dwell on this not as a doctrine but as an organizational device. For, as Eugene Kogon, author of the most penetrating analysis of the S.S. and their camps, has said, the Nazis came to power by creating a state within a state; a body with its own countermorality and its own counterlaw, its courts and its own execution of sentence upon those who did not live up to its orders and standards. Even as a movement, it had inner circles within inner circles; each sworn to secrecy as against the next outer one. The struggle between these inner circles continued after Hitler came to power; Himmler eventually won the day. His S.S. became a state within the Nazi state, just as the Nazi movement had become a state within the Weimar state. One is reminded of the oft quoted but neglected statement of Sighele: "At the center of a crowd look for the sect." He referred, of course, to the political sect; the fanatical inner group of a movement seeking power by revolutionary methods. Once the Nazis were in power, this inner sect, while becoming now the recognized agent of the state and, hence, of the masses of the people, could at the same time dissociate itself more completely from them in action, because of the very fact of having a mandate. It was now beyond all danger of interference and investigation. For it had the instruments of interference and investigation in its own hands. These are also the instruments of secrecy. So the S.S. could and did build up a powerful system in which they had the resources of the state and of the economy of Germany and the conquered countries from which to steal all that was needed to carry out their orgy of cruelty luxuriously as well as with impunity.

Now let us ask, concerning the dirty workers, questions similar to those concerning the good people. Is there a supply of candidates for such work in other societies? It would be easy to say that only Germany could produce such a crop. The question is answered by being put. The problem of people who have run aground (*gescheiterte Existenzen*) is one of the most serious in our modern societies. Any psychiatrist will, I believe, testify that we have a sufficient pool or fund of personalities warped toward perverse punishment and cruelty to do any amount of dirty work that the good people may be inclined to countenance. It would not take a very great turn of events to increase the number of such people and to bring their discontents to the surface. This is not to suggest that every movement based on discontent with the present state of things will be led by such people. That is obviously untrue, and I emphasize the point lest my remarks give comfort to those who would damn all who express militant discontent. But I think study of militant social movements does show that these warped people seek a place in them. Specifically, they are likely to become the plotting secret police of the group. It is one of the problems of militant social movements to keep such people out. It is, of course, easier to do this if the spirit of the movement is positive, its conception of humanity high and inclusive, and its aims sound. This was not the case of the Nazi movement. As Kogon puts it: "The S.S. were but the arch-type of the Nazis in general." But such people are sometimes attracted, for want of something better, to movements whose aims are contrary to the spirit of cruelty and punishment. I would suggest that all of us look well at the leadership and entourage of movements to which we attach ourselves for signs of a negativistic, punishing attitude. For once such a spirit develops in a movement, punishment of the nearest and easiest victim is likely to become more attractive than striving for the essential goals. And, if the Nazi movement teaches us anything at all, it is that if any shadow of a mandate be given to such people, they will—having compromised us—make it larger and larger. The processes by which they do so are the development of the power and inward discipline of their own group, a progressive dissociation of themselves from the rules of human decency prevalent in their culture, and an ever growing contempt for the welfare of the masses of people.

The power and inward discipline of the S.S. became such that those who once became members could get out only by death; by suicide, murder, or mental breakdown. Orders from the central offices of the S.S. were couched in equivocal terms as a hedge against a possible day of judgment. When it became clear that such a day of judgment would come, the hedging and intrigue became greater; the urge to murder also became greater, because every prisoner became a potential witness.

Again we are dealing with a phenomenon common in all societies. Almost every group which has a specialized social function to perform is in some measure a secret society, with a body of rules developed and enforced by the members and with some power to save its members from outside punishment. And here is one of the paradoxes of social order. A society without smaller rule-making and disciplining powers would be no society at all. There would be nothing but law and police; and this is what the Nazis strove for, at the expense of family, church, professional groups, parties, and other such nuclei of spontaneous control. But apparently the only way to do this, for good as well as for evil ends, is to give power into the hands of some fanatical small group which will have a far greater power of self-discipline and a far greater immunity from outside control than the traditional groups. The problem is, then, not one of trying to get rid of all the self-disciplining, protecting groups within society but one of keeping them integrated with one another and as sensitive as can be to a public opinion which transcends them all. It is a matter of checks and balances, of what we might call the social and moral constitution of society.

Those who are especially devoted to efforts to eradicate from good people, as individuals, all those sentiments which seem to bring about the great and small dirty work of the world, may think that my remarks are something of an attack on their methods. They are right to this extent; that I am insisting that we give a share of our effort to the social mechanisms involved as well as to the individual and those of his sentiments which concern people of other kinds.

32. POLICE BRUTALITY—ANSWERS TO KEY QUESTIONS

ALBERT J. REISS JR.

Reprinted by permission of Transaction, Inc. from Trans-action 5 *(July-August 1968): 10-19. Copyright © 1968 by Transaction, Inc. Albert J. Reiss, Jr., is Professor of Sociology at Yale University and has taught at the University of Michigan, Vanderbilt University, and the University of Chicago. He has made important contributions to the fields of social stratification, urban sociology, and deviant behavior. Most recently he has directed intensive research on the police and on problems of crime in urban communities.*

■ One of the clearest examples of the dirty work dynamic in operation in American society is police brutality. Individuals who have occasion to meet with police in situations when they probably will be suspected and questioned are well aware that the use of physical coercion is not uncommon. However, government officials rarely openly discuss such behavior or accept its routine nature. And, as Selection 18 indicates, most men do not consider undesirable police use of violence to keep control of situations. No wonder, then, that the police see themselves as having been given an implicit mandate to use whatever force is necessary to maintain control even when that control is more a matter of proper respect, deference, and acquiescence than of making certain they can carry out their legal mandate. Evidence also suggests that policemen often take out the peculiar frustrations of their work on the most vulnerable of its objects.

All these observations about police brutality have until recently been made on the basis of hearsay evidence of one kind or another, but in the study reported here, we have for the first time the results of systematic observation of the police in operation. Reiss' observers traveled with policemen on their rounds to learn about their jobs and how they get done. One of the things they observed was the quality of interaction between the police and those citizens with whom they came in contact. From these observations they then were able to note the number of cases in which policemen used "unwarranted," "unreasonable," or "undue" force. This study shows something of the prevalence of unnecessary force, how such behavior is socially patterned in the situations the policeman finds himself in, and the social characteristics of his victim.

Reiss has reported other results of his research on the police in *The Police and the Public* (Yale University Press, 1971). Other studies of police behavior include Jerome H. Skolnick, *Justice Without Trial: Law Enforcement in a Democratic Society* (Wiley, 1966); and James Q. Wilson, *Varieties of Police Behavior: The Management of Law and Order in Eight Communities* (Harvard University Press, 1968). See also Wayne R. LaFave, *Arrest* (Little, Brown, 1965); and Arthur Niederhofer, *Behind the Shield: The Police in Urban Society* (Doubleday, 1967). A useful contrast is found in a study of English police by Michael Banton, *The Policeman and the Community* (Tavistock, 1964). ■

"FOR THREE YEARS, there has been through the courts and the streets a dreary procession of citizens with broken heads and bruised bodies against few of whom was violence needed to effect an arrest. Many of them had done nothing to deserve an arrest. In a majority of such cases, no complaint was made. If the victim complains, his charge is generally dismissed. The police are practically above the law."

This statement was published in 1903, and its author was the Hon. Frank Moss, a former police commissioner of New York City. Clearly, today's charges of police brutality and mistreatment of citizens have a precedent in American history—but never before has the issue of police brutality assumed the public urgency it has today. In Newark, in Detroit, in Watts, in Harlem, and, in fact, in practically every city that has had a civil disturbance, "deep hostility between police and ghetto" was, reports the Kerner Commission, "a primary cause of the riots."

Whether or not the police accept the words "police brutality," the public now wants some plain answers to some plain questions. How widespread is police mistreatment of citizens? Is it on the increase? Why do policemen mistreat citizens? Do the police mistreat Negroes more than Whites?

To find some answers, 36 people working for the Center of Research on Social Organization observed police-citizen encounters in the cities of Boston, Chicago, and Washington, D.C. For seven days a week, for seven weeks during the summer of 1966, these observers, with police permission, sat in patrol cars and monitored booking and lockup procedures in high-crime precincts.

Obtaining information about police mistreatment of citizens is no simple matter. National and state civil rights commissions receive hundreds of complaints charging mistreatment—but proving these allegations is difficult. The few local civilian review boards, such as the one in Philadelphia, have not produced any significant volume of complaints leading to the dismissal or disciplining of policemen for alleged brutality. Generally, police chiefs are silent on the matter or answer charges of brutality with vague statements that they will investigate any complaints brought to their attention. Rank-and-file policemen are usually more outspoken: They often insinuate that charges of brutality are part of a conspiracy against them and against law and order.

THE MEANING OF BRUTALITY

What citizens mean by police brutality covers the full range of police practices. These practices, contrary to the impression of many civil rights activists, are not newly devised to deal with Negroes in our urban ghettos. They are ways in which the police have traditionally behaved in dealing with certain citizens, particularly those in the lower classes. The most common of these practices are: the use of profane and abusive language;

commands to move on or get home; stopping and questioning people on the street or searching them and their cars; threats to use force if not obeyed; prodding with a nightstick or approaching with a pistol; and the actual use of physical force or violence itself.

Citizens and the police do not always agree on what constitutes proper police practice. What is "proper," or what is "brutal," it need hardly be pointed out, is more a matter of judgment about what someone did than a description of what police do. What is important is not the practice itself but what it means to the citizen. What citizens object to and call "police brutality" is really the judgment that they have not been treated with the full rights and dignity owing citizens in a democratic society. Any practice that degrades their status, that restricts their freedom, that annoys or harasses them, or that uses physical force is frequently seen as unnecessary and unwarranted. More often than not, they are probably right.

Many police practices serve only to degrade the citizen's sense of himself and his status. This is particularly true with regard to the way the police use language. Most citizens who have contact with the police object less to their use of four-letter words than to *how* the policeman talks to them. Particularly objectionable is the habit policemen have of "talking down" to citizens, of calling them names that deprecate them in their own eyes and those of others. More than one Negro citizen has complained: "They talk down to me as if I had no name—like 'boy' or 'man' or whatever, or they call me 'Jack' or by my first name. They don't show me no respect."

Members of minority groups and those seen as nonconformists, for whatever reason, are the most likely targets of status degradation. Someone who has been drinking may be told he is a "bum" or a "shitty wino." A woman walking alone may be called a "whore." And a man who doesn't happen to meet a policeman's standard of how one should look or dress may be met with the remark, "What's the matter, you a queer?" A white migrant from the South may be called a "hillbilly" or "shitkicker"; a Puerto Rican, a "porkchop";

a young boy, a "punk kid." When the policeman does not use words of status degradation, his manner may be degrading. Citizens want to be treated as people, not as "nonpersons" who are talked about as if they were not present.

That many Negroes believe that the police have degraded their status is clear from surveys in Watts, Newark, and Detroit. One out of every five Negroes in our center's post-riot survey in Detroit reports that the police have "talked down to him." More than 1 in 10 says a policeman has "called me a bad name."

To be treated as "suspicious" is not only degrading but is also a form of harassment and a restriction on the right to move freely. The harassing tactics of the police—dispersing social street-gatherings, the indiscriminate stopping of Negroes on foot or in cars, and commands to move on or go home—are particularly common in ghetto areas.

Young people are the most likely targets of harassing orders to disperse or move on. Particularly in summer, ghetto youths are likely to spend lots of time in public places. Given the inadequacy of their housing and the absence of community facilities, the street corner is often their social center. As the police cruise the busy streets of the ghetto, they frequently shout at groups of teen-agers to "get going" or "get home." Our observations of police practices show that *White as well as Negro youths* are often harassed in this way.

Frequently the policeman may leave the car and threaten or force youths to move on. For example, one summer evening as the scout car cruised a busy street of a White slum, the patrolmen observed three White boys and a girl on a corner. When told to move on, they mumbled and grumbled in understones, angering the police by their failure to comply. As they slowly moved off, the officers pushed them along the street. Suddenly one of the White patrolmen took a lighted cigarette from a 15-year-old boy and stuck it in his face, pushing him forward as he did so. When the youngsters did move on, one policeman remarked to the observer that the girl was "nothing but a whore." Such

tactics can only intensify resentment toward the police.

Police harassment is not confined to youth. One in every four adult Negroes in Detroit claims he has been stopped and questioned by the police without good reason. The same proportion claim they have been stopped in their cars. One in five says he has been searched unnecessarily, and one in six says that his car was searched for no good reason. The members of an interracial couple, particularly a Negro man accompanying a White woman, are perhaps the most vulnerable to harassment.

What citizens regard as police brutality many policemen consider necessary for law enforcement. While degrading epithets and abusive language may no longer be considered proper by either police commanders or citizens, they often disagree about other practices related to law enforcement. For example, although many citizens see "stop and question" or "stop and frisk" procedures as harassment, police commanders usually regard them merely as "aggressive prevention" to curb crime.

PHYSICAL FORCE— OR SELF-DEFENSE?

The nub of the police brutality issue seems to lie in police use of physical force. By law, the police have the right to use such force if necessary to make an arrest, to keep the peace, or to maintain public order. But just how much force is necessary or proper?

This was the crucial problem we attempted to answer by placing observers in the patrol cars and in the precincts. Our 36 observers, divided equally between Chicago, Boston, and Washington, were responsible for reporting the details of all situations where police used physical force against a citizen. To ensure the observation of a large number of encounters, two high-crime police precincts were monitored in Boston and Chicago; four in Washington. At least one precinct was composed of primarily Negro residents, another primarily of Whites. Where possible, we also tried to select precincts with considerable variation in social class composition. Given the criterion of a high-crime rate, however, people of low socioeconomic status predominated in most of the areas surveyed.

The law fails to provide simple rules about what—and how much—force policemen can properly use. The American Bar Foundation's study, *Arrest,* by Wayne La Fave, put the matter rather well, stating that the courts of all states would undoubtedly agree that in making an arrest a policeman should use only that amount of force he reasonably believes necessary. But La Fave also pointed out that there is no agreement on the question of when it is better to let the suspect escape than to employ "deadly" force.

Even in those states where the use of deadly force is limited by law, the kinds of physical force a policeman may use are not clearly defined. No kind of force is categorically denied a policeman, since he is always permitted to use deadly force in self-defense.

This right to protect himself often leads the policeman to argue self-defense whenever he uses force. We found that many policemen, whether or not the facts justify it, regularly follow their use of force with the charge that the citizen was assaulting a policeman or resisting arrest. Our observers also found that some policemen even carry pistols and knives that they have confiscated while searching citizens; they carry them so they may be placed at a scene should it be necessary to establish a case of self-defense.

Of course, not all cases of force involve the use of *unnecessary* force. Each instance of force reported by our observers was examined and judged to be either necessary or unnecessary. Cases involving simple restraint—holding a man by the arm—were deliberately excluded from consideration, even though a policeman's right to do so can, in many instances, be challenged. In judging when police force is "unwarranted," "unreasonable," or "undue," we rather deliberately selected only those cases in which a policeman struck the citizen with his hands, fist, feet, or body, or where he used a weapon of some kind—such as a nightstick or a pistol. In

these cases, had the policeman been found to have used physical force improperly, he could have been arrested on complaint and, like any other citizen, charged with a simple or aggravated assault. A physical assault on a citizen was judged to be "improper" or "unnecessary" only if force was used in one or more of the following ways.

If a policeman physically assaulted a citizen and then failed to make an arrest; proper use involves an arrest.

If the citizen being arrested did not, by word or deed, resist the policeman; force should be used only if it is necessary to make the arrest.

If the policeman, even though there was resistance to the arrest, could easily have restrained the citizen in other ways.

If a large number of policemen were present and could have assisted in subduing the citizen in the station, in lockup, and in the interrogation rooms.

If an offender was handcuffed and made no attempt to flee or offer violent resistance.

If the citizen resisted arrest, but the use of force continued even after the citizen was subdued.

In the 7-week period, we found 37 cases in which force was used improperly. In all, 44 citizens had been assaulted. In 15 of these cases, no one was arrested. Of these, eight had offered no verbal or physical resistance whatsoever while seven had.

An arrest was made in 22 of the cases. In 13, force was exercised in the station house when at least 4 other policemen were present. In two cases, there was no verbal or physical resistance to the arrest, but force was still applied. In two other cases, the police applied force to a handcuffed offender in a field setting. And in five situations, the offender did resist arrest, but the policeman continued to use force even after he had been subdued.

Just how serious was the improper use of force in these 44 cases? Naturally there were differences in degree of injury. In about half of the cases, the citizen appeared little more than physically bruised; in three cases, the amount of force was so great that the citizen had to be hospitalized. Despite the fact that cases can easily be selected for their dramatic rather than their representative quality, I want to present a few to give a sense of what the observers saw and reported as undue use of force.

OBSERVING ON PATROL

In the following two cases, the citizens offered no physical or verbal resistance, and the two White policemen made no arrest. It is the only instance in which the observers saw the same two policemen using force improperly more than once.

The police precinct in which these incidents occurred is typical of those found in some of our larger cities, where the patrolmen move routinely from gold coast to slum. There are little islands of the rich and poor, of old Americans and new, of recent migrants and old settlers. One moves from high-rise areas of middle and upper income Whites through an area of the really old Americans—Indians—to an enclave of the recently arrived. The recently arrived are primarily those the policemen call hillbillies (migrants from Kentucky and Tennessee) and porkchops (Puerto Ricans). There are ethnic islands of Germans and Swedes. Although there is a small area where Negroes live, it is principally a precinct of Whites. The police in the district are, with one exception, White.

On a Friday in the middle of July, the observer arrived for the 4 to 12 midnight watch. The beat car that had been randomly chosen carried two White patrolmen—one with 14 years of experience in the precinct, the other with 3.

The watch began rather routinely as the policemen cruised the district. Their first radio dispatch came at about 5:30 p.m. They were told to investigate two drunks in a cemetery. On arriving they found two White men "sleeping one off." Without questioning the men, the older policeman began to search

one of them, ripping his shirt and hitting him in the groin with a nightstick. The younger policeman, as he searched the second, ripped away the seat of his trousers, exposing his buttocks. The policemen then prodded the men toward the cemetery fence and forced them to climb it, laughing at the plight of the drunk with the exposed buttocks. As the drunks went over the fence, one policeman shouted, "I ought to run you fuckers in!" The other remarked to the observer, "Those assholes won't be back; a bunch of shitty winos."

Not long after they returned to their car, the policemen stopped a woman who had made a left turn improperly. She was treated very politely, and the younger policeman, who wrote the ticket, later commented to the observer, "Nice lady." At 7:30 they were dispatched to check a suspicious auto. After a quick check, the car was marked abandoned.

Shortly after a 30-minute break for a 7:30 "lunch," the two policemen received a dispatch to take a burglary report. Arriving at a slum walkup, the police entered a room where an obviously drunk White man in his late forties insisted that someone had entered and stolen his food and liquor. He kept insisting that it had been taken and that he had been forced to borrow money to buy beer. The younger policeman, who took the report, kept harassing the man, alternating between mocking and badgering him rhetorical questions. "You say your name is Half-A-Wit [for Hathaway]? Do you sleep with niggers? How did you vote on the bond issue? Are you sure that's all that's missing? Are you a virgin yet?" The man responded to all of this with the seeming vagueness and joviality of the intoxicated, expressing gratitude for the policemen's help as they left. The older policeman remarked to the observer as they left, "Ain't drunks funny?"

For the next hour little happened, but as the two were moving across the precinct shortly after 10 p.m., a White man and a woman in their fifties flagged them down. Since they were obviously "substantial" middle class citizens of the district, the policemen listened to their complaints that a Negro man was causing trouble inside the public transport station from which they had just emerged. The woman said that he had sworn at her. The older policeman remarked, "What's a nigger doing up here? He should be down on Franklin Road!"

With that, they ran into the station and grabbed the Negro man who was inside. Without questioning him, they shoved him into a phone booth and began beating him with their fists and a flashlight. They also hit him in the groin. Then they dragged him out and kept him on his knees. He pleaded that he had just been released from a mental hospital that day and, begging not to be hit again, asked them to let him return to the hospital. One policeman said: "Don't you like us, nigger? I like to beat niggers and rip out their eyes." They took him outside to their patrol car. Then they decided to put him on a bus, telling him that he was returning to the hospital; they deliberately put him on a bus going in the opposite direction. Just before the Negro boarded the bus, he said, "You police just like to shoot and beat people." The first policeman replied, "Get moving, nigger, or I'll shoot you." The man was crying and bleeding as he was put on the bus. Leaving the scene, the younger policeman commented, "He won't be back."

For the rest of the evening, the two policemen kept looking for drunks and harassing any they found. They concluded the evening by being dispatched to an address where, they were told, a man was being held for the police. No one answered their knock. They left.

The station house has long been suspected of harboring questionable police practices. Interrogation room procedures have been attacked, particularly because of the methods the police have used to get confessions. The drama of the confession in the interrogation room has been complete with bright lights and physical torture. Whether or not such practices have ever existed on the scale suggested by popular accounts, confessions in recent years, even by accounts of offenders, have rarely been accompanied by such high drama. But recently the interrogation room has come under fire again for its failure to protect the constitutional rights of the suspect to remain silent and to have legal counsel.

BACKSTAGE AT THE STATION

The police station, however, is more than just a series of cubicles called interrogation rooms. There are other rooms and usually a lockup as well. Many of these are also hidden from public view. It is not surprising, then, that one-third of all the observations of the undue use of force occurred within the station.

In any station there normally are several policemen present who should be able to deal with almost any situation requiring force that arises. In many of the situations that were observed, as many as seven and eight policemen were present, most of whom simply stood by and watched force being used. The custom among policemen, it appeared, is that you intervene only if a fellow policeman needs help, or if you have been personally offended or affronted by those involved.

Force is used unnecessarily at many different points and places in the station. The citizen who is not cooperative during the booking process may be pushed or shoved, have his handcuffs twisted with a nightstick, have his foot stomped, or be pulled by the hair. All of these practices were reported by policemen as ways of obtaining "cooperation." But it was clear that the booking could have been completed without any of this harassment.

The lockup was the scene of some of the most severe applications of force. Two of the three cases requiring hospitalization came about when an offender was "worked over" in the lockup. To be sure, the arrested are not always cooperative when they get in the lockup, and force may be necessary to place them in a cell. But the amount of force observed hardly seemed necessary.

One evening an observer was present in the lockup when two White policemen came in with a White man. The suspect had been handcuffed and brought to the station because he had proved obstreperous after being arrested for a traffic violation. Apparently he had been drinking. While waiting in the lockup, the man began to urinate on the floor. In response, the policemen began to beat the man. They jumped him, knocked him down, and beat his head against the concrete floor. He required emergency treatment at a nearby hospital.

At times a policeman may be involved in a kind of escalation of force. Using force appropriately for an arrest in the field seemingly sets the stage for its later use, improperly, in the station. The following case illustrates how such a situation may develop.

Within a large city's high-crime rate precinct, occupied mostly by Negroes, the police responded to an "officer in trouble" call. It is difficult to imagine a call that brings a more immediate response, so a large number of police cars immediately converged at an intersection of a busy public street where a bus had been stopped. Near the bus, a White policeman was holding two young Negroes at gun point. The policeman reported that he had responded to a summons from the White bus driver complaining that the boys had refused to pay their fares and had used obscene language. The policeman also reported that the boys swore at him, and one swung at him while the other drew a screwdriver and started toward him. At that point, he said, he drew his pistol.

The policemen placed one of the offenders in handcuffs and began to transport both of them to the station. While driving to the station, the driver of one car noted that the other policeman, transporting the other boy was struggling with him. The first policeman stopped and entered the other patrol car. The observer reported that he kept hitting the boy who was handcuffed until the boy appeared completely subdued. The boy kept saying, "You don't have any right to beat me. I don't care if you kill me."

After the policemen got the offenders to the station, although the boys no longer resisted them, the police began to beat them while they were handcuffed in an interrogation room. One of the boys hollered: "You can't

beat me like this! I'm only a kid, and my hands are tied." Later one of the policemen commented to the observer: "On the street you can't beat them. But when you get to the station, you can instill some respect in them."

Cases where the offender resists an arrest provide perhaps the most difficulty in judging the legitimacy of the force applied. An encounter that began as a dispatch to a disturbance at a private residence was one case about which there could be honest difference in judgment. On arrival, the policemen—one White, the other Negro—met a White woman who claimed that her husband, who was in the back yard and drunk, had beaten her. She asked the policemen to "take him in." The observer reported that the police found the man in the house. When they attempted to take him, he resisted by placing his hands between the door jamb. Both policemen then grabbed him. The Negro policeman said, "We're going to have trouble, so let's finish it right here." He grabbed the offender and knocked him down. Both policemen then wrestled with the man, handcuffed him, and took him to the station. As they did so, one of the policemen remarked, "These sons of bitches want to fight, so you have to break them quick."

A MINIMAL PICTURE?

The reader, as well as most police administrators, may be skeptical about reports that policemen used force in the presence of observers. Indeed, one police administrator, indignant over reports of undue use of force in his department, seemed more concerned that the policemen had permitted themselves to be observed behaving improperly than he was about their improper behavior. When demanding to know the names of the policemen who had used force improperly so he could discharge them—a demand we could not meet, since we were bound to protect our sources of information—he remarked, "Any officer who is stupid enough to behave that way in the presence of outsiders deserves to be fired."

There were and are a number of reasons why our observers were able to see policemen behaving improperly. We entered each department with the full cooperation of the top administrators. So far as the men in the line were concerned, our chief interest was in how citizens behave toward the police, a main object of our study. Many policemen, given their strong feelings against citizens, fail to see that their own behavior is equally open to observation. Furthermore, our observers are trained to fit into a role of trust—one that is genuine, since most observers are actually sympathetic to the plight of the policeman, if not to his behavior.

Finally, and this is a fact all too easily forgotten, people cannot change their behavior in the presence of others as easily as many think. This is particularly true when people become deeply involved in certain situations. The policeman not only comes to "trust" the observer in the law-enforcement situation—regarding him as a source of additional help if necessary—but, when he becomes involved in a dispute with a citizen, he easily forgets that an observer is present. Partly because he does not know what else to do, in such situations the policeman behaves "normally." But should one cling to the notion that most policemen modify their behavior in the presence of outsiders, one is left with the uncomfortable conclusion that our cases represent a minimal picture of actual misbehavior.

Superficially it might seem that the use of an excessive amount of force against citizens is low. In only 37 of 3,826 encounters observed did the police use undue force. Of the 4,604 White citizens in these encounters, 27 experienced an excessive amount of force—a rate of 5.9 for every 1,000 citizens involved. The comparable rate for 5,960 Negroes, of whom 17 experienced an excessive amount of force, is 2.8. Thus, whether one considers these rates high or low, the fact is that the *rate of excessive force for all White citizens in encounters with the police is twice that for Negro citizens.*

A rate depends, however, upon selecting a population that is logically the target of force. What we have just given is a rate for *all* citizens involved in encounters with the police. But many of these citizens are not logical targets of force. Many, for example, simply call the police to complain about crimes against themselves or their property. And others are merely witnesses to crimes.

The more logical target population consists of citizens whom the police allege to be offenders—a population of suspects. In our study, there were 643 White suspects, 27 of whom experienced undue use of force. This yields an abuse rate of 41.9 per 1,000 White suspects. The comparable rate for 751 Negro suspects, of whom 17 experienced undue use of force, is 22.6 per 1,000. If one accepts these rates as reasonably reliable estimates of the undue force against suspects, then there should be little doubt that in major metropolitan areas the sort of behavior commonly called "police brutality" is far from rare.

Popular impression casts police brutality as a racial matter—White police mistreating Negro citizens. The fact is that White suspects are more liable to being treated improperly by the police than Negro suspects are. This, however, should not be confused with the chances a citizen takes of being mistreated. In two of the cities we studied, Negroes are a minority. The chances, then, that any Negro has of being treated improperly are, perhaps, more nearly comparable to that for Whites. If the rates are comparable, then one might say that the application of force unnecessarily by the police operates without respect to the race of an offender.

Many people believe that the race of the policeman must affect his use of force, particularly since many White policemen express prejudice against Negroes. Our own work shows that in the police precincts made up largely of Negro citizens, over three-fourths of the policemen express prejudice against Negroes. Only 1 percent express sympathetic attitudes. But as sociologists and social psychologists have often shown, prejudice and attitudes do not necessarily carry over into discriminatory actions.

Our findings show that there is little difference between the rate of force used by White and by Negro policemen. Of the 54 policemen observed using too much force, 45 were White and 9 were Negro. For every 100 White policemen, 8.7 will use force; for every 100 Negro policemen, 9.8 will. What this really means, though, is that about 1 in every 10 policemen in high-crime rate areas of cities sometimes uses force unnecessarily.

Yet, one may ask, doesn't prejudice enter into the use of force? Didn't some of the policemen who were observed utter prejudiced statements toward Negroes and other minority group members? Of course they did. But the question of whether it was their prejudice or some other factor that motivated them to mistreat Negroes is not so easily answered.

Still, even though our figures show that a White suspect is more liable to encounter violence, one may ask whether White policemen victimize Negroes more than Whites. We found, for the most part, that they do not. Policemen, both Negro and White, are most likely to exercise force against members of their *own* race.

67 percent of the citizens victimized by White policemen were White.

71 percent of the citizens victimized by Negro policemen were Negro.

To interpret these statistics correctly, however, one should take into account the differences in opportunity policemen have to use force against members of their own and other races. Negro policemen, in the three cities we studied, were far *less* likely to police White citizens than White policemen were to police Negroes. Negro policemen usually policed other Negroes, while White policemen policed both Whites and Negroes about equally. In total numbers, then, more White policemen than Negro policemen used force against Negroes. But this is explained by the fact that Whites make up 85 percent of the police force and more than 50 percent of all policemen policing Negroes.

Though no precise estimates are possible, the facts just given suggest that White policemen, even though they are prejudiced toward Negroes, do not discriminate against Negroes in the excessive use of force. The use of force by the police is more readily explained by police culture than it is by the policeman's race. Indeed, in the few cases where we observed a Negro policeman using unnecessary force against White citizens, there was no evidence that he did so because of his race.

The disparity between our findings and the public's sense that Negroes are the main victims of police brutality can easily be resolved if one asks how the public becomes aware of the police misusing force.

THE VICTIMS AND THE TURF

Fifty years ago, the immigrants to our cities —eastern and southern Europeans such as the Poles and the Italians—complained about police brutality. Today the new immigrants to our cities—mostly Negroes from the rural South—raise their voices through the civil rights movement, through Black nationalist and other race-conscious organizations. There is no comparable voice for White citizens since, except for the Puerto Ricans, they now lack the nationality organizations that were once formed to promote and protect the interests of their immigrant forbears.

Although policemen do not seem to select their victims according to race, two facts stand out. All victims were offenders, and all were from the lower class. Concentrating as we did on high-crime rate areas of cities, we do not have a representative sample of residents in any city. Nonetheless, we observed a sizable minority of middle and upper status citizens, some of whom were offenders. But since no middle or upper class offender, White or Negro, was the victim of an excessive amount of force, it appears that the lower class bears the brunt of victimization by the police.

The most likely victim of excessive force is a lower class man of either race. No White woman and only two Negro women were victimized. The difference between the risk assumed by White and by Negro women can be accounted for by the fact that far more Negro women are processed as suspects or offenders.

Whether or not a policeman uses force unnecessarily depends upon the social setting in which the encounter takes place. Of the 37 instances of excessive force, 37 percent took place in police-controlled settings, such as the patrol car or the precinct station. Public places, usually streets, accounted for 41 percent, and 16 percent took place in a private residence. The remaining 6 percent occurred in commercial settings. This is not, of course, a random sample of settings where the police encounter suspects.

What is most obvious, and most disturbing, is that the police are very likely to use force in settings that they control. Although only 18 percent of all situations involving suspects ever ended up at the station house, 32 percent of all situations where an excessive amount of force was used took place in the police station.

No one who accepts the fact that the police sometimes use an excessive amount of force should be surprised by our finding that they often select their own turf. What should be apparent to the nation's police administrators, however, is that these settings are under their command and control. Controlling the police in the field, where the policeman is away from direct supervision, is understandably difficult. But the station house is the police administrator's domain. The fact that one in three instances of excessive force took place in settings that can be directly controlled should cause concern among police officials.

The presence of citizens who might serve as witnesses against a policeman should deter him from undue use of force. Indeed, procedures for the review of police conduct are based on the presumption that one can get this kind of testimony. Otherwise, one is left simply with a citizen complaint and contrary testimony by the policeman—a situation in which it is very difficult to prove the citizen's allegation.

In most situations involving the use of excessive force, there were witnesses. In our 37 cases, there were bystanders present three-fourths of the time. But in only one situation did the group present sympathize with the citizen and threaten to report the policeman. A complaint was filed on that incident—the only one of the 37 observed instances of undue force in which a formal complaint was filed.

All in all, the situations where excessive force was used were devoid of bystanders who did not have a stake in being "against" the offender. Generally, they were fellow policemen, or fellow offenders whose truthfulness could be easily challenged. When a policeman uses undue force, then, he usually does not risk a complaint against himself or testimony from witnesses who favor the complainant against the policeman. This, as much as anything, probably accounts for the low rate of formal complaints against policemen who use force unnecessarily.

A striking fact is that in more than half of all instances of undue coercion, at least one other policeman was present who did not participate in the use of force. This shows that, for the most part, the police do not restrain their fellow policemen. On the contrary, there were times when their very presence encouraged the use of force. One man brought into the lockup for threatening a policeman with a pistol was so severely beaten by this policeman that he required hospitalization. During the beating, some policemen propped the man up, while others shouted encouragement. Though the official police code does not legitimate this practice, police culture does.

VICTIMS—DEFIANT OR DEVIANT

Now, are there characteristics of the offender or his behavior that precipitate the use of excessive force by the police? Superficially, yes. Almost half of the cases involved open defiance of police authority (39 percent) or resisting arrest (9 percent). Open defiance of police authority, however, is what the policeman defines as *his* authority, not necessarily "official" authority. Indeed in 40 percent of the cases that the police considered open defiance, the policeman never executed an arrest—a somewhat surprising fact for those who assume that policemen generally "cover" improper use of force with a "bona fide" arrest and a charge of resisting arrest.

But it is still of interest to know what a policeman *sees* as defiance. Often he seems threatened by a simple refusal to acquiesce to his own authority. A policeman beat a handcuffed offender because, when told to sit, the offender did not sit down. One Negro woman was soundly slapped for her refusal to approach the police car and identify herself.

Important as a threat to his authority may appear to the policeman, there were many more of these instances in which the policeman did *not* respond with the use of force. The important issue seems to be whether the policeman manages to assert his authority despite the threat to it. I suspect that policemen are more likely to respond with excessive force when they define the situation as one in which there remains a question as to who is "in charge."

Similarly, some evidence indicates that harassment of deviants plays a role in the undue use of force. Incidents involving drunks made up 27 percent of all incidents of improper use of force; an additional 5 percent involved homosexuals or narcotics users. Since deviants generally remain silent victims to avoid public exposure of their deviance, they are particularly susceptible to the use of excessive force.

It is clear, though, that the police encounter many situations involving deviants where no force is used. Generally they respond to them routinely. What is surprising, then, is that the police do not mistreat deviants more than they do. The explanation may lie in the kind of relationships the police have with deviants. Many are valuable to the police because they serve as informers. To mistreat them severely would be to cut off a major source of police intelligence. At the same time, deviants are easily controlled by harassment.

Clearly, we have seen that police mistreatment of citizens exists. It is, however, on the increase?

Citizen complaints against the police are common, and allegations that the police use force improperly are frequent. There is evidence that physical brutality exists today. But there is also evidence, from the history of our cities, that the police have long engaged in the use of unnecessary physical force. No one can say with confidence whether there is more or less of it today than there was at the turn of the century.

What we lack is evidence that would permit us to calculate comparative rates of police misuse of force for different periods of American history. Only recently have we begun to count and report the volume of complaints against the police. And the research reported in this article represents the only attempt to estimate the amount of police mistreatment by actual observation of what the police do to citizens.

LACK OF INFORMATION

Police chiefs are notoriously reluctant to disclose information that would allow us to assess the nature and volume of complaints against the police. Only a few departments have begun to report something about citizen complaints. And these give us very little information.

Consider, for example, the 1966 Annual Report released by the New Orleans Police Department. It tells us that there were 208 cases of "alleged police misconduct on which action was taken." It fails to tell us whether there were any allegations that are *not* included among these cases. Are these all the allegations that came to the attention of the department? Or are they only those the department chose to review as "police disciplinary matters"? Of the 208 cases the department considered "disciplinary matters," the report tells us that no disciplinary action was taken in 106 cases. There were 11 cases that resulted in 14 dismissals; 56 cases that resulted in 72 suspensions, fines, or loss of days; and 35 cases involving 52 written or verbal "reprimands" or "cautionings."

The failure of the report to tell us the charge against the policeman is a significant omission. We cannot tell how many of these allegations involved improper use of force, how many involved verbal abuse or harassment, how many involved police felonies or misdemeanors, and so on. In such reports, the defensive posture of the nation's police departments is all too apparent. Although the 1966 report of the New Orleans Police Department tells us much about what the police allege were the felonies and misdemeanors by citizens of New Orleans, it tells us nothing about what citizens allege was misconduct by the police!

Many responsible people believe that the use of physical brutality by the police is on the wane. They point to the fact that, at least outside the South, there are more reports of other forms of police mistreatment of citizens than reports of undue physical coercion. They also suggest that third-degree interrogations and curbstone justice with the nightstick are less common. It does not seem unreasonable, then, to assume that police practices that degrade a citizen's status or that harass him and restrict his freedom are more common than police misuse of force. But that may have always been so.

Whether or not the policeman's "sense of justice" and his use of unnecessary force have changed remains an open question. Forms may change while practices go on. To move misuse from the street to the station house, or from the interrogation room to the lockup, changes the place but not the practice itself.

Our ignorance of just what goes on between police and citizens poses one of the central issues in policing today: How can we make the police accountable to the citizenry in a democratic society and yet not hamstring them in their legitimate pursuit of law and order? There are no simple answers.

Police departments are organizations that process people. All people-processing organizations face certain common problems. But the police administrator faces a problem in controlling practice with clients that is not found in most other organizations. The problem is that police contact with citizens occurs in the community, where direct supervision is not possible. Assuming our unwillingness to spend resources for almost one-to-one supervision, the problem for the police commander is to make policemen behave properly when they are not under direct supervision. He also faces the problem of making them behave properly in the station house as well.

Historically, we have found but one way— apart from supervision—that deals with this problem. That solution is professionalization of workers. Perhaps only through the professionalization of the police can we hope to solve the problem of police malpractice.

But lest anyone optimistically assume that professionalization will eliminate police malpractice altogether, we should keep in mind that problems of malpractice also occur regularly in both law and medicine.

33. POLICE ENCOUNTERS WITH JUVENILES

IRVING PILIAVIN AND SCOTT BRIAR

Reprinted from the American Journal of Sociology *70 (September 1964): 206-14 by permission of the authors and the University of Chicago Press. Copyright 1964 by the University of Chicago Press. Irving Piliavin is Associate Professor of Social Work at the University of Wisconsin. Scott Briar is Dean of the School of Social Work, University of Washington at Seattle.*

■ The relationship between police and juveniles has the same characteristics as that between police and adults, but with an additional complication. Police are expected both as part of their official duties and simply as adults to take a somewhat paternal interest in youth, to represent to them the authority of the adult world, and to encourage them to conform to adult standards. Since many kinds of behavior are not considered worthy of note when engaged in by adults but are illegal for juveniles, policemen inevitably have a good deal to do with them, peace-keeping duties like those Bittner described for skid row (in Selection 21) and law enforcement functions.

In this selection Piliavin and Briar describe some of the ways in which the policeman is left on his own to exercise wide discretion in how he responds to juvenile behavior. Of particular importance is the discussion of the relationship between the deference or recalcitrance juveniles show and the likelihood that they will be arrested. Although not all subsequent research has produced such clear-cut findings, this study seems to suggest that juveniles' attitudes toward the police are as important in determining arrest as whether or not an actual violation of the law took place.

The additional readings suggested for Selection 32 apply equally here. ■

AS THE FIRST OF A SERIES of decisions made in the channeling of youthful offenders through the agencies concerned with juvenile justice and corrections, the disposition decisions made by police officers have potentially profound consequences for apprehended juveniles. Thus arrest, the most severe of the dispositions available to police, may not only lead to confinement of the suspected offender but also bring him loss of social status, restriction of educational and employment opportunities, and future harassment by law enforcement personnel. According to some criminologists, the stigmatization resulting from police apprehension, arrest, and detention actually reinforces deviant behavior. Other authorities have suggested, in fact, that this stigmatization serves as the catalytic agent initiating delinquent careers. Despite their presumed significance, however, little empirical analysis has been reported regarding the factors influencing, or consequences resulting from, police actions with juvenile offenders. Furthermore, while some studies of police encounters with adult offenders have been reported, the extent to which the findings of these investigations pertain to law enforcement practices with youthful offenders is not known.

The above considerations have led the writers to undertake a longitudinal study of the conditions influencing, and consequences flowing from, police actions with juveniles. In the present paper findings will be presented indicating the influence of certain factors on police actions. Research data consist primarily of notes and records based on nine months' observation of all juvenile officers in one police department. The officers were observed in the course of their regular tours of duty. While these data do not lend themselves to quantitative assessments of reliability and validity, the candor shown by the officers in their interviews with the investigators and their use of officially frowned-upon practices while under observation provide some assurance that the materials presented below accurately reflect the typical operations and attitudes of the law enforcement personnel studied.

The setting for the research, a metropolitan police department serving an industrial city with approximately 450,000 inhabitants, was noted within the community it served and among law enforcement officials elsewhere for the honesty and superior quality of its personnel. Incidents involving criminal activity or brutality by members of the department had been extremely rare during the 10 years preceding this study; personnel standards were comparatively high; and an extensive training program was provided to both new and experienced personnel. Juvenile Bureau members, the primary subjects of this investigation, differed somewhat from other members of the department in that they were responsible for delinquency prevention as well as law enforcement; that is, juvenile officers were expected to be knowledgeable about conditions leading to crime and delinquency and to be able to work with community agencies serving known or potential juvenile offenders. Accordingly, in the assignment of personnel to the Juvenile Bureau, consideration was given not only to an officer's devotion to and reliability in law enforcement but also to his commitment to delinquency prevention. Assignment to the bureau was of advantage to policemen seeking promotions. Consequently, many officers requested transfer to this unit, and its personnel comprised a highly select group of officers.

In the field, juvenile officers operated essentially as patrol officers. They cruised assigned beats and, although concerned primarily with juvenile offenders, frequently had occasion to apprehend and arrest adults. Confrontations between the officers and juveniles occurred in one of the following three ways, in order of increasing frequency: (1) encounters resulting from officers' spotting officially "wanted" youths; (2) encounters taking place at or near the scene of offenses reported to police headquarters; and (3) encounters occurring as the result of officers' directly observing youths either committing offenses or in "suspicious circumstances."

However, the probability that a confrontation would take place between officer and juvenile, or that a particular disposition of an identified offender would be made, was only in part determined by the knowledge that an offense had occurred or that a particular juvenile had committed an offense. The bases for and utilization of nonoffenses-related criteria by police in accosting and disposing of juveniles are the focuses of the following discussion.

SANCTIONS FOR DISCRETION

In each encounter with juveniles, with the minor exception of officially "wanted" youths, a central task confronting the officer was to decide what official action to take against the boys involved. In making these disposition decisions, officers could select any one of five discrete alternatives:

1. Outright release.
2. Release and submission of a "field interrogation report" briefly describing the circumstances initiating the police-juvenile confrontation.
3. "Official reprimand" and release to parents or guardian.
4. Citation to juvenile court.
5. Arrest and confinement in juvenile hall.

Dispositions 3, 4, and 5 differed from the others in two basic respects. First, with rare exceptions, when an officer chose to reprimand, cite, or arrest a boy he took the youth to the police station. Second, the reprimanded, cited, or arrested boy acquired an official police "record"; that is, his name was officially recorded in bureau files as a juvenile violator.

Analysis of the distribution of police disposition decisions about juveniles revealed that in virtually every category of offense the full range of official disposition alternatives available to officers was employed. This wide range of discretion resulted primarily from two conditions. First, it reflected the reluctance of officers to expose certain youths to the stigmatization presumed to be associated with official police action. Few juvenile officers believed that correctional agencies serving the community could effectively help delinquents. For some officers this attitude reflected a lack of confidence in rehabilitation techniques; for others, a belief that high caseloads and lack of professional training among correctional workers vitiated their efforts at treatment. All officers were agreed, however, that juvenile justice and correctional processes were essentially concerned with apprehension and punishment rather than treatment. Furthermore, all officers believed that some aspects of these processes (e.g., judicial definition of youths as delinquents and removal of delinquents from the community), as well as some of the possible consequences of these processes (e.g., intimate institutional contact with "hard-core" delinquents, as well as parental, school, and conventional peer disapproval or rejection), could reinforce what previously might have been only a tentative proclivity toward delinquent values and behavior. Consequently, when officers found reason to doubt that a youth being confronted was highly committed toward deviance, they were inclined to treat him with leniency.

Second, and more important, the practice of discretion was sanctioned by police department policy. Training manuals and departmental bulletins stressed that the disposition of each juvenile offender was not to be based solely on the type of infraction he committed. Thus, while it was departmental policy to "arrest and confine all juveniles who have committed a felony or misdemeanor involving theft, sex offense, battery, possession of dangerous weapons, prowling, peeping, intoxication, incorrigibility, and disturbance of the peace," it was acknowledged that "such considerations as age, attitude, and prior criminal record might indicate that a different disposition would be more appropriate." The official justification for discretion in processing juvenile offenders, based on the preventive aims of the Juvenile Bureau, was that each juvenile violator should be dealt with solely on the basis of what was best for him. Unofficially, administrative legitimation of discretion was further justified on the grounds that strict enforcement practices would over-crowd court calendars and detention facilities as well as dramatically increase juvenile crime rates—consequences to be avoided because they would expose the police department to community criticism.

In practice, the official policy justifying use of discretion served as a demand that discretion be exercised. As such, it posed three problems for juvenile officers. First, it represented a departure from the traditional police practice with which the juvenile officers themselves were identified, in the sense that they were expected to justify their juvenile disposition decisions not simply by evidence proving a youth had committed a crime—grounds on which police were officially expected to base their dispositions of nonjuvenile offenders—but in the *character* of the youth. Second, in disposing of juvenile offenders, officers were expected, in effect, to make judicial rather than ministerial decisions. Third, the shift from the offense to the offender as the basis for determining the appropriate disposition substantially increased the uncertainty and ambiguity for officers in the situation of apprehension because no explicit rules existed for determining which disposition different types of youths should receive. Despite these problems, officers were constrained to base disposition decisions on the character of the apprehended youth, not only because they wanted to be fair, but because persistent failure to do so could result in judicial criticism, departmental censure, and, they believed, loss of authority with juveniles.

DISPOSITION CRITERIA

Assessing the character of apprehended offenders posed relatively few difficulties for officers in the case of youths who had committed serious crimes such as robbery, homicide, aggravated assault, grand theft, auto theft, rape, and arson. Officials generally regarded these juveniles as confirmed delinquents simply by virtue of their involvement in offenses of this magnitude. However, the infraction committed did not always suffice to determine the appropriate disposition for some serious offenders; and, in the case of minor offenders, who comprised over 90 percent of the youths against whom police took action, the violation per se generally played an insignificant role in the choice of disposition. While a number of minor offenders were seen as serious delinquents deserving arrest, many others were perceived either as "good" boys whose offenses were atypical of their customary behavior, as pawns of undesirable associates, or, in any case, as boys for whom arrest was regarded as an unwarranted and possibly harmful punishment. Thus, for nearly all minor violators and for some serious delinquents, the assessment of character—the distinction between serious delinquents, "good" boys, misguided youths, and so on—and the dispositions which followed from these assessments were based on youths' personal characteristics and not their offenses.

Despite this dependence of disposition decisions on the personal characteristics of these youths, however, police officers actually had access only to very limited information about boys at the time they had to decide what to do with them. In the field, officers typically had no data concerning the past offense records, school performance, family situation, or personal adjustment of apprehended youths. Furthermore, files at police headquarters provided data only about each boy's prior offense record. Thus both the decision made in the field—whether or not to bring the boy in—and the decision made at the station—which disposition to invoke—were based largely on cues which emerged from the interaction between the officer and the youth—cues from which the officer inferred the youth's character. These cues included the youth's group affiliations, age, race, grooming, dress, and demeanor. Older juveniles, members of known delinquent gangs, Negroes, youths with well-oiled hair, black jackets, and soiled denims or jeans (the presumed uniform of "tough" boys), and boys who in their interactions with officers did not manifest what were considered to be appropriate signs of respect tended to receive the more severe dispositions.

Other than prior record, the most impor-

tant of the above cues was a youth's *demeanor*. In the opinion of juvenile patrolmen themselves the demeanor of apprehended juveniles was a major determinant of their decisions for 50-60 percent of the juvenile cases they processed. A less subjective indication of the association between a youth's demeanor and police disposition is provided by Table 33.1, which presents the police dispositions for 66 youths whose encounters with police were observed in the course of this study. For purposes of this analysis, each youth's demeanor in the encounter was classified as either cooperative or uncooperative. The results clearly reveal a marked association between youth demeanor and the severity of police dispositions.

The cues used by police to assess demeanor were fairly simple. Juveniles who were contrite about their infractions, respectful to officers, and fearful of the sanctions that might be employed against them tended to be viewed by patrolmen as basically law-abiding or at least "salvageable." For these youths it was usually assumed that informal or formal reprimand would suffice to guarantee their future conformity. In contrast, youthful offenders who were fractious, obdurate, or who appeared nonchalant in their encounters with patrolmen were likely to be viewed as "would-be tough guys" or "punks" who fully deserved the most severe sanction—arrest. The following excerpts from observation notes illustrate the importance attached to demeanor by police in making disposition decisions.

TABLE 33.1
SEVERITY OF POLICE DISPOSITION
BY YOUTH'S DEMEANOR

Severity of Police Disposition	Youth's Demeanor cooperative	uncooperative	Total
Arrest (most severe)	2	14	16
Citation or official reprimand	4	5	9
Informal reprimand	15	1	16
Admonish and release (least severe)	24	1	25
Total	45	21	66

1. The interrogation of "A" (an 18-year-old upper lower class White male accused of statutory rape) was assigned to a police sergeant with long experience on the force. As I sat in his office while we waited for the youth to arrive for questioning, the sergeant expressed his uncertainty as to what he should do with this young man. On the one hand, he could not ignore the fact that an offense had been committed; he had been informed, in fact, that the youth was prepared to confess to the offense. Nor could he overlook the continued pressure from the girl's father (an important political figure) for the police to take severe action against the youth. On the other hand, the sergeant had formed a low opinion of the girl's moral character, and he considered it unfair to charge "A" with statutory rape when the girl was a willing partner to the offense and might even have been the instigator of it. However, his sense of injustice concerning "A" was tempered by his image of the youth as a "punk," based, he explained, on information he had received that the youth belonged to a certain gang, the members of which were well known to, and disliked by, the police. Nevertheless, as we prepared to leave his office to interview "A," the sergeant was still in doubt as to what he should do with him.

As we walked down the corridor to the interrogation room, the sergeant was stopped by a reporter from the local newspaper. In an excited tone of voice, the reporter explained that his editor was pressing him to get further information about this case. The newspaper had printed some of the facts about the girl's disappearance, and as a consequence the girl's father was threatening suit against the paper for defamation of the girl's character. It would strengthen the newspaper's position, the reporter explained, if the police had information indicating that the girl's associates, particularly the youth the sergeant was about to interrogate, were persons of disreputable character. This stimulus seemed to resolve the sergeant's uncertainty. He told the reporter, "unofficially," that the youth was known to be an undesirable person, citing as evidence his membership in the delinquent gang. Furthermore, the sergeant added that he had evidence that this youth had been intimate with the girl over a period of many months. When the reporter asked if the police were planning to do anything to the youth, the sergeant answered that he intended to charge the youth with statutory rape.

In the interrogation, however, three points quickly emerged which profoundly affected the sergeant's judgment of the youth. First, the youth was polite and cooperative; he consistently addressed the officer as "sir," answered all questions quietly, and signed a statement implicating himself in numerous counts of statutory rape. Second, the youth's intentions toward the girl appeared to have been honorable; for example, he said that he wanted to marry her eventually. Third, the youth was not, in fact, a member of the gang in question. The sergeant's attitude became increasingly sympathetic, and after we left the interrogation room he announced his intention to "get 'A' off the hook," meaning that he wanted to have the charges against "A" reduced or, if possible, dropped.

2. Officers "X" and "Y" brought into the police station a 17-year-old White boy who, along with two older companions, had been found in a home having sex relations with a 15-year-old girl. The boy responded to police officers' queries slowly and with obvious disregard. It was apparent that his lack of deference toward the officers and his failure to evidence concern about his situation were irritating his questioners. Finally, one of the officers turned to me and, obviously angry, commented that in his view the boy was simply a "stud" interested only in sex, eating, and sleeping. The policemen conjectured that the boy "probably already had knocked up half a dozen girls." The boy ignored these remarks, except for an occasional impassive stare at the patrolmen. Turning to the boy, the officer remarked, "What the hell am I going to do with you?" And again the boy simply returned the officer's gaze. The latter then said, "Well, I guess we'll just have to put you away for a while." An arrest report was then made out and the boy was taken to Juvenile Hall.

Although anger and disgust frequently characterized officers' attitudes toward recalcitrant and impassive juvenile offenders, their manner while processing these youths was typically routine, restrained, and without rancor. While the officers' restraint may have been due in part to their desire to avoid accusation and censure, it also seemed to reflect their inurement to a frequent experience. By and large, only their occasional "needling" or insulting of a boy gave any hint of the underlying resentment and dislike they felt toward many of these youths.

PREJUDICE IN APPREHENSION AND DISPOSITION DECISIONS

Compared to other youths, Negroes and boys whose appearance matched the delinquent stereotype were more frequently stopped and interrogated by patrolmen—often even in the absence of evidence that an offense had been committed—and usually were given more severe dispositions for the same violations. Our data suggest, however, that these selective apprehension and disposition practices resulted not only from the intrusion of long-held prejudices of individual police officers but also from certain job-related experiences of law enforcement personnel. First, the tendency for police to give more severe dispositions to Negroes and to youths whose appearance corresponded to that which police associated with delinquents partly reflected the fact, observed in this study, that these youths also were much more likely than were other types of boys to exhibit the sort of recalcitrant demeanor which police construed as a sign of the confirmed delinquent. Further, officers assumed, partly on the basis of departmental statistics, that Negroes and juveniles who "look tough" (e.g., who wear chinos, leather jackets, boots, etc.) commit crimes more frequently than do other types of youths. In this sense, the police justified their selective treatment of these youths along epidemiological lines; that is, they were concentrating their attention on those youths whom they believed most likely to commit delinquent acts. In the words of one highly placed official in the department:

If you know that the bulk of your delinquent problem comes from kids who, say, are from 12 to 14 years of age, when you're out on patrol you are much more likely to be sensitive to the activities of juveniles in this age bracket than older or younger groups. This would be good law enforcement practice. The logic in our case is the same except that our delinquency problem is largely found in the Negro community, and it is these youths toward whom we are sensitized.

As regards prejudice per se, 18 of 27 officers interviewed openly admitted a dislike for Negroes. However, they attributed their dislike to experiences they had, as policemen, with youths from this minority group. The officers reported that Negro boys were much more likely than non-Negroes to "give us a hard time," be uncooperative, and show no

remorse for their transgressions. Recurrent exposure to such attitudes among Negro youth, the officers claimed, generated their antipathy toward Negroes. The following excerpt is typical of the views expressed by these officers.

They (Negroes) have no regard for the law or for the police. They just don't seem to give a damn. Few of them are interested in school or getting ahead. The girls start having illegitimate kids before they are 16 years old and the boys are always "out for kicks." Furthermore, many of these kids try to run you down. They say the damnedest things to you, and they seem to have absolutely no respect for you as an adult. I admit I am prejudiced now, but frankly I don't think I was when I began police work.

IMPLICATIONS

It is apparent from the findings presented above that the police officers studied in this research were permitted and even encouraged to exercise immense latitude in disposing of the juveniles they encountered. That is, it was within the officers' discretionary authority, except in extreme limiting cases, to decide which juveniles were to come to the attention of the courts and correctional agencies and thereby be identified officially as delinquents. In exercising this discretion policemen were strongly guided by the demeanor of those who were apprehended, a practice which ultimately led, as seen above, to certain youths (particularly Negroes and boys dressed in the style of "toughs") being treated more severely than other juveniles for comparable offenses.

But the relevance of demeanor was not limited only to police disposition practices. Thus, for example, in conjunction with police crime statistics the criterion of demeanor led police to concentrate their surveillance activities in areas frequented or inhabited by Negroes. Furthermore, these youths were accosted more often than others by officers on patrol simply because their skin color identified them as potential troublemakers. These discriminatory practices—and it is important to note that they are discriminatory, even if based on accurate statistical information—may well have self-fulfilling consequences. Thus it is not unlikely that frequent encounters with police, particularly those involving youths innocent of wrongdoing, will increase the hostility of these juveniles toward law enforcement personnel. It is also not unlikely that the frequency of such encounters will in time reduce their significance in the eyes of apprehended juveniles, thereby leading these youths to regard them as "routine." Such responses to police encounters, however, are those which law enforcement personnel perceive as indicators of the serious delinquent. They thus serve to vindicate and reinforce officers' prejudices, leading to closer surveillance of Negro districts, more frequent encounters with Negro youths, and so on in a vicious circle. Moreover, the consequences of this chain of events are reflected in police statistics showing a disproportionately high percentage of Negroes among juvenile offenders, thereby providing "objective" justification for concentrating police attention on Negro youths.

To a substantial extent, as we have implied earlier, the discretion practiced by juvenile officers is simply an extension of the juvenile court philosophy, which holds that in making legal decisions regarding juveniles, more weight should be given to the juvenile's character and life situation than to his actual offending behavior. The juvenile officer's disposition decisions—and the information he uses as a basis for them—are more akin to the discriminations made by probation officers and other correctional workers than they are to decisions of police officers dealing with nonjuvenile offenders. The problem is that such clinical-type decisions are not restrained by mechanisms comparable to the principles of due process and the rules of procedure governing police decisions regarding adult offenders. Consequently, prejudicial practices by police officers can escape notice more easily in their dealings with juveniles than with adults.

The observations made in this study serve to underscore the fact that the official delinquent, as distinguished from the juvenile who simply commits a delinquent act, is the product of a social judgment, in this case a judgment made by the police. He is a delinquent because someone in authority has defined him as one, often on the basis of the public face he has presented to officials rather than of the kind of offense he has committed.

34. NORMAL CRIMES AND THE PUBLIC DEFENDER

DAVID SUDNOW

Reprinted with permission from "Normal Crimes: Sociological Features of the Penal Code in a Public Defender Office," Social Problems 12 (Winter 1965): 255-74. David Sudnow is Associate Professor of Sociology at the University of California, Irvine. He is the author of Passing On: The Social Organization of Dying *(Prentice-Hall, 1967).*

■ For Americans one of the clearest and most broadly supported meanings of equality is that of equality before the law. An individual accused of a crime is entitled to a proper defense regardless of ability to pay; so for persons without funds, the court traditionally appoints a private attorney to serve as defense counsel.

Attorneys have generally considered this assignment to be part of their duty as officers of the court but it has been argued that this system results in young and inexperienced attorneys for indigent defendants because well-established counselors avoid this kind of service. Many jurisdictions have tried to reform the system by establishing a public defender's office. Public defenders are paid by the state, and their sole business is the defense of clients who cannot or will not retain attorneys. The argument has been that public defenders will acquire expertise as defense attorneys, and because their sole job is to provide such defense they will take it more seriously than private attorneys for whom it is a burden.

This policy response to the problem does not necessarily represent an improvement, because as David Sudnow shows, the public defender becomes part of the judicial bureaucracy and is subject to its pressures. Sudnow shows how these pressures are subtle and pervasive, perhaps even against the wishes of the public defenders themselves.

For discussions of indigent defense systems see *Equal Justice for the Accused* (Association of the Bar of the City of New York, 1959); and E. A. Brownell, *Legal Aid in the United States* (Lawyers Cooperative Publishing Co., 1951). ■

TWO STANCES toward the utility of official classificatory schema for criminological research have been debated for years. One position, which might be termed that of the "revisionist" school, has it that the categories of the criminal law—e.g., "burglary," "petty theft," "homicide"—are not "homogeneous in respect to causation." From an inspection of penal code descriptions of crimes, it is argued that the way persons seem to be assembled under the auspices of criminal law procedure is such as to produce classes of criminals who are, at least on theoretical grounds, as dissimilar in their social backgrounds and styles of activity as they are similar. The entries in the penal code, this school argues, require revision if sociological use is to be made of categories of crime and a classificatory scheme of etiological relevance is to be developed. Common attempts at such revision have included notions such as *"white collar* crime," and *"systematic* check forger," these conceptions constituting attempts to institute sociological meaningful specifications which the operations of criminal law procedure and statutory legislation "fail" to achieve.

The other major perspective toward the sociologist's use of official categories and the criminal statistics compiled under their heading derives less from a concern with etiologically useful schema than from an interest in understanding the actual operations of the administrative legal system. Here, the categories of the criminal law are not regarded as useful or not useful, as objects to be either adopted, adapted, or ignored; rather, they are seen as constituting the basic conceptual equipment with which such people as judges, lawyers, policemen, and probation workers organize their everyday activities. The study of the actual use of official classification systems by actually employed administrative personnel regards the penal code as data, to be preserved intact; its use, both in organizing the work of legal representation, accusation, adjudication, and prognostication and in compiling tallies of legal occurrences, is to be examined as one would examine any social activity. By sociologically regarding, rather than criticizing, rates of statistics and the categories employed to assemble them, one learns, it is promised, about the "rate-producing agencies" and the assembling process.

While the former perspective—the "revisionist" position—has yielded several fruitful products, the latter stance (commonly identified with what is rather loosely known as the labeling perspective), has been on the whole more promissory than productive, more programmatic than empirical. The present report will examine the operations of a public defender system in an effort to assess the warrant for the continued theoretical and empirical development of the position argued by Kitsuse and Cicourel. It will address the question: What of import for the sociological analysis of legal administration can be learned by describing the actual way the penal code is employed in the daily activities of legal representation? First, I shall consider the guilty plea as a way of handling criminal cases, focusing on some features of the penal code as a description of a population of defendants. Then I shall describe the public defender operation with special attention to the way defendants are represented. The place of the guilty plea and penal code in this representation will be examined. Lastly, I shall briefly analyze the fashion in which the public defender prepares and conducts a "defense." The latter section will attempt to indicate the connection between certain prominent organizational features of the public defender system and the penal code's place in the routine operation of that system.

GUILTY PLEAS, INCLUSION, AND NORMAL CRIMES

It is a commonly noted fact about the criminal court system generally that the greatest proportion of cases are "settled" by a guilty plea. In the county from which the following material is drawn, over 80 percent of all cases "never go to trial." To describe the method of obtaining a guilty plea disposition, essential for the discussion to follow, I must distinguish between what shall be termed "necessarily included lesser offenses" and "situationally included lesser offenses." Of two offenses designated in the penal code, the lesser is considered to be that for which the length of required incarceration is the shorter period of time. *Inclusion* refers to the relation between two or more offenses. The "necessarily included lesser offense" is a strictly legal notion.

Whether a lesser offense is included in the crime charged is a question of law to be determined solely from the definition and corpus delicti of the offense charged and of the lesser offense. . . . If all the elements of the corpus delicti of a lesser crime can be found in a list of all the elements of the offense charged, then only is the lesser included in the greater.

Stated alternatively:

The test in this state of necessarily included offenses is simply that where an offense cannot be committed without necessarily committing another offense, the latter is a necessarily included offense.

The implied negative is put: could Smith have committed A and not B? If the answer is yes, then B is not necessarily included in A. If the answer is no, B is necessarily included. While in a given case a battery might be committed in the course of a robbery, battery is not necessarily included in robbery. Petty theft is necessarily included in robbery but not in burglary. Burglary primarily involves the "intent" to acquire another's goods illegally (e.g., by breaking and entering); the consummation of the act need not occur for burglary to be committed. Theft, like robbery, requires that some item be stolen.

I shall call *lesser* offenses that are not necessarily but "only" *actually* included, "situationally included lesser offenses." By statutory definition, necessarily included offenses are "actually" included. By actual here, I refer to the "way it occurs as a course of action." In the instance of necessary inclusion, the "way it occurs" is irrelevant. With situational inclusion, the "way it occurs" is definitive. In the former case, no particular course of action is referred to. In the latter, the scene and progress of the criminal activity would be analyzed.

The issue of necessary inclusion has special relevance for two procedural matters.

A man cannot be charged and/or convicted of two or more crimes any one of which is necessarily included in the others, unless the several crimes occur on separate occasions.

If a murder occurs, the defendant cannot be charged and/or convicted of both "homicide" and "intent to commit a murder," the latter of which is necessarily included in first-degree murder. If, however, a defendant "intends to commit a homicide" against one person and commits a "homicide" against another, both offenses may be properly charged. While it is an extremely complex question as to the scope and definition of "in the course of," in most instances the rule is easily applied.

The judge cannot instruct the jury to consider as alternative crimes of which to find a defendant guilty, crimes that are not necessarily included in the charged crime or crimes.

If a man is charged with "statutory rape," the judge may instruct the jury to consider as a possible alternative conviction "contributing to the delinquency of a minor," as this offense is necessarily included in "statutory rape." He cannot, however, suggest that the alternative "intent to commit murder" be considered and the jury cannot find the defendant guilty of this latter crime, unless it is charged as a distinct offense in the complaint.

It is crucial to note that these restrictions apply only to (a) the relation between several charged offenses in a formal allegation, and (b) the alternatives allowable in a jury instruction. At any time before a case "goes to trial," alterations in the charging complaint may be made by the district attorney. The issue of necessary inclusion has no required bearing on (a) what offense(s) will be charged initially by the prosecutor, (b) what the relation is between the charge initially made and "what happened," or (c) what modifications may be made after the initial charge and the relation between initially charged offenses and those charged in modified complaints. It is this latter operation, the modification of the complaint, that is central to the guilty plea disposition.

Complaint alterations are made when a defendant agrees to plead guilty to an offense and thereby avoid a trial. The alteration occurs in the context of a "deal," consisting of an offer from the district attorney to alter the original charge in such a fashion that a lighter sentence will be incurred with a guilty plea than would be the case if the defendant were sentenced on the original charge. In return for this manipulation, the defendant agrees to plead guilty. The arrangement is proposed in the following format. "If you plead guilty to this new lesser offense, you will get less time in prison than if you plead not guilty to the original, greater charge and lose the trial." The decision must then be made whether or not the chances of obtaining complete acquittal at trial are great enough to warrant the risk of a loss and higher sentence if found guilty on the original charge. As we shall see below, it is a major job of the public defender, who mediates between the district attorney and the defendant, to convince his "client" that the chances of acquittal are too slight to warrant this risk.

If a man is charged with "drunkenness" and the public defender and public prosecutor (hereafter P.D. and D.A.) prefer not to have a trial, they seek to have the defendant agree to plead guilty. While it is occasionally possible, particularly with first offenders, for the P.D. to convince the defendant to plead guilty to the originally charged offense, most often it is felt that some "exchange" or "consideration" should be offered—i.e., a lesser offense charged.

To what offense can "drunkenness" be reduced? There is no statutorily designated crime that is necessarily included in the crime of "drunkenness." That is, if any of the statutorily required components of drunk behavior (its corpus delicti) are absent, there remains no offense of which the resultant description is a definition. For drunkenness there is, however, an offense that while not necessarily included is "typically situationally included"—i.e., "typically" occurs as a feature of the way drunk persons are seen to behave, "disturbing the peace." The range of possible sentences is such that of the two offenses, "disturbing the peace" cannot call for as long a prison sentence as "drunkenness." If, in the course of going on a binge, a person does so in such a fashion that "disturbing the peace" may be employed to describe some of his behavior, it would be considered as an alternative offense to offer in return for a guilty plea. A central question for the following analysis will be: in what fashion would he have to behave so that disturbing the peace would be considered a suitable reduction?

If a man is charged with "molesting a minor," there are not any necessarily included lesser offenses with which to charge him. Yet an alternative charge, "loitering around a schoolyard," is often used as a reduction. As above, and central to our analysis, the question is: What would the defendant's behavior be such that "loitering around a schoolyard" would constitute an appropriate alternative?

If a person is charged with "burglary," "petty theft" is not necessarily included. Routinely, however, "petty theft" is employed for reducing the charge of burglary. Again, we shall ask: What is the relation between burglary and petty theft and the *manner in which the former occurs* that warrants this reduction?

Offenses are regularly reduced to other offenses, the latter of which are not necessarily or situationally included in the former. As I have already said the determination of whether or not offense X was situationally included in Y involves an analysis of the course of action that constitutes the criminal behavior. I must now turn to examine this mode of behavioral analysis.

When encountering a defendant who is charged with "assault with a deadly weapon," the P.D. asks: "What can this offense be reduced to so as to arrange for a guilty plea?

As the reduction is only to be proposed by the P.D. and accepted or not by the D.A., his question becomes "what reduction will be allowable?" (As shall be seen below, the P.D. and D.A. have institutionalized a common orientation to allowable reductions.) The method of reduction involves, as a general feature, the fact that the particular case in question is scrutinized to decide its membership in a class of similar cases. But *the penal code does not provide the reference for deciding the correspondence between the instant event and the general case; that is, it does not define the classes of offense types.* To decide, for purposes of finding a suitable reduction, if the instant case involves a "burglary," reference is not made to the statutory definition of "burglary." To decide what the situationally included offenses are in the instant case, the instant case is not analyzed as a *statutorily* referable course of action; rather, reference is made to a *nonstatutorily* conceived class "burglary" and offenses that are typically situationally included in it, taken as a class of behavioral events. Stated again: in searching an instant case to decide what to *reduce it to*, there is no analysis of the statutorily referable elements of the instant case; instead, its membership in a class of events, the features of which cannot be described by the penal code, must be decided. An example will be useful. If a defendant is charged with burglary and the P.D. is concerned to propose a reduction to a lesser offense, he might search the elements of the burglary at hand to decide what other offenses were committed. The other offenses he might "discover" would be of two sorts: those necessarily and those situationally included. In attempting to decide those other offenses situationally included in the instant event, the instant event might be analyzed as a statutorily referable course of action. Or, as is the case with the P.D., the instant case might be analyzed to decide if it is a "burglary" in common with other "burglaries" conceived of in terms other than those provided by the statute.

Burglaries are routinely reduced to petty theft. If we were to analyze the way burglaries typically occur, petty theft is neither situationally or necessarily included; when a burglary is committed, money or other goods are seldom illegally removed from some person's body. If we therefore analyzed burglaries, employing the penal code as our reference, and then searched the P.D.'s records to see how burglaries are reduced in the guilty plea, we could not establish a rule that would describe the transformation between the burglary cases statutorily described and the reductions routinely made (i.e., to "petty theft"). The rule must be sought elsewhere, in the character of the nonstatutorily defined class of "burglaries," which I shall term *normal burglaries*.

NORMAL CRIMES

In the course of routinely encountering persons charged with "petty theft," "burglary," "assault with a deadly weapon," "rape," "possession of marijuana," etc., the P.D. gains knowledge of the typical manner in which offenses of given classes are committed, the social characteristics of the persons who regularly commit them, the features of the settings in which they occur, the types of victims often involved, and the like. He learns to speak knowledgeably of "burglars," "petty thieves," "drunks," "rapists," "narcos," etc., and to attribute to them personal biographics, modes of usual criminal activity, criminal histories, psychological characteristics, and social backgrounds. The following characterizations are illustrative.

Most ADWs (assault with deadly weapon) start with fights over some girl.

These sex fiends (child molestation cases) usually hang around parks or schoolyards. But we often get fathers charged with these crimes. Usually the old man is out of work and stays at home when the wife goes to work and he plays around with his little daughter or something. A lot of these cases start when there is some marital trouble and the woman gets mad.

I don't know why most of them don't rob the big stores. They usually break into some cheap department store and steal some crummy item like a $9.95 record player you know.

Kids who start taking this stuff (narcotics) usually start out when some buddy gives them a cigarette and they smoke it for kicks. For some reason they always get caught in their cars, for speeding or something.

They can anticipate that point when persons are likely to get into trouble.

Dope addicts do O.K. until they lose a job or something and get back on the streets and, you know, meet the old boys. Someone tells them where to get some and there they are.

In the springtime, that's when we get all these sex crimes. You know, these kids play out in the schoolyard all day and these old men sit around and watch them jumping up and down. They get their ideas.

The P.D. learns that some kinds of offenders are likely to repeat the same offense while others are not repeat violators, or if they do commit crimes frequently, the crimes vary from occasion to occasion.

You almost never see a check man get caught for anything but checks—only an occasional drunk charge.

Burglars are usually multiple offenders, most times just burglaries or petty thefts.

Petty thefts get started for almost anything—joy riding, drinking, all kinds of little things.

These narcos are usually through after the second violation or so. After the first time some stop, but when they start on the heavy stuff, they've had it.

I shall call *normal crimes* those occurrences whose typical features—e.g., the ways they usually occur and the characteristics of persons who commit them (as well as the typical victims and typical scenes), are known and attended to by the P.D. For any of a series of offense types the P.D. can provide some form of proverbial characterization. For example, *burglary* is seen as involving regular violators, no weapons, low-priced items, little property damage, lower class establishments, largely Negro defendants, independent operators, and a nonprofessional orientation to the crime. *Child molesting* is seen as typically entailing middle-aged strangers or lower class middle-aged fathers (few women), no actual physical penetration or severe tissue damage, mild fondling, petting, and stimulation, bad marriage circumstances, multiple offenders with the same offense repeatedly committed, a child complainant, via the mother, etc. *Narcotics* defendants are usually Negroes, not syndicated, persons who start by using small stuff, hostile with police officers, caught by some form of entrapment technique, etc. *Petty thefts* are about 50-50 Negro-White, unplanned offenses, generally committed on lower class persons and don't get much money, don't often employ weapons, don't make living from thievery, usually younger defendants with long juvenile assaultive records, etc.

Drunkenness offenders are lower class White and Negro, get drunk on wine and beer, have long histories of repeated drunkenness, don't hold down jobs, are usually arrested on the streets, seldom violate other penal code sections, etc.

Some general features of the normal crime as a way of attending to a category of persons and events may be mentioned.

1. The focus, in these characterizations, is not on particular individuals but offense types. If asked "What are burglars like?" or "How are burglaries usually committed?" the P.D. does not feel obliged to refer to particular burglars and burglaries as the material for his answer.

2. The features attributed to offenders and offenses are often not of import for the statutory conception. In burglary, it is "irrelevant" for the statutory determination whether or not much damage was done to the premises (except where, for example, explosives were employed and a new statute could be invoked). Whether a defendant breaks a window or not, destroys property within the house or not, etc., does not affect his statutory classification as a burglar. While for robbery the presence or absence of a weapon sets the degree, whether the weapon is a machine gun or pocket knife is "immaterial." Whether the residence or business establishment in a burglary is located in a higher income area of the city is of no issue for the code requirements. And, generally, the defendant's race, class position, criminal history (in most offenses), personal attributes, and particular style of committing offenses are features

specifically not definitive of crimes under the auspices of the penal code. For deciding "Is this a 'burglary' case I have before me," however, the P.D.'s reference to this range of nonstatutorily referable personal and social attributes, modes of operation, etc., is crucial for the arrangement of a guilty plea bargain.

3. The features attributed to offenders and offenses are, in their content, specific to the community in which the P.D. works. In other communities and historical periods the lists would presumably differ. Narcotics violators in certain areas, for example, are syndicated in dope rackets or engage in systematic robbery as professional criminals, features which are not commonly encountered (or, at least, evidence for which is not systematically sought) in this community. Burglary in some cities will more often occur at large industrial plants, banking establishments, warehouses, etc. The P.D. refers to the population of defendants in the county as "our defendants" and qualifies his prototypical portrayals and knowledge of the typically operative social structures, "for our county." An older P.D., remembering the "old days," commented:

We used to have a lot more rapes than we do now, and they used to be much more violent. Things are duller now in———. . . .

4. Offenses whose normal features are readily attended to are those which are routinely encountered in the courtroom. This feature is related to the last point. For embezzlement, bank robbery, gambling, prostitution, murder, arson, and some other uncommon offenses, the P.D. cannot readily supply anecdotal and proverbial characterizations. While there is some change in the frequencies of offense-type convictions over time, certain offenses are continually more common and others remain stably infrequent. The troubles created for the P.D. when offenses whose features are not readily known occur, and whose typicality is not easily constructed, will be discussed in some detail below.

5. Offenses are ecologically specified and attended to as normal or not according to the locales within which they are committed.

The P.D. learns that burglaries usually occur in such and such areas of the city, petty thefts around this or that park, ADWs in these bars. Ecological patterns are seen as related to socioeconomic variables, and these, in turn, to typical modes of criminal and non-criminal activities. Knowing where an offense took place is thus, for the P.D., knowledge of the likely persons involved, the kind of scene in which the offense occurred, and the pattern of activity characteristic of such a place.

Almost all of our ADWs are in the same half a dozen bars. These places are Negro bars where laborers come after hanging around the union halls trying to get some work. Nobody has any money and they drink too much. Tempers are high and almost anything can start happening.

6. One further important feature can be noted at this point. Its elaboration will be the task of a later section. As shall be seen, the P.D. office consists of a staff of 12 full-time attorneys. Knowledge of the properties of offense types of offenders—i.e., their normal, typical, or familiar attributes—constitutes the mark of any given attorney's competence. A major task in socializing the new P.D. deputy attorney consists in teaching him to recognize these attributes and to come to do so naturally. The achievement of competence as a P.D. is signaled by the gradual acquisition of professional command not simply of local penal code peculiarities and courtroom folklore but, as importantly, of relevant features of the social structure and criminological wisdom. His grasp of that knowledge over the course of time is a key indication of his expertise. Below, in our brief account of some relevant organizational properties of the P.D. system, we shall have occasion to reemphasize the competence-attesting aspects of the attorney's proper use of established sociological knowledge. Let us return to the mechanics of the guilty plea procedure as an example of the operation of the notion of normal crimes.

Over the course of their interaction and repeated "bargaining" discussions, the P.D. and D.A. have developed a set of unstated recipes for reducing original charges to lesser offenses. These recipes are specifically appropriate for use in instances of normal crimes and in such instances alone. "Typical" burglaries are reduced to petty theft, "typical" ADWs to simple assault, "typical" child molestation to loitering around a schoolyard, etc. The character of these recipes deserves attention.

The specific content of any reduction—i.e., what particular offense class X offenses will be reduced to—is such that the reduced offense may bear no obvious relation (neither situationally nor necessarily included) to the originally charged offense. The reduction of burglary to petty theft is an example. The important relation between the reduced offense and the original charge is such that the reduction from one to the other is considered "reasonable." At this point we shall only state what seems to be the general principle involved in deciding this reasonableness. The underlying premises cannot be explored at the present time, as that would involve a political analysis beyond the scope of the present report. *Both P.D. and D.A. are concerned to obtain a guilty plea wherever possible and thereby avoid a trial. At the same time, each party is concerned that the defendant "receive his due." The reduction of offense X to Y must be of such a character that the new sentence will depart from the anticipated sentence for the original charge to such a degree that the defendant is likely to plead guilty to the new charge and, at the same time, not so great that the defendant does not "get his due."*

In a homicide, while battery is a necessarily included offense, it will not be considered as a possible reduction. For a conviction of second-degree murder a defendant could receive a life sentence in the penitentiary. For a battery conviction he would spend no more than six months in the county jail. In a homicide, however, "felony manslaughter," or "assault with a deadly weapon," whatever their relation to homicide as regards inclusion, would more closely approximate the sentence outcome that could be expected on a trial conviction of second-degree murder. These alternatives would be considered. For burglary, a typically situationally included offense might be "disturbing the peace," "breaking and entering," or "destroying public property." "Petty theft," however, constitutes a reasonable lesser alternative to burglary as the sentence for petty theft will often range between six months and one year in the county jail, and burglary regularly does not carry higher than two years in the state prison. "Disturbing the peace" would be a 30-day sentence offense.

While the present purposes make the exposition of this calculus unnecessary, it can be noted and stressed that the particular content of the reduction does not necessarily correspond to a relation between the original and altered charge that could be described in the terms of either necessary or situational inclusion. Whatever the relation between the original and reduced charge, its essential feature resides in the spread between sentence likelihoods and the reasonableness of that spread—i.e., the balance it strikes between the defendant's "getting his due" and at the same time "getting something less than he might so that he will plead guilty."

The procedure we want to clarify now, at the risk of some repetition, is the manner in which an instant case is examined to decide its membership in a class of "crimes such as this" (the category *normal crimes*). Let us start with an obvious case, burglary. As the typical reduction for burglary is petty theft and as petty theft is neither situationally nor necessarily included in burglary, the examination of the instant case is clearly not undertaken to decide whether petty theft is an appropriate statutory description. The concern is to establish the relation between the instant burglary and the normal category "burglaries" and, having decided a "sufficient correspondence," to now employ petty theft as the proposed reduction.

In scrutinizing the present burglary case, the P.D. seeks to establish that "this is a burglary just like any other." If that correspondence is not established, regardless of whether or not petty theft in fact was a feature of the way the crime was enacted, the reduction to petty theft would not be proposed. *The propriety of proposing petty theft as a reduction does not derive from its in-fact existence in the present case, but is warranted or not by the relation of the present burglary to "burglaries," normally conceived.*

In a case of "child molestation" (officially called "lewd conduct with a minor"), the concern is to decide if this is a "typical child molestation case." While "loitering around a schoolyard" is frequently a feature of the way such crimes are instigated, establishing that the present defendant *did in fact loiter around a schoolyard* is secondary to the more general question "Is this a typical child molestation case?" What appears as a contradiction must be clarified by examining the status of "loitering around a schoolyard" as a typical feature of such child molestations. The typical character of "child molesting cases" does not stand or fall on the fact that "loitering around a schoolyard" is a feature of the way they are in fact committed. It is *not* that "loitering around a schoolyard" as a *statutorily referable behavior sequence* is part of typical "child-molesting cases" but that "loitering around a schoolyard" as a *socially distinct mode of committing child molestations typifies the way such offenses are enacted.* "Strictly speaking"—i.e., under the auspices of the statutory *corpus delicti* "loitering around a schoolyard" —requires *loitering, around, a schoolyard;* if one loiters around a ball park or a public recreation area, he "cannot," within a proper reading of the statute, be charged with loitering around a *schoolyard.* Yet "loitering around a schoolyard," as a feature of the typical way such offenses as child molestations are committed, has the status not of a description of the way in *fact* (*fact,* statutorily decided) it occurred or typically occurs, but "the kind of social activity typically associated with such offenses." It is not its statutorily conceived features but its socially relevant attributes that gives "loitering around a schoolyard" its status as a feature of the class "normal child molestations." Whether the defendant loitered around a schoolyard or a ball park, and whether he loitered or "was passing by," "loitering around a schoolyard" as a reduction will be made if the defendant's activity was such that "he was hanging around some public place or another" and "was the kind of guy who hangs around schoolyards." As a component of the class of normal child molestation cases (of the variety where the victim is a stranger), "loitering around a schoolyard" typifies a mode of committing such offenses, the class of "such persons who do such things as hang around schoolyards and the like." A large variety of actual offenses could thus be nonetheless reduced to "loitering" if, as kinds of social activity, "loitering," conceived of as typifying a way of life, pattern of daily activity, social psychological circumstances, etc., characterized the conduct of the defendant. The young P.D. who would object "You can't reduce it to 'loitering'—he didn't really 'loiter'," would be reprimanded: "Fella, you don't know how to use that term; he might as well have 'loitered'—it's the same kind of case as the others."

Having outlined the formal mechanics of the guilty plea disposition, I shall now turn to depict the routine of representation that the categories of crime, imbued with elaborate knowledge of the delinquent social structure, provide for. This will entail a brief examination of pertinent organizational features of the P.D. system.

PUBLIC "DEFENSE"

Recently in many communities the burden of securing counsel has been taken from the defendant. As the accused is, by law, entitled to the aid of counsel, and as his pocketbook is often empty, numerous cities have felt obliged to establish a public defender system. There has been little resistance to this development by private attorneys among whom it is widely felt that the less time they need spend in the criminal courts, where practice is least prestigeful and lucrative, the better.

Whatever the reasons for its development, we now find in many urban places, a public defender occupying a place alongside judge and prosecutor as a regular court employee. In the county studied, the P.D. mans a daily station, like the public prosecutor, and "defends" all who come before him. He appears in court when court begins, and his "clientele," composed without regard for his preferences, consists of that residual category of persons who cannot afford to bring their own spokesmen to court. In this county, the "residual" category approximates 65 percent of the total number of criminal cases. In a given year, the 12 attorneys who comprise the P.D. Office "represent" about 3,000 defendants in the municipal and superior courts of the county.

While the courtroom encounters of private attorneys are brief, businesslike, and circumscribed, interactionally and temporally, by the particular cases that bring them there, the P.D. attends to the courtroom as his regular workplace and conveys in his demeanor his place as a member of its core personnel.

While private attorneys come and leave court with their clients (who are generally "on bail"), the P.D. arrives in court each morning at nine, takes his station at the defense table, and deposits there the batch of files that he will refer to during the day. When, during morning "calendar," a private attorney's case is called, the P.D. steps back from the defense table, leaving his belongings in place there, and temporarily relinquishes his station. No private attorney has enough defendants in a given court on a given day to claim a right to make a desk of the defense table. If the P.D. needs some information from his central office, he uses the clerk's telephone, a privilege that few private lawyers feel at home enough to take. In the course of calendar work, a lawyer will often have occasion to request a delay or "continuance" of several days until the next stage of his client's proceedings. The private attorney addresses the prosecutor via the judge to request such an alteration; the P.D. talks directly over to the D.A.

Private attorney: "If the prosecutor finds it convenient your Honor, my client would prefer to have his preliminary hearing on Monday, the 24th."
Judge: "Is that date suitable to the district attorney?"
Prosecutor: "Yes, your honor."
Private attorney: "Thank you, your Honor."

Public Defender: "Bob (D.A.), how about moving Smith's prelim up to the 16th?"

Prosecutor: "Well, Jim, we've got Jones on that afternoon."

Public Defender: "Let's see, how's the 22nd?"

Prosecutor: "That's fine, Jim, the 22nd."

If, during the course of a proceeding, the P.D. has some minor matter to tend to with the D.A., he uses the time when a private attorney is addressing the bench to walk over to the prosecutor's table and whisper his requests, suggestions, or questions. The P.D. uses the prosecutor's master calendar to check on an upcoming court date; so does the D.A. with the P.D.'s. The D.A. and P.D. are on a first-name basis and throughout the course of a routine day interact as a team of coworkers.

While the central focus of the private attorney's attention is his client, the courtroom and affairs of court constitute the locus of involvements for the P.D. The public defender and public prosecutor, each representatives of their respective offices, jointly handle the greatest bulk of the court's daily activity.

The P.D. office, rather than assign its attorneys to clients, employs the arrangement of stationing attorneys in different courts to "represent" all those who come before that station. As defendants are moved about from courtroom to courtrooom throughout the course of their proceedings (both from municipal to superior courtrooms for felony cases, and from one municipal courtroom to another when there is a specialization of courts—e.g., jury, nonjury, arraignment, etc.), the P.D. sees defendants only at those places in their paths when they appear in the court he is manning. A given defendant may be "represented" by one P.D. at arraignment, another at preliminary hearing, a third at trial, and a fourth when sentenced.

At the first interview with a client (initial interviews occur in the jail where attorneys go, en masse, to "pick up new defendants" in the afternoons) a file is prepared on the defendant. In each file is recorded the charge brought against the defendant and, among other things, his next court date. Each evening attorneys return new files to the central office where secretaries prepare court books for each courtroom that list the defendants due to appear in a given court on a given day. In the mornings, attorneys take the court books from the office and remove from the central file the files of those defendants due to appear in "their court" that day.

There is little communication between P.D. and client. After the first interview, the defendant's encounters with the P.D. are primarily in court. Only under special circumstances (to be discussed below) are there contacts between lawyers and defendants in the jail before and after appearances in court. The bulk of "preparation for court" (either trials or nontrial matters) occurs at the first interview. The attorney on station, the "attending attorney," is thus a stranger to "his client," and vice versa. Over the course of his proceedings a defendant will have several attorneys (in one instance a man was "represented" by eight P.D.'s on a charge of simple assault). Defendants who come to court find a lawyer they don't know conducting their trials, entering their motions, making their pleas, and the rest. Often there is no introduction of P.D. to defendant; defendants are prepared to expect a strange face.

Don't be surprised when you see another P.D. in court with you on Tuesday. You just do what he tells you to. He'll know all about your case.

P.D.s seldom talk about particular defendants among themselves. When they converse about trials, the facts of cases, etc., they do so not so much for briefing—e.g., "This is what I think you should do when you 'get him' "—but rather as small talk, as "What have you got going today." The P.D. does not rely on the information about a case he receives from a previous attending attorney in order to know how to manage his "representation." Rather, the file is relied upon to furnish all the information essential for making an "appearance." These appearances range from morning calendar work (e.g., arraignments, motions, continuances, etc.) to trials on offenses from drunkenness to assault with a deadly weapon. In the course of a routine day, the P.D. will receive his batch of files in the morning and, seeing them for the first

time that day, conduct numerous trials, preliminary hearings, calendar appearances, sentencing proceedings, etc. They do not study
files overnight. Attorneys will often look over
a file only a half-hour or so before the jury
trial begins. . . .

As we noticed, the defendant's guilt is not
attended to. That is to say, the presupposition
of guilt, as a *presupposition,* does not say
"You are guilty" with a pointing accusatory
finger but "You are guilty, you know it, I
know it, so let's get down to the business of
deciding what to do with you." When a
defendant agrees to plead guilty, he is not
admitting his guilt; when asked to plead
guilty, he is not being asked, "Come on, admit
it, you know you were *wrong*" but, rather,
"Why don't you be sensible about this thing?"
What is sought is not a *confession* but
reasonableness.

The presupposition of guilt as a way of
attending to the treatment of defendants has
its counterpart in the way the P.D. attends
to the entire court process, prosecuting
machinery, law enforcement techniques, and
the community.

For P.D. and D.A. it is a routinely encountered phenomenon that persons in the
community regularly commit criminal offenses, are regularly brought before the courts,
and are regularly transported to the state and
county penal institutions. To confront a
"criminal" is, for D.A. and P.D., no special
experience, nothing to tell their wives about,
nothing to record as outstanding in the happenings of the day. Before "their court" scores
of "criminals" pass each day.

The morality of the courts is taken for
granted. The P.D. assumes that the D.A., the
police, judge, the narcotics agents, and others
all conduct their business as it must be conducted and in a proper fashion. That the
police may hide out to deceive petty violators,
that narcotics agents may regularly employ
illicit entrapment procedures to find suspects,
that investigators may routinely arrest suspects before they have sufficient grounds and
only later uncover warrantable evidence for a
formal booking, that the police may beat
suspects, that judges may be "tough" because

they are looking to support for higher office
elections, that some laws may be specifically
prejudicial against certain classes of persons
—whatever may be the actual course of
charging and convicting defendants—all of
this is taken, as one P.D. put it, "as part of
the system and the way it has to be." And the
P.D. is part of the team.

While it is common to overhear private
attorneys call judges "bastards," policemen
"hoodlums," and prosecutors "sadists," the
P.D., in the presence of such talk, remains
silent. When the P.D. "loses" a case—and
we shall see that *losing* is an adequate description only for some circumstances—he is
likely to say "I knew *he* couldn't win." Private
attorneys, on the other hand, will not hesitate
to remark, as one did in a recent case, "You
haven't got a fucking chance in front of that
son-of-a-bitch dictator." In the P.D. office
there is a total absence of such condemnation.

The P.D. takes it for granted and attends
to the courts in accord with the view that
"what goes on in this business is what goes on
and what goes on is the way it should be."
It is rare to hear a public defender voice
protest against a particular law, procedure, or
official. One of the attorneys mentioned that
he felt the new narcotics law (which makes
it mandatory that a high minimum sentence
be served for "possession or sale of narcotics") wasn't too severe "considering that
they wanted to give them the chair." Another
indicated that the more rigid statute "will
probably cure a lot of them because they'll
be in for so long." One P.D. feels that wire-
tapping would be a useful adjunct to police
procedure. It is generally said, by everyone
in the office, that "——— is one of the best
cities in the state when it comes to police."

In the P.D.'s interviews, the defendant's
guilt becomes a topic only when the defendant
himself attempts to direct attention to his
innocence. Such attempts are never taken
seriously by the P.D. but are seen as "innocent pitches," as "being wise," as "not knowing what is good for him." Defendants who
make "innocent pitches" often find themselves
able to convince the P.D. to have trials. The
P.D. is in a professional and organizational

bind in that he requires that his "clients" agree with whatever action he takes "on their behalf."

Can you imagine what might happen if we went straight to the D.A. with a deal to which the client later refused to agree? Can you see him in court screaming how the P.D. sold him out? As it is, we get plenty of letters purporting to show why we don't do our job. Judges are swamped with letters condemning the P.D. Plenty of appeals get started this way.

Some defendants don't buy the offer of less time as constituting sufficient grounds for avoiding a trial. To others, it appears that "copping out" is worse than having a trial regardless of the consequences for the length of sentence. The following remarks, taken from P.D. files, illustrate the terms in which such "stubborn" defendants are conceived.

Def wants a trial, but he is dead. In lieu of a possible 995, DA agreed to put note in his file recommending a deal. This should be explored and encouraged as big break for Def.

Chance of successful defense negligible. Def realizes this but says he ain't going to cop to no strong-arm. See if we can set him straight.

Dead case. Too many witnesses and . . . used in two of the transactions. However, Def is a very squirmy jailhouse lawyer and refuses to face facts.

Possibly the DA in Sup/Ct could be persuaded into cutting her loose if she took the 211 and one of the narco counts. If not, the Def, who is somewhat recalcitrant and stubborn, will probably demand a JT (jury trial).

The routine trial, generated as it is by the defendant's refusal to make a lesser plea, is the "defendant's fault."

What the hell are we supposed to do with them. If they can't listen to good reason and take a bargain, then it's their tough luck. If they go to prison, well, they're the ones who are losing the trials, not us.

When the P.D. enters the courtroom, he takes it that he is going to lose; e.g., the defendant is going to prison. When he "prepares" for trial, he doesn't prepare to "win." There is no attention given to "how am I going to construct a defense in order that I can get this defendant free of the charges against him." In fact, he doesn't "prepare

for trial" in any "ordinary" sense (I use the term *ordinary* with hesitation; what *preparation for trial* might, in fact, involve with other than P.D. lawyers has not, to my knowledge, been investigated.)

For the P.D., "preparation for trial" involves, essentially, learning what "burglary cases" are like, what "rape cases" are like, what "assaults" are like. The P.D.'s main concern is to conduct his part of the proceedings in accord with complete respect for proper legal procedure. He raises objections to improper testimony; introduces motions whenever they seem called for; demands his "client's rights" to access to the prosecution's evidence before trial (through so-called discovery proceedings); cross-examines all witnesses; does not introduce evidence that he expects will not be allowable; asks all those questions of all those people that he must in order to have addressed himself to the task of insuring that the *corpus delicti* has been established; carefully summarizes the evidence that has been presented in making a closing argument. Throughout, at every point, he conducts his "defense" in such a manner that no one can say of him "He has been negligent, there are grounds for appeal here." He systematically provides, in accord with the prescriptions of due process and the Fourteenth Amendment, a completely proper, "adequate legal representation."

At the same time, the district attorney, and the county which employs them both, can rely on the P.D. not to attempt to morally degrade police officers in cross-examination, not to impeach the state's witnesses by trickery, not to attempt an exposition of the entrapment methods of narcotics agents, not to condemn the community for the "racial prejudice that produces our criminals" (the phrase of a private attorney during closing argument), not to challenge the prosecution of "these women who are trying to raise a family without a husband" (the statement of another private attorney during closing argument on a welfare fraud case); in sum, not to make an issue of the moral character of the administrative machinery of the local courts, the community, or the police. He will not cause any serious trouble for the routine motion of the court conviction process. Laws will not be challenged, cases will not be tried to test the constitutionality of procedures and statutes, judges will not be personally degraded, police will be free from scrutiny to decide the legitimacy of their operations, and the community will not be condemned for its segregative practices against Negroes. The P.D.'s defense is completely proper, in accord with correct legal procedure, and specifically amoral in its import, manner of delivery, and perceived implications for the propriety of the prosecution enterprise.

In "return" for all this, the district attorney treats the defendant's guilt in a matter-of-fact fashion, doesn't get hostile in the course of the proceedings, doesn't insist that the jury or judge "throw the book" but, rather, "puts on a trial" (in their way of referring to their daily tasks) in order to, with a minimum of strain, properly place the defendant behind bars. Both prosecutor and public defender thus protect the moral character of the other's charges from exposure. Should the P.D. attend to demonstrating the innocence of his client by attempting to undermine the legitimate character of police operations, the prosecutor might feel obliged in return to employ devices to degrade the moral character of the P.D.'s client. Should the D.A. attack defendants in court, by pointing to the specifically immoral character of their activities, the P.D. might feel obligated, in response, to raise into relief the moral texture of D.A. and police and community operations. Wherever possible, each holds the other in check. But the "check" need not be continuously held in place, or even attended to self-consciously, for both P.D. and D.A. trust each other implicitly. The D.A. knows, with certainty, that the P.D. will not make a closing argument that resembles the following by a private attorney, from which I have paraphrased key excerpts.

If it hadn't been for all the publicity that this case had in our wonderful local newspapers, you wouldn't want to throw the book at these men.

If you'd clear up your problems with the Negro in————maybe you wouldn't have cases like this in your courts.

[after sentence was pronounced] Your honor, I just would like to say one thing—that I've never heard or seen such a display of injustice as I've seen here in this court today. It's a sad commentary on the state of our community if people like yourself pay more attention to the local political machines that to the lives of our defendants. I think you are guilty of that, your Honor.

(At this last statement, one of the P.D.s who was in the courtroom turned to me and said, "He sure is looking for a contempt charge.")

The P.D. knows how to conduct his trials because he knows how to conduct "assault with deadly weapons" trials, "burglary" trials, "rape" trials, and the rest. The *corpus delicti here* provides him with a basis for asking "proper questions," making the "proper cross-examinations," and pointing out the "proper" things to jurors about "reasonable doubt." He need not extensively gather information about the specific facts of the instant case. Whatever is needed in the way of "facts of the case" arise in the course of the D.A.'s presentation. He employs the "strategy" of directing the same questions to the witness as were put by the D.A. with added emphasis on the question mark, or an inserted "Did you really see . . . ?" His "defense" consists of attempting to "bring out" slightly variant aspects of the D.A.'s story by questioning his own witnesses (whom he seldom interviews before beginning trial but who are interviewed by the office's two "investigators") and the defendant.

With little variation the same questions are put to all defendants charged with the same crimes. The P.D. learns with experience what to expect as the "facts of the case." These facts, in their general structure, portray social circumstances that he can anticipate by virtue of his knowledge of the normal features of offense categories and types of offenders. The "details" of the instant case are "discovered" over the course of hearing them in court. In this regard, the "information" that "comes out" is often as new to him as to the jury.

Employing a commonsense conception of what criminal lawyers behave like in cross-examination and argument, and the popular portrayal of their demeanor and style of addressing adversary witnesses, the onlooker comes away with the sense of having witnessed not a trial at all but a set of motions, a perfunctorily carried-off event. A sociological analysis of this sense would require a systematic attempt to describe the features of adversary trial conduct. . . .

35. THE JUVENILE COURT SYSTEM

EDWIN M. LEMERT

Reprinted from Task Force Report: Juvenile Delinquency and Youth Crime *(Government Printing Office, 1967b), Appendix D, pp. 91-105. Edwin M. Lemert is Professor of Sociology at the University of California, Davis. We have referred throughout this book to the work of Edwin M. Lemert, who is perhaps the single most influential figure in establishing the labeling approach to the study of deviant behavior. In the 1950s his textbook,* Social Pathology *(McGraw-Hill, 1951), had a strong influence on researchers, who, in turn developed new theoretical perspectives and empirical research that substantially redirected work in this area.*

■ The juvenile court was one of the earliest social reforms to be strongly influenced by social science. In the late 19th century various reformers became concerned with the extent to which juvenile offenders were victimized and mistreated by the ordinary criminal justice system. From that concern came the juvenile court, a special court for children in which their needs and the principles of humane treatment would be central. In the early 20th century, new developments in psychology and social work were used to buttress the rationale for this reform. The juvenile court, unlike the regular court, was to have a strongly therapeutic orientation; the offender's situation was to be diagnosed and a regime of treatment decided on to help the child find more constructive avenues of self-realization. In the better juvenile court systems the judge presided over a collection of social science talent that included social workers, psychiatrists, psychologists, and professionally trained probation officers. Nothing could have seemed less punitive and more humanitarian in contrast to the regular court system, with its prosecutors and adversary process.

However, by the 1940s a few social scientists were noting that the effect of the bureaucratization of such a system was to establish a presumption of the child's guilt. The juvenile was being denied due process by not having the issue of his guilt or innocence taken seriously in the court. Further, it became obvious from studies of recidivism that the "treatment" meted out by the juvenile court system was not particularly effective. In this selection Lemert analyzes some of the social dynamics involved in the establishment of the juvenile court and provides a diagnosis of a system that might be characterized as one of "humanitarian injustice."

This analysis was originally prepared as a report to the President's Commission on Law Enforcement and the Administration of Justice. Lemert has written in greater detail about the juvenile court system in *Social Action and Legal Change: Revolution Within the Juvenile Court* (Aldine, 1970). Another recent study of the system is Robert M. Emerson, *Judging Delinquents: Context and Process in Juvenile Courts* (Aldine, 1969). For earlier writings about juvenile delinquency see Margaret K. Rosenheim, ed., *Justice for the Child* (Free Press, 1962); F. T. Gile, *The Juvenile Courts* (Allen and Unwin, Ltd., 1946); and Paul Tappan, *Comparative Survey of Juvenile Delinquency, Part 1: North America* (United Nations Department of Economic and Social Affairs, 1958). ■

ROSCOE POUND called the juvenile court one of the great social inventions of the 19th century. But the enthusiasms heralding its birth and early history have dampened considerably with the slow stain of passing time. Its later years have been those of unmet promise and darkened with growing controversy. Evidence that it has prevented crime or lessened the recidivism of youthful offenders is missing, and dour sociological critics urge that it contributes to the juvenile crime or inaugurates delinquent careers by imposition of the stigma of wardship, unwise detention, and incarceration of children in institutions which don't reform and often corrupt. The occasional early voice of the dissenting judge and of the frustrated lawyer has grown to a heavy swell of modern contention that the juvenile court under the noble guise of humanitarian conern and scientific treatment of the problems of children too often denies them the elements of justice and fair play.

Even more impressive than the mounting volume of polemic literature and responsible criticism arraigning the court are the concrete actions taken by a number of leading states, such as New York and California, Minnesota, and, indeed, the state of its origin, Illinois, which in years immediately past have substantially or drastically revised their laws dealing with the form and operations of the juvenile court. Other states have seen the appointment of committees of inquiry and new legislation introduced to amend significant aspects of their juvenile or family courts. Events as well as the literature of protest compel thoughtful persons to a searching reconsideration of the makeup and purposes of the juvenile court in a society dominated by large-scale social organization, aggressive public welfare ideologies, and mass-produced justice.

THE PHILOSOPHY AND FUNCTION OF THE JUVENILE COURT

Much has been said of the philosophy of the juvenile court and little that is definitive can be added to it, other than to note that the very preoccupation with its philosophy sets it apart from other courts. In general, American courts created for children were given broad grants of power by legislatures to protect and help children, depart from strict rules of legal procedure, and utilize kinds of evidence ordinarily excluded from criminal and civil adjudication. There have been attempts by some writers to discover historical continuity between the juvenile court and courts of equity or chancery following guardianship proceedings. But these have been held to be dubious exercises at best, and in the words of a wry English judge, little more than spurious justifications for the sometimes "highhanded methods of American judges." As he and others have noted, equity procedure clearly requires evidentiary findings within specifiable limits conspicuously lacking in our early juvenile court statutes.

It is less profitable to speculate on the philosophy of the juvenile court than to examine its historical development and the variety of its adaptations to regional and local necessities. Such an examination will benefit by heuristically distinguishing the official goals of the court from its functions, particularly those which sociologists call unintended or unanticipated consequences of purposeful action. In so doing it becomes apparent that the functions of the juvenile court in reality are several, dictated by its peculiar sociolegal characteristics. Thus while it is well known to sociologists of law that regular courts may serve a number of extralegal or nonlegal ends, such as, for example, an action for damages brought solely to embarass a business competitor, the anomalous design of the juvenile court has made its extraneous, nonlegal functions paramount.

In historical retrospect the juvenile court has the look of an agency of social control directed to raising and maintaining standards of child care, protection, and family morals, a purpose currently reinforced by its close association with social welfare organizations. At the same time the juvenile court by virtue of its inescapable identity as a court of law is an agency of law enforcement seeking to reduce and prevent crime, but also protecting legal rights. Finally, it serves purposes derived from its essentially local nature as an arena of conflict resolution, in which conflicts within and between families, between individuals, and between organizations (not excluding those within the court itself) are aired, dramatized, and sometimes turned into cold war compromises.

Despite their insular character and the cloak of independence given juvenile courts by their connection with the regular courts, they tend to reflect patterns of values and power alignments within the community or areas they service. When this is joined with the fact that there are 50 federated states, these states having 5 to 58 more or less autonomous juvenile courts each, it is painfully clear that efforts to outline the distinctive philosophy and function of the juvenile court are feckless. It is, however, possible to state that juvenile courts in action generally reveal variations in the order in which values falling within the three areas of function of the court are satisfied. This permits questions to be raised as to whether and how the juvenile court should be restructured so that certain value orders do not occur or, further, so that some of the values currently satisfied will be excluded from its decisions and patterns of action.

There are some social science propositions which can serve well enough as guides for those seeking to install new forms and methods in the juvenile court. A salient one is that the family, even though badly attenuated or disturbed by conflict, morally questionable, or broken by divorce or death, continues to be the institution of choice for the socialization of children. Neither the Spartan gymnasium, nor the Russian creches, nor the Israeli Kibbutz nurseries, nor scientifically run children's homes have been found to successfully duplicate the sociopsychological mystique which nurtures children into stable adults. Explicit recognition of this might very well preface the juvenile court codes and statutes of the land. At the same time it would be well to delete entirely from such laws pious injunctions that "care, custody and discipline of children under the control of the juvenile court shall approximate that which they would receive from their parents," which taken literally becomes meaningless either as ideal or reality. Neither the modern state nor an harassed juvenile court judge is a father; a halfway house is not a home; a reformatory cell is not a teen-ager's bedroom; a juvenile hall counselor is not a dutch uncle; and a cottage matron is not a mother. This does not mean that the people referred to should not be or are not kindly and dedicated but, rather, that they are first and foremost members of organizations, bound by institution controls and subject to its exigencies; they are enforcers of superimposed rules. Where conflicts arise between the interests of a youth and those of the organization to which these functionaries are bureaucratically responsible there is no pattern of action which can predict that they will observe an order of value satisfaction favorable to the youth's interest.

STIGMA

Social scientists familiar with the juvenile court and its problems in the main agree that one of the great unwanted consequences of wardship, placement, or commitment to a correctional institution is the imposition of stigma. Such stigma, represented in modern society by a "record," gets translated into effective handicaps by heightened police surveillance, neighborhood isolation, lowered receptivity and tolerance by school officials, and rejections of youth by prospective employers. Large numbers of youth appearing in juvenile court have lower class status or that of disadvantaged minorities, whose limited commitments to education already puts them in difficulties in a society where education increasingly provides access to economic opportunity. Given this, the net effect of juvenile court wardship too often is to add to their handicaps or to multiply problems confronting them and their families.

Lest these seem like animadversions or imprecise charges, consider the hard facts that social welfare agencies can be identified which as a matter of policy, without delving into the facts of the case, arbitrarily refuse to accept as clients youth who have been wards of the juvenile court. The reality of stigma due to wardship is also borne home by the firmed policy of the armed forces, which may make it the grounds for rejection, or most certainly the bar to officer candidacy. The paradoxical expression of stigma often colors the statements of probation and correctional officers, even judges, who at certain stages of a youth's progress through juvenile court and beyond, openly label him as a type destined for failure.

Proposals, laws, and administrative action to preserve the anonymity of juvenile court proceedings through closed hearings, sealing case records, and expunging records are probably worthy moves, but it is in vain to expect them to eliminate the stigma of wardship and contacts with the juvenile court. In smaller communities, as one judge observed, "Everyone knows about juvenile court cases anyway." In larger communities strongly organized police departments can be expected to resist rigorous controls over delinquency records detrimental to their efficiency and will search for ways to circumvent them. Employers denied information from juvenile courts often get the desired facts from the police.

Expunging records is not the simple operation it may seem. In California it requires initiative from the party concerned and usually the assistance of an attorney; the procedure necessitates a hearing, and it may be complicated or impossible if a person has been a juvenile ward in more than one county. Private and public organizations can and do protect themselves by including questions about a juvenile record on application forms for employment or for occupational licenses, indicating that perjured replies will be grounds for rejection. The applicant has the unpleasant "damned if you do, damned if you don't" choice of lying or revealing damaging facts about himself. Finally, it is doubtful whether total anonymity of juvenile court hearings and records is in the public interest.

While the successful management of stigma by individuals is not impossible, the necessary insights and social skills are not given to many people, least of all immature youth or those struggling with other status handicaps. A number of social psychologists, including the author, believe that social rejections provoked by such stigma may reinforce a self-image held by the individual that he is no good or that he can't make it on the outside. They may feed a brooding sense of injustice which finds expression in further delinquency, or they may support, strengthen, and perpetuate ideological aspects of delinquent subcultures. In this sense the juvenile court may become a connecting or intervening link of a vicious circle in which delinquency causes delinquency.

PREVENTING DELINQUENCY

The indiscriminate way in which stigma embraces juvenile court wards raises the most serious questions about an important part of the rationale for state intervention into the lives of youth and parents through the juvenile court. Reference here is to the idea that delinquency can be or will be thereby prevented. This belief rests upon uncritical conceptions that there are substantive behaviors, isometric in nature, which precede delinquency, much like prodromal signs of the onset of disease. The viability of these ideas probably can be traced to their lineal ties with older, repressive Puritan philosophy; they received new life from early 20th-century propaganda of the mental hygiene movement, which helped to birth child guidance clinics, school social work, and establish juvenile courts in many areas. Quaint examples of these views were the 19th-century convictions that smoking or drinking by youth, shining shoes, selling newspapers, or frequenting poolrooms insidiously set them on a downward path toward a life of crime. Their contemporary survivals can be seen in unproved concepts like predelinquent personality, or delinquency prone, and in laws of a number of states which make truancy, running away from home, or refusal to obey parents or school officials jurisdictional bases for juvenile court control.

Social science research and current theory in social psychology refute the idea that there are fixed, inevitable sequences in delinquent or criminal careers. As yet no behavior patterns or personality tendencies have been isolated and shown to be the antecedents of delinquency, and it is unlikely that they will be. Furthermore, youthful actions conventionally regarded as delinquent tendencies in a number of jurisdictions, such as truancy, curfew violations, incorrigibility, and running away from home on close examination are found to correspond to no behavior entities but, rather, to arbitrary definitions by school authorities, parents, and police. Truancy is defined variously, depending on the area, by anywhere from 3 to 10 days of unexplained absences. An older New York investigation into a large number of cases of truancy disclosed little or no similarity in the contingencies associated with school absences. Indeed, to a degree they were simply a measure of the willingness or availability of parents to write excuses for their children. Runaways found in juvenile court cases cover departures from home ranging from a few hours to two months, and incorrigibility may mean anything from refusing a mother's order not to see a boyfriend to attacking a parent with a knife. While curfews are useful administrative devices for policing communities, there are attorneys who argue that the associated ordinances are questionable law because they leave violations incapable of definiton.

The allegation of incorrigibility often is difficult to distinguish from that of parental neglect or unfitness, and both kinds of allegations at times arise in a welter of accusations and counteraccusations which are quieted by arbitrary fixing of the blame by a probation officer assigned to investigate the case.

The brave idea that the juvenile court can prevent delinquency is further deflated or even reduced to absurdity by sociological studies of unreported or hidden delinquency. These have brought to light that the majority of high school and college students at some time or another engage in delinquencies, not excluding serious law violations. The main difference which emerged from comparisons of delinquencies by college students and those by youths who had been made wards of juvenile courts was the greater recidivism of the latter group. While these data admit of several interpretations, on their face they demand explanation as to why the large population of youth committing delinquent acts and made court wards commit more rather than fewer delinquencies. The conclusion that the court processing rather than the behaviors in some way helps to fix and perpetuate delinquency in many cases is hard to escape.

There are other data which suggest that formal efforts by the juvenile court to shape the course of childhood and adolescent development away from hypothetically dire directions in the large may be gratuitous or self-defeating. The reference is to facts or common knowledge that most youth pass through epochs in their lives when they engage in activities definable in other than their contexts as delinquency. Children normally play hookey, help themselves to lumber from houses under construction, snitch lipstick or other items from 10-cent stores, swipe some beer, get a little drunk, borrow a car, hell around, learn about sex from an available female or prostitute, or give the old man a taste of his own medicine. Transitional deviance not only is ubiquitous in our society but universal to all societies, especially among boys turning into men—Margaret Mead's droll observations on adolescence in the South Seas to the contrary notwithstanding.

Most youth phase out of their predelinquency, so-called, and their law flaunting; they put away childish things, ordinarily as they become established in society by a job, marriage, further education, or the slow growth of wisdom. Maturation out of the deviance of adolescence is facilitated by a process of normalization in which troublesome behavior, even petty crimes, are dealt with by parents, neighbors, and law people as manifestations of the inevitable diversity, perversity, and shortcomings of human beings —in other words, as problems of everyday living calling for tolerable solutions short of perfection. This means the avoidance whenever possible of specialized or categorical definitions which invidiously differentiate, degrade, or stigmatize persons involved in the problems. The costs of "muddling through" with children who become problems have multiplied with the rising plateau of mass conformities needed for a high-energy society, but they must be absorbed in large part where the alternatives are even more costly.

THE THREE-MINUTE CHILDREN'S HOUR

The ideology of delinquency prevention is much more urban than rural. Handling problems of youthful disorders and petty crime in rural areas and small towns, characteristically by sheriffs' deputies, town police, the district attorney, and probation officer in the past and even yet today in many places has been largely informal. Sharp distinctions are drawn between less consequential moral and legal infractions—"mickey mouse stuff"—and serious delinquencies, with no implications that one conduces to the other. This is reflected in the reluctance of elective officials and those beholden to them to make records of their action, but at the same time for action in serious misdemeanors and crimes by youth to be swift and punitive. The juvenile court usually reserves formal action for real problems of families and the community; the functional context of youthful misconduct ordinarily can be realistically gauged and its consequences dealt with in a number of different situations.

A major difficulty in the large bureaucratic urban juvenile court is that the functional context of child problems directed to it easily gets lost; it has to be reconstructed by bits and pieces of information obtained through investigations and inquiries conducted under highly artificial circumstances, and communicated in written reports which easily become stereotyped as they pass from person to person. There is little or no direct community feedback of criticism and reaction which might put individual cases into a common-sense context which would encourage normalization. This plus the rapidity with which cases are heard in large courts (three minutes per case in Los Angeles circa 1959) explains why the distinction between mild and serious child problems breaks down or disappears. A notorious illustration of the tendency came to light in Orange County, Calif., in 1957 when a private attorney put his own investigator to work on a case of an eight- and nine-year-old-boy and girl accused of a sex crime against a seven-year-old girl. It was discovered that the probation officer presenting the case in court had not even investigated, and the private investigator's report swiftly pared down the charge to an imputed incident witnessed by no one and reported two days after it supposedly occurred.

While it would push facts too far to insist that the ideology of preventing delinquency is used deliberately by juvenile courtworkers and judges to justify slipshod operations which bring cases of benign youthful misbehavior before them under the duress of formal allegations, nevertheless it has allowed them to change the basis of jurisdiction from one problem to another. The practice is badly indicated in the statement of a California judge arguing for retention under juvenile court jurisdiction of simple traffic violations by juveniles.

Moreover it seems to have been demonstrated that the broad powers of the juvenile court can be helpfully invoked on behalf of children whose maladjustment has been brought to light through juvenile traffic violations. A girl companion of a youthful speeder may be protected from further sexual experimentation. Boys whose only amusement seems to be joyriding in family cars can be directed to other more suitable forms of entertainment before they reach the stage of borrowing cars when the family car is unavailable.

POLICE AND COMMUNITY DELINQUENCY PREVENTION

The ideology of delinquency prevention and statutes incorporating special laws for regulating the conduct of children have not been ill adapted to the needs and problems of police in large cities, and to some extent have been their outgrowth. It needs to be emphasized, however, that police generally are less concerned with the prevention of delinquency in individual cases than in its prevention and control as a communitywide problem variously manifested in gang violence, disturbances of public order, a rise in crime rates, or mounting property losses. The special utility to police of specious legal categories describing delinquent tendencies is most obvious when they seek to break up youthful gang activity, quell public disturbances such as occur at drive-ins or public parks, gain access to witnesses or sources of information to solve a crime series or to recover stolen property. While the arrest and detention of youth to clear up other crimes may be efficient police tactics, abuses may arise at the expense of individual youths if such methods can be pursued under diffuse charges. Unfortunately there have been and are judges willing to allow juvenile detention to be used for these purposes. It was for reasons such as these that the Juvenile Justice Commission of California, following a state-wide survey, in 1960 recommended legislation to encourage the use of citations for minor offenses by juveniles, and to require that detention hearings be held within specified time limits to act as a check on over-zealous police action.

Lest a picture be left of police as ruthless manipulators of juveniles as law enforcement ends, be it noted that in a number of areas they have sought to aid juveniles avoid clashes with the law through setting up recreation programs, Big Brother assignments, informal probation, and even police social work. However, such undertakings have declined in recent years and tend to be looked upon as too widely divergent from essential police functions. This also may point to growing disillusionment with more generalized or communitywide delinquency prevention programs. Police in some cities sharply disagree with community organizers of such projects over the issue of maintaining the autonomy of neighborhood gangs; they tend to take a jaundiced view of proposals and attempts to divert such groups from law-breaking into more compliant pursuits.

Research assessments of community programs to prevent delinquency, such as the Chicago area project, the Harlem project, and the Cambridge-Somerville youth study, have been disappointing; results either have been negative or inconclusive. Possible exceptions are community coordinating councils, especially in the western United States where they originated. However, they seem to work best in towns between 2,000 and 15,000 population; it remains unclear whether they can be adapted successfully to large urban areas. Significantly, they work chiefly by exchanging agency information and referrals of cases to community agencies, with full support and cooperation of the police. In effect they represent concerted action to bypass the juvenile court, and it might be said that their purpose if not function is prevention of delinquency by preventing, wherever possible, the adjudication of cases in the court.

TREATMENT OF CHILD PROBLEMS AND DELINQUENCY

Much of what has already been said about preventing delinquency by means of juvenile court intervention is equally applicable as criticism of intervention by the court to treat youth problems and delinquency by therapeutic means. The ideal of therapeutic treatment found its way into juvenile court philosophy from social work and psychiatry, its pervasiveness measurable by the extent to which persons educated and trained in social work have indirectly influenced the juvenile court or moved into probation and correctional officer positions. An underlying premise of therapeutic treatment of children is that scientific knowledge and techniques exist, making possible specific solutions to individual and family problems. It seeks to impose the positivism of hard science upon individual behavior.

Scientific social work, whose tenets were originally laid down by Mary Richmond in her early work, "Social Diagnosis," eventually came to lean heavily upon theories of Freudian psychiatry, taking over its psychobiological orientation and the medicinal idea that childhood problems and delinquency are symptoms of unresolved Oedipal conflicts. Updated versions of socially applied psychoanalysis conceive of delinquency as an acting out of repressed conflicts in irrational, disguised forms. Accent in treatment is laid upon the internal emotional life rather than upon external acts; the social worker or the psychiatrist is a specialist who understands the problems while the client does not; the specialist knows best, studies, analyzes, and treats, much in the manner of the authoritative medical practitioner.

A divergent, competing line of thought in social work repudiates scientific treatment in favor of a more simple conception of its task as essentially a helping process, in which problems are confronted in whatever terms the child or youth presents them; responsible involvement of the client is a sine qua non of success in this process. Needless to say, this conception of the nature of social work is much more compatible with a philosophy of democracy.

Generally speaking, social workers advocate a more curtailed dispositional function for the juvenile court and advocate assigning to other agencies many of the tasks it has assumed. Some social workers seriously doubt whether the helping process can be carried on in an authoritarian setting, and to emphasize their stand refuse as clients children who have been wards of the court. Other social workers believe that judges go beyond their competence and should use their power solely for adjudication, after which determination of treatment should pass on to social work agencies. A smaller number of social workers hold to a more sanguine view of reconciling personal help and authority within the role of the probation officer. Finally, there are some social workers who are not beyond using juvenile court power as a tool for getting access to clients, or prolonging their contacts with them because they will benefit from treatment. Experience showed that this pattern became aggravated in Utah during the period when juvenile courts there were under the administrative control of the state department of welfare.

A long-standing, ubiquitous problem of social workers and psychiatrists of whatever theoretical persuasion has been that of the noninvolvement of their clients or patients. Clients are either disinclined to seek their services or they break off contacts after they have been established, or they respond superficially without showing interest in changing their personal values or life-styles. Much of the difficulty stems from the identification of social workers with middle class values and the invidious moralistic implications of imputing defective personalities to those they try to assist. As a result, barriers to communication often become insurmountable.

Actually, comparatively few juvenile court cases are referred to social workers for treatment, and many juvenile court judges and probation officers are inhospitable toward social workers. According to a U.S. Children's Bureau study some years ago, the most frequent disposition of juvenile court cases was dismissal, followed by informal or formal supervision under a probation officer. Dismissals can scarcely be called treatment, even though the associated court appearance before an admonitory judge may have a chastening effect upon some youths. At most, such cases have a brief exchange with an intake or investigating officer who asks some questions, issues a stern warning, and says he hopes he will not see the boy again.

The consequences of supervision of delinquents by probation officers either in parental homes or in foster homes have been little studied and the outcome, even when successful, little understood. Probation practices with juveniles have little in common if the nation is taken as a whole, and often they consist of a bare minimum of office interviews and telephone or mail reports. The frequent claim of probation officers that they could give more help to their charges if they had more time for supervision must be scouted as an occupational complaint rather than an accurate prediction of treatment possibilities. What little research there is on the subject has shown that mere reduction of the size of caseloads of probation and parole officers does not in itself lower rates of recidivism of those supervised.

If the results of probation supervision of delinquents on the whole are disappointing or inconclusive, even less can be said in behalf of the treatment of juvenile offenders undertaken in institutional commitments. Sociological analysis and evaluations of correctional programs in institutional settings tend to be uniformly negative, with some writers taking a position that the goals of correctional programs in prisons and reformatories are inherently self-defeating. This follows from the very fact of incarceration, which by necessarily posing a series of problems of personal deprivation for inmates generates a more or less antithetical subculture which negates and subverts formal programs of rehabilitation. The logistics of processing delinquents or criminal populations brings large numbers of recidivists to the institutions, where they control informal communication and face-to-face interaction which importantly shapes the course of inmate socialization.

The problems of correctional institutions for delinquents have been highlighted in the popular press and literature as those of poor physical plants, niggardly appropriations, and underpaid, undereducated personnel, but to the social scientist they lie far deeper. At this writing it remains doubtful whether the generously funded and well-staffed California Youth Authority has neared its original purpose of providing individualized treatment for youthful offenders. This has not been due to a lack of dedication of its leadership but, rather, has resulted from having to assume the task of institutional administration, in which sheer numbers of commitments, contingencies, conflicting values of staff and custody people, and organizational inertia daily conspire to defeat the purpose of treatment. The top people of CYA have not been unaware of its dilemmas, which accounts for recent moves to establish large-scale community treatment projects and a probation subsidy program devised to stimulate local innovations in the supervision or treatment of juveniles as alternatives to commitment.

The less than sanguine remarks here directed to the ideology of delinquency treatment do not exclude the possibility that clinically trained and humanly wise people cannot help youth solve problems which have brought them athwart the law. Rather, the intent is to leaven professional contumely with humility, to place the notion of treatment into a more realistic perspective, and to point out denotative differences between dealing with problems of human relationships and treatment as it has evolved in the practice of medicine. The treatment of delinquency is best regarded as a kind of guidance, special education, and training, much more akin to midwifery than medicine, in which hopeful intervention into an ongoing process of maturation is undertaken. Objective criteria for the use of methods of intervening and controlled conditions necessary for predictable outcomes are neither present nor likely to be. Hence the actions of a judge, proba-

tion officer, correctional counselor, or an institutional psychiatrist at most can be small influences brought to bear among many simultaneously affecting child development and emergence of youth into adulthood. Although the power and the authority of the juvenile court can determine that certain intervenings will take place in a prescribed order in the process of socialization, they cannot control the meanings and values assigned to such occurrences.

JUDICIOUS NONINTERVENTION

The aims of preventing delinquency and the expectation of definitively treating a profusion of child and parental problems have laid an impossible burden upon the juvenile court, and they may be seriously considered to have no proper part in its philosophy. If there is a defensible philosophy for the juvenile court it is one of judicious nonintervention. It is properly an agency of last resort for children, holding to a doctrine analogous to that of appeal courts which require that all other remedies be exhausted before a case will be considered. This means that problems accepted for action by the juvenile court will be demonstrably serious by testable evidence ordinarily distinguished by a history of repeated failures at solutions by parents, relatives, schools, and community agencies. The model should be derived from the conservative English and Canadian juvenile courts, which in contrast to the American receive relatively few cases.

This statement of juvenile court philosophy rests upon the following several propositions.

1. Since the powers of the juvenile court are extraordinary, properly it should deal with extraordinary cases.

2. Large numbers of cases defeat the purposes of the juvenile court by leading to bureaucratic procedures antithetical to individualized treatment (guidance).

3. The juvenile court is primarily a court of law and must accept limitations imposed by the inapplicability of rule and remedy to many important phases of human conduct

and to some serious wrongs. Law operates by punishment, injunction against specific acts, specific redress, and substitutional redress. It cannot by such means make a father good, a mother moral, a child obedient, or a youth respectful of authority.

4. When the juvenile court goes beyond legal remedies it must resort to administrative agents or itself become such an agency, which produces conflicts and confusion of values and objectives. Furthermore, it remains problematical whether child and parental problems can be solved by administrative means.

It may be protested that the conception of the juvenile court adumbrated here is so narrow as to emasculate it or take away any distinctive purpose. However, if it can be accepted that many acts termed delinquent in reality are not equatable with adult crimes, and that many situations called dangerous for youth on close examination turn out to be functions of moral indignation by persons and groups who, to paraphrase Maitland, "Screw up standards of reasonable ethical propriety to unreasonable heights," then organized nonintervention by the juvenile court assumes a definite protective function for youth. It has become equally or more important to protect children from unanticipated and unwanted consequences of organized movements, programs, and services in their behalf than from the unorganized, adventitious "evils" which gave birth to the juvenile court. America no longer has any significant number of Fagans, exploiters of child labor, sweatshops, open saloons, houses of prostitution, street trades, an immoral servant class, cruel immigrant fathers, traveling carnivals and circuses, unregulated racetracks, open gambling, nor professional crime as it once existed. The battles for compulsory education have long since been won, and technological change has eliminated child labor—perhaps too well. The forms of delinquency have changed as the nature of society has changed; social and personal problems of youth reflect the growth of affluence in one area of society and the growth of hostility and aggression in a nonaffluent sector. Current sociological theories of delinquency stress drift and risk-taking as causes on one hand and on the other deprivation and dilapidated opportunity structures.

The basic life process today is one of adaptation to exigencies and pressures; individual morality has become functional rather than sacred or ethical in the older sense. To recognize this at the level of legislative and judicial policy is difficult because social action in America always has been heavily laden with moral purpose. However, if the juvenile court is to become effective, its function must be reduced to enforcement of the ethical minimum of youth conduct necessary to maintain social life in a high energy, pluralistic society. Given this lower level of function, it can then proceed to its secondary task of arranging the richest possible variety of assistance to those specially disadvantaged children and youth who come under its jurisdiction.

STRUCTURING THE JUVENILE COURT

A philosophy of judicious nonintervention demands more than verbal or written exhortation for implementation. Action is needed to research and redefine the jurisdiction of the court, the nature of the roles assigned to its personnel, and its procedures. Ideally it will be so structured that it will have built-in controls, feedback mechanisms, and social scanning devices which make it self-regulating and adaptive. This by no means signifies that the juvenile court should or will become inner directed; if anything, contacts and interaction with the community and its agencies will have more importance, if for no other reason than to guard its stance of nonintervention.

It follows that relationships between juvenile courts and policing agencies probably will become more critical with a shrinkage in juvenile court functions. However, it can be hoped that this will be an irritant means whereby more police departments develop juvenile bureaus and upgrade their competence for screening and adjusting cases within their own cognizance. Even now it is common practice for many police departments to dismiss large numbers of juvenile arrests or adjust them within the department. More and better trained juvenile officers and rationalizing of their procedures can greatly decrease referrals to juvenile courts. This does not mean that police should develop their own probation or social work service but, rather, will parsimoniously utilize contacts with relatives and referrals to community agencies or, at most, engage in brief, policeman-like counseling with youths where they believe it may do some good. One way to answer the cry of American police for public support is to funnel grants of aid into juvenile officer training and police consultation services.

Since police probably always will to some extent seek to employ the juvenile court for their own special purposes of keeping law and order or preventing crime in the large, the second line of defense protecting jurisdictional boundaries of the juvenile court must be manned by intake workers of the juvenile court or the probation department serving it. These ideally should be organized into an intake, referral, and adjustment division, where the maximum effort of the court is made by its most competent personnel. Organizational considerations suggest that it should have a good deal of autonomy, assuming that a high caliber of staff is reached, and be oriented toward the social welfare agencies of the community. Denial of applications for petitions should be its clear-cut prerogative.

In some large probation departments it may be possible to erect a still higher level of screening by a special division of the workers who file petitions for assuming jurisdiction by the court. Again, some organizational independence would be needed to reject petition applications sent forward by intake people. To an extent such screening already exists in many probation departments but tends to be overshadowed by functional specialization due to the heavy volume of investigations and placements in overworked courts. If probation departments were so empowered that investigations of the factual basis of law violations were a mandatory police function, more time and energy could be allocated to screening, referrals, and dispositions work.

As Paul Tappan and others have noted, referral of cases from juvenile courts to social work agencies is complicated by unwillingness of the latter to expend their resources on hostile or uncooperative clients. Believing that contact with the juvenile court fosters uncooperativeness in youth, many agencies, as previously stated, refuse their referrals. Juvenile courts which take on the treatment of children with small difficulties, which often are indistinguishable from those daily being handled in large numbers by welfare agencies, forego their opportunities to make use of referrals at a later date. For this reason, it appears that referrals should be made immediately, prior to detention, minus confrontations with youth and parents, or without investigations which go beyond the reasons for their referral to the court. Intake interviews and citation hearings should not turn into fishing expeditions to uncover and record problems to justify further action by the court.

JURISDICTION

Action to narrow and refine the functions of the juvenile court will need much greater precision than now holds in setting the jurisdictional limits to its authority, explicitly with reference to problem categories and minimum age of cases accepted. Statutes conferring jurisdiction over children on the juvenile court generally differentiate four categories: (1) those lacking care due to contingencies of family life—death, absence of a parent or parents, or their inability to provide the care; (2) those who are neglected or mistreated; (3) those who disregard, defy, or disobey authority of parents, guardians, custodians, or teachers; (4) those who violate laws. Popularly, administratively, and to some extent legally, these categories are status attributions designating the dependent child, the neglected child, and the delinquent. Although the early and primary aim of the juvenile court was to abolish the stigma of such statutes, this has not occurred, and the pall of moral questionability continues to settle over all children made wards in these categories.

It is difficult or impossible in the face of facts known about modern society to defend the locus of jurisdiction over dependent children in the juvenile court on any grounds other than convenience. Just why, for example, a child whose mother must be committed to a mental hospital should be made the ward of a court whose latent structure is criminal is not readily explainable. The same is true for children whose parents' problems stem from deficient income, or unemployability due to disability or illness; likewise for orphaned and illegitimate children. Granted that some person or agency other than parents must take custody, and that this needs legal sanction, there is no irrebuttable proof that this cannot be done by civil courts, with welfare agencies receiving custody, so long as a time limit is placed upon its duration and the rights of child and parents presumptively kept by law.

Probation officers are apt to defend juvenile court jurisdiction over dependent children in the juvenile court on any grounds linquent child and a dependent child are in the same family and to contend that duplicate supervision should be avoided. They also have defended placing dependent children in the same institution with delinquent children on these grounds and the additional one that families should not be broken up. Yet in a number of areas welfare agencies carry a large share of the supervision of dependency cases for the juvenile court, and on the whole they are probably better prepared than probation officers to supervise such cases. Unless a child presents the most serious kind of delinquency or unless welfare agencies refuse to do the job, less delinquent and dependent children in the same family should be under welfare supervision.

The arguments for retaining juvenile court jurisdiction over neglected children are somewhat stronger but still questionable, for if the child's problem is truly the fault of his parents why should he receive the stigma of wardship? The suspicion is strong that juvenile court procedure has been invoked to gain control over children where it would be troublesome or impossible to prove neglect in an adult criminal court, borne out by the fact that statutes in some states allow such cases to be tried in juvenile courts. Admittedly a knotty problem exists, but it is a problem of court procedure and law for which children should not pay the costs. If it is necessary to put parents on probation it should be done by regular legal procedures, and if a child must be removed from their custody let it be placed through a welfare agency and, as with dependent children, a time limit set to such custody carrying the presumption that parents will have mended their ways at its termination.

A less obvious but more pervasive reason why juvenile court people wish to retain jurisdiction over dependent and neglected children lies in persistent beliefs that the roots of delinquency and crime are discoverable in dependency and parental neglect. These ideas, descended from hoary Biblical notions and 19th-century, middle class moralism, and outmoded by modern sociology, still have their partisans. A 1959 annual report of a probation department strongly oriented in a psychiatric direction and serving a heavily middle class population, speaks of the function of its separate dependency and neglect unit.

Implicit in the function of this unit is the concept that it is very probable that the basis for delinquent acting out has been laid in the children and that delinquency prevention is, therefore, a prime concern.

Sociological research has discovered little durable evidence to support the contention that poverty, broken homes, and many of the charges of parental unfitness—alcoholism, sexual immorality, or cruelty—are in themselves causes of delinquency. Most delinquents come from intact homes, and various studies comparing the incidence of delinquents with broken and with unbroken homes show differences to range from 7 to 24 percent. Furthermore, for every child in a broken home who is delinquent there are on the average two or more brothers or sisters who are nondelinquent. Cruelty or alcoholism in a father can contribute to the growth of serious problems for his children, but nothing in sociological research demonstrates that they will necessarily take the form of breaking laws. The rationale for bringing dependent and neglected children under juvenile court aegis to prevent delinquency rests upon small statistical pluralities which are categorical or group differences, not predictable individual differences.

DELINQUENT TENDENCIES

Truancy, runaways, and incorrigibility already have been shown to be diffuse categories whose conversion into statutory foundation for jurisdiction by the juvenile court is made superficially plausible by unexamined assumptions that they are precursors to delinquency. If the juvenile court is to proceed with approximate uniformity which is a central attribute of law, the weakness of such statutes either as substantive law or as legislative directives for the development of administrative rules is patent. The reasons may be summarized as follows: (1) they lack common meaning from one jurisdiction to another, or between different judges' rulings in the same jurisdiction; (2) they are not derived from any fixed criteria; (3) they assign criminal responsibility to children in many instances where blame or responsibility cannot be determined or where closer investigation would reveal thir actions to have been reasonably normal responses to highly provocative or intolerable situations.

If the image of the juvenile court is to be changed from that of a multifarious problem-solving agency, and its functions circumscribed to be more consistent with available means, then its statutory jurisdiction cannot be allowed to rest upon subjective definitions. Furthermore, if it is to avoid the risk of making delinquents by a labeling process, statutes whose vagueness in some localities allow almost any child, given compromising circumstances, to be caught up in the jurisdictional net of the court, must be altered.

Highly important is the fact that when such specious legal grounds as incorrigibility and associated terms are written into statutes as warrants for juvenile court action they invite its use for extraneous conflict resolu-

tion. They allow parents, neighbors, school officials, and police—even the youth themselves—to solve their problems by passing them on to the court. No better illustration of this is at hand than the lengthy history of conflict between juvenile court workers and school officials, in which the former accuse the school people of foisting off their own failures onto the court, and the latter reply heatedly that the court is unreceptive or does nothing about really mean kids. Probation officers ruefully discover in some counties that sheriff's deputies expect them to settle all neighborhood quarrels in which juveniles are involved, and parents or relatives in juvenile court many times leave it clear that they desire their child to be punished for highly personal reasons, or that they have abdicated responsibility for no defensible reason. So long as the court allows itself to be used in these ways it creates its official problems largely by definition.

Runaways must be understood in the same interactional context as incorrigibility, with the added difference that they are proportionately more numerous among girls than boys. Often runaways have the quality of dramatic demonstrations—a little like suicide attempts by adult women—or bids for partisans in an unequal battle with parents. California girl runaways sometimes demand to be placed in detention in order to expose the "hatefulness" of their home situation or to embarrass their parents. While police action often is clearly indicated in runaways, action by the court is decidedly not. If drama is needed it should be staged under some other auspices.

A depressing sidelight is that the juvenile court itself can be a cause of incorrigibility when in effect it holds a child in contempt. Thus failure to obey an order of the court can be an official reason for a more severe disposition—even commitment to an institution. Runaways from camps may be treated in this way, without any need to inquire into the conditions or situation which led to the boy's flight. Inasmuch as the original cause for taking jurisdiction may have been minor, it can be seen how problems of children grow and aggravate in interaction within the court.

It might be said that in such cases the ego of the court causes incorrigibility.

A net conclusion is that incorrigibility, truancy, and running away should not in themselves be causes for assuming juvenile court jurisdiction over children. There is much reason to believe that the bulk of such problems can be handled successfully by referrals, demonstrated by an inquiry in the District of Columbia where it was found that noncourt agencies took responsibility for 98 percent of the total identifiable or reported runaways, 95 percent of truancies, 76 percent of sex offenses, and 46 percent of youth termed ungovernable. If disobedience, truancy, and running away are retained as bases for juvenile court jurisdiction, statutes should be rigorously drawn to require a showing of their material relevance to serious law violations, or a showing that other agencies have been incapable of containing the problems.

TRAFFIC

The heavy rise in the volume of juvenile traffic offenses in past decades and the large portion of total juvenile arrests for which they account have produced much confusion of procedures and stirred hot debates over the subject of jurisdiction. There are those who contend that ordinary traffic violations of juveniles are no different from those of adults, and since the state in licensing juveniles assumes them capable of ordinary care and caution in operating automobiles, their violations should be processed by regular courts. Opposition to removing jurisdiction over juvenile traffic offenses from the juvenile court has been strong, even fervent, among judges and others who see such proposals as part of a militant campaign to cripple or eliminate the juvenile court. Some of their arguments have validity, namely that juveniles under regular traffic courts would be liable for large and, for them, excessive fines, and that they could be sentenced to jails or road camps in the company of petty criminals and drunkenness offenders. The further claim that juveniles should not be exposed to the routinized, "cash register" justice of adult traffic courts is less convincing, and the argument that the end justifies the means—adjudication in the juvenile court of traffic offenses allows more serious problems to be detected and treated—is from the point of view here presented least defensible of all.

While separate juvenile traffic courts with limited punitive and administrative powers are well enough justified, safeguards are needed to preclude their use as formal or informal catch places to funnel youth into juvenile courts. Organization along the lines of 1959 Minnesota legislation, which spells out that traffic offenses are not to be construed as delinquency, is preferable to placing them within jurisdiction of the juvenile courts. The strongest sanction which juvenile traffic courts can apply is revocation of driver's licenses, which they must share with state motor vehicle departments. Methods and procedures inevitably bring them closer to those of administrative hearing officers dealing with adult cases there than to those of the juvenile court. Juvenile traffic courts, of course, should be able to make referrals to juvenile courts, but there they should be screened with the same rigor intake people apply to other types of cases presumed less serious. One added protection should be that no social report can be required on juveniles who disobey traffic rules.

AGE

Discussion of the minimum age for juvenile court jurisdiction is muddied by the fact that a specialized, technologically geared society generates functional rather than chronological concepts of age. Thus, in our society persons as young as 15 years can be licensed to drive automobiles in some states, leave school for adult employment by the time they reach 17 years, yet be unable to marry without parental permission until they are 21. As civilians persons may be unable to purchase alcoholic beverages until past their 21st birthdays, yet as members of the armed forces may enjoy the right at 18. Moreover, private organizations and community usages conceive responsible age in ways different from those of the law. Insurance companies select 25 years as a cutoff point for assigning high-risk premiums to automobile drivers, and many communities exist where parents see no reason why high school age boys should not be learning to drink. Automobile salesmen are not loath to sell to underage youth, or stores to issue credit to juveniles where legally there is no presumption of financial responsibility.

From such facts it must be concluded that setting a sociologically realistic minimum age for bringing youth under authority of the juvenile court is difficult or impossible if its substantive jurisdiction is pushed too far beyond law violations. Hence any discussion of age limits of jurisdiction must return to the question of the age at which responsibility for criminal actions can be assumed. Most states have settled on age 18 as the minimum below which children cannot be tried in criminal courts. However, this is qualified by statutory exceptions covering such offenses as murder or armed robbery. In highly punitive states the list of such offenses may be quite long.

Any age limit for juvenile court jurisdiction has to be arbitrary because maturation is an uneven process and varies from individual to individual. Furthermore, violation of laws symbolizing highly important social values of life, person, and property are likely to arouse public demands for formal demonstration trials and punishment, even though the offender involved is below the age limit. For example, cattlemen are apt to take it for granted that no child over 12 years raised by a rancher will be ignorant of or fail to understand the implications of rustling or shooting and butchering stray cattle. More generally the same assumption can be made about the taking of human life by any child who is over eight or nine years. The insistence on formal airing and publicity of homicides is likely to be both urgent and widespread, although with child offenders disposition can be greatly mitigated once such needs are met. The point is often missed by more sentimental juvenile court propagandists, for although history shows that a number of very young children have been tried and convicted of murder, harsh sentences seldom have been carried out.

The problems of jurisdiction and age to some extent are met by establishing concurrent jurisdiction in which offenses committed by youth in marginal age categories may be tried in either juvenile or criminal courts. California, for example, establishes 16 years as the minimum age for exclusive jurisdiction by the juvenile court, but shares jurisdiction over 17- through 21-year-old offenders with the superior court. In practice few 18-year-olds are retained by the juvenile court and very rarely those of 19 and 20. Considering that youth of 17 years coming before the courts usually have committed more serious violations and are more likely to have a lengthy juvenile court record, their retention in juvenile court in most cases is immaterial.

As a matter of fact, a youth in these borderline age groups may receive a more lenient disposition as a first-time offender in an adult court than as a last-resort offender in juvenile court. The most important requirement in concurrent jurisdictions are statutory safeguards to insure that the decision as to where cases in concurrent age categories get heard be made by the juvenile court. This guarantees that the occasional immature youth of 18 or 19 years will not get lost in routine processing by prosecutors and judges in adult courts, who have less experience to make such decisions.

If age is to be an effective means of limiting the authority of the juvenile court it may be as important to tie it to dispositions as jurisdiction. This should be observed closely for children of younger ages, whose offenses, while chargeable as law violations, qualitatively are seldom comparable to crimes. Here it may be worth recalling a Polish law of the 1920s which forbade sending any youth under 13 years of age to a correctional institution. Statutes in this vein to be meaningful would have to incorporate definitions of correctional institutions to distinguish them from those with educational or training aims, and also exclude assignment of administrative responsibility for the latter to departments of corrections. Full realization of the intent of such laws would hinge upon innovations and new means for controlling the untoward acts of administrative officials and of judges acting in administrative capacities.

PROCEDURES

The wide powers assumed by juvenile courts were more or less inherent consequences of their loose design. The origins of the juvenile courts in humanitarian social movements disposed legislators to see them primarily as child welfare agencies, with the result that early statutes specified few procedures. Subsequent statutory evolution and the growth of "living law" of juvenile courts proved to be extremely divergent, and little in the way of generally accepted case law developed to supply procedural guides, among other reasons because relatively few cases were appealed, and none of these reached the U.S. Supreme Court.

Narrowing the scope of juvenile court functions to avoid what have been its less desirable features calls for new procedures designed to modify and better fix the roles of judges and probation officers, to augment the probabilities of dismissals of cases where indicated, and to change the order of values dominant in dispositions. First and foremost are hard rules governing the number, forms, and timing of hearings, which in many courts have tended to become attenuated, ex parte, or even nonexistent. The minimum essential can be no less than provision for hearings in every instance in which the freedom of children is abridged, curtailed by detention or commitment, changed from lesser to greater restraint, or custody renewed according to law. Ordinarily this will mean a special hearing if a child is to be placed in a detention facility pending investigation, and a subsequent hearing or hearings when adjudication and disposition are made.

Significant changes in the direction of greater conservatism in juvenile courtwork can be achieved by introducing bifurcated or split hearings, in which adjudication is sharply set apart from dispositions. The first hearing should be devoted to findings of fact rich enough to authorize court jurisdiction, the second to ascertain what should be done with the child, equally rigorous in procedure but admitting the soft data and evaluations which customarily make up the so-called social report.

Split hearings have had some limited use in civil (auto accident) litigation, and research on their results disclose a large and significant increase in findings for defendants over plaintiffs. A criticism has been made that such hearings may distort the balance of substantive rights between plaintiffs and defendants, but note that this claim has yet to be advanced against criminal prosecutions of adults in which probation investigations and hearings are regularly held after trial and conviction.

The aim of bifurcated hearings in juvenile cases is to make certain that impressionistic, diagnostic, purely recorded, hearsay-type evidence will not be received by the court at the time of adjudication. However, the introduction of such hearings alone may go wide of their target if rules concerning admissibility of social reports are not also clarified. Bifurcated hearings were made mandatory in California in 1961 as part of a wholesale revision of its juvenile court law, but according to a 1965 survey by the author, a majority of judges (67 percent) continue to read the dispositional (social) report before jurisdictional hearings. A 1957 survey of New York judges showed about the same proportion of family court judges in that state read social reports before or during adjudication hearings.

California judges seem to take the position that the special work of the juvenile court could not be done without prior reading of the social report, and appellate wisdom in the state has decreed that the social report shall be received in evidence. In contrast, an older New York appellate decision struck directly at the practice as inconsistent with the rights of juveniles and parents. While dogmatic conclusions are out of place here, nevertheless the issue to a sociologist as well as to a civil rights advocate is highly critical and needs enlightenment by research rather than by opinions. It may be crucially important to learn how the one-third minority of judges in the two states, as well as English juvenile court judges, who postpone hearing dispositional evidence, manage to get their work done, and whether its quality or results are any less effective than that of judges who proceed into adjudication with knowledge of the social report.

If the contents of the social report continue to be admitted during adjudication hearings or are part of the materials on which the judge makes a finding, then the social report should be open to scrutiny by persons who are its subjects or to their representatives. Authors of statements contained therein should on request be summoned as witnesses to cross-examination in either jurisdictional or dispositional hearing if they are separated in time. As the tenor of the language here implies, the knowledge and skills of competent counsel are prerequisites to the fullest exploitation of such procedural rights and controls.

THE RIGHT TO COUNSEL

Much of the discussion of the right to counsel in juvenile court has been cast in legalistic terms, sifting through appellate decisions to uncover constitutional arguments to vindicate attorneys' claims to a place in the court procedure. The state of legal opinion seems to be that in actuality juveniles and their parents have always had the right to engage counsel to appear in court if they so desire, but that the absence of counsel per se does not imply unfairness and lack of due process; such must be demonstrated to be true on appeal. The differences of opinion lie in questions as to whether the court has a positive obligation to apprise juveniles and parents of their right to counsel and under some circumstances appoint counsel to represent their interests. The 1959 Standard Juvenile Court Act answered these questions in the affirmative, and a number of states now have statutes fixing the right to counsel.

A more generic issue underlying the legal debates revolves about the compatibility of the presence of counsel with the special philosophy of the juvenile court, which ideologically has charged the judge and the probation officer with protection of the child's interests. Rhetorical questions are posed as to whether the presence of counsel will not rob the court of its informality and open it to the possibility of regular adversary proceedings, and whether such a change does not risk converting the juvenile court into little more than a miniaturized criminal court.

The arguments that children as well as adults are entitled to full protection of constitutional rights are quite powerful when considered in the context of a society radically changed since the juvenile court was born. However, it must be heeded that the nature of law has been changing rapidly; hence it may be more informative to examine immediate questions, such as how and to what extent traditional advocacy and adversary interaction can be synthesized with a court which, although more circumscribed in function, must remain a children's court. Beyond this, a hard look must be taken at consequences of the introduction of counsel where it has occurred to see if it does engineer more constraint, preclude unnecessary wardships, or enlarge the range of alternatives for dispositions.

Research on the presence of counsel in the juvenile court has barely begun, so that any conclusions must be tentative. Research by the author in California juvenile courts has shown that advising juveniles and their parents of their right to counsel, as ordered by 1961 legislation, has indeed increased the use of counsel, but that the rate of increase and of current use varies tremendously from county to county. For all counties of the state the gain has been from about 3 percent of the cases to 15 percent. In some counties appearance of attorneys in court has risen from 0 to 1 or 2 percent, in others from a low of 15 percent to highs of 70 or even 90 percent. Generally speaking, the factors found to affect the use of counsel are the existence of a public defender's office and the attitudes of judges and probation officers at the time they advise juveniles and parents of their rights. In assigning counsel, courts tend to favor dependent and neglected children and those in which serious offenses are alleged, likely to be followed by commitment to the California Youth Authority. Thus far there is no evidence of any discrimination in assignment of counsel on the basis of social class or race.

Problems have emerged because private attorneys without experience or knowledge of the juvenile court are unsure as to what their roles should be, and often do little for their clients. Moreover, public defenders tend to be co-opted by the court and may simply stipulate to the allegations by the probation officer in order not to make his workload excessive, or even because they think a youth needs some chastening experience or punishment by the court. These tendencies are likely to be pronounced where judges indiscriminately assign counsel and assume that rights of juveniles are thereby fully protected. This leads to a conclusion that mere introduction of counsel into juvenile courts without corresponding strengthening of their intake functions to cut down the sheer numbers of cases processed may be self-defeating. They also suggest that the independent private attorney may be preferable for representing juveniles over public defenders, although the latter have fuller knowledge of the workings of the court.

Another kind of problem develops where youth deny the allegations of the petition and transform hearings into adversary proceedings. The burden of presenting the case or protecting the interests of the public tends to fall most heavily on the probation officer, who is neither legally trained nor temperamentally inclined to play what is in essence a prosecutor's role. Often he resents the assignment because it alienates the youth or parents he is expected to help subsequently— often impossible. Where judges intervene to take over the interrogation, attorneys are at a painful disadvantage because they must object to the judge's questions and then hear the judge rule on the objections.

There are those, especially in police associations, who believe that prosecuting attorneys should enter the juvenile court and present contested cases, but prosecutors show little enthusiasm for the task, and judges are not yet disposed to permit hearings to become all-out adversary struggles. Their attitude is not ill-considered to one who has seen an attorney attempt to impugn the credibility of a 15-year-old girl witness by referring to her CYA record and to sexual experiences for which she received money.

Despite the problems coming with the appearance of attorneys in juvenile court and a trend toward more formal, adversary-type hearings, the author's research on one intensively studied California juvenile court indicates that attorneys do their clients some good. A comparison of cases with and without attorneys showed that the former had a higher percentage of dismissals, fewer wardships declared, and more sentences to the California Youth Authority suspended. However, dismissals were not proportionately numerous, and, moreover, they clustered among cases alleging neglect by parents or unfit homes. Hence the main conclusion reached was that the major contribution of attorneys in the juvenile court lay in their ability to mitigate the severity of dispositions rather than disproving allegations of the petitions.

Attorneys often successfully challenged the precision of allegations in the jurisdictional hearings, causing them to be reduced in number and seriousness. This then became grounds to argue for a more lenient disposition of the cases. Specific dispositions were influenced when attorneys found relatives to take a child in preference to a foster home placement, or when they proposed psychiatric treatment or psychological counseling as an alternative to commitment to a ranch school. Sometimes they gave emphasis to reasons why a boy should be given another chance at home, and swayed an otherwise uncertain judge. Finally, attorneys sometimes protected the client, especially a parent, against himself, by persuading him to accept a condition of probation in order to avoid a more draconic order by the court.

Not all of the good work of attorneys was reflected in the outcomes of hearings; some of it was done before and after the court sessions, through convincing probation officers to change a recommendation or make some administrative modification of an order. If California findings are indicative, the adversary function of the emerging role of the attorney in juvenile court is likely to be marginal; more important is his role as a negotiator, interpreter of court decisions to child and parents, and as a source of psychic support in a new kind of court where there is greater social distance between probation officers and juveniles. Finally, the very presence of an attorney or the possibility of his entry into cases has a monitory value reinforcing the new consciousness of judges and probation officers of rights of juveniles. For this reason it may be that the New York State concept of the attorney in juvenile court as a law guardian is a most fitting description of his role.

Commentaries on the New York system for bringing counsel into family courts have been sensitive to the problem of his possible co-optation by the court and the need to preserve his independence of action. To make him an agent of the court raises a real question as to where his loyalties would lie. Yet total independence may mean disruption and loss of informality in the court proceedings. A recent proposal seeks to solve this dilemma by moving delinquency hearings from the juvenile court into the probation department, where defense officers would be assigned to juveniles, leaving the court in a supervisory or appellate position. However, administrative justice has its own unsolved problems in which the use or function of adversary contention is clouded by uncertainties as to where and how findings are made. Loyal opposition is the desideratum, but opposition remains the social mechanism which compels total and critical assessment of facts.

LEVELS OF PROOF

The clashing views over the propriety of adversary hearings in juvenile court are not dissociated from disagreements as what kind of evidence should be mandatory for its findings. When the California juvenile court law was altered in 1961, civil rules of evidence were designated for hearings in all save most serious offenses—i.e., those which would be felonies if committed by an adult. An attempt was made at the time to institute criminal rules of evidence in such cases, but legislators qualified the original recommendation of the Juvenile Justice Commission to a "preponderance of evidence legally admissible in the trial of criminal cases." This was a concession to the fears of those who felt that the juvenile court would otherwise be made into a criminal court.

Many California judges have met the thorny problem of hearsay evidence in juvenile court hearings by admitting everything, on the assumption that they can cull out that which is not competent. This tack has some support from law scholars who argue that the hearsay rule was intended for gullible juries rather than judges. However, this misses an important point that much juvenile court evidence is in the form of reports which often are little more than compilations of professional hearsay. Whether the ordinary run of judges and referees are qualified to sift this kind of evidence is questionable; many juvenile court judges appear remarkably naive about psychiatric diagnoses and the true nature of that which is easily called psychiatric treatment. Their knowledge of social science and its critical evaluations of psychiatry and social work are, at best, rudimentary.

An attractive solution to evidentiary problems of the juvenile court in the majority of its cases may be to require clear and convincing proof, which the lawbooks denote as more than a preponderance of evidence but less than proof beyond doubt demanded in criminal procedure. Clear and convincing proof is the highest order of civil evidence, which admits of only one reasonable conclusion.

For the most grievous juvenile law violations, in which protection of public interests becomes a dominant value the canons of criminal proof should prevail. However, their seriousness can be defined more meaningfully in operational terms by making them contingent upon legally possible dispositions rather than on formal allegations that the offense is analogous to a felony. By this is meant that if the youth against whom the allegations are found to be true can be committed to an institution jointly used for adult criminals, or to an institution whose correctional or security features are equal to or greater than the least correctionally oriented adult institution, then criminal rules of evidence must obtain.

One difficulty with this kind of proposal is that judges, subjected to heavy public pressures or confronted with difficulties due to lack of resources for dispositions, may simply find that for the purposes at hand a given institution is noncorrectional or otherwise meets statutory requirements. If appellate courts are unwilling to look behind such findings and evaluate the evidence rather than merely determining that the judge's finding was based on evidence, other remedies, perhaps administrative, would be necessary.

SOCIAL ACTION TO CHANGE THE JUVENILE COURT

Juvenile courts evolve and change in several ways: by legislation, rulings on appeals, administrative policy formation by regulatory agencies, and the cumulative, day-to-day actions of judges, probation officers, and correctional workers. Because the court either is a local or ecologically contained institution, the interaction within the court and between the court and the community is the most important area for sudying the processes by which it changes. Legislation, appellate decisions, and administrative programs for this reason need formulation with recognition that the corpus of juvenile court practice to be changed is highly diverse and that outcomes of intervention will not be so much the result of selected causes as products of interaction.

While law represents a striving for uniformity, it must be heeded that similar ends may be reached by a variety of means, administrative as well as legislative. The juvenile court is a prime example of an agency in which the connection between legal action and administrative action, traditionally neglected in American jurisprudence, must be coordinated. Nowhere is this more readily seen than in sparsely populated areas and resource-poor counties, or counties with

unique problems such as a large ethnic population. A more circumscribed juvenile court means that counties which previously have relied upon the court as a receptacle for child problems of all kinds must find or develop new agencies and forms of organization for their purposes. This calls for a high order of administrative ingenuity to facilitate the working juvenile court laws without provoking resistance or destroying local initiative.

On the whole, appellate court decisions have not been effective means for shaping the course of juvenile court evolution, although they may become more so with passing time. One recent exception was the supreme court decision in Utah which removed juvenile courts from control by the department of public welfare and gave them status as an independent judiciary. The history and background of this action throws considerable light on the weaknesses of vesting administrative control over juvenile courts in a state welfare agency, which in this instance had made some notable improvements but had stirred strong dissatisfaction among judges by more or less preempting their right of judicial review.

Historical materials accumulated by the author on the period during which the state department of welfare supervised juvenile probation services in California indicate that its record of achievements was not impressive. Supervisory control of juvenile probation under the regime of the California Youth Authority has been more productive of innovations in juvenile court practices, but these have had to be secured almost entirely by cooperative means. Although this agency supported the action, the impetus for the major revision of the juvenile court law came from the director of the department of corrections, a small number of dedicated private attorneys, a few judges, and several law school professors. A goodly number of judges and probation officers throughout the state resisted this change. This was in decided contrast to the Utah scene, where judges seemingly played the yeoman roles in action to change their juvenile court law.

Ordinarily bar associations may be expected to take the lead or strongly support others seeking to better adapt the juvenile court to its contemporary social setting, and this has been true for New York State and to a degree in other states. However, the California state bar has shown a singular lack of interest in problems of the juvenile court. Obviously, then, action to legislate change in the juvenile court will have to work through limitations imposed by the nature of the values or commitments of elite groups in professional associations and state power structures.

An issue which complicates any action to modify juvenile court procedures is the old one as to whether the legislature or the courts should make rules for courts to follow. Since the juvenile court is a peculiar type of court, with direct policy implications, the scales get weighted in favor of legislative action. However, legislative action pushed without a sense of full participation by judges and their probation officers risks subversion of changes by judicial indifference or noncompliance, and judges are a notoriously hard lot to discipline by direct means.

Modifying the structure and procedures of the juvenile court through legislative channels in such a way as to make it part of the living law, the implicit as well as the explicit rules of the game, is contingent on complementary communication and opinion change among judges. Such processes can be encouraged by such organizations as the National Council of Juvenile Court Judges, the National Probation and Parole Association, National Council on Crime and Delinquency, and the U.S. Children's Bureau, but differences between states make imperative some type of state administrative or regulatory agency for juvenile courts. It is probably too early to tell whether such organization should be part of judicial councils or commissions with autonomy of their own. Changes which make the fate of the juvenile courts the proprietary interests of judges should be avoided, because the police, probation officers, prosecutors, public defenders, and social workers all have solid stakes in the workings of the juvenile court.

The most important objective, so far as administrative action is concerned, is that some state body exist to continuously oversee juvenile court operations, to promote the organic growth and advise application of legal procedures, to accumulate data, and to contract for research on the court as needed. Such an agency could not review the decisions of juvenile court judges, but it might conceivably be given some power to review the acts of administrative officials in juvenile correctional institutions or some inquisitorial and injunctive power to compel them to desist from practices inconsistent with juvenile court objectives. Hopefully this might begin to establish long-needed liaison between work of the juvenile court and ministrations of state institutions for juveniles. Even more, its very existence might discourage commitments to state institutions and speed a trend toward community centered forms of guidance and training of errant juveniles, not unlike the shifts which are occurring in treatment of mentally disordered persons.

THE PLACE OF RESEARCH

Although there is a great volume of impressions, opinions, and speculative discussion published about the juvenile court, the amount of carefully designed, relevant empirical research is pitifully small. Much of the data available on the juvenile court must be culled from surveys or study reports made by state agencies or community groups attempting to document the need for new programs. While studies of the U.S. Children's Bureau to some extent have been an exception, even its publications have been colored by long-time goals of raising standards in juvenile courts. Granted that most research on the juvenile court should be action research, nevertheless it can benefit from the wider employment of social science design and methods for gathering data comparable to those put to use in sociological studies of industries and mental hospitals. There is a pressing need for some basic ethnographic or descriptive studies to discover in greater depth what are the patterns of actions in juvenile courts and then, proceeding from these, to make more comprehensive studies of the modalities and dispersions in its patterns.

Our society now has both the surplus energy and trained social science personnel to do this job; the problem is one of their reallocation. Whether this will or can occur through the research funding methods and policies of the National Institutes of Mental Health is debatable. Research into juvenile delinquency and the program innovation for juvenile courts are of sufficient importance to merit their separate husbandry by the federal government. Furthermore, it does not appear that the strong appeal of health or mental health auspices is a prerequisite to securing needed research funds, for Congress already has shown its willingness to support special research and developmental programs on delinquency and the juvenile court.

The federal government is in a much better position than state governments to stimulate and fund the independent type of inquiry needed to clarify the nature of the anomaly which has been the juvenile court. Whatever mechanisms it devises for this purpose should be sufficiently flexible to catch up the mar-ginal, lone-wolf investigators whose detachment from organizations and wariness toward their values may be especially fitting for studying the problems of the juvenile court in modern society.

In concluding, the author freely admits to his omission of any other than incidental discussion of the kinds of adaptations in the fields of public welfare, private social work, special education, and community organization which a more conservative construction of the juvenile court would entail. The changes taking place in these areas are many and rapid, but their overall directions are not easy to make out in a more general atmosphere of conflict and confusion of goals. New ways of looking at things are badly needed by social workers and educators, with a recognition that differentiation and flexibility are collateral requirements of organizational advances toward common ends.

Meantime sufficient consensus on new goals for the juvenile court has accumulated to make the times propitious for its change through social action.

36. THE CHANGING ROLE OF THE ASYLUM

DAVID J. ROTHMAN

Reprinted from The Public Interest, *no. 26 (Winter 1972), pp. 3-17. Copyright © by National Affairs, Inc., 1972. David J. Rothman is Professor of History at Columbia University. This selection is a summary of his book,* The Discovery of the Asylum: Social Order and Disorder in the New Republic *(Little, Brown, 1971). He is a member of the Committee for the Study of Incarceration and author of* Politics and Power: The United States Senate, 1869-1901 *(Harvard University Press, 1966).*

■ As we learned from Selection 1, Americans tend to regard deviance as a pervasive attribute of individuals who engage in deviant behavior, rather than as a transitory or intermittent aspect of the lives of such individuals. Therefore in American life deviance tends, when labeled, to become a master characteristic dominating other aspects of the individual's behavior and identity. The serious regard for deviance combined with a desire to protect and improve the quality of human life perhaps accounts for the particular emphasis of 19th-century American reform movements on the development of model institutions and communities for the treatment of moral disorders.

In this selection David Rothman examines the historical factors that brought about what he terms "the discovery of the asylum," the establishment of places to provide new and rehabilitative environments for those who in one way or another were not up to par. These places included penitentiaries, insane asylums, orphan asylums, houses of refuge for juvenile delinquents, and almshouses. Each such institution was to provide the order and protection from noxious influences deemed necessary to cure the criminal, the psychotic, and the pauper.

Rothman shows how this reformist zeal became routinized, how the institutions quickly became merely custodial, and how reform movements by the end of the 19th century were mounting a concerted attack on the asylum and seeking to move care outside them. An increasingly prevelant feeling was that the cure was worse than the disease. This turning away from closed institutions has accelerated in the past two decades and during this time has been particularly striking in mental hospitals; Rothman cites as an example, New York State, where the number of patients in mental hospitals declined by one-third from 1955 to 1970. No one believes that insanity in that state has declined, but new ways of dealing with mental illness have allowed much less reliance on incarceration.

A classic and contemporary analysis of the reform movement that invented the modern penitentiary is Gustave DeBeaumont and Alexis deTocqueville, *On the Penitentiary System in the United States* (Southern Illinois University Press, 1964). The development of American prisons is described in Blake McKelvey, *American Prisons: A Study of American Social History Prior to 1915* (University of Chicago Press, 1936). A similar history for mental asylums is Albert Deutsch, *The Mentally Ill in America: A History of their Care and Treatment* (Columbia University Press, 1949). Norman Dain analyzes conceptions of insanity in *Concepts of Insanity in the United States, 1789-1865* (Rutgers University Press, 1964). ■

OVER THE COURSE of the past several decades, without clear theoretical justification or even a high degree of self-consciousness, we have been completing a revolution in the treatment of the insane, the criminal, the orphaned, the delinquent, and the poor. Whereas once we relied almost exclusively upon incarceration to treat or punish these classes of people, we now frame and administer many programs that maintain them within the community or at least remove them as quickly as possible from institutions. Policymakers in each of these areas interpret their own measures as specific responses to internal developments—an advance in drug therapy or a dissatisfaction with prevailing penitentiary conditions—not as part of a general antiinstitutional movement. But such a movement exists, and it must be seen in a comprehensive way if it is ever to be understood.

The basic statistics are, themselves, most striking. Since 1955 the annual number of inmates in the nation's mental hospitals has been falling. New York state institutions, for example, held 93,000 patients in 1955; in 1966 their number dropped to 82,765; and in 1970 to 64,239. A similar decline has occurred in correctional institutions. In 1940, 131.7 prisoners per 100,000 of the population served time in federal or state penitentiaries; in 1965 the number fell to 109.6 per 100,000, and this without a concomitant drop in the number of crimes committed or criminals convicted. Dramatic changes have also affected the young. The orphan asylum has almost disappeared, and the juvenile correction center has also declined in use. As for the poor, the almshouse or traditional poorhouse is no longer a specter in their lives.

Obviously, no one would be foolish enough to predict that within the next 20 or 30 years incarcerating institutions will disappear. Some 400,000 adults and juveniles remain in correctional institutions, and a similar number fill mental hospitals. Moreover, Attorney General Mitchell is insisting that money be spent on constructing new penitentiaries and refurbishing old ones, and the Justice Department's Law Enforcement Assistance Administration spends around $29 million annually in block grants to the states for these purposes. Nevertheless, when our current practices are viewed within historical perspective, the degree to which we have moved away from the incarcerative mode of coping with these social problems is clear enough. We are witnessing nothing less than the end of one era in social reform and the beginning of another.

THE MOVEMENT FOR INCARCERATION

Institutionalization of "problem people" in the United States originated in the opening decades of the 19th century. Prior to that, colonial communities, particularly the more settled ones along the seaboard, relied upon very different mechanisms of control. Their level of expectations was very low; they did not expect to eliminate poverty or to reform the criminal. Rather, the colonists devoted their energies to differentiating carefully between neighbor and stranger. Typically, they provided assistance to the resident within his household or that of a friend—and they banished the troublesome outsider. A neighbor's poverty was not suspect—clergymen, after all, preached regularly on the virtue of charity, making little effort to distinguish the worthy from the unworthy poor. (As one cleric put it, "What if God were to refuse his mercy to those of us who do not deserve it?") Local ne'er-do-wells were fined or whipped or shamed before their neighbors through such devices as the stocks. Outsiders, on the other hand, whether honest and poor or petty criminals, were sent on their way as quickly as possible, often with a whipping to insure their continuing absence.

When these responses proved inadequate, as they often did—residents might not correct their ways or strangers might persist in returning—the community had recourse to the gallows. The frequency with which 18th-century magistrates sentenced offenders to capital punishment testified to the fragility of the system. But almost nowhere did the colonists incarcerate the deviant or the dependent. Jails held only prisoners awaiting trial, not those convicted of a crime; and the few towns that erected almshouses used them only in exceptional cases—for the sailor so ill that he could not be moved, or the resident so incapacitated that no neighbor would care for him.

Beginning in the 1820s the perspective on both poverty and crime underwent a major shift. The relatively passive attitudes of the 18th century gave way to a new, energetic program as Americans became convinced that poverty and crime, as well as insanity and delinquency, could be eliminated from the New World. Crime, it was decided, did not reflect the innate depravity of man but the temptations at loose in the society. Insanity was not the work of the devil but the product of a deleterious environment. Poverty was not inevitable but, rather, reflected the inadequacies of existing social arrangements. These interpretations revealed not only an Enlightenment optimism about the perfectability of human nature but also a nagging fear that American society, with its unprecedented geographic and social mobility, was so open and fragmented that stability and cohesion could not be maintained unless reforms were instituted. An odd marriage of ideas occurred in the young republic. The optimism of an environmentalist doctrine joined a basic concern that American society was in a state of imbalance; though the majority were coping well enough, a minority seemed unable to confront the challenges of American life. The result was a widespread belief that insanity could be cured in the New World because its causes were rooted in a social order that encouraged limitless ambition and disrespect for traditional opinions and practices. The criminal, too, could be reformed, once he was removed from a setting in which gambling halls and dens of iniquity corrupted him. Poverty would also be eliminated as soon as the poor were taught to resist the temptations loose in a free community.

Starting from these premises, reformers moved quickly and enthusiastically to a new program: the construction of asylums—new "environments"—for the deviant and dependent. Between 1820 and 1840 penitentiaries spread throughout the country, and the states constructed insane asylums. Concomitantly, they built orphan asylums, houses of refuge (for juvenile delinquents), and almshouses. The walls that surrounded these structures were intended not only to confine the deviant and dependent but also to exclude the community, for in origin incarceration was a semiutopian venture. Superintendents aimed to establish a corruption-free environment which would compensate for the irregularities and temptations existing in the larger, more turbulent society. Thus the bywords of all Jacksonian institutions became order and routine, discipline and regularity, steady work

and steady habits. The inmates would be provided with a new spiritual armor so that upon release they would go forth shielded from temptations and corruptions.

MODELS OF REFORM

In fact, the initial organization of the asylums closely approximated the reformers' designs. The institutions consistently isolated the inmates from the community. Wardens sharply limited the number of letters and visits a prisoner could receive and prohibited the circulation of periodicals and newspapers. Insane asylum superintendents instructed relatives to remove the sick patient from the family and bring him to the institution as soon after the onset of the disease as possible, and then not to visit or to write him frequently. Many child-care institutions insisted that the parents abdicate all rights to their children.

The asylums' internal organization put a premium on bell-ringing punctuality and a precise routine. Regimentation became the standard style of prison life in the popular Auburn plan, where the inmates remained isolated in individual cells during the night and worked in congregate shops during the day. Convicts did not walk from place to place, but went in lockstep, a curious American invention that combined a march and shuffle. A military precision marked other aspects of their lives. At the sound of a morning bell, keepers opened the cells, prisoners stepped onto the deck, lockstepped into the yard, washed their pails and utensils, marched to breakfast, and then, when the bell rang, stood, and marched to the workshops where they remained till the next signal. The new world set before the insane was similar in many respects. The essential ingredient in "moral treatment" was to bring discipline and regularity into chaotic lives without exciting frenetic reactions. In the well-ordered asylum, declared Isaac Ray, a prominent 19th-century psychiatrist, "quiet, silence, regular routine, would take the place of restlessness, noise, and fitful activity." One of his colleagues noted that in the asylum "the hours for rising, dressing, and washing, for meals, labor, occupation, amusement . . . should be regulated by the most *perfect precision.*" This style reappeared in the first houses of refuge. One official boasted that "a month's stay in the company with boys accustomed to systematic discipline and obedience, with a sense that there is no escape from order and regularity, generally converts the most wayward into good pupils." And a visitor to a Long Island orphan asylum was struck by the military exercises that the children followed, ostensibly "as a useful means of forming habits of order." She added that it was supposed to be "beautiful to see them pray; for at the first tip of the whistle, they all dropped to their knees. . . . Everything moves by machinery."

Under these routines American asylums became world famous as models of progressive social reform. Tocqueville and Beaumont and a host of European visitors traveled here to examine our penitentiaries, and the verdicts were almost always favorable. Americans themselves were not reluctant to boast of the glories of their insane asylums or of their almshouses. The reformers' rhetoric and these accolades from distinguished visitors sanctioned the new program, and few contemporaries objected to it. On the contrary, incarceration became the first resort as psychiatrists rushed to put patients behind walls and judges with little hesitation meted out long sentences for convicted criminals. Legislators kept commitment laws as simple as possible, reluctant to erect legal barriers between the insane and the asylum, or between the delinquent and the reformatory. With the promise of rehabilitation by incarceration so grand, safeguards were clearly irrelevant.

FROM REHABILITATION TO CUSTODY

Unfortunately, the promise turned out to be hollow, and by 1870 the asylums exhibited all their modern ills. They were overcrowded and in sad disrepair, without internal discipline, disorderly, enervating, monotonous, and cruel. Their preoccupation was with custody and security, not rehabilitation. And yet they lasted, maintaining through the 19th century their monopoly over corrections and treatment.

Both the failure and the persistence of the asylums had common causes. The environmental theories of the founders helped at once to promote and disguise the shift from rehabilitation to custody. Superintendent after superintendent succumbed to the notion that in administering a holding operation he was still promoting rehabilitation. The first proponents had so enthusiastically praised the benefits of incarceration that their successors could smugly assume that just keeping the inmates behind walls accomplished much good. Regardless of the degree of overcrowding, or the extent of corruption, or the absence of supervision, officials could still self-righteously declare that institutionalization was therapeutic.

Another critical element in both the asylums' failure and persistence was the ethnic and class composition of the inmates. By 1870, and increasingly thereafter, the lower classes and the immigrants filled the penitentiaries and mental hospitals. First it was the Irish, then the eastern Europeans, and later the Blacks. Incarceration thus became identified in the public mind as the particular fate of the outsider. To the middle and upper classes, the inmate was an outcast even before entering his ward or cell. Since institutionalization served marginal people, the conditions could be no worse than the inmates. In essence, the promise of reform had built up the asylums, and the functionalism of custody perpetuated them.

THE NEW REFORM MOVEMENT

The Progressive era marked a dividing point in public policy, giving the initial thrust to new, noninstitutional programs. Change was uneven and selective, affecting some areas more quickly than others. Nevertheless, between 1890 and 1920 care and correction of the deviant and dependent began to shift away from incarceration. The changes were most popular and complete where citizens' suspicions and fears were least intense. The first caretaker institutions to decline in importance were orphan asylums, replaced by foster homes and liberalized adoption proceedings. Public and private benevolent societies that in the 19th century had devoted their funds to administering child-care institutions transformed themselves into placing-out and adoption agencies. Simultaneously, innovations in public welfare programs decreased reliance on the almshouses, at least for some groups. State aid that allowed widowed mothers to care for their dependent children at home was first enacted in Illinois in 1911 and then spread quickly through densely populated and industrial states. No longer would these women be dispatched to an almshouse and their dependents to an orphan asylum.

New Deal legislation furthered these trends. The Social Security Act of 1935 eliminated incarceration for other segments of the poor, keeping the aged and the able-bodied unemployed out of the almshouse. The law expressly prohibited federal grants to states to expand their almshouses and refused to match state funds that went to the support of persons institutionalized. Incarceration had been the mainstay of public relief for over 100 years, and the abolition of this policy was no mean feat.

In the first decades of the 20th century, state mental hospitals also began to decline in importance. Between 1920 and 1940, outpatient facilities for the mental ill—caring for the patient during the day and returning him home at night—opened in several metropolitan centers. In the post-World War II period the program grew increasingly popular, particularly after the passage of the Community Mental Health Act of 1963, under which the federal government matches state funds for constructing community mental health facilities. As a result, institutionalization in large state mental hospitals has steadily dropped so that patients discharged now outnumber patients admitted. Indeed, the principles of antiinstitutionalism are now so widely accepted that the mental health literature is beginning to focus on the administrative question of how best to convert custodial institutions into community outpatient centers.

Other types of custodial institutions are also gradually disappearing. It was the pride of Jacksonian reformers to construct asylums for retarded and defective children, and many of these structures lasted into this century. Physicians and administrators, however, are now eager to abandon this approach and to end the isolation of these children. They organize special public school curriculums that enable many of these youngsters to live home; and where residential treatment is necessary they design small structures in the community, not large, isolated ones in a country location.

In this same spirit, states are experimenting with incentives to encourage not just foster care but adoption for orphaned and illegitimate children. Traditionally, the foster home received compensation for its effort but the adoptive one did not. Convinced that many foster families would prefer to adopt their child but cannot afford to give up the stipends they receive, officials are offering payments, based on need, to adopting parents as well. The motive is clear; the closer the surrogate family approximates the normal one, the less it resembles an institution, the better. In fact, the spread of contraceptive knowledge together with liberalization of the abortion laws makes it not unlikely that child asylums, and perhaps even adoption, will disappear within the next two decades.

THE DECLINE OF THE PRISON

Although prison walls still impose themselves massively upon the public eye, in this field, too, we have decreased our reliance upon incarceration. Correctional institutions have lost their 19th-century monopoly. Since 1961 the percentage of the population in prisons has declined annually. The most important procedure effecting this change is probation. In 1965, 53 percent of all offenders were out in the community under the periodic supervision of a probation officer.

By 1975, according to the estimates of an advisory committee to the President's Commission on Law Enforcement and the Administration of Justice, the proportion will rise to 58 percent. The most dramatic increases have been among juvenile offenders. In 1965 only 18 percent of convicted deliquents served in correctional institutions, while 64 percent were on probation. Among adult offenders, 39 percent of those convicted of a crime were institutionalized, while 49 percent (including, to be sure, misdemeanants) were on probation.

The other major alternative to prolonged incarceration is parole, whereby a convict, having completed some fraction of his sentence, is discharged from prison and obliged to report regularly to a corrections officer. Although the idea of parole is not new—it was advocated by many prison experts as early as the 1870s—it has been extensively used only in the post-1930 period. Reliance on parole, it is true, varies enormously from state to state. In New Hampshire and Washington, practically every convict leaves the state prison before completing his formal sentence; in Oklahoma, Wyoming, and South Dakota, less than 20 percent of the inmates enjoy this privilege. Still, by 1965, 18 percent of all juvenile delinquents and 12 percent of adult offenders were on parole. Among all convicts serving in American prisons in 1964, fully 65 percent won release under this program.

Several states are also experimenting with new programs to decrease the distance between correction programs and the community. The publicity given these procedures to date outweighs their actual importance, but they all look to the same antiinstitutional goal. One such effort is work release, whereby the offender leaves the prison in the morning, works at his job in the community, and then returns to confinement at night. One warden regards this innovation as "revolutionary, not evolutionary. It's going to change," he predicts, "about all of penology." For the moment, however, work release has been authorized in some 24 states and for the federal corrections systems. Important programs

operate in Wisconsin, California, Minnesota, and North Carolina; in Wisconsin, for example, it affected 30 percent of the misdemeanants in 1956, and 48 percent in 1964. And, at present, some 5 percent of all federal offenders come under it. But the scope of work release is limited, typically not covering those convicted of crimes of violence or of a morals charge, or those believed to be part of an organized crime syndicate. Some preliminary evaluations also suggest that the arrangement is expensive and cumbersome to administer. Nevertheless, some states are trying to extend the program to cover felons, and they also report a significant drop in such incarceration-related costs as welfare payments to convicts' families.

LEGAL REFORM

These developments have stimulated and in turn been furthered by an important series of legal actions intended to reduce dependence on incarceration. The most notable advances have occurred in the field of juvenile detention. In the Gault decision (1967) the Supreme Court brought some of the protections of "due process" to the juvenile courts. While the requirements that the Court insisted upon were by no means negligible—notification of charges and the right to confront witnesses—it is not only for procedural reasons that the case stands out; the *Gault* decision was premised upon a disillusionment with incarceration. Underlying the majority opinion, written by Justice Fortas, was the belief that the juvenile institution was totally inadequate to the job of reformation. As Justice Black insisted in a concurring opinion, "It is in all but name a penitentiary." And since the disposition of a juvenile case might well result in confining the offender to an essentially penal institution, the justices wanted the trial proceedings to protect the defendants' rights. A similar reason appeared in the Court's decision in the *Winship* case. In an earlier day, magistrates assumed that a reformatory would accomplish some good and were therefore content to incarcerate delinquents on the basis of the "preponderance of the evidence." Now, far less enthusiastic about these institutions, the Court ruled that juvenile convictions had to meet the standard of "beyond a reasonable doubt."

Public interest law firms and reform organizations have also launched major campaigns to extend legal protections to prison inmates and to reduce the disabilities convicts suffer after release. As a result of these efforts, lower courts have ruled that solitary confinement for juveniles violates their constitutional right against cruel and unusual punishment. They have also extended this reasoning to prohibit the use of "strip cells," in which the convict must crouch naked in a space so designed that he can neither stand nor sit down. Recent state penal codes have begun to expand convicts' procedural rights, and the courts, most notably and recently in the *Landman* decision, have also insisted on expanding the prerogatives and protection due the convict. In *Landman,* the federal district court forbade the Virginia state penitentiary system from any longer imposing a bread and water diet, from using chains or tape or tear gas except in an immediate emergency, from using physical force as a punishment; it also demanded minimum due process protections before a convict lost "good time" (that would shorten his sentence) or suffered any deprivation of his normal prison privileges (such as loss of exercise or communication with other inmates). Suits now pending are also contesting the constitutionality of prohibiting ex-convicts from obtaining trucker's or chauffeur's licenses and the restrictions on parolees' rights of association and travel. Thus, one detects not only a closing of the gap between the legal rights of citizens and those of inmates but also the beginnings of a series of changes that will make the prison system as we know it increasingly unworkable.

Another major concern of these reformers is the liberalization of bail. One of their goals is to insure that bail itself will not be set excessively high and that bonds are not difficult to obtain. But they are also experimenting with methods that eliminate bail altogether, allowing many of those awaiting trial to go free on their own recognizance. Since city detention centers and jails are filled with arrestees waiting their turns on crowded court calendars, this innovation would dramatically reduce the numbers incarcerated. One pilot project by the Vera Institute revealed that in New York City, with careful fieldwork, the percentage of those arrested on minor offenses who can be sent home without bail is substantial, and only a few of them will fail to appear at trial (4.6 percent of some 37,000 cases). Moreover, these procedures saved the city some $2.5 million in police and court costs. With such results it is no wonder that the institute is trying to expand the program to persons caught committing petty crimes, a step that would further decrease the numbers incarcerated and save additional funds.

AVOIDING NEW ILLUSIONS

Thus, over the past several decades public officials and private organizations have energetically and successfully attempted to reduce reliance upon incarceration. They have done so with considerable enthusiasm—one doesn't achieve sweeping reforms of this kind without enthusiasm. However, there is the danger that this enthusiasm could lead to exaggerated expectations and, eventually, public disillusionment.

One of the first tasks confronting the various proponents of antiinstitutional measures is a clear and level-headed definition of expectations and purposes. In the Progressive era, when many of these plans were first devised, the reform rhetoric promised breathtaking success. Advocates shared not only a disgust with the custodial practices of large state institutions but also a generally unqualified faith that the deviant and dependent, if left in the community under proper supervision, would quickly undergo rehabilitation. Incarcerating these classes, the reformers insisted, had the effect of confirming their antisocial impulses. Keeping them with society would break the pattern and promote normal behavior. But this is probably to promise too much. More important, it focuses attention on the wrong things. We do not yet know whether the antiincarceration movement will be any more effective than the original proincarceration movement—equally idealistic and enthusiastic—in effecting "cures." But there are other and very powerful arguments in its favor.

To begin with, there is the fact that many of the institutions functioning today, particularly correctional ones, are simply a national scandal, a shame to the society. They brutalize the inmates, humiliate them, and educate them in the ways of crime. Moreover, an impressive sociological literature, exemplified in the writings of Erving Goffman and Gresham Sykes, convincingly demonstrates that these characteristics are inherent in institutions, which by their very nature are infantalizing or corrupting. Moreover, while incarceration does exclude the deviant from the community for a period of time, eventually he is released; so unless one is prepared to lock up the criminal and throw away the key, institutionalization does not offer permanent security. And while public opinion may be growing tougher on the offender, we have not yet reached, and in all likelihood we are not going to reach the point where life sentences for robbers, burglars, car thieves, and embezzlers will seem like an equitable solution.

Institutionalization is also incredibly expensive. To confine 201,220 criminals in state institutions in 1965 cost $384,980,648; to administer probation programs for slightly more than twice that number of people cost $60 million. Somehow, it would seem, the vast sums expended on institutionalization could be better spent.

THE LESSON OF ATTICA

But perhaps the most compelling reason for experimenting with antiinstitutional programs is that the penitentiary has actually lost much, if not all, of its legitimacy in our society. It is not just academic students of criminal incarceration who despair of the penal system. Those in charge of the prisons, from wardens and corrections commissioners to state legislators, also share an incredibly high degree of self-doubt, ambivalence, dismay, and even guilt over prison operations. They are no longer secure in what they are doing. The depth and impact of these attitudes emerged with striking clarity and force in the recent events at Attica. Given the history of prison administration in this country, what is surprising and unusual about this revolt is not that it was suppressed harshly but that several days were spent in negotiation. Attica was not our first prison riot; all through the 1920s and 1930s bloody revolts broke out, only to be repressed immediately, even at the cost of some hostages' lives. Why was Attica different? Why were negotiators flown in, an ad hoc committee formed, proposals and counterproposals exchanged? Why did this prison riot come to resemble so closely the student uprising and the university administration's response at Columbia in 1968?

The most obvious answer, that many hostages' lives were at stake, is altogether inadequate. It is a clear rule of prison guard life, one that is conveyed immediately to recruits, that guards are not ransomable. Should one or more of them be taken hostage, no bargain will be struck for their release. The maxim is not as coldhearted as one might first think. On the contrary, it assumes that once convicts understand that guards are not ransomable they will have no reason—except for pure revenge—to take them as hostages. And, in fact, events have usually borne out the shrewdness of this calculation; for all the brutality of the prison system, guards have not often been the victims of the prisoners' anger or desperation. Then why did not officials in New York stand by this rule, move in quickly at Attica to regain control, and rationalize the entire operation as necessary to protect guards' lives everywhere?

The failure to act immediately and with confidence points directly to the prison's loss of legitimacy. Both the inmates and their keepers shared an attitude that Attica was in a fundamental way out of step with American society. Most of the convicts' demands were not obviously unreasonable in the light of public opinion today: better pay for their work, better communication with their families, rights to lawbooks and counsel. Most citizens were probably surprised to learn that these privileges were not already established. Commissioner Oswald himself had promised Attica inmates just before the riot that these changes were long overdue and would soon be enacted. How could he then act with sure and fast resolve to harshly repress a revolt when many of its aims were conceded to be sensible and appropriate and long overdue? It is one thing to sacrifice guards' lives for a system that has a sense of its own purpose; it is quite another to sacrifice them when the system is full of self-doubts. So Oswald negotiated, brought in outsiders, and tried to bargain. In the end it did not work, perhaps because not enough time was allowed, perhaps because compromise is impossible in such a charged situation. The revolt was suppressed, with a rage and force that in part reflects the urge to obliterate the questions and the ambivalence. Still, from Attica we have learned that we cannot administer penal institutions that we no longer believe in.

From Attica we have also learned how impossible it is to administer existing prisons when inmates withhold their compliance. The internal organization of penitentiaries today is an irrational mix of old rules, some relaxed, others enforced. Whereas once all prisoners spent their time isolated in a cell, now they mingle freely in the yard, communicate with one another, and move about. As a result, the cooperation of hundreds of prisoners is necessary to the smooth running of the institution. The ratio of guards to inmates is generally low; officers are able to prevent mass breakouts but are not able to prevent takeovers. As events at Attica demonstrated clearly, a group acting in concert has great power to disrupt the normal routine. Moreover, the likelihood of similar actions recurring seems very high. For one, prisoners are certain to sense the steady loss of legitimacy of incarcerating institutions in our society. For another, the convicts in state institutions are bound to be more homogeneous in terms of class (lower), color (Black),

crime (violent), and politics (radical). As White embezzlers or Blacks guilty of property offenses increasingly go out on probation or enter minimum-security prison farms, the possibilities for uprisings by those remaining in penitentiaries increases. To be sure, the state might respond to this crisis by building bigger and internally more secure prisons; we do have the managerial ability to structure settings where 20 guards can keep 1,000 men captive. But this response will probably not get very far. The courts, given their due process inclinations, will not allow such prisons, and wardens do not seem to have the inclination to administer them.

A NEW CALCULUS

The implication of this state of affairs makes clear that we must experiment with alternatives. Incarceration is at once inhumane by current standards, destructive of inmates, incredibly expensive, and increasingly losing its legitimacy. Our institutions of incarceration are 19th-century anachronisms, out of step with the other American institutions of the 1970s. This marked discrepancy among our social institutions cannot continue for very long without provoking crises more disastrous than Attica. It is time for a new calculus and a new strategy.

The dilemma we now face may enable us to progress in ways that might have been impossible in calmer times. For we no longer need to demonstrate that innovations will accomplish such grandiose goals as solving the problem of crime or reforming the deviant. Such goals are, of course, desirable. But the plain fact of the matter is that we have not yet been able to invent techniques or procedures to achieve them. The record on criminal reform, past and present, is dismal—if by reform one means transforming criminals into law-abiding citizens. That existing prisons do not rehabilitate anybody, or produce lower rates of crime, or decrease recidivism, is beyond dispute. Would newer programs like increased staff for probation, or halfway houses, or intensive prison counseling, or liberalized bail accomplish these ends? Probably not. Research findings on the effectiveness of these procedures demonstrate all too unanimously that no one procedure has a better effect in reforming the criminal or lowering recidivism rates than any other. Social science has not reached the point of being able to fulfill these aims.

Yet if we look to more simple and realizable goals, if we employ such criteria as the degree of humanity and cruelty, or the levels of financial costs, or the kinds of structures we want to live with in a democratic society, we may fare a good deal better. In essence, if we recognize that we face a choice among evils, we may do more to ameliorate existing conditions than if we cling to fanciful notions of reform.

These considerations are immediately relevant to policy decisions we now confront. Ought we to build new and better equipped prisons, with better lighting, larger cells, more schoolrooms and workshops (as Attorney General Mitchell proposes)? Ought we at the same time to construct max-max-security prisons, ostensibly to bring more intensive treatment to the hard-core recidivist, while allowing inmates in other institutions to gain greater freedom of action (a plan now under consideration in New York State)? Those pressing for these modifications invariably cloak their arguments in the garb of reform: The hard-core recidivist will receive far more personal attention than before; he will be able to visit a prison psychiatrist for counseling and have the benefit of individual instruction; in new and more commodious prisons inmates will live more comfortably, master a trade, and return, without anger or frustration, to the community as diligent, law-abiding citizens. One suspects, with much justification, that this rhetoric is really an after-the-fact rationalization for a more straightforward urge to get tough with the criminal. But even in its own terms, the program is foolhardy. One psychiatrist per maxi-

mum security prison (as in the New York plan) is not going to rehabilitate anybody; indeed, given the state of the art, even 20 or 30 of them could not do the job. Nor are workshops and classrooms automatically going to turn convicts into respectable citizens. In the name of such illusory goals we ought not to invest thousands of dollars in prison structures. At best, these changes would be temporary and shaky supports for an already crumbling system. Ultimately, when their goals prove illusory, as they surely will, we will be back where we started with brutal, expensive, and increasingly illegitimate institutions.

Instead let us invest these funds in broadening probation, parole, bail, and halfway houses, not because they offer a hope of redeeming the criminal or of ridding our society of crime but because (a) they will do no worse than our present system in terms of prevention, and (b) the price we pay for them, in terms of human and financial and social costs, will be considerably lower. The sums saved on institutional expenditures could well be used to underwrite a national crime insurance program to compensate victims (a procedure already in limited operation in six states), or perhaps to increase the number of policemen on the beat. It might prove necessary to administer a few maximum-security prisons for recidivists, rapists, and murderers, but they would function admittedly as places of last resort, without any pretense of reform.

There is no magical plan for prison reform that can promise to reduce the number of criminals or the number of crimes. We know of no correction system that can deliver on such a promise. But that is no reason to continue to suffer our present arrangements. If we scale down our expectations and rely upon such basic standards as human decency and economic costs, we will be in a better position to consider the merits of innovation and decarceration.

37. INMATE PRIDE IN TOTAL INSTITUTIONS

ROLAND WULBERT

Reprinted from the American Journal of Sociology *71, no. 1 (July 1965): 1-9. Copyright © 1965 by the University of Chicago Press. Roland Wulbert is Assistant Professor of Sociology at Columbia University.*

■ Once an asylum, a total institution, is established it takes on a social life of its own, which social commentators have consistently described as inimical to "recovery," whether that be the reformation of a criminal or the return to health of a mental patient. The dynamics of these institutions seem to move readily in directions that are destructive to the very sense of self-respect, personal responsibility, and self-confidence that they are supposed to build. For those concerned with these institutions (specialists in penology or hospital administration, for example), much can be gained from determining those characteristics of their organization and routine that are most conducive to constructive rather than destructive and degrading operation. In this selection Wulbert presents some important generalizations about the relationship between social interaction in the institution and the psychological functioning of its inmates. The concept of total institution, as we have noted, derives from the work of Erving Goffman in *Asylums* (Anchor Books, 1961).

The literature on the characteristics of mental hospitals and patients is extensive. Representative work is available in Milton G. Greenblatt, Daniel J. Levinson, and Richard H. Williams, eds., *The Patient and the Mental Hospital* (Free Press, 1957); and A. H. Stanton and M. S. Schwartz, *The Mental Hospital* (Basic Books, 1954). For prisons the reader should consult Richard A. Cloward et al., eds., *Theoretical Studies in the Social Organization of the Prison* (Social Science Research Council, 1960); Donald Klemmer, *The Prison Community* (Holt, Rinehart & Winston, 1958); and Gresham M. Sykes, *The Society of Captives* (Princeton University Press, 1958). ■

THE INTERRELATIONS of customs and dimensions of social change in total institutions can be explained by inmate pride. The following analysis begins with social change in a mental hospital. Collective behavior and its antecedents are described multidimensionally and placed in their context of custom. Inmate pride is introduced as an explanatory concept and ultimately extended to prison riots and customs.

DIMENSIONS OF COLLECTIVE BEHAVIOR

Most analyses of collective behavior in mental hospitals speculate on, rather than demonstrate, the association of variables. As a rule, it is only after the disorder is well under way, or over, that it begins to interest researchers, who are thus unable to record changes in associated variables and so simply speculate about them. The data reported here can describe changes over time because, by chance, a survey of the patients had been completed just before the disturbance. Although the survey had not been designed to study collective behavior, relevant questions were repeated when order was reestablished. The two surveys, along with observations, hospital records, and informants' reports, show changes in ward structure over time.

The scene of the collective behavior was 2 male wards on the same floor of a large psychiatric hospital that draws most of its 2,400 patients from the Chicago metropolitan area and adjoining counties. Mental patients in these two wards have common activities, interact frequently, and are represented by one patient council. They are essentially one group and will be treated as such.

TABLE 37.1

DYNAMICS OF RULE VIOLATION: FREQUENCY
OF INMATE DEVIATION BEFORE, DURING,
AND AFTER DISORDER

	Rule Violations*						
	S	E	A	D	R	To-tal	In-cre-ment
Before disorder July 5-August 5)	1	0	0	0	0	1	
During disorder (August 6-13)	1	3	3	1	1	9	+8
After disorder (August 14-September 14)	0	0	0	0	0	0	−9

* S=suicide attempts; E=elopements attempted; A=
assault; D=destruction of property; R=refusal to obey
staff.

All communicative patients on the 2 wards were interviewed, 25 before the disturbance and 22 afterward; 20 patients were interviewed both times. The first survey had been completed about a week before the collective behavior began, and the second survey, initiated about half a week after the disorder ended, took a week to complete.

Table 37.1 shows the frequency of inmate deviation before, during, and after the disorder. Deviance increased sharply, by eight acts, in the second period and then decreased just as sharply in the third. The duration of patient council meetings also expressed disruption. Table 37.2 shows that patient council meetings were disrupted slightly before hospital rules were. In the second period, when rule violations were greatest, disruption of the patient council was also greatest. In this period the length of meetings decreased by 30 minutes. And, like rule violations, patient council meetings returned to normal in the third period, increasing in length by 25 minutes.

Other symptoms of disruption in the patient council were observed but not measured precisely. Attendance decreased suddenly. Many patients chose to stay out on work details or simply did not come. Participation decreased as a few patients increasingly dominated the meetings. The week before the height of the disruption there was a suggestion that the

meetings be discontinued. During a typical meeting some patients walk around, others hallucinate or manifest bizarre symptoms; an occasional speech or question betrays pathology. All three of these symptoms increased in frequency just before and during the disruption.

Patients spontaneously mentioned that they were becoming more dissatisfied with the meetings. These sentiments ceased after the disruption. The disorder also became a topic of conversation among staff members. They speculated on causes and said that they had not seen anything like it since moving into the present building.

In summary, disorder has been described in terms of a sudden increase in deviance, deterioration of patient council meetings, and recognition of these changes. Two facts are of special interest. First, all aggression was directed against fellow patients and not 1 of the 10 deviant acts (recorded in Table 37.1) was overt aggression against the staff. Second, disorder was unorganized. It consisted of isolated individual acts. There was no hint of group formation, of influence, or of concerted action.

Collective behavior was preceded by a period of unusually high turnover among patients and staff. For a long time the ward

TABLE 37.2

DYNAMICS OF PATIENT COUNCIL MEETINGS
LENGTH BEFORE, DURING, AND
AFTER DISORDER

	Length (Minutes)	Mean	Increment
Before disorder:			
July 3	40		
July 10	50	45	
July 17	40		
July 24	40		
Week before disorder:			
July 31	20		
During disorder:		15	−30
August 7	10		
After disorder:			
August 14	40		
August 21	40	40	+25
August 28	40		

personnel had been static. The same faces followed each other in the same order every day. Then things changed. Many people left, temporarily or permanently; others would soon follow. One of the two ward physicians had been on vacation for over two weeks before the episode of collective behavior, and the other left in the middle of it. A clinical psychologist, who was active in ward affairs, went on vacation at the beginning of the disorder. One head nurse had been on vacation for a week before the disruption began. The student nurses had left earlier; they had been well liked by patients. Ten patients had left just before the disruption or were about to leave. Four of them had been discharged, and another four, who were about to be discharged, were getting month-long leaves of absence or passes to go home every weekend. Patients knew who was about to be discharged and would mention it during interviews and informal talks. One of the 10 patients had transferred to another ward, and the 10th one was about to become an aide. Total turnover involved more than one-fourth of the patients.

Patients were asked, before and after the disorder, "Is a patient discharged when he has improved, or does he have to wait a long time?" "Long time" answers imply dissatisfaction with the hospital and evaluation of its discharge policies as unfair. Table 37.3 reveals that dissatisfaction decreased after the disorder. Disorder apparently consumes the dissatisfaction aroused by high turnover.

Informal social structure among patients also changed markedly during the episode of collective behavior. Before and after the dis-

TABLE 37.3
DEPRIVATION BEFORE AND AFTER WARD DISORDER*

| | No. Inmates Who Expected Time until Discharge To Be | | Total |
	long (dissatisfaction)	not long (satisfaction)	
Before disorder	15	5	20
After disorder	7	13	20

*$\phi = 0.40$;
ϕ/ϕ Max $= .40/.91 = 0.44$; $.025 > P > .010$.

order all communicative patients were asked: among patients, (1) who are best liked by other patients? (2) who contributes most to patient council meetings? (3) who has the most influence on other patients? Each respondent named as many patients as he wished. Every patient named at least once is a "leader." "Present leaders" are those currently on the floor, not to be discharged for at least a month. "Absent leaders" had either been discharged or would be within a month. Table 37.4 shows how the informal social structure of mental patients lagged behind reality. Before the collective behavior mental patients seemed to cling to absent leaders. Afterward absent leaders were replaced.

TABLE 37.4
INMATE LEADERSHIP CHOICES BEFORE AND AFTER WARD DISORDER*

	Number of Subjects	Mean Proportion' of Choices for Present Leaders
Before disorder	25	0.37
After disorder	22	0.80

*$t = 3.95$; $P < .001$.

This association between collective behavior and turnover is not an isolated findings. Although it has not figured in theoretical formulations, it has received brief mention. Miller remarks in passing that the informal patient leader had been discharged just before the outbreak of the disruption he studied in a mental hospital. In addition, there had been considerable turnover of physicians; staff members went on vacations, and "those remaining took on extra duties. . . . Two new patients had been admitted in close succession." Caudill notes that "just prior to the collective disturbance two key members of the patient group were discharged." Two new patients were admitted at the same time. Stanton and Schwartz mention the same pattern. Immediately before the increased deviation "there was a sharp influx of patients from other wards." And "alterations among the nursing staff contributed to the tension. Absenteeism increased . . . two central figures of the nursing staff were ill." The disruption studied by Boyd, Kegeles, and Green-blatt came during the "weekend slump" when the hospital was undermanned and staff was "reduced by at least two out of five."

The following picture of collective behavior and its antecedents emerges: Abnormally high patient and staff turnover is the initial impulse; turnover is depriving to patients, motivating dissatisfaction with the discharge system, reluctance to replace informal leaders, and collective behavior which is unorganized and characterized by aggression against fellow patients rather than staff. After the disturbance, dissatisfaction diminishes and informal leaders are replaced.

The problem now is to explain these facts. That is, not to answer simply (1) why is turnover depriving? but also (2) why is aggression directed against patients rather than staff? (3) why is mental patient collective behavior a mass rather than crowd action? (4) why are patient leaders replaced so slowly? Many theories can answer any one question, but the number that can answer all four is much smaller.

LACK OF INMATE PRIDE IN MENTAL HOSPITALS

In order to avoid the degrading name of "mental patient" without giving up the security of the hospital, inmates communicate that they are only passing through. But things are not so easy. People cannot be tourists just by saying so, not even mental patients. How can this tourist myth resist time? The answer is simple enough: it cannot. Then how do we account for it in mental hospitals? Again the answer is simple: Time does not pass in mental hospitals, and so there is no problem. Patients are moved through a well-developed routine. They see the same faces and do the same things with the same people in the same order every day. They have world enough and time. But there are flaws in this conspiracy to deny reality. Anguish arises when time's illusory immobility is threatened,

when the context—the pattern of roles, the sequence of activities, the people on the ward —alters, when the iceman comes.

Turnover symbolizes the passage of time. It forces reality on patients. Time has passed, and they are still in the hospital. How can they claim tourist status? The data in Table 37.3 suggest the deprivation of time's passage. And Table 37.4 implies that patients try to hold back the clock by not replacing absent leaders. They do everything in their power to preserve the illusion that their leaders have not left and that time has not passed. But they cannot avert the painful confrontation; they can only express it in an outbreak of collective behavior.

What is more, when disturbance does occur it will certainly be unorganized. In order to band together in some sort of corporate revolt, inmates must perceive a common interest, or at the very least they must feel that the results of corporate action are worth the membership costs of communicating a common identity. But if mental patients feel that nothing outweighs the avoidance of inmate status, common identity will not develop and collective behavior will be unorganized. Mental patients do not form a social contract when they are deprived because expressive costs exceed instrumental returns. Degree of inmate pride not only determines how collective behavior is organized; it also selects the objects of aggression. In addition to venting frustration, aggression against other inmates expresses alienation from them.

Low inmate pride accounts not only for the deprivation caused by staff and patient turnover but also for intrastatus aggression, the unorganized form of collective behavior, and the reluctance to replace absent leaders. This is not to say that motives other than presence or absence of inmate pride do not exist. Each dimension of collective behavior undoubtedly has multiple motivations. In all likelihood, aggression against patients expresses general frustration as well as alienation from public status, and discharge of leaders may very well mean to patients not only time elapsed but also broken friendships and loss of a means of controlling the hospital environment.

Low inmate pride should not be regarded as the only factor underlying collective behavior but as the most pervasive one.

Up to now discussion has centered on the functional integration of social change. Turnover is depriving, at least in part, because it threatens the tourist myth, and two responses to this threat—unorganized, internally aggressive collective behavior and reluctance to replace absent leaders—maintain alienation from inmate status. The next section turns from social change to mental hospital customs. If low inmate pride is actually a fundamental factor, then it should functionally integrate customs as well as dimensions of social change. If it does not, the validity of the inmate pride hypothesis is put in question. Each additional cultural component that the model accounts for increases its usefulness.

CUSTOMS IN MENTAL HOSPITALS

When they talk to outsiders for the first time—to social scientists, student nurses, new aides—most mental patients bring up their outside status. They talk about work, family, school, or anything to communicate that their hospital status is entirely temporary, accidental, a minor digression from their true careers. More directly, Dunham and Weinberg quote dozens of patients who say that they do not really belong in a mental hospital. Some patients customarily use patient council meetings to claim they have been hospitalized by mistake and demand to be released because they are not really crazy like all the others.

In the survey made before the disturbance, patients were asked, "What do you feel you have in common with other patients?" Over one-third of those who answered said they had nothing at all in common. What is more, those who said they did have something in common usually chose only the most general attributes. A frequent answer was, "We're all human." Patients would admit they had in common what they could not help sharing with humanity.

When asked, "Do you have more friends in this hospital or out?" over two-thirds said they had more friends outside. Even though their median length of hospitalization was over a year and a half, patients insisted on their connection to the outside. Quite often a patient would say that he had more friends on the outside and then add, "Well, *right now* I'm not seeing much of them," again communicating that his occupation of inmate status was temporary.

The organization of interaction among mental patients communicates their alienation from a common identity. As Goffman observes, the mental patient "may avoid talking to anyone, may stay by himself when possible, and may even be 'out of contact' or 'manic' so as to avoid ratifying any interaction that presses a politely reciprocal role upon him and opens him up to what he has become in the eyes of others."

In short, low inmate pride is manifest in low rates of interaction, alienation from other inmates, attachment to outsiders, and absence of attempts to raise inmate rank or proclaim its superiority. "Low inmate pride" is a central tendency of mental patients, which makes internal analysis possible. It follows from the preceding discussion that higher rates of interaction and attempts to raise mental patient rank or proclaim its superiority should be correlated because both manifest higher inmate pride. And this is just what Polansky et al. found. They scaled the amount of rights mental patients felt they should have and found that members of cliques demanded more rights than did nonmembers. This intra-institutional comparison supports the inmate pride hypothesis, as does the following inter-institutional comparison between mental hospitals and prisons.

INMATE PRIDE IN PRISONS

In 1952 and 1953 a wave of remarkably similar prison riots swept America. Prisoners would capture some building in the compound, hold guards captive, and refuse to come out until prison officials had agreed to meet their demands for better food, more time to talk to the parole board, freedom from brutality of guards, and investigation of the prison by the John Howard Agency. There were occasional escape attempts and general destructive riots, in which large numbers of prisoners, ostensibly ignited by something like finding salt in their coffee, would destroy everything they could. The most striking difference between collective outbursts in prisons and mental hospitals is the amount of group organization. Prisoners organize and develop leadership; they differentiate roles, lines of communication, and authority; they define themselves as a group and formulate goals and policy. Organized collective behavior is a manifestation of high inmate pride, and so, according to the previous derivation, it should be associated with customs which attempt to raise the rank of prisoners or proclaim their superiority. And again this is just what researchers have found.

Skyes and Messinger write, "Despite the number and diversity of prison populations, observers of such groups have reported only one strikingly pervasive value system . . . the maxims are usually asserted with great violence by the inmate population, sanctions ranging from ostracism to physical violence." The code contains five maxims: (1) be loyal to your class—the cons; (2) don't lose your head; (3) don't exploit inmates; (4) be tough; be a man; (5) guards are to be treated with constant suspicion and distrust. In any situation of conflict between officials and prisoners, the former are automatically in the wrong."

Ohlin says, "In the majority of prisons throughout the country the leaders among inmates are those who embody in clearest form antiadministration and anticonventional values." Cloward also finds that the charismatic prison leader is the right guy who "gains prestige from his fellows largely because he is able to elicit a deferential response from the authorities" against whom "he is capable of mobilizing and employing violence."

The research reported here on the mental hospital included observation, formal interviews, and informal talks. Not once was anything similar to the prison code mentioned. No such code has been reported in the literature on mental hospitals. Dunham and Weinberg, in their exhaustive account of norms and values in mental hospitals, record nothing like it.

In their code and choice of leaders, prisoners manifest higher regard for their status than do mental patients. Prisoners make little distinction between private and public status; they stress the heroic, manly, colorful aspects of inmate status. Mental patients accept a dishonorable definition and so communicate the alienation of their private selves from this public status through such customs as the tourist myth. Inmate pride is greater for prisoners than for mental patients, and so prisoners, unlike mental patients, will not avoid organized or externally aggressive collective behavior simply because it identifies them as prisoners.

The reminder above that degree of inmate pride refers to a central tendency, around which there is a good deal of variation. This also holds true for prisons, of course. We would expect to find differences not only among prisoners but also among prisons—for example, between custodial and therapeutic prisons. Thus some mental patients may have greater inmate pride than some prisoners. It is this sort of variation that encourages internal analysis.

The inmate pride model can be generalized under some conditions to the encompassing society. For instance, "decadence" is what Crane Brinton calls low status pride among a traditional elite. It is integrated with noncorporate activities, just as in mental hospitals and prisons. "When numerous and influential members of such a class begin to believe that they hold power unjustly . . . or that the beliefs they were brought up on are silly . . . they are not likely to resist successfully any serious attack on their social, economic, or political position."

Amount of inmate pride may change over time, making historical analysis indispensable. Themes in Caribbean literature reveal that an increase in organized external aggression (in terms of social revolt and rejection of European culture), marking their emergence from colonial status, was accompanied by islanders' increased commitment to public identity (Afro-Cubanism and *négritude*).

But even though similarities may be striking, the inmate pride model cannot be generalized mechanically from total institutions to more complex social structures. For one thing, interpretation of aggression becomes more difficult. Unlike total institutions, more complex societies are rarely composed of two mutually exclusive castes, and so aggression against one group might mean identification with any number of others. A factory worker whose answer to the question, "When business booms, does anyone get an unfair share of the profits?" is "the upper class," may not identify with the urban working class but rather with farmers or southerners.

SUMMARY

Mental patients, like other-world-oriented religionists and Chinoy's automobile workers, are alienated from their public status. This alienation, or low inmate pride, integrates customs and dimensions of collective behavior. Mental patients are away from home, in a hotel for transients. Turnover threatens to identify them with their inmate status, but so would organized action and aggression against staff, and so a period of unusually high turnover precipitates a crisis culminating in unorganized, internally aggressive collective behavior. For the same reason, customs are characterized by low rates of interaction and attempts by patients to communicate their alienation from each other. Conversely, in such total institutions as prisons, where inmate pride runs high, customs communicating the worth of inmates and organized, externally aggressive collective behavior are associated.

38. ORGANIZATIONAL GOALS AND INMATE ORGANIZATION

BERNARD B. BERK

Reprinted from the American Journal of Sociology *71, no. 5 (March 1966): 523-34. Copyright © 1966 by the University of Chicago Press. Bernard B. Berk is a Lecturer in the Department of Sociology, University of California, Santa Barbara.*

■ This selection continues the examination, begun in Selection 37, of the relationship between the organizational characteristics and imperatives of the total institution and the life and responses of the inmates. Here the subject is prisons, more particularly variations among prisons as a consequence of institutional ideology oriented to treatment or custody and in response to differing patterns of formal and informal organization.

The readings listed for Selection 37 apply here also. The role of treatment versus custodial versus other ideologies is discussed in considerable detail for psychiatric institutions in Anselm Strauss et al., *Psychiatric Ideologies and Institutions* (Free Press, 1964). The study Berk replicates here is reported in Oscar Grusky, "Organizational Goals and the Behavior of Informal Leaders," *American Journal of Sociology* 65, no. 1 (July 1959): 59-67. A similar study dealing with juvenile institutions is reported in David Street, "Inmates in Custodial and Treatment Settings," *American Sociological Review* 30 (February 1965): 40-56; see also Donald Cressey, ed., *The Prison: Studies in Institutional Organization and Change* (Holt, Rinehart & Winston, 1961). For a study of "prisonization" see Stanton Wheeler, "Socialization in Correctional Communities," *American Sociological Review* 26 (October 1961): 697-712. ■

WHILE SOCIOLOGICAL INTEREST in informal organization dates back to the time of Cooley, there has been little exploration of the relationships between formal and informal organization. Earlier research efforts have been more concerned with documenting the existence of informal organization and demonstrating that it had an impact upon organizational functioning than with trying to establish relationships between it and the organizational context. Different conclusions have been reached in regard to its contribution to the formal organization's ability to achieve its goals, with Roethlisberger and Dixon highlighting its subversive aspect in limiting productivity in economic organizations, while Shils and Janowitz suggest it can facilitate the goals of military organizations by developing social cohesion. Reconciling these findings rests upon the notion that organizations with different goals, structures, and contexts should produce different patterns of informal organization, and informal organization would also have different effects upon the functioning of such diverse types of organizations. What is needed is specification of relationships between the parameters of formal and informal organization and identification of those aspects of organizations which generate oppositional informal organization. By limiting this investigation to one particular type of organization and by examining variation in one of its parameters—its goals—it is hoped some clarification of the problems may emerge.

Specifically, this paper examines relationships between organizational goals and informal organization in a variety of correctional institutional settings. The study had major objectives. First, we sought to replicate Grusky's study of the consequences of treatment goals for the informal organization of prison inmates. Second, we were concerned with extending existing formulations concerning the relationship between the formal and informal structure of total institutions and, in particular, the conditions which generate informal organizations that are fundamentally opposed to the existing administration.

DESCRIPTION OF RESEARCH SITES

The three institutions selected for study were minimum-security prisons which differed in their emphasis of treatment goals. The criteria used to determine the extent to which treatment goals were dominant were: (1) the presence of a full-time counselor or of treatment personnel; (2) the existence of a rehabilitative program; and (3) the active implementation of educational, vocational, or other auxiliary-type programs. The three prisons (to be called Benign, Partial, and Lock) were ranked on a continuum ranging from a strong treatment orientation to a strong custodial orientation.

Camp Benign ranked as the most treatment-oriented institution, as all three criteria were present. In addition, it was the smallest, containing only 97 inmates. This prison was characterized by considerable staff-inmate interaction, maximal opportunities for counseling and guidance, and a sincere effort directed at changing the inmate. Camp Partial was slightly larger (127 inmates) and had both a full-time counselor and a limited educational program. However, it did not have an official treatment program. Treatment techniques employed in this institution tended to be subverted to custodial ends, such as securing inmate conformity. Camp Lock, which had 157 inmates, was the most custodially oriented institution, the sole rehabilitative program being an Alcoholics Anonymous group. Its primary goal was containment, and there was little official pretense or concern about treatment or rehabilitation. The officials sought to run an institution which attracted as little attention as possible from the community.

THE FINDINGS

INMATE ATTITUDES

The first investigated was the differences in attitudes of inmates of the treatment and custodial prisons. Numerous observers have asserted that the relationship between guards and inmates in custodial institutions is characterized by hostility, mistrust, suspicion, and fear, promulgated by both the official dictates of the prison and the informal norms among the inmates. Grusky, Vinter and Janowitz, and others have argued that a positive and cooperative type of staff-inmate relationship is a prerequisite for and a consequence of treatment goals. This is due primarily to accepting attitudes on the part of the staff, the overall replacement of formal controls by more informal ones, and the general reduction of inmate deprivations.

Grusky found support for the hypothesis that more positive attitudes among inmates are found in treatment rather than in custodial institutions. By comparing attitudinal responses of inmates in three institutions, each situated in a different position along the treatment-custodial continuum, we were able to test this same hypothesis more carefully than could be done in the original case study.

As in the original study, inmate attitudes in three areas were examined: attitudes toward the prison, staff, and treatment program. Table 38.1 demonstrates a positive relationship between favorable inmate response toward the prison and the degree of development of its treatment goals. Where about 6 out of 10 of Benign's inmates were

TABLE 38.1

INMATE ATTITUDES TOWARD THE PRISON, STAFF, AND PROGRAM

	Benign (per cent)	Partial (per cent)	Lock (per cent)
Attitudes toward the prison:			
Favorable (Scale types I-II)	63.1	48.2	39.1
Attitudes toward the staff:			
Favorable (Scale types I-II	44.3	29.2	23.4
Attitudes toward the program:			
Favorable (Item response "yes")	88.8	81.9	74.8
N =	(95)	(124)	(138)

positively oriented toward the prison (63 percent), not quite 5 of 10 of Partial's inmates (48 percent) and less than 4 of 10 of the inmates at Lock (39 percent), the most custodially oriented prison of the three, had positive feelings toward their institutions. A similar pattern is revealed concerning attitudes toward the staff. At Benign, 44 percent of the men had favorable attitudes toward the staff, whereas only 29 percent at Partial and 23 percent at Lock were as positively oriented toward the staff. The third area of inmate attitudes investigated were those toward existing programs. These attitudes were also found, as expected, to be related to the goals of the prison. At Benign, 89 percent of the men felt that the program had helped them, as compared with 82 percent of the men at Partial, and 75 percent of the men at Lock who expressed similar views. Attitudes toward the programs were the most positive and reflected, in part, the salience of the program, which, in turn, was due to the official support for treatment goals. In short, Grusky's original hypothesis was strongly confirmed. Significant differences were found between the prison which was most custodially oriented and the one most treatment oriented.

THE EFFECTS OF SOCIALIZATION

In order to give a sharper test to the proposition, the length of residence in the institution was held constant. In this manner, the consequences of official socialization could be examined. It would be expected that the longer the inmate was exposed to the values and programs of the prison, the more likely he would be influenced by them; that is, inmates who have spent a long time in the prison should most clearly reflect the impact of the prison on their attitudes, and those who have been there only a short time should be least affected.

The data show a strong relationship between attitude toward the staff and length of time spent in the prison. Inmates who had spent longer times in the custodially oriented prison were more likely to hold negative attitudes than those who had only been there a few months, whereas the reverse was true at the treatment oriented prison where inmates who had spent a long time in the prison were more likely to hold positive attitudes than negative ones. When those inmates at Benign who had spent fewer than 3 months in the prison were compared with those who had spent more than 8 months there, we found that only about 1 of 3 (35 percent) of the former, as contrasted with about half (56 percent) of the latter, fell into the most favorable scale type. At Camp Lock the reverse was found true. The proportion of positive responses dropped sharply from 27 percent of the inmates who had been there less than 3 months to less than 9 percent of those who had been there 8 or more months. Camp Partial exhibited a mild positive influence, reflecting its intermediate position.

The same general relationship is revealed with respect to attitudes toward the prison, but not quite as clearly. The proportion of inmates at Lock who were favorably oriented decreased slightly from 36 percent of those whose stay was short term to 31 percent of those having a longer term stay in the prison. In contrast, the percentage of favorable responses increased at Benign from 50 percent of those having less than 3 months' experience to 64 percent of those who had 8 or more months in prison. However, in both prisons, inmates with 4-7 months' experience were most negative.

INFLUENCE OF OTHER VARIABLES

Before any conclusions could be drawn from these findings, it was necessary to control for other relevant variables, since an important obstacle to studies of this nature is that inmates are not usually randomly assigned to treatment institutions. This was true of this study as well, in that inmates at Benign were younger and likely to have been less serious offenders. However, this type of selectivity does not appear to have accounted for the results obtained in this study.

Age. Initially, it might have been argued

that the older age of the inmates at Lock and Partial would be sufficient to account for the more negative attitudes found there. Our findings, on the contrary, show age to be inversely related to negative attitude at both Lock and Benign, with the younger inmates in both camps more likely to hold negative attitudes. No difference was found at Partial. Furthermore, young inmates were more positive at Benign than were their counterparts at Lock. The same was true for older inmates. This would suggest that selectivity in regard to age would operate against the hypothesis.

Type of offender. It similarly could have been argued that inmates at Partial and Lock were more experienced and hardened criminals, well indoctrinated in the ways of crime and would, therefore, exhibit more negative attitudes. We may ask, first, whether this is true, and, second, if so, whether this factor is large enough to account for the differences obtained between the prisons. Again, the findings show, in contradiction to what is commonly believed, that the more serious offenders, by a variety of measures, did not have more negative attitudes. On the contrary, these two variables were generally unrelated. In the few cases where differences were found, they were small and variable. Furthermore, the direction of this relationship was reversed in the treatment institution, where the more serious offenders were more likely to hold more positive attitudes than the less serious offenders. And, finally, when comparable groups of types of offenders were compared in the various camps they were more positive in their attitudes at Benign than at Lock.

It would appear that the selectivity in regard to age and type of offender would not be sufficient to account for the differences obtained in this study, and certainly could not account for the differences between Partial and Lock, since there was little difference in the types of inmates sent to those two camps. It should be pointed out, however, that inmates at Benign were more positive during the early period than inmates at the other camps, which may have been partly due to

a selectivity, or may have resulted from the camp's having had an initial positive impact on inmate attitudes. In any case, whatever differences existed in the nature of the inmates in the organization initially as a result of differential recruitment procedures, inmates became more positive over time in the treatment institution and more negative in the custodial one, reflecting the differential impact of the organization upon its members.

By these tests, then, it appears that, regardless of any selectivity in input, the differences between prisons were responsible for attitudinal differences.

INFORMAL ORGANIZATION

These attitudinal differences between prisons reflected major differences in the nature of the informal organization among prison inmates.

Support for this assertion is reflected in the finding that attitudes of inmates were related to the degree of their involvement in the inmate subculture. Attitudes appeared to be acquired as a result of informal socialization and participation in prison subculture and reflected those informal standards held by its members.

Involvement and participation in the subculture was measured by the number of friendship choices the inmate received from other inmates. Three types of inmates were distinguished: the uninvolved or isolate who received no choices, the moderately involved who received from one to three choices, and the highly involved who received four or more friendship choices. At Benign isolates were the most negative and the highly involved inmates the most positive in their attitudes toward the prison. At Lock, the reverse was true with the highly involved inmates the most negative and the uninvolved inmates the most positive in their attitudes. At Partial, negative attitudes were related to both high and low involvement in the subculture. It is not immediately clear why moderately involved inmates at Partial were more positive than isolates. In all three prisons, however, favorableness of attitude was related to degree of involvement with the informal organization.

INFORMAL LEADERSHIP

Further evidence of the impact of custodial and treatment goals on informal organization among prison inmates was found in the kinds of attitudes held by informal leaders in the various prisons.

Both Schrag's and Grusky's studies dealt with the relationship between leaders and organizational goals. Schrag asserted that leaders were uniformly selected from among the most negative inmates. In contrast, Grusky hypothesized that orientation of the leader would vary with the type of total institution; specifically, informal leaders in treatment institutions were seen as more likely to be cooperative than were their counterparts in custodially oriented prisons.

Consistent with Grusky's hypothesis, leaders at Benign were more positive in their attitudes than were leaders at Partial, who, in turn, were more positive than those at Lock. However, this might have been true for any sample of inmates, because inmates were, as a whole, more positive at Benign than at Lock. By comparing the leaders with the nonleaders within each prison, a more precise test of this relationship was obtained. Leaders were more positive than the nonleaders at Benign, while the reverse was true at Lock, where the leaders were more negative than the nonleaders. This relationship was found to hold both for attitudes toward the prison and the institution's programs.

OBSERVATIONS ABOUT INFORMAL ORGANIZATION

THE FUNCTION OF INFORMAL ORGANIZATION IN TOTAL INSTITUTIONS

Having replicated Grusky's study and substantiated the hypothesis, we sought to develop a fuller explanation of the findings. Inmate attitudes reflect the nature of inmate subcul-ture and informal organization, which, in turn, is conditioned by formal organizational characteristics, such as the formal structure and the official objectives.

Informal organization develops in prison because: (1) inmates are isolated from society; (2) institutionalization generates common problems of adjustment, which require cooperation for their solution while simultaneously providing a situation with opportunity for effective interaction with others similarly situated; and (3) inmates are members of a formal organization, which by its very nature as a system of action can never fully anticipate or coordinate all behavior through the formal system alone; hence, informal organization serves to close the gaps of the formal organization.

Two kinds of informal organization have been identified in the prisons studied—one supportive of the official structure and the other in opposition to it. We submit that the goal of treatment encourages the development of the former and the goal of custody the latter.

Inmate subcultures develop as solutions to the problems and deprivations experienced by inmates in the prison situation. They would, therefore, differ in their form and content as the nature of the problems experienced by inmates, particularly those created by the institutional experience itself, differ. The two different types of informal organization developed because the inmate subsystem performed contrasting functions in the treatment and custodial institutions.

Two reasons may be suggested to explain the character of the inmate subculture in the custodial institution; first, the problems faced by inmates tend to be more severe there; in addition, inmates perceive the custodial institution itself to be responsible for their problems. As a result, they band together in opposition to the prison and its administration, which they see as the source of their frustrations. Consequently, inmate subcultures tend to become more and more dominated by the values of professional criminals which already emphasize a strict demarcation between the guards and inmates, since these groups are seen as fundamentally in opposition to one another.

The emergence of this subculture compounds an already difficult problem—a central concern, in fact, of the custodial institution—that of maintaining social control within the prison. Since techniques for insuring conformity are inadequate, guards resort to various methods of accommodation and bargaining for conformity with the means available to them. One method, as Sykes points out, is to "buy compliance at the cost of tolerating deviance." In return for the guards overlooking selected infractions of the rules, inmates are expected to comply with the rest. In this fashion, inmates begin to regulate their own behavior and, in so doing, begin to fulfill, in part, the formal organization's task of maintaining internal order. The more effectively they are able to exert control over their behavior, the more advantageous is their bargaining position vis-a-vis the guards—a process which itself has a further consolidating effect upon inmate subculture. In this manner, inmates are able to gain some degree of freedom from the demands and pressures of the formal organization, thereby increasing the relative amount of control they can exercise over the conditions of their existence. This newly gained mastery over their environmental conditions is, however, illusory. It would appear that they have merely traded their previous situation and its attendant deprivations for subjugation to an even more despotic ruling group—other inmates who have less compunctions and fewer limitations about the use of force and violence to gain compliance with their ends. Thus, in reality, freedom is usually only temporary, as inmate leaders quickly replace the official demands for conformity with new demands for conformity to new rules which sustain their dominance.

In contrast to this picture of informal organization in custodial institutions, we can view the development of informal organization in treatment institutions. While inmate organization can also be found in treatment institutions, it does not generally take on an oppositional character. It does not simply because many of the psychological deprivations of imprisonment have been reduced, and a shift in patterns of control has occurred. Inmates are treated with more respect by the organization, and as a result the institution is not perceived by inmates to be totally against them or antithetical to their interests. In addition, the treatment institution is more flexible in regard to its rules, and treatment needs of inmates are considered in its demands for conformity. Furthermore, in its attempt to regulate behavior, formal methods of controls are replaced by more informal ones, thus reducing resentment and hostility. This leads to a greater tolerance in the range of inmate conformity and, concomitantly, "control" becomes less important in the hierarchy of organization objectives. Accordingly, there is little payoff from the administration for inmates' regulation of their own behavior.

Selected aspects of the formal organization's structure also have an impact on informal organization. Particularly in total institutions, the formal authority structure serves as a model for the informal. The custodially oriented prison, which is usually highly centralized, tends to produce a similar type of informal inmate leadership; for such an adaptation serves, on the one hand, to strengthen official control and administration of the prison and, on the other, to stabilize inmate relations by focusing attention on the deprivations inflicted by the authorities. Because inmate subculture there is dominated by criminal values emphasizing a strict demarcation between guards and inmates, informal leadership must thereby justify itself by securing special concessions from the oppressors, the "screws," in return for which the leaders prevent their men from stepping too far out of line. The typical inmate in such a situation is confronted with few alternatives and usually accepts the values and the leadership as it is presented to him, thereby perpetuating the subculture.

The inmate subsystems are seen as performing within their respective institutions different functions which, as we have seen, are directly linked to the goals of the prison. In the custodial prison, even though oppositional and subversive to the organization, it also functioned to assist it in the maintenance of internal order by regulating inmate behavior, though this is usually at the cost of the "corruption of the formal authority system." In contrast, control of inmate behavior was not a primary function of informal organization in the treatment institution. Informal organization there was more compatible with the formal organization and was more oriented toward meeting the particular needs of inmates and integrating and coordinating their behavior.

The functioning of informal leaders was, in turn, directly linked to the functions performed by the inmate subsystem, and, as a consequence, the informal leaders' main task in the custodial prison was one of exercising control over the behavior of other inmates. In order to effectively implement this end, the informal leadership employed the same techniques as the formal organization and developed a highly consolidated and centralized power structure. And, like the formal organization, it also relied upon coercion and force, rather than on consensus or cooperation, to insure conformity.

In contrast, the informal leaders in the treatment institution, because the treatment goal allowed for a broader range of inmate adaptation, performed a variety of functions depending on the particular needs of the inmates, and functioned more as coordinators and integrators of behavior rather than as controllers, as they did in the custodial prison. Not only did the informal leaders play very different roles in the two types of prisons, but techniques of leadership differed as well, since the inmate subsystem in the treatment institution tended to be based more upon consensus and cooperation than was true of the custodial prison.

These speculations led to a new hypothesis about the structure and functioning of informal leadership in the different types of prisons. As we have pointed out, one of the techniques for maintaining order in the custodial prison was the *centralization of control* by informal leadership. Because this function was less important for the inmate subsystem

in the treatment institution, it was hypothesized that the more treatment oriented the prison, the less centralized the informal leadership structure would be and the proportionately greater number of inmates who would emerge as top leaders.

The data supported this hypothesis. At Benign, 9.3 percent of the inmates were chosen as top leaders (that is, received 9 or more choices), while at Partial 6.3 percent were chosen, compared with only 1.3 percent of the inmates at Lock. When inmates were asked: "Who were leaders?" similar results were obtained. At Benign 43 percent of the inmates were named, compared with 38 percent at Partial and 23 percent at Lock. Both measures indicated greater concentration of power and centralization of control in the custodial prison.

A second technique adopted by inmate leaders in the custodial prison to control inmate behavior was the use of coercion to secure conformity and to maintain power. This led to a hypothesis dealing with types of persons likely to rise to positions of leadership or influence in the two types of prisons. Because *control* was an important function of the inmate leaders in the custodial prison, individuals disposed toward such behavior would be more likely to rise to positions of leadership there than would be true of treatment prisons where a more charismatic, socioemotional, or consensus oriented type of leader would be expected to develop. Therefore, it was hypothesized that leaders in the custodial institution would be more authoritarian, reflecting their "tough-minded" orientation toward the use of power, and would be "less well liked" due to their reliance upon coercion and emphasis upon control than leaders in treatment institutions. Support for this hypothesis comes from the finding that leaders were selected from the most authoritarian inmates at Lock, whereas the reverse was true at Benign, where leaders were selected from the least authoritarian inmates. Not only was the leadership structure more decentralized at Benign but the leadership positions also were occupied there by less authoritarian persons. Furthermore, leaders at Benign were less authoritarian than those at Partial, who, in turn, were less authoritarian than the leaders found at Lock. No difference in authoritarianism was found between the general population of inmates at the three prisons. In addition to their being less authoritarian, the leaders at Benign were liked better, were friendlier, and were more approachable by other inmates than was true of the leaders at Lock. This style of leadership is reflected in the findings that leaders at Benign were more likely to be chosen by other inmates as "well liked," a "best buddy," and as someone with whom they could discuss their personal problems than was true of the leaders at Camp Lock. Camp Partial once again was found to exhibit an intermediate position with regard to its leaders.

SUMMARY AND CONCLUSIONS

The purpose of this study was twofold: (1) to replicate a study conducted by Grusky; and (2) to examine the consequences of treatment and custodial goals upon the inmate subsystem within correctional institutions, wih particular emphasis on the conditions generating oppositional informal organization. Three areas of concern were inmate attitudes, the effect of socialization, and the development of informal leadership.

1. The findings on the whole supported Grusky's major hypothesis: Inmates were more positive in their attitudes toward the institution, staff, and programs in the treatment institution than those in the custodial one. Furthermore, they became more positive or negative with the length of time they spent in the prison, depending upon the type of organizational goal, thereby suggesting that it was the prison experience which was primarily responsible for the development of negative attitudes.

2. Differences between prisons were found to be related to differences in inmate organization. Two facts suggested this: first, attitudes were found to be related to degree of involvement with inmate organization; second, leaders' attitudes were found to vary systematically with the prison's goals, being more positive in the treatment institution and more negative in the custodial one.

3. The informal leadership structure was also found to be more centralized in the custodial institution in an attempt to maintain more effective control over inmate behavior. The informal leaders among the inmates played different roles, depending upon organizational goals and contexts; and these roles were directly linked to the function of the inmate subculture within the prison. Leaders in the custodial prison were also found to be more authoritarian and less well liked than leaders in the treatment prison, reflecting the differences in their roles.

The goal of "custody," with its concomitant centralized and formal authority structure and increased deprivations for inmates, contributed significantly to the development of the hostile informal organization in the custodial prison. The disenfranchisement of inmates from possible rewards of the institution encouraged the development of negative attitudes and a hostile informal leadership.

39. THE PROSAIC SOURCES OF PRISON VIOLENCE

HANS W. MATTICK

This selection first appeared as one of a series of Occasional Papers *for the Law School, University of Chicago, March 15, 1972. It had been presented at a symposium on law and order sponsored by the Law Alumni-Association of Los Angeles in February 1972. Hans W. Mattick is Professor of Criminal Justice and the Director of the Center for Research in Criminal Justice at the University of Illinois at Chicago Circle. He served as the Sociologist-Actuary at Stateville Penitentiary, Joliet, Illinois for three years, and as the Assistant Warden of the Cook County Jail, Chicago, Illinois for four years. He is the author of many papers dealing with crime and corrections. Please contact him with any questions concerning the use of this material.*

■ Problems of prisons have been recognized among professionals and those with a serious interest in various kinds of social reform from the 19th century onward, as Rothman showed in Selection 36, but in recent times the general public's attention to the problem of the prison as an inhuman institution came as a result of a wave of prison riots in the early 1970s. In this selection Mattick relates some of the currents in the outside world concerned with the civil rights revolution and the rise of militancy to the constant instigations to violence built into the way prisons ordinarily operate. He shows that far from being a difficult-to-explain phenomenon, or simply the result of the liberal permissiveness of our time, prison riots have their genesis in the constant and inevitable characteristics of large, repressive institutions. ■

IT IS, PERHAPS, gratuitous to assert that those who have been convicted of breaking the law are most in need of having respect for the law demonstrated to them. We are, moreover, a generous people who are fond of the notion that the law includes more than a narrow legalism, ". . . for the letter killeth, but the spirit giveth life." In that view, which we all share in our more virtuous moments, the law approaches the Platonic ideal of the good, the true, and the beautiful. It is a wonderful vision where the law embodies all that is moral, all that is humane, all that is decent, and all that is civilized. But, in the age of Pendleton, Attica, San Quentin, and all the tragic rest, it may be instructive to inquire how some of those who act on our behalf have sometimes demonstrated respect for the law to those who have been convicted of breaking the law.

It may also be instructive to try to trace some of the correlates of prison violence— what are popularly referred to as "the causes" of violence—and to do it in such a way as to transcend the usual banalities. Neither the simpleminded conspiracy theories, involving inside or outside agitators, that the old-line penal administrators are so quick to espouse nor the standard complaints that inmates put forward during the course of riots are in themselves, sufficient explanations. These are important and, perhaps, necessary conditions, but they are secondary because they are constants in the prison situation. They have been present from the beginning of our experience with incarceration, and they are present today, but prison violence fluctuates sporadically and independently of these constants. Much more fundamental is a contradictory complex of utilitarian and religious ideas of 18th- and 19th-century origin, which have been slowly debased into a melange of 20th-century "high school thought," and now serve as the basis for our penal policy. It is, for the most part, a policy of isolation and punishment, accompanied by the rhetoric of rehabilitation, which results in the chronic underfinancing, inadequate staffing, deflected sexuality, and general lack of resources and poverty of imagination that characterizes our prisons and jails. But these too have been constants for the past 200 years and cannot, of themselves, explain sporadic fluctuations in prison violence. If such conditions were both necessary and sufficient, the Nazi concentration camps would have been less one-sided in their violence and in a continuous state of revolt. We know that was not the case. To try to explain prison violence, we must penetrate below the surface and get to more fundamental structures and processes.

The massacre at Attica has captured the public imagination, at least for a little while; but as bloody as it was, it is by no means the most calculated use of deadly force in a prison disturbance in recent years. That dubious distinction belongs to Pendleton. One can understand the fear, anger, and disorganization at Attica, with the lives of hostages seemingly at stake and no clear chain of command to control the situation, without condoning the tragic consequences, but there can be no moral justification for what happened at Pendleton. A short account of "the Pendleton incident" was given in the January-February 1970 issue of the *N.C.C.D. News,* an organ of the National Council on Crime and Delinquency.

According to Bruce Nelson, of the *Los Angeles Times,* on September 26, 1969, "12 white men fired repeated volleys of buckshot through a fence [at the Indiana State Reformatory] at young black men who were lying on their stomachs. They killed one and wounded 46. Very few people around the country seemed to notice." Shortly before the shooting, several hundred inmates had congregated in a fenced-in recreation area. They had several demands, including the right to read black literature and to wear their hair in the "Afro" style. Their most important demand was the release of four black inmates who, for unclear reasons, had been isolated. . . . The guards told inmates in the recreation area to leave the vicinity. Many, including all the white inmates, did so. The black inmates asked to present their grievances to [the Superintendent who] refused to talk to the inmates. On the other side of a chain-link fence were 11 white guards and at least one vocational teacher, dressed in riot helmets and carrying loaded shotguns, according to Nelson. The confrontation continued for about 10 to 15 minutes. No attempt was made to disperse the crowd with tear gas, smoke bombs or nearby fire equipment. The guards fired warning shots and then, at the command of the Captain . . . the guards began firing through the fence. . . . One witness said that some of the men were trying to rise from the ground, raising their hands in a gesture of surrender, but were told by the guards, "You've had your chance," and were shot down. After the shooting, the men were told to leave the blood-spattered court, and did so, carrying the wounded. Two men were left lying on the pavement. One of the two . . . was dead. Of the 46 wounded, estimates of those seriously injured run from eight to twenty."

It may be added that a second inmate died about five months later, and although this story was covered in the *Los Angeles Times* some 3,000 miles away, the Chicago newspapers, only 170 miles away, failed to mention it. For sheer coldbloodedness, Pendleton far surpasses the emotion-packed atmosphere of Attica.

Such seemingly one-sided incidents of prison violence, unless they are directed against the authorities, receive very uneven news coverage and slip easily from the memory if, indeed, they ever entered it. But that does not mean they are rare occurrences. Perhaps a more recent "incident," that happened after Pendleton and before Attica, will help reinforce this point. The following account was given in the April 1971 issue of *Civil Liberties,* an organ of the American Civil Liberties Union.

The mass beatings and shootings of inmates at a Florida prison have led to a massive A.C.L.U. lawsuit alleging violations of federal civil rights law and state law. . . . On February 12, about 500 prisoners were peacefully assembled in the prison yard by order of the prison officials. Guards and other officers, according to the complaint, fired on them "at point blank range," with absolutely no warning or provocation. The guards then fired into the windows of occupied cells. Five days of beatings and tear gassing of prisoners followed. At one point, officers opened fire into the windows of the prison hospital.

It might be added that February 12th in 1971 was a Friday, followed by a weekend of Saturday and Sunday, which, combined with an "emergency," is the best of all reasons to close down an institution and keep all outsiders out. A great deal can be done to prepare an institution for public scrutiny in three days.

Again, not a very pretty story and, like the affairs at Pendleton and Attica, not yet finally resolved in the courts. But, if we waited upon court determination before such matters received any comment, some of the most significant events of our time would have years of silence before they came to public notice. The Chicago Panther Party raid, the Kent and Jackson State killings, and the My Lai incident are typical examples. However the blame for violence at Pendleton and Attica may ultimately be fixed, prison violence is clearly not a simple one-sided affair, with the inmates always aggressing against their keepers. Moreover, although we had serious prison disturbances in both Ohio and Oregon in 1968, and two earlier cycles in the early 1950s and the late 1920s, the massive use of deadly force against groups of prisoners in the last three or four years seems to be a new development.

One would have thought that we could have taken notice sooner that something was seriously amiss in the prison system of the United States when such clear desperation signals as the following were manifest to many public and private observers over the past 40 years. (1) In 1968, the celebrated Davis "Report on Sexual Assaults in the Philadelphia Prison System and Sheriffs' Vans" was published. (2) In 1967, the President's Crime Commission, among other things, again revealed the appalling state of American prisons and jails. (3) Earlier in the 1960s, at the congresses of the American Correctional Association, there was some desultory, but subterranean, discussion of the novel punishment methods being used in Arkansas, Florida, and Illinois prisons. In Arkansas, the infamous "Tucker Telephone," a hand-operated electric generator that was attached to the genitals of prisoners for punishment purposes, was in frequent use. In Florida, at Raiford Prison, a new use for salt was discovered. Nude inmates, cuffed hand and foot through their cell bars, were seated in piles of salt for periods of 72 hours without relief. In Illinois' Sheridan Reformatory, the members of the inmate boxing team were being used as an indirect disciplinary method, while "shock-therapy" was being converted into punishment at the Menard Psychiatric Division. (4) In the 1950s, the inmates at Rock Quarry Prison in Georgia were breaking each other's legs with 20 pound sledgehammers to achieve transfers, and at Angola Penitentiary in Louisiana prisoners were crippling themselves for life by cutting their Achilles' tendons in a vain attempt to call attention to their conditions of imprisonment. (5) In 1931, the Wickersham Commission revealed the appalling state of American prisons and jails. (6) That was the year after 317 inmates of the Ohio State Penitentiary died, locked into their cells, in the course of a fire, said to have been set by rioting inmates, although there is some debate about whether the riot began before or after the fire. But enough is, perhaps, too much. It is clear that violence is no stranger to the prison environment.

With the potential for violence being such a characteristic feature of prison life, it may be a vain pursuit to seek for developmental patterns and explanations in what appears to be a constant. If there is a "pattern," it is a subtle and emergent process that must be stated in tentative terms. Nevertheless, looking back over the past 40 years, prison violence, like a huge, malignant amoeba, seems to have both shape and direction.

There is, to begin with, a change in the proportionate distribution of violence among the wounders and the wounded. In the earlier period (1930-1960), most of the violence was more securely contained within the walls and consisted, for the most part, of assaults between inmates. Then, in descending order of frequency, there were assaults between keepers and kept, self-mutilations by inmates, and a few suicides. Except for a few mass disturbances that came to public notice, with few casualties but some property damage, little systematic information about intramural violence exists for the early period.

In the later period (since 1960), self-mutilations seem to have diminished, and both suicides and ambiguous deaths, and the proportion of altercations between inmates and guards have increased. Rebellious inmates have also made more strenuous and self-conscious attempts to communicate their grievances beyond the walls and have begun to find a constituency there. This is, in part, a natural development of the more general civil rights movement and a reflection on the cumulative number of ex-prisoners in the free community who maintain an interest in prison affairs. For example, every year about 70,000 prisoners leave the prisons and about 3 million persons pass through local jails; to these must be added the increasing numbers of convicted persons being placed on probation, residents of halfway houses and prerelease centers, persons in community treatment programs, and organized groups of ex-prisoners, like the Fortune Society, which are multiplying rapidly. The guards, too, have begun to seek extramural support for their grievances in the form of incipient unionization, associational alliances with police organizations, and attempts to influence civil service regulations.

Population shifts and changes in sentencing procedures have also had an impact on prison violence. Geographically, there seems to have been a slow migration of prison violence in a northerly and westerly direction, as White racism has manifested itself in heretofore less tested regions. The southern prisons, in the earlier period, had a much greater tolerance for violence and a more apathetic public audience for what went on among the nether classes in the prisons, while violence that came to public notice in the North tended to generate more public indignation in passing. Thus, while northern prisons got blacker and blacker, incident to Negro migration, and as the increasing use of probation tended to weed out the less violence prone and more stable prisoners of both races, an exacerbated level of racial conflict was added to the normal level of violence in the northern prisons, while southern prisons were still segregated and able to shield their normal level of violence from adverse public scrutiny. The net effect of these population shifts, changes in sentencing practices and differences in public attitudes was to increase the actual and perceived amount of violence in northern and western prisons, while the amount of violence, actual and perceived, in southern prisons, was largely masked. Moreover, while racial conflict between guards and prisoners has a long contributory history to prison violence, with the inmates getting much the worst of it, as active recruitment of Negro prison staff belatedly gets under way, some interesting and unanticipated cross-alliances become possible. It is too early to try to determine what the relation of these new staffing patterns will be to prison violence; all contingencies are possible, but it will be a period of stress for all concerned.

Thus far, we have taken an external view of prison violence by citing some historical examples, pointing out the changing racial composition of prison inmates, indicating some regional differences and referring to changes in sentencing practices—e.g., noninstitutional alternatives, like probation, that also change the character of the residual prison population. Such factors, in themselves, do not "explain" prison violence, but they must be understood as contributory elements. We must now place these factors in context and take an internal view of prisons as unisexual, age-graded, total institutions of social control. They are closed communities where real human beings interact in both formal and informal ways, as keepers and kept go through their daily routines. It is in the real humanity of prisoners and guards, and in their mundane routines, that we will find the sources of prison violence.

In any situation where a relatively small group of men control and direct a much larger group, the controllers depend, in a very real sense, on the passive acquiescence of the controlled. Such passivity is purchased by an effective sharing of power. The maintenance of absolute controls requires such implacable social relations that few men are willing to impose them, and even fewer will abide them, for they convert life into death. Prisons are characterized by caste relations where every member of the dominant caste, regardless of personal qualifications, formally rules every member of the subordinate caste, regardless of personal qualifications. Since such personal qualities as intelligence, sophistication, experience, age, strength, and energy are differentially distributed among men, regardless of legal status, the formal rules designed to preserve caste relations tend to be subverted. And yet, unless the smaller ruling caste is willing to live in a Hobbesian "state of nature," where the hand of every man is potentially raised against every other, and this for every minute of the day, they know they must come to terms, and do so, with some of the conditions set by the more numerous subordinate caste. It is somewhat like the "social contract" that early philosophers said was necessary for men to emerge from the "state of nature."

Thus the prisoners and their keepers strike a complex bargain. It is a tacit, implicit, and informal bargain, somewhat ambiguous as to its precise limits and level, and somewhat variable as to time, place, circumstance, and personalities, but one that is unmistakably present. Like the exercise of police discretion in the free community, or plea-bargaining in the criminal courts, such informal arrangements tend to be unacknowledged in daily practice, and are denied altogether when their legitimacy is brought into question by the formal requirements of the criminal justice system, but their weight is disproportionate in the normal prison community. If the average penal administrator or guard were asked, "Who's running this prison, anyway?" they would reply with some degree of self-righteous assertiveness, "Why, we are, of course." In the last analysis, they are right; but the last analysis could mean every prisoner is locked in his cell, gagged and straitjacketed; and then some would be perverse enough to breathe at a rhythm of their own choosing. Few penal administrators want to run a prison that way, for in that direction lies inhumanity and death. It is a question of where the line is drawn, and the line must not only be drawn but accepted. Most penal administrators know where the line is drawn, some will acknowledge it, but a few entertain the delusion of absolute control.

Different prisons strike this bargain at different levels of tolerance, depending upon such factors as: the kinds of work or programs the administration wants the prisoners to participate in; the amount of intramural mobility imposed by prison architecture on the routine tasks of prison life; the intelligence and sophistication of guards and inmates; corruption through sentimentality, stupidity, laziness, or venality; the external political climate, custom, tradition, and the like. These are the human factors in prison life that make life minimally tolerable for all concerned. Once the level of this power-sharing bargain has been fairly well established, it is difficult to change its terms and limits because very complex social relations, and mutual expectations and obligations come to depend upon it. To disrupt these informal relations by sudden or extensive social changes, affecting either staff or inmates, is to disrupt prison life; and such disruptions increase the probability of violence.

In the past, when southern prisons were more strictly segregated and the northern and western prisons still had a racial balance that favored White inmates, prison violence could usually be accounted for in terms of an inadvertent or unavoidable change in the power-sharing bargain. Political elections were followed by key staff changes; groups of prisoners were transferred without notice; the normal turnover of staff and the receipt and discharge of prisoners; the implementation or discontinuance of work assignments or treatment programs; in short, many of the things that had the appearance of the routine could also have very fateful consequences for the informal set of social relations organized around the existing power-sharing bargain. When such routine changes affected important pressure points in the closed prison community, the expectations and obligations of many persons, most of whom were indirectly related to each other, were suddenly disappointed. This would raise the level of tension in an already tense environment, and a precipitating incident that would ordinarily be more easily contained would be the occasion for a sudden flaring of violence.

How was anyone to know that among the inmates who were discharged a few days ago was, for example, inmate X, who worked in the officer's dining room and was stealing food which he sold, traded, or gave away to others, who, in turn, were trading or paying off gambling debts to still others, and so on, ad infinitum? Similarly, when Captain A, a grizzled veteran who knew how to survive the prison environment, finally retired and was replaced by Lieutenant B, who tried to run the cellhouse "by the book," a subterranean chain reaction took place, affecting both guards and prisoners, that required many adjustments. Suddenly a whole host of guards who had been having their civilian clothes cleaned, repaired, and pressed in the tailor shop had to turn to outside cleaning shops. Moreover, the tailor shop inmates who had been rewarded in a variety of ways for their extracurricular work were denied the capital that enabled them to participate in the internal economy.

Such individual examples are only indicative and necessarily limited in their ramifications. Group transfers, staff shifts, prison industry contracts, elections that affect the upper echelons of prison administration, or too-rapid attempts to either "tighten up" or "loosen up" the status quo can have very serious results. Gambling debts go unpaid, borrowed goods are out of control, lovers are separated, incompetent people lose competent help, political or friendship alliances are broken up, mutual service and communication links are disrupted; in short, the social fabric, real and symbolic, is badly torn.

To an outsider, such events have a pedestrian appearance because he is used to the available alternatives and free choices that a free man can make. If a firm's bookkeeper quits his job, another can be hired; if a grocery store closes, there is another in the next block. Some of the routine disruptions of prison life are somewhat akin to the breakdown of utilities or a transportation strike in the free world. Some persons are affected at once, others experience delayed and indirect effects, but only a few have the resources or alternatives to make long-run substitutions. In the closed prison community, life is driven in on itself; there are fewer alternatives and choices, and people are more directly and

intensely related, whether they wish it or not. If the routine changes of prison administration or external politics press too frequently or too rapidly on the crucial nerve centers and disrupt the social fabric in such a way that the power-sharing bargain is threatened at too many points for too many people, the potential for violence is escalated. Moreover, the actual eruption of violence is likely to be delayed because the latent effects of routine changes take time to ramify through the prison's social structure. Much of what has been considered random or "irrational" prison violence is traceable to such routine prison processes that are simply allowed to happen instead of being carefully planned for and skillfully managed. Invariably, when the violence was "explained," the administration invoked conspiracies and the inmates voiced the ordinary grievances about food, sentences, parole policies, and the like. Both were right to some degree because both the conspiracies and the grievances were real, but they were just as real six months ago and, more than likely, would be just as real six months hence. Such "explanations" are more in the nature of rationalizations than a reflection of actual and proximate "causes."

As we approach the present and consider contemporary prison violence, everything that has been said about the power-sharing bargain still has general applicability, but with some important differences. Perhaps most important is that there is less willingness to bargain, and the bargain that is struck is struck at a much lower level, with fewer benefits for fewer inmates. As in process of time the prison population got blacker and blacker, and more Chicano and Puerto Rican as well, the parties to the traditional bargain became more hostile to each other. Much has been said in recent years about a "new breed" of prisoners and that they are the source of recent violence. A much better case can be made, however, for the existence of an "old breed" of prison guard and penal administrator who have been sheltered, much more than their prisoners, from social changes taking place in the free community. Prisons are isolated, rural, resistant to change, and, for the most part, content to remain so. Prisoners are transients who are always upsetting the status quo. Moreover, they are more urban, more influenced by current events, more socially aware, and naturally concerned about civil rights and the condition of man; but this, too, is a part of a much wider social movement concerned with equality and justice. Not even the most secure prison can keep it out. A generation ago, penal administrators were deploring the presence of a "new breed" of spoiled and overindulged youthful offenders who were the offspring of permissive parents, and they were bemoaning the absence of the old professional safecrackers and con men who "knew how to do time."

In this perspective, every generation of prisoners has been a "new breed" of prisoners. In addition, in recent years, as an accompaniment to the civil rights movement and dissent over the war in Vietnam, we have responded to social dissent by defining a part of it as criminal. The result has been a new mixture of prisoners and a new kind of exchange of information among them. Radical ideologists have been thrown together with traditional criminal types, and each has taken something from the other at the margin. Thus, the prisons have been "politicized," and some of the prisoners convicted of traditional crimes have been furnished with a radical critique of imprisonment and all of society, while some of the more radical social dissidents have been furnished with traditional criminal techniques that may be useful in the furtherance of their objectives. It is a stupid arrangement that the older European countries have learned to handle more astutely by wiser separations among these classes of prisoners. And this new mixture of prisoners is regularly delivered into the hands of a predominantly White, rural, conservative, ruling caste in the prisons —a ruling caste which, for the financial, numerical, and philosophical reasons mentioned earlier, is wholly inadequate to the task.

No wonder, then, that there is more intransigence and less willingness to compromise in the informal bargaining processes that make prison life minimally tolerable for all concerned. For a while, the guards and penal administrators were still able to bargain in the traditional way with the decreasing proportion of White prisoners, but that form of power sharing has come to an end. In the prison situation, where outside race relations are reversed, the White minority feels the mounting pressure of the darker majorities. The choice is getting narrower and the potential for violence is increasing; soon the choices will be only open hostility, repression, or compromise. This is one interpretation of what the prisoners at the Tombs, at Attica, and elsewhere meant when the cry went up: "We want to be treated like human beings." It is also one interpretation of what President Nixon meant when he sent his 13-point directive to Attorney General Mitchell on November 13, 1969. "The American system for correcting and rehabilitating criminals presents a convincing case of failure."

There is today, as there was in 1870, some evidence that we are, at long last, ready to face the prison problem. When such an unlikely group as President Nixon, Chief Justice Burger, Attorney General Mitchell, and Senator Hruska, on the one hand, and Senators Kennedy and McGovern and Congressman Mikva and former Attorney General Clark, on the other, can agree on the current necessity for penal reform, there might be some hope. Chief Justice Burger, in his State of the Federal Judiciary message last July said, "If any phase of the administration of justice is more neglected than the courts, it is the correctional systems." At the National Conference on Corrections held at Williamsburg, Virginia, on December 6, 1971, Attorney General Mitchell, citing the recommendations of the National Congress on Penitentiary and Reformatory Discipline of 1870, citing the Wickersham Commission of 1931, and referring to the findings of the President's Commission on Law Enforcement and Administration of Justice of 1967, was moved to ask: "What was the result of this century of recommendations?" And he answered: "In state after state, most of the prisons have no programs for correcting prisoners."

So there is recognition in high places that a problem exists. Moreover, recent U.S. Court decisions in Arkansas (*Holt* v. *Sarver*, 2/18/

70), Rhode Island (*Morris* v. *Travisino,* 3/11/70), California (*Clutchette* v. *Procunier,* 6/21/71), and Virginia (*Landman* v. *Royster,* 10/30/71), have held longstanding prison practices unconstitutional. Even the Quakers, who had such an enormous influence on the form of American imprisonment, have returned to the drawing board after 200 years. A working party of the American Friends Service Committee recently published a report on crime and punishment in America, *Struggle for Justice,* in which they said, in effect, "We were wrong and must begin again with a different set of premises."

Santayana has admonished that "Those who cannot remember the past are condemned to repeat it." We have been through such a repetitious cycle once before. In 1870, the National Congress on Penitentiary and Reformatory Discipline was held at Cincinnati, Ohio. It was clear to the best penal minds in the country that we had already reached a serious impasse in our methods of imprisonment. Accordingly, after a thorough review of what was wrong with American penology, this National Congress published the famous Declaration of Principles which was to give rise to a New Penology. We can ascertain some measure of what the participants of that National Congress felt they had accomplished by adverting to the sentiments of Zebulon Brockway, the foremost penal administrator of his day, who was present and active. In 1876 he was appointed Warden of the Elmira Reformatory, the "wonder prison" of the Western world. Some 17 years after the National Congress of 1870, he reflected on its accomplishments and was still able to describe it as "an experience similar to that of the disciples of Our Blessed Lord on the Mount of Transfiguration." Last December, just 100 years later, we held the National Conference on Corrections at Williamsburg, Virginia. Will we, 17 years hence, as Santayana admonished, have remembered the past, or will we reflect with Goethe that "There is nothing so frightful as ignorance in action?"

INDEX

SOCIAL PROBLEMS AND PUBLIC POLICY
Deviance and Liberty
edited by Lee Rainwater

Publisher: Alexander J. Morin
Manuscript Editor: Elizabeth Pearson
Production Editor: Janet E. Braeunig
Production Manager: Mitzi Carole Trout

Designed by David Miller
Composed by Production Type, Inc., Dallas, Texas
Printed and Bound by George Banta Company, Inc.,
   Menasha, Wisconsin